THE MEASURES OF MAN

Published to honor

WILLIAM HOWELLS

ᴘ

Photograph by Muriel Howells

W. W. Howells

The Measures of Man

Methodologies in Biological Anthropology

Edited by

Eugene Giles

Anthropology Department, University of Illinois, Urbana

and

Jonathan S. Friedlaender

Peabody Museum, Harvard University, Cambridge

𝖖𝖵𝖯

Peabody Museum Press

A current list of all publications
is available from
Publications Department
Peabody Museum, Harvard University
Cambridge, MA 02138

Foreword

Stephen Williams

The measures of a man's greatness lie not only in what he has accomplished himself but also in the effect that he has had on those around him. By both these criteria Bill Howells has achieved much. In his own way, without bombast or swagger, he has made lasting contributions to the field of anthropology, and his students have spread across the country with the seeds of wisdom and methodology that he has planted.

Bill's return to the Peabody Museum to fill Earnest Hooton's chair as the head of Physical Anthropology at Harvard coincided with my own arrival on the Cantabrigian scene in 1954. His presence here has been a joy and a reward for all of us: the Department has benefitted from his deep concern and from his Chairmanship; a generation of Harvard and Radcliffe undergraduates has been educated by his gentle wit and skillful teaching; and for myself, I've taught with him, and learned from him.

As he and his wife, Muriel, have shared their warm hospitality with endless visitors from far and wide to the pleasure of all concerned, there has been an ambiance of grace and charm that has lighted many dark corners of our existence. Happily retirement from teaching will not mean his absence from the Peabody; for that fact, we who are privileged to have worked with Bill Howells are glad.

This volume, the work of his students and friends, is a testimony to their high regard for a fine professor and a gentleman. Part of the publication costs have been provided by a subvention from the Wenner-Gren Foundation, New York City, for which we are deeply grateful. I am also happy to have been able to contribute the title of this book.

Stephen Williams,
Peabody Professor
   of Archaeology and Ethnology
Director, Peabody Museum

Contents

FIVE   **Biological Anthropology: The Cultural Context**

Preface

Eugene Giles and Jonathan S. Friedlaender

Editors ought, in a preface, to be candid about the aims of the volume they are heralding. We have two: they combined into the present book. One was to provide some special tribute to a much-honored man, Professor William White Howells, on his retirement from active teaching at Harvard University. The other was to display the vitality of biological anthropology in the seventies by bringing together a collection of original papers that demonstrate the methodological diversity in the field. Admittedly when the publication of a set of papers is contemplated (often the belated spawn of a conference), it is more orthodox now to circumscribe them severely by topic. This is supposed to save time and money in an ever-narrowing pursuit of knowledge. We have not done that, and no doubt will be chastized for it. For one thing, such relentless specialization does not represent our view of biological anthropology. Our hope for this volume is that it will not only edify by the exposition of the many expertises of the modern physical anthroplogist, but also that it will impart our enthusiasm for the subject and its extraordinary breadth of view. If this volume aids in developing or sustaining such mental nimbleness, we will have achieved a major aim.

Our concept of the book—topical breadth, methodological

emphasis—also in a sense epitomizes the man to whom it is dedicated. We two have now watched Bill Howells over two decades mold a significant number of the practicing biological anthropologists in the country. At the close of his formal teaching career—and we emphasize "formal teaching"—we were quite surprised at the number of his students and all that they were doing. They, together, seemed a sound basis for a wide-ranging methodological book and, of course, would provide an appropriate tribute to the man. The response of Bill's students to our idea has been a most gratifying experience for us. Virtually all reacted favorably when we made the first contact and carried through by submitting papers by September, 1973. Unfortunately, subsequent difficulties have delayed publication.

We should mention here that all of the senior authors of papers are students of Bill Howells. Some contributors, particularly Paul Baker, George Holcomb, Dave Horr, Don Lathrap, Tom McKern, Don Mitchell, Jill Nash, Gene Ogan and Hal Ross, did not have Bill as their primary advisor during most or all of their doctoral student years, but they, like the rest of us, were much affected by him. Two, Phil Rightmire and Mike Crichton, were his undergraduate students (those who think only of novels like *The Andromeda Strain* or *The Terminal Man* or movies like *Binary* or *West World* in connection with Mike ought to scan vol. 57, no. 1, *Papers of the Peabody Museum* or vol. 23, no. 1, *American Journal of Physical Anthropology*). Only three of our principal contributors, Hal Movius, Harry Shapiro and Steve Williams, are "merely" appreciative colleagues.

In addition to expressing our thanks to our authors for their patience as well as their contributions, we also must acknowledge our obligation to Michael Crichton, James B. Stoltman, and the Peabody Museum Director of Publications, Richard Bartlett, for assistance along the way. We are particularly grateful to the Wenner-Gren Foundation for Anthropological Research for their support of this publication. But our deepest appreciation does go to our teacher.

Eugene Giles
Jonathan S. Friedlaender

Urbana, Illinois and Cambridge, Massachusetts, June, 1976

xi

The Measure of a Man:
William White Howells

Eugene Giles
Hallam L. Movius, Jr.
Harry L. Shapiro
George R. Holcomb
Michael Crichton

A long-recognized and special characteristic of American anthropology has been the embracement of its prehistorical, biological and social elements in one comprehensive discipline. From this tradition many intellectual leaders have emerged to influence its course of development. Quite understandably such an all-encompassing view of anthropology has nurtured very few outstanding figures who have dominated the entire field. To excel in any one of anthropology's branches is a worthy goal, but to be an important figure in all three is almost inconceivable in this day and age. Yet consider this singular accomplishment: writing celebrated texts in the two subareas of anthropology other than one's own, and underscoring a laudable career in biological anthropology by publishing *three* books in that subfield during one's year of retirement. This volume honors a great General Anthropologist: William White Howells.

A salute now to Bill Howells obviously catches him in full

forward motion. But his retirement from Harvard last year is an event worth demarking in a way that reflects the closure it is: as a formal mentor of graduate students in biological anthropology. Bill's advice and counsel will undoubtedly benefit many students to come as it has in the past; nevertheless, his influence as a teacher has already ramified to an extent that does him great credit. This collection of papers by his students, focusing on methodology, makes manifest the direct influence his teaching has had on anthropological theory and practice.

Of Bill the man this section offers five reminiscences through the eyes of students and colleagues. William Howells was born in New York City on November 27, 1908, the son of John Mead and Abby Macdougall White Howells. His secondary education at St. Paul's School in Concord, New Hampshire was followed by Harvard College. A classmate, Hallam L. Movius, Jr., recalls those student days.

In the class of 1930 at Harvard there were seven of us who decided to concentrate in anthropology, which at that time constituted a record number of undergraduate concentrators in the Department. Bill Howells was the only one amongst us, however, who had taken enough courses to be granted leave of absence during our senior year thereby making it possible for him to go to Graduate School and to marry Muriel Gurdon Seabury in June of 1929. Thus the distinction of having the Class Baby, a daughter, belongs to them. In 1934 Bill received his Ph.D. having completed his thesis under Earnest Hooton.

Bill's professional career began as a Research Associate of the American Museum of Natural History in New York, where he conducted research particularly on the racial types of the Pacific. He spent the summer of 1935 in County Offaly, Ireland, exhuming and studying a large number of Early Christian monks for the Harvard-Irish Survey. I visited him during the course of his field-work and remember his telling me that his preliminary study demonstrated that the population of Ireland had remained essentially unchanged since the Early Bronze Age, Ireland not having been influenced by the various racial elements which penetrated England during the millenium and a half or so in question.

xiii

In 1939 Bill became an Assistant Professor at the University of Wisconsin. Then in early 1943 he was commissioned a lieutenant (j.g.) in the U.S. Navy, and for three years he was assigned to ONI in Washington where he kept track of Japanese ships afloat and sunk. Returning to Wisconsin in 1946 as an Associate Professor, he was made a full Professor of Anthropology there in 1948. With Earnest Hooton's sad and untimely death in May of 1954, Bill was appointed to succeed him at Harvard.

It cannot be very often that one finds one's close, intimate friend and classmate as a member of the same Department as the one in which he is serving. Nevertheless, this is what has happened in the case of Bill Howells and myself. As a Palaeolithic archaeologist I do not pretend to understand the significance and importance of the particular research on which he has embarked, and doubtless the reverse is likewise true. But we do come together in one very exciting area of mutual interest—i.e. new discoveries of fossil man. However, this almost seems irrelevant in contrast with the deep personal affection and respect which both my wife and I share for Bill and Muriel. Bill's retirement will in no way modify our personal relationship, which has been developing now over a period of some 46 years. As a member of our Department or of any of the committees on which we have served together, Bill has always been the most open-minded, even-tempered and sympathetic colleague I have ever had.

Bill and Muriel's first child, Muriel Gurdon (now Mrs. Richard E. Metz) was born during Bill's days at Harvard. Their second child, William Dean II, was born during the beginning of the first of Bill's three major institutional affiliations. Harry L. Shapiro remembers that period at the American Museum of Natural History.

Writing about an old friend can be both a delight and an embarrassment. If one is honest and can in truth find only the most charming things to say, one's pleasure is great. But one does thereby run the risk of offending the privacy and modesty of a cherished friend, for public encomia can be embarrassing to

xiv

*some of us. Well, this is the chance that both Bill Howells and I
must take for I find that I can only write about him in warm and
glowing terms.*

*I have known Bill for about 45 years. In fact, I first met him at
a dance in his honor to which I was invited by his aunt Miss
Elizabeth White. Muriel was there too, so my acquaintance and
attachment began with both of them. The next encounter that I
recall was a visit to both Muriel and Bill at their apartment in
Cambridge. It was Bill's last graduate year at Harvard, and he
was to me, still a bachelor, the picture of domesticity, with little
Gurdon in her crib at one end of the living room. It was shortly
after this visit that we began discussing an arrangement I was
organising for Bill to join me at the American Museum of Natural History after completing his obligations at Cambridge.*

*Although there was at the time no staff vacancy at the Mu-
seum, Bill was prepared to come, as a volunteer assistant, partly
I suspect because he was still enough of a New Yorker to welcome a return to the fold. His and Muriel's families and their
numerous friends were in New York, they had been raised there
and it must have appealed to them strongly as a comfortable
home base. But perhaps as influential was the professional opportunities that the Museum and its resources provided at the
outset of an anthropological career.*

*The following year Bill joined us, technically as my assistant,
but in reality pretty much on his own as far as research was
concerned. His quiet charm and sense of humor made him immediately a part of the warm intimacy that existed in the Department of Anthropology at the Museum. Pretty much contemporary with him were George Vaillant,Wendell Bennett and
myself. But in actual appearance he made the rest of us seem like
gray-beards. Besides this there was in addition a Harvard cluster
with Clarence Hay in conjunction with Vaillant and myself.
Whenever Alfred M. Tozzer was in New York and visited us at
the Museum he always took great pleasure in figuratively em-
bracing his Harvard sons.*

*These years when Bill was at the American Museum I look
back on with a deep nostalgia. Not only had a warm friendship
developed between us with the usual social overtones of evening
parties, but for me it was stimulating to have a professional col-*

league in the department who spoke my particular anthropological dialect, for up to Bill's arrival I was a lone physical anthropologist in a nest of archeologists and ethnologists. It is, after all these years, impossible to remember the kind of technical discussions we had, but they were frequent, casual and always rewarding. It became quickly evident to me that Bill had a sharp critical sense that not only got to the core of a particular problem, but that also gave him a balanced assessment of the current literature. In his quiet way he could be very firm in his convictions and not easily shifted. But this determination never led to acrimony. Often he could turn a discussion that threatened to become a bit tense into quieter channels by his delightful humor.

It was at this period that he became interested in a project that I suspect played a part in his later pioneering research in multivariate analysis. We had at that time a cranial collection of some 12,000 specimens representing all parts of the world. It was, of course, invaluable for comparative purposes and general reference. A large segment of it had recently been acquired by the generosity of Mr. Otto Warburg who had purchased the famous Von Luschan Collection that Mrs. Von Luschan had decided to sell after her husband's death.

Bill was looking for a sample large enough to provide statistical reliability and at the same time sufficiently localised to represent a distinctive population. After some debate, he settled on a collection coming from a Melanesian island. This turned out to be his first major population study and in the light of his subsequent researches opened for him a field of investigation that proved to be highly productive.

Although it was published after he had left the Museum to go to Wisconsin, I suspect that he had already begun Mankind So Far before he left or at least had made his preliminary explorations of the ground work for it. With its publication it became evident that Bill had an exceptional gift for literary expression. I had been aware that he was meticulous in his writing and was sensitive to the turgidity of much of the professional literature, but I had not until then sensed his own natural talents for highly felicitous prose.

The years at Wisconsin and later at Harvard made our inter-
course much more sporadic. But the now relatively infrequent
encounters continued, at least for me, to be occasions for the re-
newal of friendship and common interests.

And now in joining Bill's students in honoring him I can
only say that I have been the gainer from a long and rewarding
friendship.

Bill and his family left New York City in 1939 to take up a
position at the University of Wisconsin in Madison. His time
there was interrupted by service in the U.S. Navy during World
War II. The Wisconsin period witnessed the recognition of his
teaching prowess by his being appointed, in 1948, Professor of
Integrated Liberal Studies in addition to his continuing Anthropology professorship. George R. Holcomb was a Wisconsin
student after the War.

I came to know William Howells when I was an undergrad-
uate student at the University of Wisconsin and I enrolled in his
course entitled Human Evolution and Racial History. I was ma-
joring in another field and it was my exposure to Professor
Howells and this particular course that determined my subse-
quent graduate school career. My experience recalls the state-
ment Bill Howells made when asked by W. L. Straus how he
happened to become interested in physical anthropology and
his reply was that Hooton stimulated his interest and that was
about the long and short of it. I venture to say that many stu-
dents, as I did, turned their interest to physical anthropology
because of the influence of W. W. Howells.

While William Howells was at Wisconsin he taught both be-
ginning and advanced courses in physical anthroplogy. The ad-
vanced physical course was a "bone course" and the students
spent many afternoons identifying bits and pieces of osteologi-
cal specimens. The culmination of their efforts came when they
were expected to identify fragments covered by a large blanket.
Needless to say, they came away from the course with an appre-
ciation of skeletal anatomy. His major seminar was entitled
Race and Variation and it was an extensive review of the litera-

ture dealing with analyses and methods that covered the study of individual and group variation. During this time of the early '50's, Professor Howells became interested in factor analysis and I often encountered him as he walked from Sterling Hall to a classroom in another building where he became the conscientious student of factor theory.

The breadth of William Howells' anthropological knowledge and interests is illustrated by noting three successful books he authored while at the University of Wisconsin. In 1944, he published Mankind So Far, a textbook widely used in introductory anthropology courses. This text, a classic example of a book that is both scientifically sound as well as easy to read and understand, was followed by The Heathens in 1948 and Back of History in 1954. The latter book was adopted by the University for its curriculum in Integrated Liberal Studies, a pioneering attempt to bring the interdisciplinary approach to undergraduate teaching. Naturally, one of the first faculty members to be asked to participate in this venture was Bill Howells. His lectures to large sections of bright young students were very much like his books: stimulating, challenging and graced with a wit that made learning an enjoyable experience.

William Howells was a distinguished faculty member at Wisconsin and the University can be proud of his many accomplishments while he was in residence there. He joined the faculty as an assistant professor in 1939. His academic career at Madison was interrupted by service in the United States Navy from 1943 to 1946. After returning to Wisconsin, he became a full Professor in 1948 and served as chairman of the Department of Sociology and Anthropology in 1953.

During his Wisconsin years, Bill Howells was the Secretary-Treasurer of the American Association of Physical Anthropologists (1939-1943) and editor of the American Journal of Physical Anthropology (1949 to 1954.) His many contributions to anthropology were recognized by his colleagues who elected him to the presidency of the American Anthropological Association in 1951. He was also honored by being selected as the Viking Fund Medalist for 1954.

William Howells left the University of Wisconsin in 1954 to

return to Harvard where he assumed the faculty position left vacant by the passing of his former teacher E. A. Hooton. I left Madison the same year and I consider myself very fortunate to have been a student of this scholarly and literate gentleman. I'm only sorry that other generations of Wisconsin students did not share my good fortune. Wisconsin's loss was certainly to be Harvard's gain.

In April of 1954 Earnest Hooton hailed me, then a Harvard Junior and the merest tyro in physical anthropology, on the Peabody Museum steps, and declaimed against the dun-colored curtains just hung in the new herbarium building across from the Museum. The focus of awe among Harvard undergraduates had not yet turned upon themselves, and I was vastly impressed by this sign of professorial camaraderie. Two weeks later Hooton was dead; who would—or could—follow him? I was elated when I discovered near the beginning of my Senior year that it was to be William Howells.

Bill (and I must not neglect the good efforts of Edward Hunt as well) awakened in me during that year an abiding interest in numerical analysis applied to problems of morphological interpretation. After a year's "flyer," as Hooton would say, in vertebrate paleontology at Berkeley, and two years' worth of rethinking time, courtesy the U.S. Army, the lure of working with Bill Howells in physical anthropology became irresistable. I was delighted when he encouraged me to return to Harvard for graduate study; I did so with never a regret.

In my mind several things made Bill superlative in his approach to graduate students at Harvard. He was, above all, incomparably fair in his dealings. Students were not "his" to do his bidding, to assist him in his endeavors, rather he was there to assist them in theirs. And what they chose ultimately to do for a dissertation was precisely what he then assisted them in. This freedom of choice, rather eloquently displayed in this volume, was a great benefit of studying with Bill. Bill thought, simply enough, that what students wanted to do most they would do best. It was an approach well suited to Harvard and the post-Sputnik sixties, but it took a person with Bill's exceptional ability to translate it into a teaching program. For his graduate students it was an exhilarating experience, but one where one's own limitations, for better or worse, had to be realistically assessed.

Bill's support of his graduate students was quiet but effective, often behind the scenes. When the U.S. Air Force was being sticky about releasing some topographical maps of New Guinea essential for my fieldwork there, I recall discovering Bill had sought, with eventual success, the assistance of his Maine Senator, Margaret Chase Smith. Students of his were able to undertake remarkable research projects, and sometimes, I'm afraid, may have temporarily undervalued the tremendous amount of overt and covert support he provided.

Because of the catholicity of his interests in anthropology, there is no topical area that categorizes his students. But Bill's attention to the acquisition of data and above all their proper analysis comes through in his students' concern with methodology in their research. Bill's recent monograph, *Cranial Variation in Man: A Study by Multivariate Analysis of Patterns of Difference Among Recent Human Populations,* exemplifies the ideals he has set for his students. He does not deny the imperfections of either anthropological data nor statistical methods, even multivariate ones. But the volume shows a man willing to spare no effort in obtaining the best possible sets of data and developing and utilizing the most appropriate numerical analytic tools. That done, he goes ahead; his work is hardly programmatic. He is interested in attacking anthropological problems, in providing sound, substantiated answers to questions; not in glossing over data accumulation with superficial manipulations nor in justifying technique modification by vacuous applications. His brilliant inquiry establishes convincingly that morphological variation in the crania of human populations— so long a rather sterile preserve of physical anthropology—is "not merely having a taffy-pull with the skeleton of the head," as Bill puts it, but obviously biologically meaningful once the methodological key is turned. The vindication of such a persistent tenet of physical anthropology would more than cap a distinguished career, but—thankfully—we can see positive signs that his productivity is not abating. Indeed, it makes us, his students, all the more convinced that

        . . . 'tis our life

   To drag slow footsteps after the far mind—

to excerpt, if I may be excused the genealogical liberty, from *Poems of Two Friends* by my great-grandfather's brother, John J. Piatt and Bill's grandfather, William Dean Howells.

But Harvard University is, after all, Harvard College, and undergraduate teaching is sovereign. In our final measure of the man, Michael Crichton conveys the style in which Bill Howells discharged that imposing responsibility.

One must account first for his popularity, which was extraordinary, and extended far beyond the Department of Anthropology. At Harvard, he always scored high marks in the Confy Guide, *a generally vitriolic undergraduate poll of professors and courses; indeed, during the years that he taught Anthropology 1a, that course was considered the best-taught and best-liked introductory course in the University. His textbooks were always singled out for their clarity, salience and wit. His lectures were described in superlatives. His examinations were considered difficult but fair.*

There was another aspect to his popularity which is more elusive. Howells was the focus of enormous fascination among undergraduates who had never laid eyes on him, much less taken a course from him. I knew a mathematics student who collected Howells stories, most of them apocryphal. One anecdote related how Howells had had his hat shot off by a gangster when he was an undergraduate; I remember it chiefly because it was so unbelievable. Yet people in the dining halls listened to these stories eagerly. Students avidly consumed the most trivial details of his mannerisms, tastes, and attitudes. The fact that he drove a Jaguar sedan, for example, assumed some sort of major significance at a time when nobody knew or cared what car other professors drove.

I never thought much about any of this at the time. I was preoccupied with Howells, and it seemed perfectly reasonable that everyone else was, too. Besides, I enjoyed enormous status as one of his students, and I was not above playing on that status. I knew when someone in his family was getting married; I knew when he was travelling out of the country; I knew when he'd returned with a suntan from somewhere or other. All this made me very important at the Lowell House dining hall. I was close to somebody Significant.

The significance of Howells, I should add, was peculiarly Cantabrigian. Other professors commuted to Washington or resigned to work for the Kennedy Administration, or were broadly public figures in one sense or another. Howells was not. Instead, he was a model for an Old New England family member carrying on a tradition of dress, manner, attitude and work which fascinated undergraduates looking for such models. He was, in a sense, the archetypal Harvard professor. And consistent with that archetype was the fact that he apparently favored undergraduates over graduate students, whom we all regarded as our natural enemies.

In retrospect, I think it is also true that Howells was popular among undergraduates because he seemed to make so few concessions to our life style. Undergraduate society is really a postadolescent grouping, and it perpetuates the adolescent anxiety about the right way to look and act. We were always suspicious of professors who dressed and talked as we did, who showed too much interest in football, or who gave easy examinations. There was never any question about that with Howells, who dressed and acted in his own way, and who taught courses which were demanding and difficult. He was comfortable with the position that he was the professor and we were the students, and there was a clear boundary between us.

I could never be sure whether Howells knew that his actions were followed by students of mathematics and government and history; he never let on, and I never felt free to broach the subject. In any case, I was content with the attention derived from being quizzed in detail every week or so by my fellow undergraduates about what Howells had recently said or done.

As a lecturer—which was the way most undergraduates experienced him—Howells was extraordinary. The famous lecturers at Harvard at that time were all well known to students; men like Frank Freidel in History, Gerald Holton in physics, George Wald in biology, Jerome Bruner in psychology. They were all men who spoke well, moved well, and lectured with conviction and insight. They shared a common element of showmanship, and they conveyed a contagious enthusiasm for their field of study.

Even among this group, Howells was exceptional. His style was disarming: he lectured quietly, in a relaxed conversational manner, with occasional long pauses to look at his notes. The effect was one of complete spontaneity. He was also a master of what Noel Coward once called "coming out of a different hole each time"—he played on the unexpected element in his lecturing. One never knew whether Howells was going to lecture for an hour behind the podium, or whether he was going to say five words and then run a film, or whether he would talk with slides, or what. He kept his audiences off balance, and they adored him.

One should mention that part of their adoration had to do with the way he presented his material. Harvard students are a hard-headed lot, and flash without substance was always denigrated. He was always superbly organized; it was easy to take clear notes in his lectures. Nor was he arbitrary. He was careful to explain the reasons behind his organization.

He was a gifted performer, and his imitations of primate gaits were justly famous. But those imitations, like the jokes and puns and anecdotes and newspaper stories sprinkled through his lectures, all made a certain point and were all the more appreciated.

His examinations were interesting, an odd comment unless one reflects how stupefyingly dreary and tedious most exam questions are. Howells subscribed to the notion that an examination question ought not only to test knowledge but the ability to use that knowledge. His questions often implied an intriguing new perspective on information. They were also frequently funny.

His textbooks were unique. Any one who opens The Heathens and reads the first sentence will immediately recognize a new academic voice—informed, bemused, serious but not self-important. *The very fact that Howells, a physical anthropologist, would choose to write about religion is itself noteworthy. He did not seem to respect traditional academic boundaries, but would conduct raiding parties outside his territory if it interested him to do so, and he conveyed the reasons for his interest extremely well.*

His texts were always praised for not reading like textbooks, and that is probably the best compliment one can bestow upon them. They reflected the strengths of his lecturing style—a conversational manner, a tentative attitude toward facts that might be re-evaluated in the future, and a quiet, dry wit. He was the master of two dangerous and little-used devices in his writing. One was puns, which he dropped in an utter deadpan fashion. The other was aphorisms and cliches, carefully and often humorously employed to deflate any sense of academic pomposity. His writing implied that while the information was interesting and sometimes complex, there was no reason to get stuffy about it. Otherwise you ran the risk of throwing out the baby with the bath water.

In person, Howells was so easygoing that it was possible to misconstrue the depth of his seriousness about his work. I did precisely this during my first junior tutorial session with him. There were three physical anthropology students that year; at our first meeting, he assigned a book to each of us, and requested that we report to him two weeks hence.

That seemed a liberal time to read a book and write a short paper. I was assigned Simpson's The Major Features of Evolution, *a book I now remember chiefly because a footnote gave me the idea for* The Andromeda Strain. *But I found the major features of the book hard going, and Howells had been so relaxed at our initial meeting that I assumed him to be a soft touch.*

I returned to his office on the fifth floor of the Peabody Museum armed with a quick glance at the contents of the book, and an even quicker paper. Howells asked me to summarize the main arguments of the book. I did so haltingly. He began to frown. I began to perspire. He asked a few questions. I had no idea what he was talking about. I finished lamely, and he re-

marked pleasantly that I might benefit from a more attentive reading of the assigned book.

He then summarized the volume in an extraordinary fashion, making Simpson's arguments, giving the outstanding supporting evidence, tying it neatly together in three or four quick minutes. All the time he was talking, I kept thinking that that book had been written in 1953, and this was now 1963, and he probably hadn't read the book since it was published. And I thought, "So this is the way it's going to be."

I left the session angry as only the guilty can be angry; I had been caught at my deception. To add insult to injury, when my paper was returned (with a C- grade) I found he had circled a number of split infinitives and dangling participles. I was at that time enormously vain about my writing style; by now I was so mad I could hardly see straight.

I vowed that I would show him. For my next paper, I read far beyond the required reading, and I wrote the best prose I was able to put together. He gave me an A, but he circled some typos. Typos! Was I not even allowed a few typographical errors here and there? The man was impossible.

I swore that he would never find another typo, and redoubled my efforts.

And that really set the pattern for the next two years. Howells was always modest, always relaxed; he spurred me on in what were—in retrospect—the most extraordinarily subtle ways. I tried to make jokes; I tried to polish my prose as well as my scholarship; I tried to write as well and as cleverly and as succinctly as he did.

Once, he wrote on a paper, "Very interesting. I enjoyed reading this." And it was the only comment. Nothing else in red pencil, for page after page. I was in heaven for weeks afterward. I also relaxed my efforts. The next paper came back with the comment, "Fuzzy thinking in parts. B." He also caught two split infinitives, and several spelling errors. But he seemed principally annoyed by two redundancies in my paper. "Once is enough," said the red-pencil comment in the margin.

There was no escaping the pressure he exerted. I cannot imagine, in retrospect, that he was unaware of what he was *doing. I remember looking at another student's paper, and realizing that Howells hadn't circled the dangling participles in that person's writing. Why was he picking on me? But I also understood. In some way I was telling him I thought I was a hell of a writer, and so he was responding to that as well as to the intellectual content of my papers.*

As it happens, I've saved all those papers, and it is enlightening to reread them now. Howells' forbearance is extraordinary. The author of those papers is unmistakably a 20 year-old hotshot who needs to be slapped down and put in his place. The narcissism in the prose is excruciating. It is also the kind of writing that dares rebuke from the reader, almost as if I were saying, "You write in unconventional academic terms, so I will, too. Are you going to criticize me for it?"

Howells never did. Sometimes he would circle a particularly idiotic passage and ask in the margin, "What is the relevance?" And I was often left looking at the circled paragraph, wondering the same thing.

Howells seemed to subscribe to the belief that a good teacher helps his students become whatever they want to become. At the end of my junior year, he contrived for each of his three students to go abroad—two went to South Africa, and I went to Europe. I had told him straight out that I wanted to be in Europe to travel with a girl I was interested in, and incidentally to do some research. He helped me decide upon a thesis topic that would require only a few weeks work in England. He seemed perfectly comfortable with the idea that I was more interested in women than research.

I remember very little about writing of my thesis the following year. For one thing, I panicked and wrote it in the most turgid academic prose—he later lightened it when it was published in the Peabody Museum Papers. For another, I was preoccupied with the question of getting into medical school. Howells seemed to approve of that decision, although he said he was sorry to lose me to anthropology. He once asked me what I really wanted to do. I said I didn't know, but that I had met Robert Gardner who was working on the New Guinea film,

Dead Birds, *and I was impressed with movies. Howells just nodded. I couldn't tell what the nodding meant.*

Shortly before graduation, I attended a garden party given by Master Perkins of Lowell House. It was a hot April afternoon, and I was well on my way to being drunk. Some old alumnus was introduced to me as a friend of Howells, and he asked me how I had fared as his student. I said it had been a wonderful experience.

"I'm sure it was," the man said. "Bill is absolutely brilliant."

I remember being surprised by the comment. It had never occurred to me to consider whether Howells was brilliant, just as it had never occurred to me to think of him as "Bill." On reflection, I supposed that quite a lot of people knew him as Bill, and recognized that he was brilliant. I had never thought of him that way. I considered trying to explain to this man that for several years I had been locked in an intricate relationship with a professor who chided, goaded and cajoled me to some point of intensity in my work, which had nothing to do with anybody casually named "Bill." I was not acquainted with Bill Howells. I was a student of one Professor Howells, the man who wrote "WWH" in red on my papers and to the extent that his Bill Howells was the same as my Professor Howells it was confusing and I didn't want to know about it.

With the perspective of more than a decade, I am fascinated by the fact that I didn't want to know about that person named Bill Howells. I suppose no student sees his teachers accurately. The relationship is at the same time too complex and too narrow, too heavily overlaid with parental images and too involved with breaking free of those images. I resolved the whole situation by extricating myself from that alumnus as quickly as possible. I remember the puzzlement on his face: but how could I explain to him that he and I were discussing two different people?

He was, of course, many different people. During the early sixties, he was the Chairman of the Department, an administration position he professed to dislike but carried off smoothly. The Anthropology Department at Harvard was small and had its minor tensions; I remember one Professor saying to me with relief, "Thank God Howells is going to be Chairman of the Department next year."

He was also engaged in his own research, carrying on graduate programs, writing an occasional popular article or book review, bringing out new editions of his texts, lecturing in introductory and advanced courses. He was also a father and husband and presumably a great many other things that I never knew about at all.

He carried this enormous and diverse load with apparent effortlessness, and certainly with a great deal of grace. People often wondered how he did it. I wondered, too, but never for long. The very fact that he could do it meant that it was possible that other people could do it as well. Or at least try. And in any case, I had my hands full.

Bibliography of William White Howells

1974   L'homme de Neanderthal. La Recherche, 5: 634-642. July-August, 1974.

1974   Neanderthals: names, hypotheses and scientific method. American Anthropologist, 76: 24-38.

1973   Cranial Variation in Man: A Study by Multivariate Analysis of Patterns of Difference Among Recent Human Populations. Peabody Museum Papers, vol. 67, 259 pp.

1973   Evolution of the Genus *Homo*. 188 pp. Reading, Massachusetts: Addison-Wesley.

1973   Measures of population distances. In M. H. Crawford and P. L. Workman, eds., Methods and Theories of Anthropological Genetics, pp. 159-76. Albuquerque: University of New Mexico Press.

1973   More on Polynesian origins. Pacific Islands Monthly, February 1973, vol. 45, no. 9, p. 60.

1973   The Pacific Islanders. 299 pp. London: Weidenfeld and Nicholson. (Published 1973 in Wellington, A. H. & A. W. Reed; 1974 in New York, Scribners).

1972   *Homo sapiens:* 20 million years in the making. UNESCO Courier, August-September, 1972, pp. 5-13.

1972   Computerised clues unlock a door to Polynesia's past. Pacific Islands Monthly, vol. 43, no. 5, May, pp. 67-69.

1972   The importance of being human. In Judith M. Tanur, ed., Statistics: a Guide to the Unknown, pp. 92-100. San Francisco: Holden-Day.

1972   Analysis of patterns of variation in crania of recent man. In R. Tuttle, ed., The Functional and Evolutionary Biology of Primates, pp. 123-151. Chicago: Aldine-Atherton.

1971   The meaning of race. In R. H. Osborne, ed., The Biological and Social Meaning of Race, pp. 3-10. San Francisco: Freeman.

1971   Applications of multivariate analysis to cranio-facial growth. In R. E. Noyers and W. M. Krogman, eds., Cranial-facial Growth in Man, pp. 209-218. New York: Pergamon Press.

1971   With R. H. Osborne, G. A. Harrison and R. Singer. Graduate training in physical anthropology: report of the AAPA Study Committee. American Journal of Physical Anthropology, 34: 279-306.

1970   Anthropometric grouping analysis of Pacific peoples. Archaeology and Physical Anthropology in Oceania, V: 192-217.

1970   Multivariate analysis for the identification of race from crania. In T. D. Stewart, ed., Personal Identification in Mass Disasters, pp. 111-121. Washington: Smithsonian Institution.

1970   Mount Carmel Man: morphological relationships. Proceedings, VIIIth International Congress of Anthropological and Ethnological Sciences, Tokyo and Kyoto, 1968. Vol. I, Anthropology, pp. 269-272.

1970   Multivariate analysis of human crania. Proceedings VIIIth International Congress of Anthropological and Ethnological Sciences, Tokyo and Kyoto, 1968. Vol. I, Anthropology, pp. 1-3.

1970   With the assistance of Hermann K. Bleibtreu. Hutterite age differences in body measurements. Papers, Peabody Museum of Archaeology and Ethnology, vol. LVII, no. 2, pp. 1-123.

1970   Recent physical anthropology. Annals of the American Academy of Political and Social Science, 389: 116-126.

1970   Anthropology. In Irving A. Falk, ed., Prophecy for the Year 2000, pp. 46-48. New York: Julian Messner.

1969   Comment on D. S. Marshall, review of Craniometry and Multivariate Analysis (papers by W. W. Howells and J. M. Crichton), Papers, Peabody Museum of Archaeology and Ethnology vol. LVIII, no. 1, 1966, in Human Biology, 14: 295-296.

1969   Multivariate analysis of human crania (preliminary report, dittoed), 379 pp.

1969   The use of multivariate techniques in the study of skeletal populations. American Journal of Physical Anthropology, 31: 311-314.

1969   Criteria for selection of osteometric dimensions. American Journal of Physical Anthropology, 30: 451-458.

1968   The beginnings of man. 1968 Year Book (Supplement to Collier's Encyclopedia), pp. 42-51.

1968   Measurement and analysis in anthropology. In D. K. Whitla, ed., Handbook of Measurement and Assessment in Behavioral Sciences, pp. 393-418. Reading, Massachusetts: Addison-Wesley.

1968   Ainus in Prehistoric Japan: a study by discriminant analysis. Proceedings, 7th International Congress of Anthropological and Ethnological Sciences, Moscow, 1964, Vol. III, pp. 22-28.

1967   With B. Patterson. Identification by discriminant function of the humerus fragment of Kanapoi Hominoid I. Newsletter of Computer Archaeology, Vol. III, No. 1, pp. 3-4.

1967   Editor: Ideas on Human Evolution: Selected Essays, 1949-1961. College edition. 555 pp. New York: Atheneum.

1967   Mankind in the Making. Harmondsworth, England: Penguin.

1967   Mankind in the Making. Revised edition. 384 pp. New York: Doubleday.

1967   With B. Patterson. Hominid humeral fragment from early Pleistocene of northwestern Kenya. Science, 156: 64-66.

1966   Population distances: biological, linguistic, geographical, and environmental. Current Anthropology, 7: 531-540.

1966   Homo erectus. Scientific American, 215 (5): 46-53.

1966   The Jomon population of Japan. A study by discriminant analysis of Japanese and Ainu crania. Peabody Museum Papers, LVII/1:1-3.

1966   Variability in family lines vs. population variability. In J. Brozek, ed., The Biology of Human Variation, Annals of the New York Academy of Sciences, 134 (art. 2): 624-631.

1965   Age and individuality in vertebral lipping: notes on Stewart's data. In Homenaje a Juan Comas en su 65 Aniversario, II: 169-178.

1965   Détermination de sexe du bassin par fonction discriminante: étude du matérial du Docteur Gaillard. Bulletins et Mémoires de la Société d' Anthropologie de Paris, XI série 7:95-105.

1965   Some present aspects of physical anthropology. Annals of the American Academy of Political and Social Science, 357: 127-133.

1965   Ma Waraa Altarikh (translation of Back of History). 588 pp. Cairo: Nahdet Miser Press.

1965   Människans Härstamning (translation of Mankind in the Making). 298 pp. Stockholm: Prisma.

1964   Mensheid in Wording: Het Verhaal van de Menselijke Evolutie (translation of Mankind in the Making). 372 pp. Hilversum: Paul Brand.

1963   De Godsdienst der Primitieve Volken (translation of The Heathens). 217 pp. Utrecht: Spectrum.

1963   Back of History. The Story of Our Own Origins. Natural History Library revised edition. 384 pp. New York: Anchor Books, Doubleday.

1963   Die Ahnen der Menschheit (translation of Mankind in the Making). 544 pp. Ruschlikon-Zürich: Albert Muller.

1962   Mas Allá de la Historia: El Maravilloso Relato de Nuestros Orígenes (translation of Back of History). 419 pp. Barcelona: Editorial Labor, S. A.

1962   An aberrant primate? In E. Lucas, ed., What is a Man? A symposium from Makerere, pp. 15-25. London: Oxford University Press.

1962   The Heathens. Primitive Man and His Religions. Natural History Library edition. 302 pp. New York: Anchor Books, Doubleday.

1962   Editor: Ideas on Human Evolution: Selected Essays, 1949-1961. 555 pp. Cambridge: Harvard University Press.

1961   With K. P. Oakley. Age of the skeleton from the Lagow Sand Pit, Texas. American Antiquity, 26: 543-545.

1960   With D. L. Oliver. Bougainville populations studied by generalized distance. Actes du VIe Congrès International des Sciences Anthropologiques et Ethnologiques, 497-502.

1960   The distribution of man. Scientific American, 203(3):112-127.

1960   Constitutional types. Encyclopedia of Educational Research, 3rd ed., pp. 333-336. New York: Macmillan.

1960   Estimating population numbers through archaeological and skeletal remains. In R. F. Heizer and S. F. Cook, eds., The Application of Quantitative Methods in Archaeology, Viking Fund Publications in Anthropology, No. 28, pp. 158-185.

1960   Would other "humans" look like us? Science Digest, 47: 53-58 (February).

1959   Boas as statistician. In W. Goldschmidt, ed., The Anthropology of Franz Boas, Memoirs, American Anthropological Association, No. 89: 112-116.

1959   Mankind in the Making. 382 pp. New York: Doubleday.

1957   Variation in external body form in the individual. 116 pp. Dittoed.

1957   With D. L. Oliver. Micro-evolution: cultural elements in physical variation. American Anthropologist, 59: 965-978.

1957   The cranial vault: factors of size and shape. American Journal of Physical Anthropology, 15: 19-48.

1957   La Race Humaine: de la Préhistoire à la Civilisation Gréco-Romaine (translation of Back of History). 383 pp. Paris: Payot.

1957   E. A. Hooton. Encyclopedia Britannica supplement.

1956   Man in the Beginning (English edition of Back of History). London: G. Bell and Sons.

1956   With A. P. Slowey. "Linkage studies" in morphological traits. American Journal of Human Genetics, 8: 154-161.

1955   Universality and variation in human nature. In W. L. Thomas, ed., Yearbook of Anthropology, 1955, pp. 227-236. New York: Wenner-Gren Foundation.

1954   Memorium—Earnest Albert Hooton. American Journal of Physical Anthropology, 12: 445-453.

1954   Back of History: The Story of Our Own Origins. 384 pp. New York: Doubleday.

1953   Correlations of brothers in factor scores. American Journal of Physical Anthropology, 11: 121-140.

1953   Birth interval and body size. Human Biology, 25: 13-20.

1953   The origins of races. UNESCO Courier VI: 5.

1952 A factorial study of constitutional type. American Journal of Physical Anthropology, 10: 91-118.

1952 The study of anthropology. American Anthropologist, 54: 1-7.

1951 Factors of human physique. American Journal of Physical Anthropology, 9: 159-191.

1950 Origin of the human stock: concluding remarks of the chairman. In Origin and Evolution of Man, Cold Spring Harbor Symposia on Quantitative Biology, Vol. XV: 79-86.

1950 Les Païens (translation of The Heathens). 335 pp. Paris: Payot.

1950 Ningen no kita michi (The Road Mankind Has Come—Japanese translation of Mankind So Far). 454 pp. Tokyo: Sogensha.

1949 Body measurements in the light of familial influences. American Journal of Physical Anthropology, 7: 101-108.

1948 Birth order and body size. American Journal of Physical Anthropology, 6: 449-460.

1948 Oracles and omens. Atlantic Monthly, 181: 78-82.

1948 Préhistoire et Histoire Naturelle de l'Homme (translation of Mankind So Far). 331 pp. Paris: Payot.

1948 The Heathens: Primitive Man and His Religions. 306 pp. New York: Doubleday. (English edition, 1949, London: Victor Gollancz).

1946 Man a million years from now. Coronet, 20:39-41 (July).

1946 Can we catch up with our world? New York Times Magazine, July 7.

1946 Editor: Early man in the Far East. A Symposium of the American Association of Physical Anthropologists and the American Anthropological Association, December 28, 1946. Studies in Physical Anthropology, No. 1. 157 pp.

1946 Physical types of the Northeast. In Frederick Johnson, ed., Man in Northeastern North America, Phillips Academy, Robert S. Peabody Foundation of Archaeology Papers, Andover, Vol. 3, pp. 168-177.

1946 El Hombre: Su Origen y Evolución (translation of Mankind So Far). Argentina: Ediciones del Tridente, S. A. C. e I.

1944 Mankind So Far. 319 pp. New York: Doubleday. (Armed Services Edition, 1944; English edition, 1947, London: Sigma Books.)

1943 The racial elements of Melanesia. In C. S. Coon and J. M. Andrews, eds., Studies in the Anthropology of Oceania and Asia. Peabody Museum Papers, XX: 38-49.

1943 Physical anthropology as a technique. American Journal of Physical Anthropology, 1: 355-361.

1942 Head height. Anthropological Briefs, No. 1: 13-15.

1942 The age of Homo sapiens. Scientific Monthly, 54: 552-556.

1942 Fossil man and the origin of races. American Anthropologist, 44: 182-193.

1941 The early Christian Irish: the skeletons at Gallen Priory. Proceedings of the Royal Irish Academy, XLIV, Section C, No. 3: 103-220.

1940 The origins of American Indian race types. In G. C. Vaillant, ed., The Maya and Their Neighbors, pp. 3-9. New York: Appleton-Century.

1940 Physical determination of race. In H. E. Harnes, H. Becker, F. B. Becker, eds., Contemporary Social Theory, pp. 264-278. New York: Appleton-Century.

1938 The prehistoric craniology of Britain. Antiquity 12: 332-339.

1938 The techniques of measuring auricular height in the living. American Journal of Physical Anthropology, XXIV: 185-198.

1938 Crania from Wyoming resembling "Minnesota Man." American Antiquity, 3: 318-326.

1937   The iron age population of Great Britain. American Journal of Physical Anthropology, XXIII: 19-29.

1937   The designation of the principal anthropometric landmarks on the head and skull. American Journal of Physical Anthropology, XXII: 477-494.

1937   Anthropometry of the natives of Arnhem Land and the Australian race problem: analysis and discussion. Peabody Museum Papers, XVI/1: 1-97. Cambridge, Mass.

1936   Some uses of the standard deviation in anthropometry. Human Biology, 8: 592-600.

1936   With H. Hotelling. Measurements and correlations on pelves of Indians of the Southwest. American Journal of Physical Anthropology, XXI: 91-106.

1933   Anthropometry and blood types in Fiji and the Solomon Islands. American Museum of Natural History, Anthropological Papers, XXXIII/IV: 279-339. New York.

1933   Notes on blood-groups and race in the Pacific. Proceedings of the National Academy of Sciences, 19: 494-497.

1932   The skeletal material. In The Swarts ruin, a typical Mimbres site in southwestern New Mexico. Report of the Mimbres Valley expedition seasons of 1924-27. Peabody Museum Papers, XV/1: 115-178. Cambridge, Mass.

The Contributors

Howard L. Bailit is Chairman of the Department of Behavioral Sciences and Community Health in the School of Dental Medicine at the University of Connecticut Health Center in Farmington.

Paul T. Baker is Professor of Anthropology at The Pennsylvania State University and past President of the American Association of Physical Anthropologists.

Hermann K. Bleibtreu is Director of the Museum of Northern Arizona at Flagstaff.

C. Loring Brace is Professor of Anthropology and Curator of Physical Anthropology in the Museum of Anthropology at the University of Michigan.

Mary L. Brace collaborates with her husband in anthropological research.

William Chasko, Jr. is a doctoral student in the Department of Anthropology at the University of New Mexico.

Michael Crichton received his A.B. and M.D. degrees from Harvard University and is a writer and movie director.

Gloria Jean Edynak is an Assistant Professor of Anthropology at Boston University.

Michael Ester is a doctoral student in the Department of Anthropology at Brandeis University.

Jonathan S. Friedlaender is Associate Professor of Anthropology and Associate Curator of Somatology in the Peabody Museum of Archaeology and Ethnology at Harvard University.

J. W. Froehlich is Assistant Professor of Anthropology at the University of New Mexico.

Edward I. Fry is Professor of Anthropology at Southern Methodist University and past President of the American Association of Physical Anthropologists.

Eugene Giles is Professor of Anthropology and Head of the Department at the University of Illinois at Urbana.

Laurie Godfrey is Assistant Professor of Anthropology at Hartwick College, Oneonta, New York.

Henry Harpending is Assistant Professor of Anthropology at the University of New Mexico.

George R. Holcomb is Dean of Research Administration and Professor of Anthropology at the University of North Carolina at Chapel Hill.

David Agee Horr is Assistant Professor of Anthropology at Brandeis University.

Thomas Mercer Hursh is on the staff of the Lawrence Hall of Science at the University of California at Berkeley.

Donald W. Lathrap is Professor of Anthropology at the University of Illinois at Urbana.

A. Vincent Lombardi is Research Associate in Physical Anthropology at the University of Pittsburgh.

Henry M. McHenry is Assistant Professor of Anthropology at the University of California at Davis.

Thomas W. McKern was Professor of Physical Anthropology in the Department of Archaeology at Simon Fraser University.

Donald Mitchell is Assistant Professor of Anthropology at the State University of New York at Buffalo.

Hallam L. Movius, Jr. is Professor of Anthropology and Curator of Palaeolithic Archaeology in the Peabody Museum of Archaeology and Ethnology at Harvard University.

Jill Nash is Assistant Professor of Anthropology at the State University of New York at Buffalo.

Melvin Neville is Assistant Professor of Anthropology at the University of California at Davis.

Eugene Ogan is Associate Professor of Anthropology and Chairman of the Department at the University of Minnesota.

Douglas L. Oliver is Professor Emeritus of Anthropology at Harvard University and Professor of Anthropology (Chair of Pacific Islands) at the University of Hawaii at Honolulu.

G. P. Rightmire is Associate Professor of Anthropology at the State University of New York at Binghamton.

Harold M. Ross is Associate Professor of Anthropology at the University of Illinois at Urbana.

Frank P. Saul is Associate Professor of Anatomy in the Medical College of Ohio at Toledo.

Henry W. Seaford, Jr. is Associate Professor of Anthropology at Dickinson College, Carlisle, Pennsylvania.

Harry L. Shapiro is Chairman Emeritus of the Department of Anthropology at the American Museum of Natural History and Adjunct Professor of Anthropology at Columbia University.

David K. Taylor is a doctoral student in the Department of Anthropology at the University of Arizona.

Stephen Williams is Peabody Professor of American Archaeology and Ethnology and Director of the Peabody Museum of Archaeology and Ethnology at Harvard University.

Mary Anne Whelan is a resident in pediatrics at the Massachusetts General Hospital in Boston.

ONE

Primates: Prolegomena to a Biological Anthropology

With almost the sole exception of C. R. Carpenter, the productive study of the behavior of free-ranging primates is a post-World War II phenomenon, coming into prominence only in the late fifties. From Earnest Hooton's *Man's Poor Relations* (1946) to the present, such research has been considered of great importance to biological anthropologists. Syntheses such as Hooton's and later Irven DeVore's *Primate Behavior: Field Studies of Monkeys and Apes* (1965) become mandatory reading for biological anthropologists and their students. As though making up for lost time when compared with the primate morphological literature, research in the behavior of unfettered primates has become a cottage industry in itself. Yet the basic question—the significance of nonhuman primate behavior in the elucidation of man's own behavior evolution—remains, if not unanswered, at least posing as many difficulties as the interpretation of morphological change through time.

In this section the methodologies of primate evolutionary morphology are discussed in a paper (Godfrey's) which shows that one point we often take for granted about dental reduction in primate evolution may not be so. Among the three behavior papers, the emphasis in Neville's is on field methodology in the collection of observational data and the direct estimation of howler monkey social parameters, while Horr and Ester delineate a computer simulation technique to model the social structure of a quite different primate, the orang-utan. The Braces put forward a stimulating if heterodox "next stage" method of utilizing behavioral data to help understand ourselves.

1. Orang-utan Social Structure: a Computer Simulation

David Agee Horr and Michael Ester

Introduction

In assessing the social behavior and organization of a species, it is important not only to demonstrate how the behaviors are functionally interrelated but also to understand how the particular organization of behaviors serves to adapt the biology of the species to its environment. Within such constraints as reproductive rates, population density and distribution, food consumption, and the resources and limitations of

NOTE: The following paper is an application of computer simulation techniques to a socio-ecological problem; the structure and adaptive function of orang-utan social organization and behavior. The objective of this study is to investigate further a model proposed by Horr (1972, 1975) of the interrelation between orang-utan social behavior, biology, and environment using a simulation strategy and program developed by Ester.[1]

[1]Field research for this project was sponsored by NIMH grant MH-13156 and the Milton Fund of Harvard University. The field work was made possible by the Sabah Game Branch, Stanley de Silva, Game Warden, and the *Dinas Perlindungan dan Perhutaanan Indonesia*, Walman Sinaga, Chief.

The work on computer simulation was made possible by support from a NSF graduate fellowship and the computing time generously provided by the Feldberg Computer Center, Brandeis University, Donna Haverford, Director.

the environment, it is assumed that selection will favor that set of social behaviors which best fits the species to its environment over other such possible sets of behavior. Crook (1969) contains several essays devoted to this topic.

In the study of non-human primates such socio-ecological models are normally generated by and examined in light of large amounts of data collected on the species in its natural habitat. Such studies of the "socio-demographic" system are often easiest to do on those troop-living species where numbers of individuals of all age-sex categories are readily observed interacting together. Thus, many of the findings of primate socio-ecology have been worked out on baboons, macaques, langurs, and other highly visible, troop-living species. Computer simulation techniques can be very important in evaluating socio-ecological models of troop-living primates by offering data of a type and quantity difficult or impossible to obtain in the field, in particular data relating to the operation of a social system over a long period of time. However, in those species that do not live in large, cohesive groups, the problem of understanding how social behavior, biology, and environment intermesh can become much greater, and it may be even more important for the researcher to explore alternate strategies such as simulation to test out his hypotheses.

The orang-utan *(Pongo pygmaeus)* represents an extreme degree of social dispersal for a higher non-human primate (Horr 1972, 1975). Not only are orangs rather widely dispersed in their habitat, but seldom are more than two or three orangs together for any length of time, so that cohesive close-knit troop structure as normally understood for primates is not present. A further complication is that the orang life span is relatively long so that longitudinal data on development are difficult to obtain from individual orang-utans. Even cross-sectional data on development and longevity are sparse due to the small numbers of individuals in any age-sex category within a particular area.

In view of this situation, the researcher is faced with a difficult, sometimes insurmountable, problem. Field work with orang-utans — locating them, habituating them, and observing them — represents a formidable investment of money, time and effort. Gathering field data on a large sample is a lengthy and expensive undertaking. To determine how accurately initial hypotheses portray actual conditions, it is necessary to pursue highly controlled observation of a large number of individuals. Given the nature of orang-utan social organization this would require study over a large spatial area. Also, while some observation through time is possible and cohort analysis can be used, it would be necessary to collect data over generations of orang-utans to determine whether the postulated nature of social contact has the proposed adaptive implications over time. Finally, supposing that a correlation between a specific kind of social organization and a population level could be demonstrated, this would only establish co-occurrence, an insufficient basis to claim that the social pattern described is more adaptive than any other. The problem of collecting demographic and developmental data on orangs, then, makes it useful to have techniques which allow testing of hypotheses that would otherwise require large amounts of long-term data for validation.

One such strategy for dealing with this situation is the use of computer simulation to test whether the social system as constructed from original data will function to maintain a viable population over relatively long periods of time. In this method the researcher constructs a model of behavior and ecology using actual field data and observed or inferred relationships among behavior, biology, and habitat. The computer runs a corresponding program of this model in a series of fixed time intervals or iterations over a specified duration. In the present study each iteration of the model represents behavioral and ecological activities during one month and to test the feasibility of our model these operations continue until 600 iterations (fifty years) have been completed. If, at the end of the simulation period, population results are produced which are inconsistent with what we know to be the case in the field, this would imply that certain of the postulated assumptions or relationships are in error. If population results conform to what would be a realistic outcome, we have increased our confidence that our conception of this system is correct.

Beyond this test of a basic model of behavior, biology, and ecology, however, computer simulation is useful as an experimental technique. The assertion that a behavior is adaptive unfortunately often relies on the ultimate justification that it is adaptive because it is there. With the opportunity to alter behavioral patterns in a model it is possible to test the hypothesis that the species' organization and behavior as represented by the model is the most adaptive arrangement for its biology and habitat. By altering certain aspects of the original model, such as range size, birth rates, or food supply, one can test to see the effects of such changes. In this paper, for example, inspection of the results after fifty-year simulation periods has given us an indication of what size male range is essential for population survival and whether significantly increasing or diminishing male range size produces a more or less adaptive arrangement.

Before proceeding to a discussion of the simulation strategy and program developed by Ester, it is necessary that we give a very brief summary of the salient characteristics of orang-utan social structure.

Orang-Utan Social Structure

The simulation model developed in this paper is based on a socio-ecological model constructed by Horr from data he collected during more than 1,450 hours of direct observation on free-ranging orang-utans in primary lowland dipterocarp forests at two sites in eastern Borneo (Fig. 1). Orang-utans here have a widely dispersed and diffuse social organization. In Borneo, they are typically encountered singly or in small groups amounting to three or four individuals at the very most. Not only is group size small, but, unlike gibbons, for example, persisting groups are not complete breeding units containing an adult male, adult female and offspring. Instead, the normal persisting unit is either a solitary individual or an adult female with one or more still-dependent offspring. In addition to being small in numbers, these primary population units are not normally in daily contact with each other, and in fact the number, frequency and duration of contacts between primary population units is very small when compared with troop-living primates. This scattered organization is in some ways reminiscent of chimpanzees. However, adult orang males do not travel in groups at any time under normal conditions, and in general all of the primary units remain more or less isolated from each other most of the time, though contacts of a few to several hours may occur infrequently. The longest contact times between otherwise independently ranging units are between mating pairs when an adult male and female may stay together for several days, traveling and foraging. However, even such contacts may be brief in duration.

There are three basic types of orang-utan population unit. The

Figure 1. Map of Borneo showing study areas, 1967-1971

largest is the adult female and her still-dependent offspring. Plate 1. This group numbers from two to possibly four individuals. Solitary-ranging adult males, Plate 2, and independent juveniles, Plate 3, of either sex are the other two types of population unit.

Each unit has a characteristic range size and area. Ranges may have considerable overlap, and there is no "territory" in the ethological sense of the term, though adult males often displace each other through threat or other aggressive behavior. There are two basic range patterns: females range over small areas, not more than about 1/4 square mile in size, while males have much larger ranges. Although the size of adult male ranges is not precisely known, two kinds

Plate 1: Adult female with older female infant.

of evidence point to a much larger range than that of adult females. The first is the infrequency with which an adult male reappears in the range of a given female and the relatively short time he spends there. Second, when males were followed, they moved relatively rapidly over an area covering more than one female range, and in one instance a male was followed for a straight line distance of nearly two miles in 8 days. That males do not travel infinite distances in the jungle was shown by their periodic reappearance every few months in the same adult female's range. In the original interpretation of these data, it was estimated that a male range must be considerably larger than that of a female, probably at least as much as two square miles (not two miles square). Old adult males have considerably restricted ranges, apparently as a result of lessened agility and perhaps of diminished sexual activity.

As described below, the breeding cycle of adult female orangs is rather long. One factor contributing to the larger size of the adult

Plate 2: Fully mature adult male.

male range is probably his search for receptive females in order to maximize his breeding potential. Since female ranges are conservative, in the sense that they remain in the same relatively small area throughout the annual cycle, males can maximize their breeding potential by moving through several adult female ranges. As the males move, they announce their presence through loud contact vocalizations so that any receptive female can know that an adult male is present, and adult females have been observed to respond enthusiastically to such calls.

Plate 3: Young semi-independent juvenile female.

The development cycle of orang-utans is relatively long. Adult females begin breeding at about age 7 and thereafter breed approximately 2½ to 3 years after the birth of their last offspring, including a 275-day gestation period (Napier and Napier 1967). Adult males are probably sexually competent around age 8. For the first 18-24 months after birth young orangs cling to their mother through most of the day, certainly when the female is moving. During the second and third year developing orangs become more independent, including learning how to make their own sleeping nests, and it is this growing physical independence which allows the adult females to reproduce again.

Independent juveniles adopt the ranging pattern characteristic of their sex. Juvenile females move from a nearly co-terminous range with their mothers to a partly or largely contiguous one. By age seven they have set up their own independent range and begin to breed to create their own female-offspring units. Juvenile males, Plate 4, beginning around age 3 to 3½ stay in much less close association with

Plate 4: Young semi-independent juvenile male.

their mothers and range over increasingly wider areas in anticipation of their own adult male ranges.

Life span in the wild is not known. The *Orang-Utan Studbook* (Yerkes Regional Primate Research Center, 1969) lists the four oldest captive orangs of known age as a male 50, a female 50, a female 32 and a male 20. This does not necessarily tell us very much about life expectancy in the wild but it makes it unlikely that, subjected to the exigencies of free-ranging conditions, orangs live much more than 35 to 40 years.

The orang-utans in this study inhabit primary lowland rain forest. Their diet consists primarily of fruits and leaves plus a large amount of bamboo shoots and inner bark. Flowers, insects, and other items constitute a much smaller portion of their diet. Meat or egg eating was never observed in the wild. Although the bulk of the diet is leaves and other vegetable matter, fruits are very important because of the specialized nutritive elements they provide. Part of the answer to the dispersed social group pattern of orangs is certainly the distribution of tropical vegetation and the nature of equatorial fruiting patterns. Unlike northern environments where vegetation is normally represented by many individuals of relatively few species, tropical forests are characterized by having many hundreds of plant species, but relatively few examples of a given species in a particular area. In addition, lack of marked seasonality does not produce strongly concentrated fruiting seasons or seasons devoid of fruit. This has two effects on orangs: basic vegetable foods and fruit are available throughout the year, but fruits are usually thinly scattered although during any given month some species may be in fruit somewhere within the orang's range. Since orangs can strip a tree of fruit in a short period of time, the most adaptive organization is one which spreads orangs around and does not concentrate them in small areas as would be the case with troop organization. This pattern is modified to some extent by the existence, in Sabah, of two "seasons" during which fruiting is more intense than other times. The most prominent takes place between November and January, while a lesser "season" takes place between April and June, roughly six months apart. These "seasons" are determined by periods of increasing wetness as opposed to the temperature and light-related alternations found in temperate and northern climates.

An additional contributing factor to the lack of troop structure in Bornean orangs is the lack of predators large enough to threaten females and young. The only predators of sufficient size to be of danger are terrestrial, and hence there is no protective function to be served by adult males and little need for them to associate permanently with adult females. Predation is a factor for younger juvenile males who are moving away from their mothers, since a large clouded leopard *(Felis nebulosa)* might kill an unwary juvenile, but this would not materially affect population size or the breeding rate since males range through the areas of several females and thus can insure that they become impregnated when receptive.[2]

To summarize, the distribution of Bornean orangs can best be visualized as a series of adult female-offspring units in nearly invariant 1/4 square-mile ranges scattered through the jungle with a certain amount of overlap of ranges in some instances. When overlap occurs, female offspring units may be in contact with each other briefly — usually for periods of less than half a day. Adult males travel greater distances through the jungle, so that they appear in the range of a given adult female at periodic intervals, stay for one or several days, and then move on to the ranges of other adult females, so that several weeks or months may elapse before the same adult male reappears in the range of any given female. These adult male ranges, or ranging patterns, overlap in space though infrequently in time. Occasionally two adult males will appear in the same female's range at the same time, but this was less frequently observed.

The pattern of organization described above, in particular the lack of tight-knit troop structure, is unusual for a higher non-human primate. Horr has postulated that this is adaptive because the dispersal reduces the possibility of habitat overload in rainforest environment allowing females and young to restrict their movements to relatively small areas which increases survival and maximizes female reproductive success. The wide range of the adult male prevents him from overloading the female areas and allows him to maximize his reproductive success by contacting the largest possible number of adult females, and this is important both due to the dispersed nature of the females and their long reproductive cycle.

The above model is consistent with the available orang field data from Borneo. Two basic questions remain: 1) Would such an organization function over time to maintain population size at an appropriate level, and 2) can one show that this postulated biological system is more adaptive for orang-utans than one in which one or more factors are different. The simulation techniques used in this paper are particularly well suited to answering these questions. However, since simulation is still a recent method, before we move to a discussion of the de-

[2]In Sumatra, where predation danger is greater, there is evidence that adult males associate more closely with adult females and offspring. MacKinnon, pers. comm.

tails of our model we will furnish a brief discussion of the technique itself.

Computer Simulation

Within the last decade, advances in technology and applied mathematics have made simulation techniques available for complex problem solving. Shubik (1960: 909) provides a definition:

> A simulation of a system or an organism is the operation of a model or simulator which is a representation of the system or organism. The model is amenable to manipulation which would be impossible, too expensive, or impractical to perform on the entity it portrays. The operation of the model can be studied and, from it, properties concerning the behavior of the actual system or its subsystems can be inferred.

Our discussion will be limited to simulation that 1) employs mathematical and logical models, 2) can be performed on digital computers, and 3) characterizes dynamic systems (as opposed to static or equilibrium alternatives).

The momentum of development behind computer simulation has in large part stemmed from its potential to substitute for one or more of the procedures associated with scientific inquiry: observation, theory formation, prediction, and experimentation. In the study of social behavior, it is often not possible to fully complete these steps: observation of certain real world events may be extremely difficult or impossible, social phenomena have been notoriously resistant to the concise elegance of analytic solutions, and prediction and verification are scarce commodities because the luxury of experimentation to test competing hypotheses is rarely if ever afforded in the field. The orang problem discussed previously presents an excellent example of these problems.

If processes or events can be approximated by computer models, it is possible to compensate in part for the absence of the above procedures by turning to simulated results. For example it is possible to generate a large data base for inductive types of analysis. Computer simulation can also be of considerable heuristic value in theory construction. Rather than working under constraints of a strictly mathematical model, computer simulation permits more freedom both in the complexity of the model and the nature of its construction.

Finally, if one is willing to accept a computer model of social behavior, almost any variable within the modeled system may be modified so that results from testing alternative assumptions can be collected. From this standpoint simulation provides much the same opportunity available in the laboratory—the manipulation of data abstracted from the real world in an ideal context.

It would be misleading in the extreme to leave the impression that computer simulation is a problem-free approach that can somehow displace traditional methods of investigation. Obviously, simulation is very much dependent on the store of data and operational concepts that are available.

What do simulations simulate? It is perhaps most accurate and useful to say that simulations simulate theories. This departs from a popular attitude that simulations replicate the real world. The only way this latter position seems tenable is if one is willing to ignore the role of the basic assumptions on which selection, measurement and explanation are based. Where the *consensus* of instrumentation may permit the "hard sciences" (including their applied derivatives) to do precisely this, behavioral science cannot so easily do the same. Such fundamental endeavors as recognition and definition are still characterized by reformulation and constant controversy. What this means in the present discussion is 1) a great number of research problems are concerned with making qualitative distinctions, a line of inquiry for which computer simulation is wholly inappropriate and 2) when simulation is applied it may be extremely difficult to achieve mutual agreement about how to operationalize basic variables and concepts.

A comparable situation arises when we come to a key term in simulation: system. Virtually all simulations are directed at modeling systems. A system can be defined as "an aggregation or assemblage of entities joined in some regular interaction or interdependence" (Gordon 1969:1). Though the ability to deal with the vast complexities which systems can display is a distinct advantage, it is also a limitation. As a general rule of thumb, the success of simulation will be proportional to the systematization of the object of study. As basic as this characteristic is to simulation, the existence of a system cannot be asserted, but is rather a speculation about the subject of study open to verification (Buckley 1967). Again, social scientists should not simply dismiss this problem. Frequently it has been pointed out that many social phenomena lack such interconnections and interdependence (i.e., Sahlins 1968), and many subjects which interest social and behavioral scientists may not conform to a systems approach and would not be profitably explored through simulation.

Systems and Variables. Simulation emphasizes the importance of explicit problem formulation. This is nowhere more evident than in setting out the system and its environment, and choosing variables to be included in a model. Since in the orang-utan problem we are interested in the relationship between demographic, social, and ecological factors, the study will require such biological data as birth rate, gestation period, sexual receptivity, habitat structure, and other factors. Knowledge of individual ability for change of location and specific subsistence needs will also play a part. Contact between individuals must also be accounted for. At the broadest boundary of the system, there is the network defined by a number of interacting individuals and their habitat. At the opposite extreme are certain organically fixed attributes of the animal itself. In making this dichotomy between system and environment, nothing has been ruled out of bounds for the study. What goes on within and without the system are still both important. However, in examining environmental variables, we will only consider them with respect to their impact on the system; the impact of the system on the environment is not of prime importance.

The more painstaking judgments of inclusion and exclusion arise at the next juncture, the selection of variables. Depending on the evaluation of a variable, three things may be done with it: include it, pool it with other variables, or exclude it. We are not seeking to label a variable as absolutely relevant or irrelevant. Rather, we are looking for a list of variables whose completeness and assignment of importance is appropriate to answering the questions posed by our research interests. How far down along the list one is willing to go towards lower level, contributing variables, hinges on the resources one is willing to mobilize for the sake of increased precision and control over the set of known variables.

We may divide the variables that are used in simulation into three types: (1) Constants, whose values remain invariant during simulation; (2) Constant-dependent variables whose values may differ at any point in simulation as a result of the arithmetic or logical transformation of constants; and (3) stochastic, or probabilistic variables.

Deterministic models are constructed using only the first two types of variables. Given the same model and the same initial conditions, a deterministic simulation will produce exactly the same results every time it is run. However, there are many instances when a deterministic solution would not be satisfactory or possible. The most obvious example in the orang-utan case is the sex identity of an offspring. No deterministic explanation can be offered to assure whether a mother will produce a male or female. The same is true for the mortality of any individual. In both cases the variable behaves randomly. Further, an outcome may not be inherently random, but still be impossible to treat in a deterministic fashion. Male orang-utans have been inferred to maintain a two-square mile or greater range. But no comparable information is available to determine which particular location in his range he will occupy at any point in time. There might be fixed rules for this behavior, but such information is not available. The outcome must be treated as a random variable. Supposing that a deterministic solution were available for male location and other movement and search activities, introducing the order of complexity necessary to reduce these to fixed variables may not be worth the trouble. Under certain conditions then, one will want to consider the case where a single variable has not one but a number of possible outcomes.

Monte Carlo is the term often used for those methods which deal with stochastic variables. Since stochastic variables lead us to probability theory, some elementary first principles of probability may be helpful.

Let R denote the entire range of value positions of a variable X, and let R_1 be a subset of those positions. Suppose that n observations are made, v of which belong to R_1. The ratio or frequency of the event where X belonged to R_1 would be v/n. A peculiar and valuable regularity is that as n increases the relation v/n becomes more or less constant. The idea behind this is that as the sample of observations from the population size N increases, v/n comes closer to the population V/N. This tendency is called the Central Limit Theorem.

V/N is of course the ideal or true frequency of X occurring in subset R_1. But with only our sample n, we would still like a number to represent this ideal value. We call this number the *probability* of X belonging to R_1 and express it $P(R_1)$. Going back to R, we can maintain that the ratio of X belonging to R is 1, since R is all the possible values. Hence $P(R)=1$. This being the case, for R_1, it can always be expected that: $0 \leq P(R_1) \leq 1$.

We can apply these rudiments of probability to the sex identity of an orang-utan offspring. R consists of two subsets, Males (M) and

Females (F), so that P(M)+P(F)=1. Expressed differently F=$\overline{\text{M}}$, and P(M)+P(M)=1. Assuming there is an even chance for either sex, then P(M)=.50. If we let all values less than and including .50 represent males, and larger values stand for females, a random selection of X between 0 and 1 inclusive would characterize the determination of sexual identity as we have defined it — each offspring has an equal likelihood of being male or female. This method would likewise be applicable for mortality or male position within his range. In the latter case, we would simply assign each Location a subset of 1/9 of the total 2¼ square mile area.

We can next ask what happens when we introduce the factor of time? For sex differentiation, the answer is nothing. The probability remains fixed, regardless of the state of the model. This is not true of mortality. As the individual orang-utan changes age, the chances of his survival change also. In this instance, we know that the mortality probability will vary, but we have only a rough idea of what the values should be. Estimation is one solution to the problem. For females, the chances of death increase with age. Early years have a characteristically low rate of mortality up to the point of maturity.

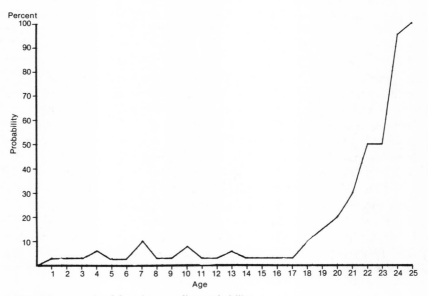

Figure 2. Graph of female mortality probability

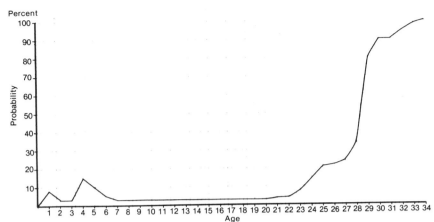

Figure 3. Graph of male mortality probability

Mortality then begins to oscillate, corresponding to the occurence of childbirth. Finally it slopes upward as they approach a maximum age.

From the important points of birth, child-bearing, and maximum age, shown in Figure 2, an intervening slope between the points has been drawn. The same has been done for the males in Figure 3, though their case is somewhat different. Young adolescent males are already free ranging though inexperienced. Falls, possible predation by clouded leopards, and general problems caused by competition with other males might take a larger toll on male lives at this age. With increasing age these dangers diminish, consequently reducing the mortality probability. There is a final upswing in mortality as males reach old age and approach a maximum age. In fixing these curves to the absolute values shown in Figures 2 and 3, we have arbitrarily selected a base mortality rate of 3% probability that an orang-utan will die in any given year. This must be considered only a rough approximation, not directly obtained from orang-utan material, but from the very meager comparative data on other non-human primate species and mammals.

Time figures in another important way. Male position within his range, for instance, depends heavily upon the iteration interval selected. As it is, we have chosen monthly intervals. Not only could a male be anywhere in his range, but since this variable is an input to food demand and birth rate, the presence of a male should be felt

at several locations for each iteration. Had we chosen a weekly interval, the same would have been true, but on a reduced scale. Had we
found it desirable to proceed on a day by day basis, where his movement would have been less than the total range, the nature of the
probability problem itself would have changed, and we would have
modeled the progression of events as a Markov chain.

INITIAL CONDITIONS.

In addition to operating values of the model, we must specify
starting values. In terms of the real world system, this means breaking into the process at some point in time, and using the state of the
system at that juncture as the initial conditions for the performance of
the model. For some situations this is quite simple. In factory production models, for example, this involves no more than starting from an
idle state. In behavioral situations, the issue of initial conditions is
not so obvious or straightforward. Clearly in the orang-utan case, an
idle or empty starting condition is impossible, since zero population
begets no additional population. Likewise, a condition where males
and females are located so that they would fail to come into contact
would produce the same undesirable result; a result that not only is
uninteresting in terms of model performance, but would yield unrealistic data to compare with existing, real-world orang-utan populations.

Consequently, we use whatever observations can be marshaled to
approximate initial values. Although we are injecting estimation into
the working of the model, there are relatively good data for setting
the initial conditions for the orang-utan model. Data on the population, sex, identity, and ages are available for three square miles.
Before a computer run of the program, a corresponding "animal"
composition was read into a central three square miles of the simulated territory based on observed distribution of real orang-utans.

The ORANG Model

A flowchart of the ORANG program is presented in figs. 4-7. It is
divided into three principal blocks, one corresponding to each of the
three main components of the program: the Location, Male, and Female subsystems. The job of each block is to process all the existing
entities of its type. Thus, for example, the Female block handles all

operations relating to adult females such as updating a female's age, determining her sexual receptivity, etc., as well as all those operations pertaining to any still-dependent offspring. Though the flowchart and actual program used are divided in this manner, this does not mean that the blocks are independent of one another. Attributes that change in one block are available and crucial to the operations of other blocks.

Several conventions are used in the flowchart: diamonds represent computer controls, ovals decision processes, rectangles equivalence and mathematical operations, and circles program markers. It is worth noting that this is not a "working" flowchart (i.e., a flowchart which could translate directly into a programming language), but rather is the clearest way in which to convey the program structure. To augment the flowchart, the following discussion will elaborate on the major sections of the program and the most important variables.

A. LOCATIONS (FIG. 4)

1. *Definition*   The model uses a matrix 28 squares by 28 squares in size. Each square is a "location," defined as the home range of an adult female or female-infant unit, and the size of this location is estimated to be ¼ square mile. All spatial operations are built around these locations or combinations of locations. For example, in our original model, an adult male range is estimated as nine locations in size. The total size of the matrix is 784 locations or 196 square miles. Only a small portion of this matrix is used by the initial condition. However, the program checks each location in every iteration whether the location is occupied or not.

2. *Food supply in location*   The model is designed to simulate uniform, "normal" habitat conditions. It is assumed that a location contains adequate food supply for year-round maintenance of an adult female and her offspring plus occasional visits by other animals; adult males, other females (where ranges overlap) and juveniles.

The food supply in any given location is determined by two factors. First, as orangs eat, plants continue to grow, producing leaves, new bark, etc. More important, however, is the question of fruit supplies. As mentioned earlier, fruits are a much more limited resource than leaves and bark, and they are relatively more important to the orang diet. Fruit, then, is depleted at a faster rate than leaves, and it does not regenerate at continuously high levels. However, at the Lokan

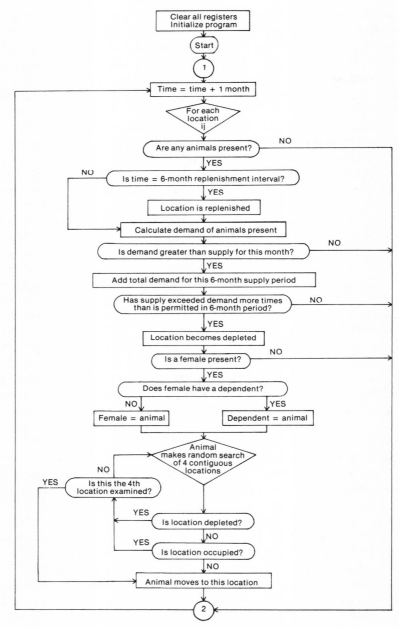

Figure 4. Flowchart of ORANG model. Section 1, Locations Block

site there were two times of the year when fruit tended to reappear in abundance. These fruiting "seasons" were approximately six months apart. To simplify this complex situation for purposes of the model, we allow a location to deplete over six-month periods at rates based on the numbers and kinds of orang-utans present.

Where no orang-utans are present, there would be a zero demand on a location. As orangs inhabit a location they contribute to a drain on the available food in that location at a given rate estimated for each type of animal.

3. *Depletion rates* Demand values are estimated for each type of orang-utan and are applied against locations on monthly schedules.

Adult males and females are each given values of .50. Pregnancies, infants, or dependents, are each given .25.

These demand values are useful only in terms of the depletion rules given below.

4. *Depletion rules* For each month, the kinds of orangs present in a location are determined and the sum of their demand values are calculated. Total demand values of 0-0.75, 1.00-1.50, and 1.75+ have corresponding depletion values of 0, 1, and 2. Depletion values are summed over a six month period. If, for any monthly iteration of the program, the sum of the depletion values since the last time the location was replenished becomes 8, the location is depleted and will remain depleted until the next "fruiting season," at which point it is reset to zero. Should a location remain undepleted by the time a new six month replenishment occurs, the location is still reset to zero, that is, savings from one six-month period are not applied to the subsequent period. If a location does not deplete, there is no effect on the animals resident there, and the program moves on to the next location. If a location becomes depleted, however, this does affect resident animals by requiring some form of relocation.

5. *Relocation rules* If a location is depleted this implies that it can no longer support the animals resident there. In a real world system, two outcomes would be likely: one or more animals would leave or, in the extreme case, one or more would die. Since mortality due to starvation was not observed in the field study, and we have no other knowledge of the circumstances under which this would occur, this model is limited to the consequence of emigration in instances of location depletion. The matrix used is of sufficient size to permit nearly unlimited emigration over the relatively short, 50-year simulation cycle in response to pressures of overpopulation.

If a location depletes during a six-month supply period, the program searches the age-sex composition of the resident animals. Adult males are disregarded because they leave at the end of the month in any case. If a resident female has a dependent offspring greater than 2½ years old with her, the dependent is evicted and it moves randomly one location away from her. Its demand value would then be calculated for the new location in the next monthly iteration.

If the female has no dependent, she then makes a random search of four locations contiguous to her own. If the first such location is neither depleted nor occupied, she will occupy it henceforth. If the location is either depleted or occupied, she will continue to search up to four such locations. If none of these modifications is available, she will occupy the fourth such location until the next monthly iteration. If the location replenishes or can continue to support her, she will remain there; if not, she will resume her search of four new contiguous locations.

Once the supply status of each location is determined, and any habitat-dependent changes in animal location are made, the computer then moves on to a new set of considerations.

Under normal conditions, of course, we would expect that location-hopping by females will be unnecessary. This does, however, allow us to assess the effects of overpopulation on spatial distribution, since at the end of each run the computer prints out the matrix showing actual locations of orangs.

B. ADULT MALE RANGE AND REPRODUCTIVE STRATEGY (Fig. 5)

1. *Range size* Unlike the adult female, whose range is reliably fixed at ¼ square mile, the range of the adult male is only estimated. For purposes of simulation, a fixed size is estimated for adult males of 2¼ square miles, or 9 locations. Although the original estimate of minimum male range was 2 square miles, 2¼ square miles is chosen because it permits a square range, three locations on a side. Although in the wild male orangs most certainly do not move in quadratic ranges, this is the best approximation possible for our matrix.

2. *Ranging pattern and effects* In this model adult males basically do one thing: search for receptive females. In this process a number of things happen to males or are caused by them which in the program occur at various points in each monthly iteration.

a. *Mortality probability* The first stochastic process occurs when the male's age is computed for the iteration. If adding one month to the

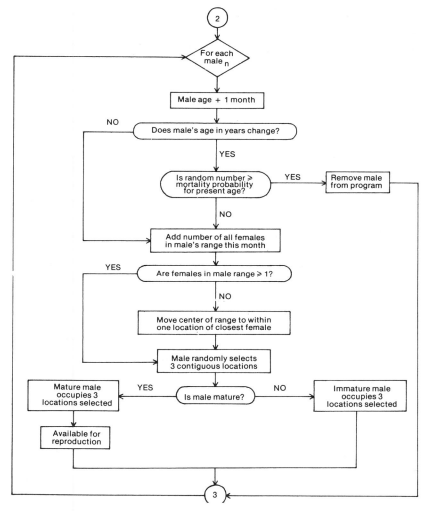

Figure 5. Flowchart of ORANG model. Section 2, Male Block

male's present age causes a change in his age in years, a random number is chosen and this is compared against the probability of his dying at that age. If the number is less than or equal to the probability of death, he is removed from the program and recorded as a death for that simulation year. Male mortality probability is estimated in Figure 3.

b. Searching behavior   If the male is still alive, the computer searches his 9-location range and adds up the number of adult females present. If the sum is 1 or greater, the male then chooses 3 locations randomly whether a female is present in one of the three or not. If the sum is 0, the male then searches the entire matrix for the female nearest him, moves the center of his 9-location range randomly 1 location away from that female and then chooses 3 locations randomly from his new range, whether the new female happens to be in one of those 3 locations or not.

This approximates postulated behavior in the wild. If males do not locate females within their normal range, then it is likely that they would move their ranges to incorporate another adult female.

It should be noted that male-male competition is not built into this model so that in addition to possible male range overlap, males may occupy the same square upon occasion without displacing one another.

c. Demand and reproduction   The final step in this portion of the program is to register the effect of the male's new position within his location. The computer checks the male's age. If he is of breeding age he is now available to any female in the locations he now occupies and his demand value of .50 is registered. If he is not yet of breeding age, he simply registers his .50 demand value. Male breeding age is estimated as 96 months birth age, again disregarding differential reproductive potential in this first-generation simulation model.

Once all of the living males have been processed in this iteration, the computer moves to the females.

C. FEMALE – OFFSPRING OPERATIONS (Figs. 6 and 7)

This section of the program is in many ways the most complicated since it involves not only the fate of the adult females, but determines most of the changes in population composition and size as well. As with the adult males, the computer searches the living females in numerical order and completes this operation for all females before moving on.

1. *Female range*   Female-offspring units, like males, range as independent units, although normally they remain within a single location unless forced to move by depletion as described earlier. Female ranges are not exclusive. Not only are males allowed, but two females may occupy the same location, though such overlap would be limited in time due to ultimate depletion.

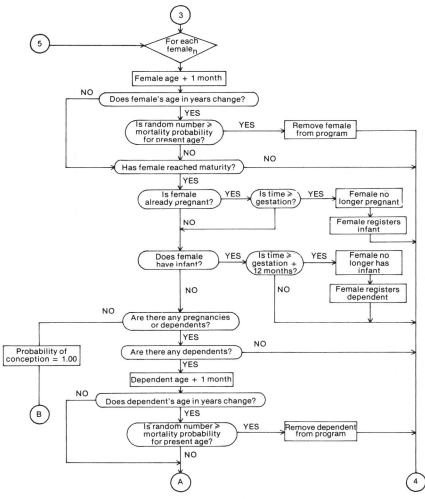

Figure 6. Flowchart of ORANG model. Section 3, Female Block, part 1

As stated earlier, the model implies that a location is adequate to the support of a female-offspring unit on a permanent basis. However, the model also implies that male-female association within a single location is not feasible on a permanent basis due to depletion, as well as male reproductive strategy.

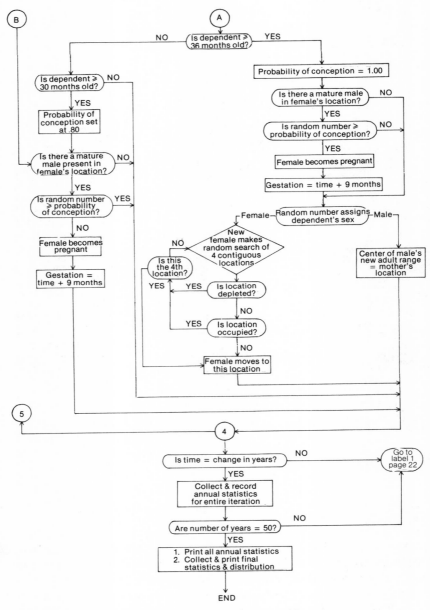

Figure 7. Flowchart of ORANG model, Section 3 (cont'd)

Based on birth spacing as built into this model, a resident female-offspring unit may have the following compositions.

An adult female alone

A pregnant female

A female and infant

A female and dependent juvenile

A female with infant and dependent juvenile

A pregnant female with a dependent juvenile

None of these combinations would exceed a depletion value of 1.00 per month or a depletion value of 6 per 6-month period, well within the depletion value limit of 8 per 6-month period.

2. *Female mortality* Mortality for living females is determined in exactly the same way as for males, with some females stochastically removed from the program at this point. The estimated mortality probabilities for females are given in figure 2.

Once the female's age and viability are determined, the program then determines if she is of reproductive age. If not, her demand value of .50 is registered against her location and the program moves to the next female.

3. *Gestation and birth* If the female is of breeding age, the computer checks whether she is pregnant. If so it adds the present month to the number of months she has been pregnant. If this equals 9 months, the pregnancy is changed to an infant although the demand value does not change.

If the female is not pregnant the program determines whether she already has an infant (in this model the two are mutually exclusive since birth rates are based on a minimum of 39-month lapses between conceptions). If she has an infant and its new month age is greater than one year, the infant is registered as a dependent, if not it remains an infant.

If the female does not have an infant the program determines whether she is pregnant or has a dependent. If neither is the case and a mature male is present in her location, she will conceive and her demand value for the succeeding month would change from .50 to .75. If no male is present, the program will move to the next female.

If the female is pregnant but has no dependent she registers her total demand value and the program moves on.

If the female has a dependent, the dependent's new monthly age is computed and its mortality probability is checked. If the dependent survives, the program determines whether the dependent is three years old or greater. If it is not, the program continues directly onto the next step. If the dependent is three years or greater, the program assigns a sex identity to the dependent and performs the necessary operations of defining a range appropriate for a juvenile of that sex.

Finally, breeding and conception are possible if certain conditions are met. One requirement, of course, is that a mature male be present at a female's location. If this should be the case and the female has no offspring at this time, she then becomes pregnant. If a female has a dependent that is 30 months of age or older, breeding with a mature male is again permissible. Pregnancy is not completely automatic in this instance, however. The probability of conception is set so that there is a .80 probability of conception.[3]

Completing the female section of the program brings the computer to the end of the behaviors we have attempted to model. After recording appropriate information pertaining to the changes that have transpired during the present iteration, the program returns to 1 and repeats this above cycle for succeeding "months." Once 600 monthly iterations (50 years) are completed the computer collects and prints annual population data for the 50 years and also prints the final population position within the matrix as well as an actual distribution matrix (Figs. 16 and 17).

Results

THE ORIGINAL MODEL

Using the ORANG model just described, six runs were made on a PDP-10 computer. The duration of each simulation was fifty years, or roughly four generations of orang-utans. Though it might have been desirable to gather additional samples of the model's behavior, the considerable size of the program[4] and the necessity of testing alternative versions of the model made this impossible without over-taxing the facilities available to us. None-the-less our results represent considerable experience with the model's performance. Though statistics were gathered only at annual intervals, the simulation proceeded on

[3]We are aware that this model "loads the dice" in favor of reproduction and that no account is taken of an expected reproductive success differential for individual males.

[4]The program is comprised of more than 500 executable Fortran IV statements. Through the computing time for a simulation of fifty years varied with the population size that was maintained through time, most runs took about 20 minutes.

monthly intervals so that a fifty-year run amounted to 600 iterations of the flow chart shown in figs. 4-7. The six runs of the original model, taken together, constitute 3,600 such monthly cycles.

The change in each simulated population over time for the initial runs of the original model may be seen in Figure 8. It should be repeated that each of these six runs employed both the same model and initial animal conditions. The only difference between runs is a change in the random numbers that are used by the various stochastic operations. Thus the variation of outcomes from run to run may be attributed solely to this modification. As can be seen, at fifty years, three of the populations are roughly the size of the initial population, two are somewhat larger, while only one shows a consistent trend towards smaller numbers. As a reasonable characteristic of a normal orang-utan system, we would expect population size to be relatively stable with persistent tendencies towards increasing or decreasing population being absent.

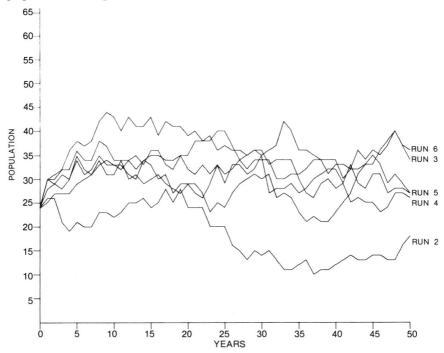

Figure 8. Graph of population over time: six runs of the original model

The general impression given by the population trends indicate that the model conforms to this expectation. Similarly a graph of the mean populations for the six runs (Figure 9) would lead us to believe that the original model we have constructed produces population figures that would be realistic in an actual orang-utan system.

In addition to what may be understood from inspection of the graphs, we can provide a more precise basis for our conclusions if we statistically assess whether the fluctuations in population size over the 50-year periods indicate actual positive or negative trends, or whether they may be attributed to the elements of chance introduced by the stochastic processes in the model design. Two relatively simple tests have been applied: 1) a test of the means to determine if the total change through time is significant and 2) a "runs" test to monitor the appropriateness of the test of the means.

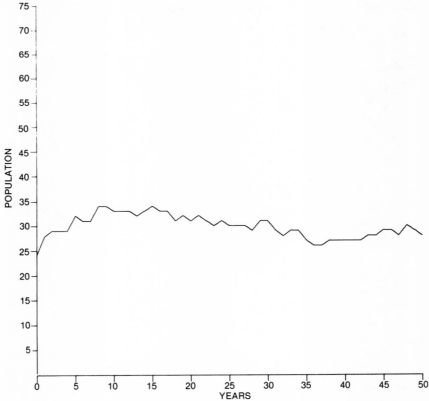

Figure 9. Graph of population over time: mean of runs for original model

In analyzing change through time, however, we run into the problem that annual population values are not independent from one another. The population in year ten, for example, is dependent upon the population in previous years. As a result, it would be inappropriate directly to compare the values we have graphed between intervals or between runs. The method we have used to standardize the data is to convert the population figures to a table of first differences (Table 1). This table was constructed by subtracting the population at any given time in a run from the population at the year preceding it. Hence, for the first run, the value for the first year shows that there was an increase of one orang-utan over the population at the beginning of the run. Similarly we find that during year nine of the same run, there was a decrease of three animals since year eight.

With reference to Table 1 an important question we can ask is whether the total change in time is significant. If our expectancy that there should be very minor change is correct, then the mean of the annual fluctuations for each run should be close to zero. If, on the other hand, we are dealing with either a substantial positive or negative trend, then the mean should be either greater or smaller than zero respectively.

For each sample, then, we tested the null hypothesis

$$H_0 : \overline{X} = 0$$

against the alternative hypothesis

$$H_1 : \overline{X} \neq 0$$

where $\overline{X}$ is the mean of the first differences. Since in this case we actually favor $\overline{X} = O$, we wanted to minimize the chance of accepting the null hypothesis when it was false. Consequently, instead of adopting the classic .05 significance level, we increased the area of rejection by setting the rejection region at one standard deviation from the mean, or $\alpha = 0.32$. Using the test statistic

$$Z = \frac{\overline{X} - \mu}{\sigma_{\overline{x}}}$$

any value outside $-Z_{0.08} = -1.4$ and $Z_{0.08} = 1.4$ would indicate a tendency for increasing or decreasing population.

TABLE 1

Year	Run 1	Run 2	Run 3	Run 4	Run 5	Run 6
1	1	2	4	6	6	6
2	2	0	1	0	−1	1
3	0	−5	−1	2	2	1
4	0	−2	2	4	−1	0
5	2	2	5	2	4	4
6	1	−1	−3	−1	−3	−2
7	1	0	−1	1	1	0
8	3	3	2	4	3	4
9	−3	0	1	2	−2	−1
10	0	−1	−1	−1	0	−3
11	3	1	−1	−3	0	0
12	−4	2	2	3	−2	0
13	1	0	1	−2	−1	−2
14	−2	1	−2	0	4	2
15	1	−2	3	2	−1	1
16	1	1	0	−4	−3	0
17	−2	3	−3	3	1	−1
18	−1	−3	−1	−1	−4	0
19	−1	3	3	0	2	1
20	2	−4	−3	−2	0	0
21	−2	0	−1	1	0	3
22	−1	0	2	−2	−2	0
23	3	−4	−2	1	−4	0
24	4	0	2	−3	2	2
25	−2	0	−4	1	−1	0
26	1	−4	4	−1	3	−3
27	2	−1	0	0	2	−3
28	1	−2	−2	−1	1	−2
29	1	2	1	1	1	2
30	0	−1	3	−1	−1	0
31	−3	1	1	−8	1	0
32	1	−2	1	1	−5	−4
33	0	−2	5	0	1	0
34	0	0	−2	1	−1	1
35	−4	1	−4	−2	−3	0
36	−3	1	0	1	−2	1
37	−1	−3	−1	2	1	2
38	3	1	−1	1	−1	0
39	1	0	−3	1	0	0
40	−2	1	2	0	2	0
41	1	1	0	−3	2	−4
42	4	1	−1	−4	2	2
43	−4	−1	4	1	4	0
44	−1	0	−2	−1	2	1
45	3	1	2	0	2	0
46	0	0	−1	−2	−2	3
47	−4	−1	2	1	−4	2
48	1	0	3	3	2	2
49	0	3	−3	0	−2	−3
50	−1	2	−3	−1	−2	−1
SAMPLE						
MEAN	.04	− .16	.12	− .08	− .06	.12
S.D.	2.13	1.43	2.42	2.39	2.41	2.03
Z SCORE	.13	.59	.35	− .23	− .17	.42

The lower set of figures in Table 1 are the sample means, standard deviations, and Z scores for each run. It can be seen that none of the Z scores even approach these critical levels. Therefore from the results of the test of means we conclude that no directional trend is evident and the net change over the 50-year intervals may be at-, tributed to chance.

Although the magnitude of population change over the 50-year runs does not appear significant this does not, by itself, warrant the conclusion that population size is relatively stable through time. For example, accentuated population growth or decline at the end of a run would be missed in a simple test of the means of fluctuations, if fluctuations in previous years were sufficiently low. More importantly, a test of the means of fluctuations would be insensitive to radical oscillation above and below a central value, since positive and negative values could cancel each other out and this might not be readily apparent from a graph of population size over time. To contend with these possibilities of erratic behavior we can investigate the way absolute change varies over time. For example, concentrations of high or low fluctuation values, whether positive or negative, in any part of the run might make us suspicious that the fluctuation mean summarizes more than just a steady trend so that the mean by itself would give us a distorted impression of the model's behavior.

While several methods exist to detect the patterning of values, a fairly simple, non-parametric test that is effective and easy to understand, is a "runs" test. A "run" in this context is not to be confused with a computer simulation run, but is merely a succession of identical outcomes.

For each sample, we took the absolute values of yearly changes from Table 1 and found their median. For any year a value could be either above, below, or equal to the median. If it was above we assigned it an "A", if below we assigned it a "B", and if equal to the median an "O". The results of this operation appear in Table 2.

Ignoring the zeros, an individual "run" would be a consecutive series of A's or B's within a particular sample. We can use the total number of such "runs" as an index of patterning of fluctuation size. The statistical problem is a test for randomness. We would like to show that the distribution of the magnitude of change does not occur in a regular order. The alternative of too few "runs" would indicate that there are non-random periods of greater and smaller amplitude during the fifty years. The test to put this question of randomness on a more precise basis utilizes the fact that for arrangement of Na letters of one kind and Nb of another kind, the sampling distribution of U, the total number of "runs", has the mean

$$\mu_u = \frac{2\ \text{Na Nb}}{\text{Na} + \text{Nb}} + 1$$

and the standard deviation

$$\sigma_u = \frac{\sqrt{2\ \text{Na Nb}\ (2\ \text{Na Nb} - \text{Na} - \text{Nb})}}{(\text{Na} + \text{Nb})^2\ (\text{Na} + \text{Nb} - 1)}$$

The sampling distribution of this statistic can be approximated with a normal distribution, and we can base our decision on the statistic

$$Z = \frac{u - \mu_u}{\sigma_u}$$

If Z is outside of $-Z_{0.08} = -1.4$ and $Z_{0.08} = 1.4$, we can reject the null hypothesis at the level of significance of $\alpha = 0.32$. At the bottom of Table 4, we give the number of years higher and lower than the median, the number of "runs", and Z.

For four of the six samples in the original model the null hypothesis cannot be rejected, that is, there is no indication that the absolute size of the fluctuations is not random.

Two computer runs, numbers 4 and 5, have Z values considerably larger than one would expect if the size of the fluctuations was distributed randomly (Table 2). Curiously, they show up as non-random, not because there are too few series of A's and B's as one might have supposed, but because there are too many "runs" (i.e., the Z value assumed a positive value). This outcome would imply an alternating pattern of smaller and larger deviations through time. Since larger fluctuations are in effect compensated by a return to smaller ones, the detrimental effects of this pattern are not as clear as with the case of too few "runs". As a logical possibility, however, one could suggest that if the values above the median grew larger through time and/or if the values below the median grew smaller, an eventual change from a mean close to zero could be predicted.

Although one could reapply the "runs" test to the few values that fell above the median, it is doubtful whether this exercise could tell us much more than inspection of Table 1. Looking at the first differences for each run, the largest changes occur in the beginning and the middle of the fifty-year interval, and if anything, the fluctuation towards the end of the run appears to have settled down considerably. Hence, while it cannot be claimed that the absolute fluctuations of simulation runs 4 and 5 are distributed randomly, nothing leads us to believe that effects from this particular pattern suggest a departure from the stability indicated by their first-difference mean.

The above findings, the test of the means and the "runs" test lend confidence to what could be seen in Figure 9; that the ORANG model produces population trends that change very little through time.

USE OF THE SIMULATION MODEL TO TEST ALTERNATIVE MODELS

Our interest in pursuing computer simulations centered on two main objectives. On the one hand we wanted to show that a model in accordance with our conception of orang social behavior and structure exhibited only slight population changes through time. To be able to argue that the postulated social strategy is adaptive, however, requires that we show other behaviors to be less adaptive. It could well be, for example, that a behavior is irrelevant to population size.

One intriguing question about orang-utan spacing is the size of the adult male range. As stated earlier, the area of an adult male range was estimated on the basis of the distance which they traveled when followed and the observed frequency of return to a given locale. The figure which seemed most consistent with the data was approximately 2 square miles, but our level of confidence for this figure is much lower than for the estimate of adult female range since it was never possible to follow adult males consistently for months or even weeks at a time. In constructing the ORANG model, therefore, we used $2\frac{1}{4}$ square miles since this would make a male range be square in shape. This range is then equal to 9 female ranges.

In the initial papers on orang social structure (Horr, 1972, 1975) it was suggested that such a large area in comparison with a female range is adaptive in terms of reproductive success and habitat structure. The question has been raised as to whether it is really necessary that males cover such a large area relative to female range, the alternative being that they move much more slowly through a more confined area.

TABLE 2

Year	Run 1	Run 2	Run 3	Run 4	Run 5	Run 6
1	O	A	A	A	A	A
2	A	B	B	B	B	O
3	B	A	B	A	O	O
4	B	A	O	A	B	B
5	A	A	A	A	A	A
6	O	O	A	O	A	A
7	O	B	B	O	B	B
8	A	A	O	A	A	A
9	A	B	B	A	O	O
10	B	O	B	O	B	A
11	A	O	B	A	B	B
12	A	A	O	A	O	B
13	O	B	B	A	B	A
14	A	O	O	B	A	A
15	O	A	A	A	B	O
16	O	O	B	A	A	B
17	A	A	A	A	B	O
18	O	A	B	O	A	B
19	O	A	A	B	O	O
20	A	A	A	A	B	B
21	A	B	B	O	B	A
22	O	B	O	A	O	B
23	A	A	O	O	A	B
24	A	B	O	A	O	A
25	A	B	A	O	B	B
26	O	A	A	O	A	A
27	A	O	B	B	O	A
28	O	A	O	O	B	A
29	O	A	B	O	B	A
30	B	O	A	O	B	B
31	A	O	B	A	B	B
32	O	A	B	O	A	A
33	B	A	A	B	B	B
34	B	B	O	O	B	O
35	A	O	A	A	A	B
36	A	O	B	O	O	O
37	O	A	B	A	B	A
38	A	O	B	O	B	B
39	O	B	A	O	B	B
40	A	O	O	B	O	B
41	O	O	B	A	O	A
42	A	O	B	A	O	A
43	A	O	A	O	A	B
44	O	B	O	O	O	O
45	A	O	O	B	O	B
46	B	B	B	A	O	A
47	A	O	O	O	A	A
48	O	B	A	A	O	A
49	B	A	A	B	O	A
50	O	A	A	O	O	O
NO. OF A'S	23	20	17	22	13	21
NO. OF B'S	8	13	20	8	20	19
NO. OF "RUNS"	12	17	21	16	21	21
Z SCORE	−.50	.08	.54	1.57	1.57	.01

To investigate this possibility, we first conducted six runs reducing the male range to one square mile (four adult female ranges) and letting males randomly occupy one ¼ square mile locale (equal to a female range) for a month at a time. These conditions were the only ones changed so that a male's ability to move his range to always include at least one female remained intact.

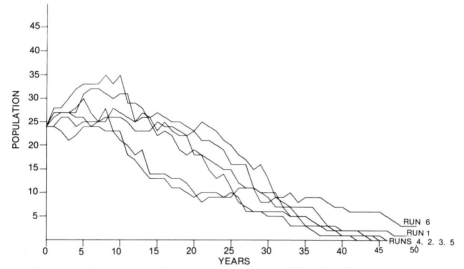

Figure 10. Graph of population over time: six runs with reduced male range

The population curves that resulted are given in Figure 10. The consequences of this alteration seem quite consistent between runs. In every case, an eventual decline of population size to an inviable level is characteristic of the simulated time series.

As with the original model, Table 3 gives the first differences of these runs and the tests of their means. Since, in this instance, we would like to reject the null hypothesis that the means are not significantly different from zero, we have reduced the significance level from $\alpha = 0.16$ used for the original model to $\alpha = 0.05$. Since the net effect of all the runs of this modified model is negative, we are interested in the one-tailed alternative that $\overline{X} < 0$. The corresponding critical value is -1.64 and values below this figure may be taken as significant. All of the Z scores corroborate the impression given by Figure 10, that the mean values represent a considerable departure from zero and a downward trend.

TABLE 3

Year	Run 1	Run 2	Run 3	Run 4	Run 5	Run 6
1	2	4	3	0	3	0
2	1	0	0	2	0	−1
3	0	2	0	0	0	−2
4	−1	2	0	−2	1	1
5	0	1	4	1	2	2
6	−2	1	1	0	−3	0
7	1	0	0	0	−2	0
8	0	2	−1	3	1	−1
9	3	−2	−1	−5	0	0
10	−1	2	1	0	0	−2
11	−1	−6	0	−5	−1	−1
12	−1	0	−6	−1	−2	−2
13	2	−1	1	−2	0	1
14	−1	−3	0	−2	0	−5
15	−3	−3	1	0	2	0
16	2	1	−1	0	−1	0
17	−2	−1	−1	−2	0	−1
18	−1	−3	0	0	−1	0
19	0	−1	−1	−1	−1	−1
20	−4	1	−1	−1	1	−2
21	0	−1	2	1	−2	−2
22	−1	−3	−1	0	0	1
23	−1	−2	−1	0	−1	0
24	−1	1	−2	−1	−1	0
25	0	−3	−1	1	−3	0
26	−3	−3	−2	−1	0	2
27	−1	−1	−1	−3	0	0
28	0	−1	−2	0	−5	0
29	−1	0	1	0	−1	−3
30	−1	0	−3	−1	0	0
31	−2	0	−4	0	0	1
32	0	0	−1	0	−3	0
33	0	−1	−1	−2	−2	1
34	−2	0	0	0	0	−2
35	0	0	0	0	−2	1
36	−1	−1	0	−1	0	0
37	−1	−1	−2	−1	0	0
38	0	0	−2	0	−1	−1
39	0	−1	−1	0	0	−1
40	−1	−1	0	0	0	0
41	0	0	0	0	0	−1
42	0	0	0	−1	0	0
43	0	0	−1	0	−1	0
44	0	−1	0	0	0	0
45	0	0	−1	0	0	0
46	0	0	0	0	−1	−1
47	−1	0	0	0	0	−1
48	0	0	0	0	0	−1
49	0	0	0	0	0	0
50	0	0	0	0	0	0
SAMPLE MEAN	−0.50	−0.57	−0.55	−0.49	−0.55	−0.42
S.D.	1.27	1.66	1.56	1.37	1.36	1.23
Z SCORE	−2.79	−2.41	−2.48	−2.50	−2.84	−2.41

The altered model, then, indicates that an adult male range of one square mile is not sufficient to maintain a self-perpetuating population even though the male can move his range to include a female as long as even one remains "alive."

In contrast to this possibility, we then constructed a new version of the original model which increased the adult male's range to four square miles—this being the next largest area which would result in a square range on our matrix (16 adult female ranges) and also one which would perhaps place a maximum demand for movement by the male to cover. Since this larger range would mean that more males would contact a given female, it would serve to increase the opportunity for her to conceive just as soon as she becomes receptive by reducing the time required for a male to arrive in her particular area. Figure 11 shows the population curves resulting from six computer runs using the four square mile range and Table 4 shows the first differences of these runs. Although the increase of the male

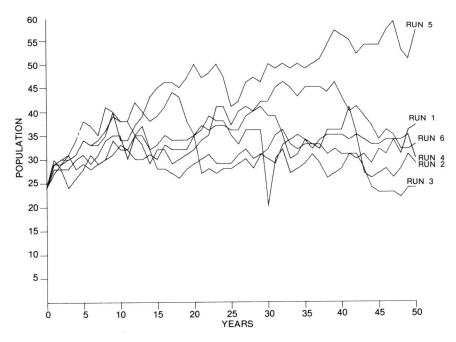

Figure 11. Graph of population over time: six runs with increased male range

TABLE 4

Year	Run 1	Run 2	Run 3	Run 4	Run 5	Run 6
1	5	4	3	5	5	6
2	0	0	2	1	1	−2
3	2	−4	1	1	0	0
4	3	2	1	− 3	1	2
5	4	2	3	1	3	1
6	−1	3	−1	− 1	−1	−2
7	−2	−2	1	1	0	2
8	6	1	2	1	2	3
9	−1	1	3	4	−6	1
10	−2	−2	−1	−2	−6	−0
11	0	−1	0	0	0	−5
12	−3	−2	4	3	3	5
13	2	0	−2	0	2	−2
14	−5	1	−2	− 3	4	−4
15	−4	−1	1	1	2	3
16	0	3	2	2	1	0
17	−1	−1	3	− 1	0	−3
18	−1	0	−1	0	−1	1
19	2	0	−5	0	2	1
20	1	3	−3	1	3	1
21	1	2	−8	1	−3	2
22	1	−1	1	3	1	1
23	−2	1	−1	− 1	2	6
24	0	0	1	0	−3	0
25	0	−1	0	− 3	−6	−4
26	2	0	1	− 2	1	3
27	1	3	1	3	4	1
28	−2	1	−2	0	1	−1
29	1	1	3	0	−1	2
30	1	−2	−1	−16	4	0
31	3	0	−1	10	−1	3
32	1	−4	4	2	1	1
33	−3	−5	1	− 5	−1	−1
34	−1	1	1	1	1	−2
35	1	3	−1	1	−1	2
36	0	−2	−1	2	1	0
37	−1	2	0	− 2	1	0
38	4	1	−2	− 3	3	−1
39	0	0	1	1	3	2
40	0	0	−1	1	−1	−3
41	5	−1	0	3	−1	−3
42	−6	1	0	− 1	−3	1
43	−1	−8	−3	1	2	−2
44	−1	−1	−4	− 2	0	−2
45	0	1	−1	3	0	−3
46	1	1	0	− 1	3	2
47	0	−2	0	3	2	−1
48	−3	2	−1	0	−6	−3
49	5	3	2	1	−2	0
50	1	−2	0	− 5	6	1
SAMPLE MEAN	.16	.02	− .06	.02	.56	.06
S.D.	2.52	2.29	2.28	3.45	2.67	2.48
Z SCORE	.45	.06	− .19	.04	1.48	.17

range to 4 square miles does yield a slightly higher rate of population growth, it is clear that the differences are not strikingly significant.

Although one might expect an increase in population proportional to an increase in male range, a moment's reflection will show why our results were not surprising. Once a critical frequency of male contact with females is achieved, increased contact would not significantly raise the birth rate since a female can conceive only once for any given gestation period. Once she is virtually assured of conceiving at a maximum rate, additional males contacting her are superfluous. Hence while we supposed that there was a minimally viable size for male range, that there was not too marked a change from increasing the male range, was not unexpected.

Since the net effect in all the runs was either equal to or greater than the original population, we concentrated on the possibility that the mean was greater than zero. Hence, for the means test, a Z-value above 1.00 for a one-tailed test would point to a trend of increasing population (see Table 4). Only run 5 (Z=1.48) exceeds this critical value.

Again, we used the "runs" test (Table 5) to determine the appropriateness of basing our judgment on the means test. In five cases, the null hypothesis (Z = 0) cannot be rejected. It should be noted that since the "runs" test is aimed solely at raising our confidence in the test of the means, in the case of run 5, the only information the "runs" test adds is that population growth is a gradual trend and not the byproduct of larger fluctuations through time. Similar to the original model, the one run (run 4) that exceeds the critical value does so in a positive direction, implying that there are too many runs. Referring back to the first difference (Table 4) there is a rather dramatic leap in years 30 and 31, but both before and after this peak, the magnitude of the fluctuations seem relatively steady.

Figure 12 shows a comparative graph of the means of the three models which vary only with respect to the size of the adult male range. On the basis of these data we can say that adult male orangutans most probably range over at least 2 to 3 square miles to maximize breeding potential and maintain an adequate level of population. Although four square miles or more could further insure stable population levels, an area of 2 square miles is already reasonably vast for an arboreal animal in tropical rainforest. Two square miles would also adequately spread out the adult male's drain on the food resources of the environment.

TABLE 5

Year	Run 1	Run 2	Run 3	Run 4	Run 5	Run 6
1	A	A	A	A	A	A
2	B	B	A	O	B	O
3	A	A	O	O	B	B
4	A	A	O	A	B	O
5	A	A	A	O	A	B
6	O	A	O	O	B	O
7	A	A	O	O	B	O
8	A	O	A	O	O	A
9	O	O	A	A	A	B
10	A	A	O	B	A	B
11	B	O	B	B	B	A
12	A	A	A	A	A	A
13	A	B	A	B	O	O
14	A	O	A	A	A	A
15	A	O	O	O	O	A
16	B	A	A	B	B	B
17	O	O	A	O	B	A
18	O	B	O	B	B	B
19	A	B	A	B	O	B
20	O	A	A	O	A	B
21	O	A	A	O	A	O
22	O	O	O	A	B	B
23	A	O	O	O	O	A
24	B	B	O	B	A	B
25	B	O	B	A	A	A
26	A	B	O	B	B	A
27	O	A	O	A	A	B
28	A	O	A	B	B	B
29	O	O	A	B	B	O
30	O	A	O	A	A	B
31	A	B	O	A	B	A
32	O	A	A	B	B	B
33	A	A	O	A	B	B
34	O	O	O	O	B	O
35	O	A	O	O	B	O
36	B	A	O	B	B	B
37	O	A	B	B	B	B
38	A	O	A	A	A	B
39	B	B	O	O	A	O
40	B	B	O	O	B	A
41	A	O	B	A	B	A
42	A	O	B	O	A	B
43	O	A	A	O	O	O
44	O	O	A	B	B	O
45	B	O	O	A	B	A
46	O	O	B	O	A	O
47	B	A	B	A	O	B
48	A	A	O	B	A	A
49	A	A	A	O	O	B
50	O	A	B	A	A	B
NO. OF A'S	22	23	20	16	18	15
NO. OF B'S	10	9	8	15	24	22
NO. OF "RUNS"	15	13	12	21	21	20
Z SCORE	.11	−.42	−.20	1.65	−.18	.40

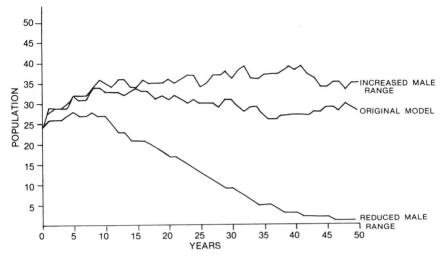

Figure 12. Graph of population over time: mean of runs for original model, reduced male range, and increased male range

Although the test of male range yields results which conform to prediction based on field data, there remains the nagging question of whether this is actually the case since we can not "prove" the model by comparing with firmly known size and boundaries of adult male ranges in the wild. Accordingly, we have performed another manipulation of the model using a variable the results of which are virtually predictable in advance. If the model performs according to prediction in this case as well, we again have increased confidence in the original model, as well as in the altered models' statements about adult male range.

We chose to alter birth rate to see what impact this would have on simulated population trends. Since we are more interested in seeing what affects maintenance of minimum population levels, we tested birth rate against the model in which adult male range is 4 square miles to ensure that adult females had ample opportunity to be contacted by adult males when the females became receptive.

As described earlier, the original model allows females to conceive again only after their offspring is 2½ years old. From conception to conception this meant that a female was first receptive 39 months after her last conception. As one extreme, we made three runs in

which females were permitted to breed only if they had no dependents at all, or once every 45 months. As a lower extreme, we made an
equal number of runs in which a female could conceive when their
dependent was but a year old, or once every 21 months. Though in
either instance the simulation could run for the normal 50-year
period, a run was terminated if the population climbed above 100
individuals or fell to zero.

Figure 13 shows the population curves for the three runs where
conception was permitted only every 45 months and Figure 14 shows

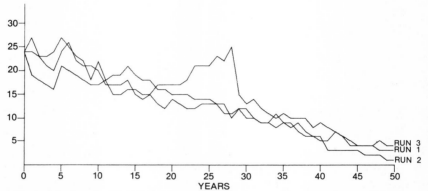

Figure 13. Graph of Population over time: three runs with conception possible every
45 months

the results when conception could take place every 21 months. Finally,
Figure 15 compares the mean curve of each of the altered birth rates
with that of the original model. As would be expected, the longer
interval between conception not only curtailed population growth,
but in fact brought each population to below survival levels within
the fifty year period. As a complementary development the shorter
interval led to a steep grade of population growth which exceeded the
computer design well before fifty years was reached.

Two inferences may be drawn from these results. First we would
maintain that the manipulation of birth rate demonstrates that a
wide range of outcomes are possible, and therefore that the stability
of our original formulation is not due to the model's inability to produce other types of population trends. Second, the results show that
the model reacts in a manner that is highly consistent with what one
might expect if comparable changes in the birth rate could be im-

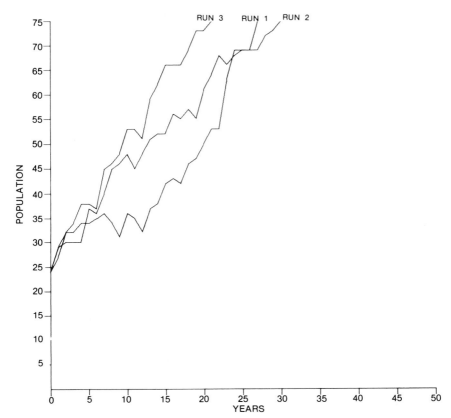

Figure 14. Graph of population over time: three runs with conception possible every 21 months.

posed on a living population of orang-utans without altering death rates. We would like to remark, however, that while it would have raised grave doubts about the model if the changes in birth rate had failed to affect population size, the effects of manipulating such a basic variable as the supply of new individuals should come as no great surprise, nor would it have been worth creating a simulation model with only this goal in mind.

Of the model variations tested, only the increased birth rate version has significantly increased the number of individuals in a population. It is interesting to note that, on the spatial distribution of final populations, in the case of greatly increased population numbers, the animals have spread out over a much larger area than the initial population or

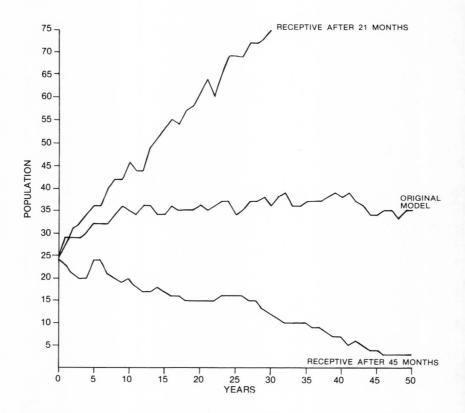

Figure 15. Graph of population over time: mean of runs for conception possible every 39 months (original condition), every 45 months, and every 21 months

any of the other final populations. In fact, the area they occupy is proportionally larger so that, although their movement is in no way curbed within the 128 square matrix, they have approximately the same population density.

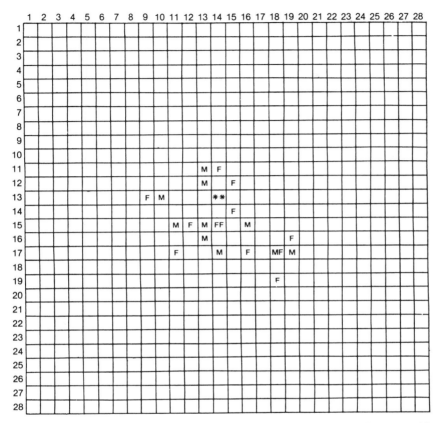

Figure 16. Distribution matrix of adult orang-utans: population equals 26, asterisk signifies more than two adults.

Figure 16 shows an output matrix with the location of each of the adult animals in a final population of 26 adults. The distribution in a run of the increased birth rate model culminating in a population of 100 adult orang-utans is shown in Figure 17[5]. This effect is most likely the result of the anticipated factor of habitat overload and the concomitant displacement of animals, and it further increases our confidence that the model tends to predict what a real population in the wild would do.

[5]Infants and juveniles are not shown on the distribution although they are included in population totals on the graphs.

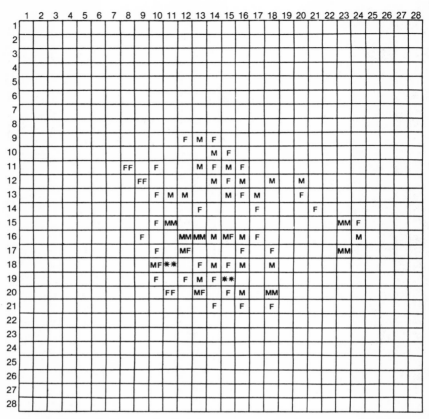

Figure 17. Distribution matrix of adult orang-utans: population equals 100 adults.

Conclusions

A primary interest in our initial efforts to apply computer simulation to a socio-ecological problem was assessing the model of orangutan social behavior first proposed by Horr (1972, 1975) on the basis of field data. Both the graphs for population trends over time and the statistical consideration of these time series data point to the interpretation that orang-utans conforming to the behaviors represented in the model would maintain their population at adequate levels and in appropriate age-sex ratios. Since this interpretation rests on the ability of the model to produce divergent outcomes, we examined the sensitivity of the simulation by introducing the variations of increased and decreased birth rate. The consequences of these variations were untenable population overload and depletion respectively.

Another major goal was to employ data in which we had a good deal of confidence based on repeated observations, (e.g., female range size, mother-offspring relations, breeding rates, habitat structure, etc.) to derive information about aspects of orang behavior that were based on fewer observations or only indirectly substantiated, such as male range size. Two interrelated questions were asked: was estimated male range size viable in terms of maintaining population size and does male range size have a significant effect on population size.

Halving the male range size clearly had a detrimental impact on the simulated populations over time. There was, however, far less effect on population size from doubling male range size, although some evidence for an initially higher population growth rate did appear. Our interpretation is that the male range as originally estimated represents nearly maximal conception probability for females. Since females can conceive only once per pregnancy, increasing the range did not have much effect on birth rate.

We emerge with the following picture: the size of the male range *is* a critical component in the maintenance of orang-utan population size, and the most adaptive range size from the standpoint of maintaining optimum and even population levels and minimizing male effort is close to the 2¼ square mile range originally estimated.

These tests strengthen our confidence in the model of social organization and social behavior originally proposed. The model is more than an idealized functional system which operates because of internal consistency alone. All behavioral and biological data are based on actual field observations or known biological relationships. The ultimate adaptiveness of these is checked against environmental factors of space and food supply which is independent of orang-utans. In so far as possible, the model is based upon the conditions and constraints of the real world. As such it can be a valid tool in evaluating hypotheses.

The simulation refines our concepts of orang social behavior. For example, the minor effect of increasing male range generates an hypothesis that by ranging over much more than 2¼ square miles, a male is wasting reproductive effort. This in itself does not prove that males do not range over areas larger than 2¼ square miles. However, it does show that in terms of female reproductive capacity, such a large range is probably superfluous. This not only increases the acceptability of the 2¼ square mile range as correct, but, should further field data indicate that males do in fact travel over a 4 square mile range, we would not assume that this was due to female birth rate potential. Rather we would look to some other factor, probably male-male competition, which would force some males to circulate more widely to maximize their reproductive efficiency.

There are many other modifications which would be desirable in this first simulation of orang-utan social organization. This is very characteristic of simulation, where one thinks in terms of "generations" of models, successive versions of a model that represent closer approximations of reality. We have assumed for purposes of simplicity that the supply value of all locations is the same. In fact, there is evidence that the habitat is not uniform in terms of food supply, and these spatial variations could be incorporated into a subsequent model using food quantities by area.

Although we deal with non-human primates, data from human social systems could also be investigated using a simulation strategy. An ecological study of human hunter-gatherer groups might utilize a simulation program to test the effects of certain variations over long periods of time. Not only could socio-ecological adaptive models and "biological" or habitat variations be subjected to the test of simulated time, but the long-range effect of cultural practices might be examined as well. Birdsell's (1968) article using equilibrium models from recent hunters and gatherers to predict Pleistocene conditions is one context in which a simulation strategy could be used to good effect.

Finally, we want to stress that the existence of a "working" computer simulation of a living system in no way substitutes for thinking about that system. However, if carefully monitored, computer simulation can be a very useful tool in assisting the researcher to evaluate his conceptions of how an observed animal system functions. The computer should never substitute for the intellect of the scholar, but it can provide a powerful technique in the development of his hypotheses.

References

Birdsell, J.B.
    1968 Some predictions for the Pleistocene based on equilibrium systems among recent hunter-gatherers. In: Lee, Richard B. and Irven DeVore, eds. Man The Hunter, Aldine, Chicago, pp. 229-240.
Buckley, Walter
    1967 Sociology and Modern Systems Theory. Prentice-Hall, Englewood Cliffs, New Jersey.
Crook, J. H. (ed.)
    1969 Social Behavior in Birds and Mammals. Academic Press, London.
Gordon, G.
    1969 System Simulation. Prentice-Hall, New Jersey.
Horr, David Agee
    1972 The Borneo orang-utan. The Borneo Research Bulletin, 4:46-50.

    1975 The Borneo orang-utan: population structure and dynamics in relationship to ecology and reproductive strategy. Primate Behavior, 4: 307-323, Leonard Rosenblum, editor.
Kuhn, T.
    1962 The Structure of Scientific Revolutions. University of Chicago Press, Chicago.
Napier, J. R., and P. H. Napier
    1967 A Handbook of Living Primates. Academic Press, London.
Sahlins, M.
    1968 Evolution: general and specific. In: Theory in Anthropology. R. Manners and D. Kaplan, eds. Aldine Publishing Co., Chicago.
Shubik, M.
    1960 Simulation of the industry and the firm. In: Economic Review, 50: 908-919.

2. Monkey Business and Bird Brains

C. *Loring Brace and Mary L. Brace*

Introduction

In spite of some of the rumors that have been circulating, it is not our intention to demonstrate that man descended from the birds. On the contrary, we reaffirm the standard view that the hominid line evolved from the Tertiary primates by way of the Australopithecines.

The ideas which we report on here were not the result of deliberate research pursued with the aim of casting light on specific, recognized problems. They derive, instead, from the unplanned but fortunate accident of circumstances. Specifically, they come from the experiences we have had with our own personal zoo. The justification for having a zoo in the house might be because of the basic biological insights which it can afford, and in the present instance these have certainly been forthcoming, but at bottom our real reason simply has been because it is fun.

From our observations, it has gradually dawned on us that the order

NOTE: Aside from the standard published sources, we owe an enormous debt of gratitude to the many people who have given us immeasurable aid, both in the actual gifts of valuable birds and animals and in the stores of information which have helped in their care and understanding. Heading our list are the manager and the assistant manager of our favorite pet store, Tim Bowsher and Ben Sieg of the

Primates cannot, as a whole, claim uncontested the designation as the "brightest" or "most advanced" creatures in the world. If the existence of such a category can be defended at all — a matter about which there is more than a little doubt — it is clear that the Primates must share it with the members of another order. Furthermore, that order, Psittaciformes, is not even mammalian but avian, and is comprised of parrots and parrot-like birds.

If this conclusion may seem a bit startling, even to those who appreciate the sterling qualities of parrots as pets, we suspect that this is partially because the pre-nineteenth century expectations embodied in the *scala naturae* continue to shape the way we look at things. While the latter may not be quite comparable to the Great Chain of Being view where each living form was assigned a position on a line leading up to Divinity itself, there is a continuing tendency to regard living things as higher or lower on a putative scale of evolutionary development. And our general judgment is that mammals are more advanced than birds. The use of the old epithet, "bird-brain," to suggest the extreme of stupidity is a case in point.

If a surviving strain of the *scala naturae* has given us, as primates and mammals, a somewhat patronizing assessment of the intellectual capabilities of non-mammalian organisms, this has been reinforced by the accident of a particular set of historical circumstances. Ever

Ann Arbor Pet Supply. Among the many others we should mention Ray and Carol Blatt of Denver, Colorado; Arthur Edson of Grand Rapids, Michigan; and James Wesley of New York. For help with the illustrations, we are indebted to Dr. Richard J. Kaplan of the Department of Psychology and the Highway Safety Research Institute at the University of Michigan. We should also credit the continuing interest and stimulation provided by the members of the Ann Arbor Zoological Club. Last, but certainly not least, we should acknowledge the contributions, witting and unwitting, of the furred and feathered denizens of the zoo which has served as the focus of the club and its activities.*

*Dedicated to the memory of Papagaj and Lolita. Read at the 71st annual meetings of the American Anthropological Association at Toronto, Canada, December 2, 1972.

since the food-producing revolution, the bird group with which people have been most familiar has been the Galliformes. And it so happens that the gallinaceous birds fall right at the bottom of the avian scale in whatever index of encephalization one might choose. Whether it be brain-stem proportion (corrected for body weight), or brain weight divided by spinal cord weight, it would appear that no bird is less brainy than the barnyard chicken. By the same criteria, the Psittaciformes display the greatest degree of cerebral development in the avian spectrum (Pearson 1972, Tables 77-82). To generalize about the intellectual endowment of the entire avian world from the case of the domestic fowl would be comparable to using the rhinoceros to typify the mammalian condition.

It is not our primary intent to stress relative encephalization as a necessary indication of "intelligence," however that may be defined, since, in fact, our conclusions were initially derived from observations of behavior and, following that, the realization that from an ecological and evolutionary perspective, we should have expected all along that the basic parrot adaptation is directly comparable to the basic primate adaptation. Scientists have long recognized the fact that the development of the phenomenon of man owed an enormous debt to the shaping effect which the tropical arboreal ecological niche exerted on the hominid ancestral line through much of the Cenozoic. Certainly the proliferation of primate studies in the recent past has been stimulated by the expectation that these could increase our understanding of the bio-behavioral substrate from which the human condition evolved, and the circumstances that operated to shape it. If the accepted faith in the shaping power of those circumstances is justifiable, then we should welcome independent demonstrations of their efficacy. It is our contention here that the systematic study of parrot populations, in addition to being interesting in its own right, can yield just such an independent check, and that it can enrich our understanding of the bio-behavioral nature of primates, and, ultimately, human beings as well.

Unfortunately, however, we can do little more than suggest the benefits that might accrue from such a course of study since there has been no ornithological counterpart as yet to the primate field study program that has grown to such prominence within the last generation. In fact, there has been only one brief field study published (Hardy 1965). Most of the available information, then, comes from the pet or avicultural trade, and this is of the "care-and-feeding" nature rather than from the perspective of evolutionary biology. In fact, the basis for our own insight stems from the non-professional observation of pet birds and monkeys from which, after the fact, we have tried to articulate the larger implications. In the portion of this paper that follows, we shall present the parrot-primate parallels that we have observed.

Habitat

The majority of both primates and psittacines are denizens of the tropical rainforest canopy. In both groups, a few species have become adapted to more temperate climates. Such deviations from the typical locale are accompanied by a tendency to depart from the characteristic frugivorous diet as well as an extension into a terrestrial or semi-terrestrial habitat. In this latter concern, the primates may have achieved greater, or at least more visible, success. Gorillas, baboons and patas monkeys as terrestrial primates have commanded more attention, and probably represent a greater biomass, than their psittacine counterparts: slender-billed cockatoos, Keas, grass parakeets, and ground (or swamp) parakeets (Figure 1). One of the things that has allowed the primates to make more effective use of a terrestrial habitat is the less stringent limitation on bulk. Chimpanzees and orangs can remain in their arboreal niche should they so choose, but are large enough so that the ground holds fewer threats to them than it would to a cebus monkey. Baboons, in fact, are large enough to deter much potential predation. But about the only thing one could say when confronted with a fifty pound bird — particularly one without an evolutionary history as a running form — is that it could never get off the ground. Evidently the stricture of maintaining the capacity for flight has placed a limit on how large a bird can get. Not surprisingly, the terrestrial and semi-terrestrial psittacines inhabit those parts of the world where mammalian predators are inefficient or absent — Australia and New Zealand for example.

Diet

Obviously diet and the other attributes we shall consider are dependent variables which cannot be considered completely apart from the category of habitat. The basic dietary focus of both parrots and primates is concentrated on the resources most widely available in the rainforest canopy—namely the fruits and nuts or seeds of flowering trees (Figure 2). There are some slight differences in emphasis, however, and among the parrots—being birds with gizzards—there are many more groups which can thrive on a diet consisting of large quantities of grain seeds. But for the most part, fruit is a major item in common (Figure 3). The grape, long used as a "reward" in laboratory studies on primates, is just as much a treat for a parrot! In the rainforest canopy, the problems of perceiving and reaching food items have resulted in striking parallel developments in monkeys and parrots.

Perception

In both groups vision is the dominant sense. Depth perception is excellent and the retina is richly supplied with cones. Consequently, the ability to perceive color is highly developed (Figure 4). This obviously is the result of selection for the ability to perceive from a distance the existence and relative ripeness of fruity food sources. On the other hand, both primates and psittacines are relatively night

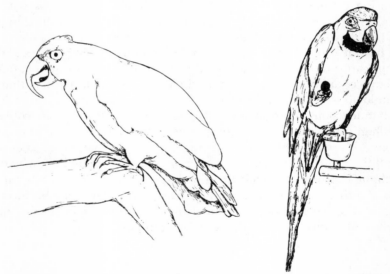

Figure 1. Slender-billed cockatoo *(Kakatoe tenuirostris)*, A semi-terrestrial parrot from Australia with a beak adapted for digging out roots, tubers and grubs. Drawn after Bates and Busenbark (1969: 332).

Figure 2. Blue-and-gold macaw *(Ara ararauna)*, "Sultan," holding a grape.

Figure 3. Squirrel monkey *(Saimiri sciureus)*, "Lolita," holding a grape.

Figure 4. Hyacinthine macaw *(Anodorhyrchus hyacinthinus)*, demonstrating the ability to match both shapes and colors. Drawn after Rogers (1969: 73).

blind. We first became aware of this when tracing the flight of a cockatiel which had been frightened off its perch in the middle of the night, and tried to fly through the darkened house. The trail of thumps and crashes was remarkably similar to that which a human would produce if it tried to run through the house in the dark. Most parrots, like most primates, are thoroughly diurnal creatures—again the result of the shaping effects of the environment which nurtured them both.

The development of the auditory sense also appears to be equivalent in both groups—that is, it is less acute than that usually found in typical terrestrial quadrupeds, whether herbivores or carnivores. On the other hand, the ability to perceive the import of specific sound combinations is well developed. We shall return to this matter when we discuss social organization. Olfaction is clearly of less importance than either vision or hearing.

Manipulo-Locomotor Development

To reverse the common phrase, the similarities in this area are more real than apparent. The obvious fact that parrots can fly and primates cannot tends to obscure the real similarities in their capabilities. Again, one can surmise that the exigencies of getting along in the rainforest canopy have been responsible.

Fruit and nuts tend to be pendulous phenomena, dangling from the tips of slender branches and twigs. The problem of access, for a creature of more than insectile size, involves fixation upon a limb of sufficient dimensions to allow support, and then the employment of some mechanism for reaching the goodies suspended from the less substantial branchlets. This problem is solved in the hornbills and toucans by the development of very long, strong but lightweight beaks (Figure 5). Parrots and primates, on the other hand, have solved it by the development of extraordinary acrobatic capabilities. Members of both groups can hang beneath a limb, suspended by a foot or two, and reach with the remaining grasping organ(s) for the object of the gastronomic quest. This suspensory feeding posture has been developed to such an extent in one group of psittacines, *Loriculus*, or the hanging parakeets, that the characteristic mode of perching is bat-like, or what we would regard as upside down.

Arboreal primates are perhaps more visibly spectacular in their acrobatics. With four grasping appendages rather than three and with their mobile and elongated limbs, the grace and speed with which they move elicits admiration from the human observer, enhanced by the realization that one slip could have disasterous consequences. Parrots too are capable of remarkable arboreal gyrations but without the accompanying leaps. The obvious counterpart, however, is the ability to fly across spaces of any size. Once at the feeding site, however, a parrot will typically clamber towards the food object using its feet and its beak for grasping and for support. The foot-beak-eye coordination demands a degree of decision-making fully comparable to the analogous activities among primates, and if this can be accepted as the key to understanding the relative intellectual development of the primates, then it follows that we should expect to find a similar degree of intellectual development among the parrots (Figure 6).

Arboreal feeding tends to be a messy and wasteful process, as anyone who has had to clean the bottom of a monkey or a parrot cage can testify. Items of food are easily dropped, pieces break off and fall, and much is lost as far as the eater is concerned. As a means of increasing food-getting efficiency, both parrots and monkeys have evolved a high degree of grasping and manipulative skill (Figure 7). Even those who have never owned a pet monkey are well aware of the mischief that can be perpetrated by their clever little fingers. Less well known is the fact that a parrot can do everything and even more than a monkey of equivalent size (Figure 8). Parrots regularly hold up objects with a foot for further inspection or processing, but the real organ for skillful treatment is the beak-tongue complex. Our primate

Figure 5. Sulphur-breasted toucan *(Ramphastos sulfuratus)*, "Tikal."

Figure 6. Green-winged macaw *(Ara chloroptera)* raising the flag at Parrot Jungle, Miami, Florida. Drawn after Rogers (1969: 82).

heritage is so implicit that we refer to such operations as "handling" or "manipulating" since we normally associate it with the hand or manus. In parrots where it is done with the mandibles and tongue, we might be justified in saying that they "mandiblate" objects. It would be a trifle precious to insist on this, however, and having recognized our primatocentrism, we shall continue to use the word manipulate.

The beak of a parrot, consisting of separately hinged upper and lower mandibles, can exert considerably more force than the hand of a monkey of comparable size (Figure 9). The largest members of the parrot family, the macaws and cockatoos, can bite with a force equalled only by the bite of a primate many times their size—gorilla, orang, chimpanzee, baboon—and not surprisingly. After all, the adaptation exists to allow access to the hard-shelled nuts and heavy-rinded fruits of the tropical rainforest. The ease with which a five-pound macaw can crush an unshelled brazil nut is impressive indeed.

But power in biting or aid in climbing are not the only functions of the beak. It can hold things which are then delicately manipulated with the tongue (Figure 10). The tongue of a parrot is not dry, horny,

Figure 7. Squirrel monkey *(Saimiri sciureus)* holding a grasshopper. Drawn after Eimerl and DeVore (1965: 48).

Figure 8. Blue fronted Amazon parrot *(Amazona aestiva)*, "mandiblating" a stick. Drawn after Rogers (1969: 114).

leathery or some of the other words that have sometimes been applied to it. It is firm, warm and soft — in fact, it has precisely the consistency of the flesh at the ball of a human finger. With its combination of sensitivity and power, a parrot's beak can shell a peanut, peel a grape; and drawing on our experiences, we note that it can also unplug an electric coffee pot, set an egg timer, destroy woodwork with the enthusiasm of a teething puppy, unsnap food dishes and throw them on the floor to get attention, and open any kind of snap-hook devised by the mind of man and used for the purpose of keeping said parrot in its cage. In short, a large parrot is capable of fully as much monkey business as our primate relatives who gave their name to the phrase.

Behavior and Social Organization

At the beginning of this paper we noted that our conclusions derive more or less accidentally from observations made on our own pet parrots and monkeys. In one sense, however, this opportune "accident" was partially predetermined. We have parrots as pets because parrots make very good pets, and the reason they make good pets is because they are social creatures with a large capacity for learned and modifiable behavior (Figure 11). Starting with young birds, it is relatively easy to substitute human companionship for their usual dependence upon other members of the flock for stimulation, reinforcement and apparently for some needed sense of identity (Figure 12). Deprived of avian or close human associations, some parrots sicken and die (Dilger 1960:660).

Under normal circumstances in the wild, psittacines exist in organized flocks. Unfortunately, very little attention has been paid to flock or troop organization, and no effort has been made to compare the various kinds of parrots either with one another or with other birds or mammals. Partially this is because it is very difficult to distinguish and sex individuals in a wild flock short of trapping and banding or marking the entire group. Consequently our knowledge of parrot social organization is principally based on the two existing studies of flocks in captivity (Dilger 1960; Hardy 1963, 1965). The two genera in question, *Aratinga canicularis* the half-moon conure, and *Agapornis pullaria* the red-headed lovebird, do not appear to have the capacity for learned behavior that characterizes the large parrots, macaws and cockatoos (Figure 13). Furthermore, the flocks were artificially made up. That is, they were constituted of whatever birds

Figure 9. Blue-and-gold macaw *(Ara ararauna)* showing the size and robustness of the beak of one of the largest members of the parrot family. Drawn after Bates and Busenbark (1969: 368).

Figure 10. Cockatiels *(Nymphicus hollandicus)* showing the position of the tongue in relation to the beak. Drawn after Bates and Busenbark (1969: 364).

Figure 11. Greater sulphur crested cockatoo *(Kakatoe galerita)*, riding a bicycle on a tightrope at Parrot Jungle, Miami, Florida. Drawn after Rogers (1969: 78).

Figure 12. "Peanuts," orange-winged Amazon *(Amazona amazonica)*, the mascot of the Ann Arbor Pet Supply store, showing the companionable relationship which can develop between a person and a parrot.

Figure 13. Scarlet macaws *(Ara macao)*, pulling chariots at Parrot Jungle, Miami, Florida, showing the learned-behavior capabilities of large parrots. (See also Figures 6 and 11). Drawn after Rogers (1969: 68).

of the species in question happened to get trapped and put in the same cage. As a result, conclusions based on their study may be no more accurate than the generalizations about baboon behavior that Zuckerman made from his observations at monkey hill in the London Zoo (Zuckerman 1932).

Given these qualifications, there are a few points that can tentatively be offered. A dominance hierarchy, or in this case—literally—a pecking order is a normal part of group organization. What its dynamics are over time and in the light of sex, age and individual experience is a problem yet to be investigated. Unlike most primates, it seems that many psittacines form a very strong and permanent pair bond. The mated pair then acts as a unit in terms of group organization, and if the pair is disrupted by the removal of one member, the dominance rank of the other may change drastically.

In captivity, the potential for pair bonding may be transferred to birds of other species, to people, or even to dogs or cats (Figure 14). The phenomenon of the "one-man-bird" is commonly recognized in the avicultural trade. The converse of this is the fact that genuine pairs in captivity make poor pets from the human point of view. A series of behavior elements reinforce the social bond between members of a flock in general but especially between pair members. Ritual fluffing and tail wagging indicate general satisfaction as do certain "chuckling" vocalizations. More specifically, head-bobbing and nape presentation are important aspects of social bond reinforcement behavior. Head-bobbing derives from the regurgitation technique whereby infants are fed (Figure 15). In adults, it becomes part of courtship behavior which continues as a sort of ritual mutual feeding

Figure 14. A military macaw *(Ara militaris)* preening a hyacinthine macaw *(Anodorhyncus hyacinthinus)*, showing the mutual attachments that can occur between parrots of different genera. Drawn after Bates and Busenbark (1969: 369).

Figure 15. Leadbeater's Cockatoos *(Kakatoe leadbeateri)* engaging in mutual feeding. Drawn after Bates and Busenbark (1969: 378).

during incubation. Nape presentation is an invitation to preening or grooming, and mutual preening is as important for maintaining psittacine social relations as is mutual grooming among primates (Figures 16 and 17).

Psittacine agonistic display has also been well documented in the few available studies. Beak-gaping, siddling, lunging, neck-stretching, tail-spreading, voluntary pupil-contraction, and a crowing kind of threat vocalization are all part of agonistic behavior although the specifics evidently vary from group to group. In the actual studies that exist, the gradation of agonistic behavior off to defensive behavior has been noted, but, so far, we have little knowledge concerning the relative importance of these behavioral elements in within-versus between-group situations.

No consideration, however brief, of parrot behavior would be complete without a mention of vocalization (Figures 18 and 19). It is legendary that parrots are capable of extraordinary feats of mimicry. What is less well known is the fact that many are also extraordinarily

Figure 16. Nape presentation and subsequent preening response in hyacinthine macaws *(Anodorhyncus hyacinthinus)*. Drawn after Rogers (1969: 136).

Figure 17. Mutual grooming between baboons *(Papio cynocephalus)*. Drawn after Napier and Napier (1967: 248, Plate 82).

Figure 18. Yellow-fronted Amazon parrot *(Amazona ochrocephala)* in full voice. Drawn after Bedford (1969: 114).

Figure 19. Howler monkey *(Alouatta seniculus)*, howling. Drawn after Napier and Napier (1967: 48, Plate 7).

loud. The loudest would appear to be the large, heavy-beaked and specifically fruit-oriented forms. One would suspect, then, that their capacity for sheer sound production might share something of the explanation offered for some of the fruit-eating primates. Particularly we have chimpanzees in mind. The identification of food sources at some distance from the troop by itinerant members is announced at a decibel level sufficient to bring the others from distances of over a mile. This may well have survival value where fruiting trees ripen spotted over a considerable area and at unpredictable intervals. Perhaps also the ability to learn specific sound patterns is of value in maintaining flock identity when the constituent birds are invisible from each other in the rainforest canopy. Whether vocalization plays a role in defending territory or in group versus group confrontation remains unstudied and unknown.

Primate and Parrot Distributions

We want to conclude this paper with a brief consideration of the ecological interaction of primates and psittacines. If in fact they are occupants of the same ecological niche, we would expect that the two groups as a whole would display an inverse or complementary aspect to their distribution throughout the world. Such indeed appears to be the case. Figure 20 shows the relative density of parrots and primates throughout the world and it is evident that parrots are few in Africa where primates are most diversified, South America is intermediate in both categories, and in Australia, New Guinea and New Zealand where there are no native primates, the psittacines achieve their greatest variety.

In order to demonstrate the inverse nature of the primate-psittacine distributions, we have not counted numbers of species or population densities. Rather we have tried to focus on numbers of adaptive categories of the two groups under consideration. As one index of the number of such categories, we have plotted their distribution by noting the numbers of genera in major geographic blocs (Figure 21; see Table 1). Since we are aware that the traditions for establishing generic identity differ between primatologists and ornithologists, we made up our own assessment of adaptive categories or kinds and plot-

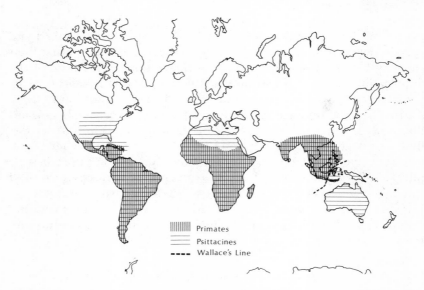

Figure 20. Map showing the comparative distributions of primates and psittacines. The relative densities are derived from the numbers of adaptive categories as indicated in Table 1.

TABLE 1

NUMBERS OF TAXONOMIC AND ADAPTIVE CATEGORIES OF PRI-
MATES AND PSITTACINES FOR THE VARIOUS GEOGRAPHIC BLOCS
OF THE WORLD BASED ON DATA IN NAPIER AND NAPIER (1967)
AND PETERS (1937, VOL. 3). SINCE THERE IS ONLY ONE FAMILY OF
THE PARROTS, PSITTACIDAE, THE SUBFAMILIAL DIVISIONS ARE
COMPARED WITH THE FAMILIAL DIVISIONS OF THE PRIMATES.

		Australia New Guinea Oceania	Africa	Madagascar	New World	India S.E. Asia
No. of Categories	Parrots	8	4	2	5	4
	Primates	1	7	6	4	6
No. of Genera	Parrots	44	4	2	29	6
	Primates	1	23	12	16	18
No. of Families or Subfamilies	Parrots	6	1	1	1	2
	Primates	1	3	3	2	6

ted their distribution in Figure 22. Our categories consist of such
attributes as insect-eating, fruit-and-nut-eating, terrestrial, nocturnal,
seed-eating, nectar-eating, leaf-eating and the like. Admittedly, there
is as much of the arbitrary about this as there is about the use of
genera, but it is interesting to note that the patterns in Figures 21 and
22 display the same kind of complementary distribution. Despite the
crudities of this approach, we feel that it sustains the substance of our
convictions.

And so we end where we began. As many a granting agency in the
past has felt that the investigation of monkey business was mere
frivolity, so have many others felt that the study of bird behavior was
brainless—bird-brained, if you will—when the issue concerned the
development of the more complex aspects of learned behavior as
exemplified in the higher primates. On the contrary, we suggest that
the study of parrot biology and behavior can have value for the understanding of the basic primate condition. Perhaps nothing new or
startling will emerge, but at the very least it could provide inde-

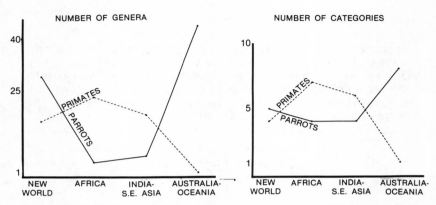

Figure 21. Graphic representation of the numbers of genera of primates compared with psittacines, region by region throughout the world, based on data in Napier and Napier (1967) and Peters (1937, Vol. 3).

Figure 22. Graphic representation of the numbers of adaptive categories of primates compared with psittacines, region by region throughout the world.

pendent verification and perspective on what we have gained from primate studies so far.

References

Bates, Henry, and Robert Busenbark
    1969   Parrots and Related Birds. T.F.H. Publications, Jersey City, N.J.
    512 pp.
Bedford, The Duke of
    1969   Parrots and Parrot-Like Birds. T.F.H. Publications. Jersey City,
    N.J. 210 pp.
Dilger, W.C.
    1960   The comparative ethology of the African genus *Agapornis*.
    Zeitschrift für Tierpsychologie, *17:* 649-685.
Eimerl, Sarel, Irven DeVore and the Editors of "Life"
    1965   The Primates. Life Nature Library, Vol. 23, Time Incorporated,
    New York. 200 pp.
Hardy, John W.
    1963   Epigamic and reproductive behavior of the orange-fronted para-
    keet. *Condor,* 65: 169-199.

    1965   Flock social behavior of the orange-fronted parakeet. Condor,
    67: 140-156.

Napier, J.H., and P.H. Napier
    1967   A Handbook of Living Primates: Morphology, Ecology and Behavior of Nonhuman Primates. Academic Press, London. 456 pp.
Pearson, Ronald
    1972   The Avian Brain. Academic Press, New York. 658 pp.
Peters, James Lee
    1937   Check List of Birds of the World, Volume 3, Harvard University Press, Cambridge, Mass. 311 pp.
Rogers, Cyril H.
    1969   Pet Library's Parrot Guide. The Pet Library, London. 250 pp.

3. The Red Howler Monkey Troop as a Social Unit

Melvin Neville

Introduction

Individuals in primate species tend to aggregate into social groupings, the structuring of which varies among and even within the species. Attempts to analyze these groupings as units have consisted primarily of assigning them to various nominal categories and then relating these categories statiscally to environmental categories, taxonomic position, and various behavioral features. Kummer (1971: 33-34) uses three categories: the multi-adult male and adult female group with young (*Alouatta* would belong here) is most common; groups with one adult male, adult females and young are fairly frequent; and a group of an adult heterosexual pair with young is very infrequent. Common correlates of the first two categories are

NOTE: The study was financed by NSE grant (GS-2057 after a preliminary investigation of the sites in the summer of 1967, sponsored by the University of California. I am deeply grateful to my friends Tomas and Cecilia Blohm of Caracas and Hato Masaguaral for their immeasurable assistance and to the Trinidad Regional Virus Laboratory and especially its former Director, Dr. L. Spence, the Acting Director during my Bush Bush work. Dr. A. Jonkers, and Dr. E. Tikasingh. I wish also to thank our many other friends and associates in Trinidad and Venezuela.

all-male groupings, more-or-less related to the heterosexual groupings. The first two categories may occur even within the same species,
as in the famous example of *Presbytis entellus* (Yoshiba, 1968).

Crook (1970: 106-107) suggests that "variations are probably best
envisaged as continua in relation to gradients in environmental conditions, but for practical purposes we may use a preliminary cate-
gorization into five main types." These types, as presented, are *directly* related to spacing behaviors:

(1) Relatively small groups with one adult male, one or more adult
     females with young: forest species with defended territories,
     examples being *Colobus guereza, Presbytis cristatus, Callicebus
     moloch,* and *Hylobates.*

(2) Larger groups of one or more adult males with adult females
     and young: forest or forest-fringe species with home ranges or
     territories and group vocal displays. Examples include
     Alouatta palliata (the most-studied howler monkey, now more
     commonly placed within *A. villosa* [Hall and Kelson, 1959])
     and *Cerocebus albigena.*

(3) Multi-adult male and female groups, females preponderating,
     with young: forest fringe to savanna species with large home
     ranges, and intertroop avoidance more important than terri-
     torial defense. Examples include *Cercopithecus aethiops, Papio*
     other than *P. hamadryas, Macaca mulatta,* and *M. fuscata.*

(4) Single adult males with adult females and young, correlated
     with all-male groups: grassland and arid savanna groups with
     very divergent intergroup behavioral relations in the three
     examples: *Erythrocebus patas* with antagonistic groups in large
     home ranges (perhaps with territory from Hall's 1965 report);
     Papio hamadryas with the one-male groups collected into bands,
     the latter more loosely gathered into "troops"; and *Theropi-
     thecus gelada* with the association of the one-male groups into
     "troops" being variable-dependent on ecological conditions.

(5) Temporary associations of decidedly social animals with the
     basic, and perhaps only, permanent social relations expressed
     through bonds developed between mother and offspring and
     among siblings during maturation of the young: the savana
     species, *Pan troglodytes* (Crook uses "*P. satyrus*").

The specialized behaviors of *Callicebus* and *Hylobates,* which limit
the basic social unit to an adult heterosexual pair with immature off-

spring, demarcate these animals from Crook's group 1, members of the latter bearing in terms of the structure of the basic social unit at least a superficial similarity to his group 4. The orang-utan, in which the most frequent multiple-animal unit seems to be a female with immature offspring (Davenport, 1967; Silva, 1971) does not fit neatly into his scheme.

An even more detailed model relating social structure to (among other factors) intergroup relations has been proposed by Denham (1971). Denham moves from a basic premise of rapid adaptability to energy requirements and predation danger in a habitat through causational arguments to the proposal of the relationship of socionomic sex ratio, group size, mating habits, and "territoriality" to food distribution, food density, and choice of predator defense method.

It is obvious that the relationship of social structure to intergroup relations is of major importance in primate behavior. Relationships between primate groups can range from positive attraction with acceptance (within limits), as in hamadryas and gelada baboons; to a watchful neutrality coupled with avoidance, such as that described for savanna baboons at water sources (DeVore and Hall, 1965: 38); to hostility manifest either through visual or vocal displays or more aggressive threats including attacks; to a combination of these latter features related to definite geographical locations in a manner describable as classical territoriality (see Bates, 1970, for possible territorial primates).

The strategy employed for land usage or resource partitioning among primates is often described in terms of home range, core area within a home range, and territory (usually in the defended-boundary sense implied above). Core areas as described by DeVore (1965) and DeVore and Hall (1965) are areas of intense usage within the home range boundaries. (The authors noted that though home ranges of their savanna baboons could overlap significantly, core areas were much more exclusive.) It is interesting to note that such restriction could result not only from classical territoriality within a larger, undefended home range boundary, but also from simple avoidance. Pitelka (1959: 253) chose to emphasize the ecological result of territoriality, but as Mason (1968: 202), Ripley (1967: 237-238), and Bates (1970: 272) observe, the behavioral mechanisms involved in land-partitioning are also of interest. Specifically, we want to know ultimate cause (selective advantage) of the species' partitioning mechanisms, the workings or the mechanisms themselves, including the proximate causes releasing or inducing the behaviors, and how individual animals ontogenetically acquire the related behavioral repertoire.

The land-usage and intergroup behaviors of the black howler monkey *(Alouatta villosa)* have been studied by a number of authors on Barro Colorado Island in Gatun Lake of the Panama Canal Zone. Carpenter (1934), in the original monograph, used the term "territory" in essentially the same sense as we currently use "home range," but in his recent summary he clearly indicates range partitioning through signalling and avoidance with an emphasis on defense of a mobile space around the group rather than that of a fixed geographical area (1965: 273-275). The overlapping character of the howler ranges has been noted by a number of authors, and Chivers (1969) in particular establishes the shifting nature of those ranges resulting in an apparent increase in overlap as the observation period increases. My observations of red howlers are very similar to those made on the Barro Colorado animals. After a brief resume of the animals and their environment, the bulk of this paper will consider the nature of intertroop relations in *A. seniculus*, concentrating on the prominent dawn chorus, though some attention will be given to the reaction of the troop to other stimuli.

"Troop" will be used to designate the social grouping of howler monkeys characterized by stability of membership, proximity of individuals, and friendly or neutral interindividual behavior. Neville (1972, tables I and III) showed that 31 troops of red howler monkeys (from the Venezuelan locality of Hato Masaguaral to be described below) had an average composition of 2.5 adult and subadult males, 2.9 adult and subadult females, and 3.2 youngsters. In that paper I suggested that the parameters of troop composition may differ consistently among various *Alouatta* species and even within a population from year to year—the latter has been well documented from Barro Colorado (Chivers, 1969: 82-86). "Extra-troop howler(s)" or "extra-troop monkey(s)" will refer to monkeys which are either solitary or members of a troop other than the subject troop.

Methodology and Locations

The following synopsis is drawn from Neville (1972a), while Neville (1972) contains a fuller description of the study location of Bush Bush Forest in Trinidad and Hato Masaguaral in the "llanos" (plains) state of Guarico, Venezuela.

"Bush Bush Forest is based on but not limited to slightly raised ground in the middle of Nariva Swamp, an extensive feature on the east side of Trinidad. The Trinidad Regional Virus Laboratory protected the area and maintained paths and several buildings. The forest resembles Beard's (1946) classification of the "evergreen Seasonal Forest." The rainy season lasts from approximately June to January, but all parts of the year could be termed hot and humid (Trinidad lies at about 10° N. latitude). Despite similarity to Hato Masaguaral in timing of seasonal rain and temperatures, Bush Bush vegetation was strikingly different. The fauna of Trinidad is closely related to that of mainland Venezuela: Vuilleumier (1971: fig. 2) indicates that the island may have been connected to the mainland during glacial periods with the accompanying sea-level lowering.

"Hato Masaguaral, a cattle-raising ranch of over 3000 ha, is 50 km south of Calabozo at about 8.5° N. latitude and at an elevation of less than 100 m (Myers, 1933). The dry season lasts from approximately December till May and is characterized by a gradual, variable increase in temperature; the maximum recorded on the ranch was 40.0° C. The wet season induces a lowering of temperatures and the relatively impermeable savanna soil becomes flooded, in places to depths exceeding 0.5 m. The vegetation varies between savannas, palm-tree savannas, and thorny forests, but about 3 km east of the highway passing through the ranch is a tall, deciduous forest accessible only during the dry season, bordering the Caracol Stream and Guarico River."

The Bush Bush data resulted from 49 days of field work during the summer of 1968 resulting in only 51.5 hr of direct observation. There were 3 major reasons for the small amount of the latter: (1) the howlers normally moved in a canopy about 15 to 25 m above the ground, (2) all but three troops regularly took prompt evasive action when they saw me (probably an indication of past hunting), and (3) WHT troop, the troop utilizing Restan, the most conditioned to my presence and the easiest to find during the first portion of the study, during the latter portion spent most of its time in the northern, forested portion of Petit Bush Bush Swamp (Neville 1972: Figs. 1 and 5) into which I could not follow.

Part of the purpose of the summer 1968 Bush Bush work was to try out equipment and techniques. Observations were made with 7x50 binoculars and a 9-30 power zoom spotting scope, but these were changed to 10x40 binoculars and a 15-60 power zoom scope for Venezuela. At both locations a Uher 4000 Report-L tape recorder equipped with an Electrovoice 666 cardioid microphone was used to tape vocalizations at 7.5 ips, and photographs were made with a 50 mm Honeywell Pentax Spotomatic camera equipped with 28, 55, and 200 mm lenses.

The Venezuelan work extended from July 1969 to August 1970 and resulted in 603 hours of direct observation, most of which occurred on Hato Masaguaral. Observational conditions were much better than in Bush Bush as trees were lower and tended to be discontinuously clustered (to the extent that howlers were sometimes forced to the ground for crossings), but with rare exceptions the scattering of the trees and thickets forced approach to within 100 m, so that the animals were usually aware of my presence.

WHT troop on Bush Bush could often be located by means of the dawn chorus, and this method also proved useful on the Hato, as did the technique of stationing myself before dawn in the same locality where a troop had been seen the previous evening. Howls during the day at both locations frequently resulted from the interaction of two troops. Both locations were mapped by means of a Brunton pocket transit mounted on a tripod. See Neville (1972) for further details on methodology and for the population structure and ranges of the troops.

Behavior Toward Extra-Troop Howlers

THE DAWN CHORUS

Notes on Vocalization Terminology The terminology I attempted to use was based on the descriptions and classifications of Altmann (1959) on the Barro Colorado species. However, taped vocalizations from both my locations differ somewhat from each other and from those recorded by Altmann (1966). That the two species should differ is not remarkable given the difference in the degree of hyoid elaboration, the most highly developed *Alouatta* hyoid being that of *A. seniculus* (Hershkovitz, 1949: 99), but the difference between the two localities of *A. seniculus* may reflect primarily behavioral, even traditional differences rather than anatomical. There is, however, no evidence on the latter point other than that implied by the evidence for possible gene flow: Andel and Postma per Rouse (1945: 500) have claimed that Trinidad was attached to Venezuela until ca. 6000 B.C., while Vuilleumier (1971: fig. 2) indicates connection during the South American analogue of the Würm glaciation.

I heard analogues to Altmann's "roar or howl" (type A1), "incipient roar" or "pops" (A2), and "roar accompaniment" (B: "wailsome in tone"), but not his "high roar coda" (A3). The A vocalizations were performed by adult and occasionally subadult males, the B vocalization appeared to be evoked from the females during particularly emphatic howls by the males.

With respect to Altmann's other vocalizations, I heard the "male bark" (C1 or C2, which differ in his terminology by the mouth being open or closed—this difference was difficult to perceive), and the "female bark" (D1 or D2, comment as with type C). I did not hear the clucking noise reported by Collias and Southwick (1952) as perhaps functioning to maintain group contact. Bernstein (1964) heard this vocalization as well as all of Altmann's. Altmann could not match 6 of Carpenter's (1934) 9 vocalizations, but he succeeded in identifying some new ones and subdividing some of Carpenter's types. Chivers (1969: 77) suggests differentiating Altmann's A1 category into howls and roars, "the one according to form and function) evoked as a spacing call, the other as an aggressive one." While I do not follow his distinction in this paper, it is possible that a more careful analysis might substantiate it for *A. seniculus*. Altmann (1968: table II) summarized the systems of Altmann (1959), Carpenter (1934), and Collias and Southwick (1952); the discrepancies emphasize the difficulty of matching the vocalization perceptions of different workers, even on the same species. I am preparing sonograms from the red howler locations.

Alouatta is famous for the vigorous howling (Altmann's vocalizations A1 and A2) performed by adult and subadult males, sometimes accompanied by females (B vocalizations), in the period during or shortly after dawn. In some cases a particular adult male will be the sole vocalizer, while at other times other animals may join him. The term "chorus" naturally arises in two ways: (1) one could use the term to designate the howlings of the various groups participating on a given morning—this is the sense in which Chivers (1969) uses it in his analysis of the parameters involved in morning howls—or (2) one could use it to designate the bout of howling performed by a particular troop. This latter usage is suggested by the subjective chorusing effect of distant howls. This paper will use the term in both senses; context should render the meaning unambiguous.

As a convention, a chorus will only be registered as a "dawn chorus" if it falls between 0500 and 0700 and is the first chorus for a particular troop on that morning. This focuses attention on the time period in which the bulk of howling occurs (fig. 1) and removes from the analyses choruses stimulated by other troops subsequent to the first chorus. However, one of the questions which will be considered is whether the first chorus ("dawn chorus") is often a result of near howling.

THE DAWN CHORUS – BUSH BUSH

Howling in Bush Bush appeared to be routinely performed by the troops in the early morning and consisted of a sequence of alternating A1 and A2 vocalizations by the males and, usually toward the end of the howling, B wails by the females. My field house ("We House" in Restan: Worth, 1967) was within the estimated 6.6 home range of WHT troop: Thus I was frequently in position to know whether WHT troop did or did not howl on a particular morning. This occurred on 22 of 23 sample mornings, which compares well with the 22 of 22 mornings for Altmann's (1959: 322) laboratory group and 23 of 25 mornings for Collias and Southwick's (1952: 144) laboratory clan. Chivers (1969: 77), however, reports variation between 81% and 47% in frequency of morning howls for four troops on Barro Colorado.

The average onset time was 0529, the earliest call being at 0448, and the length of duration of WHT troop's dawn choruses ranged for 19 observations from 3 to 12.5 min with a mean of 7.75 min. Either an A1 or a series of A2 "pops" began the howling. There was considerable variation in the proportion of A2 pops to A1 roars, even during the same howling bout: frequently there were 2 to 4 A2 pops, but once I counted 66 between sequential A1 roars. An A1 howl lasted from 3 to 13 sec, while A2 pops were about 3 sec. During the long roars an effect can be heard which suggests that the howler is alternately inhaling and exhaling.

Fig. 1 gives the frequency of onset of howling bouts within half-hour periods for WHT troop, with the frequency adjusted for the number of times I was so positioned as to be able to detect the presence or absence of howling by the troop during the period. (Number of times I was correctly positioned for the various half-hour periods varied from 26 to 38). The peak of the onset of howling occurred during 0500-0600, which emphasized again the importance of tim-

ing in this vocalization. Similar curves for Barro Colorado can be
seen in Altmann (1959: fig. 3), Carpenter (1965: fig. 8-6), and
Chivers (1969: fig. 9).

I attempted to relate the onset of howling to the amount of light
present, though light conditions varied on the forest floor according
to location and weather conditions. I first noticed dawn between 0500
and 0524; it then took about 26 minutes to become light enough to
read (in the same sense as Chiver's "light time" [1969: 68], but less
precise in that Chivers used a standard location). WHT troop began
howling an average of 23.4 min after the first signs of dawn on 12 occasions (standard error = 5.6 min). On one occasion (not included
in the above statistics as dawn time was not noted) WHT troop com-
menced howling at 0448, possibly 23 min before I would normally

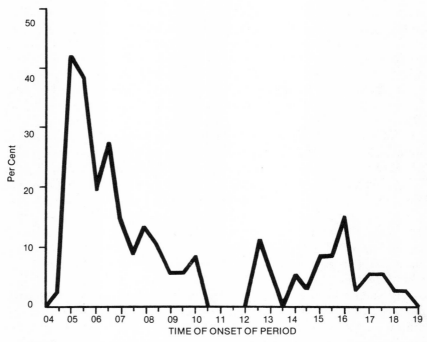

Figure 1. Frequency of onset of howling bouts within half-hour periods for WHT
troop, Bush Bush. Frequency is adjusted for the number of observation opportunities
for each half-hour period; minimum such number for any period = 26.

have begun to perceive dawn. If instead of using the actual perceived or noted first signs of dawn on a given day we use a linear regression approximation, then the sample size expands to 22 and the average delay after the beginning of dawn was 19.6 min (s.e. = 4.7 min). Analysis of variance demonstrates an added delay in onset of howling by WHT troop on days with as opposed to without rain at the critical time at better than the 2.5% significance level, though this does not take into account changes in absolute dawn time. Adjusting for the latter by using the linear regression approximation for first perceptible dawn, the delay in howling by WHT troop on days with dawn rain is significant at better than the 5% level. I restricted the analysis to WHT troop, as rain drastically reduced my ability to hear most distant troops.

THE DAWN CHORUS – HATO MASAGUARAL

Howling was much more sporadic on the Hato, and characteristics of the choruses also differed somewhat. Thus, B-wails were much more infrequent, and though one gained the impression of extensive howling each morning (the flat, partially open llanos being conducive to long-distance transmission of howls), investigation showed that a given troop very frequently did not vocalize. Thus troop 1 failed completely to howl on 18 of 22 mornings on which I was correctly situated during the critical time. On one of the other mornings the troop howled at 0704, which is really too late to be considered part of the dawn chorus, and on another occasion there was what amounted to a false start (giving the impression of throat-clearing) 10 minutes before the onset of dawn. On the remaining two occasions the troop genuinely howled (at 0644 and 0548) on successive mornings, but the situation was unusual for troop 1 in that on the first morning an extra-troop adult male was in a tree 75 meters away: troop 1 was rarely within view of another troop despite the fact that other howlers were sometimes found within its range (Fig. 2). I hypothesize that the howling on the succeeding morning was due to the stimulation of the male on the previous day (searching located no howlers near the troop).

The frequency of howls was higher for troops in the more densely settled East and Eastern Middle Forests of the Hato (Table 1). These statistics are not directly comparable to those for troop 1 nor for WHT troop in Bush Bush, for the frequency is biased toward the

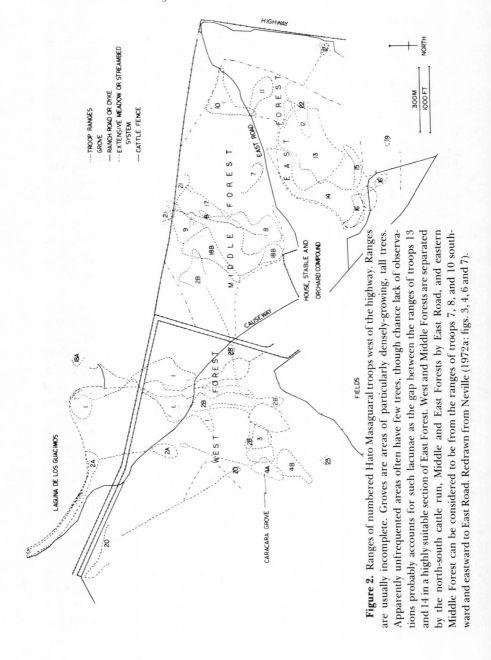

Figure 2. Ranges of numbered Hato Masaguaral troops west of the highway. Ranges are usually incomplete. Groves are areas of particularly densely-growing, tall trees. Apparently unfrequented areas often have few trees, though chance lack of observations probably accounts for such lacunae as the gap between the ranges of troops 13 and 14 in a highly suitable section of East Forest. West and Middle Forests are separated by the north-south cattle run, Middle and East Forests by East Road, and eastern Middle Forest can be considered to be from the ranges of troops 7, 8, and 10 southward and eastward to East Road. Redrawn from Neville (1972a: figs. 3, 4, 6 and 7).

high side. My technique in Middle and East Forest involved stationing myself before dawn in one of several special locations, taking compass fixes on the direction of morning howls, and trying to track some or all of these down. In many cases I could not be sure if a particular troop had howled, in which case no entry is made in Table I; also, the more distant the troop, the more likely entry of a datum about that troop was likely to result from having tracked it down after it had howled.

As in Bush Bush I judged the progress of dawn by two criteria: the first noticeable signs of lightening to the east and the time when I could first read my notebook. Fig. 3 shows the curves drawn through these two series of markers; the actual times varied from day to day depending on weather conditions location. The retardation of the maxima of the curves until after the winter solstice may be due to 3.2 mm of rain and accompanying weather conditions occurring in early January in the middle of a dry season. As can be seen from

TABLE 1

FREQUENCY OF DAWN CHORUSES BY PARTICULAR TROOPS IN
EAST AND EASTERN MIDDLE FORESTS, HATO MASAGUARAL[a]

Troop[b]	Dawns on which the howl/not howl datum entered	Dawns on which the troop howled	%
7	14	4	28
8	3	3	100
10	7	4	57
11	8	2	25
12	4	2	50
13	7	6	86
14	10	3	30
15	7	3	43
16	6	5	83
Total	66	32	49

[a] Based toward increased frequency of howling: see discussion in text. Howls after 0700 not counted: only one chorus per troop per dawn period included.

[b] For ranges see fig. 2.

Fig. 3, the spacing between the two curves varies from ca. 23 to 27 min (though a greater variation could occur on given days), which is comparable to Bush Bush.

The first detectable howls were often shortly after or even before the first signs of dawn, but, because of potential variability in transmission conditions, I have placed on Fig. 3 only the time of onset of howls judged to be from East or eastern Middle Forests. These data begin in January 1970, for prior to that time I had not begun to work those areas intensively. These regional choruses began very variably, averaging for 24 mornings 22.4 min after the first signs of dawn as given by the lower curve in fig. 3 (s.e. = 3.4 min); on 5 other mornings there were probably no howls from this region prior to 0700.

Although the probability of a troop howling during a given dawn differs between the two sites, the distribution of delay after the first detectable signs of dawn (as determined from the regression equations) is about the same. The two "populations" of dawn choruses are, strictly speaking, not founded on the same basis, for the Bush Bush sample is based on only WHT troop, while the Hato sample is based on the first call of any troop in the East Forest and eastern Middle Forest area, which should, if anything, reduce the average delay. The F-test indicates that the two populations variances are not significantly different at the 10% level for a two-tail test, and analysis

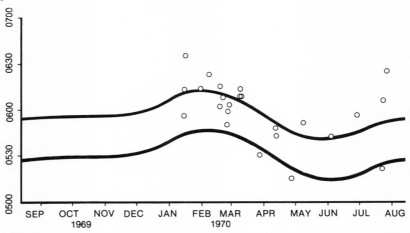

Figure 3. The relation of the first detected dawn choruses from the area of East and Eastern Middle forests. Hato Masaguaral, to the regression curves for the first signs of dawn and the achievement of enough light for reading.

of variance shows that the means of the two populations are not significantly different (50% significance level).

Factors inducing Dawn Choruses The determination of causal factors for dawn choruses is exceedingly difficult, for the ground-level observer cannot be sure what the arboreal troop is perceiving or has perceived. Some of the most important possible hypotheses are:

(1) *Alouatta* troops always howl around dawn.

(2) A troop's dawn chorus is stimulated by physical interaction with or visual proximity of howlers not of that social group. (This could be subdivided in terms of time of the stimulus, e.g., whether such interaction on the previous day sufficient to increase the probability of chorusing the next morning.)

(3) The probability of howling is dependent on the degree of acquaintance of the troop with neighboring troops. (Thus, one could ask about the history of the groups and the stability of group membership in an area.)

(4) The probability of howling is increased by a nearby chorus and/or by the numbers of howls heard that morning.

(5) The probability of howling is dependent on the density of troops.

(6) The probability of howling is dependent on the age and sex composition of the troop.

The above hypotheses are not independent or mutually exclusive; thus, density might increase howling through an increase in visual and vocal contacts. However, one could in theory record data directed toward any of the particular questions. I emphasize "in theory," for certain types of data would be very difficult or expensive to obtain. Thus, establishment of common ancestry for two troops would require observing a troop split either through luck or a very extended study.

The data from Hato Masaguaral and Chivers' results from Barro Colorado disprove the universality of (1), though it remains as a possibility for some species or populations.

Hypothesis (2) is suggested by the data for troop 1. In a similar incident troop 7 howled vigorously beginning at 0637 on the morning of February 27th: troop 7 rarely gave dawn choruses (4 of 12 observations), but this chorus was evidently evoked by the presence of an extra-troop male in the same grove less than 100 m away. Certainly the proximity of extra-troop monkeys stimulated howling at other times of the day (discussed later).

Hato Masaguaral troops did not chorus automatically at the sight or sound of nearby extra-troop monkeys. On 12 of 21 occasions (57%) when I ascertained the presence of extra-troop howlers within 100 m of a troop in eastern Middle or East Forests during the critical dawn period, the troop gave a dawn chorus. On an additional 28 mornings the closest known extra-troop howlers to a troop in the same area were between 100 and 200 m distant; the subject troops howled on 16 of these days (also 57%). On 10 of 15 occasions (67%) when extra-troop monkeys within 100 m were probably visible to a subject troop, that troop howled. On an additional 10 of 15 occasions when the nearest extra-troop howlers, between 100 and 200 m away, were probably visible the subject troop also chorused. Lack of an increase in frequency of dawn choruses when the closest extra-troop howlers are less than 100 m away as opposed to being between 100 and 200 m is surprising and probably accidental. There is an increased trend toward howling when the nearest known extra-troop monkeys are, firstly, within 200 meters and, secondly, if less than 200 meters away, probably visible as opposed to non-visible (Table 2); chi-squares of these two trends are just significant at the 5% level ($x^2_{(d_1)} = 2.79$ and 2.97 respectively) for one-tail tests (justified in Blalock, 1960: 218).

Therefore proximity of extra-troop howlers, both at dawn and later in the day was evocative of howling, but this was not the only govern-

TABLE 2

FREQUENCY OF DAWN CHORUSING BY SUBJECT TROOPS WITH REGARDS TO NEARNESS AND VISIBILITY OF CLOSEST-KNOWN EXTRA-TROOP HOWLERS (ETH): EAST AND EASTERN MIDDLE FORESTS.

Subject troop	Closest-known ETH>200 m	*Closest known ETH ≤ 200 m* "Not visible"[b]	"Visible"[b]
Choruses	7	8	20
Does not chorus	13	11	10

[a] Totals 69; difference from Table 1 results from inclusion of some cases wherein the identity of a subject troop could not be specified.

[b] Text discusses difficulty of determining this distinction.

ing factor. In some cases location of suitable trees grouped several troops in a small area with almost constant visual contact, yet howls could be rare. An example would be the "Caracara Grove" (Fig. 2): troops 3, 4a and 4b were often in or close to this grove, and troops 3 and 4a were frequently separated by less than 70 m throughout the day, and yet choruses at any time including, apparently, dawn were infrequent. ("Apparently" results from the distance of the grove from the Causeway where I was usually stationed and the resulting infrequency of the occasions on which I could be sure of the occurrence or non-occurrence of dawn choruses from the grove.) This, of course, could be a result of common ancestry or habituation (hypothesis 3). On at least one afternoon, however, about 30 min of roaring was heard from that general locality.

Hypothesis (4) can be examined by looking at the time lapse in onset of dawn chorus between two troops in relation to the distance separating them. The following procedure was used: the assumption was made that one chorus tended to stimulate another. After one troop had howled the next howling heard was analyzed as to whether the second troop was "near" (ND), "middle-distant" (MD), or "far" (FD) from the first. This sorting was primarily evaluated by sound cues, the observer being located by one of the two troops, and was therefore approximate, but those checks which could be made indicated that ND corresponded roughly to distance up to ca. 200 m and MD to a range of ca. 200 to 400 m. If indeed nearby choruses tend to stimulate chorusing, one could expect that the mean separation time for the howling of ND pairs would be less than that of MD pairs; furthermore, one could expect that the standard deviation of the MD pairs' separation times would exceed that of the ND pairs on the grounds that MD pairs might have vocalized without reference to each others' calls. (FD pairs were not analyzed because it was unclear whether the howlers would be perceiving the same set of choruses which I perceived.) Table 3 indicates that both predictions obtained. My impression is that an ND troop's chorus was more likely to stimulate a chorus than that of an MD troop, but if the MD troop was stimulated, the time lapse was distributed as for ND troops. The increased onset time difference for MD pairs would therefore be due to unrelated howling.

In the above analysis it should be remembered that the constraints of 0500-0700 were used in determining whether a troop's first chorus

TABLE 3

COMPARISON OF THE DIFFERENCE IN ONSET TIMES OF SEQUEN-
TIAL DAWN CHORUSES WHEN SEPARATED INTO "NEAR" (ND)
AND 'MIDDLE-DISTANT" (MD) PAIRS.

Statistic	ND pairs	MD pairs	Probability (one-tail)
Number of pairs	11	29	
Mean onset time difference (min)	5.1	12.1	$p = 0.019$ [a]
Standard deviation	6.3	11.9	$p < 0.025$

[a] Wilcoxon two-sample test.

could be evaluated as a dawn chorus; furthermore, on many occasions troops did not howl despite the sight and/or sound of a nearby
troop chorusing. I have not done an analysis of cumulative effects
of howling.

Hypothesis (5) is probably true but is a result of (2) and (4). This
provides part of the mechanism for possible self-regulation of density;
one would also wish to establish some reaction to frequent dawn
choruses through a correlation with decreased birth frequency, increased emigration, or some other population-regulating phenomenon. Chivers (1969: 73-78) presents and discusses evidence that his
group tend to move away from close troops (in the sense of shifting
night positions). However, an alternate interpretation might be that
troops tend to gravitate back toward the center of their range after
being on the peripheries, and two neighboring troops will of course
be closer if they are located in adjacent portions of the peripheries
of their current ranges than if located elsewhere. Admittedly, among
the stimuli inducing a troop to move away from its periphery might be
near-by howling!

Population densities in the tall, deciduous forest bordering the
Caracol Stream and Guárico River were probably much higher than
in the main study areas west of the highway. I unfortunately worked
too briefly in this area to be sure of home ranges, but I estimate that
5 known troops totalling 48 monkeys had ranges probably largely
contained within a circle with 300 m radius; even not allowing for

the solitaries and non-associated pairs seen in this area, this would be a population density of ca. 1.7 monkeys/hectare. The comparison in Table 4 to estimates of density from other areas indicates that, even considering the possibility of considerable inaccuracy, in Puente Caracol population density was probably significantly higher than in the shorter sparser Hato Masagural forests. On the 3 mornings on which I was in the area throughout the critical period 055-0700 the earliest choruses occurred 1.5 min prior to the regression line for first signs of dawn from East and eastern Middle Forests (Fig. 3), 9.5 min after (though "rumbles" — very incomplete A1's — began 10 minutes before the regression-line dawn), and 26 minutes after. On the first two days several social groups within a 100 m radius circle were interacting strongly (Table 5), while on the 3rd morning the only troop I could locate first howled at 0702 and the only other chorus that might have come from a troop within the Puente Caracol study area was judged "middle-distant."

Together with the data on the infrequency of howling of individual troops, hypothesis (5) indicates that a survey for presence as opposed to absence of *Alouatta* cannot depend solely upon sampling for dawn choruses on one morning.

Hypothesis (6) will be difficult to test, though it is implied by the

TABLE 4

ESTIMATES OF POPULATION DENSITY.[a]

Region	Population of troops	Area (ha)	Population density (monkeys/ha)
HATO Masaguaral			
Puente Caracol	48	25.2	1.7
East and Middle Forests	104.75	97.2	1.08
West Forest	61.25	93.4	0.61
Bush Bush			1.14
Barro Colorado in 1967	926-1278	1554	0.60-0.82

[a] See Neville (1972) for calculation of the Bush Bush, East and Middle Forest, and West Forest figures, which, however, do not include solitaries and, in the case of Bush Bush, are based on WHT troop's range and size. Barro Colorado figures are from Chivers (1969).

TABLE 5

PUENTE CARACOL: PROTOCOL OF "NEAR" AND "MIDDLE-
DISTANT" CHORUSES BETWEEN 0500 AND 0700 ON THE MORNINGS
OF APRIL 23RD AND APRIL 25TH.

April 23rd: Troops PC1, PC2, and PC3 within a circle of ca. 100 m radius;
strong and close interaction between PC2 and PC3; the fourth troop not seen
but "near" or "middle-distant."

Troop PC1	*Troop PC2*	*Troop PC3*	*Troop PC4 (?)*
0521.5-0531			
	0522.5- ?		
			0523.5-0532
	0537.5-0544.5		
0538.5-0544			
			0546.5-ca. 0552
	0546.5-0554		
0546.5-ca.0552			
	ca.0554-0558 [b]		
		0606 (a few roars)	
			0650.5- ?
	0650.5-0705 [c]		

[a] Troops PC2 and PC3 began physically so close to each other that I could
not exclude the possibility that PC3 was also howling at the time of the early
choruses. At 0648 PC2, which had begun withdrawal at 0613 to ultimately ca.
100 meters away, reapproached PC3.
[b] PC2 recommences its roars after a distant-sounding chorus begins.
[c] PC2 ceases howling at my approach and starts C vocalizations ("male bark").

April 25th Troop PC1 and PC3 separated by 150 meters, plus intense interaction with an extra-troop male and two extra-troop females. The other vocalizing troops not seen, though PC4, apparently silent, encountered less than 300
m from PC3.

Troop PC1	*Troop PC2 (?)*	*Troop PC3*	*Two middle-distant troops*
	0512 (rumble)		
		0517-0529 (rumbles)	
			0530 (rumbles)
		0531.5-0537.5	
0534-0551.5 [a]			
0554.75-0602			
0603.25			
			0627 (rumbles)
0629.75-0630.75			
0634 (rumble)			
		0637.5-0644.25	
0644.25-0657 [b]			

[a] Chorus may have been stimulated by PC3's chorus, but continuing vocalizations are due to proximity of two extra-troop females and (separately) an extra-
troop male.
[b] Vocalizations continue after 0700, and the protocol is continued from the
perspective of troop PC1 in Table 7. The extra-troop monkeys also later interact with PC3.

observation that howling by one member of the troop stimulated others. As noted earlier, the female B vocalization occurred only during periods of intense vocalization by males. If several adult or sub-adult males were in the troop, they often approached each other and their pattern of head bobbing and A1 and A2 vocalizations were frequently synchronized in phase or in opposite phases (Fig. 4). (The howling of two interacting troops is apparently not synchronized, however, and this provides a clue to the nature of the circumstances in distant howling.)

The high rate of howling in Chivers' YY troop despite its relative degree of isolation compared to his other Barro Colorado Troops AA, Ab or XX might be due to having 5 adult males (Chivers, 1969: table 1, and p. 73); Chivers attributed the excessive howling of YY to its instability (p. 70).

Behaviors other than the Dawn Chorus

TROOP INTERACTIONS

The basic features of howling at other times of the day are similar to those occurring during the dawn chorus period, though there is never a peak as extreme as in the early morning (Fig. 1). However, howling outside of the context of the dawn chorus is more easily related to stimuli, e.g., proximity of another troop or a solitary howler, rainstorms, humans.

In Bush Bush the howling resulting from close interactions could last for over 1/2 hour: duration of the exchanges between the troops and the non-synchronization of howling by the males of the two troops were audible differences from the chorus of a single troop. On the Hato, as mentioned in the discussion of hypothesis (2) for dawn howling, some troops were forced into proximity by the disposition of suitable trees, and these appeared to habituate to some extent to each other. The following example from East Forest demonstrates the interaction of the factors involved in intertroop relations. On the dawn of July 23rd troop 14 was located 100 m northwest of troop 15, but no howling occurred. In the afternoon when I returned to the locality, I found that troop 14 had approached to a position 50 m west of troop 15, and, in addition, troop 16 had appeared about 15 m west of troop 14. Troop 16 vocalized while I was there, including A1's and C and D barks, but these vocalizations appeared to be with

Figure 4. Troop PC1 bunched and howling at an extra-troop male (not visible) at 0949 on April 25.

reference to me rather than the other two troops. The dawn of the succeeding day found the positions of the three troops unchanged, and at least one of the troops gave a dawn chorus before my approach stimulated other reactions. (Shortly thereafter I was driven from the area by insects.)

The Puente Caracol area, being the most densely populated, was the location of frequent interactions. Troop PC2, the largest of my red howler troop at probably 16 monkeys, manifested signs of instability through widely varying troop counts and through spatial separation of subgroups, especially during close interaction with other troops. As well as adult and subadult males, advance portions of a troop in interaction with another could include adult and subadult females and juveniles, the latter appearing particularly adventuresome. In addition to male and female howling, sudden darts forward by a grouping of one troop corresponded with retreats of a few meters by the other troop. No contact nor fighting was seen; as indicated in Neville (1972:73) I interpreted wounds on howlers as probably resulting mainly from minor predatory activity rather than intraspecies fighting. Close, interacting troops tended to be separated by ca. 20-50 m.

Troop Constituency Fluctuations Occasionally solitary animals or pairs would be seen in an area. The ultimate fate of these animals was almost never known; one female that subsequently was seen in a troop was interpreted as having been separated from that troop at the time of the earlier sighting. Indeed, the lack of vocalizations at the onset of and during a red howler troop move probably frequently led to the separation of inattentive members. This is in sharp distinction to the reports on the Barro Colorado howlers: Carpenter's (1934) type 2 vocalization presumably matches Altmann's type H (1959, 1968) and is reported as "a deep metallic cluck repeated at irregular intervals" which "initiates progression, controls its direction and rate and coordinates the animals of the clan." The vocalization is heard "precurrent to group progression and during movement of the clan" and is given by "the leading male." (Carpenter, 1934: Table 4). As mentioned earlier in the section on vocalization terminology, Bernstein (1964: 95) likewise heard Altmann's type H, and Collias and Southwick (1952: 150) also reported clucking by females (in group progression?) and another female vocalization presumably functioning as a contact call at dusk, "somewhat similar to clucking, but . . . less audible to the observer, higher pitched, and less rhythmic."

Lack of movement noise with resulting involuntary separations may be the explanation for most of the day-to-day alterations in my troop counts and is a possible mechanism for troop fission. Males were much more likely to move independently of their troop (Table 6), and the only two known recruitments to troops other than by births were an adult male to troop 4b and a subadult or adult male to troop 9. Male mobility may be a behavioral phenomenon causing genetic exchanges between groups in a way similar to that reported for many Old World monkeys, e.g., classically rhesus monkeys (Lindburg, 1969, 1971; Neville, 1968), though for rhesus the phenomenon is concentrated in a mating season. Badly needed are extended studies on changes in howler troop membership with marked animals (unscarred howlers are difficult to distinguish).

Apparent attempts by solitary males to associate with a troop were seen in both Bush Bush and Hato Masaguaral. In Bush Bush on two successive days a male (or males) was seen attempting to approach WHT troop. On both occasions his presence evoked howling

TABLE 6

NONAPPEARANCE OF AGE/SEX CATEGORIES IN APPARENTLY GOOD
TROOP COUNTS IN WEST, MIDDLE, AND EAST FORESTS, HATO
MASAGUARAL.[a]

Adult		Subadult		Juvenile		Infant		
Male	*Female*	*Male*	*Female*	*Male*	*Female*	*Male*	*Female*	*Unsexed*
Frequency of absences from sequential counts:								
13	7	3	0	1	2	0	6[b]	0
Frequency permanent disappearance from troop:[c]								
5	0	0	0	0	2	0	0	2

[a] Analysis includes all but troops 6, 18a, 19, 22, 23, and 25 of the 26 troops recorded in Neville (1972: table 1). When the age/sex category of the apparently missing animal(s) was not ascertained, the fluctuations are not recorded.

[b] On several occasions an infant and its mother were simultaneously absent.

[c] In the cases of the infants and possibly the juveniles, the disappearances indicate deaths.

by males and females in the troop (i.e., A1, A2, and B vocalizations), and he was chased away by a sudden rush of one adult male and one big and one small howlers (unsexed) from a position of 15 m from the troop on one occasion and by 3–4 howlers on the next. On the first occasion the extra-troop male rubbed his chin and neck against a branch during his approach toward the troop. During this period the principal male of WHT troop appeared to be in a consort relationship with one of the adult females, although no copulation was seen, and several times he rubbed his neck back and forth on a branch while near or before approaching the female (Neville, 1972). Both the neck-rubbing and the fact that the extra-troop male was interested in the troop may therefore have something to do with the female's physiological state. A gular gland field similar to that of *Pithecia* and *Lagothrix* is described by Epple and Lorenz (1967:109-110) for *A. seniculus* in 3 males and 1 female, although Hill (1962) does not comment on it.

Solitary monkeys on the Hato could evoke the same type of vocalization response from a troop as did another troop. In one chasing incident it was not clear if the male chased were not part of troop 1:

1247.5   A male climbs up the troop's tree to adult female F1, who had moved closer to the others. He touches her, she wakens, chirps angrily, and chases him down the tree. The rest of the troop moves with her, with grunting and occasional A1 vocalizations. I see 7 monkeys in the tree looking down and one briefly on a vine below the tree looking up. Both male and female barks are to be heard. The intruder moves off to the north and disappears.

1259.0. The vocalizations end. All adults in the troop seem to have been involved, but I do not know if the intruder vocalized.

From 1300-1300.75 there were male A2's and A1's and accompanying female barks (D), the troop then subsiding. One hour later I obtained the first full troop count of 9, and it is possible that the intruder was adult male M4, who was the young male least active socially in the troop. Shortly after the chasing incident an infant was born to female F1, so the approach to her may not have been sexually motivated. However, adult female F2 was in a consortship with the principal male of the troop, male M2, and was seen copulating with that male 10 days later.

"Solitary" animals were also seen in the Puente Caracol area. One "marked" adult male (patch of fur missing next to his right eye) was seen following closely and interacting with troop PC1 on April 22, 23, 25, and 27.

On the mornings of the first three days the extra-troop male (ETM) was sometimes as close as 15 meters to the troop and either gave ground slowly before it or moved after it. Occasionally members of the troop would make little sallies after the ETM:

0940. The troop lets out a roar—as does the ETM, who was foraging. An adult female with a small infant ventrally carried leads a pursuit burst of the ETM which carries both parties ca. 6 meters. The troop and the ETM are now separated by 15 meters.

The troop on this morning (April 25) had been slowly following two extra-troop females (one adult and the other perhaps a large juvenile), and the ETM had been following after it; this led to occasional alterations of orientation in roaring troop males (roaring was not, however, continuous) between the direction the troop was headed and the following ETM. The unusual frequency and duration of roars from troop PC1 is recorded in Tables 5 and 7 and Fig. 4 shows the troop howling at the ETM. The "squeaky-door screech" was heard

TABLE 7

PUENTE CARACOL: INTERACTIONS OF TROOP PCI WITH EXTRA-
TROOP MONKEYS ON THE MORNING OF APRIL 25TH: A CONTINUA-
TION OF TABLE 5 FROM 0700 TO 1040 FROM THE PERSPECTIVE
OF TROOP PCI.

Roars by Troop PC1	Probable cause	Comments
0704-0711	The ETM[a], 15 m from PC1.	During troop's roars ETM yawns, may vocalize.

0713-0830: interruption in observations on troop PC1.

0841.5 (one)	An ETF[a] or the rumbles of PC3.	PC3 had left out a few rumbles at 0841, at which time the ETF, between PC1 and PC3 and 20 m from the former, looked at the latter. ETF looks at PC1 when it roars.
0855 - ?0905	Roars of troop PC3.	PC1 moves toward the ETF and PC3; by 0902 PC1 has moved 45 m and dislodged the ETF.
0905 - 0916	Response to the ETM, who roared once while following PC1.	PC1 halts progression and alternates direction of roars. The ETF and another ETF retreat over the road.
0940 - 0947	The ETM, who also roars.	Adult female with ventrally-carried infant leads sally after the ETM (see quote in text). PC1 silences as I approach to photograph.
0949 - 0958	The ETM, who is moving around the troop.	Troop silences only after the ETM withdraws an additional 6 m. Allogrooming within the troop follows.

[a] ETM = extra-troop male; ETF = extra-troop female.

occasionally from the roaring troop, this vocalization testifying to the
tenseness of the situation (Neville, 1972: Table V) as did an unusual,
antagonistic-sounding screech with which a mother interrupted her
B1-vocalizations at ca. 0957 every time one of the roaring troop males
came down the branch toward her.

On the afternoon of April 27th the ETM was seen together with an adult female with a subadult (juvenile?) female ca. 6 m away. The male reacted to my approach with first C barks and then A1/A2 howls. A close but invisible troop almost immediately replied. I and the extra-troop monkeys approached them, but my progress was so impeded by the swamp that I returned to the road, where after 1/2 hour I saw the younger extra-troop female, troop PC1, and, following ca. 15 m after the others, the ETM. The female first seen with the ETM may, of course, have been a member of the troop. On two subsequent returns to the Puente Caracol area, troop PC1 was not seen and the ETM not positively identified (two extra-troop males were seen on May 15th, but possible fur regrowth may account for negative identification), and subsequently rains terminated access to the area.

Such incidents as the extra-troop male's pursuit of troop PC1 may be the beginning of the recruitment of the male to the troop and appears quite similar to the behavior described by Carpenter for troop relations with "complementary males" (1934: 69-72). We can examine a more advanced stage in the recruitments mentioned earlier. During a 3-month hiatus in observations toward the end of my study a second adult male joined troop 4b. While the two males could not be distinguished with certainty, one of the males when first seen on the day the troop was again encountered was with an adult female and this pair was more closely associated with the other 2 adult females and 3 juveniles of the troop than was the 2nd male. However, while vocalizing at me the pair entered the same tree as the 2nd male and the 2 males stood side-by-side for a few seconds while giving an A1 vocalization. The 2nd male was with the troop over the last month of the study, and the two males continued to co-operate on A1 vocalizations and one of the males to be interested in an adult female.

On July 12th in Middle Forest after an observation gap of about 2 months a subadult or adult male was spotted separated from troop 9 by less than 5 meters though he was in a different tree. On August 5, the next and last time that I saw the troop, the count still included an extra subadult or adult male, and he was cooperating with the troop in the repulse of two extra-troop males (who were perhaps temporarily separated from troop 18b). For at least 110 minutes the two extra-troop males were 15 m or less from the troop, and one of the males even entered a tree containing a juvenile female approaching to within 2 m of her. The two largest troop males, one of whom was probably the recruit, joined in A1 vocalizations, and once they were joined by the troop's large subadult male, a smaller subadult male remaining quiet. The two extra-troop males, one adult and the other subadult, occasionally cooperated on A1 vocalizations as well as independently giving A2 or C vocalizations. The main male of troop 9 was suffering from the major wounds described in Neville (1972), and the presumed recruit also had a tooth exposed by a cut in his upper lip; however, as I indicated in the earlier publication, I suspect that the wounds should be ascribed to a small predator.

Thus troop membership in respect to proximity and troop defense participation can be attained within 3 months or less.

Troop Reactions toward Other Stimuli

MAN

Carpenter (1934) describes the reactions of Panama howlers as ranging from ignoring an accustomed, neutral observer, to giving initial burst of vocalizations followed by usual activities when contact with man is frequent and non-harmful, to continued aggressive vocalizations when contact is infrequent, to quick and silent disappearance when the animals have been hunted. The major vocalizations would seem to be (using Altmann's [1959] terminology) C and D barks with A and B roars and wails indicating greater excitement; these correspond roughly with Carpenter's types 9 and 1 (1934: table 4).

Howler troops in Bush Bush with few exceptions disappeared rapidly when they sighted me, though this was usually accompanied by barks. Troop SST in the Restan Neck area (Neville, 1972: Figs. 1 & 5). with more contact with official Trinidad Regional Virus Laboratory personnel and presumably less with hunters, remained uneasy and frequently vocalized while I was near, but WHT troop, whose range included the area most frequented by and hence protected by official personnel, after the first few weeks usually did not alter their behavior in my presence other than by frequently looking at me. Vocalizations C and D were given by howlers disturbed by my presence, with C barks sometimes changing into A1 and A2 vocalizations and D barks into B wails; this also matches my experience in Hato Masaguaral and the reports from Barro Colorado.

A two-stage yawn was often directed at me: the mouth would open in a relatively circular "o"; the vertical dimension would then be increased into what resembled a yawn. This two-stage yawn had con-

siderable visual effect because the inside of the lips outlined the expression in white. The tongue inside the mouth was often visible.

General reaction in Hato Masaguaral was more mixed. The same
types of vocalizations occurred, with the A and, very rarely, B vocalizations correlating with apparently greater stimulation. However,
flight was more infrequent, in some cases probably because the low,
discontinuous canopy rendered it less effective except when the troop
was in a particularly thorny area. Even regularly visited troops had a
tendency to gradually move away from me, and no troop habituated
to consistent neutrality. On many occasions I was alerted to the
presence of a troop by barks from a male or female. Hunting of howlers did not occur on the ranch proper, and howlers were not used as
food in this part of Venezuela (this was probably due to the abundance of cattle and the possibilities for poaching pigs or deer instead),
but I was told about a troop which had been shot along the highway,
presumably for "sport," and a howler male who had been run down
on the ground and castrated by the peons a few years previously
(T. Blohm, personal communication).

I did not see in Bush Bush two types of antagonistic behavior recorded on Barro Colorado (Carpenter, 1934: 21): my howlers did not
break off dead limbs and drop them nor defecate nor urinate with
reference to me. (The breaking-off of limbs was common with the
Bush Bush cebus monkeys while staring at me and chirping. They
let the branches fall from where they were, but there was a tendency
of some — only males? — to approach and perhaps to get overhead.)

In Hato Masaguaral, however, both apparently defensive defeca-
tion/urination and branch-breaking ("branching") behavior were seen.
I interpret the defecation and urination as being only incidentally
aggressive, however, as it seemed to result from tension. On occasion
the monkeys would approach rather than retreat, and the combination of a monkey moving overhead and eliminating under tension
could produce the same effect as intentional attack. I did not note
evidence for purposeful delay in elimination when an animal did
make an approach. Branching was more evidently part of the defensive behaviors of the howlers. The behavior consisted in breaking
off and letting drop branches which could vary in size from small
twigs to meter-long clubs. The energy involved ranged from that
expended by relatively unexcited animals limply detaching loose
branchlets to an instance when an adult female almost fell as a result

of her violent tugging. The tendency of interested or excited animals to occasionally approach overhead and the fact that my degree of closeness correlated with their degree of excitement sometimes led to the branches falling quite close, however, there did not seem to be purposeful movement to maximize the probability of hitting me. Indeed, on one occasion an adult male (who was the most consistent brancher) started branching while I was still 60 m from the base of his tree. Furthermore, the probability of branching varied among the troops and among the animals within a troop. Branching was noted in 14 of the 26 troops west of the highway recorded in table I of Neville (1972), in troop PC2 from the Puente Caracol area, and twice by extra-troop males, one found with a female and the other interacting with a troop. If we take as an "occurrence" of branching the detaching of one or more branches or twigs as part of defensive behavior by a particular animal during a bout of uninterrupted observations on a troop, there were 64 clear-cut occurrences: 36 by adult males, 22 by adult females, 4 by unsexed, presumed adults, and 2 by male juveniles (on the same day and at the same time). In addition there were a few other incidents by juveniles that could also be interpreted as play, as the stick was chewed on before being allowed to drop. Often branching was characteristic of one particular animal in a troop; thus in the 7 branching occurrences in troop 11, 6 were by one of the two adult females and the other by the other adult female. Some idea of the intertroop variability can be gained by comparing the "rate" for troop 1 and troop 3: troop 1 had 5 clear-cut occurrences during 290 hours of observation while troop 3 had 21 occurrences (almost all by the alpha male) during 58 hours. Pooling the two rates gives expected values for troops 1 and 3 of 21.7 and 4.33 respectively, almost the reverse of those obtained!

There thus appears to be considerable variation among and within populations of howlers as to branching behavior. The literature contains a debate concerning the significance of agonistic instrumental actions by non-human primates, mostly dealing with chimpanzees and Cercopithecoidea and revolving around questions of "innateness" and the evolution of such behaviors; for reviews including the New World monkeys see Hall (1963) and Kortlandt and Kooij (1963). As with so many distinctive behaviors, local tradition, individual personality, and some genetic base permitting and encouraging development of the pattern seem to be involved.

OTHER STIMULI

In general, the howlers in both localities appeared to ignore other animals. Interactions with cebus monkeys were not seen. Insects were usually ignored but occasionally slapped at. Birds were occasionally watched but often ignored, even when a flock of "zamuros" *(Coragyps atratus* per Rohl, 1959) would land in the same tree a few meters away, though these large black vultures are said to destroy young pigs in the forest (A. Palma, p.c.) and hence could kill a young monkey. That birds could produce alarm is shown by an incident in which, when a flight of birds thundered by me, a juvenile female looked around and gave a grimace; of course, the monkey was probably sensitized by my presence. The reaction of a troop to a small feline, perhaps a "gato cervantes" *(Herpailurus yaguarondi* per Rohl, 1959), on the ground was not clearly discriminated from reaction toward me but at the most consisted in attention and barks.

Carpenter (1934) and Bernstein (1964) describe rainstorms and airplane noise as releasers of howling. In Bush Bush the approach of a rain-front could be roughly followed by the commencement of howling of distant troops, but there was no reaction to five occurrences of airplane noise (quite loud on at least 4 of these occasions). On the Hato rain had only the effect of reducing activity, and 14 instances of planes or helicopter produced no reactions. I suspect variability among the localities to be primarily due to local traditions. From occasional reactions, howlers are capable of perceiving many stimuli which they appear to ignore; given the right situation, a reaction will be made.

Summary and Concluding Discussion

Both *A. seniculus* and *A. villosa* have open social groups in the sense that recruitments may occur. I have shown that males are probably most responsible for troop composition fluctuations in red howlers. However, the groups—despite their potential openness—interact as units with stereotyped patterns of hostility (as do many primates including, frequently, man). Of these patterns, the most obtrusive is howling and especially the concentration of howling at daybreak which produces the "dawn choruses." The analysis in this paper shows that factors increasing the probability of howling include the howling, proximity, and visibility of another troop or of a solitary;

these factors of course correlate with population density. Howling may also be dependent on the constitution and personality of individual members of a troop. Light and rain conditions apparently effect the timing of the onset of dawn chorusing. The effect of various stimuli (such as rainstorms and airplanes) and the frequency of certain reactions (such as branching) vary among and within species and even within populations: factors such as individual personality and tradition as well as general genetic predisposition must contribute.

While the stimuli for howling are becoming better known, the immediate results and selective basis for this behavior are not so clear-cut. Most students agree that howling serves a spacing function, but as previously discussed, the second part of the following assertion of Chivers (1969: 78) "that the nearer two groups are the more intensive is the howling, and the stronger is the tendency to move apart" may be also interpreted on the basis of movements within an accustomed range. Marler, in his analysis of primate dispersion signals as distance-increasing, distance-maintaining, distance-reducing, or proximity-maintaining, suggests that *Alouatta* howls ("hoots") may function as both distance-maintaining and distance-increasing signals (1968: 429). However, both in Bush Bush and on the Hato excited troops occasionally approached each other rather than retreated, an effect also noted by Chivers (1969: 78) and attributed by him to an intrusion of the groups on each others' space ("that intangible area around a group within which conspecifics cannot be tolerated"):

"Interactions of this kind occur when one group becomes aware of the close presence of another (up to about 150 yards), usually by auditory stimuli, of which the most frequent is the dawn chorus. So it was observed that when the day range of a group brought it close to another by nightfall, following the dawn chorus the two groups would either move towards each other . . . or one would heed the signal of the chorus and move away."

One could argue that a close chorus induces approach. Marler (1968: 427-428) suggests that for some primates approach as opposed to distance-maintenance depends "on the position of the calling group in space. If a neighboring group located the source of the call outside the area they occupy, they are likely to reply in kind. If they locate it close to the edge of their area, or within it, they may approach the source as a prelude to the use of distance-increasing signals." It is not clear whether the area he refers to is relatively fixed geographically or is "group space," but Bates (1970: 280) suggests that this implies "a relationship between intergroup contacts and core areas." In any case, for howlers dawn and other calls would then simply contribute to the troops' information about conspecific distributions, and subsequent movement by the individual troops would be compounded from such factors as closeness of other troops, food sources, routes, and perhaps whether or not other troops were infringing on some particular (but gradually changing—Chivers, 1969: table III) geographically-defined area.

As brought out in the introduction most authors are attempting to correlate primate behavioral patterns (such as territoriality) and troop structure with ecological constraints. Considerable intraspecies variation some of which is indicated for red howlers in this paper and in Neville (1972), indicates the potential adaptability of primates and the importance of local "traditions"; in addition, differences in troop composition parameters between *A. seniculus* in Bush Bush and *A. villosa* on Barro Colorado Island, two habitats with at least superficial physical similarity, suggest that closely-related animals may develop different effective strategies in dealing with similar environmental problems. If one studies less closely related species living in the same habitat, as Chivers (1969: 91-97) has done for *Cebus capucinus* and *A. villosa* on Barro Colorado, one can see even more striking differences. Chivers (1969: 87, 89-90) even suggests that the effectiveness of howling in spacing the Barro Colorado troops has increased during this century, i.e., that we are witnessing rapid alteration in behavior with change in population density. Longitudinal studies of such alterations will clearly be one of the most important approaches used in future primatology.

Given the variability of habitats in time and space, it is unlikely that selection has fine-tuned the behavioral and social-structural features of a species to its environment throughout its range. One result of intertroop hostility and presumably the resulting spacing besides that of limiting demands on habitat may be that of increasing the probability of groups or individuals emigrating and colonizing new areas. This not only leads to geographic dispersion of the species but increases its chances of surviving, interrelated features which may be more susceptible to mathematical analysis (perhaps analogous to MacArthur and Wilson's [1967] treatment of island colonization) than analyses of fit to habitat. The dispersive colonizing effects of "territoriality" have been emphasized by others — see the listing of advocates and suggested functions in Carpenter (1968) — but have not been considered in any systematic way for the Primates.

Marler (1968: 429) notes "that those species with the best developed distance-maintaining signals live in the high forest"; this may relate to the potentially greater danger of attention-drawing signals to terrestrial animals. He goes on to suggest that high-forest monkeys are enjoying a stable environment and therefore have not been forced to maintain "opportunistic capacities" comparable to those of more terrestrial monkeys and "may be much more vulnerable to change in the environment." However, the tremendously wide distribution of *Alouatta*, from northern Argentina to Vera Cruz, Mexico (Hill, 1962: 93, 95), and the fact that it is still to be found in many parts of this range despite being a large, edible, and slow moving animal, indicates that arboreal monkeys can be adaptable and also successful at colonization (see also Hershkovitz, 1949: 385). The latter feature in *Alouatta* is perhaps due to the "spacing behaviors" described in this paper and to its willingness to come to the ground if necessary (Neville, 1972:75). As Chivers (1968:91) says:

"It can . . . be argued, and the present-day distribution of howling monkeys supports this, that until the advent of man (at least) the response to overcrowding was further dispersion, with the South American rain-forest providing an almost unlimited area for expansion."

I suggest that the howlers' sense of overcrowding is part of the colonizing mechanism.

Bibliography

Altmann, S.A.
 1959   Field observations on a howling monkey society. Journal of Mammalogy, *40:* 317-330.

 1966   Vocal Communication in howling monkeys (7.5 ips tape). Library of Natural History Sounds, Laboratory of Ornithology, Cornell University.

1968   Primates (Communication in selected groups). In: Animal Communications: Techniques of Study and Results of Research. T. Sebeok, ed. Indiana University Press, Bloomington, pp. 466-522.
Bates, B.C.
1970   Territorial behavior in Primates: a review of recent field studies. Primates, *11:* 271-284.
Beard, J.S.
1946   The Natural Vegetation of Trinidad. Oxford Forestry Memoirs No. 20, 1945, Clarendon Press, Oxford.
Bernstein, I.S.
1964   A field study of the activities of howler monkeys. Animal Behaviour, *12:* 92-97.
Blalock, H. M., Jr.
1960   Social Statistics. McGraw-Hill, New York.
Brunk, H. D.
1960   An Introduction to Mathematical Statistics. Ginn and Co., Boston.
Carpenter, C. R.
1934   A field study of the behavior and social relations of howling monkeys. Comparative Psychology Monographs, *10*(2): 1-168. (Page citations as reprinted in 1964 in: Naturalistic Behavior of Nonhuman Primates. C. R. Carpenter, ed. Pennsylvania State University Press, University Park, pp. 3-92.)

1958   Territoriality: a review of concepts and problems. In: Behavior and Evolution. A. Roe and G. G. Simpson, eds. Yale University Press, New Haven, pp. 224-250.

1965   The howlers of Barro Colorado Island. In: Primate Behavior: Field Studies of Monkeys and Apes. I. DeVore, ed. Holt, Rinehart & Winston, New York, pp. 250-291.
Chivers, D. J.
1969   On the daily behaviour and spacing of howling monkey groups. Folia Primatologica. *10:* 48-102.
Collias, N., and C. Southwick
1952   A field study of population density and social organization in howling monkeys. Proceedings of the American Philosophical Society, *96:* 143-156.
Crook, H.
1970   The socio-ecology of Primates. In: Social Behavior in Birds and Mammals. J. H. Crook, ed. Academic Press, New York, pp. 103-166.
Davenport, R. K., Jr.
1967   The orang-utan in Sabah. Folia Primatologica, *5:* 247-263.

Denham, W.
    1971   Energy relations and some basic properties of primate social organization. American Anthropologist, *73:* 77-95.

DeVore, I.
    1965   Changes in the population structure of Nairobi Park baboons, 1959-1963. In: The Baboon in Medical Research. H. Vagtborg, ed. University of Texas Press, Austin, pp. 17-28.

    _____, and K. R. L. Hall
    1965   Baboon ecology. In: Primate Behavior: Field Studies of Monkeys and Apes. I. DeVore, ed. Holt Rinehart and Winston, New York, pp. 20-52.

Epple, G., and R. Lorenz
    1967   Vorkommen, Morphologie und Funktion der Sternaldruse bei den Platyrrhini. Folia Primatologica, *7:* 98-126.

Hall, E. R., and E. R. Kelson
    1959   The Mammals of North America, Vol. I. Ronald Press Co., New York.

Hall, K. R. L.
    1963   Tool-using performances as indicators of behavioral adaptability. Current Anthropology, *4:* 479-494.

    _____
    1965   Ecology and behavior of baboons, patas, and verbet monkeys in Uganda. In: The Baboon in Medical Research. H. Vagtborg, ed. The University of Texas Press, Austin, pp. 43-61.

Hershkovitz, P.
    1949   Mammals of Northern Colombia. Preliminary report no. 4: monkeys (primates), with toxonomic revisions of some forms. Proceedings of the United States National Museum, *98:* 323-427.

Hill, W. C. O.
    1962   Primates: Comparative Anatomy and Taxonomy. Volume V, Cebidae Part B. Edinburg University Press, Edinburg.

Kortlandt, A., and M. Kooij
    1963   Protohominid behaviour in Primates. In: The Primates. Symposia of The Zoological Society of London, Number 10. J. Napier and N. A. Barnicot, eds. London Zoological Society, London, pp. 61-88.

Kummer, H.
    1971   Primate Societies. Aldine, Chicago.

Lindburg, D. G.
    1969   Rhesus monkeys: mating season mobility of adult males. Science, *166:* 1176-1178.

    _____
    1971   The rhesus monkey in North India: an ecological and behavioral study. In: Primate Behavior: Developments in Field and Laboratory

Research, Volume 2. L. Rosenblum, ed. Academic Press, New York, pp. 1-106.

MacArthur, R. H., and E. O. Wilson
1967 The theory of Island Biogeography. Princeton University Press, Princeton.

Marler, P.
1968 Aggregation and dispersal: two functions in primate communication. In: Primates: Studies in Adaptation and Variability. P. Jay, ed. Holt, Rinehart & Winston, New York, pp. 420-438.

Mason, W. A.
1968 Use of space by Callicebus groups. In: Primates: Studies in Adaptation and Variability. P. Jay, ed. Holt, Rinehart & Winston, New York, pp. 200-216.

Myers, J. G.
1933 Notes on the vegetation of the Venezuelan llanos. Journal of Ecology, *21:* 335-349.

Neville, M. K.
1968 Male leadership change in a free-ranging troop of Indian rhesus monkeys *(Macaca mulatta).* Primates, *9:* 13-28.

1972 The population structure of red howler monkeys *(Alouatta seniculus)* in Trinidad and Venezuela. Folia Primatologica, *17:* 56-86.

1972a Social relations within troops of red howler monkeys *(Alouatta seniculus).* Folia Primatologica, *18:* 47-77.

Pitelka, F. A.
1959 Numbers, breeding schedule, and territoriality in pectoral sandpipers of northern Alaska. Condor, *61:* 233-264.

Ripley, S.
1967 Intertroop encounters among Ceylon gray langurs *(Presbytis entellus).* In: Social Communication among Primates. S. Altmann, ed. University of Chicago Press, Chicago, pp. 237-253.

Röhl, Eduardo
1959 Fauna Descriptiva de Venezuela. Nuevas Graficas, Madrid, 4th ed.

Rouse, I.
1964 Prehistory of the West Indies. Science, *144:* 499-513.

Silva, G. S. de
1971 Notes on the orang-utan rehabilitation project in Sabah. Malayan Nature Journal, *24:* 50-77.

Vuilleumier, B. S.
1971 Pleistocene changes in the fauna and flora of South America. Science, *173:* 771-780.

Worth, C. B.
    1967   A Naturalist in Trinidad. J. B. Lippincott, Philadelphia and New York.
Yoshiba, K.
    1968   Local and intertroop variability in ecology and social behavior of common Indian languer. In: Primates. Studies in Adaptation and Variability. P. Jay, ed. Holt, Rinehart and Winston, New York, pp. 217-242.

4.   Dental Reduction in the Indriidae

Laurie Godfrey

Introduction

My purpose in this paper is to bring together a number of lines of evidence bearing on tooth reduction in the Indriidae, and to dispel the widespread but erroneous notion that premolar reduction in primates has always proceeded in serial order mesiodistally. Many authorities (e.g. Le Gros Clark, 1971, Simons, 1972) assume general applicability among primates of Gregory's hypothesis of premolar reduction from $P\frac{1234}{1234}$ of the primitive eutherian dentition to the hypothetical advanced $P\frac{34}{34}$. Yet there is much evidence that in the Indriidae the second lower premolar of the primitive eutherian dentition was never lost. The most striking evidence comes from studies of the ontogeny of living Indriinae contained in the European literature of decades ago and earlier. These studies will be reviewed here, and supplemented by observations on the adult dentitions of extant and fossil lemurs and lorises.

Dental reduction began early in primate history with the loss of one incisor from upper and lower dentitions and the reduction or loss of the anteriormost premolar. The dental formula was therefore quickly reduced from the primitive eutherian $\frac{3.1.4.3}{3.1.4.3}$ (incisors, canines, premolars, molars) to $\frac{2.1.4.3}{2.1.4.3}$ or even $\frac{2.1.3.3}{2.1.3.3}$. According to recent interpretations of the dental formulae of the Plesiadapoidea (dominant primates of the Paleocene era in Europe and North America) (Szalay, 1972b), apparently none had three incisors nor

109

four premolars. Four premolars did exist in some members of the predominantly Eocene families Adapidae (e.g. *Pelycodus, Notharctus, Adapis, Pronycticebus*) and Omomyidae (e.g. *Teilhardina*) and, possibly, in members of the extinct subfamily Microchoerinae of the Tarsiidae (e.g. *Necrolemur*). Even in these animals it is a very reduced anterior premolar which persists, a tooth which, in those animals for which we have developmental information such as the Adapidae (Bennejeant, 1935), erupts with the milk dentition and persists without replacement. In fact, as Zeigler (1971) points out, this is the normal condition for "$P\frac{1}{1}$" (or the first milk molars, as these teeth should be called) in mammals where these teeth persist, and it can be argued (Zeigler, 1971) that the adult first premolars were lost as early as Mid-Cretaceous in a portion of the ancestral eutherian stock. One can state categorically that no primate, living or fossil, retains a functionally important first premolar and that no primate, living or fossil, retains three incisors either in the upper or lower dentitions.[1] The dental formula of the Tupaiidae is, of course, $\frac{2.1.3.3}{3.1.3.3}$ but it is becoming increasingly apparent that homologies of various parts of the anatomy of tree shrews and primates (including the ear region) were misinterpreted by Le Gros Clark (1971) and others, and the tree shrews should be excluded from the order Primates.[2]

Initial snout recession and dental reduction (i.e. the loss of one pair

[1] The literature contains a number of references to fossil primates with three incisors in either maxilla or mandible (e.g. Teilhard de Chardin, 1921, Hill, 1953) but these claims are equivocal. Simons (1972), for instance, has shown that *Pseudoloris* does not have three upper incisors, contrary to claims made by Teilhard de Chardin (1921). Unfortunately the anterior dentitions of a number of early Tertiary primates are still poorly known.

[2] It is not the purpose of this paper to discuss the taxonomy of the tree shrews, a subject on which there is an extensive literature (e.g. Van Valen, 1965, McKenna, 1966, R. D. Martin, 1968a, 1968b, Sorenson, 1970, etc.). Whether or not they are called primates, it is clear that tree shrews are more distantly related to living primates than are the plesiadapoids, which are included in the order because of dental and basicranial similarities. (See references by Szalay.) Cartmill (1972) has argued that even these should be excluded from Primates on the grounds that they do not share with living primates important "primate" adaptations resulting from the invasion of a specific ecological niche. This is one of the reasons for preferring a tripartite division of the order Primates, and separating the Plesiadapoidea from the more lemur-, loris- and tarsier-like fossil prosimians (i.e. the adapids, omomyids and anaptomorphids). The latter alone should be included with modern prosimians and their closer fossil relatives in the Suborder Prosimii.

of incisors and the first pair of premolars) are said to have coincided with a behavioral shift from snout to hand procurement of foods. This is clearly the case for modern prosimians and their Eocene relatives but not necessarily for plesiadapoids. Napier and Napier (1967) have shown that modern prosimians and anthropoids share anatomical prehensility (i.e. the ability to grasp an object securely in one hand), and that this can be correlated with single-handed feeding. Single-handed feeding is, of course, advantageous in an arboreal milieu, whether the animal is feeding on insects, fruit or leaves, since it allows for greater postural stabilization while feeding. Cartmill (1972) has attempted to relate a whole complex of adaptions we associate with "primates" (including snout recession but also prehensility, orbital convergence and the development of a postorbital bar) to an early primate invasion of a particular niche *within* the arboreal setting, that is, to "nocturnal, visually directed predation on insects in the terminal branches of the lower strata of tropical forests" (p. 121). According to this hypothesis the "basal" prosimian was a *Cheirogaleus-Microcebus-Galago*-like creature, similar to Crook and Gartlan's (1966) "Grade 1" primate or Charles-Dominique and Martin's (1970, 1972) hypothetical ancestor of the lemurs and lorises. Presumably prosimians only secondarily entered a frugivorous-herbivorous niche, or did so immediately but without abandoning their predaceous habits. If Cartmill is correct, early dental reduction would be related not merely to single-handed feeding in an arboreal milieu, but to the invasion of a very specific niche within that milieu. Initial dental reduction in the plesiadapoids cannot be explained in this manner. *Plesiadapis,* whose postcranial and cranial skeleton is well-known (Simpson, 1935, Russell, 1964) was a clawed squirrel-like creature lacking marked orbital convergence and a post-orbital bar. The aberrant dentitions of plesiadapoids suggest herbivorous and frugivorous diets (Szalay, 1968, 1972). While it is impossible to state that dental reduction was not correlated with more effective hand use in plesiadapoids (clearly, efficient hand use is of value to herbivorous and frugivorous as well as insectivorous primates in a terminal branch setting) it is perhaps more likely that dental reduction in plesiadapoids was correlated with specific feeding habits rather than any major change in hand function. Certainly there were major shifts in food procurement and preparation technique as is evidenced by the unusual form of the plesiadapoid incisors.

Additional premolar loss (loss of a second and occasionally a third pair of premolars) occurred repeatedly within the primates. It occurred independently in all four plesiadapoid families, and in the Eocene prosimian family Anaptomorphidae. It also occurred in the Cercopithecoidea, Hominoidea, Daubentoniidae, and, finally, in the Indriidae.

The family Indriidae contains a number of extinct as well as living forms, and can be divided into three subfamilies: Indriinae (containing all of the living forms as well as an extinct genus, *Mesopropithecus*[3]), Palaeopropithecinae and Archaeolemurinae. The classification of the Indriinae is given in Table 1.

The living Indriinae form a phylogenetically "tight" group; these animals resemble one another in details of their dental, cranial and postcranial anatomies, and in locomotor and dietary behavior.[4] Only one, *Avahi*, is nocturnal, but as Martin (1972) points out, the others possess a tapetum (reflecting membrane), an indicator of nocturnal ancestry. All three are strict vegetarians. *Indri* and *Avahi* consume large quantities of leaves. *Propithecus* consumes large quantities of fruit as well as leaves. All three are "vertical clingers and leapers" (Napier and Walker, 1967). Finally, all living Indriinae have no canine (or only one incisor and a canine) in the lower jaw and have only two premolars in the upper and lower jaws.

Extinct members of the indriid family do not form a phylogenetically "tight" group. Of the extinct forms, *Mesopropithecus* resembles the living Indriinae the most, especially in features of its cranial and dental anatomy, but postcranially it is aberrant. Walker (1967b) has demonstrated that the limb bones of *Mesopropithecus* show some resemblances to bones of the koala bear, a marsupial, and he has suggested that, like the koala bear, *Mesopropithecus* probably exhibited a kind of modified sedentary vertical clinging and leaping, with quadrupedal "frog-like" leaping on the ground instead of bipedal hopping.

[3]The taxonomy of this genus has recently been revised, Tattersall (1971b), and materials previously classified as *Neopropithecus* have been included in *Mesopropithecus* on the basis of cranial similarities. Postcranial distinctions were emphasized by Walker (1967b) based on Lamberton (1939, 1946), but having seen materials upon which Lamberton based his claims I would affirm that the differences do not warrant generic separation.

[4]The social behavior of only one genus, *Propithecus*, is well known, but all three indriines are social animals living in small family groups. See Petter (1962), Jolly (1966) and Jolly (1972).

TABLE 1

CLASSIFICATION OF THE INDRIIDAE

Family Indriidae
   Subfamily Indriinae
      Indri
      Avahi
      Propithecus
      Mesopropithecus
   Subfamily Palaeopropithecinae
      Palaeopropithecus
      Archaeoindris
   Subfamily Archaeolemurinae
      Archaeolemur
      Hadropithecus

The Palaeopropithecinae and Archaeolemurinae are phylogenetically further removed from living Indriinae than is *Mesopropithecus*. As Tattersall (1971a) points out, it is difficult to determine (in the absence of any fossil evidence) which of the two subfamilies diverged first from the common indriid stock. It is generally assumed that the Archaeolemurinae diverged first (Figure 1) because they exhibit the more primitive dental formula, $\frac{2.1.3.3}{2.0.3.3}$ or possibly $\frac{2.1.3.3}{1.1.3.3}$, (as opposed to the palaeopropithecene-indrine $\frac{2.1.2.3}{2.0.2.3}$ or possibly $\frac{2.1.2.3}{1.1.2.3}$) and because they exhibit divergent dental specializations. The dentition of *Archaeolemur* converges in certain respects with that of cercopithecoids, and that of *Hadropithecus* converges with dentitions of gelada baboons and hominoids (Jolly, 1970, Tattersall, 1971).[5] Cranially, Archaeolemurinae closely resemble the Indriinae.

[5]In 1970 Cliff Jolly published an interesting and, on the whole, excellent article concerning *Hadropithecus*. The essential point of this article, that there are parallelisms in dental morphology and certain cranial features of *Hadropithecus*, *Theropithecus*, *Gigantopithecus* and *Ramapithecus* is well brought out and valid. However, in dealing with the postcranial skeletons of *Archaeolemur* and *Hedropithecus*, Jolly makes factual errors and assertions which are, in my view, highly contestible. Jolly calculates the "humero-femoral" indices of *Archaeolemur* and *Hadropithecus* and concludes that *Archaeolemur* exhibits an index "within the normal range for cercopithecoid monkeys" and that the humero-femoral index of *Hadropithecus* closely matches that of Pleistocene "representatives" of *Theropithecus* (i.e. "*Simopithecus*"), an extremely terrestrial baboon. In fact Jolly mistakenly uses Walker's (1967b) figures for the radius and tibia of *Archaeolemur* instead of those for the humerus and femur, resulting in a "humero-femoral"

114   *The Measures of Man*

The Palaeopropithecinae do not exhibit unusual dental specializations, but features of their cranial anatomy are divergent. Both Palaeopropithecinae and Archaeolemurinae possess postcranial distinctions. *Palaeopropithecus* had elongated forelimbs unlike those of any other prosimian (except, perhaps, *Archaeoindris*, a close relative of *Palaeopropithecus* about which we know very little). Walker (1967b) has compared *Palaeopropithecus* to the orang. The Archaeolemurinae converged postcranially with semiterrestrial cercopithecoids (Godfrey, in prep., Jouffroy, 1963, Walker, 1967b). I have taken the somewhat arbitrary position in Figure 1 that the Archaeolemurinae diverged first since the dental evidence is most simply explained in this manner. If, in reality, the Palaeopropithecinae left the common stock first (and one can argue on the basis of their cranial and postcranial anatomy that they did), premolar reduction would have occurred twice in the Indriidae.

Whether premolar reduction occurred once or twice within the Indriidae, the evidence is strong that it occurred in both the Palaeopropithecinae and the Indriinae in a unique fashion, with the loss of P^2 in the upper dentition and P_3 in the lower dentition. One cannot assume, *a priori*, that premolar reduction occurred in the same fashion in the Anthropoidea, or indeed, in any other group of the primates. Evidence for premolar reduction in monkeys should be examined independently.

Before beginning a thorough analysis of the available evidence, let us examine the relationship between premolar morphology and the morphology of the anterior dentition in lemurs and lorises. All

---

index of 96.2 instead of the correct value 82. The correct value is higher than that exhibited by *Galago* (ca. 62-63) or *Cheirogaleus* (ca. 71-73) or *Lemur* sp. (mid-60's) or *Lemur variegatus* (ca. 70), but not unusual for animals like *Aotus, Cebus* or *Colobus*. In fact, the intermembral index of *Archaeolemur* is closer to that of baboons than is the humero-femoral index. With regard to the humero-femoral index of *Hadropithecus*, it is probably unwise to calculate this figure at all. There are no associated forelimb and hindlimb materials of *Hadropithecus*, and total sample size is very small. The possibility exists, moreover, that some of the hindlimb bones attributed to *Hadropithecus* by Lamberton (1937) really belong to *Archaeolemur*. Furthermore it can be shown, based on *associated forelimb* bones of *Hadropithecus* in the Vienna Museum that *Hadropithecus* had an unusually low brachial index (radius length x 100/humerus length = mid 80's). Therefore any substitution of a humero-femoral index for an intermembral index will give figures which are misleadingly high.

members of the superfamilies Lorisoidea and Lemuroidea[6] (except *Daubentonia*) possess a toothcomb or some modification thereof.[7] The toothcomb is a scraper which is used primarily in grooming, and occasionally (in Malagasy lemurs but apparently not lorises) in feeding (i.e. to scrape bits of fruit from rinds or seeds from pods, to "pick at" food objects, or, in *Propithecus*, to gouge out chunks of bark from trees) (Buettner-Janusch and Andrew, 1962, Jolly, 1966, A. Richard, personal communication). It is reasonable to assume that for animals lacking "fine control" of the hand and "true opposability" of the thumb (Bishop, 1964, Napier and Napier, 1967), an efficient grooming device would have provided definite selective advantages. In addition, it is evident that the switch from snout to hand snatching of food matter would have aided the development of the toothcomb because the necessity to retain incisors as food-getting devices was eliminated (Cartmill, 1972).

The toothcomb (Figure 2) is composed of laterally compressed and procumbent central and lateral lower incisors and lower canines (except in the Indriidae where the lower canines or one pair of incisors are missing entirely). The tips of these teeth are pointed and exhibit no blunted cutting edge. Variation is greatest in relative size of the toothcomb and degree of procumbency (angle of implantation of the roots and angulation of the crowns). The opposing upper incisors are usually reduced and in some cases *(Lepilemur* and *Megaladapis)* they are gone. Right and left pairs of upper incisors are usually separated by a wide median gap. Central and lateral incisors may be tiny peg-like teeth, or long, vertical, pin-like teeth. The latter are found in most of the insectivorous prosimians. There is a tendency in some of the herbivores (such as *Indri* and especially

[6]The superfamily Lemuroidea includes the Lemuridae (Cheirogaleinae and Lemurinae), the Indriidae, Daubentoniidae and Megaladapidae. The superfamily Lorisoidea includes only one family, the Lorisidae (Galaginae and Lorisinae).

[7]The lemur-loris toothcomb has been compared with that of the tree shrew. Certainly these structures are analogous but they are not homologous. As is well known, the lemur-loris toothcomb consists of two pair of incisors and one of canines whereas the tupaiid toothcomb consists of three pair of incisors. In *Tupaia* the lower canine occludes normally with the upper canine (in front of the upper canine) whereas in lemurs and lorises the mandibular caniniform tooth occludes behind the upper canine and is therefore, clearly, the anteriormost premolar. Since one pair of incisors was lost early in the history of Primates, the conclusion that the outermost tooth of the lemur-loris toothcomb is the canine is inescapable.

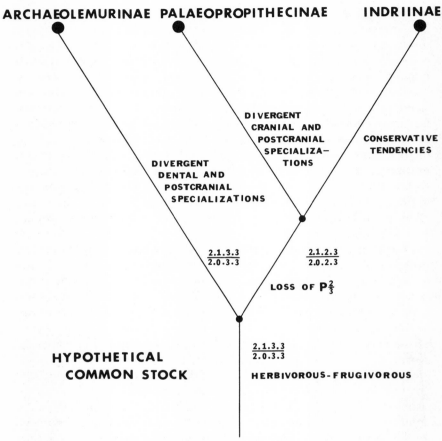

Figure 1. Hypothetical phylogenetic tree of the Indriidae.

Propithecus) to develop spatulate upper incisors with definite blunted biting surfaces. This tendency is carried to the extreme in *Archaeolemur* where the central incisors are enlarged to such an extent that the median gap is completely closed. The tips of the somewhat procumbent lower incisors are brought into active occlusion with the uppers, becoming nipping or biting devices paralleling those of Anthropoidea.

Despite moderate structural variation in the form of the toothcomb and the opposing upper incisors, living and fossil lemurs and lorises obviously share significant dental specializations. In terms of its consequences for subsequent premolar loss, the altered function of the lower canine is most important. The lower canine has lost its primitive occlusal relationship with the upper canine (and hence its primitive eutherian function as a piercing, dagger-like killing or tearing instrument). It has been either lost or incorporated into a grooming device. This means that *if* the animal is to retain a well-developed dagger-like upper canine, the occlusal relationship between the upper canine and the anteriormost lower premolar becomes quite important. The anteriormost lower premolar (P₂) tends to become caniniform, and there is often extensive wear on the posterior surface of the upper canine and the tip and anterior surface of P₂. A diastema often develops in the maxilla between the upper canine C^1 and the anteriormost premolar P^2 for the reception of P₂.

In Paleocene and Eocene primates the upper and lower canines are hardly consistently high-crowned dagger-like teeth. They are sometimes reduced or lost, especially within the Plesiadapoidea. But the particular configuration that we find in the lemurs and lorises, that is, deviation or loss of the lower canine *without marked reduction in the upper canine*, is not present in plesiadapoids, adapids, omomyids

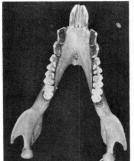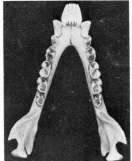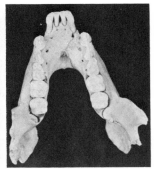

Figure 2. Mandibles of: a. *Lemur macaco* b. *Indri indri* c. *Archaeolemur majori.* The toothcomb of *Lemur* (and all lemurids and lorisids) contains six teeth: two incisors and one canine on right and left sides. That of *Indri* contains four teeth (all incisors or two canines and two incisors). Note the two permanent premolars in the jaw of *Indri,* as compared to three in the jaw of *Lemur,* and the caniniform shape of the anteriomost premolar. Figure 2c. shows an immature *Archaeolemur* (British Museum of Natural History M7739), with its full deciduous dentition (deciduous incisors or one deciduous incisor plus the deciduous canine, dm₂, dm₃ dm₄) plus M₁ and M₂. Note the blunted cutting edge on the deciduous incisiform teeth.

or anaptomorphids. With such a development the normal occlusal relationship between C^1 and P_2 acquires secondary importance. In the adapids, in contrast, the lower canine is a vertically implanted tooth which occludes in front of the upper canine, and $P\frac{1\text{-}2}{1\text{-}2}$ are reduced.

It can be assumed, then, that the ancestor of the indriid stock in which premolar reduction was to occur possessed an enlarged and somewhat caniniform P_2. Given selective pressure toward additional foreshortening of the skull (associated with extensive use of the manus in food gathering and the mechanical demands of a largely herbivorous diet) the question becomes, would such an animal lose $P\frac{2}{2}$?

The Evidence: Studies of the Ontogeny of Living Indriids

Before presenting the most convincing evidence that such an animal would not (and indeed did not) lose $P\frac{2}{2}$, it will be necessary to review some dental terminology. The deciduous dentition and permanent adult molars comprise what is often called the "primary dentition." The deciduous incisors, canines and "molars"[8] are replaced by adult incisors, canines and premolars, that is, the "replacement" dentition. Usually the number of deciduous teeth corresponds to the number of adult teeth minus the molars, but there are exceptions. These are cases in which the deciduous dentition is more complete than the adult dentition, closely approximating or reproducing the ancestral adult condition. Such dentitions represent an intermediate stage of dental reduction or loss. Prior to complete loss of a tooth, there is normally:

   a) a progressive reduction in size of both the milk tooth and its permanent successor,
   b) a slowing in the relative speed of ontogenetic development and eruption of both the milk and replacement teeth, usually resulting in the disappearance of the replacement tooth first, followed by the disappearance of the milk tooth (Zeigler, 1971).

One can see such an intermediate stage of tooth loss in the Adapidae.

[8]Deciduous "molars" (or deciduous "premolars," as they are sometimes called), may be caniniform, premolariform, or molariform, depending upon their position within the "field" (Butler, 1939, 1963), but in any case they are replaced by the corresponding adult *premolars*. Dm^2 is replaced by P^2, dm_3 by P_3, etc.

But whereas in these animals the unreplaced first milk molars are not shed after the permanent dentition has erupted, in numerous other cases of mammals possessing unreplaced milk teeth, these teeth are lost (or crowded out) as the jaw grows and the permanent dentition erupts. Even in animals which normally do not retain deciduous molars, there are reports in the literature of unreplaced deciduous teeth found in the jaws of adult animals.

Clearly, deciduous dentitions which are more complete than the corresponding replacement dentitions provide unique opportunities to reconstruct dental reduction and retrace dental homologies. Living Indriidae present us with exactly this kind of opportunity. In the mandible of all three living indriids (Milne-Edwards and Grandidier, 1875) there are two teeth which are not present in the adult dentition. Proper identification of these unreplaced teeth is essential to our understanding of indriid dental homologies. For this reason a number of investigators have studied the deciduous dentitions of living indriids (Leche, 1897, Friant, 1935a and 1935b, Bennejeant, 1935, Lamberton, 1938, Spreng, 1938, cited in Hill, 1953). Unfortunately these studies, while known to various authorities (Weber, 1928, Remane, 1960) have been largely ignored by others.

The jaws of young indriines present a number of problems of interpretation. We will begin with the maxilla, which is more easily interpreted than is the mandible. According to the figures published in Milne-Edwards and Grandidier (1875), each of the living indriines has two deciduous incisors, one deciduous canine, and two deciduous molars, corresponding exactly to the number of replacement incisors, canines and premolars. Leche (1897) noted the presence of a third milk molar in the upper jaw of a young *Propithecus*, a tiny, pin-like tooth located between the deciduous canine and the anterior-most of the two "normal" deciduous molars. A similarly located tooth has been reported in an adult *Propithecus* (Bennejeant, 1935) and an adult *Indri* (Friant, 1935 a and b). From its position one must conclude that this is either a remnant dm^1 or dm^2. If one makes the reasonable assumption that dm^1 was lost early in primate history (prior to the loss of a second premolar in the upper jaw of indriids) one must conclude that the pin-like tooth noted by Leche (1897) is dm^2. The fact that this tooth is usually not present in prepared specimens (no matter how immature) indicates that either it is normally absent but retained as an atavism in occasional specimens, or, possibly it is normally present but usually lost very early in ontogenetic development. Careful study of serial sections of indriine foetuses would resolve the problem, and establish the normal primary maxillary dental formula for indriines at either 2.1.3.3 (milk incisors, milk canines, milk molars, true molars) as reported by Leche (1897) Weber (1928) and Friant (1935a), or 2.1.2.3 as reported by Milne-Edwards and Grandidier (1875) and Lamberton (1938).

In the mandible there are four deciduous teeth distal to the deciduous toothcomb, and of these four, two are rudimentary. These are the first and third. Milne-Edwards and Grandidier (1875), Leche (1897) and Friant (1935a) believed the anteriormost rudimentary tooth to be the unreplaced deciduous canine, and accordingly believed the toothcomb in both deciduous and permanent dentitions to be composed of incisors. Gregory (1920) favored an alternative interpretation of the adult indriid toothcomb (cf. Flower and Lyddeker, 1891). He believed the lateral teeth of the toothcomb to be canines (adult dental formula $\frac{2.1.2.3}{1.1.2.3}$ rather than $\frac{2.1.2.3}{2.0.2.3}$), the rudimentary tooth just distal to the deciduous toothcomb to be "P_1" (i.e. dm_1) rather than dc_1, and the lateral incisiform tooth belonging to the deciduous toothcomb to be dc_1.

The difficulty in interpreting the anterior teeth of indriids is due to the extreme crowding in the deciduous dentition. The main occlusal relationship of the upper deciduous canine is clearly with the caniniform (second) deciduous molar. However, Gregory noted that his "P_1" also occludes *behind* the upper deciduous canine, an observation which was recently confirmed by J. Schwartz (personal communication) for very immature specimens of *Propithecus*. (The upper deciduous canine occludes posteriorly and inferiorly with *both* the anteriormost rudimentary tooth and the second deciduous molar.) Schwartz suggests that Gregory may have been correct in refusing to call this tooth a deciduous canine. In somewhat older specimens the anteriormost rudimentary tooth lies just lateral to the erupting teeth of the permanent toothcomb, suggesting that it is a deciduous canine. In any case, solution to this problem is not of paramount importance to the solution of the primary problem being considered here, the loss of the second pair of premolars in the Indriidae.

Leche (1897) and then Friant (1935a, 1935b) stressed the significance of premolar replacement in the Indriidae. Friant observed that of the three deciduous molars which are (sometimes) present in

the upper dentition, it is the *first* which is rudimentary and not replaced, but of the three distal deciduous molars in the mandible of
Indri it is the *second* which is rudimentary and not replaced(Figures
3 & 4). If we label these deciduous molars $dm\frac{2}{2}$, $dm\frac{3}{3}$, and $dm\frac{4}{4}$, assuming that $P\frac{1}{1}$ was lost early in eutherian history in at least part of
this stock and its predecessor dm¹ (at least) and maybe also dm₁ was
lost early in primate history, it becomes clear that dm² and dm₃ are
unreplaced. Therefore the permanent mandibular molars in *Indri*
are the homologues of the primitive eutherian P₂ and P₄, whereas
the upper premolars are the homologues of the primitive eutherian
P³ and P⁴. Living indriids have lost $P\frac{2}{3}$ in their adult dentitions.

Similar conclusions were reached by Bennejeant (1935) who examined a mandible of a young *Propithecus diadema* (Figure 5). Here
again there are three deciduous molars, dm₂₋₄, and it is the intermedi-

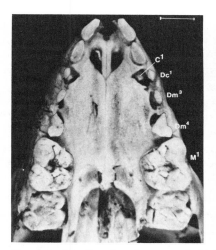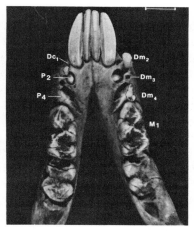

Figure 3. Maxilla of an immature *Indri indri* (Laboratoire d'Anatomie Comparée
1934-583, Paris). M¹ and the adult incisors are fully erupted. Dc¹ is being replaced by
C¹. Dm³ is being replaced by P³, dm⁴ by P⁴. A photograph of a similar specimen (Figure 12d) appears in Warwick-James (1960). The tooth labeled P² is really the deciduous canine being replaced by the permanent canine.   SCALE = .5 cm.

Figure 4. Mandible of an immature *Indri indri* (Laboratoire d'Anatomie Comparée
1934-583, Paris), showing the partially erupted permanent toothcomb, dc₁ or dm₁ on
the left side (alveolus only on the right side), caniniform dm₂, alveoli for dm₃ on both
sides, and dm₄ on right side only. The replacement premolars can be seen. In
Warwick-James (1960) Figure 12e shows all three deciduous molars in the mandible of
an immature *Indri*.   SCALE = .5 cm.

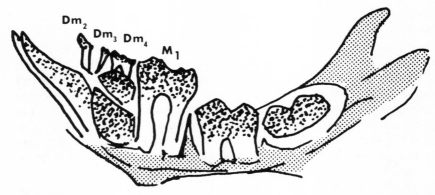

Figure 5. Mandible of an immature *Propithecus diadema* (drawn from a photograph of an X-ray, Bennejeant, 1935). The three deciduous molars and two permanent premolars (unerupted) can be seen. The adult incisors and anterior permanent molars have erupted.

ate deciduous molar which is tiny and has no successor. In Figure 5 the three deciduous molars and the entire replacement dentition can be seen. The caniniform adult premolar replaces the caniniform dm$_2$. P$_4$, near eruption, replaces the most distal of the deciduous molars.

Loss of P$\frac{2}{3}$ can hardly be called an unusual pattern of tooth loss; P^2 and P$_3$ are as much of a "functional pair" as are P^2 and P$_2$, or P^3 and P$_3$. Since each lower tooth generally occludes slightly in front of the corresponding tooth in the upper jaw, an occlusal relationship of varying importance develops between the lower tooth in question and the slightly more mesial tooth in the upper jaw — between M$_1$ and P^4, for instance. Thus, for example, P^4 may become partially molarized while P$_4$ does not, and molarization of premolars may be described as proceeding in a series of stages involving first P^4/M$_1$, then P^3/P$_4$, then P^2/P$_3$, and so on (Slaughter, 1970). Occlusal relationships between teeth can change, as is illustrated clearly by the fact that, in lemurs and lorises possessing three premolars, P$_2$ occludes with C^1 whereas, primitively it must have occluded with P^1 or dm^1. Such changes in occlusal relationships can occur only with loss or reduction of the intervening tooth to such a point that it ceases to interfere with the new occlusal relationship.

Clearly, studies in the ontogeny of living indriines all point to the same conclusion. It is instructive, at this point, to turn to other methods of inquiry, which tend to substantiate conclusions reached above.

Fossil Evidence

Fossil evidence is clearly the most direct means to establish the course of dental reduction, if relevant historical materials exist. Unfortunately, despite the abundance of fossil prosimians in the Paleocene and Eocene deposits of Europe and North America, direct fossil evidence regarding the history of lemurs and lorises is sorely lacking. The fossil Adapidae which, of all Eocene prosimian families, resemble the lemurs and lorises the most, are still of little help in deciphering the *specific* history of modern families. There is, in fact, wide disagreement over such basic issues as whether a common African lemur-loris stock existed in the early Tertiary, or whether various lemuroid and lorisoid lines originated independently from different adapid ancestors, and the resemblances between the modern forms (including those of the anterior dentitions) developed in parallel (Simons, 1962a, 1962b, Charles-Dominique and Martin, 1970, 1972). Gregory (1920), for instance, believed that the Lemuridae and Indriidae, as well as the Lorisidae, could be derived independently from the Adapidae. Charles-Dominique and Martin (1970, 1972) have argued most convincingly in favor of an ancient African lemur-loris stock, although some of the supposed homologies of the middle ears of Cheirogaleinae and Galaginae have been challenged by Szalay (1972a).[9] The problem is that vital palaeontological materials which would help to solve these problems are missing; there are no known fossil lemurids or lorisids in Africa prior to the Miocene, when the first fossil (and essentially modern) lorisids, *Progalago* and *Komba*, appear (see Simpson, 1967, on the form of the toothcomb, and Szalay, 1972a, on the structure of the middle ear). Fossil lemurs of Madagascar are, in reality, representatives of the fauna of the present geological epoch; none are more than several thousand years old (Walker, 1967a). We know from a consideration of the facts of

[9]Charles-Dominique and Martin (1970) contested the then widely accepted notion (Le Gros Clark, 1959) that lorises are more monkey-like (more "advanced") than lemurs and their close relatives, the adapids. These authors pointed out numerous similarities of lemurs and lorises when Cheirogaleinae are compared with Galaginae, and they postulated a common lemur-loris stock with a *Microcebus-Cheirogaleus*-like common ancestor. It is becoming increasingly clear that the old "tree shrew- lemur- loris- tarsier- higher primate" progression is far too simple (Szalay, 1972a) but the lack of fossil evidence for the African early Tertiary makes it difficult to determine whether "common" features of Cheirogaleinae and Galaginae are ancestral (lemur-loris) homologues, parallelisms or advanced features of an independent cheirogaleid-lorisid stock.

palaeogeography and biogeography that Africa possessed a prosimian stock or stocks in the early Tertiary, during the period of most intensive colonization of Madagascar, and that during this time Africa was enjoying a paleogeographic autonomy (see Keast, 1972, Cooke, 1972, Walker, 1972), being separated from Eurasia and North America by the Tethys Sea, and from South America by the Atlantic Ocean.[10] Faunal exchanges between Africa and any other continent were severely limited and intermittent. *Adapis* and its relatives were, at least *geographically*, one step removed from the ancestors of the Malagasy lemuroid stock, and their true phylogenetic proximity cannot be determined at present.

Gregory (1920, 1921) used an adapid model in reconstructing the history of premolar reduction in Primates. His concept of serial mesiodistal reduction of the premolar series is based on the morphology of premolars in such animals as *Adapis*, *Notharctus* and *Pronycticebus*, where $P\frac{1\text{-}2}{1\text{-}2}$ are always consistently smaller than $P\frac{3\text{-}4}{3\text{-}4}$. One must pose the following question: at the time or times of premolar reduction in the ancestral indriid stock, does *Adapis* or *Notharctus* represent a good structural model for conditions of the anterior dentition? Certainly, if *Notharctus* itself were to lose two premolars in the upper and lower dentitions, we would expect it to loose $P\frac{1\text{-}2}{1\text{-}2}$. But *Notharctus* did not possess a caniniform P_2. It possessed, rather, a caniniform C_1, which was not lost or incorporated into anything resembling a toothcomb. The question then becomes, did the loss of a second set of premolars in the Indriidae precede or follow the development of a toothcomb and possible loss of C_1? If it is likely that the development of the toothcomb preceded the loss of the second set of premolars, then the adapids do not represent good structural ancestors with regard to this trait. If, on the other hand, it is likely that the indriid toothcomb

[10]Walker (1972) postulates a late Cretaceous land link between Africa and "Laurasia" (Eurasia and North America) followed by no major periods of faunal exchange until the closing of the Tethys Sea (Miocene). The palaeoposition of Madagascar throughout this period is still disputed (Walker, 1972, Heirtzler and Burroughs, 1971, Green, 1972, Andriamirado, 1971, cited by Mahé, 1972), but the African character of the Madagascan fauna is not disputed (Bigalke, 1972, Millot, 1972, and other articles in the latter book). Although Simpson (1943, 1973) disputes the notion that the fauna of Madagascar is archaic, and although the fauna does contain some recent arrivals, its overall character *is* archaic (Walker, 1972, Millot, 1972). One can safely presume that the founding prosimian stock or stocks rafted to Madagascar in the early Tertiary, when the paleopositions of Madagascar and Africa favored such raftings.

and associated changes evolved after the loss of the second set of pre-molars, then an *Adapis-Notharctus*-like structural ancestor cannot be ruled out. It is evident from a comparison of living and subfossil indriids alone that the former is the far more likely possibility. Despite subsequent dental specializations (i.e. the development of bilopho-donty, a premolar shearing edge, and morphological changes in the upper and lower anterior dentitions) the Archaeolemurinae demon-strate beyond question that the loss of the lower canine and the development of a caniniform P2 preceded the loss of a second pre-molar from upper and lower jaws of indriids. Given the importance of P2 in the hypothetical common ancestor, it was not this tooth that was subsequently lost but the functionally more expendable P3. P^2 was functionally expendable, and so it was lost.

It is important to separate the loss of P$\frac{1}{1}$ from the loss of a second of the original eutherian four premolars. These were two separate events which occurred at substantially different times in the history of the Indriidae (and of the Anthropoidea, for that matter). One can safely presume that the loss of the first set of premolars in the early Tertiary lemuroid stock was as Gregory (1920, 1921) described. In fact the adapids were in the process of such a change, and, as Gregory so amply demonstrated, there is good reason to believe that the Adapidae were at least close to the stem from which lemurs and lorises can be derived. For the loss of P$\frac{1}{1}$ in the early Tertiary pro-simian stock ancestral to the modern Malagasy lemurs, an animal like *Notharctus* probably does represent a good structural model.

But Gregory used *Notharctus* as a model not only for the loss of P$\frac{1}{1}$ but the loss of $\frac{2}{2}$. The following general remarks are exemplary of his views on the subject:

"The adult dental formula of *Notharctus* is (I$\frac{2}{2}$ C$\frac{1}{1}$ P$\frac{4}{4}$ M$\frac{3}{3}$) x 2 = 40. This is undoubtedly the primitive formula for Primates and it differs from that of the most primitive placental mammals only in the reduction of the incisor formula from I$\frac{3}{3}$ to I$\frac{2}{2}$. In later Primates this formula suffers various reductions, as by the loss of some of the incisors (Indrisidae, Chiromyidae), of the anterior pre-molars (P$\frac{1}{1}$) (most lemuroids, New World monkeys), of P$\frac{1}{1}$ and P$\frac{2}{2}$(Indrisidae, Old World monkeys, great apes, man)."

(Gregory, 1920, P. 225)

"The Indrisidae also afford an instructive example of the reduction in the number of premolars from four to two, a reduction which has occurred inde-pendently in many other groups of primates. Even in the Notharctidae, the first and second premolars, both in the upper and lower jaw, remained retarded in development, while the third and fourth premolars were more progressive. This tendency, for the premolar series to differentiate into two contrasting parts, the anterior part consisting of the small or reduced P^1 and P^2, and the posterior part consisting of the progressive P^3 and P^4, is highly developed, not only in the Indrisidae, but also several other groups, such as the Old World primates, including man. In the final stage of this evolution, the first and second premolars disappear entirely and the remaining premolars are homologous with the third and fourth of the primitive placental dentition."

(Gregory, 1921, p. 261)

Actually, Gregory's account of premolar reduction in Indriidae is decidedly confusing and contradictory. Whereas several times he refers to the Indriidae the general "principle" of premolar reduction stated above, in discussing the deciduous dentition of *Propithecus* as figured by Milne-Edwards and Grandidier in 1875, Gregory (1920, p. 215) comes to the inevitable conclusion that dm3 is unreplaced and P3 lost. In 1915, he implies that $P\frac{3}{3}$ is lost in Indriidae. His labeling of figures of the anteriormost premolars of Indriidae possessing only two premolars is inconsistent (1920, 1921, 1951).

Retrogressive Changes in Adult Dentitions of Close Relatives of the Indriidae

Retrogressive changes in the morphology of specific teeth in the adult dentitions of close relatives of the animals exhibiting dental reduction, where such close relatives can be presumed to reflect the ancestral condition, may help in deciphering the course of dental reduction.

We can assume that the ancestor of the Indriid stock in which premolar reduction was to occur possessed:

1. no lower canine or a procumbent incisiform lower canine
2. a caniniform P2
3. three permanent premolars in upper and lower jaws.

One might ask whether we can also assume retrogressive changes in $P\frac{2}{3}$, that is, whether there is any evidence of reduction in $P\frac{2}{3}$ in the relatives of the living Indriidae? The only fossil indriids with three premolars in upper and lower permanent dentitions, the Archaeolemurinae, exhibit no particular retrogression of these premolars. But *Archaeolemur* and *Hadropithecus* have clearly undergone unique dental specializations away from the ancestral condition in the development of a cutting edge in the entire premolar series of *Archaeolemur* and the reduction of the entire anterior dentition of

Hadropithecus. In order to answer the question posed, we must seek information from outside the Indriidae.

Outside the Indriidae, we do find evidence of reduction of $P\frac{2}{3}$, but not in all lemurs and lorises. There is strong evidence that the entire indriid radiation was an herbivorous-frugivorous one, and it can be assumed that the common ancestor of all living and fossil indriids was an herbivore-frugivore. Accordingly I have divided the living

TABLE 2

GROUPS I AND II LEMURS AND LORISES

a. Niche preferences of living lemurs and lorises.

GROUP I	GROUP II
DESCRIPTION: Primarily insectivorous (also frugivorous), nocturnal, "solitary."	Herbivorous and frugivorous. Primarily diurnal or crepuscular. Primarily social.
GENERA:	
Cheirogaleus	*Lemur*
Microcebus	*Lepilemur*
Phaner	*Hapalemur*
Loris	*Indri*
Nycticebus	*Avahi*
Arctocebus	*Propithecus*
Perodicticus	
Galago	

b. Presumed niche preferences of fossil lemurs and lorises. (Based on inferences drawn from crania and dentitions.)

GROUP I	GROUP II
Komba	*Lemur (Pachylemur)*
Progalago	*Megaladapis*
	Mesopropithecus
	Palaeopropithecus
	Archaeoindris
	Archaeolemur
	Hadropithecus

lemurs and lorises into two groups based on preferred diet. The in-sectivorous-frugivorous Cheirogaleinae and Lorisidae constitute Group I, and the herbivorous-frugivorous Lemurinae and Indriinae constitute Group II (Table 2). Group I is similar to Crook and Gart-lan's (1966) adaptive Grade I except that *Daubentonia* and *Lepilemur* are excluded. *Daubentonia* is excluded from this discussion entirely because its aberrant specializations are irrelevant to the point under consideration. *Lepilemur* is included in Group II because it is a leaf-eater and my emphasis is on diet rather than daily cycle or social patterns.

If we look at the dentitions of Group I and Group II primates, a general pattern emerges (Figure 6). With the exception of the gen-erally more frugivorous *Microcebus*, which may retain the primitive condition, members of Group I exhibit a tendency to develop a high-crowned or even caniniform P². This, then, becomes part of an effec-tive piercing device in many of these animals, composed of three caniniform interlocking teeth: C¹-P2-P². This pattern is found in its most exaggerated form in *Galago (Euoticus) elegantulus, Phaner furcifer* and *Perodicticus potto*, but also in other insectivorous lemurs and lorises. P3 is also high-crowned in some forms (e.g. *Periodicticus potto*). There is no trend in this group toward reduction of P $\frac{2}{3}$, a trend

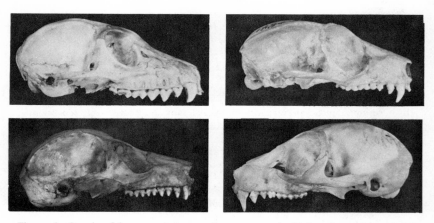

Figure 6. Crania of four prosimians: a. *Lemur macaco* b. *Cheirogaleus major* c. *Galago crassicaudatus* d. *Arctocebus calabarensis*. Only the first, *Lemur macaco*, belongs to Group II. For photographs of Group I primates which exhibit a more extreme enlargement of P², refer to Warwick-James (1960).

which is found, however, in members of the vegetarian Group II, notably the genus *Lemur*. There is no tendency in members of the vegetarian Group II, on the other hand, to develop high-crowned or caniniform premolars distal to C^1 and P_2. Rather, they exhibit immediate premolar reduction. One can assume that the ancestral indriid possessed the latter adaptation.

Pattern of Dental Eruption and Eruptive Retardation

Groups I and II lemurs and lorises share important occlusal antagonism between C^1 and P_2, and a caniniform or semi-caniniform P_2, but in the morphology of premolars distal to the "C^1-P_2" unit these animals are not alike. We have seen that the development of the caniniform P_2 is related to the evolution of the toothcomb and the concomittant change in function of the lower canine, and that differences in premolar crown-height are related to dietary divergences. These relationships are further emphasized if one looks at the pattern of dental eruption in the two groups.

Dental eruption proceeds in an orderly fashion in mammals. Firstly, teeth in functional occlusion generally erupt simultaneously or follow one another in rapid succession. For instance, in most primates C^1 and C_1 erupt simultaneously or in succession but in *Lemur* C^1 and P_2 erupt ninth in each jaw whereas C_1, which belongs to the toothcomb, erupts in association with the incisors, i.e. fifth. The pattern of eruption therefore reflects the pattern of occlusal antagonism, and there exists a definite pattern of "developmental" antagonism. Superimposed upon this pattern of developmental antagonism is a pattern of sequential eruption. Dental eruption in any specific portion of the tooth row usually follows a serial order, i.e. distomesial or mesiodistal. Permanent molars consistently erupt in mesiodistal order as the jaw grows, but the order is variable for deciduous molars and permanent premolars. It tends to be mesiodistal in higher primates, and distomesial in many prosimians. There are intermediate cases (in which premolars do not erupt in serial order) as well.

If we look at the order of eruption of the permanent dentition of lemurs and lorises[11] (Bennejeant, 1935, Lamberton, 1938) (Tables 3 and 4), we find that:

[11]Reports of the pattern of dental eruption in primates are usually based on only a

a) C^1 and P_2 tend to erupt as a unit or in direct succession.

b) In the Cheirogaleinae and Lorisidae, that unit tends to erupt early, followed by the eruption of the permanent premolars, in mesiodistal order (Bennejeant, 1935).

c) In the Lemurinae and Indriidae (including the fossil forms), this unit erupts late following distomesial eruption of the premolars.

d) C^1 and P_2 do not erupt as a unit in Eocene prosimians, such as *Adapis*, nor in the higher primates. In these animals the important occlusal relationship is between C^1 and C_1. In *Adapis* the premolars erupt in distomesial order after the eruption of the permanent canines. In the Anthropoidea premolars generally erupt in mesiodistal order before the eruption of the upper and lower canine.

These data reemphasize the importance of the C^1-P_2 relationship in lemurs and lorises in general, and, incidentally, the differences between Group I and Group II primates in certain properties of their dentitions. The importance of the C^1-P_2 relationship in lemurs and lorises contrasts with its unimportance in animals like *Adapis*, which cannot be considered a good model for premolar reduction in lemurs and lorises. In *Adapis*, $P\frac{2}{2}$ bears no relation in its eruptive pattern to the anterior dentition.

As discussed earlier, one may expect to find signs of eruptive retardation or delayed tooth germ formation of $P\frac{2}{3}$ *specifically* in relatives of the living indriines which retain three primitive upper and lower premolars. Eruptive retardation and retarded tooth germ formation have been interpreted as signs of evolutionary retrogression preliminary to evolutionary loss (Bennejeant, 1935, Butler, 1963). A familiar example is $M\frac{3}{3}$ which experiences frequent aegenesis and eruptive retardation in man. Bennejeant (1935) attempted to apply the indriid premolar homologies to monkeys, citing retardation of P_3 in marmosets. But for the same reasons that adapids are not relevant to premolar loss in indriids, callithricids are not relevant to premolar loss in cercopithecoids and hominoids.

Apparently *Lepilemur* alone among lemurs and lorises (Table 4) exhibits a pattern of eruptive retardation of $P\frac{2}{3}$ specifically (Lamber-

---

few specimens per species; therefore the possibility of individual variation must be taken into account. A statistical study should be done but it is difficult in most cases to obtain sufficient relevant materials.

TABLE 3

ERUPTION ORDER OF C^1, C_1, AND P_2 IN VARIOUS PRIMATES.

(Data from Bennejeant, 1935, Lamberton, 1938)

Genus	C^1	C_1	P_2
Adapis	6	6	9
Lemur	9	5	9
*Galago**	5	5	6
Ateles	8	8	5
Callithrix	7	7	4
Colobus	7	7	5
Homo	6	6	4

*The eruptive coincidence of C^1 and C_1 in *Galago* is an artifact of the fact that the C^1-P_2 unit erupts immediately after the eruption of the incisors. The eruption of C_1 follows the eruption of the central and lateral incisors. All of these teeth contribute to the formation of the toothcomb.

TABLE 4

DENTAL ERUPTION IN VARIOUS PROSIMIANS.

(Data from Bennejeant, 1935, and Lamberton, 1938)

Genus	Maxilla									Mandible								
	I^1	I^2	C^1	P^2	P^3	P^4	M^1	M^2	M^3	I_1	I_2	C_1	P_2	P_3	P_4	M_1	M_2	M_3
Adapis	3	4	6	9	8	7	1	2	5	3	4	6	9	8	7	1	2	5
Lemur	3	4	9	8	7	6	1	2	5	3	4	5	9	8	7	1	2	6
Hadropithecus	3	4	9	8	7	6	1	2	5	3	4	—	8	7	6	1	2	6
*Indri**	2	3	8	—	6	5	1	4	7	2	3	—	6	—	5	1	4	7
*Propithecus**	2	3	8	—	6	5	1	4	7	2	3	—	6	—	5	1	4	7
*Lepilemur**	—	—	7	6	5	4	1	2	3	4	5	6	8	9	7	1	2	3
Galago	3	4	5	6	7	9	1	2	8	3	4	5	6	7	9	1	2	8

*Asterisk represents animal with uneven numbers of teeth in the maxilla and mandible. These data must be reviewed carefully. For instance, if we presume that the maxillary incisors in *Lepilemur* should have erupted 4th and 5th, then P^4 through C^1 would have erupted 6th through 9th. Thus, taking the gap into consideration, C^1 again erupts in association with P_2 and not C_1.

ton, 1938). The Archaeolemurinae exhibit the normal lemurine-indriine pattern of distomesial premolar eruption.

Simons (1972) has asserted that primates have universally lost the primitive incisors and premolars on either side of the canine (presumably I$\frac{3}{3}$ and P$\frac{1\text{-}2}{1\text{-}2}$) in the course of dental reduction. He bases this conclusion on a paper written by Butler in 1963. Butler demonstrates an apparent correlation between late tooth germ formation of I$\frac{3}{3}$ and P $\frac{1\text{-}2}{1\text{-}2}$ in "primitive" mammals such as *Talpa*, the mole, and loss of these teeth in primates. The validity of Butler's assertion that primates show "loss of those teeth on either side of the canine that were last to develop in the mole" (Butler, 1963, p. 6) clearly depends upon whether or not the assumed homologies are correct. The apparent correlation does not prove them to be correct. Of course, *Talpa* has even less to do with dental eruption in primates than does *Callithrix* with cercopithecoids, or *Adapis* and *Notharctus* with Indriinae. The comparison is valid only to the extent to which all animals involved retain the primitive pattern of developmental retardation.

Neither eruptive retardation nor delayed tooth germ formation in close relatives of lineages exhibiting tooth loss appears to be a reliable tool for predicting tooth loss. The loss of the upper incisors in *Lepilemur* and *Megaladapis* is not anticipated by eruptive retardation in extant or subfossil relatives of these animals. There is no indication of eruptive retardation in C_1 in extant lemurs and lorises, yet this tooth is missing from the jaws of indriids. Once a tooth is lost completely, i.e. the germ never forms, it is, of course, possible to say that germ formation and dental eruption are "retarded." But such "retardation" may be anticipated by changes in the epithelial growth rate effecting retrogressive morphological changes rather than actual eruptive retardation. Rudimentary deciduous teeth may form and erupt rapidly, then be lost rapidly. In *Tarsius*, as Butler himself points out, neither dm^2 nor its successor P^2 are retarded in development, yet P^2 is a rudimentary, "vestigial" tooth. Thus, although there may be a general correspondence between order of tooth germ appearance, order of dental eruption, and the size of the final product, as Butler implies, this is far from consistently the case.

Diastemata

Occasionally, if foreshortening of the skull and crowding of the permanent dentition do not obliterate it, a diastema will occupy the spot on the dental arcade formerly occupied by the lost permanent tooth. Diastemata are not, of course, reliable criteria for dental reduction, often resulting from active occlusion (in which case the gap is occupied by an enlarged usually caniniform tooth from the opposing jaw). Diastemata may also result from secondary elongation of the dental muzzle without tooth loss. Such diastemata are, however, of interest here, in that they reflect the relative importance of various occlusal relations. If a gap develops in the middle of the toothrow, two teeth, one from the upper and one from the lower jaw, will lose their primitive occlusal antagonism. For instance, in *Megaladapis* a large diastema develops between P2 and P3 in the lower jaw, C^1 and P^2 in the upper jaw. The primitive occlusal antagonism between P^2 and P2 is lost, but the primitive antagonism between C^1 and P2, and between P^2 and P3 retained. Once again the functional importance of the C^1-P2 relationship is clear. One might note, in addition, that *Megaladapis,* like *Lemur* exhibits a reduction of P^2-P3, which is consistent with its inferred highly heribivorous diet (Table 2).

Of the indriids which have actually undergone premolar reduction, diastemata are present only in *Palaeopropithecus* and *Archaeoindris.* All others exhibit sufficient crowding to conceal any sign of tooth loss. In *Palaeopropithecus* and *Archaeoindris* there is a distinct diastema between the two premolars in the lower jaw, and sometimes a slight gap between the upper canine and anterior premolar in the upper jaw. These diastemata occupy the normal positions of P^2 and P3, and support the hypothesis that these teeth, indeed, are gone.

Conclusion

Parallel reductions in the number of cheek teeth have occurred frequently in primates. In reconstructing the course of particular trends in particular lineages, it is essential that probable ancestral conditions be considered. Since the starting materials will influence the course of subsequent change, no trend can be divorced from those circumstances anticipating its development. Gregory's *Notharctus* is a poor representation of conditions anticipating the loss of the "second" set of premolars in the Indriidae. The data clearly refute the hypothesis of serial mesiodistal premolar loss for these animals.

The data warrant careful reconsideration of some of Gregory's interpretations. The alternative hypothesis favored by this writer can be outlined as follows:

Early in the history of the African prosimian (lemur-loris?) stock, or independently in several early Tertiary prosimian stocks, the primitive lower canine ceased to act in important occlusal relation with the upper canine, thereby increasing the functional importance of the occlusion between the anterior lower premolar (P₂) and the upper canine. In various evolving lines the lower canine was either lost or incorporated into the toothcomb. When further premolar reduction occurred (as it did in the living Indriinae *Indri, Propithecus* and *Avahi,* and the subfossil *Mesopropithecus, Palaeopropithecus* and *Archaeoindris*) it did so without disrupting this important occlusal relationship.

Bibliography

Bennejeant, C.
  1935   Discussion sur les observations de Mlle. M. Friant (De l'interpretation de prémolaires chez les Primates). Bulletin du Museum National
  d'Histoire Naturelle, 2 série, 7: 343-347.
Bigalke, R. C.
  1972   The contemporary mammal fauna of Africa. In: Evolution,
  Mammals and Southern Continents. A. Keast, F. C. Erk and B. Glass,
  eds. State University of New York Press, Albany. pp. 141-194.
Bishop, A.
  1964   Use of the hand in lower primates. In: Evolutionary and Genetic
  Biology of the Primates. J. Buettner-Janusch, ed. Academic, New York,
  2: 133-225.
Buettner-Janusch, J., and R. J. Andrew
  1962   The use of the incisors by primates in grooming. American
  Journal of Physical Anthropology, 20: 129-132.
Butler, P. M.
  1939   Studies of mammalian dentition. Differentiation of the post-
  canine dentition. Proceedings of the Zoological Society of London,
  Ser. B., 109: 1-36.

  ───────────

  1963   Tooth morphology and primate evolution. In: Dental An-
  thropology: Symposia of the Society for the Study of Human Biology.
  D. R. Brothwell, ed. Macmillan, New York, 5: 1-13.
Cartmill, M.
  1972   Arboreal adaptations and the origin of the order Primates. In:
  Functional and Evolutionary Biology of Primates: Methods of Study and
  Recent Advances. R. H. Tuttle, ed. Aldine, Chicago. pp. 97-218.

Charles-Dominique, P., and R. D. Martin
1970   Evolution of lorises and lemurs. Nature, *227:* 257-260.

1972   Behavior and Ecology of Nocturnal Prosimians. Advances in Ethology, Supplements to the Journal of Comparative Ethology 9. Paul Parey, Berlin and Hamburg.

Cooke, H. B. S.
1972   The fossil mammal fauna of Africa. In: Evolution, Mammals and Southern Continents. A. Keast, F. C. Erk and B. Glass, eds. State University of New York Press, Albany. pp. 89-139.

Crook, J.H., and J. S. Gartlan
1966   On the evolution of primate societies. Nature, *210:* 1200-1203.

Flower, W. H., and R. Lydekker
1891   An Introduction to the Study of Mammals, Living and Extinct. Adam and Charles Black, London.

Friant, M.
1935a   Description et interprétation de la dentition d'un jeune *Indris.* Bulletin de l'Association des Anatomistes, Comptes Rendus, *38:* 205-213.

1935b   De l'interprétation des prémolaires chez les Primates. Bulletin du Museum National d'Histoire Naturelle, 2 série, *7:* 340-342.

Green, A. G.
1972   Seafloor spreading in the Mozambique Channel. Nature Physical Science, *236:* 19-21, 32.

Gregory, W. K.
1915   I. On the relationship of the Eocene lemur *Notharctus* to the Adapidae and to other Primates. II. On the classification and phylogeny of the Lemuroidea. Bulletin of the Geological Society of America, *26:* 419-446.

1920   On the structure and relations of *Notharctus,* an American Eocene primates. Memoirs of the American Museum of Natural History, *3:* 49-243.

1921   The origin and evolution of the human dentition, Part II. Journal of Dental Research, *2:* 215-273.

1951   Evolution Emerging. Vols. 1 and 2. Macmillan, New York.

Heirtzler, J. R., and R. H. Burroughs
1971   Madagascar's paleoposition: new data from the Mozambique Channel. Science, *174:* 488-490.

Hill, W. C. O.
1953   Primates. I. Strepsirhini. Edinburgh University Press, Edinburgh.
Jolly, A.
1966   Lemur Behavior. University of Chicago Press, Chicago.
Jolly, A.
1972   The Evolution of Primate Behavior. Macmillan, New York.
Jolly, C. J.
1970   *Hadropithecus:* A lemuroid small-object feeder. Man, *5:* 619-626.
Jouffroy, F.-K.
1963   Contribution à la connaissance du genre *Archaeolemur* Filhol, 1895. Annales de Paléontologie, *49:* 129-155.
Keast, A.
1972   Continental drift and the evolution of the biota on Southern Continents. In: Evolution, Mammals and Southern Continents. A. Keast, F. C. Erk and B. Glass, eds. State University of New York Press, Albany. pp. 23-87.
Lamberton, C.
1937   Contribution à la connaissance de la faune subfossile de Madagascar. Note III. Les Hadropithèques. Bulletin de l'Academie Malgache, nouvelle serie, *20:* 127-170.

1938   Contribution à la connaissance de la faune subfossile de Madagascar. Note II. Dentition de lait de quelques lemuriens subfossiles Malgaches. Mammalia, *2:* 57-80.

1939   Contribution à la connaissance de la faune subfossile de Madagascar. Note IV. Nouveaux lemuriens fossiles du groupe des Propithèques. Memoires de l'Academie Malgache, *27:* 9-49. Planches I-V.

1946   Contribution à la connaissance de la faune subfossile de Madagascar. Note XX. Membre posterieur des Neopropithèques et des Mesopropithèques. Bulletin de l'Academie Malgache, nouvelle serie, *27:* 30-34.
Leche, W.
1897   Untersuchungen über das Zahnsystem Lebender und Fossiler Halbaffen. Festschrift zum Siebenzigsten Gerburtstage von Carl Geganbaur am 21. August 1896. Vol. 3. Wilhelm Engelmann, Leipzig. pp. 125-166 plus plate.
Le Gros Clark, W. E.
1959   The Antecedents of Man. Edinburgh University Press, Edinburgh.

1971   The Antecedents of Man. Quadrangle Books, Chicago.

Mahé, J.
    1972 The Malagasy subfossils. In: Biogeography and Ecology of
    Madagascar. R. Battistini and G. Richard-Vindard, eds. Junk, The
    Hague. pp. 339-365.

    1968a Towards a new definition of primates. Man, *3:* 377-401.
Martin, R. D.
    1968b Reproduction and ontogeny in tree-shrews *(Tupaia belangeri)*
    with reference to their general behavior and taxonomic relationships.
    Zeitschrift fur Tierpsychologie, *25:* (4 and 5): 409-495, 505-532.

    1972 A preliminary field-study of the lesser mouse lemur *(Microcebus
    murinus* J. F. Miller 1777). In: Behavior and Ecology of Nocturnal
    Prosimians. (op. cit.) Advances in Ethology, Supplements to the Journal
    of Comparative Ethology (Zeitschrift fur Tierpsychologie), *9:* 43-89.
McKenna, M.
    1966 Paleontology and the origin of primates. Folia primatologica,
    4: 1-25.
Millot, J.
    1972 In conclusion. In: Biogeography and Ecology of Madagascar.
    R. Battistini and G. Richard-Vindard, eds. Junk, The Hague. pp. 741-
    756.
Milne-Edwards, A., and A. Grandidier
    1875 Histoire naturelle des Mammiferes. Ordre des Lémuriens,
    Famille des Indrisinés. In: Histoire physique, naturelle et politique de
    Madagascar. A. Grandidier, ed. Vol. 6. Texte 1. Vol. 9. Atlas 1. (Plates
    14, 35, 44). Imprimerie Nationale, Paris.
Napier, J. R., and P. H. Napier
    1967 A Handbook of Living Primates. Academic Press, New York and
    London.
Napier, J. R., and A. C. Walker
    1967 Vertical clinging and leaping—a newly recognized category of
    locomotor behaviour of Primates. Folia primatologica, *6:* 204-219.
Petter, J. J.
    1962 Recherches dur l'ecologie et l'ethologie des Lémuriens malgaches.
    Mémoirs du Museum Nationale d'Histoire Naturelle. Ser. A. *27:* 1-146.
Remane, A.
    1960 Zahne und Gebiss. In: Primatologia, Handbook of Primatology.
    III (2). H. Hofer, A. H. Schultz and D. Starck, eds. S. Karger, Basel
    and New York. pp. 637-846.
Russell, D. E.
    1964 Les Mammiferes Paleocene d'Europe. Memoirs du Museum
    Nationale d'Histoire Naturelle, nouvelle serie *13:* 1-324.

Simons, E. L.
1962a A new Eocene Primate genus, *Cantius*, and a revision of some allied European lemuroids. Bulletin of the British Museum of Natural History *7:* 1-36.

1962b Fossil evidence relating to the early evolution of primate behavior. In: Relatives of Man: Modern Studies of the Relation of the Evolution of Nonhuman Primates to Human Evolution. J. Buettner-Janusch, ed. Annals of the New York Academy of Science, *102:* 282-293.

1972 Primate Evolution Macmillan, New York.
Simpson, G. G.
1935 The Tiffany fauna, upper Paleocene II. Structure and relationships of *Plesiadapis*. American Museum Novitates, *816:* 1-30.

1943 Mammals and the nature of continents. American Journal of Science, *241:* 1-31.

1967 The tertiary lorisiform primates of Africa. Bulletin of the Museum of Comparative Zoology (Harvard), *136:* 39-61.

1973 Book Review: Minicontinent. Science, *180:* 1163-1164.
Sorenson, M. W.
1970 Behavior of Tree Shrews. In: Primate Behavior: Developments in Field and Laboratory Research. A. Rosenblum, ed. Academic Press, New York and London. pp. 141-193.
Slaughter, B. H.
1970 Evolutionary trends of chiropteran dentitions. In: About Bats. B. H. Slaughter and D. W. Walton, eds. Southern Methodist University Press, Dallas. pp. 51-83.
Szalay, F. S.
1968 The beginnings of primates. Evolution, *22:* 19-36.

1969 Mixodectidae, Microsyopidae, and the insectivore-primate transition. Bulletin of the American Museum of Natural History, *140:* 193-330.

1972a Cranial morphology of the early Tertiary *Phenacolemur* and its bearing on primate phylogeny. American Journal of Physical Anthropology, *36:* 59-76.

1972b Palaeobiology of the earliest primates. In: Functional and

Evolutionary Biology of Primates: Methods of Study and Recent Advances. R. H. Tuttle, ed. Aldine-Atherton, Chicago. pp. 3-35.

Tattersall, I.

1971a Crania and Dentitions of Archaeolemurinae (Lemuroidea, Primates). Ph. D. Dissertation, Yale University, New Haven.

1971b Revision of the subfossil Indriinae. Folia primatologica, *16:* 257-269.

Teilhard de Chardin, P.

1921 Les Mammiferes de l'Eocène inférieur français et leur gisements (fini). Annales de Paléontologie, *11:* 1-108.

Van Valen, L.

1965 Treeshrews, primates and fossils. Evolution, *19:* 137-151.

Walker, A.

1967a Patterns of extinction among the subfossil Madagascan lemuroids. In: Pleistocene Extinctions: the Search for a Cause. P. S. Martin and H. E. Wright, Jr., eds. Yale University Press, New Haven. pp. 425-432.

1967b Locomotor adaptation in recent and fossil Madagascan lemurs. Ph. D. Dissertation, University of London.

1972 The dissemination and segregation of early primates in relation to continental configuration. In: Calibration of Hominoid Evolution. W. W. Bishop and J. A. Miller, eds. University of Toronto Press, Toronto. pp. 195-218.

Warwick-James, W.

1960 The Jaws and Teeth of Primates. Pitman Medical, London.

Weber, M.

1928 Die Saügetiere. Vol. 2. Gustav Fischer, Jena.

Zeigler, A.

1971 A theory of the evolution of Therian dental formulas and replacement patterns. Quarterly Review of Biology, *46:* 226-249.

TWO

Biological Anthropology: The Life Cycle

Explaining "why we differ" comprises the research activity of a large number of biological anthropologists. People as well as populations are both different and alike, and they become so by means of the growth process. Biological anthropologists begin to study this process nine months after conception (usually) and see it through to old age. Whelan's paper shows how the examination of growth processes within a population can be a window, perhaps a somewhat opaque one, on the genetic basis for ontogenetic development. Interpopulational variation in ontogenetic measures seems to appeal to anthropologists particularly. Fry's contribution documents the growth process in the teeth of Polynesian children. But methodologies in growth studies are not restricted to subadult applications. Friedlaender and Oliver have grasped a rare opportunity to assess secular changes in body size over a large part of the adult life cycle in a remote, preliterate group. In the final article, Bleibtreu and Taylor use a sequence of multivariate techniques to examine the way in which thirty-three physical measurements of the body can be combined to show how boys and girls in three different ethnic/racial groups become physically differentiated quite apart from overt sexual characteristics. Though diverse, the methodologies illustrated in this section are only a fraction of those that can be used to indicate just how we grow up.

5. Effects of Aging and the Secular Trend in Bougainville Males

Jonathan S. Friedlaender and Douglas L. Oliver

Introduction

It is undeniable that older people are generally shorter than young adults who have recently reached full size. At least in contemporary European, Japanese, and American populations, this is the result of two well-documented biological phenomena, with the possibility that a few more factors may be at work as well.

The first clear fact is that successive generations living in these industrialized societies over the past century or more have attained larger and larger average statures and weights. The differences over time have been considerable. Generally speaking, the increase has

NOTE: This research has been supported in part by NSF Grant GS3088; NSF fellowships and dissertation improvement awards; a Population Council post-doctoral fellowship; Grant GM 13482 from NIGMS; and a W.H.O. Visiting Investigator award from the Population Genetics Laboratory, University of Hawaii.

R. H. Osborne originally suggested the possibilities of a follow-up survey in Siwai. Of the many others who have given advice or assistance in this project, we would like to mention William Howells, Albert Damon, Eugene Ogan, Nancy Lubin, Susan Groisser, the Marist Mission on Bougainville, the Department of Public Health and of Native Affairs, Territory of New Guinea, and the people of Bougainville, especially M. Mandaku and Maneha.

142

been on the average about one inch per generation of 33 years, for a variety of different industrialized societies and socioeconomic groups.[1] There is also some indication that the change has been generally more abrupt and marked in men than in women (e.g., Froehlich, 1970), probably for a wide variety of reasons.

This increasing size of new generations has not been going on for ever. There is some evidence that in Classic and Renaissance times, people were bigger than their descendants in the 16th and 17th centuries (Tanner, 1968). Also, the trend seems to be stopping in some groups which have long been economically and socially in a favorable position.

The most obvious explanation for the so-called secular increase in stature (referring to its documented 100-year extent in Europe and America) has been nutritional improvement. Inadequate nutrition, simply measured in caloric deficiency, may lead to both slow growth, retarded maturation time, and small final adult stature (Newman, 1961). Takahashi (1966) established a correlation between the consumption of milk and eggs with the greater attained stature of higher socioeconomic groups in Japan. Especially for the European working classes during the 18th and early 19th centuries, there is the strong suggestion that the diet was worse than it had been during the pre-industrialized era, and that only in the middle of the century did the real income of the workers increase substantially (Tanner, 1968). Conversely, there are recorded instances when periods of relative starvation have been associated with a temporary reversal in the trend; for example, in Moscow during the Second World War (Vlastovsky, 1966), and in European Russia following World War I (Ivanovsky, 1923). Japan during the early 1940's also seems to have undergone a similar reversal.

Geneticists have suggested a second possible cause for the increase in stature, and that is heterosis or hybrid vigor. It is a common phenomenon, in animals and plants, that crosses between members of two relatively inbred strains produce offspring which attain larger sizes than either of the parental strains, at least during the first

---

[1]For example, French soldiers increased on the average by 4.6 cm. between 1880 and 1960 (Chamla, 1964), American recruits increased an average of 3.1 cm. between World War I and 1958 (Karpinos, 1961), Harvard families gained an average of 3.5 cm. between 1855 and 1915 (Bowles, 1932), and Japanese students, aged 21 and 22, averaged a 6.5 cm. increase between 1900 and 1960 (Takahashi, 1966).

generation. Attempts to separate out this effect from the explanation of improved nutrition are quite difficult, and have given equivocal results. Hulse (1957), in studies of Swiss immigrants and isolates, has the most convincing study, while Trevor (1953), in a survey of a number of different hybrid populations, finds possible evidence of heterosis only among the Norfolk Islanders. Damon (1965a) suggests the possible combined effects of heterosis and nutritional improvement in Italian immigrants living in Boston.

Improved medical care, or lack of disease in childhood, is sometimes mentioned as a possible contributing factor to the secular trend as well. However, Tanner found that in Tanganyika, the eradication of chronic disease had no discernible effect on growth, and that minor illnesses seem to have had no effect on long-term growth of normal children (Tanner, 1966; same, 1962).

The second confounding biological phenomenon which causes young adults to be larger than the aged is that at some age people do begin to shrink, at least in most societies. The likely causes of this diminution with age are degenerative processes in the intervertebral discs, osteoporosis (Bourne, 1956), and increasing curvature of the spine and the concurrent inability to stand erect (Kleemeier, 1959). Other differences in bony dimensions after the attainment of full stature can be caused by arthritic lipping of various articular margins (Krogman, 1962) and appositional bone growth (Lasker, 1953). Conversely, as Damon (1968) has shown for most American groups, weight tends to increase steadily with age, at least until the sixth decade of life.

It has been extremely difficult to estimate the real size of this decrease in stature, principally because of the confounding effect the secular increase in stature has on all cross-sectional studies. Longitudinal studies, following the same individuals over the span of their adult lives, are difficult to carry out, but are by far the best indicators of age effects. But even the few good studies are not unanimous in their findings, as Froehlich was quick to point out. Lipscomb and Parnell (1954) found no significant decrease in stature to age 72 among 44 retired British servicemen, and Damon saw no difference in 187 Columbia College men who were remeasured at age 56 (Damon, 1965b). Two overlapping cohort studies, where people of different ages are measured at two or more time intervals, have shown the opposite. Miall and others (1967) have evidence that a decrease from a maximum height attained around age 35 to age 70 is of the order of magnitude of three centimeters in males, and even greater in females living in two Welsh communities. For Swiss, Gsell (1966) and Büchi (1950) obtained largely the same results, with stature being about one centimeter less at age 64 than at age 20, and considerably less than at the maximum, around 35.

One likely conclusion is that there are marked differences among human populations in the timing and extent of aging processes, just as there are for developmental processes, which have been more adequately documented (Malcolm, 1970; Tanner, 1968).

Other possible contributing explanations for the apparent decrease in size with age in cross-sectional studies revolve around differential fertility and mortality. If taller people had more offspring, or if shorter people tended to live longer, this might contribute to the apparent result. These notions have been impossible to substantiate in most instances, but must be kept in mind in any study.

Here we wish to present an overlapping cohort study of a group of men from Bougainville Island, Papua-New Guinea, who provide a unique examination of the secular trend and aging effects in a non-Western society in transition from self-sufficiency to dependence on the world market and cash cropping.

The Bougainville Sample

Bougainville Island, although geographically and culturally part of the Solomon Island chain, is administered as part of Papua-New Guinea (see Figure 1). The people are dark-skinned Melanesians, and the coastal dwellers are related in culture and language to neighboring islanders, but the villagers living in the interior of the island speak a group of languages which share only very distant relationships with any others known off the island. The people who comprise the main focus of this study belong to the Siwai, who live on the relatively heavily populated southwestern plain. Their traditional cultural and social patterns have been described by Oliver (1955).

During his ethnographic field study, Oliver measured and weighed approximately 1300 men from various parts of the island, but principally the Siwai (See Oliver, 1954, Oliver and Howells, 1960; and Howells, 1966). As part of a more recent survey on the island which included not only anthropometrics but also examinations of finger and palm prints, blood polymorphisms, and dental casts, Friedlaender tried to remeasure as many of the men covered by Oliver in 1938-39

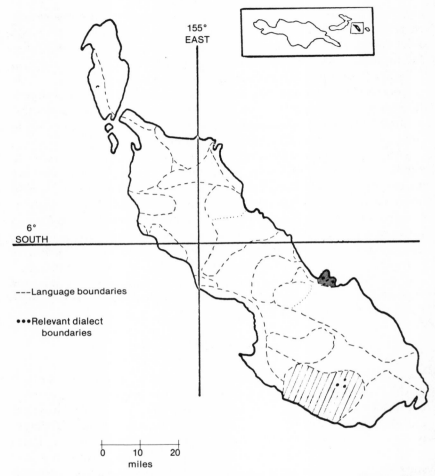

Figure 1. Bougainville Island, Papua New Guinea, Siwai Area denoted by Hatching, Melanesian Area of the study denoted by shading.

as possible. The results of this entire survey are presented in Fried-laender (1969; 1971; 1975).

Two villages were surveyed by Friedlaender where Oliver had lived for extended periods of time and also word was sent to other villages of northeast Siwai that he wanted to measure anyone who had been measured by Oliver 28 years previously. In this way, he was able to include 45 Siwai in a follow-up survey; 17 from the two villages covered intensively, and 28 from the immediately surrounding area. Their ages varied from 40 to over 70 in 1967. Identification of remeasured individuals was not an insuperable task. Oliver had taken photographs of all the men he measured, and these were available along with the original measurement blanks. Only four men who claimed to have been measured by Oliver were finally excluded from the tabulations either because they could not be positively identified with photographs, or because their old measurement records could not be found in Peabody Museum. Oliver had also visited Arawa and Rorovana villages on the east coast, which Friedlaender also surveyed, so that, in a similar manner, 17 additional men were located and re-measured from that very different area of the island. Undoubtedly, many more men previously measured by Oliver could have been located, especially in central Siwai and Nagovisi. About half of Oliver's 1,300 subjects lived in these two language areas, which were sampled fairly exhaustively.

Table 1 and Figure 2 compare the cross-sectional results of Oliver's and Friedlaender's surveys for stature in northeast Siwai, the area most intensively covered by Oliver, and with the most overlap in both

TABLE 1

HEIGHT — CROSS-SECTIONAL RESULTS OF
OLIVER'S (1939) AND FRIEDLAENDER'S (1967) SURVEYS

	OLIVER			FRIEDLAENDER			
Age	Mean Ht. (cm.)	σ	N	Mean Ht. (cm.)	σ	N	$\overline{\Delta}$
10-14	148	7	4				
15-19	158	7	16				
20-29	162	6	95	164	4	7	−2
30-39	161	5	83	164	6	19	−3
40-49	161	6	56	162	6	15	−1
50-59	161	6	29	162	7	31	−1
60-69	160	3	5	157	4	5	4
70-80				155	7	3	
			288			79	

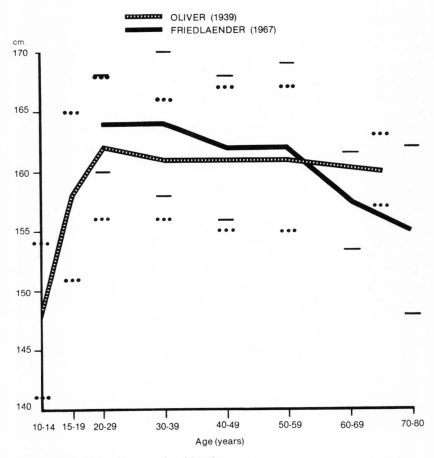

Figure 2. Height — Cross-sectional Results.

surveys. Oliver's series is remarkably uniform over the adult cohorts, with the twenty to twenty-nine cohort being a centimeter taller than the succeeding three. Quite to the contrary, Friedlaender's smaller series shows a pronounced difference in stature in those adult males younger than 49 as opposed to those 50 and over, who average at least two centimeters shorter. It should be noted that the oldest two cohorts have such small numbers that their interpretation is questionable in such a cross-sectional comparison. Note that there is no difference between the average stature of the 20-29 year cohort in

Oliver's series and Friedlaender's 40-59 year cohorts, which include many of the same individuals.

The most obvious preliminary interpretation of this comparison is that there has been a secular trend in Siwai populations, at the least, and that this increase may well have begun initially among those males born during 1910-1919, and subsequently increased another two centimeters. It is also possible that the anthropologists measured the subjects in different ways or had a significantly different set of subjects in ways they did not realize. Differential mortality with regard to height, with taller people dying earlier, might be one other possible explanation.

Figure 3 and Table 2, with the restudy results of the 62 subjects measured both in 1938-39 and 1967 largely answer these questions. These men, 45 from Siwai and 17 from Rorovana and Arawa, have been grouped according to their ages in 1938-39. The dotted line represents the average values of this select group in 1938-39, and the solid line gives their height 28 or 29 years later, in early 1967. The empty circles are the cross-sectional values for the corresponding classes in Oliver's study taken from the previous figure for reference.

TABLE 2

HEIGHTS OF INDIVIDUALS MEASURED 28 YEARS APART BY OLIVER AND FRIEDLAENDER

| Age in '38 | OLIVER (1939) | | | FRIEDLAENDER (1967) | | | |
	Mean Ht. (cm.)	σ		Mean Ht. (cm.)	σ	N	$\overline{\Delta}$
10-14	147.7	6		159.2	2	3	−11.5
15-19	157.5	8		160.3	7	6	− 2.8
20-24	164.8	6		165.8	6	15	− 1.0
25-29	161.1	7		160.4	7	22	.7
30-39	163.1	5		160.5	5	12	2.6
40 and over	159.5	8		156.7	7	4	2.8

62

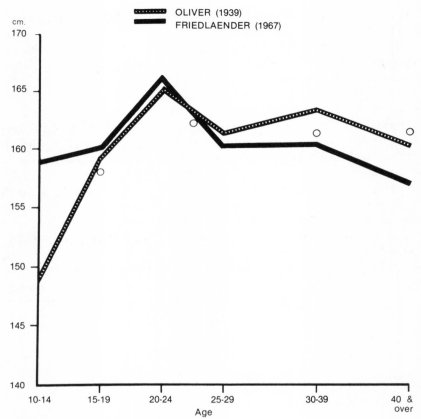

Figure 3. Height — Longitudinal Results.

In this figure (3), the two lines cross. That is, the men Oliver measured who were younger than 25 were generally taller in the restudy, while those 25 and older when Oliver measured them (and who were 53 and older when remeasured) generally had lower values the second time around. These differences grow with each age class, from .7 to 2.8 centimeters. This graph indicates that there is little difference in measuring technique. The results from men who were fully grown in 1939 and who were still in their early 50's in 1967 correspond quite closely, indicating that the secular trend explanation for the differences in the cross-section graph is the correct one. Also, there is good evidence for real "shrinkage" beginning in the late 50's and increasing thereafter.

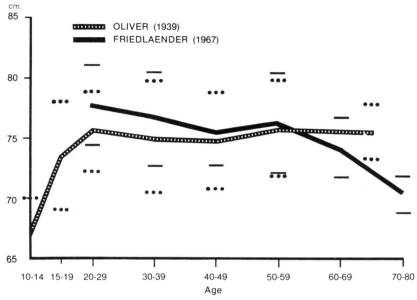

Figure 4. Upper Extremity Length — Cross-Sectional Results.

TABLE 3

UPPER EXTREMITY LENGTH — CROSS-SECTIONAL RESULTS
OF OLIVER'S (1939) AND FRIEDLAENDER'S (1967) SURVEYS

	OLIVER			FRIEDLAENDER			
Age	Mean Arm Lgth. (cm.)	σ	N	Mean Arm Lgth. (cm.)	σ	N	$\overline{\Delta}$
10-14	67.3	2.7	4				
15-19	73.5	4.5	16				
20-29	75.6	3.3	94	77.8	3.3	7	−2.2
30-39	75.0	4.5	83	76.6	3.9	19	−1.6
40-49	74.7	4.0	56	75.6	2.9	15	− .9
50-59	75.6	4.2	29	76.2	4.2	30	− .6
60-69				74.1	2.5	5	
	75.4	2.3	5				2.7
70-80				70.3	1.4	3	

TABLE 4

UPPER EXTREMITY LENGTHS OF INDIVIDUALS MEASURED
28 YEARS APART BY OLIVER AND FRIEDLAENDER

	OLIVER (1939)		FRIEDLAENDER (1967)			
Age in '38	Mean Arm Length (cm.)	σ	Mean Arm Length (cm.)	σ	N	$\overline{\Delta}$
10-14	68.6	1.3	73.5	.9	3	-4.9
15-19	72.2	4.2	75.1	3.4	6	−2.9
20-24	76.7	3.8	77.7	4.1	15	−1.0
25-29	74.8	3.5	75.9	4.1	21	− .4
30-39	75.8	3.5	76.0	3.1	12	− .2
40 and over	75.2	5.9	75.5	4.8	4	− .3

TABLE 5

SITTING HEIGHT – CROSS-SECTIONAL RESULTS
OF OLIVER'S (1939) AND FRIEDLAENDER'S (1969) SURVEYS

	OLIVER			FRIEDLAENDER			
Age	Mean Sitting Ht. (cm.)	σ	N	Mean Sitting Ht. (cm.)	σ	N	$\overline{\Delta}$
10-14	75.1	3.2	4				
15-19	80.5	4.9	16				
20-29	82.5	3.7	95	84.7	1.1	7	−2.2
30-39	82.5	3.4	83	84.7	2.8	19	−2.2
40-49	82.7	4.3	55	82.3	3.0	15	.4
50-59	81.6	4.7	29	83.0	4.0	31	−1.4
60-69				80.2	1.9	5	
	77.1	8.5	5				−1.8
70-80				76.8	3.4	3	

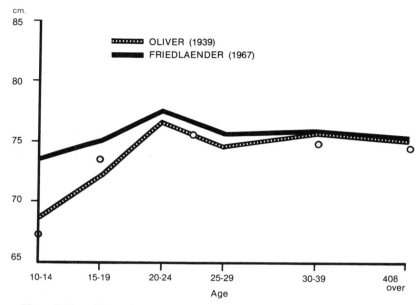

Figure 5. Upper Extremity Length — Longitudinal Results.

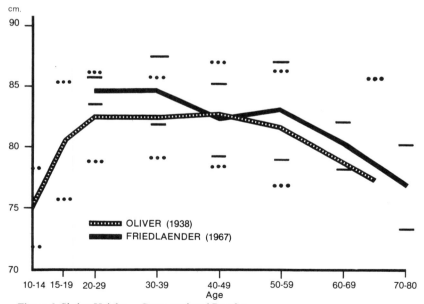

Figure 6. Sitting Height — Cross-sectional Results.

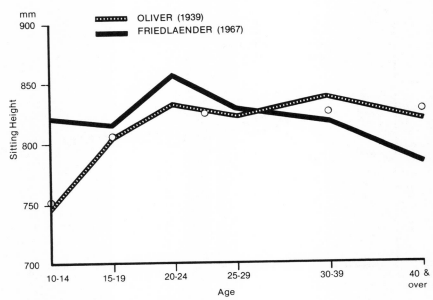

Figure 7. Sitting Height — Longitudinal Results.

TABLE 6

SITTING HEIGHTS OF INDIVIDUALS MEASURED 28
YEARS APART BY OLIVER AND FRIEDLAENDER

	OLIVER (1939)		FRIEDLAENDER (1967)		
Age in '38	Mean Sitting Ht. (cm.)		Mean Sitting Ht. (cm.)	N	$\overline{\Delta}$
10-14	74.3	4.8	82.4	2.6	3	−8.1
15-19	80.4	5.5	81.5	4.2	6	−1.1
20-24	83.1	6.1	85.6	2.9	15	−2.5
25-29	82.1	3.5	82.8	3.5	22	− .7
30-39	83.8	2.8	81.8	2.3	12	2.0
40 and over	81.8	3.2	78.4	4.4	4	3.4

Another point—comparing the dotted line with the open circles, it is clear that the 62 men were fairly close to the average values for their age classes in 1939, or if anything, slightly taller. Therefore, differential survival of shorter men into later life does not seem to be a likely explanation for the sharp drop in stature for later age classes.

The other measured trunk and limb lengths (upper extremity length and sitting height) given in Tables 3-6 and Figures 4-7 suggest that by far the largest portion of the "shrinkage" occurs within the trunk, but that the younger generation attains longer trunk and limb lengths. Measurement error is a distinct possibility here, however.

The cross-sectional curves for weight (Figure 8, Table 7), a variable which reflects many different cross-currents and influences, are generally similar to those for stature, although the differences are more pronounced. Except for those men in their fourth decade, the values for the 1967 survey cohorts are all about five pounds greater than for the corresponding cohorts in Oliver's survey.

There is a technical question here, as two different scales were used, but again in this instance, the longitudinal results make large technical differences unlikely. Figure 9 and Table 8 show that the re-weighed men tend to be fairly consistently lower in weight than they were in 1939 (except for the first group) as opposed to the cross-sectional results, where the newer means for all groups are higher. In the restudied subsample, the average difference between the first and second weighings increases gradually up to 10 pounds for men 68 to 72 years old, a large weight loss by any reckoning.

As with stature, the most reasonable interpretation is that there has been an increase in the maximum attained weight in the new post-war generation, and that there continues to be a decrease in weight in later life, which appears to take place earlier than does the shrinkage in stature. Vines (1970) interpreting cross-sectional studies in New Guinea, believes this weight loss to be most pronounced and earliest in females, beginning even in their mid-thirties.

This pattern is, of course, contrary to the pattern for industrialized populations, where the later years of adulthood up to the sixth decade are generally characterized by weight gain, although variation from individual to individual in this gain is great.

The results from other measurements included in the battery are generally less interesting. There is good evidence for the so-called "senile chest"; that is, chest breadth decreasing sharply with increasing age, and chest depth, at least in this case, increasing only slightly.

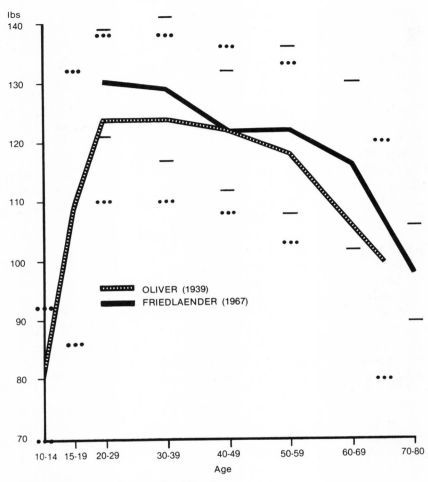

Figure 8. Weight — Cross-sectional Results.

In the head, there are only some minor differences between curves in both cross-sectional and follow-up studies. Nose length and breadth tend to increase in later life, but total face height declines, most likely because of tooth loss.

In summary, there is good evidence for "shrinkage," particularly in the vertebral column, and for an accompanying loss in weight. This shrinkage occurs rather earlier in life than seems the case in modern industrialized societies. It is also clear that at least the post-war generation of Siwai and Torau and Arawa males are bigger than their fathers by an appreciable amount, at least a centimeter. The cause of this increase is most likely improved nutrition although improved health conditions might have contributed.

There is the distinct possibility that, at least in part, the differences in the cross-sectional curves may be due to differential survival of men in the 28-year interval between 1938-39 and 1967. Note that, particularly in weight (Figure 9), the 61 "surviving" males were, on the average, more than 5 pounds heavier than the mean for their entire cohort in 1938-39. To explore this matter, we have compared "recovered" and "unrecovered" groups of both Siwai and Melanesian speakers by ten-year age cohorts.

In northeast Siwai, where the sampling was very close to complete in both 1938 and 1967, almost half of the teenagers, and almost a third of the men in their twenties who were measured by Oliver, were recovered and measured in 1967 (see Table 9). For the smaller series of Melanesian speakers from Rorovana and Arawa, the recovery rate was better for men in their twenties, and much better for

TABLE 7

WEIGHT – CROSS-SECTIONAL RESULTS OF
OLIVER'S (1939) AND FRIEDLAENDER'S (1967) SURVEYS

	OLIVER			FRIEDLAENDER			
Age	Mean Weight (Lbs)	σ	N	Mean Weight (Lbs)	σ	N	$\overline{\Delta}$
10-14	81	11	4				
15-19	109	23	16				
20-29	124	14	94	130	9	7	−6
30-39	124	14	83	129	12	19	−5
40-49	122	14	56	122	10	15	0
50-59	118	15	29	122	14	30	−4
60-69				116	14	5	
	100	20	5				−9
70-80				98	8	3	

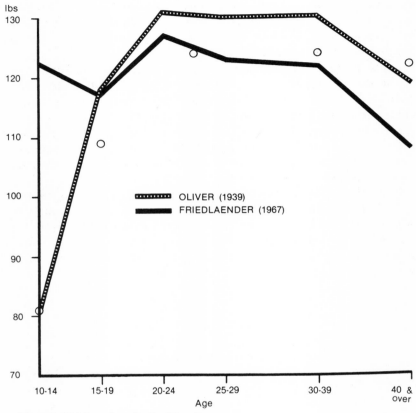

Figure 9. Weight — Longitudinal Results.

men in their thirties. Almost no men in their forties in 1938-39 were recovered in 1967.

Comparing the "recovered" and "unrecovered" males for the two language areas, we have found, among other things, that the "recovered" males in both Siwai and Melanesian speaking groups do tend to outweigh the "unrecovered" groups in the early decades. This is reflected in Figure 9, although only Siwai teenagers show this

TABLE 8

**WEIGHTS OF INDIVIDUALS MEASURED 28
YEARS APART BY OLIVER AND FRIEDLAENDER**

Age in '38	OLIVER (1939) Mean Wt.	σ	FRIEDLAENDER (1967) Mean Wt.	σ'	N	$\overline{\Delta}$
10-14	80	13	123	2	3	−43
15-19	118	22	117	17	6	1
20-24	131	16	127	15	15	5
25-29	130	21	123	17	21	8
30-39	130	18	122	15	12	8
40 and over	119	15	108	17	4	11

61

TABLE 9

**RECOVERY RATE OF NORTHEAST SIWAI
AND ROROVANA AND ARAWA MALES**

Age	SIWAI Number Measured by Oliver	Number Recovered in 1967	MELANESIAN SPEAKERS Number Measured by Oliver	Number Recovered in 1967
10-14	5	2	0	0
15-19	15	6	6	0
20-24	43	11	14	4
25-29	52	17	10	5
30-34	49	5	9	2
35-39	32	1	11	4
40-44	31	2	8	2
45-49	24	0	5	0

clearly, while Melanesians up through their thirties have this pattern. In the fourth decade (and also third for Siwai), it was the lighter male who tended to "survive" to be remeasured at age 70 or so. As for differences in height, these are less distinctive, but they parallel the pattern of weight differences in both groups.

All this suggests that the bigger, especially heavier young men survived the war and the rest of the intervening 28 years between 1938-39 and 1967 in greatest numbers, but that the very few middle-aged men who attained age 70 or thereabouts in 1967 were shorter and lighter than their age mates in 1938-39. This switch in survival differential set in earlier in the hard-pressed Siwai than among the eastern beach people, who generally seem to have enjoyed lower mortality rates. Perhaps bigger adolescents and young men survived the wartime depridations more successfully, but now die at increasingly high rates after the onset of middle age.

References

Bourne, G.
1956 The biochemistry and physiology of bone. Academic Press, New York.

Bowles, G. T.
1932 New types of old Americans at Harvard and at eastern women's colleges. Harvard University Press, Cambridge, Massachusetts.

Büchi, E. C.
1950 Änderungen der Körpferform beim erwachsenes Menschen. Anthrop, Forsch, *1*.

Chamla, M. C.
1964 L'accroissement de la stature en France de 1880 à 1960; comparison avec les pays d' Europe Occidentale. Soc. d' Anthrop. Paris Bull. et Mém., *6*: 201-278.

Damon, A.
1965a Stature increase among Italian-Americans: environment, genetic, or both? American Journal of Physical Anthropology, *23*: 401-408.

————
1965b Discrepancies between findings of longitudinal and cross-sectional studies in adult life: Physique and Physiology. Human Development, *8*: 16-22.

————
1968 Secular trend in height and weight within old American families at Harvard, 1870-1965. I. Within twelve four-generation families. American Journal of Physical Anthropology, *29*: 45-50.

Friedlaender, J. S.
1969 Biological Divergences over Population Boundaries in South-Central Bougainville. Ph.D. thesis, Harvard University, Cambridge, Massachusetts.

————
1971 The population structure of south-central Bougainville. American Journal of Physical Anthropology, *35*: 13-25.

————
1975 Patterns of Human Variation. Harvard University Press, Cambridge, Massachusetts.

Froehlich, J. W.
1970 Migration and the plasticity of physique in the Japanese-Americans of Hawaii, American Journal of Physical Anthropology, *32*: 429-442.

Gsell, O.
    1966   Longitudinale Alterforschung über 10 Jahre: Basler Studien
    1955-1965. Schweizer. Med. Wochenschrift, *96:* 1541-1548.
Howells, W. W.
    1966   Population distances: biological, linguistic, geographical, and
    environmental. Current Anthropology, *7:* 531-540.
Hulse, F. S.
    1957   Éxogamie et hétérosis. Arch. Suisses d' Anthrop. Gen., *22:*
    103-125.
Ivanovsky, A.
    1923   Physical modification of the population of Russia under famine.
    American Journal of Physical Anthropology, *6:* 331-353.
Karpinos, B. D.
    1961   Current height and weight of youths of military age. Human
    Biology, *33:* 335-354.
Kleemeier, R.
    1959   Behavior and the organization of the bodily and the external
    environment. In: Handbook of Aging and the Individual. J. E. Birren,
    ed. University of Chicago Press, Chicago.
Krogman, W. M.
    1962   The Human Skeleton in Forensic Medicine. Thomas, Spring-
    field, Illinois.
Lasker, G. W.
    1953   The age factor in bodily measurements of adult male and female
    Mexicans. Human Biology, *25:* 50-63.
Lipscomb, F. M., and R. W. Parnell
    1954   The physique of Chelsea pensioners. J. Royal Army Med. Corps,
    100: 247-255.
Malcolm, L.
    1970   Growth and development of the Bundi child of the New Guinea
    Highlands. Human Biology, *42:* 293-328.
Miall, W. E., M. T. Ashcroft, H. G. Lovell, and F. Moore
    1967   A longitudinal study of the decline of adult height with age in
    two Welsh communities. Human Biology, *39:* 445-454.
Newman, M. T.
    1961   Biological adaptation of man to his environment: heat, cold,
    altitude, and nutrition. Ann. N. Y. Acad. Sci., *91:* 617-633.
Ogan, E.
    1969   Changing Nasioi Economics: An Ethnographic Study. Ph.D.
    thesis. Harvard University, Cambridge, Massachusetts.
Oliver, D. L.
    1954   Somatic Variability and Human Ecology on Bougainville Island,
    Solomon Islands. Ms. Harvard University, Cambridge, Massachusetts.

1955   A Solomon Island Society. Harvard University Press, Cambridge, Massachusetts.

Oliver, D. L., and W. W. Howells
1960   Bougainville populations studied by generalized distance. Actes, VIᵉ Congres International des Sciences Anthropologiques et Ethnologiques, Paris, France, *1:* 497-502.

Takahashi, E.
1966   Growth and environmental factors in Japan. Human Biology, *38:* 112-130.

Tanner, J. M.
1962   Growth at Adolescence. Thomas, Springfield, Illinois.

1966   Growth and physique in different populations of mankind. In: The Biology of Human Adaptability. P. T. Baker, and J. S. Weiner, eds. Clarendon Press, Oxford.

1968   Earlier maturation in man. Scientific American, *218:* 21-27.

Trevor, J.
1953   Race Crossing in Man: The Analysis of Metrical Characters. Cambridge University Press, London, United Kingdom.

Vines, A. P.
1970   An Epidemiological Sample Survey of The Highlands, Mainland, and Island Regions of the Territory of Papua and New Guinea. Bloink, Port Moresby.

Vlastovsky, V. G.
1966   The secular trend in the growth and development of children and young persons in the Soviet Union. Human Biology, *38:* 219-230.

6. Dental Development in Cook Island Children

Edward I. Fry

Introduction

This study reports the dental conditions of 85 Polynesian boys from Rarotonga, Cook Islands, South Pacific. Rarotonga is a "high" island, in the Southern Cook group, with volcanic peaks up to 2,100 feet, a fringing reef enclosing a shallow lagoon, and 16,500 acres of land area. It is 20 miles in circumference, and supports a population of 6,000, some 5,700 of whom are Polynesians. It is located in the center of the Polynesian triangle, at 159° 45' east longitude, and 21° 15' south latitude. With reference to other well known land masses, Rarotonga is 2400 miles due south of Hawaii, 600 miles southwest

NOTE: This work was carried out while the author was a Fullbright Fellow to Auckland University College, New Zealand. The cooperation of Mr. E. G. Budge of the United States Educational Foundation in New Zealand is gratefully acknowledged. I am particularly indebted to Dr. F. M. MacKenzie, the Cook Island Dental Officer and his staff, and to the Cook Island Administration. All dental examinations were made in the Cook Island Dental Clinic by F. M. MacKenzie. Dr. Charles Carothers, of Lincoln, Nebraska, deserves mention for his assistance. Finally, I am indebted to the people of Titikaveka village in ways beyond words.

of Tahiti, 700 miles southeast of Samoa, and 1600 miles northeast of New Zealand.

The 85 Rarotongan boys who were examined ranged in age from six to sixteen years. They comprised the total schoolboy population of the village of Titikaveka, a small settlement of 750 people in Rarotonga. These children were of mixed parentage, some 60 per cent of them showed physical evidence of recent mixture with Europeans, Negroes or Mongoloids. They are representative of the present-day population of the Cook Islands, a group of Polynesian peoples who have been mixed with other populations for more than 100 years (Simmons *et al.*, 1955).

Results

The basic results of the dental examinations are shown in Table 1. They are analyzed in detail in the following sections of this paper.

TOOTH ERUPTION

Studies of the eruption time of the permanent teeth of non-

TABLE 1

FEATURES OF THE RAROTONGAN DECIDUOUS
AND PERMANENT DENTITION

Feature	Deciduous		Permanent		Total	
	N	Per cent	N	Per cent	N	Per cent
Carious	21	4	3	0.2	24	1.0
Missing Teeth						
Trauma	0	0	4	0.2	4	0.18
Congenital	0	0	3	0.2	3	0.14
Caries	101	19	7	0.4	108	5.0
Filled	215	40	342	21.0	557	25.0
Erupting	0	0	149	9.0	149	6.8
Impacted	0	0	2	0.1	2	0.09
Hypoplastic	0	0	14	0.8	14	0.6
Displaced	1	0.2	14	0.8	15	0.7
Fractured	0	0	1	0.06	1	0.04
Rotated	0	0	16	1.0	16	0.7
Normal	203	38	1178	71.0	1381	63.12
Total Present	531		1657		2188	

Europeans show them to be earlier than standards for Europeans (Garn and Moorrees, 1951; Hurme, 1946; Hurtate and Scrimshaw, 1955; Spier, 1919; Steggarda and Hill, 1942). Data on the eruption dates of 149 teeth from 51 Rarotongan subjects are presented in Table 2, where the mean eruption ages in years are compared to composite mean ages given by Hurme (1949) for over 93,000 White children.

The eruption dates of the Rarotongans are ahead of those of Hurme's Whites by an average of 0.76 years in the maxilla and 0.28 years in the mandible. These differences are significant at the 1 per cent level for the maxilla ($Z = 5.70$), and the 5 per cent level for the mandible ($Z = 1.96$). In general, then, the teeth of Rarotongans erupt earlier than those of Whites. When the individual teeth are considered, however, a slightly different picture is seen. The differences between the eruption times of the Rarotongans and the White group are shown in Table 3.

Statistically significant Z scores were recorded for five teeth which erupted earlier in the Rarotongans than in the North Americans. In the maxilla, these teeth are the canines and first and second premolars, and in the mandible, the lateral incisors and second molars. With the exception of these five teeth, the differences between the groups are not statistically significant.

In general, the Rarotongans are significantly early in their tooth

TABLE 2

MEAN ERUPTION AGES OF PERMANENT TEETH OF RAROTONGANS
AND NORTH AMERICAN WHITES

Tooth	N	Maxilla		N	Mandible	
		Rarotongans	North Americans		Rarotongans	North Americans
I_1	11	7.18	7.47	11	6.10	6.54
I_2	6	8.50	8.67	13	7.15	7.70
C	10	9.60	11.69	2	11.50	10.79
PM_1	16	9.44	10.40	12	10.17	10.82
PM_2	9	9.56	11.18	10	10.90	11.47
M_1	9	6.33	6.40	6	6.62	6.21
M_2	20	13.21	12.68	14	11.28	12.12

TABLE 3

DIFFERENCES BETWEEN RAROTONGAN AND NORTH AMERICAN
PERMANENT TOOTH ERUPTION

Tooth	Maxilla (Years)	Mandible (Years)
I_1	+0.29	+0.44
I_2	+0.17	+0.55*
C	+2.09**	−0.71
PM_1	+0.96**	+0.65
PM_2	+1.62**	+0.57
M_1	+0.07	−0.41
M_2	−0.53	+0.84*
Mean	+0.76	+0.28

+ = Rarotongan eruption earlier.

− = Rarotongan eruption later.

* = Significant at the 5 per cent level.

**= Significant at the 1 per cent level.

eruption, but this significance is primarily due to the five teeth mentioned above. Since non-European children have earlier eruption dates than Europeans, a finding of early eruption times for the Rarotongans agrees with previous reports. Hurme (1946) has cited Steggerda and Hill (1942) and Spier (1919) in stating that:

> The findings . . . strengthen the impression that the populations native to hot climates generally erupt their permanent teeth earlier than those native to cooler regions. (Hurme, 1946, p. 134).

The Rarotongan data confirm this general impression.

Qualitative Observations

A number of qualitative features were observed on the teeth and mouths of these subjects. Some of these features are summarized in Table 4.

Since these subjects are young, it is difficult to postulate what "average" tooth wear would be. Certainly these children's teeth are not badly worn. Attrition shows only a slight tendency to increase with age. All of the six-year-olds show slight wear, but heavy wear is restricted to an eleven and a thirteen-year-old.

TABLE 4

QUALITATIVE FEATURES OF RAROTONGAN DENTITION

	Number of Cases				
Feature	None	Slight	Medium	Heavy	Not Applicable
Attrition	14	69	2	0	0
Shovel-shaped Incisors	32	36	4	0	13
Calculus Deposits	85	0	0	0	0

Figures on the Rarotongans indicate that 53.5 per cent of the incisor teeth are shovel-shaped, and that 10.3 per cent of the incisors have medium to marked shoveling. Riesenfeld (1956) has published evidence showing that 79 per cent of eighty Polynesian incisors are shovel-shaped, and that 34 per cent show medium and marked shovel-shaping. There is thus a broad range in the incidence of shovel-shaped incisors in Polynesians.

No subjects of the Rarotongan group had visible calculus deposits. Davies (1956b), however, found 115 cases (23 per cent) in his Pukapuka sample, which ranged in age from zero to more than seventy years. No individual had erupted his third molars, so that it is impossible to determine the incidence of impaction for these teeth. Davies also found that 21 per cent of the third molars which were present in the Pukapukans were impacted. Two impacted second premolar teeth were seen in the Titikaveka group and belonged to a ten-year-old and a thirteen-year-old subject. Visual examination did not reveal any supernumerary teeth in the Rarotongan children, although Davies found twelve supernumerary teeth in ten (2 per cent) of his subjects. There were no cases of Carabelli's cusp in the Rarotongan group. Moorrees (1957) in summarizing the data on the incidence of the cusp of Carabelli, has shown that Mongoloid dentitions are marked by a low incidence of this feature.

Occlusion

This feature was observed using a modification of Angle's classification (Angle, 1899; Knutson, 1955) which considers the relationship between the first permanent molars of the mandible and maxilla as the significant criterion of occlusal relationships. The resulting categories are defined as follows: Class I, the maxillary and mandibular first molars are in their normal relationship with the maxillary slightly distal to the mandibular; Class II, the mandibular is abnormally distal to the maxillary; Class III, the mandibular is abnormally mesial to the maxillary.

For the Titikaveka children, those with normal occlusions and Class I malocclusions were grouped together, so that observations of this feature were based solely on the occlusion of the mandibular and maxillary first molars and did not take into account the degree of anterior occlusion or malocclusion and open or cross bite. Data from reports by Davies on Pukapukans, and McDowell (1953) on Rarotongans were similarly combined to facilitate comparison (Table 5).

There are no differences between the Titikaveka and Rarotongan samples and both groups have low percentages of Class II and Class III malocclusions. The differences between the Rarotongans and the Pukapukans were tested for statistical significance by the use of X^2, and were found to be significant at the 1 per cent level ($X^2 = 14.39$). There is a real difference between these groups, and the Pukapukans have significantly more malocclusions than the Rarotongans.

TABLE 5

MALOCCLUSION AND NORMAL OCCLUSION IN POLYNESIANS

| | Normal and Class I | | Class II | | Class III | | Total |
	N	Per cent	N	Per cent	N	Per cent	N
Mixed Dentition							
Pukapuka	66	84	5	6	8	10	79
Titikaveka	43	98	0	0	1	2	44
Permanent Dentition							
Pukapuka	275	82	12	3	48	14	335
Titikaveka	39	98	1	2	0	0	40
Total							
Pukapuka	341	82	17	4	56	14	414
Titikaveka	82	98	1	1	1	1	84
Rarotonga	338	98	8	2	4	1	350

Most of the differences between the children from Titikaveka and the children from Pukapuka are in the incidences of Class III malocclusions. Fourteen per cent of the Pukapukans, and only 1 per cent of the Rarotongans have Class III malocclusions.

Davies concluded that the high incidence of malocclusions in the Pukapukans resulted from natural selection operating on a series of genetic mutations. Function, as measured by the degree of attrition of the teeth, was not a significant cause of malocclusion. If these conclusions are correct, similar mutations do not seem to have occurred in Rarotonga.

Further comparisons between the Titikaveka group and Wisconsin Whites and Indians (Foster, 1942) are shown in Table 6. In this table, the permanent and mixed dentitions are not separated, and the Normal and Class I malocclusions have been combined.

The Whites and the Indians are seen to have appreciable incidences of Class II malocclusions, and low incidences of Class III malocclusions. The Rarotongans, however, have only 1 per cent of each of these types. A X^2 test was applied to these differences, and in each case found to be significant at the 1 per cent level. For the Rarotongan-White differences, $X^2 = 18.66$; for the Rarotongan-Indian differences, $X^2 = 12.43$. Hence, the Rarotongans have a significantly smaller number of malocclusions than either Wisconsin Whites or Indians.

In summary, Rarotongans have a very low incidence of malocclusions. The Rarotongan incidence of Class II and Class III malocclusions is significantly lower than the incidences of these malocclusions in Polynesians from Pukapuka, and Whites and Indians from Wis-

TABLE 6.

MALOCCLUSION IN THE RAROTONGANS AND OTHER GROUPS

	N	Normal and Class I Per cent	N	Class II Per cent	N	Class III Per cent
Whites	148	79	34	18	6	3
Indians	230	84	31	11	13	5
Rarotongans	82	98	1	1	1	1

TABLE 7.

PERIODONTAL DISEASE IN THREE POLYNESIAN GROUPS

	N	Arorangi Per cent	N	Pukapuka Per cent	N	Titikaveka Per cent
None	272	55	202	59	20	24
Mild	62	12	50	15	63	74
Moderate	68	14	39	11	2	2
Severe	40	8	36	10	0	0
General Periodontitis	55	11	17	5	0	0
Total	497	100	344	100	85	100

consin. If malocclusion is a genetically controlled trait, the gene frequency of this trait is low on Rarotonga.

PERIODONTAL DISEASE

Comparative material on this feature is summed up in Table 7 which compares the Pukapukan material and that from Arorangi village on Rarotonga (Davies) with the result from the examination of Titikaveka school children.

For Titikaveka, 76 per cent of the children had gingivitis, compared to 41 per cent for the children from Arorangi, and 35 per cent for Pukapukans. McDowell (1953) found that 45 per cent of 200 Rarotongan children had gingivitis. The children measured in the present survey have a significantly higher percentage of gingivitis than any of the other groups. The possibility exists, however, that these differences are the result of different standards used in making the examinations, and these comparisons may not be valid.

In a large scale cross-sectional study of children from seven to seventeen years of age, Massler, Cohen and Schour (1952) found that 48 per cent of Negro children from Philadelphia, 54 per cent of White children from Philadelphia, and 66 per cent of White children from Chicago had gingivitis. These figures are significantly below the 76 per cent recorded for the children from Titikaveka village.

The cause of this disease is unknown, although such diverse items as diet and bacterial infection have been mentioned (Glickman, 1953). Massler *et al.* suggested that the differing percentages of gingivitis which they found in a Negro and two White groups may be the result of racial factors. Davies found no association between food impaction and gingivitis in Pukapukans, so that the lack of oral hygiene in the Polynesians is not a contributing factor. The geographically isolated Pukapukans eat fewer European foods than the Rarotongans, yet, except for the Titikaveka sample, the Polynesian groups are about equal in percentages of periodontal disease. For this reason, diet does not seem to be a significant cause of gingivitis.

In view of the different percentages of gingivitis in White children from Chicago and Philadelphia, the differences between the children from Titikaveka village on the one hand, and children from Rarotonga, Arorangi and Pukapuka on the other, are not surprising. We may conclude that the Polynesians as well as the Whites show a broad incidence of gingival disease.

DMF Rates

There are a number of different methods of calculating the incidence of decayed, missing and filled (DMF) teeth all yielding different DMF indices.

The first method of calculating the DMF index of Rarotongan teeth considers the number of teeth in the subject's mouth at the time of examination. This method allows consideration of individual and racial factors in tooth eruption, and the resulting rate gives an accurate picture of the tooth conditions of these children. The formula for this index (Table 8) is:

$$\frac{\textit{Number of decayed, missing and filled teeth}}{\text{Number of teeth present}}$$

In every case where deciduous teeth are present, their index is consistently higher than that for the permanent teeth. The average deciduous rate is over two and one-half times the average permanent rate. These data confirm the work of Davies (1952) who found a higher DMF index during the mixed dentition period in Cook Island children from Pukapuka.

The trends of these rates show wide fluctuations. The deciduous dentition shows a sharp spurt from six to eight years, with a slight drop at nine and ten, and reaches a maximum value of 100 per cent

TABLE 8

DMF RATE FOR PERMANENT AND DECIDUOUS TEETH
OR RAROTONGAN CHILDREN

Age	N	DMF Deciduous	DMF Permanent	DMF All Teeth
6	7	34.8	0.0	28.2
7	12	58.8	10.3	43.4
8	6	84.6	20.0	49.0
9	8	82.7	24.0	46.4
10	8	68.2	20.5	31.3
11	5	95.0	19.1	30.8
12	6	100.0	21.6	22.1
13	10		23.4	23.4
14	11	71.4	18.6	19.8
15	7		20.9	20.9
16	5		35.0	35.0
	—			
Total	85			

at twelve years. By this time only one deciduous tooth was still present, and the DMF rate for the deciduous dentition no longer applied.

The rate for the permanent dentition also shows a rapid increase. From zero at six years, when thirty-one permanent teeth were found, the rate climbs to a high of 24 per cent at nine years. It remains close to this level until sixteen years when it again jumps, reaching a terminal peak at 35 per cent at sixteen years. There is a plateau of DMF conditions from eight to fifteen years, which seems to indicate that: 1) The first permanent molars which erupt between six and seven years in the Rarotongans (Table 2) are the main ones under attack. They become carious after several years, and the DMF rate is not greatly altered by eruption of the other teeth; and 2) when the second permanent molar erupts, the rate again increases, although there is a lag in the DMF rate at this time. In the Rarotongans, this tooth erupts between eleven and thirteen years, and the maximum decay rate is delayed by three to four years. This delay is a result of the greater resistance of the second molar to decay.

Polynesian comparisons using this same DMF formula can be made on material gathered in 1951-52 by McDowell. In this study, dental examinations were made on children aged six to fifteen years from Avarua and Titikaveka villages on Rarotonga, and on children from the Southern Cook Islands of Atiu, Mauke, and Mitiaro. Additional data from New Zealand Maoris and Whites (Hewat, Eastcott and Bibby, 1952) are included in Table 9 which shows these computations.

The Titikaveka group examined in the present survey shows slight but not significant reductions of their indices when compared to McDowell's data. The differences between the Titikaveka group and the others are not statistically significant, except for the Titikaveka-Mitiaro comparison, where Z = 2.40 and is significant at the 5 per cent level. We may conclude, that with the exception of the children from Mitiaro, there are no significant differences between children from islands in the Southern Cook group on the incidence of DMF rates.

The DMF rates of the Rarotongans can be compared for each age to the rates from the large-scale Hagerstown study (Klein, Palmer and Knutson, 1938). That study, which observed 5,722 White school children in the age ranges from six to sixteen years, reported the

TABLE 9

DMF RATES OF POLYNESIANS

Group	N	DMF Deciduous	DMF Permanent	DMF All Teeth
Titikaveka*	85	61.8	23.4	32.7
Titikaveka**	100	66.3	25.6	35.8
Avarua	100	67.8	28.7	39.1
Atiu	50	56.5	21.8	37.2
Mauke	50	59.8	18.3	30.3
Mitiaro	50	34.2	6.1	15.4
New Zealand Maori	1317	50.8	x	x
New Zealand White	2191	46.8	x	x

*   This study
**   McDowell

data at each year level with the two sexes combined. The DMF formula used in the Hagerstown study was:

$$\frac{Number\ of\ decayed,\ missing\ and\ filled\ teeth}{\text{Number of subjects}}$$

These data are listed in Table 10. The differences between the Rarotongan and Hagerstown rates were tested using the normal test of the difference between means (Edwards, 1946), and no statistically significant differences were found.

A small amount of additional comparative material using the same DMF formula is available from an earlier survey of Rarotongan children by Faine and Hercus (1951). Their material is based on a sample of 84 boys and girls aged six to twelve years from Arorangi village, a large settlement about 4 miles from Titikaveka. These comparisons are given in Table 11.

The Titikaveka children have a lower rate of decayed and missing teeth, and a higher rate of filled teeth, suggesting that they are receiving better dental care than the children from Arorangi. Both groups have high DMF rates, indicating that there is a high incidence of dental decay for these Polynesians. This high rate of decay exists in spite of the fact that the Rarotongan water supply contains 2.2 parts per million of fluorine.[1]

The Rarotongan water supply comes from a catch-water basin and streams in the interior. There are no wells on the island. This water is not filtered or chemically treated to remove impurities, and is circulated to the whole island by a piping system.

In the United States, areas with fluorine amounts as high as the 2.2 parts per million found in Rarotonga show low dental caries rates and high fluorosis rates. For example in Colorado Springs, Colorado, where the water supply has a natural fluorine level of 2.6 parts per million, 28.5 per cent of the children did not have caries, and 73.8 per cent had fluorosis (Arnold, 1948). A study on children from Galesburg, Illinois where the fluorine content is 1.9 parts per million, revealed that 27.8 per cent of the children were caries-free and 47.6 per cent of them had fluorosis (Dean, 1946).

On Rarotonga, where the fluorine content is high, only 2.4 per cent

[1]Based on a sample of tap water secured by the author, and analyzed by the Texas State Department of Health, Austin, Texas.

TABLE 10

DMF RATES FOR PERMANENT TEETH OF ARORANGI AND TITIKAVEKA CHILDREN

Age	Raro-tonga	Hager-stown	RATE							
			Decayed		Filled		Missing		DMF	
			Raro-tonga	Hager-stown	Raro-tonga	Hager-stown	Raro-tonga	Hager-stown	Raro-tonga	Hager-stown
6	7	327	0	.2	0	.04	0	.003	0	.3
7	12	403	0	.6	0.8	.1	0	.03	.8	.7
8	6	487	0	.9	0.8	.2	0	.05	2.7	1.2
9	8	493	.1	1.4	3.5	.4	0	.2	3.6	2.0
10	8	529	0	1.6	3.5	.6	.4	.3	3.9	2.0
11	5	531	0	1.7	4.2	.8	0	.3	4.2	2.9
12	6	596	0	2.1	5.8	1.1	0	.5	5.8	3.7
13	10	565	0	2.5	6.2	1.5	.3	.7	6.5	4.6
14	11	695	0	3.1	5.0	1.8	.1	.8	5.1	5.7
15	7	651	0	3.1	5.7	2.6	.1	1.1	5.8	6.8
16	5	445	.2	2.9	9.2	3.3	.4	1.2	9.8	7.4
Total	85	5722								

TABLE 11

DMF RATES FOR PERMANENT TEETH OF ARORANGI AND
TITIKAVEKA CHILDREN

Group	Ages	N	Decayed	Missing	Filled	DMF
Titikaveka	6-12	52	0.01	0.06	2.9	3.0
Arorangi	6-12	84	4.3	0.2	1.4	5.9

of the children are caries-free, and there are no cases of dental fluorosis. These Rarotongan data represent a contradiction to all known investigations.

Since only one sample of Rarotongan water was tested, it is possible that the fluorine content of the Rarotongan water supply is not as high as reported. Nevertheless, large quantities of fluorine are ingested in the Rarotongan dietaries. All foods contain small amounts of fluorine, and tea which contains from 75-100 parts per million of fluorine, and sea foods, which contain from 5-15 parts per million of fluorine (Shaw, 1960) are foods which are taken in large quantities by Rarotongans of all ages (Fry, 1957). The Rarotongans, then, appear to have an adequate supply of fluorine from their drinking water and from their diets.

There are two conclusions which may be reached from these data: 1.) the Rarotongan caries rate would be higher if they did not have adequate amounts of fluorine. 2.) there are factors which act to diminish the caries-retarding effect of fluorine.

A genetic factor may be involved. Hodge and Sognnaes (1946) have suggested that susceptibility to tooth mottling may be a familial trait. It is possible, however, that neither fluorosis nor a reduction of caries occurs because of a genetically controlled biochemical reaction. This genetic factor may be a trait of this population. This hypothesis would then explain the high incidence of caries and nonexistence of fluorosis for the Rarotongan children, although ample fluorine is available to them. Dean (1946) has shown that mottled enamel is not a necessary consequence of a high fluorine intake. From the foregoing discussion, it seems possible that a low caries rate is not a necessary consequence of a high fluorine intake.

Conclusions

Tooth eruption in Rarotongans is early by White standards, particularly for the maxillary canines and pre-molars. The incidence of malocclusions is lower in Rarotongans than in Polynesians from Pukapuka, Negroes from Philadelphia, or Whites from Chicago and Philadelphia. A high percentage of gingival disease, but no calculus formation was seen. A fair to poor prognosis was indicated for most of these children.

The DMF rates of the Rarotongan children are not significantly higher than those of American White children. The Rarotongans receive large amounts of fluorine in their diets and water supply, yet exhibit neither dental fluorosis nor low caries rates.

References

Angle, E. H.
    1899   Classification of malocclusion. Dental Cosmos, *41:* 248-350.
Arnold, F. A.
    1948   Fluorine in drinking water: its effect on dental caries. Journal of the American Dental Association, *36:* 28-36.
Davies, G. H.
    no date   Dental Disease Among the Polynesians of Pukapuka or Danger Island. Thesis for D. D. S. degree, Otago College, New Zealand.

    1956a   Dental conditions among the Polynesians of Pukapuka (Danger Island). I. General background and the prevalence of malocclusion. Journal of Dental Research, *35:* 115-131.

    1956b   Dental conditions among the Polynesians of Pukapuka (Danger Island). II. The prevalence of periodontal disease. Journal of Dental Research, *35:* 734-741.
Dean, H. T.
    1946   Epidemiological studies in the United States. Dental Caries and Fluorine, pp. 5-31, American Association for the Advancement of Science, Washington.
Edwards, A. L.
    1946   Statistical Analysis. Rinehart and Co., Inc., New York.
Faine, S., and C. E. Hercus
    1951   The nutritional status of Cook Islanders. British Journal of Nutrition, *5:* 327-343.

Foster, L. W.
    1942   Dental conditions in white and Indian children in Northern Wisconsin. Journal of the American Dental Association, *29:* 2251-2255.
Fry, P. C.
    1957   Dietary survey on Rarotonga, Cook Islands. II. Food consumption in two villages. American Journal of Clinical Nutrition, *5:* 260-273.
Garn, S. M., and C. F. A. Moorrees
    1951   Stature, body-build and tooth emergence in Aleutian children. Child Development, *22:* 261-270.
Glickman, I.
    1953   Clinical Periodontology. W. B. Saunders Co., Philadelphia.
Hewat, R. E. T., D. F. Eastcott, and J. B. Bibby
    1952   The prevalence of dental caries in deciduous teeth of New Zealand children. New Zealand Dental Journal, *49:* 19-24.
Hodge, H. C., and R. F. Sognnaes
    1946   Experimental caries and a discussion of the mechanism of caries inhibition by Fluorine. Dental Caries and Fluorine, pp. 53-73, American Association for the Advancement of Science, Washington, D. C.
Hurme, V. O.
    1946   Decay of the deciduous teeth of Formosa Chinese. An analytical summary and interpretation of certain statistics published by Maruyama. Journal of Dental Research, *25:* 127-136.

    1949   Ranges of normalcy in the eruption of permanent teeth. Journal of Child Dentition, *16:* 11-15.
Hurtate, E. A., and N. S. Scrimshaw
    1955   Dental findings in a nutritional study of school children in five Guatemalan highland villages. Journal of Dental Research, *34:* 390-396.
Klein, H., C. E. Palmer, and J. W. Knutson
    1938   Studies on dental caries. I. Dental status and dental needs of elementary school children. Public Health Report, *53:* 751-765.
Knutson, J. W.
    1955   Surveys and the evaluation of dental programs. Dentistry in Public Health, 2nd ed., pp. 11-45, W. B. Saunders Co., Philadelphia.
Massler, M., A. Cohen, and I. Schour
    1952   Epidemiology of Gingivitis in children. Journal of American Dental Association, *45:* 319-324.
McDowell, B. H.
    1953   A Survey of dental conditions among the Cook Island natives. New Zealand Dental Journal, *49:* 19-24.
Moorrees, C. F. A.
    1957   The Aleut dentition. Harvard University Press, Cambridge.

Riesenfeld, A.
    1957   Shovel-shaped incisors and a few other dental features among
    native peoples of the Pacific. American Journal of Physical Anthro-
    pology, *14:* 505-521.
Shaw, J. H.
    1960   Nutrition in relation to dental medicine. Modern Nutrition in
    Health and Disease, 2nd edition, pp. 558-601, Lea and Febiger, Phila-
    delphia.
Simmons, R. T., J. J. Graydon, F. N. Semple, and E. I. Fry
    1955   A blood group genetical survey in Cook Islanders, Polynesia,
    and comparisons with American Indians. American Journal of Physical
    Anthropology, *13:* 667-690.
Spier, L.
    1919   The growth of Puerto Rican Boys with special reference to the
    relation between their stature and dentition. Journal of Dental Re-
    search, *1:* 145-157.
Steggerda, M., and T. J. Hill
    1942   Eruption time of teeth among whites, Negroes, and Indians.
    American Journal of Orthodonty, *28:* 361-370.

7. The Channel and the Grid: the Canalisation of Growth

Mary Anne Whelan

In 1966, Howells called attention to a neglected aspect of the problem of assessing intra-familial correlations. He pointed out that there are two sources of variance to be considered: the general population variance, and intra-familial variance proper. Howells always speaks best for himself:

> Our estimates of population variance in measured traits in man have always been very crude. There may be found, in the literature, standard deviations of frequently taken measurements, such as stature or head length, for a great many populations, often represented by large samples. It is difficult to see in such figures much of a tendency to converge on something like a typical degree of variation for that trait. One would expect a reduction in the fluctuation of variances as sample size rises, followed by an increase in the value of the variance or standard deviation, as samples become very large and represent something like "U. S. Army" or "English males," i.e. not an actual population but a conglomerate of populations, with disparate gene pools and affected by differing cultural and environmental factors. Such effects do seem to occur in the figures available, but I know of no study in recent years exploring the matter systematically. Yet it seems to me that data bearing on it are necessary to the advancement of quantitative genetics in man.

NOTE: Supported in part through Project 928, Maternal and Child Health Service, Department of Health, Education and Welfare, and by National Institute of Dental Research Grant # 5-PO1-DE-02873-05.

> Similarly, we have all too little information on relative intrafamily variation . . .
> Sibling correlation is theoretically .50, for a continuous variable under au-
> tosomal polygenic control, without dominance and without assortative mating
> . . . This value, .50, should not be substantially exceeded, but in fact considerably
> higher correlations for brothers have been reported . . . Unless assortative mat-
> ing by itself is very effective, this excess can only be due to a lack of homogeneity
> in the 'population' from which the sample is drawn, with respect to ethnic
> origins, diet, etc. (which of course involves assortative mating as well). This is
> doubtless usually overlooked in the case of the very populations (i.e. western)
> in which family studies are normally carried out. (Howells, 1966).

This paper is concerned with the extension of Howells' ideas on variability to the problems of defining and quantifying the "canalisa-tion" of growth in children, and in distinguishing this process from what is called "catch-up" growth. Although the difficulty which Howells identified in assessing sibling correlations has not been satis-factorily resolved it may be partially circumvented, and the derivation of sibling correlations remains uniquely useful for some purposes. It is suggested that the definition of canalisation which is offered may be usefully generalized to the study of a spectrum of developmental processes.

Waddington (1957) credits Galton with the origin of the concept of canalisation, presented in *Natural Inheritance* (1899) as the idea of "Organic Stability." Central to this idea is the assumption of limited variability. As Howells identifies two sources of variability in human metrical traits, so we may infer two sources of restriction of the limits of variability. One source of limitation is indigenous to the population or, more broadly, to the genetic construction of the species in its universally shared aspects. Such genetic bases may indeed go beyond the species level in proportion as they represent fundamental processes; for example, of cell growth. This notion is close to what Galton meant by Organic Stability, which he felt resulted in "the existence of a limited number of frequently recurring forms" (Galton, 1899). Although Galton's concept is excessively Platonic for the tastes of most contemporary biologists, we may say that there is, for all practical purposes, a finite limit to the amount of variability a species may exhibit in certain traits. For height in man, the range of variation of normal persons is roughly 150 cm. from Pygmy to Nilote. The observation that upward secular trend in height has come to an end in consistently well-nourished and healthy populations (Bakwin and McLaughlin, 1964; Damon, 1968) suggests that under reasonably constant selection pressures and environmental circumstances an upper bound may be reached.

In 1942 Waddington extended Galton's concept of Organic Stability to include specific embryological processes. At a later date he wrote: " . . . The whole course of development from the initial stage in the egg up to the final adult condition is a 'most favored path'; that is to say if a mass of material is developing along one such path and is at some time during the course of development forced out of it by some experimental means, it will exhibit 'regulative behavior' and tend to return to the normal path. To express this character I have spoken of such paths as being 'canalised' or 'buffered' (Waddington 1941, 1942)" (Waddington, 1957). It is the concept of the path which is critical to the idea of canalisation, and this path may be identified with a second source of the restriction of variability.

The second source of restriction of the range of variation is one which proceeds from a more intimate level of genetic determination, and which is specific to the individual through his family context. The restrictions on intra-familial variation, relative to the variability of a given population of reference, are indicated by whatever values are obtained as coefficients of correlation between family members. Since such correlations are known to exist for a number of metrical traits, we may say that the intra-familial variation is a subset of the population or species variation and that as such it too will have a practicably identifiable upper limit. It is this level of genetic determination which we may identify as the channel through which population members reach what Waddington (1942) referred to as the "standard end-product"; with regard to height, a person somewhere within the expected range of the family and of the population to which he belongs. The expected values and limits of variability which familial correlations may be used to predict for an individual provide a means of defining the channel through which we expect the developing organism to proceed. This, in turn, gives a prospective advantage to the concept of canalisation: by use of it, we may test hypotheses concerning developmental homeostasis in populations or in individuals. The problems of assessing growth in children make an illustrative case.

Although the term "catch-up growth," referring to increased velocity and greater than expected increments in size for a given period of time, is loosely interchanged with the phrase "canalisation of growth," it is advantageous to distinguish the two. The tendency for children to grow at an increased rate after release from a variety of growth-retarding circumstances has been well documented and Tanner, in particular, has concerned himself with models of control systems which might account for a return to a predetermined pattern of growth (Tanner, 1963a, 1963b). A major difficulty, however, lies in finding a defensible *a priori* definition of the proper channel for a particular child. Although Tanner reports an excellent fit for 3 to 9 year old children to a height curve of $h = a + bt + c \log t$, where $t =$ time, the constants in the equation are empirically derived from the child's own measurements. For children who have not been measured regularly and over a substantial period of time while in good health, the prediction of the normal pathway will be compromised. For children whose growth is already deviant at birth (a not infrequent concommitant of a variety of pediatric problems), no normative channel specific to the child can be predicted by empirical curve-fitting. If such a child enters a period of increased velocity of growth compared to others of his age and sex, we may certainly say that he is showing "catch-up" growth. There is, however, no way to be sure from this observation alone that his growth is "canalised" in the sense that it has returned to the particular pathway set for him by his familial genetic context. A similar problem arises in the use of the Wetzel grid (Wetzel, 1943) or any conventional set of growth standards for the purpose of determining a track appropriate to a given child. Moreover, the limits of the expected variation about the track are not defined with the finesse we might wish. Reference to growth charts derived from studies of various populations may be deceptive, since it may be "normal" for a member of a particular family to be above the 97th or below the third percentile. Inclusion within these limits cannot be assumed to represent canalisation of growth, and exceeding these limits need not rule it out. Here we may take advantage of obtained familial correlations to solve the problems of defining a familial pathway and of determining its boundaries.

Although empirically obtained parent-child correlations have found some application as predictors of size at maturity and at a given age (Galton, 1899; Garn and Rohmann, 1967), predictions based upon sibling correlations have not been offered to date. When predictions are based upon sibling correlations, several advantages accrue. First, siblings represent in themselves a test of the mid-parent hypothesis: they compensate, in their own beings, for the hazards to the expression of the genetic potential for growth that may have befallen a parent and which might obscure the potential genetic contribution. If the sib himself has been prey to such a phenomenon, this will usually be known; in any event, such information will, on the whole, be more readily available for siblings than for parents. Second, siblings typically share closely similar nutritional and other environmental circumstances, and these similarities will contribute to increased familial non-genetic correlations. Third, the effect of assortative mating will be represented in a sibling (the results of assortative mating under various genetic arrangements have been reviewed by Tanner in Sorsby, 1953). Finally, in the case where we may wish to evaluate a group of children with regard to canalisation of their growth processes, the problems of assessing the source of restrictions on variability that are indicated by familial correlation coefficients may be somewhat ameliorated by the use of their own sibling correlations. In order to obtain normal values for fraternal correlations, the raw scores of the siblings of the children whose growth we wish to analyze may be converted into scores standardized for age and sex over some population of reference, and the results entered as pairs in a product-moment correlation. Thus each family will have had some share in contributing to the variance of the population as a whole, and is by definition represented in that population. The possibility of entering multiple sibling pairs from the same families may serve to increase sample size without introducing extra-familial new sources of variability.

This method of analysis was applied to a population of 42 children known to be at risk for growth failure secondary to congenital rubella (Lundstrom, 1962; Naeye and Blanc, 1965; Michaels and Kenny, 1969). An attempt to study the canalisation of their growth processes was made in the following manner.

The scores for height of 63 pairs of siblings of the rubella children were entered into a Pearson product-moment correlation, together with the scores of an additional 57 pairs of siblings whose data was kindly furnished by Dr. Coenraad Moorrees of the Forsyth Dental Infirmary. The age range of the sibling pairs was restricted to 24-119 months, in an effort to avoid the irregularities in growth pattern that might be introduced by prematurity or insufficient intra-uterine nutrition, at the one end, and the vagaries introduced by the onset of

186   *The Measures of Man*

the adolescent growth spurt, at the other. The raw scores for each child had been converted to standard scores for age and sex: the standards for the reference population on which the converted scores were based, were furnished by Dr. Robert Reed and Dr. Isabelle Valadian of the Harvard School of Public Health. The results are presented in Table I.

TABLE 1

CORRELATIONS OF THE STANDARD SCORES IN HEIGHT OF
IMMATURE SIBS AGED 24-119 MONTHS

n pairs	120
r^2	0.19
r	0.44
error	0.81
value of t	5.13

The value of r is significant (p $=<.01$) when tested by the statistic

$t = \dfrac{Z}{\sqrt{1/n-3}}$ where Z refers to Fisher's statistic for testing the hypothesis

pothesis r=any value, here 0.

On the assumption of normal distribution, the relationship between standard deviation and percentile on the growth curve generated by the reference population is a straight-forward one. Two standard deviations in either direction from the mean represent the 2.5th and 97.5th percentiles, depending on their location with regard to the mean (or 50th percentile). If no correlation existed between sib pairs, the best guess about the location and permissible range for a child would be the 50th percentile (point location) and between the 2.5th and 97.5th percentiles (range). In making use of the information derived from sibling correlations, however, it is possible to narrow this range, and also to derive a more exact prediction for his point location. We may predict both a location on the curve and a permitted range for sib B from the score of his sibling, A, in the following manner. Given that sib A has a standard score of +1.0 in height, he is one standard deviation above the mean of the reference population. We would predict sib B to be at (.44) x (1) above the population mean in terms of standard deviations, with a range around this prediction of twice the standard error (.81) on either side of the point prediction (see Table I). A standard score of -1.5 for sib B, while within normal limits of the population as a whole, would not be expected in his family context. A shift in growth pattern which placed the child within the limits predicted by his family context would properly be termed an effect of canalisation. Thus we have a way of predicting both a point of value for a child at any given age, and also a way of predicting the limits of expected (in contrast to abnormal) deviation from the point prediction, in a manner which takes into account the familial context of the child and hence the most probable channel for his growth as determined by that context.

When initially studied the ages of the rubella children ranged from 3 to 4½ years. Thirty-five percent of these children had growth failure, as defined by standard scores more than two s.d. below the mean height of the population of reference, while this was true of only 6 percent of their randomly selected normal siblings. However, the patients showed a definite and positive trend in the direction of change of their standard scores with time: this was not true of their siblings, who showed no trend in either direction. Table 2 presents the experience of the rubella cohort in this respect over the period 1968-1970, with measurements made at yearly intervals. The increasing standard deviations of the males are of some interest, and reflect pleuralistic behavior of these children with respect to their growth patterns.

It is possible, however, to distinguish between the apparent catch-up growth and the phenomenon of increasingly canalised growth. At the time of the initial visit, the correlation (r) in height between rubella child and normal sibling was found to be .37. Two years later, despite clear evidence of catch-up growth, this correlation was .34. Although it is not possible to test the difference between the correlations of $r = .37$ (patient-sib) and $r = .44$ (normal siblings) because of the overlapping membership of the groups, the numbers suggest that patients are less closely correlated with their siblings than is usual and that canalisation processes have been disturbed. Canalisation of growth processes would be expected to be manifested as an increasing coefficient of correlation between patient and sibling, up to the limit of that normally obtained, even in the presence of continued growth failure. No such trend is apparent, and by our definition of canalisation we are not entitled to say that such a process has been responsible

TABLE 2

CHANGES IN STANDARD SCORES OF RUBELLA CHILDREN
OVER TIME

Visit 1: 1968
  males
  n   18
  X   −1.88
  S.D.   1.07

  females
  n   24
  X   −1.69
  S.D.   1.27

Visit 2: 1969
  males
  n   17
  X   −1.55
  S.D.   1.20

  females
  n   24
  X   −1.60
  S.D.   1.29

Visit 3: 1970
  males
  n   11
  X   −1.44
  S.D.   1.28

  females
  n   21
  X   −1.46
  S.D   1.17

for the catch-up growth observed: the patients grow increasingly, but they do not grow increasingly like their siblings. The fact that catch-up growth nonetheless occurs implies the presence of regulatory mechanisms which are independent of familial factors: this effect we may call "buffering" of the genotype at a population or species level.

A second application of this definition of the canalisation of growth may be as follows. We may suppose that growth processes are normally canalised, not only in terms of the "standard end product" observed at maturity, but also in terms of the status of an organism at any given moment. This assumption is supported by documentation of familial correlations in rate of maturation as well as of size at maturity (Reynolds, 1943; Hewitt, 1957; Garn *et al.*, 1960; Tanner, 1962; Garn and Rohman, 1966) and of course by the correlations of standard scores of immature siblings measured at different ages (Hewitt, 1957); Whelan, 1972), or the raw scores of immature siblings measured at the same age (Garn, 1966). At any point, then, we may use the concept of canalisation to narrow the permissible range for the status of an individual, provided we know (or can reasonably extrapolate) the size of his siblings at that age and the expected correlations between them. The problem of age differences at the time of measurement may be solved by conversion of raw to standardized scores, as before. However, in the case in which a pediatrician is concerned about the growth of a particular child under his care, whatever advantage (probably very small) may be gained by having the siblings of the patient entered into the determination of the normative coefficients of correlation will be lost: some "typical" value of correlation will have to be accepted, and the difficulties emphasized by Howells cannot be avoided. Table 3 presents values of fraternal correlations in height which have been obtained to date.

Despite this increased liability which, like Baudelaire's coat, is probably more ideal than real, the method has a useful application in determining whether or not a given child is within a channel appropriate to his family context. When applied to the rubella population (whose siblings were, however, entered into the determination of normal r and the permissible variation for family members), 20 percent of the patient population were found to be either within normal limits but outside the expected family range, or outside "usual" limits (below the third percentile of the reference population) but within the family range. This represents a substantial gain in information concerning the growth status of the child involved, and revealed a significant percentage (18) with a derangement of growth which would be missed by the more conventional analysis of simply plotting the child on a standard growth chart. Reasonable values of *r* for working pediatricians to adopt might be .50 for the same-sexed sibs and

TABLE 3

SUMMARY OF SIBLING CORRELATIONS IN HEIGHT

Author	*n pairs*		*r*
Pearson and			
Lee (1903)			
brother-brother:			.51
sister-sister:			.54
brother-sister:			.53
Bowles (1932)			
brother-brother:	79		.57
Howells (1949)			
brother-brother:	96		.47
Howells (1953)			
brother-brother:	76		.57
Hewitt (1957):			.63
Schreider (1961)			
brother-brother:	32		.35
Garn (1966)			
brother-brother:	67	at	.51
sister-sister:	52	age	.70
brother-sister:	114	7	.46
Garn (1966)			
brother-brother:	31	at	.10
sister-sister:	25	age	.58
brother-sister:	48	17	.40
Howells (1966)			
siblings of			
both sexes:			.47
Whelan (1972)			
siblings of			
both sexes:	120		.44

.40 for opposite-sexed sibs, with a range in standard score units of 1.5 on either side of the point prediction derived from using the suggested values.

Given definition based upon the major source of the restriction of variability, then, the concepts of canalisation and catch-up growth may be usefully distinguished. We may choose to apply the term "buffering" to either process — no real advantage is apparent in restricting it to one phenomenon or the other — but we should be aware that the buffering of the genotype at a population level may not be synonymous with the familial canalisation of growth. In the data presented on the height gains of children with congenital rubella they would appear to be noncongruent. It may be argued from these data that familial pathways are more easily displaced, and population pathways somehow more indurated in the genetic make-up of an immature organism. Because the discrepancy between patient-sib and normal sibling correlations is slight and the values from these data refractory to analysis, further study would be required to settle this point.

The definition of canalisation as a shift towards an ontogenetic pathway determined by the immediate familial genetic context of the developing organisms distinguishes this process from other regulatory mechanisms. This concept may also provide an *a priori* definition of normative metrical gains for a variety of traits where sibling correlations are known and where siblings are available for measurement. Although difficulties are introduced by the non-linearity of gains for certain traits or at certain ages, as well as by the interplay of familial vs. population factors, such a method should find both clinical and heuristic application.

Bibliography

Bakwin, H. and McLaughlin, S. M.
    1964   Secular increase in height. Is the end in sight? Lancet, *ii:* 1195-1196.
Bowles, G. T.
    1932   New Types of Old Americans at Harvard and at Eastern Women's Colleges. Cambridge, Mass.
Damon, Albert
    1968   Secular trend in height and weight within Old American families

at Harvard, 1870-1965. I. Within twelve four-generation families. American Journal of Physical Anthropology, *29:* 45-50.

Galton, F.
1899   Natural Inheritance. London.

Garn, S. M.
1966   Malnutrition and skeletal development in the pre-school child. Pre-School Child Malnutrition. National Academy of Sciences National Research Council, Washington, D.C.

Garn, S. M., Lewis, A. B., and Polacheck, D. L.
1960   Sibling similarities in dental development. Journal of Dental Research, *39:* 170-175.

Garn, S. M. and Rohmann, B. A.
1966   Interaction of nutrition and genetics in the timing of growth and development. Pediatric Clinics of North America, *13:* 353-379.

————————
1967   Midparent' values for use with parent-specific, age-size tables when paternal height is estimated or unknown. Pediatric Clinics of North America, *14:* 283-284.

Hewitt, D.
1957   Some familial correlations in height, weight and skeletal maturity. Annals of Human Genetics, *22:* 213-221.

Howells, W. W.
1949   Body measurements in the light of familial influences. American Journal of Physical Anthropology, *7:* 101-108.

————————
1953   Correlations of brothers in factor scores. American Journal of Physical Anthropology, *11:* 121-140.

————————
1966   Variability in family lines vs. population variability. Annals of the New York Academy of Science, *134:* 624-631.

————————
1962   Rubella during pregnancy. A follow-up study of children born after an epidemic of rubella in Sweden, 1951. Acta Paediatrica, *51:* Supplement 133.

Michaels, R. H. and Kenny, F. M.
1969   Postnatal growth in congenital rubella. Pediatrics, *43:* 251-259.

Naeye, R. L. and Blanc, W.
1965   Pathogenesis of congenital rubella. Journal of the American Medical Association, *194:* 1277-1283.

Pearson, K. and Lee, A.
1903   On the laws of inheritance in man. I. Inheritance of physical characters. Biometrika, *2:* 357-462.

Reynolds, E. L.
    1943   Degree of kinship and pattern of ossification. American Journal of Physical Anthropology n.s., *1:* 405-416.
Schreider, E.
    1961   Anthropometric correlations between adult brothers. Nature, *192:* 1311.
Sorsby, A. (ed.)
    1953   Clinical Genetics. London.
Tanner, J. M.
    1962   Growth at Adolescence, London.

    1963a   The regulation of human growth. Child Development, *34:* 817-847.

    1963b   Regulation of growth size in mammals. Nature *99:* 845-850.
Waddington, C. H.
    1942   The canalisation of development and the inheritance of acquired characters. Nature, *150:* 563.

    1957   The Strategy of the Genes. London.
Wetzel, N. C.
    1943   Assessing the physical condition of children. Journal of Pediatrics, *22:* 82-110.
Whelan, M. A.
    1972   The bulk of the measured: sibling correlations in selected measurements of growth and their application to the problem of relative growth failure. Unpublished doctoral dissertation. Harvard University, Cambridge.

8. Sexual Dimorphism in Children: a Multivariate Study

Hermann K. Bleibtreu and David K. Taylor

Introduction

In the study of multivariate relationships, many of the multiple and partial correlation and regression techniques have been used. These are really multivariable rather than multivariate (Kendall, 1957). We concentrate on the use of canonical variate-canonical correlation techniques for such studies as described by Hotelling (1936), Bartlett (1947) and Rao (1952).

Additionally, these canonical techniques are valuable aids in the area of multivariate classification problems. Our interest in this area is not that of classifying males and females or Anglos and Indians on the basis of biometrical variables. Such classification is better done by other means. Rather, we use canonical techniques and discriminant function analysis: 1) to find what variables, in what relationships, weighted in what ways distinguish the groups in our analyses; 2) to discover how various combinations of variables are abstracted into a few latent axes of biologically meaningful interpretation which "explain" the variation within and among groups described by the original variables; and 3) to develop "distance" measures such as Mahalanobis D^2 to describe the relationships of groups within each period of measurement and throughout the growth period.

McKeon (1966) and others have noted that canonical methods have several desirable properties:

1)   Results of canonical analysis are invariant with respect to the unit of measurement (i.e., one variable may be a volume, one a length, or one may be a score). Canonical analysis has even been successful using presence-absence data (Maxwell, 1961, and Claringbould, 1958).

2)   Canonical variate analysis may be viewed as a generalization of principal components analysis and multiple groups discriminant analysis in that any number of groups may be compared simultaneously as opposed to taking them pairwise.

3)   Experience with these techniques suggests that the number of relevant dimensions required for comparison of (n) groups of (p) variate observations will be less than the number required for summarizing any one such group by principal component analysis.

4)   These methods not only assist in the reduction of dimensionality, elucidation of multivariate relationships, and discrimination among groups, but also they are easily interpretable as multivariate analysis of variance, one-way classification (MANOVA) through the natural breakdown of variability into "among" and "within" components.

Our use of canonical variate methods will usually be preceded by a stepwise discriminant analysis so as to select the most diagnostic variables of groups differences for use in canonical analysis. For this purpose, we have used certain of the approaches outlined by Rao (1952), Anderson (1958), Majumdar and Rao (1960), Seal (1964), McKeon (1966), Morrison and Art (1967), and Blackith and Reyment (1971); and our slightly altered versions of such familiar computer programs as BMD07M ("Stepwise Discriminant Analysis," Dixon, 1970), ORNTDIST (Discriminant function analysis, Reyment et al., 1969), CANVR2 (Canonical variate analysis, Reyment and Ramden, 1970), and EIDISC ("Stepwise Multiple Discriminant Analysis," Morrison and Art, 1967).

Discriminant-Canonical Analysis of Sexual Dimorphism

Studies of sexual dimorphism are quite common in biology and anthropology. In humans, such studies have been directed towards the study of adult differences, especially among skeletal populations. One development of this study has been the use of the linear discriminant function techniques developed by Fisher (1936) in the construction of statistical methods of "sexing" skeletal specimens of unknown sex (e.g., Martin, 1936; Pons, 1955; Giles and Elliot, 1963; Howells, 1966, 1969). The use of discriminant functions has also been applied in the study of sexual dimorphism among the living (Tanner, 1951), but it has not been applied repeatedly to a cohort of growing children.

We use these traditional discriminant methods with the canonical techniques described above so as to elicit the best combination of measurements that distinguishes boys from girls and to construct from these variables via canonical analysis the latent axis of variation between male and female children. As our longitudinal cohort ages, it is interesting to see which anthropometric measurements are the best discriminators in each measurement period and to note how the discriminatory power of such variables changes from one period to another. Moreover, it should be possible to determine the nature of ethnic group differences in the discriminatory power of growth variables to distinguish sexes. Our results to date suggest that at the same chronological age, the "best" metric predictors of sex will differ among ethnic groups. We are currently investigating whether these differences are due to inequalities in growth rates of our samples or to some innate differences which may prove to be independent of growth rate.

Boys and girls of four ethnic groups (N = 637) and three age cohorts have been analyzed for those variables which made the best discrimination between sexes using an altered version of BMD07M (Dixon, 1970:214 and Afifi and Azen, 1972:252-259). Biometric variables are placed in discriminant functions of sex by a stepwise selection procedure based on F ratio tests (maximum variance between sexes, minimum variance within sex). In successive steps, consideration is given to the conditional distribution of each variable not entered given those in the function. Through the use of one-way analysis of variance F tests, selection of the next variable to enter is made for that variable whose mean value in the conditional distributions of the two sexes is "most different." The stepwise procedure ceases when no additional variables contribute significantly to discrimination among the populations. Up to this step, the included variables' power to discriminate boys from girls will change with each stepwise entry to the function towards better discrimination, but due to correlation, any one variable's discriminatory power may change drastically depending upon which variables are in the function. A variable may, in the first several steps, be a good discriminator and then, when more variables are added to the function, it may become very poor in its discriminatory power. When this occurs, the variable is deleted (*) from the function (Tables 1-4). Similarly, should further variables be added, it may occur that a previously deleted variable will be reintroduced into the function because its power to separate the sexes has again risen to significant levels. Such reintroduced variables are designated with a plus sign (+). The efficiency of the discriminant function in distinguishing boys and girls based upon biometrical variables may be judged from the number of misclassified individuals. While the variables included in the function are taken in order by univariate F tests, once all such variables have been entered into the function, their relative importance can be quite different. Such "relative importance" may be judged from 1) construction of scaled vectors corresponding to the canonical coefficients associated with each included variable, and 2) comparison of the absolute value of these scalar elements. These scalars are produced by multiplying each canonical coefficient by the pooled within-group standard deviation associated with its corresponding variable. These scalars of "relative importance" are shown in the body of Tables 1-4 next to their corresponding variables.

Next in Tables 1-4, the results of a multivariate analysis of variance (MANOVA) are presented. The null hypothesis (H_o) that the mean vectors of the two sexes are equal (i.e., that the population Mahalanobis distance, $\Delta^2 = 0$) is tested against the alternate hypothesis (H_1) that the mean vectors are unequal ($\Delta^2 \neq 0$) by F ratio approximations to the U-statistic developed for such tests by Anderson (1958) and Rao (1952). The sample Mahalanobis distances, D^2, between the sexes for three periods of measurement are included. If

TABLE 1

DISCRIMINATORY-CANONICAL ANALYSIS OF SEXUAL DIMORPHISM

Anglo Children. 70 Males, 76 Females

	Cohort I (6-7 yrs.)		Cohort II (7-8 yrs.)		Cohort III (8-9 yrs.)	
	Stepwise Order of Variable Inclusion-Deletion	Relative Importance to Discrimination	Stepwise Order of Variable Inclusion-Deletion	Relative Importance to Discrimination	Stepwise Order of Variable Inclusion-Deletion	Relative Importance to Discrimination
	Bicondylar Femur	5.455	Bimalleolar	–	Bimalleolar	–3.403
	Wrist Breadth	–8.319	Triceps Skinfold	– .047	Cristal Height	–
	Head Length	1.522	Waist Circumf.	.668	Chest Depth	– .707
	Nose Breadth	3.765	Bicristal	–	Weight	.023
	Head Circumf.	– .285	Head Length	2.727	Cristal Height (*)	–
	Hand Length	.827	Bicondylar Femur	4.436	Waist Circumf.	– .044
	Bicristal	– .268	Bimalleolar (*)	–	Head Length	–1.073
	Waist Circumf.	.044	Weight	– .020	Bigonial	–2.399
	Calf Circumf.	– .208	Bicristal (*)	–	Bicondylar Femur	–2.512
	Bicondylar Humerus	1.904	Bicondylar Humerus	5.706	Nose Length	2.581
			Head Breadth	2.800	Bicondylar Humerus	–3.641
			Head Circumf.	– .384		

$H_0: \mu$ males $= \mu$ females

$H_1: \mu$ males $\neq \mu$ females

	$F_{[10,135]} = 39.297$		$F_{[8,137]} = 38.375$	$F_{[9,136]} = 48.983$	
Decision	Reject Null at 5%		Reject Null at 5%	Reject Null at 5%	
Mahalanobis D^2 between sexes:	11.506		8.856	12.810	

Misclassifications:

Males:	3/70 (4.3%)	1/70 (1.4%)	2/70 (2.9%)
Females:	4/76 (5.3%)	6/76 (7.9%)	4/76 (5.3%)

TABLE 2

DISCRIMINATORY-CANONICAL ANALYSIS OF SEXUAL DIMORPHISM

Mexican-American Children. 179 Males, 186 Females

	Cohort I (6-7 yrs.)		Cohort II (7-8 yrs.)		Cohort III (8-9 yrs.)	
	Stepwise Order of Variable Inclusion-Deletion	Relative Importance to Discrimination	Stepwise Order of Variable Inclusion-Deletion	Relative Importance to Discrimination	Stepwise Order of Variable Inclusion-Deletion	Relative Importance to Discrimination
	Head Length	2.261	Bimalleolar	3.518	Bimalleolar	-2.240
	Head Breadth	2.046	Triceps Skinfold	-.035	Triceps Skinfold	.045
	Head Circumf.	-.428	Bicondylar Femur	3.452	Bicondylar Femur	-4.659
	Bicondyla- Femur	4.603	Bimalleolar (*)	—	Bimalleolar (*)	—
	Weight	-.010	Stature	-.042	Stature	.049
	Bigonial	1.018	Head Length	2.875	Chest Depth	-.171
	Calf Circumf.	-1.76	Head Breadth	2.998	Head Length	-2.750
	Bimalleolar	3.531	Head Circumf.	-.674	Head Breadth	-2.180
	Bicristal	-.258	Bimalleolar (*)	—	Head Circumf.	.572
	Waist Circumf.	.019	Bigonial	1.098	Tibial Length	-.229
	Upper Facial Ht.	2.363	Arm Length	.074	Sitting Height	-.052
	Nose Length	-1.479	Hand Length	-.727	Bicristal	.237
	Bicondylar Humerus	1.980	Foot Breadth	1.689	Bigonial	-1.004
	Biacromial	-.132	Calf Circumf.	-.087	Bimalleolar (*)	—
			Sitting Height	.047	Calf Circumf.	.090
					Waist Circumf.	-.011

Ho: μ males = μ females

H1: μ males ≠ μ females

	Cohort I	Cohort II	Cohort III
	$F_{[14,350]}$ = 42.962	$F_{[13,351]}$ = 49.475	$F_{[14,350]}$ = 57.781
Decision:	Reject Null at 5%	Reject Null at 5%	Reject Null at 5%
Mahalanobis D² between sexes:	6.839	7.292	9.198

Misclassifications:

	Cohort I	Cohort II	Cohort III
Males:	15/179 (8.4%)	13/179 (7.3%)	13/179 (7.3%)
Females:	25/186 (13.4%)	15/186 (8.1%)	16/186 (8.6%)

TABLE 3

DISCRIMINATORY-CANONICAL ANALYSIS OF SEXUAL DIMORPHISM

Black Children. 41 Males, 51 Females

	Cohort I (6-7 yrs.)		Cohort II (7-8 yrs.)		Cohort III (8-9 yrs.)	
	Stepwise Order of Variable Inclusion-Deletion	Relative Importance to Discrimination	Stepwise Order of Variable Inclusion-Deletion	Relative Importance to Discrimination	Stepwise Order of Variable Inclusion-Deletion	Relative Importance to Discrimination
	Head Length	2.620	Head Length	-3.921	Head Length	-1.426
	Head Circumf.	-.360	Cristal Ht.	.030	Triceps Skinfold	.035
	Head Breadth	2.885	Bimalleolar	–	Bicondylar Femur	-4.369
	Total Facial Ht.	2.096	Triceps Skinfold	.049	Stature	.021
	Stature	-.042	Chest Depth	.558	Chest Depth	-.579
	Bicondylar Femur	5.083	Bicondylar Humerus	–		
	Calf Circumf.	-.366	Bimalleolar (-)	–		
	Foot Breadth	1.974	Head Breadth	-5.344		
	Sitting Height	.082	Head Circumf.	.724		
			Hose Length	-3.590		
			Bizygomatic	3.223		
			Bicondylar Femur	-3.387		
			Bicondylar Humerus (*)	–		

Ho: μ males $= \mu$ females

H1: μ males $\neq \mu$ females

Decision:

Mahalanobis D^2 between sexes:

Misclassification:

	Cohort I	Cohort II	Cohort III
	$F_{[9,82]} = 29.938$	$F_{[9,82]} = 20.817$	$F_{[5,86]} = 29.803$
	Reject Null at 5%	Reject Null at 5%	Reject Null at 5%
	13.011	9.047	6.861
Males:	1/41 (2.4%)	2/41 (4.9%)	2/41 (4.9%)
Females:	2/51 (3.9%)	2/51 (3.9%)	7/51 (13.7%)

TABLE 4

DISCRIMINATORY-CANONICAL ANALYSIS OF
SEXUAL DIMORPHISM

Indian Children. 14 Males, 20 Females

	Cohort I (6-7 yrs.)		Cohort II (7-8 yrs.)		Cohort III (8-9 yrs.)	
	Stepwise Order of Variable Inclusion-Deletion	Relative Importance to Discrimination	Stepwise Order of Variable Inclusion; Deletion	Relative Importance to Discrimination	Stepwise Order of Variable Inclusion-Deletion	Relative Importance to Discrimination
	Bicondylar Femur	10.371	Foot Breadth	-9.209	Foot Breadth	-.044
			Triceps Skinfold	.186	Triceps Skinfold	4.568
			Waist Circumf.	—	Cristal Height	4.388
			Hand Length	3.323	Chest Breadth	-1.366
			Chest Breadth	-1.410		
			Waist Circumf. (*)	—		
			Wrist Breadth	-17.824		
			Nose Breadth	-15.534		

H_1: μ males = μ females

H: μ males $\neq$ μ females

	Cohort I	Cohort II	Cohort III
	$F_{[1,32]}$ = 5.478	$F_{[6,27]}$ = 16.763	$F_{[4,29]}$ = 14.087
Decision:	Reject Null at 5%	Reject Null at 5%	Reject Null at 5%
Mahalanobis D^2 between sexes:	0.665*	14.475	7.550
Misclassifications:			
Males:	4/14 (28.6%)	0/14 (0%)	2/14 (14.3%)
Females:	7/20 (3.5%)	1/20 (5.0%)	3/20 (15.0%)

*We realize that D^2 values based upon fewer variables than groups are of questionable utility.

one compares this distance with the number of misclassifications, he gains an idea of the density of the individual dispersion about the group mean vector or the discriminant-canonical axis score.

We do not include the discriminant-canonical coefficients or the equations for each group and period. As was previously mentioned, identification of sex is obviously much better accomplished by non-biometrical means. It is our task rather to elicit the relevant discriminating variables, their relationships, and the manner of their change in time within each group.

The variables used as discriminators of sex are shown in Tables 1-4 and were chosen from the following:

1.	Weight	18.	Wrist Breadth
2.	Sitting Height	19.	Hand Breadth
3.	Stature	20.	Hand Length
4.	Acromial Height	21.	Bicondylar Femur
5.	Cristal Height	22.	Bimalleolar
6.	Tibial Length	23.	Foot Breadth
7.	Arm Length	24.	Head Length
8.	Biacromial	25.	Head Breadth
9.	Bicristal	26.	Bizygomatic
10.	Chest Breadth	27.	Bigonial
11.	Chest Depth	28.	Head Circumference
12.	Foot Length	29.	Biceps Circumference
13.	Total Facial Height	30.	Chest Circumference
14.	Upper Facial Height	31.	Waist Circumference
15.	Nose Length	32.	Calf Circumference
16.	Nose Breadth	33.	Triceps Skinfold Thickness
17.	Bicondylar Humerus		

Anglos (Table 1), Mexican-Americans (Table 2), Blacks (Table 3), and American Indians (Table 4) have been analyzed for sexual dimorphism in Cohorts I, II and III. For example, in Cohort 1 (aged 6-7 years), Anglos (Table 2) were distinguished for sex by biometrics. The more important discriminators were wrist breadth followed by bicondylar femur, nose breadth and bicondylar humerus as may be seen from comparing the absolute value of the scalars labeled "Relative Importance to Discrimination." The sign associated with the scalars distinguishes variables whose mean values were larger in one sex or the other. In this case, the negative sign of the scalar associated with wrist breadth means that girls had larger diameters on the average. There is no rule as to which sex is assigned which sign. In Cohort III, girls had larger means on weight and nose length; the only variables whose scalars had positive sign. Thus, in Cohort I, Anglo boys and girls are separated by a linear "discriminating function" of 10 variables which contrasts wrist breadth, head circumference, bicristal breadth, and calf circumference against bicondylar femur, nose breadth, bicondylar humerus, head length, etc. The variables used in discriminating functions, their relationships and relative importance in other groups and cohorts may be likewise inspected (Tables 1-4).

It should be noted that the multivariate analysis of variance of sexual dimorphism demonstrates that the sexes of all four ethnic groups in all three periods had significantly different mean vectors. This may be restated by saying that the sample Mahalanobis D^2 distance between sexes was in all cases significantly different from zero. It must be noted that each of the D^2 estimates was calculated from different covariance matrices and usually on different sets of variables; they are not comparable in the strict sense.

Misclassification of children by the discriminant functions is surprisingly low for children of pre-pubescent ages. Generally, boys are more tightly clustered about their mean producing less than 10% misclassifications. Small sample sizes in American Indian children may explain some of their unique results. We find the following to be of particular interest:

1) Variables directly reflecting body size or mass are not important discriminators of sex during the ages 6-9 years for this cohort.

2) Over 69% (38/55) of the discriminating variables for all groups and cohorts are transverse diameters of the body, especially joint diameters of the limbs.

3) Except in American Indians, the only important sex discriminators are variables measuring limb joint diameters, and dimensions of the head and face. No trunk measurements, circumferences of trunk or limbs, or linear dimensions of the axial skeleton are very important. The only important linear measurements are of the cranium and face.

4) Except in American Indians, the two variables, bicondylar femur and head length, are important discriminators of sex in all groups and cohorts.

5) Anglos have three variables found as "more important discriminators" in all three periods; bicondylar femur, head length, and bicondylar humerus. Mexican-American children have five such variables; bicondylar femur, head length, bimalleolar, head breadth, and bigonial. Blacks have but two; bicondylar femur and head length. American Indians have no variables common to all three cohorts.

6) The more important discriminators of Indian boys and girls are fewer in number and of a different character than in other groups especially in Cohort III; the only instance of a trunk diameter, axial length, and skinfold thickness being important discriminators.

7) Black children through five periods of measurement appear to be decreasingly dimorphic. By Cohort III, the sexes differ in fewer variables, the distance between sexes has decreased, and the number of misclassifications has increased.

We believe that the marked changes seen in the important discriminants in Cohort III for Blacks and Indians are but the precursors of rather dramatic shifts in sexual dimorphism that may occur as girls approach puberty. We expect boys to "lag" behind, marking time as it were, in their pre-pubescent patterns relative to changes soon to be seen in girls. Only further study will show how and when these groups will change their patterns, and which variables will prove to be important discriminators of ethnic-specific sexual dimorphism in the future growth of these children.

Certain preliminary indications of changes in the patterns of sexual dimorphism among four groups of children may be seen in Figures 1 and 2. Stepwise discriminatory canonical analysis, as described previously, was applied to four ethnic groups in Cohorts I-III so as to produce three possible latent or canonical axes upon which each group's mean score is arranged. Figures 1 and 2 represent two dimensional plots of group centroids with reference to the first two

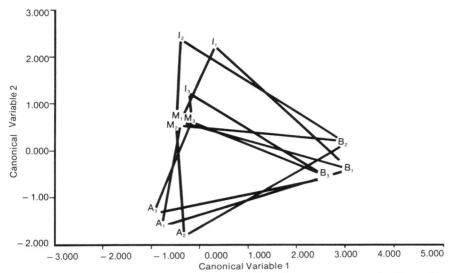

Figure 1. GROUP DISTANCES, MALES — Plot of group means on the first and second canonical variate axes in cohorts 1, 2, and 3. The square of the euclidean distance between any two means is approximately their Mahalanobis squared distance. Anglos=A. Mexican-Americans=M, Blacks=B, and American Indians=I.

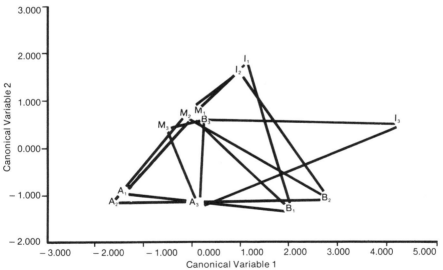

Figure 2. GROUP DISTANCES, FEMALES — Plot of group means on the first and second canonical variate axes in cohorts 1, 2, and 3. The square of the euclidean distance between any two means is approximately their Mahalanobis squared distance. Anglos=A, Mexican-American=M, Blacks=B, and American Indians=I.

205

canonical variate axes. The third possible canonical axis is significant
only in Cohort III in either sex, but even then, it "explains" only
4-8% of the total dispersion. Very little information relevant to these
groups' multivariate relationships is lost by not plotting their centroids
in three dimensional space. Thus, within any cohort or sex, the square
of the length of the line segment connecting any two groups of
centroids is approximately equal to their Mahalanobis D² distance.

Both males and females of the four ethnic groups in Cohorts I
and II are represented in two dimensions by an approximately equila-
teral triangle. Blacks, American Indians and Anglos are arranged at
the vertices with Mexican-Americans positioned about halfway
between Anglos and American Indians.

In Cohort III, males change only to the extent that Mexican-
Americans and American Indians are statistically indistinguishable.
Spacially, the American Indian males have "migrated" towards the
size and shape of Mexican-American males. Blacks, Anglos and
Mexican-Americans have remained in essentially stable positions over
a two-year period.

The longitudinal sample of females demonstrates very different
changes. In Cohorts I and II, females have the same pattern of relationships as do the males, albeit they are "closer" in a distance
sense. In Cohort III, very drastic changes are noted among females.

The relationships of Chicana and Indian females are exactly opposite that of their male peers. These females are the furthest removed groups in Cohort III, whereas the boys were indistinguishable.
Note also that Chicana females have not moved from their previous
positions, but that Indian females have "migrated" quite far. Most of
this change is attributable to vastly different scores on the first
canonical variate axis. The variables of importance in this axis include for the first time in Cohort III, those with larger environ-
mental-genetic interaction components which have not previously
been important in discrimination. Recall that Chicanas and Anglos
are increasingly sexually dimorphic whereas Indian children are not
(Tables 1, 2 and 4). Thus, if Indian girls in Cohort III are separated
from other groups by variables which measure certain aspects of
sexual maturation in females and are still very similar to Indian boys
in size and shape, then it must be that Indian girls are "delayed" in
expressing incipient "femaleness" patterns compared to other
females. Anglo, Black and Chicana girls appear to be approaching

puberty-related growth patterns faster than are Indian girls. This indication is revealed some 3½ to 4 years prior to the average age (circa 12½ years) for the onset of menarche among American females.

The changes in variables and their relationships in the important discriminators in Cohort III has shown other important group relationship changes. Black and Anglo females have nearly identical scores on the first canonical axis. Heretofore, they were maximally separated by the first axis and barely distinguishable on the second. In Cohort III, this has been reversed. Anglo females differ greatly from other groups on the second axis in Cohort III while the latter are almost indistinguishable, contrary to the patterns in Cohort I and II. The ways in which Black and Chicana females are changing appear to have become very similar in Cohort III. Anglos appear as if they are becoming more feminine at a similar rate, but in a different manner. Indian girls appear to be changing in ways more similar to Blacks and Chicanas but at a much slower rate. Perhaps more insightful relationships and dramatic differences in growth pattern differences among groups differing in sex, ethnic group, residence, and socio-economic status will be seen as these groups approach puberty.

Morphological Ranking of Maleness and Femaleness

The discriminatory-canonical analysis described previously can be used in the construction of maleness-femaleness scores for individual members of our longitudinal cohort as analyzed within ethnic groups. A similar technique has been described by Defrise-Gussenhoven (1966) who used discriminant function rankings upon osteological materials.

Each individual will be ranked within his ethnic group and measurement cohort for maleness or femaleness relative to the mean of males or females on the canonical axis of sexual dimorphism. During the course of growth, an individual's position relative to the mean for his sex may change. These "migrating" individuals are then analyzed for the important features of their shape and size which distinguishes them from individuals who migrate differently or who remain stable for sexness rating. Ethnic groups may show different patterns in the manner of timing and rate of migration and in the proportion of in-

dividuals who remain stable relative to the several possible patterns
of "migration." Moreover, in an individual, different body parts or
complexes may show different degrees of maleness and femaleness.

The stepwise discriminant-canonical variate analysis of sexual
dimorphism as described above produces a canonical axis associated,
naturally, with sexual dimorphism. If the individual members of the
groups analyzed within each cohort and the sample means of each
sex are placed on this axis, one can produce a ranking of maleness
for boys and femaleness for girls. This is accomplished by ranking
each individual's canonical variate score relative to the mean score
of his sex. This ranking may be made comparable across periods if
the canonical scores are transformed such that the two sexes' mean
scores are assigned values of −1.0 and +1.0, and the discrimination
boundary score between sexes is assigned as zero. For example, a
female at point A who had a canonical axis score of −.29

	Females			Males	
C	$\overline{X}$	A		B	$\overline{X}$
/	/	/		/	/
−1.5	−1.0	−.29	0.0	.40	+1.0

Transformed Sexual Dimorphism Canonical Axis

would be ranked relative to the mean for girls (−1.0) so as to produce
a femaleness ranking of +.29 (= −.29/−1.0). Similarly, a female C
whose score was −1.5 would be ranked as a +1.5 (= −1.5/−1.0) for
femaleness. However, a female B, whose score placed her at +.40
on the male side of the boundary between males and females, would
be misclassified as a boy due to biometrical relationships. Her ranking
for femaleness would be −.40 (= +.40/−1.0), i.e., she would be ranked
as having negative femaleness.

Anglo, Mexican-American and Black children in a longitudinal
cohort (n = 603, Indians were excluded) were so ranked from measurement of Cohorts I, II and III. Some of these children remained
stable in their sexness rankings, some oscillated about the range of
their sex's scores, and some demonstrated a consistent trend in sexness scores toward or away from the boundary line. Among the more
significant findings of the analysis are:

1) Black males of "increasing sexness ranking" trend (those becoming less like females) were heavier and taller than were those of decreasing rankings. However, Anglos and Mexican-Americans show no significant size difference between the increasing and decreasing sexness trend groups; in fact, the "decreasing" trend groups tended to be larger in size.

2) While mass-volume variables were important in distinguishing the opposite trend groups of Black males, these variables were not important discriminators of sex in Black children. Black females are larger than or as large as Black male children in all three cohorts.

3) Size differences were not found as discriminators between sexes in any group. Thus, "femaleness" or "maleness" in these ages and groups are not functions of body size; rather, the shape of the body is all important.

4) Black females show much less "migration" in sexness rankings than do other females. They appear to be more "stable" than the other groups, and the differences between their two opposite trend groups are very slight.

5) The time frame is too brief to determine whether a consistent pattern of migration will develop for groups or individuals. If such patterns emerge, their biological and/or environmental significance must be sought.

Bibliography

Afifi, A.A. and S.P. Azen
    1972   Statistical Analysis. A Computer Oriented Approach. Academic Press, New York.
Anderson, T.W.
    1958   An Introduction to Multivariate Statistical Analysis. Wiley, New York.
Bartlett, M.S.
    1947   Multivariate Analysis. J. Roy. Statist. Soc. B, *9:* 176-197.
Blackith, R.E. and R.A. Reyment
    1971   Multivariate Morphometrics. Academic Press, New York.

Claringbould, P.J.
1958 Multivariate Quantal Analysis. J. Rcy. Statis. Soc. B, *20:* 113-121.
Defrise-Gussenhoven, E.
1966 A masculinity-feminity scale based on a discriminant function. Acta Genet., Basel, *16:* 198-208.
Dixon, W.J.
1970 BMD – Biomedical Computer Programs. University of California Press, Los Angeles.
Fisher, R.A.
1936 The use of multiple measurements in taxonomic problems. Ann. Eugen., London, *7:* 179-188.
Giles, E. and O. Elliot
1963 Sex determination by discriminant function analysis. Amer. J. Phys. Anthrop., *21:* 53-68.
Hotelling, H.O.
1936 Relations between two sets of variates. Biometrika, *28:* 321-377.
Howells, W.W.
1966 Craniometry and multivariate analysis: The Jomon population of Japan. Pap. Peabody Mus., *57:* 1-43.

1969 The use of multivariate techniques in the study of skeletal populations. Amer. J. Phys. Anthrop., *31:* 311-314.
Kendall, M.G.
1957 A Course in Multivariate Analysis. Griffin, London.
McKeon, James J.
1966 Canonical analysis: some relations between canonical correlation, factor analysis, discriminant function analysis, and scaling theory. Psychometric Monographs, No. 13, pp. 43.
Majumdar, D.N. and C.R. Rao
1960 Race Elements in Bengal: A Quantitative Study. Indian Statistical Institute. Asia Publ. House, London.
Martin, E.S.
1936 A study of an Egyptian series of mandibles with special reference to mathematical methods of sexing. Biometrika, *28:* 148-178.
Maxwell, A.E.
1961 Canonical variate analysis when the variables are dichotomous. Educ. Psychol. Measur., *21:* 259-271.
Morrison, D.G. and R. C. Art Jr.
1967 A Fortran Program for Stepwise Multiple Discriminant Analysis. mimeo. Vogelback Computing Center. Northwestern University, Evanston, Ill., pp. 112.

Pons, J.
   1955   The sexual diagnosis of isolated bones of the skeleton. Hum.
   Biol., *27:* 12-21.
Rao, C. Radhakrishna
   1952   Advanced Statistical Methods in Biometric Research. Hafner,
   Darien, Conn. (Reprint, 1970).
Reyment, R.A. and H. Å. Ramdén and W.J. Wahlstedt
   1969   Fortran IV program for the generalized statistical distance and
   analysis of covariance matrices for the CDC 3600 computer. Computer
   Contribution No. 39, State Geol. Survey, Lawrence, Kansas.
Reyment, R.A. and H. Å. Ramedén
   1970   Fortran IV program for canonical variates analysis for the CDC
   3600 computer. Computer Contribution No. 47. State Geol. Survey,
   Lawrence, Kansas.
Seal, H.
   1964   Multivariate Statistical Analysis for Biologists. Methuen, London.
Tanner, J.M.
   1951   Current Advances in the Study of Physique. Lancet, March 10,
   1951, 574-579.

THREE

Biological Anthropology: Variation in Populations

The basis for our evolution has been adaptation. But clearly our success in adapting became polytypic as our conspecifics penetrated virtually all land areas save Antarctica. How these adaptations came about is a question that has stimulated a wide range of research, and the papers in this section provide a sampling of methodologies that attempt to assess that adaptation. Bailit's paper illustrates the first requisite: establishing the variation in a specific trait. His paper deals only with dental eruption, but an emphasis on analyses "back home" should not obscure the importance of getting the basic data in the field correctly.

The overview provided by Baker shows how environmental stress affects individuals and groups of individuals—they adapt. Baker's methodologies concentrate on the adaptation, while the methodologies in the remaining two papers focus on the genetic results of past adaptation. In Baker's physiological studies the nature of the adaptation—genetic, long-term acclimatization, or a combination of the two—is elusive, while in the research outlined by Harpending and Chasko and by Froehlich the populational variation has been established, but by what evolutionary adaptation? The latter two articles evidence a common methodological opposition in population genetic analysis. The single-gene, discrete-trait data base available to Harpending and Chasko allows a remarkable interpretation but one not applicable to the quantitatively varying traits utilized by Froehlich. Each of these papers, dealing with qualitatively different human variation, in its own way shows just how much information can now be extracted from such material.

9. Heterozygosity and Population Structure in Southern Africa

Henry Harpending and William Chasko, Jr.

Introduction

Recent work in human population breeding structure and its genetic consequences has been concentrated either upon local micro-taxonomy (Ward and Neel, 1970; Lalouel and Morton, 1972; Weiner and Huizinga, 1972) or upon the minor departures from regional Hardy-Weinberg equilibrium due to finite population size, subdivision and the Wahlund effect, or non-random mating within small groups. We wish to call attention to a surprising and potentially more interesting aspect of some material gathered in the course of an ongoing study of gene distributions in southern Africa (Jenkins, 1972; Harpending and Jenkins, 1973; Jenkins et al., 1973). Genetic distances and F-statistics depend on relative heterozygosity in a region; we describe a striking effect of population structure on absolute heterozygosity in a range of southern African groups.

NOTE: Part of the data collection was supported by NIH grant MH 13611. The computations were supported by the research allocation committee of the University of New Mexico. The data were provided by Dr. Trefor Jenkins and by Dr. George Nurse, both of the Human Sero-genetics unit of the South African Institute for Medical Research. We have benefitted from comments by J. N. Spuhler and M. Nei.

214

Relative Heterozygosity

Statistics in common use in human population genetics have an underlying simplicity which is often obscured by terminology and minor statistical considerations, such as how best to weight information from different alleles when there are more than two at a locus. It is worth outlining the form of these statistics in order to clarify our approach to absolute heterozygosity.

If a certain allele has a gene frequency q in a large region, then the fraction of the population which would be heterozygous for the allele under Hardy-Weinberg conditions should be:

$$2q(1-q)$$

In fact we observe a fraction j to be heterozygous, and we write

$$j=2q(1-q)(1-F) \qquad (1)$$

F as defined here is rarely more than five per cent. There are two principal contributors to the observed value of F; one is regional variation of gene frequencies and the other is non-randomness in local mating practices.

Consider a region containing N local groups, assumed to be of equal size for algebraic convenience, with local gene frequencies q_1, q_2, ...etc. If mating were random within each one, average heterozygosity within the region would be

$$(1/N) \sum_i 2q_i (1-q_i)$$

which can be written

$$2q(1-q) - 2var(q_i)$$

where $var(q_i)$ is the variance of the gene frequency among the local groups. Writing

$$R_{st} = var(q_i) / q(1-q) \qquad (2)$$

we predict regional heterozygosity of

$$j = 2q(1-q) (1-R_{st})$$

This is the familiar Wahlund effect. R_{st} as defined here has several disguises in the literature; F_{st}, F_w in Cavalli-Sforza (1967), ϕ_0 in Morton et al. (1971) and later papers from Morton's group (but beware, in the reports from that group on the Brazilian study and others earlier the same symbol was used for a very different quantity, akin to the F in equation 1).

The form of equation (2) suggests that we define for any population i its contribution to R_{st} as

$$R_{ii} = (q_i-q)(q_i-q) / q(1-q)$$

and, since this looks like a variance, it is natural to define a covariance between populations i and j:

$$R_{ij} = (q_i - q)(q_j - q) / q(1-q)$$

These quantities can be given an interpretation in terms of the theory of genetic drift or in simple geometric terms (Harpending and Jenkins, 1973).

Most current genetic statistics can be written closely as functions of these quantities or, rather, as functions of estimates of these quantities. For example, the quantity ϕ_d which Morton and his colleagues call "kinship" is simply an average over all alleles of R_{ij} for all pairs of populations which are some distance d from each other. Genetic distances between populations i and j are some kind of average of

$$R_{ii} + R_{jj} - 2R_{ij}$$

whether they are Sanghvi's (1953) distance, Morton's θ (Morton et al., 1971), or the statistic used by Cavalli-Sforza which is an approximation to these (Cavalli-Sforza and Bodmer, 1971). These distances may differ in whether they take q to be a regional mean gene frequency of an allele or whether they simply use the mean of q_i and q_j for q. They also vary, as we mentioned before, in the way that they combine information from many alleles and many loci; here we have defined each in terms of the frequencies of a single allele.

Many of the arguments in the literature about the merits of one kind of genetic distance over another are probably silly, since each in its own way is unfit to handle the behavior of real populations. For example, the measure of Edwards and Cavalli-Sforza (1964) assumes that human micro-evolution proceeds among populations of exactly equal size which never exchange genes, thus neglecting, as N.E. Morton has put it, the basic fact of sexual reproduction. In spite of these reservations genetic distances have led to much lovely micro-taxonomic work.

The F in equation (1) can be regarded very roughly as the sum of R_{st} and a value f which measures the way local subpopulations do not mate at random within themselves. The contribution from f is distinguished by its very erratic behavior both in real populations (Harpending, Workman, and Grove, 1973: Workman and Niswander, 1970) and in computer populations (MacCluer, 1973).

Altogether, the value of F in equation (1) rarely exceeds five per cent for any region. Few have ventured to claim much evolutionary significance for such an effect (but see Neel, 1970), for five per cent is not very much; it depends on many irrelevant quantities such as the sample size and hence the budget of the project, and it is not very important anyway (Ewens, 1968). These are only Hulse's "ripples on a gene pool".

Absolute Heterozygosity

The aspect of population structure, inbreeding and random genetic drift which should have significant evolutionary consequences is absolute heterozygosity, the j of equation (1). This depends much more on the gene frequencies q than upon the ripples F. If, for example, the familiar polymorphisms in man are involved in resistance to infectious disease then variation among populations in heterozygosity—the percentage of the population which is heterozygous at the relevant loci—would be directly reflected in variation in health and ultimately reproductive success of these populations.

Dobzhansky (1970) cites several experiments with Drosophila where populations of flies made polymorphic for various chromosome arrangements showed higher rates of population increase than the corresponding monomorphic populations. He also describes experiments showing higher mating efficiency and lower mortality for flies heterokaryotypic for certain chromosomes. The well studied sickle-cell polymorphism is a familiar case of fitness overdominance in man, and many believe that such a mechanism is involved in the maintenance of a large proportion of human serological polymorphisms. This is a controversial area, however; while we lean toward a neutralist viewpoint we wish to mention the possible biological significance of variation in heterozygosity.

Nei (1972) provides an excellent introduction to the changing concept of inbreeding in population genetics. He discusses the distinction between relative and absolute heterozygosity in terms of the difference between a "fixed-allele" and a "variable-allele" model of inbreeding and population structure. Under the fixed-allele model there is some stable central tendency for a gene frequency, defined by recurrent mutation or migration. This central tendency is in practice unknowable if it exists at all, so it is not clear what the evolutionary meaning of studies of the Wahlund effect is.

The variable-allele model was motivated by the realization from molecular genetics that most mutations are probably to new and different alleles, that many of these may be selectively neutral (King and Jukes, 1969), and that recurrent mutation must be very rare. In this framework no central tendency for a gene frequency is assumed and identity of alleles by descent (inbreeding) is equivalent to homozygosity. Most of the theory of inbreeding and relationship is directly applicable to this model.

Absolute heterozygosity has been examined by zoologists in various species including man. The classic papers by Lewontin (1967) and Harris (1969) pointed out that total heterozygosity was considerably greater than had generally been suspected. Nei and Roychoudhury (1972) considered the three major human races and showed that average heterozygosity at the loci they studied was approximately the same in each race. Lewontin (1972) used a related statistic, Shannon-Weaver information, to examine what in effect was the magnitude of the Wahlund effect among races within the human species as had been done previously by Cavalli-Sforza (1967).

Southern Africa

We wish to examine the consequences of population breeding structure for the amount of heterozygosity in various southern African populations. Data for the study consist of gene frequencies of 51 alleles at 17 polymorphic loci in fifteen populations in southern Africa (Figure 1). Among the seventeen loci (Table I) are eight blood groups, five enzymes, two serum proteins, and the Gm and Inv loci of the immunoglobulin molecule. In the ABO system in addition to the four common alleles the "A-Bantu" allele was found in significant frequencies. In the Rhesus system five allelic frequencies were estimated. The Gm system had nine alleles, more than any other, while nine loci were diallelic.

Southern Africa is ideal in many ways for the study of human population structure and population genetics. There are isolated hunting and gathering peoples living at a band level of organization, several Bantu-speaking peoples at various stages of acculturation, large populations of recent European origin, and the heterogeneous Coloured populations which are mixtures of the above along with Asian peoples. We give here a short overview of the populations we include in this study; more information on these populations can be

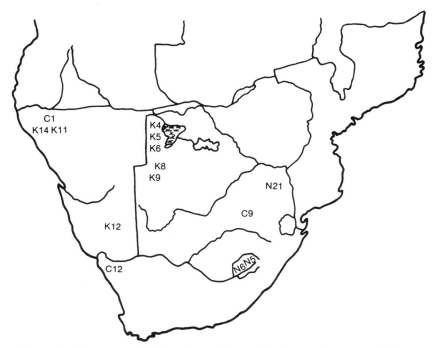

Figure 1. The geographical location of the 15 Southern African populations included in the present study.

Key (after Jenkins et. al. (1973))

C1	Sesfontein Coloured	K5	/Ai/ai !Kung
C9	Johannesburg Coloured	K6	/Du/da !Kung
C12	Kuboes Coloured	K8	Kaukau
N2	Herero	K9	Naron
N5	Sotho-a	K11	Sesfontein Khoikhoi
N6	Sotho-b	K12	Keetmanshoop Khoikhoi
N21	Pedi	K14	Damara
K4	Dobe !Kung		

found in Harpending and Jenkins (1973), Nurse et al (1973), and Jenkins (1972). For comparison we have included a pseudo-population, "Negroes", which is a compilation of gene frequencies from various large African samples in Cavalli-Sforza and Bodmer (1972) along with a few from Jenkins (1972).

The populations labelled /Du /da, /Ai /ai, Dobe, and Kau Kau are !Kung speakers, of which there may be five to ten thousand in Africa. /Du /da is the most isolated group since there are no reliable water sources in the area to support cattle owned by Bantu-speakers intrusive into the area. There are more people and more Bantu-speakers at /Ai /ai, but the largest concentration of both in Ngamiland is in the Dobe region. None of these groups is in as cosmopolitan a setting as the Kau Kau, about one hundred miles south, who are settled on cattle ranches in association with several Bantu-speaking peoples, with European ranchers, and with the Naron. The latter speak a language closely related to Nama and completely unrelated to !Kung, but otherwise the subsistence of the two groups on the farms is very similar. There seems now to be very little gene flow into any of these groups, but what there has been should have been greatest among the Kau Kau and Naron, less at Dobe and /Ai /ai, and least at /Du /da. The observed ranking by heterozygosity corresponds to this order except for the Naron who

TABLE 1

DIVERSITY BY LOCI

LOCUS	# OF ALLELES	$\overline{d}$	$\overline{h}$
ABO	5	.469	1.28
MNSs	4	.626	1.61
He	2	.104	.295
Rh	5	.341	.951
K	2	.0118	.041
Fy	2	.268	.602
Le	2	.476	.965
Se	2	.466	.946
Gm	9	.639	1.80
G-6-PD	3	.158	.449
PGD	3	.0577	.170
AK	2	.0816	.241
PGM$_1$	2	.221	.518
PGM$_2$	2	.0322	.112
Hp	2	.455	.933
Tf	2	.020	.270
Inv	2	.431	.895

would appear from this to be more endogamous and isolated than the neighboring Kau Kau. It is of interest that the Wahlund variance among these San groups is very small, .01 to .02, so that much gene flow must occur among them.

The Bantu-speaking groups in our sample all represent considerably larger tribal populations. The Herero sample was taken in northwest Ngamiland in Botswana in the same region as the /Ai /ai and Dobe samples from the San. The Herero were quite traditional and endogamous, probably more so than the Sotho and Pedi groups from South Africa and Lesotho. The Sotho samples were taken at altitudes of 5000 and 7000 feet in Lesotho, while the Pedi samples are from the northern Transvaal of South Africa. According to Murdock (1959) the Herero should number considerably more than 25,000, the Pedi about 800,000 and the Sotho about 1,400,000. These are certainly underestimates today considering the appreciable rate of increase of southern African populations.

In the Khoi and Coloured group three different samples were taken at Sesfontein, a settlement in northern Namibia. The Sesfontein Khoi are people who claimed four Khoi grandparents, the Damara claimed four Damara grandparents, and the rest of the population from Sesfontein was labelled Coloured. The Damara are phenotypically Negro but their gene frequency configuration is unlike southern African Bantu-speaking groups (Harpending and Jenkins, 1973). They speak Nama and are thought to have been slaves of the Khoi in pre-contact times.

The Keetmanshoop population is from a small town in southern Namibia where, again, the sample consists of individuals claiming four Khoi grandparents. There is evidence that there has been considerably more admixture of non-Khoi genes into this group.

The Kuboes Coloured sample is from a small and semi-isolated population in the northwestern Cape Province of South Africa, where the residents are descendants of a mixed group of Khoi, San, and Afrikaner farmers.

The Johannesburg Coloured population is a very large urban population of mixed genetic origins; it is usually thought to have incorporated more Negro genes than the other Coloured groups of South Africa and Namibia. There has been until recently much population movement among the various Coloured populations in South Africa.

Methods

We compute heterozygosity (d) of a population at a given locus simply as

$$d = 1 - \sum_{k=i}^{t} P_k^2$$

where t is the number of alleles at the locus and p_k is the frequency of the k*th* allele at the locus. The overall heterozygosity of a population (D) is computed as the mean for all loci

$$D = (1/N) \sum_{i=1}^{N} d_i$$

This measure, then, is strictly a property of the gene frequencies and is unaffected by the vagaries of local mating practices. It gives the heterozygosity to be expected under Hardy-Weinberg conditions. For comparison we have computed Shannon-Weaver information; for a single locus it is

$$h = \sum_{k=1}^{t} p_k \log p_k$$

The information (H) in a population over N loci is the mean

$$H = (1/N) \sum_{i=1}^{N} h_i$$

Table 2 gives computed values for both of these statistics. They are very highly correlated. Miller and Madow (1954) derive bias and sampling variance for the Shannon-Weaver measure estimated from multinomial samples. These are both small enough to be inconsequential for us since our smallest sample is on the order of fifty people (or one hundred alleles). Since heterozygosity has the more direct biological interpretation, we will concentrate our discussion on it.

Nei and Roychoudhury (1973) derive bias and sampling variance for heterozygosity. The bias is on the order of $1/2N$ and so is small for our samples. These authors show that the direct estimate (d) will usually have smaller mean squared error than the unbiased form.

We can obtain a simple but fairly accurate idea of the effects of sample size on the heterozygosity measure as follows. Assume that the true gene frequencies at some locus in a population with K alleles are $\pi_1, \pi_2 \ldots \pi_k$, and that we estimate the frequencies to be $P_1, P_2 \ldots, p_k$. We form the statistic

$$d = 1 - \sum_{i} p_i^2$$

TABLE 2

DIVERSITY BY GROUPS

GROUPS	D	H	σd
/Du/da	.259	.604	.0065
Naron	.263	.651	.0075
Damara	.264	.624	.0081
/Ai/ai	.274	.638	.0063
Herero	.281	.681	.0089
Dobe	.287	.683	.0032
Sesfontein Khoikhoi	.288	.697	.0089
Kaukau	.288	.703	.0053
Sotho-a	.297	.746	.0079
Pedi	.297	.745	.0054
Kuboes Coloured	.299	.741	.0045
"Negroes"	.299	.737	.0044
Sotho-b	.299	.745	.0070
Keetmanshoop Khoikhoi	.308	.761	.0045
Sesfontein Coloured	.336	.763	.0069
Johannesburg Coloured	.336	.847	.0056

We write this statistic as a Taylor series around the true frequencies and keep only first order terms. Then

$$d \approx (1 - \sum_i \pi_i^2) + \sum_i \frac{\partial d}{\partial p_i} (p_i - \pi_i)$$

Transferring the first term on the right to the left side and squaring both sides we have

$$[d - (1 - \sum_i \pi_i^2)]^2 \approx \sum_i \sum_j (p_i - \pi_i)(p_j - \pi_j) \left.\frac{\partial d}{\partial p_i}\right|_{\pi_i} \left.\frac{\partial d}{\partial p_j}\right|_{\pi_j}$$

The expected value of the term on the left is the sampling variance of the statistic d; the right side has expected value

$$\sum_i \sum_j \frac{\partial d}{\partial p_i} \frac{\partial d}{\partial p_j} \text{cov} (p_i, p_j)$$

Substituting the observed values p_i for the true values π_i and assuming multinomial sampling with

$$\text{cov} (p_i, p_j) = \begin{cases} p_i (1 - p_i)/2N & (i = j) \\ -p_i p_j /2N & (i \neq j) \end{cases}$$

we obtain

$$\text{var} (d) \approx \frac{2}{N}[\sum_i p_i q^3 - \sum_{i \neq j}\sum p_i p_j q_i q_j]$$

writing q_i for $(1-p_i)$. For moderately large N (>20) this is very close to the more exact expression given by Nei and Roychoudhury. The sampling variance of D can be computed by averaging these and dividing by the number of loci. The corresponding standard deviations are given in table 2.

Ewens (1972) shows that the number of different alleles in a given size of sample can be used to construct a sufficient statistic for a parameter which is, for selectively neutral alleles, the product of four times the effective size with the mutation rate to new selectively neutral alleles at a single locus. This quantity, plus one, is the reciprocal of the expected homozygosity at the locus. We have not used his procedure because it is not certain how robust it is to violation of the assumptions and because we are more interested in examining heterozygosity per se. Further, for many of these loci the number of different alleles observed in a sample will depend first on the diligence with which the laboratory checks the occasional anomalous typing, which makes this an unsatisfactory approach.

Results

The average heterozygosity in our sample, thirty percent, is about the same as that of the "Negro" pseudo-population. If we take the generalization (Dobzhansky 1970; Nei and Roychoudhury 1972) that one third of all loci are polymorphic and that mean heterozygosity per individual is ten percent, then in a sample of polymorphic loci mean heterozygosity should be about one third, in good agreement with our findings.

The range of heterozygosity in our populations, twenty-six to thirty-four percent, is quite large. As a robust check on the significance of these differences we may ask a question, phrased in terms of the analysis of variance, as follows: for a random polymorphic locus do "treatments" by these various population structures result in consistent differences in heterozygosity? To check this we subjected

Additional Acknowledgments:

Institutional support toward illustration and
publication costs was provided by:

The College of the Liberal Arts of
The Pennsylvania State University

The University Museum of Michigan

The Dental School of the University
of Connecticut

Hartwick College

Erratum, p. xxxix

Drs. Donald Mitchell and Jill Nash are at
the State University College of New York
at Buffalo.

the seventeen by sixteen matrix of heterozygosity measures to a non-parametric two-way analysis of variance by ranks (Bradley, 1968). For each locus populations were ranked according to heterozygosity and the sum of ranks then taken for each population. These sums are used to construct a statistic which is approximately chi-square with degrees of freedom equal to the number of treatments ₋ss one if there are in fact no differences among treatments. For our data the statistic was equal to 34.03 which has a probability of occurrence of less than .005. Thus these populations do have significantly different effects if our sample can be considered a random sample of polymorphic loci. This means that membership in one or the other of these populations is a strong determinant of the genetic variability within the genome of an individual and, conversely, that heterozygosity of a population is a meaningful indicator of the effective size and the structure of gene flow into a population.

The differences among the populations are clearly referable to population structure. The lower values are associated with breeding populations which are more endogamous and of smaller size; we suspect that endogamy may be the more important parameter. The Damara and the Sesfontein Khoi, chosen from the total population at Sesfontein on the basis of statements about their grandparents, are significantly less heterozygous than the outbred fraction of the population. It is a surprise that the Naron are much less heterozygous than the neighboring Kau Kau. We do not know very much about the population structure of the Naron, but on the Ghanzi farms they are not as prominent as the Kau Kau, and oral tradition has the Kau Kau expanding into Naron territory and displacing them at the time of European settlement around the turn of the century. Much of the low heterozygosity of the San groups may reflect the way that offspring of San-Bantu matings are usually defined to be Bantu. Hence there is gene flow from the San into the Bantu groups but almost none from the Bantu into the San.

The Bantu populations occupy the middle range of heterozygosity and are equivalent in this measure to the "Negroes" from Cavalli-Sforza and Bodmer (1971). This is an interesting check on the validity of our results. The set of gene frequencies for "Negroes" is derived from various locations over the whole African continent, probably mostly from tribal societies. This section yields a mean heterozygosity precisely in the middle of the values for a series of populations in a continuum from isolated band level societies to large urban mixed populations.

The most heterozygous populations are two recently mixed out-breeding Coloured populations and the Khoi group from Keet-manshoop. The high value for the Keetmanshoop Khoi, who are in a region of Namibia more densely settled by non-Khoi groups than Sesfontein, indicates that they are not as isolated as the latter group. Jenkins et al (1973) report finding both non-African phenogroups $Gm^{1,2}$ and $Gm^{3,5,13,14}$ at Keetmanshoop, although the former was also found in the Sesfontein Khoi group. Harpending and Jenkins (1973) found the Keetmanshoop Khoi to have a higher score than the Sesfontein Khoi on a principal component which they identified with extra-African admixture.

We have looked at the first several principal components of the covariance matrices of heterozygosity among loci and among groups. These indicate that the Khoi/Coloured groups are distinguished by excess heterozygosity primarily in the blood groups and the Gm locus, while the San and Bantu-speakers are differentiated by differences in the enzymes, the serum proteins, and the Inv locus. We don't know what to make of this.

The range of heterozygosity in our populations is approximately plus or minus twelve per cent of the mean. If heterozygosity at these loci is generally due to natural selection, either as overdominance or as transient directional selection, then this amount of variation could have important consequences for general health or for susceptibility to sporadic infectious disease or other environmental insult. If these are transient polymorphisms, then the magnitude of the differences we have found together with the small sampling uncertainty of the statistic show that the comparison of absolute heterozygosity may be an interesting and fruitful approach to the elucidation of genetic consequences of human population structure.

While human population genetics suffers from excessive specula-tion and unwarranted generalization, it is tempting to consider the implications of an effect of population structure and heterozygosity on population fitness in human evolution. The advent of settled vil-lage life probably brought both larger regional populations and higher local endogamy. The former may have been more important for heterozygosity, but the concomitant change in the relationship of human populations to nutritional stresses and to infectious diseases make the implications for fitness unclear. But when these settled populations interacted with neighboring foraging peoples, so that the latter were exposed to the same infectious agents and, often, the same nutritional stresses, the settled peoples would have had a significant fitness advantage due to the greater amount of genetic variability they could maintain.

A more interesting implication of this study is that heterozygosity may lead to a method of objective assessment of the genetic consequences of breeding structure valid in comparisons among very disparate groups. Large numbers of loci are required for these studies, since heterozygosity varies widely from locus to locus. This is in contrast to the Wahlund effect where variance among loci should be and is much smaller, and meaningful microtaxonomic work and comparisons of F-statistics can be done with five to ten loci. We include table 1, which gives mean heterozygosity for each locus in our sample, to facilitate comparisons with other groups. We expect that different parts of the world will show large differences in the way that the various loci contribute to heterozygosity. Hence, for global comparisons data from very many loci will be required. However, the high significance in our analysis of variance implies that the differences among populations in southern Africa are very real consequences of variation in breeding structure, so that this approach can be an objective means for world-wide population structure comparisons. The Wahlund approach, depending as it does on sample size and on the way local groups are defined by the investigator, cannot offer a similar hope for objective comparisons.

Bibliography

Bradley, J. V.
    1968   Distribution free statistical tests. Prentice-Hall, Englewood Cliffs, New Jersey.
Cavalli-Sforza, L. L.
    1967   Human populations. In A. Brink, ed., Heritage from Mendel. University of Wisconsin Press, Madison.
Cavalli-Sforza, L. L. and W. F. Bodmer
    1971   The Genetics of human populations. W. H. Freeman, San Francisco.
Dobzhansky, T.
    1970   Genetics of the evolutionary process. Columbia University Press, New York.

Edwards, A. W. F. and L. L. Cavalli-Sforza
    1964   Reconstruction of evolutionary trees. In V. E. Heywood and J.
    McNeill, eds., Phenetic and Phylogenetic Classification. The Systematics
    Association, London.
Ewens, W. J.
    1968   Population genetics. Methuen, London.

———

    1972   The sampling theory of selectively neutral alleles. Theoretical
    Population Biology, *3:* 87-112.
Harpending, H., P. Workman, and J. Grove
    1973   Local genotypic disequilibrium in a generalized island model.
    Human Biology, *45:* 359-362.
Harpending, H. C. and T. Jenkins
    1973   Genetic distance among Southern African populations. In M.
    H. Crawford and P. L. Workman, eds., Method and theory in anthro-
    pological genetics. University of New Mexico Press, Albuquerque,
    pp. 177-199.
Harris, H.
    1969   Enzyme and protein polymorphism in human populations.
    British Medical Bulletin, *25:* 5-13.
Jenkins, T.
    1972   Genetic polymorphisms in Southern Africa. Thesis presented to
    the University of London.
Jenkins, T., H. C. Harpending and G. T. Nurse
    1973   Genetic differences among certain Southern African popula-
    tions. In press.
King, J. L. and T. H. Jukes
    1969   Non-Darwinian evolution. Science, *164:* 788-798.
Lalouel, J. M. and N. E. Morton
    1973   Bioassay of kinship in a South American Indian population.
    American Journal of Human Genetics, *25:* 62-73.
Lewontin, R. C.
    1967   An estimate of average heterozygosity in man. American Journal
    of Human Genetics, *19:* 681-685.
Lewontin, R. C.
    1972   The apportionment of human diversity. Evolutionary Biology,
    6: 381-398.
MacCluer, J. W.
    1973   Monte Carlo simulation: the effects of migration on some
    measures of genetic distance. In J. F. Crow, C. Denniston and P. O'Shea,
    eds., Genetic Distance. Plenum Press, New York.
Miller, G. A. and W. G. Madow
    1954   On the maximum likelihood estimate of the Shannon-Wiener

measure of information. AFCRC-TR-54-75, Air Force Cambridge Research Center, Bolling Air Force Base, Washington, D. C.

Morton, N. E.
1969 Human population structure. In H. L. Roman, L. M. Sandler, and A. Campbell, eds., Annual Review of Genetics, Annual Reviews, Palo Alto, Calif., *3:* 53-74.

Morton, N.E., S. Yee, D. Harris, and R. Lew
1971 Bioassay of Kinship. Theoretical Population Biology, *2:* 507-524.

Murdock, G. P.
1959 Africa: its peoples and their culture history. McGraw-Hill, New York.

Neel, J.V.
1970 Lessons from a "primitive" people. Science, *170:* 815-822.

Nei, M.
1972 The theory and estimation of genetic distance. In N. E. Morton, ed., Genetics of Population Structure. University of Hawaii Press, Honolulu, pp. 45-51.

Nei, M. and A. K Roychoudhury
1972 Gene differences between Caucasian, Negro, and Japanese populations. Science, *177:* 434-436.

1973 Sampling variances of heterozygosity and genetic distances. In press.

Nurse, G.T., H. Harpending, and T. Jenkins
1973 Biology and the history of southern African populations. In press.

Sanghvi, L. D.
1953 Comparison of genetical and morphological methods for a study of biological differences. American Journal of Physical Anthropology, *11:* 385-404.

Ward, R. H. and J. V. Neel
1970 Gene frequencies and microdifferentiation among the Makiritare Indians. IV. A comparison of a genetic network with ethnohistory and migration matrices; a new index of isolation. American Journal of Human Genetics, *22:* 538-561.

Weiner, J. S. and J. Huizinga
1972 The Assessment of Population Affinities in Man. Clarendon Press, Oxford.

Workman, P. L. and J. Niswander
1970 Population studies on Southwestern Indian tribes. II. Local genetic differentiation in the Papago. American Journal of Human Genetics, *22:* 24-49.

10. Research Strategies in Population Biology and Environmental Stress

Paul T. Baker

Introduction

The various researchers concerned with human population biology were for the first half of this century generally satisfied with describing *how* human populations vary in their genetics, morphology and physiology, but recent investigators have made increasing efforts to find out *why* populations vary. A major problem is the development of research strategies capable of testing the hypotheses that are raised.

In our current efforts to understand why human populations vary in physical and physiological characteristics most recent thinking has stressed the effects of environment. When the biological difference under consideration is presumed to have a strong genetic base the assumption is often made that at some time in the past natural selection set in operation by environmental conditions produced the

NOTE: The list of professional and technical workers who have contributed to the Andean program is too long for full recognition here but I would like to thank Drs. J. M. Hanna, J. D. Haas, M. A. Little and R. B. Thomas for permission to use some of the illustrations found in the paper. Financial support for this research came from many sources including U. S. Army Research and Development Command Contract DA-49-193-MD-2260, Public Health Service Grant 5 TO1 GMO 1748 and grants from the Wenner-Gren Foundation.

variation under study. Such assumptions are not always the case since stochastic processes as exemplified by genetic drift are often interpreted as causal, and the cultural environment, with its multiple intricacies of mating proscription, can also alter gene frequencies. Nevertheless, most human biologists find it hard to accept that the large genetic variation which is found among the human subpopulations could have developed and persisted without environmentally mediated natural selection as a major factor (Baker, 1966a). While specific genetic differences may have other sources, differences in traits which are developmentally labile are universally attributed to environmental variation. Thus, if a known Swedish population in Brazil weighs less in Brazil than in Minnesota it is assumed that it must be caused by some simple environmental variable, such as nutrition.

Despite this implicit faith in environmental forces the evidence remains incomplete, and knowledge of how the environmental forces operate on populations is almost never clear. Among the primarily genetic traits which differentiate populations only a few, such as skin color and some abnormal hemoglobins, seem satisfactorily related to environmental forces. Even among the more developmentally labile traits it cannot be said that we know with any precision the exact forces at work. When populations vary in an obvious manner in their physical growth rates we usually resort to a simple cause such as nutrition. This occurs in spite of the fact that we know or suspect that such factors as infectious disease, temperature and chronic hypoxia can all affect the rates and specifics of growth and development.Certainly we can predict with fair accuracy how children in Yellow Springs, Ohio and some other places are likely to grow if their environment remains similar but why this growth is quite different from a group of Nilotic children in Africa or Quechua children in highland Peru remains very inadequately explained.

While child growth is a rather obvious example many better ones could be cited. Thus, populations vary in completed female fertility from 2 to 11 and most explanations deal in social causes without reference to the host of environmental factors which are known to affect basic fecundity.

Populations vary substantially in work capacity and the common explanation is that they vary in habitual exercise levels even though it is known that genetic factors, disease, and nutrition can all affect individual capacities.

Examples could be greatly multiplied but perhaps the point is made and we can proceed to the more important question of why several decades of strong interest in how environment affects populations have not produced more satisfactory answers. The answer is, of course, complex and includes the limited number of investigators and funds as well as the known difficulties of working with humans as test subjects. Even so, it seems to me that the basic problem has been one of research design and method. The animal experimentalists have developed designs which permit them to answer rather definitively how a given population will respond to an environmental variation. Cut off from these basic methods because man cannot be subjected to long term control, human biologists, whatever the particular discipline, have spent much of their time in simple normative research. Alternately they have been forced into less effective groping for answers with techniques such as statistical association or short term experimentation.

I do not know of any simple solution to this methodological impasse but during the past ten years some progress has been made and in the remainder of this paper I will explore the strengths and weaknesses of four research strategies which we have applied in our Andean research program. These four strategies are not at the moment well enough described or documented to have standard nomenclature so for convenience I will designate them as the: (1) One Stress–One Population Model; (2) Multiple Stress–One Population Model; (3) One Stress–Multiple Population Model; and (4) Multiple Stress–Multiple Population Model.

Research Strategies

ONE STRESS–ONE POPULATION

A number of years ago I suggested that one strategy of understanding man's relationship to his environment was to pick a single rather obvious environmental stress and then attempt to elucidate all of the cultural, developmental and genetic traits which contributed to the survival of a given population in the presence of such a stress (Baker, 1965).

The basic approach in this method is to pick a rather obvious environmental variable such as temperature or oxygen pressure and study a group which is living in ambient conditions which are known to be potentially stressful to the biological organism. As used in this paper stressful means a force which distorts the homeostatic process sufficiently to constitute a health hazard. Once a stress and population is chosen it is well to determine whether the material and nonmaterial culture so shields the population as to create a nonstressful micro-environment. With the exception of modern culture this is rarely the case and instead the culture usually only reduces the stress to biologically tolerable levels. It is also usually the case that the level of cultural protection varies by age, sex, and social structure.

The next step in the method is a full exploration of the population's biological responses to the stress with an appraisal of the adaptive and adjustment value of the response. Finally, one may explore the extent to which the population's and subpopulation's responses are unique and inquire into the mechanisms which produce these responses.

THE COLD STRESS EXAMPLE.

Several environmental stresses have been explored in this manner in our Andean studies but the responses to cold are probably the best example. A number of studies have now been completed to determine the extent and forms of cultural protection against the normally low environmental temperature (Baker, 1966b; Hanna, 1968, 1970; Larsen, 1973). In order to complete such studies it was necessary to measure various microenvironmental and body temperatures in houses, under clothes, and on people throughout their daily and life cycles in our study area, Nuñoa, Peru. A result from one such study is illustrated in Figure 1. This study, conducted on a number of families during their normal sleep cycle in their homes, illustrated a lack of stress during the sleep period but showed that children seemed to suffer some total body cooling prior to sleep. Along with many related conclusions we can now say that the adult female Nuñoan is almost completely protected from total body cold by cultural mechanisms. Adult males receive only sporadic total body cold exposure but young children are frequently so stressed. All Nuñoans receive frequent cold stress to the extremities. We do not as yet know to what extent intrapopulation variation in material culture, wealth or social position produces variation in cold exposure.

Proceeding with controlled experimental studies, the biological responses of Nuñoans and the factors which affect these responses were explored (Baker et al., 1967; Mazess et al., 1969; Mazess and Larsen, 1972; Weitz, 1969). As illustrated in Figure 2, studies of their

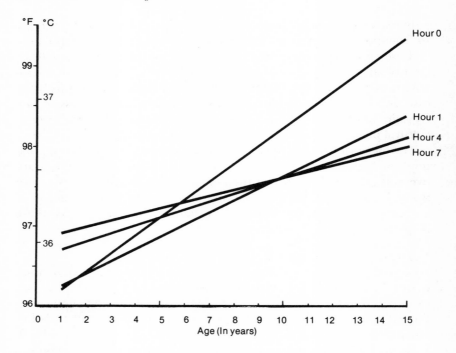

Figure 1. Relation between rectal temperature and age after various hours of sleep: based on statistical regression.

response to total body cooling during both a wakeful period and a stressed sleep period showed this population to have different responses from U.S. whites. Most of this difference appeared related to the maintenance of high peripheral temperatures and as a consequence subsequent studies emphasized this aspect (Little, 1969). As shown in Figures 3 and 4 the Nunoans do maintain very warm extremities. Other studies of the same nature illustrated a developmental aspect to this response (Little et al., 1971).

By using similar techniques it was possible to show (Fig. 5) that the Nuñoan habit of chewing cocoa leaves certainly did not produce the unique high peripheral temperature response. Instead it may produce some vasoconstriction which increases core temperatures during inactive periods (Hanna, 1971; Little, 1970) but the frequent consumption of alcohol (Fig. 6) by adults did elevate peripheral temperatures and probably dispels any feeling of cold even during the nights (Little, 1970; Mazess et al., 1968).

ADVANTAGES.

This strategy seems to me to offer a number of advantages over the traditional descriptive study in which the behavior or the results of single experiments on populations are reported. First, it permits over-simplified single cause explanations to be discarded. Thus, in Nuñoa we can reject the hypothesis that coca chewing causes the physiological uniqueness of the population's cold responses. Second, it illustrates that man does not generally adjust to environmental stress by cultural mechanisms alone as many social scientists have believed. Indeed in the cold example from Nuñoa it appears that the mechanisms which provide adjustment are a complex interaction of material culture, behavior, developmental biology and quite possibly some genetically unique characteristics. Of course, the greatest possibilities of the method are that it may allow the development of models with their predictive capabilities on how a population adjusts to a given stress.

DISADVANTAGES.

A clear disadvantage to the one stress—one population strategy

	Whites N = 19	Nuñoans N = 26	Lowland Indians N = 10
Heat Production (KCAL/m²)			
1st 60 min.	51.5	58.1	54.7
2nd 60 min.	62.2	65.5	65.5
Total time	113.7	123.6	120.2
Heat loss (not replaced by metabolic activity — KCAL/m²)			
1st 54 min.*	29.6	51.0	30.1
2nd 60 min.	11.8	12.9	14.7
Total time	41.4	63.9	44.8

* Because perfect equivalence in pre-exposure body temperatures was not achieved, heat loss in the first 4 minutes of exposure has been excluded from this calculation.

Figure 2. Body heat exchange as exemplified in heat production and loss of body heat content. Average values for two exposures at 10°C. expressed on the basis of body surface area.

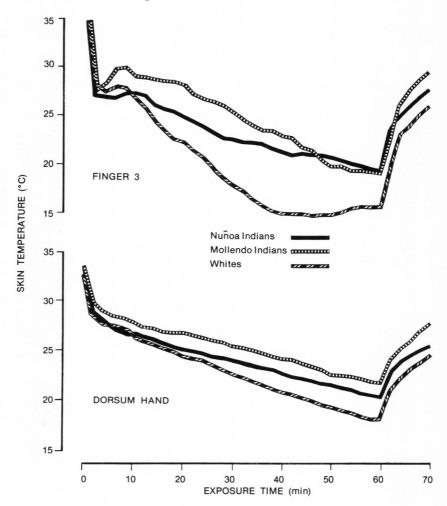

Figure 3. Skin temperature of the third finger and dorsal hand surface during 60 minutes of cold air exposure at 0°C. and 10 minutes recovery at 24°C.

occurs from the need for comparative data. For some stresses such as cold enough is known about selected aspects so that judgments can be made by reference to published work. Thus, the stress of a given micro-climate can be judged from simple temperature measurements,

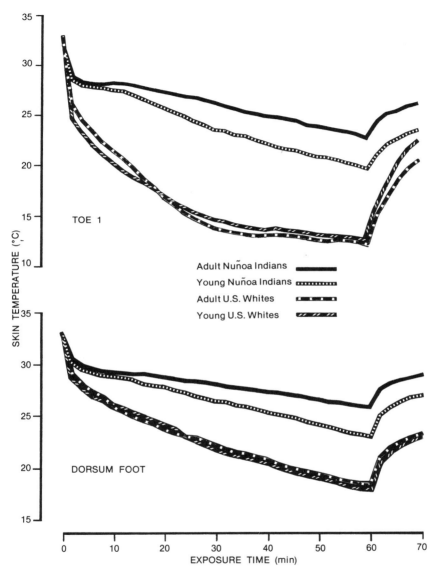

Figure 4. Skin temperature of the large toe and dorsal foot surface during 60 minutes of cold air exposure at 0°C. and 10 minutes of recovery at 24°C. Notice age change in Nuñoans.

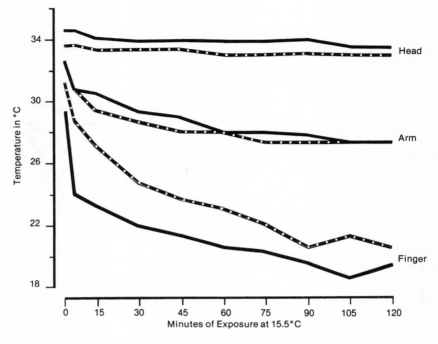

Figure 5. Relationship between body surface temperature and coca chewing during two hour exposure to 15.5°C. Solid lines are trials with coca chewing; broken lines are trials without coca chewing.

but even for cold studies research techniques vary so much that the discovery of how physiological responses to cold vary from other populations usually requires that some members of another population be transported to the location and tested. For other stressors such as nutrition or hypoxia it may be impossible to find appropriate comparative material and experimental studies may be limited to intrapopulation comparisons. This is particularly the case when one wants to study development or aging.

MULTIPLE STRESS – ONE POPULATION
One of the major research strategies which has developed in the public health branch of medicine is the epidemiological techniques for discovering the underlying causes of certain diseases (MacMahon and Pugh, 1970). By this strategy it has often been possible, within a

single population, to define the causative environmental factors in a specific disease and even quantify how the factors interrelate in their contribution to the disease. The lung cancer and smoking linkage is, of course, the most obvious recent example of the technique's capabilities. In our Andean studies we arrived at a somewhat similar strategy by a different route. As we explored the responses of the Nuñoa population to a single stress such as cold and hypoxia it became apparent that responses to these stresses interact. Thus increased peripheral circulation in the cold also facilitates oxygen pickup in peripheral body cells. When the stress responses under study are multiplied it becomes economical and reasonable to reverse the procedure and start asking different kinds of questions. One may ask how the stresses and their interaction affect growth or how growth rates affect mortality, etc.

The approach is fundamentally a shotgun one in which one attempts by regression analysis to relate the various biological and social processes to each other in the hope that serendipity will provide an

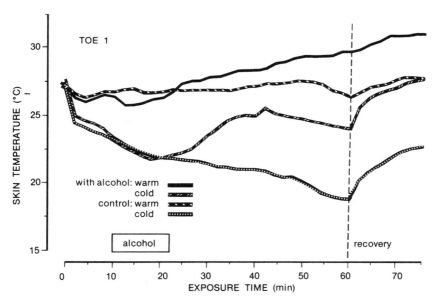

Figure 6. Skin temperatures of the large toe during cold exposure (0°C.) and exposure to room temperature (24°C.). Solid figures signify experiments when alcohol was consumed.

organizing principle. The probability of success is quite strongly related to quantity and variety of the data. By such techniques we arrived at the very strong hypothesis that growth was slowed by hypoxia (Frisancho, 1970; Frisancho and Baker, 1970) and that fertility might be reduced by the same factor (Baker and Dutt, 1972). However, probably the most significant of results which developed simply because of the mass of data collected was the development of an energy flow model for the population (Thomas, 1973).

THE ENERGY FLOW MODEL.
Nuñoa, the area of the Andes where much of our research effort was concentrated, is not an area rich in floral and faunal resources. As shown in Figure 7 only a part of the district can be used for agriculture and even in these areas only specialized frost resistant crops can be grown. Most of the area is suitable only as marginal pasture land. This led one of our investigative teams to feel that energy availability might itself be a stress on the population to which biological as well as cultural adaptations had been made. In some two years of work using some assistants and the field laboratory facilities, he was able to develop a rather complete picture of energy flow for the native population. Figure 8 shows the flow in the natural system while Figure 9 reflects how the maintenance system works for a representative family. As can be seen from the latter figure the family is very much dependent upon the external economic value of the animals for survival. As was suspected energy availability is a serious problem. For every calorie of human energy expended agriculture yields 11.7. However, only limited crops can be grown in restricted areas and year to year yields are quite unreliable. For herding the direct caloric return would only be 1.6 calories per human calorie invested were it not for the high trade value of the animals.

While these results within themselves would be of considerable anthropological interest it is the further analysis of the adaptive mechanisms by which the population has adjusted to their energy flow problems which is unique. These adaptations are summarized in Figure 10, and while some of the adaptive responses can be only partially quantified I feel most of them have been quite carefully documented in the study and the energy saving is well quantified. This study points out very nicely not only the significant research rewards which can accrue from holistic approaches to a population but also

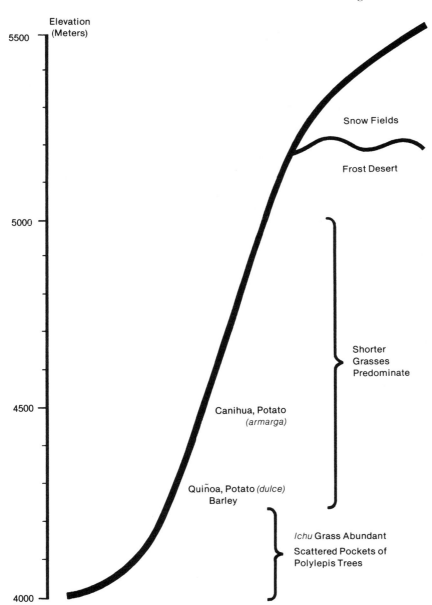

Figure 7. Altitude limits of cultigen production and natural flora in Nuñoa district.

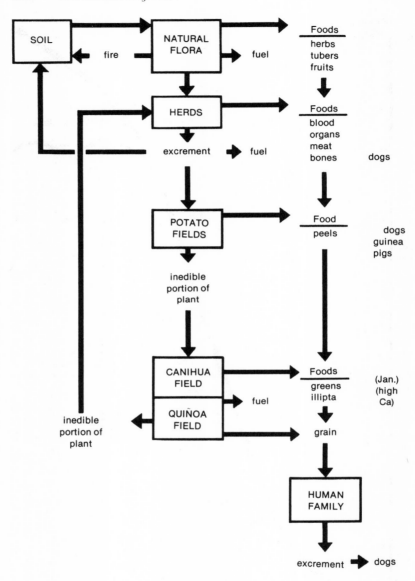

Figure 8. A simplified diagram of nutrient cycling in Nunoa.

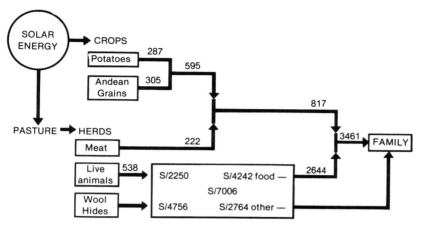

Figure 9. Annual energy flow and cash flow through a typical Nuñoa family. Figures without S/ are thousands of kilocalories.

indicates the massive quantity of data required to obtain results. The adaptive analysis could not have been accomplished without the depth information already available for the population on its nutrition, demography, growth, physiology, etc.

ADVANTAGES.

The collection of detailed interlocked biological information on a single population has many obvious advantages. As in the case of the energy flow analysis it is often possible to ask and answer many questions which were not planned at the beginning of the research. Furthermore, statistical manipulation of the data can and often does generate hypotheses even when the information is not precise enough to permit a definitive answer. Perhaps most importantly it allows the generation of community models. While the study of responses to a single stress such as cold permits the creation of a detailed model of response to the particular stress, the multiple stress analysis offers the possibility that we may one day model how the various genetic and environmental factors interact to produce a given mortality, growth, and fertility pattern, etc. I hasten to add that this is obviously no more than a hopeful prediction since at this point energy flow and some infectious diseases are probably the only traits which can be even crudely modeled for some human populations.

I. Socio-Technological Adaptations
   A. A spatially dispersed, multiple resource base of energetically efficient crops and
      domestic animals.
   B. An interzonal exchange system whereby resources produced in the Nunoa ecosystem
      are exchanged for high energy foods from lower regions.
   C. A division of labor heavily reliant upon child participation.
   D. An activity pattern in which a large portion of the day is spent performing sedentary
      subsistence tasks.

II. Demographic Adaptations
   A. Familial attempts to maximize fertility.
   B. High infant mortality.
   C. Temporary and seasonal emigration.

III. Biological Adaptations
   A. Slow and prolonged growth pattern.
   B. Small adult body size.

Figure 10. A summary of the major adaptations to the Nuñoan energy flow system.

DISADVANTAGES.

Two primary disadvantages are inherent in this research strategy. First, if carried out without hypotheses based on sub-structures it may often cost a great deal of effort without necessarily producing significant results. I am sure most readers can think of several instances where this has happened. Second, even if successful models are created these usually are not applicable to more general human biological problems unless comparative data already exist. As a personal opinion it seems to me that a common fallacy in medical research is the assumption that an epidemiological discovery in one segment of the human species is applicable to other environments and other subpopulations. Thus, this strategy seems best justified when a large data base already exists or the model required is of great scientific merit.

ONE STRESS—MULTIPLE POPULATIONS.

Single population research strategies always have major flaws if one is attempting to dissect precisely environment and genetic contributions to a trait. Thus no animal experimentalist would feel safe in generalizing about how mice adapt to cold from a set of experiments in which temperature was varied but genetic and other environmental variables were not controlled. For human research such control is not possible but genetically similar populations live under dissimilar environmental conditions and genetically dissimilar groups live in similar environmental conditions. Therefore, a careful search for appropriate groups can sometimes uncover the kinds of natural human populations required to fulfill at least in major part the experimentalist's requirements. The complexities of this research strategy are too great to develop in a short essay but can be illustrated by one of our research efforts in Peru.

INFANT GROWTH AND HYPOXIA.

From our research in Nuñoa we had hypothesized that hypoxia was a factor in slowing the growth and development of Nuñoa infants. Indeed we had surmised on the basis of a cross-sectional sample that they were among the slowest growing infants in the world and also showed very late development in tooth eruption and motor development (Baker, 1969). While hypoxia was an attractive answer it was quite apparent that many alternative causes could be suggested and some of these must contribute to the small birth sizes and slow growth of these infants. Just to list a few, mal- or undernutrition was possible for at least some of the mothers and infants; the lack of any medical care implied infectious disease possibilities; and finally the population was both culturally and genetically different from the ones on whom comparative data were available. To progress further in this type of question it would be necessary either to find a specific mechanism by which reduced atmospheric oxygen tension could affect infant growth or develop a research design similar to the experimentalist which would manipulate the significant variables. While experimental research on other animals has shown that a hypoxic environment can slow growth in some species the mechanism of this action in mammals is not known (Frisancho and Baker, 1970). Thus, an appropriate research design for man was the most feasible method for answering the question.

Since the Andean region contains a substantial interpopulation variation in all of the mentioned variables it might be possible to fulfill the exact design requirements. However, the cost of locating the samples with measured differences in nutrition, disease, genetic structure, etc. would be prohibitive. Instead, another of our research group felt the design problem could be simplified by sample choices which were based on the easily identified variables of altitude, rural-urban residence, ethnic designation and social class. His design is shown in Figure 11.

This design has variable power in determining the importance of

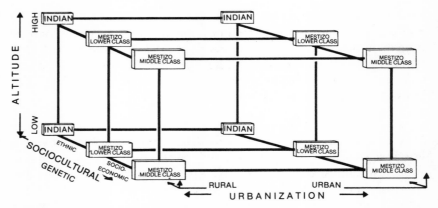

Figure 11. Idealized research design in graphic form for analysis of the effect of altitude on infant growth.

the independent variables to the dependent ones. It is most powerful in resolving the effect of altitude while it is less effective in determining the relative effects of nutrition and medical care since these are measured indirectly in the comparison through rural-urban residence and social class. Finally, it is least effective in measuring the relative effects of child care versus genetic differences since the socio-cultural scale is one which movement within the scale reflects changes in Indian-European gene admixture and variation from the Indian to Peruvian cultural form.

Even with this simplification of design the problem of finding and measuring all the groups proved too difficult so that the research finally completed was a cross-sectional study based on eight of the originally proposed 12 populations (Haas, 1973). The rural *mestizo* middle classes and the *mestizo* lower classes at altitude were not included. Despite these several limitations the research strategy proved an effective one. As can be surmised from a perusal of Figures 12 and 13 it, in my opinion, proved that regardless of nutrition, health care or socio-cultural status, the infants in the Andean region at least are slow in their prenatal and infant growth. The analysis also revealed that the slow motor development which we had found in Nuñoa was not altitude-related but instead varied with the socio-cultural scale. This unfortunately leaves the relative contribution of the genetic and cultural factors to motor development unresolved.

With the eight samples it was, of course, possible to go beyond the

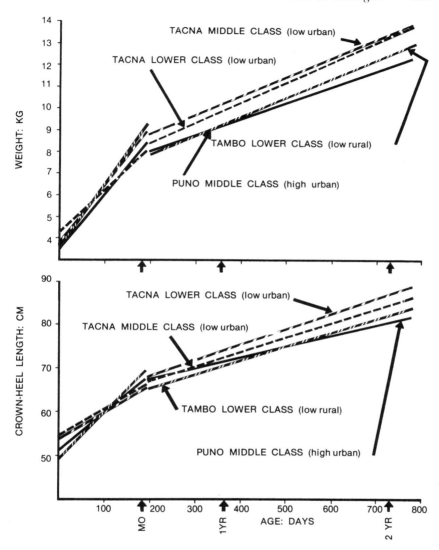

Figure 12. Regressed age trends in weight and crown-heel length: comparison of four Peruvian *mestizo* male infant groups.

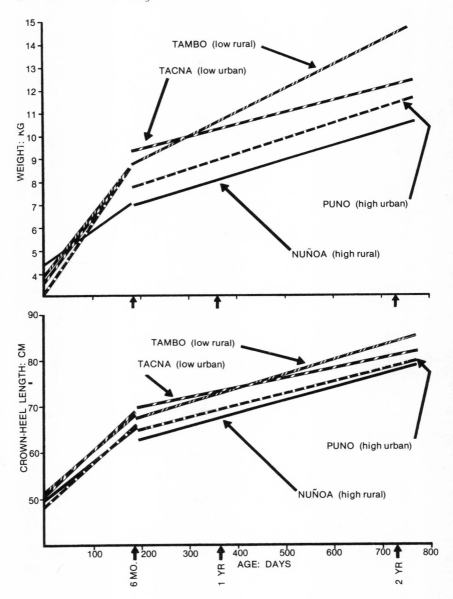

Figure 13. Regressed age trends in weight and crown-heel length: comparison of four Peruvian Indian male infant groups.

straightforward conclusions and look for interactions. How this was possible is illustrated in Figure 14. While these results must be considered somewhat more tentative it appears that among other findings *mestizo* birth weights are more affected by altitude than Indian ones, and it appears the poor nutrition and health care may have a more severe affect on growth at high altitude.

ADVANTAGES.

The prime value of this research strategy is its ability to provide rather direct causal linkage. While the previous strategies based on single populations can provide depth information on how populations have adapted to their environments they are quite weak in providing causal links for determining why the populations respond as they do. Even when comparative published data are available or samples of other populations brought for experimental testing the answers obtained can often only define that the groups do or don't differ, not why they differ. The experimentalist format is, of course, the basic strategy of biologists to answer causal relationships and since many of the human biological questions noted in the introduction to this paper were causal it seems that human biologists would do well to pursue a

INFANT WEIGHT AT 15 MONTHS
COMBINED SEXES

		Weight Means in Kilograms				Significance of Difference			
		LOW ALTITUDE		HIGH ALTITUDE		Rural-urban		Altitude	
		Rural x	Urban x	Rural x	Urban x	Low	High	Rural	Urban
INDIAN		1 10.58	2 10.69	3 8.23	4 9.27	1-2 ns	3-4 .001	1-3 .001	2-4 .001
MESTIZO	LOWER CLASS	5 9.79	6 10.70			5-6 .01			
	MIDDLE CLASS		7 11.22		8 9.77				7-8 .001

SIG. OF DIFF.	ETHNIC	1-5 .01	2-6 ns		4-8 .05					
	SOC-EC		6-7 ns							

Figure 14. A comparison of infant weights at 15 months sexes combined.

more experimentalist approach using carefully chosen natural populations as their experimental groups.

DISADVANTAGES.

As the experimentalist well knows the major disadvantages of this strategy is first the large amount of work involved to answer a single question. More importantly, many experiments fail. While it may be economically feasible to test hundreds of compounds for their toxicity on mice any attempt at mass screening studies using naturally occurring human populations is not feasible. The question to be tested should be backed by a rather strong hypothesis otherwise one may end the study with nothing to say. On the other hand, it appears that in human biology we more commonly create designs which can only reprove what is already known and we should be a little more adventurous in our hypothesizing.

MULTIPLE STRESS—MULTIPLE POPULATIONS

In 1964 Harrison again using the experimentalist strategy provided a design for studies which would definitively answer how altitude affected the genetic and development aspects of man's biology (Harrison, 1966). A condensation of this design and what the comparisons could provide are shown in Figure 15. The same design can with

---

1. HAN — A group living at high altitude and native to altitude, in the sense of having a long generational history of high altitude residence.
2. HAN↓ — A subdivision of group 1 (one) who live under identical conditions but who have migrated down to sea level.
3. LAN — A group living at low altitude with other conditions similar to those of groups 1 (one) and 2 (two).
4. LAN↑ — A subdivision of group 3 (three) which migrated up to the same altitude and conditions of group 1 (one).

With these populations intergroup comparisons would provide the following information.

HAN — LAN = total differences caused by altitude
HAN — LAN↑ = genetic features of altitude adaptation
LAN — LAN↑ = ontogenetic and physiological adaptations to altitude (acclimatization) plus detrimental effects of altitude
HAN — HAN↓ = ontogenetic and physiological adaptation (acclimatization) to downward migration plus detrimental effects of downward migration
LAN — HAN↓ = differences in response to sea level pressure produced by genetic differences

---

Figure 15. Abbreviated Harrison research design description showing deductive possibilities.

modifications provide similar answers for other causal questions. Thus, high and low caloric intake, presence and absence of a disease, etc. would be substituted for altitude and many of the basic answers we seek in human biology could be provided. The impossibility is, of course, the discovery of the human populations which fulfill the rather exacting requirements set forth. While this makes the certainty and depth of the conclusions which could be derived from this approach less satisfactory, I do not think that it makes it necessary to abandon entirely this quite promising strategy. In attempting to modify this design to our Andean research it appeared that some of the required basic populations could be found and while it was impossible to find groups in the different locations who lived under identical cultural and physical conditions, other than altitude, it was possible to take partial account of the other stresses by applying previous information on their probable effects. I am sure that similar groups might be found in relation to other causal questions and it may, therefore, be helpful to illustrate our rather limited effort to modify and utilize this basic strategy in our Andean program.

DESIGN AND POPULATION CHOICES.

Referring to the groups outlined in Figure 15 we already had rather complete information on a group which satisfied the requirements for population 1 (HAN). It did not seem possible to obtain any population which came close to satisfying the requirements for group 4 (LAN↑) since the few migrants who have arrived in the high Andes in recent generations are almost entirely part of the upper social classes and are primarily European in ethnic origin. However, the highland Quechua from nearly identical altitudes and life styles to the Nunoan (HAN) population had been migrating in large numbers to both the coastal and jungle faces of the Andes. This made possible at least a partial fulfillment of requirements for group 2 (HAN↓) and group 3 (LAN). In addition group 2 could be studied under two sets of environmental conditions. Several studies were conducted using the migrants on the jungle side (Garutto, 1973; Hoff, 1972) but a larger effort was made on the coastal side since there it was more nearly possible to fulfill the requirements for groups 2 and 3.

We found that on the coast of southern Peru in an area called the *Vallé de Tambo* nearly 50 percent of the population were migrants with about one-half of these coming from the high altitude area while the other half had moved from areas low enough not to produce altitude related physiological effects. The *Vallé* climate while not as cold as Nuñoa is quite cool for much of the year and the standard of living not dramatically higher than Nuñoa. While medical care and nutrition are somewhat better than in Nuñoa these differences could in part be compensated for by sample choice and segment analytical manipulation.

The data collected on the population in the *Vallé de Tambo* are not as complete as they were in the Nuñoa area. Instead research efforts were concentrated on a series of biological differences which had been found in Nuñoa and on those traits which we could presume might be modified by downward migration. Some of the results illustrate the power and limits of this research strategy.

SOME REPRESENTATIVE RESULTS.

An unresolved question from previous studies has been the potential effect of altitude on fertility. As shown in Figure 16 it was possible from these studies to collect samples which allowed a fairly detailed comparison of the effect of downward migration versus low altitude migration on fertility. Other data collected on these populations allowed at least a partial analysis of how other cultural factors in the various areas might affect fertility and in sum allowed us to consider the results strong supporting evidence that altitude does tend to reduce fertility in even native high altitude residents (Abelson et al., 1974).

| | Non-Migrant | | | Low Altitude Born Migrants | | | | | | High Altitude born Migrants | | | | | |
| | Tambo Valley | | | Before Migration | | | After Migration | | | Before Migration | | | After Migration | | |
Age Group	N	$\bar{X}$	S.D.	N	$\bar{X}$	S.D.	N	$\bar{X}$	S.D.	N	$\bar{X}$	S.D.	N	$\bar{X}$	S.D.
15-19.9	56	0.79	1.02	36	0.44	0.65	19	0.95	0.91	57	0.37	0.69	23	1.08	0.99
20-24.9	54	1.87	1.23	18	1.28	1.13	30	1.70	0.99	33	1.12	1.11	39	2.00	0.75
25-29.9	44	1.89	1.20	—			34	1.65	1.07	17	1.41	1.12	38	1.76	1.10
30-34.9	34	1.53	1.37	—			29	1.34	0.97	—			31	1.84	1.03
35-39.9	28	1.21	1.37	—			24	1.00	1.14	—			21	1.14	1.01
40-44.9	16	0.75	0.86	—			19	1.05	1.47	—			14	0.64	1.09
Total		8.04						7.69						8.46	

No births were reported for the 11 women non-migrants for the age group 45 to 49: 4 were reported for 13 migrants born at low altitude, and three for five migrants born at high altitude, after migration.

Figure 16. Births by five year age intervals, *Vallé de Tambo*.

In another study on the same groups we tested the hypothesis that downward migration increased the frequency of respiratory disease. The results based in part on an index of respiratory symptoms shown in Figure 17 appeared to support this hypothesis (Austin, 1973; Beall, 1972).

Several other studies were conducted but I will restrict discussion to one further study which may help show the potential of this strategy (Baker, in press). In our work on the Nuñoa (HAN) group we had been struck by the lack of hypertension and the apparent correlate of infrequent old age cardiovascular disease. Therefore, we examined the groups in the *Vallé de Tambo* in order to see how migration affected systemic blood pressure. As shown in Figures 18 and 19 the downward migration seemed to have little effect and although our samples are rather small for very firm conclusions it seems that early development at high altitude may confer some form of permanent immunity to hypertension.

As will be noted the examples given from this strategy are piecemeal and specific rather than population comprehensive in nature such as the energy flow example. This is related in major part to the smaller quantities of data we have available from the *Vallé de Tambo*.

Group	Mean Index No.
Sedente male	14.4
Sedente female	15.9
Low altitude migrant male	15.7
Low altitude migrant female	19.7
High altitude migrant male	21.1
High altitude migrant female	22.8

T-Tests for Significance Between Means

Group Comparison	Male	Female
SED-LA	ns	sig. .02
LAM-HAM	sig. .02	ns
SED-HAM	sig. .001	sig. .001

Figure 17. a. Group means for respiratory symptom index. b. T-tests for significance between means.

| | High Altitude Migrants | | Other Migrants | | Low Altitude Sedente | |
| | N = 54 | | N = 20 | | N = 15 | |
	Mean	S.D.	Mean	S.D.	Mean	S.D.
Age	33.1	8.2	36.5	10.3	36.3	9.6
Systolic	109.5	15.9	114.0	14.5	128.0	24.2
Diastolic	68.0	12.4	74.5	10.6	86.7	15.1

Figure 18. Comparison of adult female blood pressure for group in the *Vallé de Tambo,* Peru.

| | High Altitude Migrants | | Other Migrants | | Low Altitude Sedente | |
| | N = 42 | | N = 22 | | N = 16 | |
	Mean	S.D.	Mean	S.D.	Mean	S.D.
Age	35.9	8.1	40.7	13.9	40.6	11.9
Systolic	127.5	13.6	132.6	16.9	138.6	20.2
Diastolic	75.8	11.3	77.3	11.7	85.4	10.9

Figure 19. Comparison of adult male blood pressures for group in *Vallé de Tambo, Peru.*

Although we have more data than the results I have cited they are by no means as complete as the data on Nuñoa and considering also the fact that the *Vallé de Tambo* actually consists of three populations we are not in the position to develop the kinds of models possible for Nuñoa. This seems to me a pity in the sense that for this particular research strategy to develop its full potential of explanatory power it would be desirable to develop general population models which could be compared to each other.

ADVANTAGES.
    The advantages of this general research design are rather obvious if one could fulfill all of the sample requirements. Given that this is impossible it still appears that the potential of modified application are rather great. How good such strategies could be in answering basic human biological questions remains to be proved since I do

not think that anyone has as of yet fully explored the potential. The forced total population relocations which has occurred in parts of the world should offer such possibilities but so far they remain opportunities which have not been fully exploited. To cite but one example, Tibetans who left during the Chinese occupation of Tibet have resettled in almost every conceivable type of physical and cultural environment. It appears that comprehensive studies of the biology of these various groups could not help but give us profound insights into the nature of how populations with the same genetic system adapt themselves to a wide variety of environmental stresses.

DISADVANTAGES.
The full exploitation of this research design must be an enormously difficult process yet perhaps an essential one. To obtain information on how the groups respond in a single biological parameter such as fertility or nutrition or growth does not yield satisfactory answers. As noted in the beginning of this paper it then becomes too easy to attribute the differences to already known mechanisms without recognizing alternative or interacting causes. With such massive design and cost requirements the basic strategy may require a planning and financing beyond the kinds of organizations of present research groups.

Final Words

While normative descriptive research will always have a role in any science the study of population biology can and should move beyond this type of study. In this paper I have outlined four research strategies which, while producing normative data, also provide better insights into how and why populations biologically adapt to their environments. These are by no means a complete catalog of the available strategies although they cover elements of most strategies. A possible exception is the current use of mathematical and simulation modeling which at least varies somewhat in problem solving strategy from the data-collection-first approach. How many alternative strategies could be developed is impossible to predict but I feel that human biologists continue to pay far too little attention to what should be our first concern. How do we develop definitive answers to the many questions we ask.

A final note on the pragmatics of the strategies we have used may also be useful. Human population biologists have generally conducted their research as lone investigators with a few assistants. Even the larger research groups have generally been based in a single institution with no more than three or four principle investigators involved. Such an investigative mode will find the first and third strategies the most attractive since even one man with the right questions and populations can often provide significant answers to limited problems. Research strategy two is not beyond the resource capacity of a small group if they are willing to invest a number of years in the effort or if as with our efforts the pursuit of problems outlined in strategy one allows sufficient data collection so that one can move forward into some types of population modeling.

The problems associated with an attempt to make the multiple stress—multiple population strategy work are indeed formidable. The only hope I can see is that a large number of research groups would have to pool their resources and be willing to work together. It was hoped that the human adaptability project of the International Biological Program might provide such an administrative vehicle. I feel that it has provided some worthwhile answers and has moved in this direction. Nevertheless, it is clear that neither the scientist's attitude nor the financial resources have been appropriate to the testing of this last strategy.

With such difficulties it may be that the ambitious fourth strategy will not be given a test for a while. This may deprive us of an important tool since I strongly suspect the basic question of how and why human populations adapt as they do may be like a Chinese puzzle. The function of the component parts may not be apparent until the whole has been assembled.

Bibliography

Abelson, A. E., T. S. Baker and P. T. Baker
    1974   Altitude, migration and fertility in the Andes, Social Biology, Soc. Biol. *21* (1): 12-27.
Austin, D. M.
    1972   Some aspects of pulmonary function in Peruvian high altitude migrants to the lowlands and lowland natives (abstract). Am. J. Phys. Anthrop., *37* (2): 429.
Baker, P. T.
    1965   Multidisciplinary studies of human adaptability: Theoretical

justification and method. In: International Biological Programme: A Guide to the Human Adaptability Proposals. J. S. Weiner (ed.). Handbook IBP No. 1. ICSU Special Committee for the International Biological Programme.

1966a Human biological variation as an adaptive response to the environment. Eugenics Quart., *13:* 81-91.

1966b Micro-environment cold in a high altitude Peruvian population. In: Human Adaptability and its Methodology. H. Yoshimura and J. S. Weiner (eds.). Japan Society for the Promotion of Sciences, Tokyo, Japan.

1969 Human adaptation to high altitude. Science, *163:* 1149-1156.

A study of biological and social aspects of Andean migration. In: Man in Geographic and Cultural Transition: Proceedings of the Symposium on Human Migration of the Fifth IBP General Assembly. E. S. Lee (ed.). National Academy of Sciences, Washington, D.C. In press.

Baker, P. T., E. R. Buskirk, J. Kollias, and R. B. Mazess
1967 Temperature regulation at high altitude: Quechua Indians and U.S. whites during total body cold exposure. Hum. Biol., *39:* 155-169.

Baker, P. T. and J. S. Dutt
1972 Demographic variables as measures of biological adaptation: A case study of high altitude human populations. In: The Structure of Human Populations. G. A. Harrison and A. J. Boyce (eds.). The Clarendon Press, Oxford.

Beall, C. M.
1972 Respiratory diseases in migrant populations in a Peruvian coastal valley. M. A. Thesis. The Pennsylvania State University, University Park, Pennsylvania.

Frisancho, A. R.
1970 Developmental responses to high altitude hypoxia. Am. J. Phys. Anthrop., *32* (3): 401-408.

Frisancho, A. R. and P. T. Baker
1970 Altitude and growth: A study of the patterns of physical growth of a high altitude Peruvian Quechua population. Am. J. Phys. Anthrop. *32* (2): 279-292.

Garruto, R. M.
1973 Polycythemia as an adaptive response to chronic hypoxic stress. Ph.D. Thesis. The Pennsylvania State University, University Park, Pennsylvania.

Hanna, J. M.
   1968   Cold stress and microclimate in the Quechua Indians of southern Peru. Ph.D. Thesis. University of Arizona, Tucson, Arizona.

   1970   A comparison of laboratory and field studies of cold response. Am. J. Phys. Anthrop. *32* (2): 227-232.

   1971   Responses of Quechua Indians to coca ingestion during cold exposure. Am. J. Phys. Anthrop., *34* (3): 272-278.
Haas, J. D.
   1973   Infant growth and development at high altitude, Ph.D. Thesis. The Pennsylvania State University, University Park, Pennsylvania.
Harrison, G. A.
   1966   Human adaptability with reference to the IBP proposals for high altitude research. In: The Biology of Human Adaptability. P. T. Baker and J. S. Weiner (eds.). Oxford University Press, Oxford and New York.
Hoff, C. J.
   1972   Preliminary observations on altitudinal variations in the physical growth and development of Peruvian Quechua. Ph.D. Thesis. The Pennsylvania State University, University Park, Pennsylvania.
Larsen, R. M.
   1973   The thermal microenvironment of a highland Quechua population: Biocultural adjustment to the cold. M. A. Thesis. University of Wisconsin, Madison, Wisconsin.
Little, M. A.
   1969   Temperature regulation at high altitude: Quechua Indians and U.S. whites during foot exposure to cold water and cold air. Hum. Biol., *41* (4): 519-535.

   1970   Effects of alcohol and coca on foot temperatures of highland Peruvians during a localized cold exposure. Am. J. Phys. Anthrop., *32* (2):233-242.
Little, M. A., R. B. Thomas, R. B. Mazess, and P. T. Baker
   1971   Population differences and developmental changes in extremity temperature responses to cold among Andean Indians. Hum. Biol., *43* (1): 70-91.
MacMahon, B. and T. F. Pugh
   1970   Epidemiology: Principles and Methods. Little, Brown and Co., Boston.
Mazess, R. B. and R. Larsen
   1972   Responses of Andean highlanders to night cold. Inter. J. Biometeor., *16* (2): 181-192.

Mazess, R. B., E. Picon-Reategui, R. B. Thomas, and M. A. Little
  1968   Effects of alcohol and altitude on man during rest and work. Aerospace Med., *39* (4): 403-406.

_____

  1969   Oxygen intake and body temperature of basal and sleeping Andean natives at high altitude. Aerospace Med., *40* (1): 6-9.
Thomas, R. B.
  1973   Human adaptation to a high Andean energy flow system. Occasional Papers in Anthropology No. 7, Department of Anthropology, The Pennsylvania State University, University Park, Pennsylvania.
Weitz, C. A.
  1969   Morphological factors affecting responses to total body cooling among three human populations tested at high altitude. M. A. Thesis. The Pennsylvania State University, University Park, Pennsylvania.

11. The Quantitative Genetics Of Fingerprints

J. W. Froehlich

Introduction

The genetic study of continuous traits in man is fraught with difficulties. Lacking discernible discrete categories, the variables of morphology and psychology are not appropriate for Mendelian analysis. Such characters are thought to have a polygenic basis and the techniques of biometrical genetics have been designed to study them. But these techniques of heritability estimation have been principally developed by applied geneticists and they aim at the practical

NOTE: This work is part of a research project by the Peabody Museum and Department of Anthropology, Harvard University, supported by Grant No. Gm 13482 of the National Institute of General Medical Sciences, U. S. Public Health Service. It is also part of the Human Adaptability section of the International Biological Program. Computational support was generously provided by the Milton Fund and the Hooton Fund of Harvard University. The work was conducted with the permission and kind assistance of the Administrations of the British Solomon Islands Protectorate and the Territory of Papua and New Guinea, Commonwealth of Australia. The tedium of ridge counting was unwaveringly performed by P. Froehlich, R. Grayson, and C. Hitt. The text profited from the comments of A.

assessment of relative amounts of heritable and environmental variation for use in animal and plant breeding (Mather and Jinks, 1971). Biometrical methods do not provide information regarding the number, location and frequency of specific genes, and, hence, *preclude* a detailed understanding of evolutionary change in many of the most important aspects of continuous human variation (Thoday, 1967). A lack of knowledge of specific genes also prevents an accurate comparison of populations on the basis of continuous variables; for various combinations of *different* polygenes can theoretically produce *identical* phenotypes.

In addition, Howells (1953) has pointed out that the traditional measurements of continuous human variation are not necessarily a direct representation of its hereditary basis. It is possible, therefore, that heritability estimates based on these measurements do not give an accurate reflection of the relative amounts of genetic and environmental control over the underlying continuous human variables. If this is so, then the traditional measurements of anthropology are not wholly adequate for genetic comparisons of human populations. Howells suggested factor analysis as a means of transforming the original measurements into more genetically specific characters. He found that heritability estimates based on these new factor traits were more consistent and suggested more genetic validity than those from direct measurements. Recently, Howells (1970) successfully used such factor measurements in an analysis of anthropometric groupings among Pacific islanders.

The transformation of the original measurements is similar to the method of somatic character analysis in applied genetics (Mather and Jinks, 1970). This method assumes that subcharacters of continuous variables are under separate genetic control and that subdivision will lead to a simpler genetic analysis. Mather and Jinks warned, however, that such a divide and conquer strategem would not necessarily simplify the analysis. After the subdivision of continuous traits, we

Damon and W. W. Howells and from numerous discussions with R. W. Thorington, Jr. The text was completed while the author was supported by a Postdoctoral Fellowship from the Smithsonian Institution. Special gratitude is reserved for the patient subjects, who provided their hand prints and family histories to make this study possible.

must still deal with complex systems of genes affecting each sub-division, and the extent to which these systems are still interlocked is unknown.

The genetic comparison of human populations using continuous variables is also hampered by an uncertainty as to the general applicability of heritability estimates from within one population to other populations (Thoday, 1969). The relative importance of environmental causes of variation may vary among populations, so that a genetically determined trait in one population may not be equivalent to an environmentally produced phenocopy in another group. Thoday cited examples of plant populations where the same apparent difference can sometimes have purely genetic causes and at other times have major environmental influences. The only way to distinguish these is by transplant experiments, which have their drawbacks in human studies. Even with similar heritability estimates from all groups compared, there is still no certainty of equivalent genetic causes, since nutritional and behavioral patterns can themselves be socially inherited and included in the hereditary component of the variance.

The uncertainty of genetic equivalence between populations is less a problem with finger print comparisons than it is with some other continuous human variables. Finger prints have the advantage that they are completely formed by the fourth fetal month, and so are not susceptible to the environmental and social influences which affect many physical and behavioral traits. Nevertheless, it is still conceivable that purely environmental factors, such as the consumption of a drug or nutrient, may influence finger print ontogeny in a consistent and nonheritable manner, thereby producing dissimilar group heritability estimates and non-genetic population differences. Various combinations and frequencies of the same genes may also interact in different ways with environmental variables to produce different degrees of genetic control in human populations and confound their comparison.

As a further complication, Howells (1966) has proposed that inflated heritability estimates for body measurements may be the result of increased interfamilial variances, due to a lack of homogeneity in the sampled population. Families tend to share many genes and provide a common environment for developing offspring; consequently the intrafamilial variance is little affected by the ethnic heterogeneity of large conglomerate populations. Since heritability estimates usually involve the ratio of the among (inter-) to within (intra-) family variances, the degree of heterogeneity in the reference population has a direct effect on the estimated heritabilities. It therefore seems likely that the heritability estimates for finger prints will vary with respect to population, even though the time of environmental exposure is brief.

An Introduction to Finger Print Methods

In order to discuss the genetics of finger prints, it is first necessary to acquaint the reader with the terminology and rudiments of dermatoglyphic analysis. The dermal ridges on the volar surfaces of the hands and feet form patterns by recurring back upon themselves. Each time this occurs, a triangular landmark, or triradius, is formed. Stated the other way around, a triradius is a point defined by the convergence of three convex ridge systems. The complexity of dermal ridge configurations can therefore be quantified by counting the triradii. For the digital patterns this is known as the pattern intensity index.

The presence of zero, one, or two triradii on a digital pad is associated with the three basic pattern types—the arch, loop, and whorl. These pattern categories represent the modes of a continuous distribution, along which transitional patterns have been variously subdivided and categorized. The present analysis used an ordinal scale of zero to five (namely arches, loops, double loops, whorled loops, true whorls, and complex patterns with more than two triradii). The index finger was additionally subdivided into radial and ulnar loops, depending on which side of the hand the loop opens. These basic pattern types are schematically illustrated in Figure 1; they were selected after an analysis of more detailed category frequencies in the populations under study, with an effort to eliminate insignificant rare events and facilitate population comparisons.

The ridge count is an enumeration of all the ridges crossed by a line drawn from the triradius to the center of the pattern. It is defined as radial or ulnar, depending on the direction this line takes from the pattern's center. When two triradii were present, both counts were made and recorded by the conventions described in Holt (1968). In all statistical analyses, the largest of these two counts was used as a measure of pattern size.

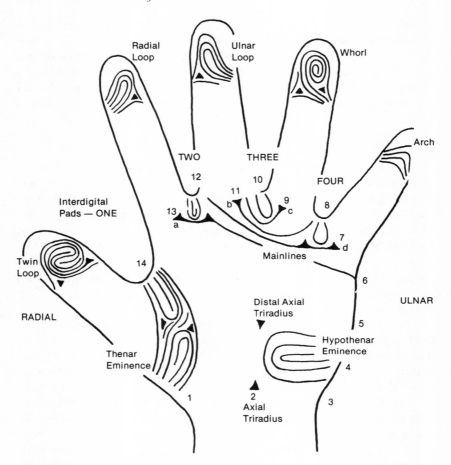

Figure 1. A schematic drawing of the principal dermal ridge systems on the human hand, showing the numbered zones for mainline terminations. The mainlines shown have a score of 6, 8, 10, 12.

On the palms, the mainlines are defined as the proximal radiants from the four triradii located below the four ulnar digits. From radial to ulnar, these triradii are labeled a, b, c, and d. The mainlines, labeled A, B, C, and D, are traced to their terminations in a particular landmark or along the border of the hand, following the conventions described by Cummins and Midlo, (1961). The areas of termination are scored as shown in *Figure 1*. These scores describe the relative transversality of the palmar ridges. It should be noted that these numbers deviate slightly from convention, wherein areas 5 and 6 are coded as 5' and 5" and all the higher categories are reduced by one. The reason for this change is the obvious difficulty of coding five prime on a computer card. It has always been necessary in the past to make this change when calculating the mainline index. This index is a sum of the A and D mainline scores, after reducing D to the same scale as A. As with the digital patterns, the scores of mainlines B and C were consolidated, while D was recoded from 8-13 to 1-8 for inclusion in the mainline index.

The pattern categories for the hypothenar, thenar, and interdigital pads of the palm *(Figure 1)* followed an ordinal scale similar to that of the fingers. For the hypothenar, there were five categories (absent, ulnar loop, radial and carpal loops, double loops and whorls, and complex patterns). The thenar was similar, with six classes and the addition of vestigial patterns, which are sharply angled ridges lacking any recurvature or triradii, but with the superficial appearance of patterning. The interdigital patterns were classed as absent, simple, and complex (i.e. with an extra or accessory triradius).

The presence of an extra triradius at the center of the palm is related to certain patterns on the hypothenar and is called the distal axial triradius. One way of measuring its position is by an angle subtended by the a and d triradii. Angle *atd* is also used to measure the proximal axial triradius, at the base of the palm. In the present analysis both are used. The proximal angle is a measure of position for the axial triradius alone, while the maximal *atd* angle measures the distal axial triradius, when it is present, and therefore involves both the position of the axial landmark and its interaction with hypothenar patterning. A second variable, the relative ad/t height was used to measure the position of the axial triradius. A linear measurement was made from the axial triradius to a line connecting the a and d triradii, perpendicular to the latter and expressed as a ratio of the total hand length. This new measure of the axial triradius is unaffected by the breadth of the hand and the distance between the a and d triradii, as is the *atd* angle. For this reason, the ad/t height is less affected by age differences.

This description of methods is not intended to be comprehensive, but only to give a rough idea of definitions and analysis procedures. For general descriptions of dermatologlyphic analysis the reader may consult Cummins and Midlo (1961) and Holt (1968). For more specific details of methods used here see Froehlich (1973).

The Genetics of Human Finger Prints —
Review and Comment

QUALITATIVE STUDIES

As a result of the multifactorial nature of finger prints and the large intragroup variation they exhibit, attempts to ascertain the exact mode of inheritance of specific dermatoglyphic patterns have been inconclusive and often mutually inconsistent. Nevertheless, qualitative pedigree studies have demonstrated a high degree of inheritance for finger prints, even though their failings have shown a lack of single gene processes. The outset of this investigation harks back to Galton (1892), who found a significant pattern resemblance between siblings compared to unrelated pairs. Similarly, Parsi and Di Bacco (1968) noted a much higher concordance of pattern type between monozygotic twins than in dizygotics. However, while the finger patterns of identical twins are very similar, they are never identical (Holt, 1961).

For the palm, Weninger (1965b) studied the incidence of thenar and hypothenar patterns in the parents and children of 290 families. By grouping these families according to which parents had patterns and how many, she found a corresponding progression of higher incidence among the children. Kumbnani (1968) reached similar conclusions for hypothenar patterns, finding a pattern incidence of 17.7%, 43.9%, and 57.7% in three sets of children, where neither parent had patterns, one had patterning, or both had patterns, respectively. While these studies show a strong hereditary component, they had many exceptions, such as children with complex patterns where both parents had none; Weninger concluded that these heritable traits could not be explained by single-gene inheritance. For a more detailed survey of this literature, see Holt (1968).

As a possible exception to the lack of single gene inheritance, Bansal and Rife (1962) found strong evidence for a simple dominant gene with 88% penetrance in the determination of accessory triradii in the second and fourth interdigital areas of 53 Indian families. Weninger (1965a) noted that her experience would place this penetrance percentage somewhat lower; but at whatever level it occurs, incomplete penetrance still indicates a greater degree of genetic complexity. Weninger concluded that there was no decisive evidence of a particular mode of inheritance for any dermatoglyphic pattern, and that all we know from such studies is, "just the fact that they are inherited" (1965a, p. 991). With the possible exception of a major gene effect on the interdigital pads, no genes have been identified or counted; indeed qualitative studies have not accurately measured the relative amount of hereditary control.

THE QUANTITATIVE GENETICS OF DIGITAL RIDGE COUNTS

For the estimation of the hereditary and environmental components of phenotypic variance, quantitative approaches to dermatoglyphic inheritance have been more successful than qualitative studies. The foundation for the study of biometrical genetics is a paper by R. A. Fisher (1918). On the basis of Mendelian inheritance, Fisher demonstrated a relationship between the hypothesis of multifactorial inheritance of morphological traits and the correlations found between relatives. When variation is continuous in a totally inherited trait with no dominance and no assortative mating, he proved that the regression of one relative on another was equal to the proportion of genes in common by descent (Holt, 1968). Since the mutual regressions of relatives are theoretically the same, the correlation coefficients are equivalent to the regressions. In the case of siblings, this is obvious, since it does not matter which enters the correlation table first. The correlation coefficient and the degree of genetic relationship are therefore equivalent when a number of coequal, additive genes explain the total variation of a trait. Stated the other way around, this means that a correlation of .5 between sibs or between parents and offspring is an indication that the trait in question is totally inherited in a polygenic manner with no dominance and no significant association between parents. Dominance will lower the correlations (about twice as much for parent-child pairs as for sibs) and assortative mating will increase them (Holt, 1968). Armed with Fisher's theoretical support, applied geneticists have used familial correlations extensively to measure the amount of hereditary variation subject to breeding manipulation (Mather and Jinks, 1971), and more generally to study the hereditary basis of complex characters.

For several decades, these methods have been applied to the investigation of finger ridge counts. Most of the techniques of ridge counting were defined by Bonnevie (1924), who found a correlation of .60 ± .13 between 30 pairs of brothers and sisters for a "quantitative value" based on the sum of average finger ridge counts. These counts are recoded on an ordinal scale of 1-10, with all actual values over 20 being included in the last category. With 16 pairs of fraternal twins, she obtained a correlation of .54 ± .08, and for 15 identical twins, .92 ± .04. Later, Newman (1930) used a similar summed ridge count, coded on a scale of 1-17, to find a correlation of .95 ± .01 between 50 monozygotic twins and .46 ± .08 for 50 dizygotics. These values do not differ significantly from the expected values of .5 for sibs and 1.0 for identical twins. They indicate that the genetic component of ridge counts is very large and follows a polygenic additive model.

By far the most extensive work on ridge count inheritance has been by Holt (1968), who studied various pairs of relatives and used the additional theories of Penrose (1949) to define more accurately the mode of inheritance for this trait. Penrose showed that the expected correlation between the average parental value for a continuous trait and the offspring is .71, based on the fact that the child has all of his genes from both parents but each parent shares only half of the child's genes.

When there is no dominance, the theoretical regression of offspring on mid-parents is 1.0 and linear. Deviations from linearity are an indication of dominance. With large British samples, Holt (1956, 57) studied the relationship between parent-child and sib pair correlations for the total maximum ridge count (i.e. the largest count summed over ten fingers) and tested these for dominance. In addition to using males and females separately, she combined the sexes by adding to female scores the difference between means to the nearest whole number.

The results of Holt's studies are reproduced in Table 1. The estimated kinship correlations are in nearly perfect agreement with expectations, indicating strong hereditary determination by non-dominant additive genes for the total ridge count. The correlation between parents is not significant, showing that mating is random for this trait (Holt, 1961). The absence of dominance was also demonstrated by the midparent-child values of .64 ± .05 and .71 ± .04 for males and females, respectively. In addition, the regressions of both sexes on midparents did not significantly deviate from linearity or a value of 1.0 (Holt, 1956). Holt (1968) concluded that only 5% of the variability was environmental (from the twin-twin correlation) and this was from *in utero* influences. The remainder of the variability was due to a number of coequal additive genes.

While these results have been frequently cited as the best example of agreement between the expected and observed results for an additive polygenic trait (McKusick, 1969; Cavalli-Sforza and Bodmer, 1971), it has also been contended that the results are too perfect. Weninger (1964) argued that the individual fingers show variation independent of the total count. Their means and distributions vary, as do the correlations between fingers. The differences between the fingers of individuals also range from large to small. All of these characteristics indicated to Weninger that the individual fingers showed environmental effects not shared by the sum; in other words, the parts were not equal to the whole. She concluded that there was no one set of polygenes controlling ridge counts.

Holt (1968) also noted independent variations in the finger ridge counts, but she argued that there is a general quantitative tendency expressed in the total count which is masked in the fingers by random fluctuation. These variations were shown by the calculations of correlations between sibs for individual fingers. The sib-sib correlations are shown in Table 2, together with those of Parsi and Di Bacco (1968) for dizygotic twins. The similarity between these two studies (i.e. the low values for the thumb and high values for middle and ring

TABLE 1

THE CORRELATIONS BETWEEN PAIRS OF RELATIVES FOR THE TOTAL MAXIMUM DIGITAL RIDGE COUNT, WITH FISHER'S EXPECTED VALUES (HOLT, 1968).

Relationship	Number of Pairs	Estimated Correlation	Expected Correlation
Mother-child	405	$0.48 \pm .04$	0.50
Father-child	405	$0.49 \pm .04$	0.50
Sib-sib	642	$0.50 \pm .04$	0.50
Fraternal twins	92	$0.49 \pm .08$	0.50
Monozygotic twins	80	$0.95 \pm .01$	1.00
Parent-parent	200	$0.05 \pm .07$	0.00

TABLE 2

THE CORRELATIONS BETWEEN SIBLINGS FOR THE MAXIMUM
RIDGE COUNTS OF INDIVIDUAL FINGERS
(THE EXPECTATION IN ALL CASES IS 0.50).

Digit	British Siblings[1] (Right + Left)	Italian Dizygotic Twins[2] Right	Left
Thumb	.31	.26	.12
Index	.42	.38	.21
Middle	.46	.55	.45
Ring	.47	.53	.54
Little	.41	.44	.33
Number of Pairs	169	50	50

[1]Holt, 1968.
[2]Parsi and Di Bacco, 1968.

fingers) indicates that perhaps more is involved than random fluctuations. Holt appears to draw a distinction between maternal environmental effects, which produce 5% of the variation in the total count,
and random processes which act as noise in the determination of
inheritance for the individual ridge counts. This erroneous distinction probably stems from the use of the term "environmental variance" (Falconer, 1960) to refer to all nonheritable variation. In
reality, the non-heritable variation is likely to be a composite of the
indeterminacy of genotypic recombination (Mayr, 1963), developmental chance fluctuations, environmental influences, and even observer bias and measurement errors. Mather and Jinks (1971, p. 39)
noted that a portion of non-heritable variation "appears to spring
from chance internal upsets of development rather than from differences in the environment external to the organism."

Regarding the random fluctuations to which Holt attributes the
presumably inaccurate heritability estimates of the fingers, it might be
asked why chance processes should affect the heritability of individual
finger ridge counts and not the sum of those ridge counts? Perhaps
these random fluctuations are a basic part of the developmental
system and not simply noise in the estimation of heritability. A related question is, what accounts for the individual differences be-

tween twins and other close relatives when the trait is so highly heritable? Holt (1968) cited the fact that identical twins "*sometimes* have patterns strikingly similar in type and size on different fingers" (p. 60, italics mine) as evidence for her almost completely heritable quantitative tendency in the total count. But *sometimes* the opposite is true as well.

Variable conditions in the same womb at the same time do not seem sufficient to explain these non-genetic variations. Indeed the complex and indirect relationships between polygenes and the phenotype might lead to an expectation of chance ontogenetic variations and heritability estimates below 100%.

I would argue that her explanation should be the other way around. The random fluctuations are the major component of the non-heritable variance and the act of summing the individual ridge counts artificially smooths these out. As Weninger (1964) noted, the total ridge count is a coarse measurement; it conceals much. Parsi and Di Bacco (1968) called it an "artificial cumulative value, with a reduced random variability" (p. 344). Therefore, the kinship correlations for the individual fingers are probably a more accurate measure of relative genetic control over ridge count variation.

The intraclass correlation coefficient can be estimated from a ratio of the variance among sibships to the variance within sibships. The summing of several traits may affect one of these variances more than the other and change the correlation coefficient. If summing reduces the variance within sibships while leaving the among sibship variance unchanged, then the correlation will be elevated. Likewise, increased heterogeneity of the population (among sibship variance) will also increase the correlation (Howells, 1966). By definition, sibships share many genes by common descent. Many of their differences are *non-genetic*. In a trait like finger prints with only a brief exposure to the environment before it is fixed, most of this non-genetic variance is probably random. By analogy to the central limit theorem, adding several ridge counts which fluctuate randomly will normalize or smooth the resulting sum, thereby cancelling out some of the non-heritable random variance. On the other hand, the among sibship variance is that of the general population. The differences are more *genetic* and therefore probably less affected by the summing of individual traits.

In this argument over which set of data gives more accurate in-

formation on heritability, I would contend that the genetic assessments of the individual fingers are closer to reality. The total count
gives an inflated estimate due to a statistical artifact, rather than a
"general quantitative tendency." This is not to say that finger prints
are not highly heritable, nor to disagree with Holt's conclusions regarding additivity and the lack of dominance; but only to assert that
very little in biology is perfect. I would conclude that averages of the
individual finger correlations might provide a useful estimate of the
relative amount of genetic determination in the "general quantitative
tendency." These averages must be determined by using Fisher's
z-transformation, for the distribution of correlation coefficients is
not normal. For Holt's sib data this average correlation is .42. With
the dizygotic twins of Parsi and Di Bacco the figure is .41, which is
remarkably close. According to these estimates and arguments, the
heritability of ridge counts would be somewhere in the range of 80%
to 85%, rather than close to 100%.

QUANTITATIVE GENETIC APPROACHES TO
OTHER FINGER PRINT TRAITS

In recent years, several other dermatoglyphic traits have been
genetically analyzed by biometrical methods. These data are summarized in Table 3. Mukherjee (1966) studied the pattern intensity
indices on the fingers and palms of 63 Bengali Brahman families.
The pattern intensity of the palm was defined as the total number of
accessory triradii associated with patterns. The correlations for digital
pattern intensities of parent-child (.40 ± .04) and sib-sib pairs (.42 ±
.05) were close, indicating about 80% heritability and no dominance.
For the palms, however, the figures were .19 ± .05 and .31 ± .06,
respectively. While indicating moderately high heritability, they also
showed some evidence of dominance in the lower parent-child correlation. It should be noted, however, that Mukherjee used ordinary
product-moment correlation methods rather than specialized intraclass techniques. Since each parent is entered in the table several
times, once with each child, the pairs are not strictly independent
and the estimates of standard error may be distorted (Holt, 1956).
Therefore, the difference between parent-child and sib-sib correlations for palmar intensity may be due to sampling error rather than
dominance.

Loesch (1971) also calculated kinship correlations for digital and

TABLE 3

A SURVEY OF PUBLISHED KINSHIP CORRELATIONS FOR DERMATOGLYPHIC CHARACTERS. EXCEPT WHERE NOTED THESE CORRELATIONS ARE FOR SIB-SIB PAIRS.

Author	Population	N[1]	Pattern Intensity Fingers	Pattern Intensity Palms	Mainline Index	A-d Ridge Count	Interdig. Count	Interdig. Three Pattern	Interdig. Four Pattern	Thenar Pattern	Hypothenar Pattern	Maximum atd Angle
Mukherjee (1966)	Bengali Brahman	312	.42	.31								
Loesch (1971)	Polish	1342	.33	.31				.25	.18	.16	.25	
Barnicot, et al. (1972)	Hadza of Tanzania	230	.31	.04								
Keiter (1950)	German	246	.40[3]								.26[2]	.19
Pons (1959)	Spanish	284			.48							
Glanville (1965a)	Cleveland White	351				.44						
Glanville (1965b)	Cleveland White	412					.41[4]					
Penrose (1954)	British	623										.37
Wyslouch (1964)	Polish	61										.31[5]

[1]Refers to the number of pairs.
[2]Radial loops only.
[3]Mother-child pairs; index different but close.
[4]Female siblings only.
[5]Fraternal twins.

palmar pattern intensities in 201 rural Polish families. For the palms of parents and children she obtained a correlation of .24, and for sib-sib pairs it was .31. These values are close and show little evidence of dominance. Loesch did not calculate standard errors because of their inaccuracy when using product-moment correlations. For the fingers, the parent-child and sib-sib correlations of .33 and .33, respectively, were lower but close to Mukherjee's results. Barnicot et al. (1972) found a similar value of .31 for the sib-sib correlation of finger pattern intensity; but for the palmar intensity index their sib-sib correlation was virtually zero. They suggested sampling errors and the possible inclusion of half-sibs for the latter low value. Alternatively, the palmar intensity index is such a composite of several independent characters that it may be inappropriate to treat as a single trait. Finally, for a complexity index similar to pattern intensity of the fingers, Keiter (1950) found correlations of .40 for mother-child and .57 for father-child pairs. The figure of .67 for midparent-child indicated a lack of dominance. These examples show that quantitative genetic techniques can be usefully applied to ordinal dermatoglyphic variables; they demonstrate a high degree of heritability for patterns as well as ridge counts.

Another ordinal trait with impressive heritability estimates is the mainline index of the palms. Pons (1959) studied 113 sib-ships from Spain and found parent-child and sib-sib correlations of .52 and .48, respectively. A small sample of 29 monozygotic twins showed a correlation of .95 ± .02. Assortative mating was discounted by a parent correlation of .001. In addition, a lack of dominance was demonstrated by a midparent-offspring value of .72 ± .05 and a regression of child on midparent that was not significantly deviant from linearity (P>.20). Therefore, a major portion of the variation of this trait is also accounted for by a number of additive polygenes. This conclusion was corroborated in a study of mainline A by Glanville (1965a). He quantified the transversality of this character by counting the ridges between the d triradius and line A at a fixed distance from the a triradius. The A-d ridge count measures both the position of line A and the density of ridges. In 115 Cleveland White families, he calculated a parent-child correlation of .48 ± .03 and for sib-sib pairs, .44 ± .04. Similarly, mother-father pairs and monozygotic twins showed values of .06 ± .09 and .94 ± .02.

For other traits on the palms, heritability has been demonstrated by these techniques, but not always at such high levels. Glanville

(1965b) quantified the patterning of the interdigital pads by counting ridges. He summed these, with adjustment to equate means, and derived correlations of .41 ± .08 and .38 ± .07 for female sib and mother-daughter pairs. Similar values were obtained in male comparisons. Monozygotic twins showed .88 ± .04, while parent-parent correlations were not significant at .10 ± .09. Loesch (1971) tabulated these traits by a more qualitative technique and found correlations of .27 and .25 in parent-child and sib-sib comparisons for interdigital III. These values were .13 and .18, respectively, for interdigital IV. Similarly, she studied thenar patterning and found correlations of .14 and .16; for hypothenar patterning, she found .25 and .25, respectively.

Another way of measuring the patterning of the hypothenar area is by the total *atd* angle (i.e. the sum of the maximum angles in both hands). Penrose (1954) corrected this trait for age and sex and found a correlation of .63 ± .09 for 48 monozygotic twin pairs. Correlations of .37 ± .04 for sibs and .29 ± .04 for parent-child pairs led him to suggest dominance for the depression of the latter. This difference is not significant, however, by a t-test (p > .15) using a z-transformation (my calculation). No significant dominance was found by Wyslouch (1964) in 107 Polish families. Her figures for mother-child and fraternal twin pairs were .39 and .31. For identical twins she found .89. In the Hadza of Tanzania, Barnicot, et al. (1972) obtained a sib-sib correlation of .19 for the total maximum *atd* angle, suggesting a somewhat lower heritability than in the above two studies. Their value of .21 for parent-child pairs was close to the sib-sib correlation and suggested no dominance. The lower kinship correlations for this trait in the Hadza may reflect the association between the maximal *atd* angle and hypothenar patterning, with different population frequencies in the latter.

While many of these palmar dermatoglyphic characters show lower heritability estimates than the finger ridge counts, they also show little evidence for dominance by the similarity between parent-child and sib-sib correlations. It would seem, in conclusion, that virtually every trait used in dermatoglyphics has a moderate to high level of genetic determination.

NON-HERITABLE FACTORS IN FINGER PRINT ONTOGENY

The fact that some traits show less than 50% heritable variation makes it necessary to define further the non-heritable influences on the variance of dermatoglyphics. Since the traits are established early in ontogeny, what are the sources of the "environmental variation?" Consistent maternal influences do not offer much of an explanation. Monozygotic twins can be different, while dizygotic twins do not show any greater similarity than other siblings. In addition, there is no greater resemblance between offspring and mothers than between offspring and fathers. Therefore, there appears to be no maternal cytoplasmic effect. Whatever maternal effect there is, it appears to be largely random.

Stern (1960) discussed some of these processes. Maternal factors include the connection of the placenta and the chemical agents allowed to cross it, the amount of activity, the presence of a twin, and the position of the fetus. Biswas (1968) felt that the position and pressure placed on the fetal fist might turn the fingers toward the radial side and produce a preponderance of ulnar loops. However, many of the non-heritable factors determining finger print characters are probably intrinsic to the embryo itself.

As a useful concept Stern has defined the "internal environment" as differences in the milieu of the growing structures within an organism. A related concept is Keiter's (1960) "phenogenetic milieu." Stern cited as an example the fact that some dermal features are apparently associated with the arrangement and ramifications of digital nerve fibers as they grow out from the spinal cord into the finger rudiments. The details of this growth and branching are sufficiently flexible to be affected by non-genetic influences, somewhat like the effects of rocks and trees in the rapid formation of a desert stream (Stern, 1960). The differences in nerve growth appear in part to be due to differences in the environment of the growing structure itself. Some of these differences in growing structure may be the finger pattern variations themselves, for the dermal papillae, which house nerve endings, develop into the spaces between epidermal ridges during the seventh month (Hale, 1952; Walker, 1954), long after the patterns are established.

As evidence for the effects of developmental chance and internal environment, Stern discussed bilateral asymmetries of finger prints. Since all cells are assumed to have the same genes, homologous parts of the same individual should be genetically identical. He concluded that bilateral differences are the result of non-heritable factors. Mather and Jinks (1971) apparently share this view, for they stated

It [non-heritable variance] may also, especially where variation is between repetitive parts of the same individual, reflect accidents and chances of development. (pp. 57-58)

The data on the ontogeny of finger print patterns provide useful information for the understanding of the non-genetic influences. These data have recently been reviewed and interpreted by Mulvihill and Smith (1969). The patterns are largely determined by the mechanical factors in the growth and topography of the fetal hand between 13 and 19 weeks. The parallel ridges are alligned at right angles to the plane of surface growth stress. The curvilinear patterns are influenced by the height and form (asymmetry) of the fetal pads, which are mound shaped clusters of tissue beneath the epidermis. These fetal pads develop between 6 and 9 weeks and subside thereafter. Mulvihill emphasized the indirect genetic determination of finger prints. A long chain of developmental pathways in polygenic traits has been discussed by Mather and Jinks (1971). They noted,

The complexity of relations between gene and character is thus attributable to the multiplicity of stages between initial action and final expression. (p. 36)

This aspect of polygenic inheritance can lead to "an ill regulated system of development, so poorly buffered against external hazard as to be pushed around . . ." (Mather, 1954, p. 22). Accidents and chance events during development may therefore be a major contributing factor to the large non-heritable components of some dermatoglyphic characters. The question of heritability of finger prints is probably not so much a question of nature versus nurture as it is of the relative degree of canalization exhibited by the trait. Some finger print characters appear to be more developmentally flexible and more subject to chance variations than others.

THE GENERALITY OF HERITABILITY ESTIMATES AMONG POPULATIONS
    With a rudimentary understanding of the non-genetic factors and data on most dermatoglyphic characters showing at least moderate amounts of genetic determination, it must be asked whether this knowledge is applicable to all populations of man. Most of the kinship correlation estimations cited above are based on no more than two samples. With the exception of the pattern intensity assessments of Bengalis (Mukherjee, 1966) and the Hadza (Barnicot et al., 1972),

all of these samples are of European white populations. For anthropometric variables, Vandenberg (1962) found a close agreement in heritability estimates between six different populations. As with the finger print data, all were "western European" populations, however. Regarding the use of these results in unrelated populations, Thoday (1969) has asserted,

> But even if they [heritabilities] are high, as with fingerprint ridge counts, we are already in difficulties with population comparisons, for *there is no warrant for equating within group heritabilities and between group heritabilities.* (p. 5, italics his).

The relevance of this caution by Thoday to finger print studies can be examined in the several populations whose heritability of total ridge count has been estimated. These data are compared in Table 4. All seven of these populations show a high degree of heritability, but

TABLE 4

A COMPARISON OF SIB-SIB CORRELATIONS FOR
THE TOTAL MAXIMUM RIDGE COUNT IN SEVERAL POPULATIONS.

Author	Population	Number of Pairs	Sib-sib r
Bonnevie (1924)	Norwegian	30	.60[1] ± .12
Newman (1930)	Chicago White	50[2]	.46[1] ± .08
Lamy, et al. (1957)	French	185	.46 ± .08
Holt (1957)	British (mixed)	642	.50[3] ± .04
Parsi and Di Bacco (1968)	Italian	50[2]	.53 ± .10[4]
Hunt and Mavalwala (1964)	Yapese	40	.40 ± .13
Loesch (1971)	Polish (rural)	1342	.38[3] ± .03

[1]"Quantitative value."
[2]Dizygotic twins.
[3]Significantly different at .01 level.
[4]My calculation of standard error.

there is a clear dichotomy between the small isolated populations and the broad cosmopolitan samples. For the comparison between Holt's (1957) British sample and Loesch's (1971) rural Polish sample, this difference is significant using Fisher's z-transformation (P < .01). Other comparisons, though of similar dimensions, are not significant because of much smaller sample sizes. The Yapese sample, while small, is in accord with the Polish heritability estimate. Loesch explained this difference by the fact that her sample was less heterogeneous, coming from isolated villages; while Holt's (1956) broad sample of 100 families included 10 Jewish and 21 Welsh. Less variability in the Polish sample was demonstrated by a significant difference in the standard deviations of the two populations (Loesch, 1971).

In a comparison of anthropometric heritability estimates for a religious isolate with those of previous studies, Howells (1966) also ascribed the higher correlations than expected in the latter to ethnic heterogeneity and environmental differences between families in broad samples. His results showed no correlations over .50, in contrast to the other studies.

From both of these examples, it may be concluded that heterogeneity acts to increase the among sibship variance while leaving the within sibship variance essentially unchanged. This will result in inflated correlation coefficients and unrealistic heritability estimates. If anything, the genes shared by descent from inbreeding would reduce the variability within sib pairs in the small isolated populations. The reduced within sibship variance in inbred groups might also cause an overestimate of heritability. In man, where inbreeding is usually not great, this probably is not as important a factor as the heterogeneity of cosmopolitan populations. The lower values of Loesch (1971) and Hunt and Mavalwala (1964) for smaller, more homogeneous populations, may therefore represent more valid estimates of ridge count heritabilities around 80%, in accord with previous arguments. A second conclusion to be drawn from these comparisons supports Thoday; for it does not seem safe to equate heritability estimates between unrelated populations.

The Biometrical Genetics of Melanesian Finger Prints

SUBJECTS AND METHODS

Since there are questions regarding the validity and mutual consistency of past heritability studies and serious doubts about the general applicability of their results to other populations, a thorough quantitative analysis of genetic determination was undertaken on finger print samples from the Solomon Islands. These data were collected in 1968 and 1970 by Muriel Howells and myself as part of two biomedical expeditions, organized and directed by A. Damon and W. W. Howells. The Solomons are a double chain of volcanic islands running for some 1500 miles in a southeast direction about 600 miles east of New Guinea. Bougainville is one of the northern-most and largest of these islands. In an area of 3500 square miles, it is inhabited by 63,000 Melanesians who speak 17 mutually unintelligible languages and exhibit marked morphological and serological diversity (Friedlaender et al., 1971). Many of the languages spoken on Bougainville are called Papuan and are considered to represent the indigenous substratum of Melanesia before the Pacific dispersal of the widespread Austronesian Phylum of languages. The Aita of north Bougainville speak one of these Papuan languages. They are a population of some 900, living from about 2000 to 3800 feet on the slopes of Mt. Balbi (10,171 feet). They subsist mainly on taro, supplemented by local greens and seasonal produce. They are one of the most isolated groups on Bougainville; until the 1950's they were almost totally unaffected by the outside world.

In contrast to the situation on Bougainville, most of the Solomon Islanders to the southeast speak Melanesian languages, a family of Austronesian. On Malaita, near the southern end of the chain, the Lau and Baegu speak two dialects of a fairly widespread Melanesian language. The Baegu, who number between 1200 and 1500, reside from the coastal plains up to about 3300 feet. Their staples are sweet potatoes and taro, supplemented by trade products such as fish from the coast. Nearby, the 5000 Lau live in coastal villages and on small natural and artificial islands in a lagoon. They are essentially fishermen, with coastal gardens providing taro and sweet potatoes.

Of these groups, only the Lau are reasonably well nourished. There are variations in the degree of Western contact and isolation from neighbors, especially for the Aita, and in the amount of protein consumption where fish is eaten by the Lau and Baegu; but in the main all of the people are basically swidden agriculturists. More importantly for present purposes, there has been little outbreeding, even with neighboring populations. These people are relatively isolated and homogeneous; they should accord more with the heritability estimates

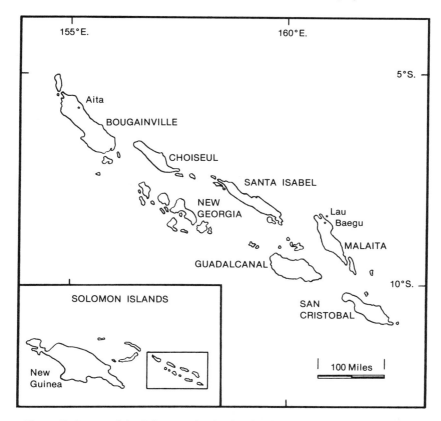

Figure 2. A map of the Solomon Islands, showing the locations of the three population samples used in the present study.

of Loesch (1971) in rural Poland, than with Holt's (1956) cosmopolitan British sample.

In part, the Aita and Baegu were selected for biometrical analysis because they represented samples from both the Papuan and Melanesian language groups; but they were also among the largest samples with adequate geneologies. The Aita data, in particular, were collected with quantitative genetic studies in mind. A photographic device designed by N. J. Harrick (1962), which used the internal reflection of a glass prism to relay the image to Polaroid film, made possible the inclusion of virtually every child in the present 52%

sample of all living Aita. In cases of poor prints, I classified the actual
hands and fingers in the field with the aid of a large magnifying glass
and a fluorescent lamp. These special collection efforts resulted in
564 sib pairs. On the other hand, the Baegu sample resulted in only
289 sib pairs, due to the difficulties of classifying children's prints
made by conventional methods.

This number of sib pairs represents a combined sample of both
mixed-sex and like-sex pairs. In order to insure that this maximiza-
tion of information from combining the data was not distorted by sex
differences, the males and females were each standardized on the
sex-population means and these z-scores were then used in all heritability estimations. By reducing both sexes to a mean of zero and a
standard deviation of one, they were effectively equalized. The sibship correlations were also calculated for each sex separately, and
these estimations were not divergent from the combined correlations in actual value. The gain in precision of estimation by combining sexes was noteworthy, for their standard errors were close to
one-half those of the separate sex estimates.

The intraclass correlations between sibs given here were estimated
by an analysis of variance technique which corrects for varying sibship size. The following formula is from Holt (1957):

$$r = \frac{1 - \left(\frac{msq_w}{msq_b}\right)}{1 + \left(\frac{N^2 - \Sigma n_i^2}{N(k-1)} - 1\right)\left(\frac{msq_w}{msq_b}\right)},$$

where msq_w refers to mean squared deviations within sibships,
msq_b = mean squared deviations between sibships, n_i = number of
sibs in i^{th} sibship, $N = \Sigma n_i$ = total number of sibs, and k = number
of sibships. Only the sib-sib correlations were calculated in this way.
Correlations for midparent-offspring, parent-child, and spouses
were calculated for most traits using the regular product-moment
method and treating all possible pairs of values as if they were independent. This is not strictly accurate, except for spouses, since
parents are included repeatedly when they have more than one child.
There is no reason to believe that this inaccuracy will bias the cor-

relation results unduly (Holt, 1956), but it may lead to grossly under-estimated standard errors (Loesch, 1971). Consequently, these crude results are presented without standard errors in the Appendix.

For the combined sex sibship correlations presented here, standard errors have been calculated using the method of Falconer (1960). The following formula for the error variance of the intraclass correlation takes into consideration the number and size of sibships:

$$S_r^2 = \frac{2\ [1\ +\ (n-1)r]^2(1-r)^2}{n(n-1)\ (N-1)},$$

where N = number of sibships and n = average size of sibship so that Nn = total number of subjects. The standard error was then taken as the square root of this value.

Neither the correlation coefficient nor its standard error are normally distributed. The latter can be seen by the fact that the standard error values decrease with the increasing value of r. For correlations between .00 and .50, the range dealt with in these heritability estimates, the decrease of the standard error is slight (.056 to .051 for the Aita), but at higher correlations the standard error becomes very small (for an r of .95, the SE_r would be .008 in the Aita). The distribution of r is also negatively skewed, requiring an adjustment in the value of the standard error for each side of a correlation coefficient, when calculating confidence limits.

Because of this distribution, it is usually recommended that Fisher's z-transformation be used for estimating the confidence intervals of individual correlation coefficients and the significance of differences between them. However, a problem was encountered in trying to do this, for the formula of the standard error of z is,

$$SE_z = \frac{1}{\sqrt{n-3}},$$

where n is the number of pairs used in the computation of r (Sokal and Rohlf, 1969). Since the number of sib pairs is not used in the analysis of variance technique, the SE_z had to be approximated from the SE_r of Falconer's formula. Even if the actual number of pairs were known, it would not give an accurate standard error because individuals are included repeatedly when they have more than one sibling. The approximation of the SE_r was made by using the usual formula for the standard error of r when the sample pairs are independent,

$$SE_r = \frac{1 - r^2}{\sqrt{n}},$$

to calculate the value of n where r and SE_r are known. By this procedure a value of n was found which was roughly equivalent to the number of pairs needed to obtain the known r and SE in a hypothetical product-moment situation. This n value for the total ridge count correlation in the Baegu (r = .463 ± .062) was found to be 161. The difference between this value and the actual number of pairs (289) underscores the necessity of using a special formula for the standard error of intraclass correlations. If the standard error had been calculated by the conventional methods it would be about 27% lower, which in this case would mean a false reduction in the confidence limits of ± .031.

By the z-transformation method, 95% confidence limits were calculated for the Baegu total ridge count correlation of .463. The results were .333 and .576. At these levels of r and n, it was found that the cumbersome z-transformation method made almost no difference, for the same 95% confidence interval was from .341 to .585 by the conventional method of using the SE_r. The shift due to a correction for skew was only .008! Since at lower levels of r and higher values for n, the SE_r approximation is even closer to the SE_z (Moroney, 1965), I concluded that this increase in precision was not worth the effort. Hence, in most subsequent statistical comparisons of the correlation data, the SE_r is used instead of the SE_z.

DIGITAL CHARACTERS

The genetic correlations of sibs for the digital finger print traits are presented in Table 5. The reason for limiting this discussion to sib pair correlations, and referring the parent-child and other kinship correlations to the Appendix, is that my purpose is only to establish realistic estimates for the relative percentage of genetic control over each trait, rather than to explore the ramifications of dominance. There is some question of efficacy regarding the available methods for determining dominance in continuous variables, given the large confidence ranges of correlations. With few exceptions, previous

TABLE 5

THE GENETIC CORRELATIONS FOR THE DIGITAL TRAITS OF SIBS
IN THE AITA AND BAEGU. THE SEXES HAVE BEEN POOLED BY
STANDARDIZATION. CORRELATIONS ARE ALL SIGNIFICANT AT
THE .05 LEVEL EXCEPT THOSE MARKED WITH a*.

	Aita		Baegu	
Number of Sibships	120		106	
Number of Sibs	396		285	

	Mean	Standard Error	Mean	Standard Error
Right 1 Pattern	.260	.055	.354	.067
Left 1 Pattern	.307	.055	.214	.069
Right 2 Pattern	.214	.055	.160	.069
Left 2 Pattern	.164	.054	.312	.067
Right 3 Pattern	.136	.053	.276	.068
Left 3 Pattern	.281	.055	.276	.068
Right 4 Pattern	.271	.055	.184	.069
Left 4 Pattern	.343	.055	.290	.067
Right 5 Pattern	.174	.054	.128*	.068
Left 5 Pattern	.106*	.052	.189	.069
Right Intensity	.347	.055	.348	.067
Left Intensity	.395	.054	.367	.067
Total Pattern Intensity	.424	.054	.385	.066
Right 1 Max. Count	.313	.056	.394	.066
Left 1 Max. Count	.315	.056	.368	.066
Right 2 Max. Count	.277	.056	.282	.067
Left 2 Max. Count	.304	.056	.325	.067
Right 3 Max. Count	.268	.056	.349	.067
Left 3 Max. Count	.345	.055	.410	.064
Right 4 Max. Count	.335	.055	.276	.068
Left 4 Max. Count	.319	.056	.285	.067
Right 5 Max. Count	.368	.055	.321	.067
Left 5 Max. Count	.328	.055	.439	.064
Total Maximum Count	.416	.054	.463	.062

biometrical genetic analyses of dermatoglyphics concluded that
there was no evidence of dominance and that these traits appeared to
be strictly additive. They often disagreed, however, in estimating
an absolute level of genetic determination and there was evidence

that this might be variable in populations. The present data, both here and in the Appendix, show no significant evidence of dominance. Most of the parent-offspring correlations are similar to the sib-sib values, and those parent values which are lower do not deviate significantly. Similarly, most of the midparent-child correlations are higher than the single parent levels.

The emphasis here is on the level of significance in discussing comparisons between correlation coefficients. Differences between parent-offspring and sib-sib correlations do not establish dominance if these differences are not significant. This does not mean that there is no dominance, even on a small scale, but only that present methods and small samples cannot possibly show it. A similar comment applies to the often stated conclusion that quantitative genetic correlations around .4 do not deviate significantly from the expected level of .5. Again this does not mean that the lower estimate shows the same degree of genetic determination, but only that sample sizes are too small to demonstrate a difference. Indeed, correlation coefficients in the range of .3 to .5 have relatively high standard errors even with moderate sized samples, so conclusions based on small differences among these coefficients are certainly hazardous.

The difficulty of establishing significant differences can be shown in the present data by several means. The 95% confidence range for the Baegu total ridge count of .33 to .58 has already been mentioned. For the Aita, this range is .30 to .52, again calculated by the z-transformation method. Describing this high sampling variation in a different way, it can be shown that the minimal significant difference ($P < .05$) between any two Baegu correlations is approximately .19. This approximation was made by using the average standard error twice to estimate the standard error of a difference and then multiplying this by 1.96, the normal deviate for a probability of .05. This approximation is a fairly good one, since the standard errors shown in Table 5 are all roughly the same. For the Aita this minimal difference is still quite large at around .16. Applying these minimal differences to Table 5, they mean that none of the individual finger ridge count correlations is significantly different from the total ridge count figure. Still another way of demonstrating the large error dispersion of these correlation coefficients is by finding the levels at which a value can be considered significantly different from the expected level of .50. For the Baegu, a coefficient of .37 is on the borderline ($p < .05$)

of significant departure from .5, while the equivalent value in the Aita is .39. With a lack of precision of this magnitude, it is only possible to discuss the degree of genetic determination in a general way, not in terms of specific modes such as dominance.

Strictly speaking, it should be noted that the use of the term "heritability" is different from that of the degree of genetic determination (Cavalli-Sforza and Bodmer, 1971). Heritability refers to the amount of genetic variability available for the applied geneticist to use in selective breeding. As such, it excludes the variability expressed by heterozygotes called the dominance variance, since this is not recognizable in potential parents and cannot be predicted in the progeny. When an estimate of heritability is made by doubling the parent-child correlation, the residual "non-heritable" component includes both environment and dominance variances. On the other hand, correlations between sibs include both additive and dominance variances, and the residual is strictly environmental. If dominance is present, both parent-child and sib-sib correlations are used to estimate the three components of phenotypic variance. When there is no evidence of dominance as may be the case with dermatoglyphics, then the sib-sib correlation is simply doubled to estimate both the heritability and the degree of genetic determination.

The weaknesses of the correlation technique are compounded when it is used to define the level of genetic determination. Based on Fisher's (1918) theory, the parent-offspring correlation is customarily doubled to obtain an estimate of the additive genetic proportion of the total variance. A correlation of .5 means, by definition, that a trait is totally determined by several nondominant, additive genes and has a heritability of 100%. When an intraclass correlation is doubled, its confidence range is also doubled so that the estimate of heritability is even less precise. For example, the Aita sib correlation for the total ridge count is .416 and the confidence interval is .30 to .52. Doubling both, the estimate of genetic determination for this trait is about 83% with a confidence range of from 60% to 100%!

Because of the lack of precision in the present intraclass correlations, an attempt was made to combine the ridge count data from each finger after the correlations were obtained. This averaging of the individual finger correlations does not have the disadvantage of statistically inflating the estimate of genetic variance as appears to be the case with the total count (see above). In addition, the average correlations have the advantage of a reduced standard error, making statistical comparisons and estimates of genetic determination more precise. Correlation coefficients can only be averaged, however, if they appear to come from the same statistical universe and therefore can be considered as sample estimates of the universal correlation. A test of homogeneity (Sokal and Rohlf, 1969) was therefore applied to the ten sibling ridge count correlations for each population. The test used z-transform values and their squares to obtain a chi-square measure of heterogeneity. For both populations this chi-square was extremely nonsignificant (P < .9), indicating a high degree of homogeneity. The ten correlation coefficients were therefore averaged, using the z-transform values, to obtain an estimate of the genetic component of general finger print complexity and size. The standard error of this average correlation coefficient was obtained by dividing the standard error of the individual correlations by the square root of 10, since the sample size had been increased by a factor of 10 and the standard error varies as the square root of the sample size.

This averaging procedure yielded new genetic correlations for digital pattern size of .33 ± .02 for the Aita and .36 ± .02 for the Baegu. Their confidence ranges are .30 to .36 and .32 to .40, respectively. They are neither significantly different from each other, nor from the total ridge count correlations of their respective populations. The increase in precision is shown by the fact that with these standard error values, any value under .46 for the Aita and .45 for the Baegu is a highly significant (P < .01) departure from the expected level of .50. Having eliminated both the statistical bias of large heterogeneous populations and the artificial inflation of using the total ridge count, these more precise genetic correlations for pattern size probably indicate a realistic estimation of genetic determination in the vicinity of 70%, with a confidence range of less than 60% to 80%.

Table 5 also shows the correlations for pattern intensity. The values for the right, left, and total pattern intensity indices are on the same order as the ridge counts and none deviate significantly from the genetic correlations for total ridge count, indicating comparable genetic control for the number of triradii. These values are also similar to those reported in Table 3. Since the same statistical inflation suspected of total ridge count may apply to the additive nature of these indices, it might be more realistic to use the average correlations of the individual finger pattern complexities. These, however, were coded in a more detailed manner than the count of triradii and therefore are not exactly comparable. They also are likely to have non-normal distributions and a greater degree of subjectivity in assessment. As a compromise, the average value for right and left pattern intensities might be taken as the best estimate of genetic determination of this trait. These average pattern intensity correlations are .37 ± .04 for the Aita and .36 ± .05 for the Baegu; and they are not significantly different from the average correlations for finger ridge counts. A comparable level of hereditary control around 70% is indicated for this trait.

The genetic correlations for the individual pattern complexity traits are neither as large nor consistent as the intensity indices and ridge counts. Nevertheless, with the exception of the Aita left fifth and Baegu right fifth fingers all intraclass correlations are significant. Except that the thumb tends to have high values, these correlations do not show a consistent pattern. For a useful approximation of the general level of genetic control of these traits, they were averaged in the same manner described for finger ridge counts. For both populations, the chi-square test showed no significant heterogeneity, though the actual values indicated far more relative heterogeneity than was found in the ridge counts. The average correlation for the Aita is .23± .02 and for the Baegu .24 ± .02, indicating a proportion of genetic control in the range of 45% to 50%. These correlations are both significantly lower than the average ridge count correlations (P< .001). The amount of genetic determination of pattern type is considerably less than for ridge counts. There apparently is a greater developmental flexibility in the form of the pattern than in its absolute size.

PALMAR CHARACTERS

Table 6 shows the sibship intraclass correlations for the palmar traits. In general they demonstrate far less genetic control than the digital traits. The total mainline index has the highest values and is perhaps best described as an average of right and left. These average correlations are .31 ± .04 and .24 ± .05 for the Aita and Baegu, respectively. They indicate a proportion of genetic determination of about .5, which is far less than the value reported by Pons (1959). His sample may have been more heterogeneous, but the size of the

TABLE 6

THE GENETIC CORRELATIONS FOR THE
PALMAR DERMATOGLYPHIC TRAITS OF SIBS
IN THE AITA AND BAEGU. THE SEXES
HAVE BEEN POOLED BY STANDARDIZATION.
NON-SIGNIFICANT CORRELATIONS
AT THE .05 LEVEL HAVE BEEN OMITTED.

	Aita		Baegu	
Number of Sibships	120		106	
Number of Sibs	396		285	
	Mean	Standard Error	Mean	Standard Error
Right Mainline A	.219	.055	.210	.069
Left Mainline A	.285	.056	.144	.069
Right Mainline B	.174	.054	.146	.069
Left Mainline B	.231	.055	.203	.069
Right Mainline C			.202	.069
Left Mainline C	.149	.053		
Right Mainline D	.215	.055	.239	.069
Left Mainline D	.282	.056	.225	.069
Right Mainline Index	.257	.056	.235	.069
Left Mainline Index	.355	.055	.236	.069
Total Mainline Index	.346	.055	.265	.069
Right Interdigital 3			.164	.069
Left Interdigital 3	.194	.055		
Right Interdigital 4			.209	.069
Left Interdigital 4	.131	.053		
Total Hypothenar	.140	.053		
Total Thenar	.268	.056	.186	.069
Total *atd* Angle	.182	.054	.265	.069

discrepancy may indicate a real population difference in the heredity of this trait. For the individual mainlines, all but one in each population show a significant sibship correlation. A and D have the highest values while C appears to be the least genetically determined. Generally the individual mainlines show a genetic determination on the order of 35% to 55%.

The interdigital patterns show inconsistent and relatively low correlations. Only half of the values are significant. These would not appear to be very useful genetic characters as they are presently classified. The same conclusion applies to hypothenar patterning. Only in the Aita did this trait show a significant value and this was low. These results are lower than those of Loesch (1971). Although her methods of classification were different, this discrepancy may indicate a greater proportion of genetic determination of radial loops than other traits on the hypothenar, and these are relatively rare in Melanesia. Loesch advocated the separate inheritance of different hypothenar loops. Combining them as in the present study may distort the results. In any case, the hypothenar region and the interdigital areas do not appear to be useful for genetic comparisons of populations.

This is not true of the thenar region, where the correlations are moderate in size. They are also higher than those presented by Loesch. They indicate around 45% genetic determination and the possibility that this may be a useful trait for genetic comparisons.

For the angular measurement of the axial triradius, it was necessary to adjust the data for age differences. Since angle *atd* is affected by the relative breadth of the hand, young children have very wide angles. As the hand grows more in length than breadth, this angle is reduced until it is fairly close to adult values at age 15. At ages between 11 and 15, the angle is frequently not significantly different from adult values, but it is usually higher. Below age 11, however, the angle increases at an accelerating rate as age decreases. This relationship is shown by a correlation of $-.49$ between age and left proximal angle *atd* in the Aita. Since this regression is non-linear, an approximate adjustment was made by subtracting from each age a value equivalent to the difference in means between that age and age 15. This resulted in a non-significant correlation of $-.02$ for the same comparison made above. With these adjustments, the total proximal angle *atd* showed moderate correlations in both populations, indicating a level of genetic control of 40% to 50%.

The conclusions of this biometrical genetic analysis of two Melanesian populations confirm many of the previous studies, but tend to set the levels of genetic control slightly lower. It is assumed that these lower levels are due to greater homogeneity in the populations and to the avoidance of summary statistics which may bias the estimated correlations upward. In some cases the discrepancies may show population differences in heritability between Europe and Melanesia.

These data show high degrees of genetic determination (around 70%) for ridge counts and the pattern intensity index; moderate levels (40% to 50%) for finger pattern traits, mainline terminations, thenar patterning, and angle *atd;* and relatively slight genetic influence on interdigital and hypothenar patterning. The last mentioned do not appear useful for genetic population comparisons. Finally, no significant differences were found between the Aita and Baegu results. In most cases the heritability estimates were quite close. Since these two populations represent both the Papuan and Austronesian language groups, it would appear that these estimates are applicable to all Melanesian populations.

A Factor Analytic
Approach to Finger Print Genetics

Howells (1953) has suggested factor analysis as a means of transforming morphological measurements into more genetically specific characters. Factor analysis is a technique which seeks to explain as much as possible of the observed systematic variation in terms of a small set of new variables. It does this by determining rotated axes from a correlation matrix such that new variables, defined as linear combinations of the original variables, each have a maximum variance (Tatsuoka, 1971). The process is sequential and the principal components extracted after the first are uncorrelated with the others and explain a maximum of the residual variance. A varimax rotation of these new components defines factors which have large correlations with a few of the original variables and close to zero correlations with the others. The orthogonality of the principal components is maintained in this solution (i.e. the factors are uncorrelated with one another). These rotated factors are therefore more biologically interpretable than the principal components, since they define small interrelated sets of the original variables.

In addition to providing a possibly more direct representation of the underlying gene structure than the original variables, a factor analytic transformation of finger prints should provide a parsimonious explanation of the overall variation (Tatsuoka, 1971). Factor analysis may offer more realistic definitions and descriptions of such gross characters as digital pattern complexity and size than the arbitrarily summed pattern intensity index and total maximum ridge count. By defining the gross characters of finger prints in terms of the correlations among the individual traits, factor analysis eliminates the redundancy of dermatoglyphic characters which makes additive indices artificial and possibly inflated (Knussman, 1971). In turn, these factors should give valid heritability estimates for the gross traits and confirm some of the above conclusions regarding the level of heritability in ridge counts.

Furthermore, a factor analysis of finger print traits should also subdivide the total variation into its important components as expressed in the relationships among the measurements (Howells, 1970). This may demonstrate the artificial nature of the summary traits, such as the total pattern intensity index, by dividing them into more basic units of genetic variation. If a group of fingers share higher correlations with each other than with other fingers, then the factor explaining the covariance of this partially independent unit should define its shared genetic component and provide a better overall picture of finger print genetics than the total summary traits or each individual character alone (Knussman, 1971).

BAEGU FACTORS

Nine varimax rotated factors are presented in Table 7 for the combined finger and palm traits of the Baegu. Both sexes and all ages were included in this analysis. The entries in each column are factor loadings (correlations) of the successive original variables on each factor; they show the amount of variance of the original variables which is explained by each factor, because the square of a correlation coefficient gives the percent of shared variance between two variables. For ease in reading this table, only the loadings above .15 are entered, a level recommended by Anderson et al. (1969).

The communalities, at the right of the table, are the total proportions of each character's variance, which are explained by the nine factors. The difference between 1.0 and the communality is the unexplained proportion, presumably unique to each variable. At the bottom of the table are sums of squares and the percents of trace based on these. The latter show the percentages of the total variance in the sample, which are explained by each factor and by the entire factor matrix.

Even though only about 63% of the total finger print variance is

TABLE 7

VARIMAX ROTATED FACTOR LOADINGS FOR NINE FACTORS EXTRACTED FROM THE DERMATOGLYPHIC VARIABLES OF 445 BAEGU. VALUES BELOW .15 ARE OMITTED FOR CLARITY. THE PERCENTS OF TRACE SHOW HOW MUCH OF THE TOTAL VARIANCE IS ACCOUNTED FOR BY EACH FACTOR AND THE TOTAL FACTOR MATRIX. THE COMMUNALITIES ARE THE PROPORTIONS OF EACH VARIABLE'S DISPERSION THAT ARE ACCOUNTED FOR BY THE NINE FACTORS.

	Rotated Factor Loadings									Communality
	1	2	3	4	5	6	7	8	9	
Right 1 Pattern	.28				-.64	.32				.62
Left 1 Pattern					-.72	.28		-.19		.64
Right 2 Pattern	.26				-.34	.58				.55
Left 2 Pattern	.30				-.37	.58				.59
Right 3 Pattern	.30					.71				.62
Left 3 Pattern	.27					.74				.63
Right 4 Pattern	.32					.59		-.26		.54
Left 4 Pattern	.26					.60		-.35		.55
Right 5 Pattern	.15					.30		-.65		.58
Left 5 Pattern	.17							-.71		.57
Pat. Intensity	.48				-.39	.70		-.26		.94
Right Mainline A		.32	.31	.22			.17		.42	.48
Left Mainline A		.28	.21	.37			.16		.43	.49
Right Mainline B		.80		.21					.22	.76
Left Mainline B		.44		.63					.27	.71
Right Mainline C		.78							-.21	.68
Left Mainline C				.64	.15				-.18	.49
Right Mainline D		.81		.24					.19	.76
Left Mainline D		.50		.64					.21	.74

294

Right Angle *atd*			.20					.20	-.78	.70
Left Angle *atd*			.49						-.66	.68
Maximum Right *atd*			.17	.22			.15		-.78	.68
Maximum Left *atd*				.38				-.32	-.61	.69
Right ad/t Height			-.82							.69
Left ad/t Height			-.88						.16	.81
Right Hypothenar			-.17	.40				-.24	-.24	.31
Left Hypothenar				.54				-.42		.51
Right Thenar							.80			.65
Left Thenar							.83			.71
Right Interdig. 2									.22	.12
Left Interdig. 2							-.20			.11
Right Interdig. 3		.86							-.17	.78
Left Interdig. 3				.67						.52
Right Interdig. 4	.16	-.66			.20					.52
Left Interdig. 4		-.17		-.43	.27					.33
Right 1 Count	.63				-.55					.71
Left 1 Count	.58				-.61					.73
Right 2 Count	.64				-.36	.38				.72
Left 2 Count	.65				-.32	.39				.70
Right 3 Count	.74					.40				.71
Left 3 Count	.70					.49				.73
Right 4 Count	.81					.15				.69
Left 4 Count	.83					.27				.77
Right 5 Count	.77							-.20		.64
Left 5 Count	.79							-.22		.69
Total Max. Count	.90				-.28	.32				.99
Sum of Squares	6.93	3.81	2.04	2.87	2.58	4.25	1.60	1.84	2.92	28.84
Percent of Trace	15.06	8.29	4.44	6.23	5.61	9.23	3.47	4.01	6.35	62.69

explained by this nine factor matrix, additional factors were not rotated because they each added less than 3% to the explained variance and they appeared to be unique, describing only the left and right expressions of a single trait. Since the purpose of this analysis was to find clusters of traits, the nine factor analysis was judged sufficient. The eigenvalue or root for the last factor extracted was 1.42, well above the 1.0 level sometimes recommended for a complete analysis (Tatsuoka, 1971).

Factors 1, 5, 6, and 8 describe the interrelationships of the finger traits. The first is a total quantitative tendency or size factor for the digital patterns. It explains 81% of the variance of the total ridge count and from 33% to 69% of the individual ridge counts, with an emphasis on the ulnar fingers (ring and little). The pattern traits of various fingers and the pattern intensity index are also partially explained on this factor, but at moderately low levels (23% of the variance of the pattern intensity index is the highest of these). This factor should accord well with the total ridge count, or at least with what the latter is designed to show.

The fifth factor expresses the relationships between the two thumbs and, to a lesser extent, between the thumb and index finger. This factor explains from 30% to 50% of the variance in the ridge counts and pattern complexities of the thumbs, with a slight emphasis on the patterns. The variances of the second digit and the pattern intensity index are less than 15% explained by this factor. Basically, therefore, this is a thumb factor.

The sixth factor expresses the covariance among the middle three digital patterns, and to a lesser extent, their ridge counts. From 35% to 56% of the pattern variance of the index, middle, and ring fingers is explained, with a strong emphasis on the middle finger. The loadings for the middle finger ridge counts show 16% and 25% explained variance. Because of the involvement of several digital pattern traits in this factor, 49% of the pattern intensity index variance is explained. This, then, is a middle finger(s) pattern factor.

The eighth factor explains 42% and 50% of the little finger pattern variance. This factor also shows a slight involvement with the fourth finger pattern (less than 12.5%), but very little with the ridge counts of the fifth. There is also some noise in this factor from the left hypothenar and maximal *atd* angle (17% and 10% explained variance). This is based on correlations of less than 0.1; undoubtedly it is a statistical artifact of rotation.

The four finger factors are in close agreement with those of Luu-Mau-Thanh (1965) and Knussman (1967; 1969), for French and German subjects, respectively. The congruence between these European populations and the Melanesian data demonstrates a general validity for the factors. In turn, this generality suggests common mechanisms of genetic control for finger print traits in all human populations.

Luu-Mau-Thanh (1965) made the intriguing suggestion that the congruence between the three digital pattern factors and the sensory innervations of the ulnar, median, and radial nerves showed one possible mechanism of genetic control. While this idea leads one to recall Stern's suggested association between nerve growth and ridge patterning (see above), the congruence is not perfect, for the radial nerve inervates the radial side of the hand's dorsum up to the second phalange, it does not reach the distal ventral surface. At best, this suggestion of Luu-Mau-Thanh points the way for further research.

In any event, it is more parsimonious to explain equivalent associations between traits in diverse populations by similar genetic processes than to seek common non-genetic causes. This commonality of genetic mechanisms supports the hypothesis that the factors of interrelated fingerprint traits may be one step closer to the genetic basis than the characters themselves.

Some of the five palm factors in Table 7 also comply with the results of Knussman (1967; 1969). In particular, the mainlines are represented by right (No. 2) and left (No. 4) factors, which emphasize the B, C, and D lines. The variances of the A lines are only about 12% explained by these factors. Furthermore, the A lines are only slightly more explained by the ninth factor (about 18%), and their communalities show less than 50% total explanation by the nine factors. This indicates that the A lines have a considerable unique component, while the other lines are bilaterally distinct and integrally related.

The right and left BCD mainline factors also include high loadings for the corresponding third and fourth interdigital patterns. These factors quite clearly describe two trait complexes, which are similar in Melanesia and Germany. Not so clear is the inclusion of the hypothenar pattern in the left BCD factor. This factor explains 16% and 28% of the hypothenar variance. The correlations for this association are all less than 0.2, so presumably further factor analysis might separate the hypothenar as a unique factor.

The remaining three factors are also fairly unique and add little more to the definition of trait interrelatedness. The third factor is essentially an axial triradius factor, with major loadings on the two ad/t heights and a secondary loading for the left *atd* angle. In addition, the A mainline has a slight influence (4% and 9%) on this factor. The seventh factor is strictly based on the thenar pattern, indicating that it is a completely autonomous trait.

Finally, the ninth factor is principally based on the *atd* angles, with secondary loadings for the A mainlines. Again this factor is largely unique, since the correlations between the A mainlines and the *atd* angles are at or below 0.1. It appears that two fairly independent traits are dumped together in this final rotated factor.

THE HERITABILITY OF BAEGU FACTORS

Since three of the nine Baegu factors, described above, are fairly specific, a second rotation was made with only six factors. The aim was to find more general factors, whose heritabilities could be compared with those from indices and sums of original variables. These six factors are presented in Table 8. The first four of these are quite similar to their counterparts in the nine factor rotation.

Factor 1 is still a size factor, it expresses the total quantitative tendency of the ridge counts and pattern complexities. It is only different from the previous first factor by having higher loadings for some fingers and for the pattern intensity index; it no longer has an ulnar emphasis. Since it explains 92% of the total ridge count's variance, it should compare favorably with the latter in terms of heritability estimates.

The second factor describes all of the mainlines, with an emphasis on the right hand. The third and fourth interdigital patterns of the right hand are also included. This is principally a total mainline factor and it should accord well with the mainline index in heritability comparisons.

Factor 3 describes the position of the axial triradius, including both the ad/t height and the *atd* angles. It is independent of the hypothenar patterns, whose loadings are well below 0.1. This factor should accord well with the total *atd* angle in heritability assessments.

The fourth factor, which previously described the left mainlines and interdigital patterns, now focuses principally on the hypothenar pattern. The left C mainline has a high loading, but the B and D

TABLE 8

VARIMAX ROTATED FACTOR LOADINGS FOR SIX FACTORS
EXTRACTED FROM THE DERMATOGLYPHIC VARIABLES OF
445 BAEGU. VALUES BELOW .15 ARE OMITTED FOR CLARITY.

| | Rotated Factor Loadings | | | | | | Commun-ality |
	1	2	3	4	5	6	
Right 1 Pattern	.41				−.53	−.25	.53
Left 1 Pattern	.26				−.59	−.29	.51
Right 2 Pattern	.46				−.45		.45
Left 2 Pattern	.50				−.47		.51
Right 3 Pattern	.46				−.49	.16	.49
Left 3 Pattern	.45				−.43	.23	.44
Right 4 Pattern	.41				−.53	.25	.52
Left 4 Pattern	.36				−.56	.26	.51
Right 5 Pattern	.15				−.58	.22	.43
Left 5 Pattern		−.20			−.46	.22	.34
Pat. Intensity	.65				−.70		.93
Right Mainline A		.44				.47	.44
Left Mainline A		.45	−.20		.16	.37	.43
Right Mainline B		.84					.74
Left Mainline B		.65	−.15	.38	.15	.19	.65
Right Mainline C		.66	.22				.50
Left Mainline C		.26		.57			.44
Right Mainline D		.84					.73
Left Mainline D		.70		.41			.70
Right Angle *atd*		.75				−.21	.61
Left Angle *atd*		.81					.67
Maximum Right *atd*		.67		.38		−.18	.63
Maximum Left *atd*	−.16	.55		.56			.66
Right ad/t Height		.58		.16		−.28	.48
Left ad/t Height		.64		.15		−.31	.53
Right Hypothenar				.53			.29
Left Hypothenar				.65			.44
Right Thenar						.39	.18
Left Thenar						.29	.09
Right Interdig. 2						.21	.07
Left Interdig. 2		.16					.07
Right Interdig. 3		.75	.19				.61
Left Interdig. 3		.24		.59			.43
Right Interdig. 4	.16	−.64			.15		.48
Left Interdig. 4		−.33	.19	−.31		.20	.29
Right 1 Count	.70				−.17	−.29	.61
Left 1 Count	.66				−.30	−.28	.61
Right 2 Count	.78				−.26		.70
Left 2 Count	.77				−.26		.69
Right 3 Count	.80				−.17	.16	.70
Left 3 Count	.78				−.25	.16	.70
Right 4 Count	.79						.65
Left 4 Count	.83					.18	.72
Right 5 Count	.73						.55
Left 5 Count	.75						.61
Total Max. Count	.96				−.22		.98
Sum of Squares	8.72	4.55	3.06	2.41	3.76	1.84	24.33
Percent of Trace	18.93	9.88	6.66	5.24	8.16	4.00	52.89

loadings show less than 17% explained variance. Associated with this mainline C involvement is a high loading for the third interdigital. In comparison with the original fourth factor, this new one de-emphasizes the mainlines and explains up to 42% of the hypothenar pattern variance. The maximum *atd* angles are included with the hypothenar in this factor, especially on the left hand.

The fifth factor combines the previous three finger pattern factors (5, 6, and 8) in a fairly equal fashion that approximates the total pattern intensity. 50% of the variation in the intensity index is explained by this factor. This is quite high, since the size factor already explained 41% of the variance of the pattern intensity index. In a sense, factor 5 more purely describes total pattern quality than the index or individual traits, for the influence of pattern size has already been removed by the first factor. This is shown by the loadings up to .50 for finger patterns on the first factor and by relatively low loadings for ridge counts on the fifth factor. Factors 1 and 5 are orthogonal by definition and therefore appear to express the independent attributes of pattern size and pattern quality better than any variable heretofore obtained.

The sixth and final factor of this second rotation explains a variety of unrelated traits. Again, the last factor in a varimax rotation seems to group all of the unrelated traits removed from the other factors, for the communalities must still be the same as for the original principal components. This factor shows principal, but relatively low loadings for the A mainlines and the thenar pattern. There is a lot of noise, however, from completely unrelated sources such as finger pattern types, ridge counts, and the axial triradius. This factor is therefore difficult to interpret and heritability estimates for it may not be informative.

The kinship correlations for these six rotated factors are presented in Table 9, together with the corresponding heritability estimates for the original variables, which are most associated with each factor. The last factor shows a moderately high kinship correlation of .30, but it is such a composite of various finger and palm traits that there is no single original variable with which it is comparable. It is therefore presented alone in the table. These kinship correlations were calculated in the same manner described previously, with the sexes equalized by standardization. They are based on six derived factor scores for each individual.

The first four heritability comparisons between factors and original

TABLE 9

A COMPARISON OF SIB PAIR CORRELATIONS
BETWEEN SIX BAEGU FACTOR SCORES
AND THE ORIGINAL VARIABLES OR INDICES WITH WHICH
EACH FACTOR IS MOST ASSOCIATED.
FACTOR 6 HAS NO COMPARABLE VARIABLE.

| | | Kinship Correlations | |
Factor Number	Original Variable	Factor	Original Variable
1	Total maximum ridge count	.43 ± .06	.46 ± .06
2	Mainline index	.31 ± .07	.26 ± .07
3	Summed *atd* angles	.28 ± .07	.26 ± .07
4	Total hypothenar pattern	.06 ± .07	.02 ± .07
5	Pattern intensity index	.21 ± .07	.38 ± .06
6		.30 ± .07	

variables show no statistical differences and in an absolute sense, they are quite close. This similarity supports previous conclusions regarding the heritabilities of pattern size, mainlines, axial triradius position, and the hypothenar pattern. It also demonstrates that these factors are no closer to the genetic substructure in terms of their heritabilities than the original variables.

The fifth factor, however, shows a significantly (P < .05) lower kinship correlation than the pattern intensity index, which is designed to measure the same attribute of pattern quality. Quite clearly, the heritability estimate for the pattern intensity index is strongly inflated by pattern size, as reflected in the total ridge count. This factor, then, gives a purer description of the total pattern quality than the traditional index. In this sense, it is closer to the genetic basis of pattern determination, and factor analysis does indeed offer a clearer genetic description of finger print variation than one of the traditional variables.

The heritability estimate of 42% for digital pattern quality, based on the fifth factor, is similar to the heritability approximated previously by averaging the kinship correlations of the separate digits. The average kinship correlation was .24 ± .02, which is indistinguishable from the correlation of .21 ± .07 for the pattern quality factor.

This corroboration supports the averaging technique as a useful approximation of the underlying heritability.

In the nine factor analysis of finger prints, the thumbs, middle fingers, and fifth fingers were described as partially independent complexes of interrelated traits. There was some noise from the palm traits, however, in the factor loadings for the fifth finger factor. This suggested an analysis of the finger patterns alone, to define the three factors more clearly. The successful definition of a relatively genetically pure factor of total pattern quality encouraged the heritability assessment of these three particular pattern quality factors.

The Aita were used for this analysis to confirm that the factors were the same in a Papuan population. Table 10 presents the varimax rotated factor loadings for the three digital pattern factors. The loadings for a factor analysis of similar, French data by Luu-Mau-Thanh (1965) are included for comparison. In the present factor analysis of ten pattern traits, only the first three eigenvalues of the principal components were greater than 1.0, indicating that the analysis was complete. Since no further significant factors can be extracted from the finger pattern data, the three factors appear to show the fundamental units of shared genetic control. Since the analysis explained about 64% of the total variance, it would seem that 36% of the finger pattern variation is unique to each finger.

The first factor shows the relationship among the middle three fingers. As in the previous analysis, the third digit is slightly emphasized in this factor. From 37% to 61% of the variance of the middle three pattern traits are explained by this factor. This range is close to that for the same factor in the previous analysis (35% to 56%). Less than 6% of the variance of the thumb and little finger patterns is explained by this factor. It is almost purely a factor of the middle three digits.

The second factor is almost completely restricted to the thumbs. About 75% of the thumbs' pattern variance is explained, while other fingers show less than 10% explanation and this is mainly on the index fingers. Similarly, the third factor is confined to the fifth finger, with slight loadings (less than 5%) on the ring finger. The little finger factor expresses 67% and 72% of the pattern variances for these digits.

TABLE 10

VARIMAX ROTATED FACTOR LOADINGS FOR THREE FACTORS EX-
TRACTED FROM THE DIGITAL PATTERN TRAITS OF 460 AITA. VALUES
BELOW .15 ARE OMITTED FOR CLARITY. THE OBLIQUE ROTATED FACTOR
LOADINGS FOR THREE DIGITAL PATTERN FACTORS FROM A STUDY OF
6000 FRENCH PRISONERS (LUU-MAU-THANH, 1965) ARE INCLUDED FOR
COMPARISON.

	Aita Factor Loadings				French Factor Loadings		
	1	2	3	Communality	1	2	3
Right 1 Pattern	.26	.84		.78	.73		
Left 1 Pattern		.88		.81	.76		
Right 2 Pattern	.66	.25		.50		.71	
Left 2 Pattern	.61	.32		.48		.75	
Right 3 Pattern	.78			.63		.74	
Left 3 Pattern	.70	.32	.15	.62		.68	
Right 4 Pattern	.72		.21	.56		.25	.47
Left 4 Pattern	.68		.23	.52		.19	.58
Right 5 Pattern	.24		.82	.74		−.21	.86
Left 5 Pattern		.18	.84	.76		−.22	.80
Sum of Squares	3.05	1.79	1.55	6.39			
Percent of Trace	30.48	17.87	15.54	63.89			

The trait complexes defined by these factors are quite similar to
those in the Baegu analysis. They also show close agreement with the
three finger pattern factors found by Luu-Mau-Thanh (1965) in
the French. He used just three finger pattern categories and an
oblique rotation to define factors for the thumb, index-middle, and
ring-little fingers. The loadings for these factors are shown in Table
10. An oblique rotation passes the new axes through the centers of
gravity of the three variable groups. It is not an orthogonal solution
and the factors are therefore correlated with one another at fairly
high levels from .51 to .78. The only discrepancies between the Aita
and French factor analyses are a shift in the ring finger loadings from
the middle finger factor to the little finger factor, and a corresponding greater emphasis on the index finger in the middle finger factor
of the French. The shift in the interrelatedness of the digital patterns may be analogous to Butler's (1937) field theory for dental

genetics. Alternatively, this shift may relate to the different rotational solution of Luu-Mau-Thanh's analysis, for an examination of his correlation table shows higher correlations between the middle and ring fingers (.46 and .50) than between the ring and little fingers (.40 and .42). In any event, the two populations show a close similarity in their factors and presumably a shared pattern of genetic control.

THE HERITABILITY OF DIGITAL PATTERN FACTORS

Table 11 presents the kinship correlations for the three finger pattern factors of the Aita. For comparison, the means of the individual correlations for the relevant fingers are shown. These were calculated by the z-transformation method described above.

The three pattern factors each have higher heritabilities than their counterparts in the table, but these differences are not great nor significant. This agreement further supports the averaging technique as a valid approximation for the combined heritabilities of several traits. The thumb factor appears to show the most genetic determination, followed closely by the middle finger factor. The little finger, however, shows somewhat less heritability, below 40%. All of these heritability estimates are consistent with the total pattern factor of the Baegu.

The consistency of these heritability estimates, and the agreement between populations as diverse as the French and Melanesians, support the hypothesis that factors are related to the shared genetic

TABLE 11

A COMPARISON OF THE KINSHIP CORRELATIONS FOR THE DIGITAL PATTERN FACTORS OF THE AITA WITH THE MEAN KINSHIP COR-RELATIONS FOR THE RELEVANT INDIVIDUAL FINGER PATTERNS.

Factor Number	Original Pattern Traits	Factor Kinship r	Mean Kinship r for Original Pattern Traits
1	Index, middle, ring	.29 ± .06	.24 ± .02
2	Thumbs	.30 ± .06	.28 ± .04
3	Little fingers	.18 ± .05	.14 ± .04

components of interrelated variables. The conclusion that these factors describe the fundamental genetic units of finger print variation is further supported by the fact that the Aita factor analysis was statistically complete and the factors so produced were orthogonal. The factor analysis shows that the variation in digital pattern type is about 50% inherited, and that this genetic control is divisible into three main, partially independent units.

The genetic separation of the individual finger patterns into three units emphasizes the artificial nature of an index like pattern intensity. Since six of the ten fingers are involved in the middle finger factor, the total pattern index will largely reflect this genetic component and ignore the thumb and little finger factors. This relationship is shown in the correlations between the three pattern factors and the pattern intensity index. The middle finger factor has a correlation of .73, while the thumb has a .53 and the little finger has only a .32. Population comparisons with the pattern intensity index will therefore give a more artificial and biased result than the factors or individual traits.

The factor analysis and heritability study of dermatoglyphics suggests the use of individual traits in the comparison of populations, rather than indices or other summary statistics. The genetic validity of many of the traditional traits is confirmed by similar heritability estimates for factors. Some traditional characters, such as ridge counts and mainlines appear to be a close representation of the underlying genetic control. In the case of pattern quality, independent of pattern size, factor analysis offers a clearer genetic description of finger print variation than any of the traditional variables.

The Identification of Specific Loci
By Genetic Associations

Even though factor analysis offers a more refined genetic definition of finger pattern characters, the new traits are still controlled by complex, polygenic systems. Defining the heritability of these traits gives a vague notion of the relative amounts of genetic influence on each; but it provides no information on the number and identity of specific genes. Even the presumed additive behavior of these genes is only a theoretical model which the data seem to support. Other, more complicated models are possible (Livingstone, 1972). Most probably, the additive appearance of polygenic systems is due to a complex averaging, balancing, and reciprocal suppression of various unequal genes. In order to test effectively the additive model of gene action, the identity and combined effects of specific genes must be established.

Thoday (1967) has defined the direction he thinks future human genetic research should take. Speaking particularly of the normal range in psychometric variables, he emphasized that a knowledge of specific genes, and of their genetic and environmental interactions, is required if there is to be any real genetic knowledge of fundamental human characters which are continuous. He said,

> This is asking for knowledge of specific genes affecting continuous variables in human populations. It is in fact asking a lot.   (p. 341)

Thoday urged the search for major genes with large effects on continuous variables. He found evidence that these exist in recent research on *Drosophila* sternopleural chaetae

> . . . because so far whenever serious attempts have been made to study polygenic variation in terms of specific genes, a few handleable genes have proved to mediate a large part of the genetic variance under study.   (p. 342)

Difficulties in the identification of specific genes arise because the heritability of the continuous variable may be small and the number of genes may be unmanageably large. Successful analysis techniques must maximize the effective heritability and limit the number of genes under study. For the former, Thoday suggested the statistical abstraction of components with higher heritabilities from the complex variables. The factor analysis of finger prints however, has shown that the components are no more heritable than the original variables. Nevertheless, finger prints show very high heritabilities to begin with, so this abstraction technique is not necessary.

For the isolation of a limited number of genes, Thoday suggested the identification of suitable single locus markers through studies of genetic association. The genes of continuous variation are identified and followed by the precise definition of the associated characters used to track them. Pollitzer (1958) suggested a similar approach. In man, of course, this effort is limited to segregating markers as they are found in existing populations.

Hesch (1932) thought he saw a possible linkage between the ABO blood group and finger print patterns. His association was in a small sample from the Loyalty Islands, and did not include segregating sibships. Linkages can only be shown within families, they do not necessarily appear as associations in the entire population (Penrose, 1939). More recent and detailed studies by Mohr (1953) and Weninger (1965b) have rejected this association. Similarly, Pons (1956) found no associations between taste sensitivity to phenylthiocarbamide and dermatoglyphic traits. Mohr (1953), however, showed a significant linkage association (P< .05) between ridge counts and the Lewis blood group, in a detailed study of segregating sib pairs. Recently, Singh (1968) suggested a further exploration of these techniques for understanding finger print inheritance.

Following Thoday's (1967) suggestion, a preliminary effort was made to identify marker loci for finger print variation in Melanesia. This preliminary study only scratched the surface in two populations, the Aita and Lau; but it yielded the very promising possibility of a pleiotropic association between the size of digital patterns and the haptoglobin locus.

In the first step of this study, general population associations between possible marker loci and finger print characters were sought by chi-square and analysis of variance tests. This was not the best attack to take, since linkages do not usually appear as associations in the general population because of crossing over (Penrose, 1939); but it was the only one available given limited time and resources.

Nevertheless, significant associations in both populations were found between finger ridge counts and the three polymorphic expressions of the haptoglobin locus. The latter are established by different electrophoretic patterns. Table 12 shows the Aita mean total ridge counts by sex for each of the three haptoglobin genotypes. Clearly, the fast moving genotype (1 - 1) and the heterozygote (1 - 2) show higher means than the slow genotype (2 - 2). An analysis of variance confirmed the significance of this association (P < .006). Similarly, Table 13 shows a significant association (P< .001) between the summed thumb ridge counts and haptoglobins.

An examination of the mean values in these two tables reveals a tendency for the sexes to differ in the expression of the haptoglobin association. For females, there is a progression from the slow to the fast genotypes, with the heterozygote group clearly intermediate. In

TABLE 12

THE MEANS AND AN ANALYSIS OF VARIANCE FOR THE ASSOCIA-
TION BETWEEN THE TOTAL MAXIMUM RIDGE COUNT AND THE
HAPTOGLOBIN LOCUS IN THE GENERAL AITA POPULATION.

TOTAL MAXIMUM RIDGE COUNT MEANS

Haptoglobin Genotype

	1 - 1	1 - 2	2 - 2
Males	161.5	160.5	146.5
Females	159.0	144.2	130.0
N	142	135	49

ANALYSIS OF VARIANCE

Source	Degrees of Freedom	Mean Square	F	Sig.	% Total Sum of Squares
Sex	1	8912.4	4.3	.038	1.3
Haptoglobin	2	10687.6	5.2	.006	3.1
Interaction	2	1362.9	0.7	.5	0.4
Unit	320	2050.1			95.2

the males, however, the heterozygote group is not clearly intermediate. Nevertheless, these apparent sex interactions are significant by the analysis of variance tests ($P < .009$).

The apparent sex interaction is shown more clearly in the Lau.
Table 14 presents the means and analysis of variance for the total
ridge count-haptoglobin association. Here the females follow the
same progression seen in the Aita; but the males show a much higher
ridge count mean for the heterozygote group, while the fast genotype group has an intermediate mean. Here this interaction with sex
is not significant; but the haptoglobin-finger print association is highly
significant ($P < .004$).

Similarly, Table 15 shows the means and the analysis of variance
for the Lau summed ring finger ridge count. The male haptoglobin
heterozygote group again shows a higher mean than either homozy-
gote group, while in the females, the heterozygote group is intermediate. The haptoglobin association with the fourth finger ridge
count is highly significant ($P < .002$), and in this case, the hapto-
globin-sex interaction is marginally significant ($P < .05$). Similar sig-

TABLE 13

THE MEANS AND AN ANALYSIS OF VARIANCE FOR THE ASSOCIA-
TION BETWEEN THE SUMMED MAXIMUM THUMB RIDGE COUNTS
AND THE HAPTOGLOBIN LOCUS IN THE GENERAL AITA
POPULATION.

THUMB RIDGE COUNT MEANS

		Haptoglobin Genotype	
	1 - 1	1 - 2	2 - 2
Males	34.2	33.2	28.1
Females	32.5	26.9	22.5
N	142	134	49

ANALYSIS OF VARIANCE

Source	Degrees of Freedom	Mean Square	F	Sig.	% Total Sum of Squares
Sex	1	1321.3	6.9	.009	2.0
Haptoglobin	2	1389.9	7.3	.001	4.3
Interaction	2	135.0	0.7	.5	0.4
Unit	319	191.1			93.3

TABLE 14

THE MEANS AND AN ANALYSIS OF VARIANCE FOR THE ASSOCIA-
TION BETWEEN THE TOTAL MAXIMUM RIDGE COUNT AND THE
HAPTOGLOBIN LOCUS IN THE GENERAL LAU POPULATION.

TOTAL MAXIMUM RIDGE COUNT MEANS

		Haptoglobin Genotype	
	1 - 1	1 - 2	2 - 2
Males	155.6	171.3	148.9
Females	167.5	159.8	142.7
N	120	146	74

ANALYSIS OF VARIANCE

Source	Degrees of Freedom	Mean Square	F	Sig.	% Total Sum of Squares
Sex	1	295.3	0.1	.5	0.0
Haptoglobin	2	11366.0	5.7	.004	3.3
Interaction	2	3890.0	2.0	.142	1.1
Unit	334	1980.9			95.6

TABLE 15

THE MEANS AND AN ANALYSIS OF VARIANCE FOR THE ASSOCIA-
TION BETWEEN THE SUMMED MAXIMUM RING FINGER RIDGE
COUNTS AND THE HAPTOGLOBIN LOCUS IN THE GENERAL LAU
POPULATION.

RING FINGER RIDGE COUNTS MEANS

Haptoglobin Genotype

	1 - 1	1 - 2	2 - 2
Males	36.2	41.2	35.0
Females	41.0	38.4	33.7
N	120	146	74

ANALYSIS OF VARIANCE

Source	Degrees of Freedom	Mean Square	F	Sig.	% Total Sum of Squares
Sex	1	4.4	0.0	.5	0.0
Haptoglobin	2	851.3	6.4	.002	3.6
Interaction	2	430.5	3.2	.042	1.8
Unit	334	133.6			94.6

nificant haptoglobin-ridge count associations were found on the middle ($P < .005$) and index fingers ($P < .008$).

Although the sex interaction pattern shown by the haptoglobin-ridge count associations is slightly different in the two populations, the Lau can be viewed as a more extreme expression of the sex difference seen in the Aita. The basic agreement between the two populations adds strength to the suspected genetic association of a continuous finger print trait and a single locus polymorphism.

There are two possible explanations for these highly significant general population associations. The first is pleiotropy (Penrose, 1939). By this explanation, the haptoglobin locus, or a gene very closely linked to it, is also a genetic determinant of finger ridge counts. There needs to be no physiological association between haptoglobin and ridge ontogeny, for the locus itself may have two independent effects. Nevertheless, in view of the fact that there seems to be no functional association whatsoever between the two traits, the very close linkage explanation may be more parsimonious.

Alternatively, the population association could be the fortuitous result of the isolation and inbreeding of subsets within the populations (Penrose, 1939). Since the Aita are totally unrelated linguistically and markedly separated geographically from the Lau, this suggestion seems less likely, for similar associations between haptoglobins and ridge counts are found in two populations. In addition, the populations are small and homogeneous, so it is unlikely that subsets within each are isolated and inbred, with congruent and fortuitous trait associations. Nevertheless, the samples include large families, and these are inbred to some extent, so there could be a fortuitous family association between the two traits.

Such fortuitous associations, due to relative isolation, however, would not occur within sibships (Mohr, 1953). As a confirmation of the suspected genetic association between finger pattern size and the haptoglobin locus, an analysis of the association was consequently made within the Aita sibships. Since the hypothesis for the association was pleiotropy, and therefore unidirectional in its expression, a paired t-test was used to confirm whether pairs of siblings, with segregation at the haptoglobin locus, showed a consistent and significant difference in their ridge counts.

These results are presented in Table 16. Comparisons are shown both for the 1-1 versus 1-2 pairs of siblings and the 1-1 versus 1-2 or 2-2 pairs. In order to pair siblings of different sex, the finger print characters were equalized for sex by standardization to a mean of 50 and a standard deviation of 10. The mean differences in the table are therefore in these standard units. For the total ridge count, the paired t-tests are highly significant (P < .001), and in actual ridge counts the mean sib difference amounts to nearly 20 ridges. The left thumb shows a more striking difference (P < .0001), which amounts to nearly 4 ridges, or about one-third of the population mean for this trait. The largest mean paired differences are found on the thumb and little fingers, while the middle fingers show smaller and frequently non-significant differences. The genetic determinations of both the thumb and little finger factors, described above, are therefore influenced by this association. The pattern intensity index shows a significant difference (P < .002), which further corroborates the genetic association between haptoglobins and finger pattern size.

TABLE 16

PAIRED T-TESTS FOR THE WITHIN SIBSHIP GENETIC ASSOCIATION
BETWEEN DIGITAL RIDGE COUNTS AND THE HAPTOGLOBIN
LOCUS IN THE AITA. THE MEAN DIFFERENCES ARE IN STANDARD
UNITS (MEAN OF 50 AND A STANDARD DEVIATION OF 10). COM-
PARISONS ARE SHOWN FOR THE HAPTOGLOBIN 1 - 1 VERSUS 1 - 2
PAIRS OF SIBLINGS AND THE 1 - 1 VERSUS 1 - 2 OR 2 - 2 PAIRS.

	1 - 1 Versus 1 - 2				1 - 1 Versus 1 - 2, 2 - 2			
	Mean Diff.	N	t	Sig. Level	Mean Diff.	N	t	Sig. Level
Right 1 Maximum Count	3.15	69	2.41	.01	2.65	84	2.30	.025
Left 1 Maximum Count	5.30	69	3.94	.0001	5.12	84	4.31	.0001
Right 2 Maximum Count	3.49	69	2.77	.005	3.64	84	3.04	.002
Left 2 Maximum Count	1.88	69	1.43	.10	2.01	84	1.75	.05
Right 3 Maximum Count	2.33	69	1.52	.10	1.87	84	1.40	.10
Left 3 Maximum Count	1.04	69	0.64	.30	0.94	84	0.68	.25
Right 4 Maximum Count	2.58	69	1.88	.05	2.09	84	1.76	.05
Left 4 Maximum Count	2.78	68	1.82	.05	2.66	83	1.91	.05
Right 5 Maximum Count	2.30	69	1.88	.05	3.68	84	3.02	.002
Left 5 Maximum Count	4.17	69	2.63	.005	4.20	84	2.92	.005
Total Maximum Count	3.80	68	3.18	.001	3.74	82	3.50	.0005
Pattern Intensity Index	3.93	68	3.01	.002	3.81	83	3.27	.001

Since this association occurs both in the general population and
within sibships, pleiotropy seems the best explanation. This is further
supported by the fact that the difference between sibs is significantly
unidirectional, indicating that the occurrence of haptoglobin 1-1 is
always associated with higher ridge counts. If this is not a pleiotropic
association, then linkage is so close that crossing over has not been
observed. The only way to determine close linkage would be to find a
population where crossing over has occurred and the association is in
the opposite direction. In any event, in behavior if not in actual fact,
there appears to be a pleiotropic association between finger pattern
size and the haptoglobin locus; a single gene seems to have two totally
different effects.

If one assumes for the moment that ridge counts are a completely additive trait, then a byproduct of this analysis of genetic association is an estimate of the number of co-equal genes involved. In the analysis of variance for the general population associations between haptoglobins and finger prints, it is possible to determine the percentage of the total variance (i.e. total sum of squares) which is accounted for by the haptoglobin segregation. These numbers were given in Tables 12-15, and they range from 3% to 4% in both populations. Assuming that about 70% of the ridge count variance is heritable, then an extrapolation from the haptoglobin locus leads to the conclusion that 20 to 25 genes of comparable effect are involved in the genetic determination of the total ridge count.

Obviously, the additive assumption is simplistic and major genes with greater effects or complex interactions probably exist, but the above is a ball park estimate that probably has heuristic merits. Holt (1968) considered the negative skew of the total ridge count distribution to be an indication of relatively few genes, since many genes would lead to a completely normal curve. However, the categorical difference between arches and loops interferes with the expression of pattern size (Luu-Mau-Thanh, 1965). This interference, causing sharp drops in the total ridge count at the lower end of its distribution, is probably a better explanation for negative skew. The above 20 to 25 gene estimate is also not altogether out of line with estimates for the number of genes involved in the determination of bristle number, or chaetae, on the bodies of *Drosophila*. Mather and Jinks (1971) emphatically stated that the minimum number was 18 and "the true number may be much larger than this" (p. 24).

A pleiotropy between haptoglobins and digital pattern size is only a single case of a genetic marker for finger prints, and by itself, it offers little further understanding of dermatoglyphic genetics. But it is a start, and it demonstrates that while Thoday (1967) was "in fact asking a lot," his suggestion is nevertheless possible. Even with a marker gene of only 4% effect on a human continuous variable, it has been possible to demonstrate a highly significant statistical association.

With just one more pleiotropic marker, it will be possible to demonstrate the additive inheritance of fingerprints in man (Howells, 1972). Perhaps this study of polygenic markers will show more complex genetic interactions, such as suppressions or combinations of two genes adding to three or more. There is already some indication of interaction with the genes that control dermatoglyphic sex differences in the haptoglobin population associations discussed above. Ridge counts are just as minute and insignificant as *Drosophila* bristle numbers; but perhaps dermal ridges will supply for man as useful a genetic tool as chaetae have been for fruit fly studies.

Bibliography

Anderson, G. J., H. J. Walberg, and W. W. Welch
    1969   Curriculum effects on the social climate of learning: A new representation of discriminant functions. Am. Educ. Research J., *6:* 315-328.
Bansal, P. and D. C. Rife
    1962   The inheritance of accessory triradii on palmar interdigital areas II and IV. Acta Genet. Med. Gemell., *11:* 29-38.
Barnicot, N. A., D. P. Mukherjee, J. C. Woodburn and F. J. Bennett
    1972   Dermatoglyphics of the Hadza of Tanzania. Human Biol., *44:* 621-648.
Biswas, P. C.
    1968   Recent advances in and further scope of dermatoglyphics. Int. Symp. Dermatoglyphics. Proceedings, 3-6.
Bonnevie, K.
    1924   Studies on papillary patterns of finger prints. J. Genet., *15:* 1-112.
Butler, P. M.
    1939   Studies of the mammalian dentition. Differentiation of the postcanine dentition. Proceedings Zool. Soc. London, *109:* 1.
Cavalli-Sforza, L. L. and W. F. Bodmer
    1971   The Genetics of Human Populations. Freeman, San Francisco.
Cummins, H. and C. Midlo
    1961   Finger Prints, Palms and Soles. Dover, New York.
Falconer, D. S.
    1960   Introduction to Quantitative Genetics. Ronald Press, New York.
Fisher, R. A.
    1918   The correlations between relatives on the supposition of Mendelian inheritance. Trans. Royal Soc. Edinburgh, *52:* 399-433.
Friedlaender, J. S., L. A. Sgaramella-Zonta, K. K. Kidd, L. Y. C. Lai, P. Clark, and R. J. Walsh
    1971   Biological divergences in South-central Bougainville: An analysis of blood polymorphism gene frequencies and anthropometric measurements utilizing tree models, and a comparison of the variables to linguistic, geographic, and migrational "distances." Am. J. Hum. Genet., *23:* 253-270.

Froehlich, J. W.
1973 The Usefulness of Dermatoglyphics as a Biological Marker of Human Populations in Melanesia. Ph.D. Thesis, Harvard Univ., Cambridge.

Galton, F.
1892 Finger Prints. Macmillan, London.

Glanville, E. V.
1965a Heredity and line A of palmar dermatoglyphics. Am. J. Hum. Genet., *17:* 420-424.

1965b Heredity and dermal patterns in the interdigital areas of the palm. Acta Gen. Med. Gemell., *14:* 295-304.

Hale, A. R.
1952 Morphogenesis of volar skin in the human fetus. Am. J. Anat., *91:* 147-181.

Harrick, N. J.
1962 Fingerprinting via total internal reflection. Philips Technical Review, *24:* 271-274.

Hesch, M.
1932 Papillarmuster bei Eingeborenen der Loyalty Inseln. Zeitschr. Rassenphysiol., *5:* 163-168.

Holt, S. B.
1956 Genetics of dermal ridges: Parent-child correlations for total finger ridge-count. Annals of Eugenics, *20:* 270-281.

1957 Genetics of dermal ridges: Sib pair correlations for total finger ridge-count. Annals of Eugenics, *21:* 352-362.

1961 Quantitative genetics of finger-print patterns. British Med. J., *17:* 247-250.

1968 The Genetics of Dermal Ridges. Charles C. Thomas, Springfield.

Howells, W. W.
1953 Correlations of brothers in factor scores. Am. J. Phys. Anthrop., *11:* 121-140.

1966 Variability in family lines vs. population variability. N. Y. Acad. of Science. Annals, *134:* 624-631.

1970 Anthropometric grouping analysis of Pacific peoples. Archaeol. Phys. Anthrop. in Oceania, *5:* 192-217.

1972 Personal communication.

Hunt, E. E. and J. D. Mavalwala
1964   Finger ridge counts in the Micronesians of Yap. Micronesica, *1:* 55-58.

Keiter, F.
1950   Uber Zehenbeerenmuster und Komplizientheitsindex. Zeitschr. Morph. Anthrop., *42:* 169-183.

1960   The problems of multifactorial genetics in man. In: Biometrical Genetics. Oscar Kempthorne, ed. Pergamon Press, New York.

Knussman, R.
1967   Interkorrelationen im Hautleistsystem des Menschen und ihre faktoranalytische Auswertung. Humangenetik, *4:* 221-243.

1969   Biostatische Familienuntersuchen zur Hautleistenvariabilität des Menschen. Humangenetik, *8:* 208-216.

1971   Biostatische Methoden im Dienst der Hautleistenforschung. In: Hautleisten und Krankheiten. W. Hirsch, ed.

Kumbnani, H. K.
1968   Inheritance of configurations on the palmar hypothenar area. Int. Symp. Dermatoglyphics. Proceedings, 105-112.

Lamy, M., J. Frézal, J. DeGrouchy, and J. Kelley
1957   Le hombre de dermatoglyphes dans un enchantillon de jumeaux. Ann. Hum. Genet., *21:* 374-396.

Livingstone, F. B.
1972   Genetic drift and polygenic inheritance. Am. J. Phys. Anthrop., *37:* 117-126.

Loesch, D.
1971   Genetics of dermatoglyphic patterns on palms. Ann. Hum. Genet., *34:* 277-293.

Luu-Mau-Thanh
1965   Étude de structure digitale des 6.000 inculpés francais par les emprientes digitales. Bull. Mém. Soc. d'Anthrop. Paris, Series 11, *8:* 23-38.

Mather, K.
1964   Human Diversity: The Nature and Significance of Differences Among Men. Oliver and Boyd, Edinburgh.

Mather, K. and J. L. Jinks
1971   Biometrical Genetics: The Study of Continuous Variation. Cornell Univ. Press, Ithaca.

Mayr, E.
1963   Animal Species and Evolution. Belknap Press, Cambridge.

McKusick, V. A.
  1969   Human Genetics. Prentice-Hall, Englewood Cliffs, New Jersey.
Mohr, J.
  1953   A Study of linkage in man. Opera ex Domo Biol. Hered. Hum. Univ. Hafniensis, 33.
Moroney, M. J.
  1956   Facts from Figures. Penguin Books, Baltimore.
Mukherjee, D. P.
  1966   Inheritance of total number of triradii on fingers, palms, and soles. Ann. Hum. Genet., *29:* 349-353.
Mulvihill, J. J. and D. W. Smith
  1969   The genesis of dermatoglyphics. J. Pediatrics, *75:* 579-589.
Newman, H. H.
  1930   The finger prints of twins. J. Genet., *23:* 415-446.
Parsi, P. and M. Di Bacco
  1968   Fingerprints and the diagnosis of zygosity in twins. Acta Genet. Med. Gemell., *17:* 333-358.
Penrose, L. S.
  1939   Some practical considerations in testing for genetic linkage in sib data. Ohio J. Sci., *39:* 291-296.

  1949   The Biology of Mental Defect. Sidgwick and Jackson, Ltd., London.

  1954   The distal triradius *t* on the hands of parents and sibs of mongol imbeciles, Ann. Hum. Genet., *19:* 10-38.
Pollitzer, W. S.
  1958   The Negroes of Charleston (S. C.): A study of hemoglobin types, serology, and morphology. Am. J. Phys. Anthrop., *16:* 241-263.
Pons, J.
  1953   Herencia de las lineas principales de la palma. Contribución de la genética de los caracteres dermopapilares. Trab. Inst. Ber. de Sahagún de Antropol. y Etnol., *14:* 35-50.

  1956   Data on linkage in man: P. T. C. tasting and some dermatoglyphic traits. Ann. Eugenics, *21:* 94-96.

  1959   Quantitative genetics of palmar dermatoglyphics. Am. J. Hum. Genet, *11:* 252-256.
Singh, S.
  1968   The dermatoglyphics of two groups of indigenes in New Guinea — Kundiawa (Chimbu) and Lake Kopiago. Archaeol. Phys. Anthrop. in Oceania, *3:* 116-122.

Sokal, R. R. and F. J. Rohlf
    1969   Biometry: The principles and practice of statistics in biological research. W. H. Freeman, San Francisco.
Stern, C.
    1960   Principles of Human Genetics. W. H. Freeman, San Francisco.
Tatsuoka, M.
    1971   Multivariate Analysis: Techniques for Educational and Psychological Research. John Wiley, New York.
Thoday, J. M.
    1967   New insights into continuous variation. In: Proceedings Third International Congress of Human Genetics. J. F. Crow and J. V. Neel, eds. Johns Hopkins Univ. Press, Baltimore.

    1969   Limitations to genetic comparison of populations. J. Biosoc. Science, Suppl., *1:* 3-14.
Vandenberg, S. G.
    1962   How "stable" are heritability estimates? A Comparison of heritability estimates from six anthropometric studies. Am. J. Phys. Anthrop., *20:* 331-338.
Walker, N. F.
    1965   The current status of research on dermatoglyphics in medical constitution. Proceedings XI Int. Cong. Genet., *3:* 981-990.
Weninger, M.
    1964   Zur "polygenen" (additiven) Vererbung des quantitativen Wertes der Fingerbeerenmuster. Homo, *15:* 96-103.

    1965a   Questioned paternity in the field of dermatoglyphics. Proceedings XI Int. Cong. Genet., *3:* 391-1000.

    1965b   Dermatoglyphic research. Human Biol., *37:* 44-57.
Wyslouch, B.
    1964   Variability, age changes and interfamilial correlations in the atd angle of the palm. Materialy I Prace Anthropologiczne, *70:* 157-162.

APPENDIX TABLE 1

THE GENETIC CORRELATIONS FOR THE DIGITAL TRAITS OF
PARENT-OFFSPRING AND SPOUSE PAIRS IN THE AITA AND BAEGU.
THEY ARE BASED ON ORDINARY PRODUCT MOMENT ESTIMA-
TIONS, AND HENCE ARE PRESENTED WITHOUT STANDARD ERRORS
OR SIGNIFICANCE EVALUATIONS. THEY ARE CRUDE ESTIMATES
PRESENTED ONLY TO SUPPLEMENT AND CORROBORATE THOSE
BASED ON SIB DATA GIVEN IN THE TEXT.

	Aita			Baegu		
	Mid-Parent Off-Spring	Like Sexed Parent Off-Spring	Spouse Pairs	Mid-Parent Off-Spring	Male Parent Off-Spring	Spouse Pairs
Right 1 Pattern	.41	.34	.18	.35	.34	−.00
Left 1 Pattern	.44	.32	.16	.31	.24	.06
Right 2 Pattern	.21	.20	.04	.18	.23	−.06
Left 2 Pattern	.38	.27	−.14	.38	.46	−.01
Right 3 Pattern	.36	.25	.02	.43	.25	.23
Left 3 Pattern	.47	.30	.15	.53	.30	.03
Right 4 Pattern	.35	.37	.01	.34	.16	−.11
Left 4 Pattern	.30	.17	.05	.44	.40	.04
Right 5 Pattern	.41	.30	.01	.24	.30	.16
Left 5 Pattern	.31	.28	−.07	.14	.12	.23
Right Intensity	.43	.37	.07	.43	.35	.13
Left Intensity	.49	.41	.06	.23	.41	.05
Total Pattern Inten.	.52	.44	.08	.52	.44	.12
Right 1 Max. Count	.47	.33	−.09	.30	.24	.02
Left 1 Max. Count	.48	.24	−.13	.38	.26	−.01
Right 2 Max. Count	.39	.25	.05	.40	.31	.09
Left 2 Max. Count	.37	.26	−.16	.46	.44	.08
Right 3 Max. Count	.41	.26	.03	.54	.34	.05
Left 3 Max. Count	.42	.30	.10	.54	.34	.06
Right 4 Max. Count	.38	.26	.05	.37	.29	−.09
Left 4 Max. Count	.38	.24	.08	.37	.30	−.03
Right 5 Max. Count	.44	.40	.14	.47	.44	.10
Left 5 Max. Count	.39	.38	.16	.42	.31	−.07
Total Maximum Count	.56	.40	.06	.45	.45	.04
Number of Pairs	212	250	62	114	96	63

APPENDIX TABLE 2

THE GENETIC CORRELATIONS FOR THE PALMAR TRAITS OF
PARENT-OFFSPRING AND SPOUSE PAIRS IN THE AITA AND BAEGU.
THEY ARE BASED ON ORDINARY PRODUCT MOMENT ESTIMATIONS,
AND HENCE ARE PRESENTED WITHOUT STANDARD ERRORS OR
SIGNIFICANCE EVALUATIONS. THEY ARE CRUDE ESTIMATES
PRESENTED ONLY TO SUPPLEMENT AND CORROBORATE THOSE
BASED ON SIB DATA GIVEN IN THE TEXT.

	Aita			Baegu		
	Mid-Parent Off-Spring	Like Sexed Parent Off-Spring	Spouse Pairs	Mid-Parent Off-Spring	Male Parent Off-Spring	Spouse Pairs
Right Mainline A	.40	.26	.06	.24	.24	−.10
Left Mainline A	.51	.36	.10	.27	.11	−.12
Right Mainline B	.27	.16	−.10	.40	.21	.08
Left Mainline B	.25	.19	.22	.49	.23	.09
Right Mainline C	.08	.00	−.05	.10	.24	.07
Left Mainline C	.09	.02	.09	.10	.39	.13
Right Mainline D	.31	.21	−.02	.43	.20	.00
Left Mainline D	.31	.22	.19	.49	.20	.15
Right Mainline Index	.40	.23	−.05	.36	.22	−.04
Left Mainline Index	.48	.34	.14	.28	.18	.02
Right Interdig. 3	.15	.11	−.09	.11	.20	−.02
Left Interdig. 3	.27	.08	.04	.20	.32	−.17
Right Interdig. 4	.22	.14	.24	.26	.36	−.14
Left Interdig. 4	.16	.14	−.12	.35	.09	.02
Total Hypothenar	.24	.25	−.06	Not		
Total Thenar	.27	.16	−.16	Calculated		
Number of Pairs	212	250	62	114	96	63

12. Variation in Tooth Eruption: a Field Guide

Howard L. Bailit

Introduction

The physical anthropologist undertaking a field study of human variation must consider restrictions of time, cost, subject cooperation and personal interests and training in deciding upon the battery of tests and observations. One often overlooked but useful measure of physiological development is the eruption of the teeth. Practically speaking this may be the only feasible index of physiological age to include because other measures such as bone age or sexual age are often impossible to determine because of the difficulties taking radiographs of the wrist in the field or making qualitative developmental assessments of secondary sex characteristics. The major disadvantage of dental age is that it is not highly correlated with bone or sexual maturation so that a child could be retarded skeletally but not dentally. However, dental age is still better than such gross indirect measures of physiological age as height or weight and should be one of the somatic characters evaluated in field studies.

The purpose of this paper is to present a brief field guide for the human biologist when collecting data on the eruption of teeth. It does not assume any special background in dental anthropology or dentistry.

In addition to giving some basic guidelines for field work, it reviews the literature, citing many of the "key" studies related to dental

In addition to giving some basic guidelines for field work, it reviews the literature, citing many of the "key" studies related to dental eruption. Emphasis is placed on variation within rather than between populations. The former literature comes mainly from clinical journals which human biologists may not often read but may find interesting because of its relevance to understanding interpopulation differences. The first section of the paper considers methods for collecting and analyzing data, followed by a discussion of the local factors which can influence the age of eruption and limit the conclusions drawn from the study. Next, the relative variance in the eruption age of individual teeth is described, as well as the variation in the sequence of eruption. Finally, the last sections briefly consider inter-population and inter-sex differences.

DEFINITION OF ERUPTION

The eruption of a tooth is defined as the first appearance of the incisal or occlusal surface of the crown in the oral cavity. It is an all or nothing phenomenon: either the tooth is present or it is not. In most cases, even an inexperienced layman would have little difficulty in determining whether or not a tooth has erupted. The only problem comes when the tooth first breaks through the gingiva and is difficult to see. In these cases, a legitimate difference in opinion could arise, but fortunately, this is a relatively fleeting event and will not be a major source of error.

The only other potential difficulty is being able to identify the tooth that has erupted. However, if both the position of the tooth relative to the other teeth and the morphology of the crown are considered, there is little concern for error.

For those who have not had a standard course in osteology or a laboratory in physical anthropology, the best way to learn the basic forms of the teeth is working with a knowledgeable tutor for two or three hours. Also, there are several books on dental anatomy which can be helpful (Wheeler, 1965). It may be safe to say, then, that population studies of tooth eruption can be done with a minimum of formal training.

To determine the age of eruption, it is, of course, absolutely necessary to know the age of the subjects being examined. This is the main reason most studies of tooth eruption deal with societies where birth records are available.

COLLECTION OF DATA

There are no required pieces of specialized equipment for obtaining data on tooth eruption. Providing there is good natural light, the most sophisticated tool that can be useful is a wooden throat stick for keeping the subject's mouth wide open and retracting the cheek from around the posterior teeth. Most commonly, subjects are seated on a chair or stool, high enough so that the examiner will not get a sore back resulting from leaning over. The sun should be behind the examiner's back but not facing directly into the subject's eyes. Then the patient's mouth is examined; the examiner notes the teeth erupted on the left side of the arches, and this is recorded by an assistant. Since teeth erupt fairly symmetrically, it is not necessary to do both sides of the mouth.

If only the permanent teeth are considered, then the forms to record the data are easily constructed and used with the assistant merely checking off which of the sixteen teeth on the left side have erupted. If the deciduous teeth are to be included, the same form can be used but there should be a special section on the primary teeth. Thus after the permanent teeth that are present have been identified, the same thing can be done for the deciduous teeth. With cooperative subjects, it should not take more than five minutes to assess an individual.

STATISTICAL METHODS

The most common measures of central tendency for tooth eruption are the arithmetic mean and median. Of the two, the median is preferred because the frequency distribution curves for age of tooth eruption are slightly skewed to the right because there are more children with abnormally late rather than early erupting teeth. Thus, the mean age of eruption tends to be older than the median, since the latter is less affected by extreme values.

Several methods are available for determining the median age of eruption. The arithmetic solution is only feasible when the frequency of erupted teeth in successive age groups increases in a linear manner, since the estimate is made by linear interpolation from a cumulative frequency curve. Generally, such a distribution will rarely be found, so that this method has little practical importance. Another arithmetic method is that of Karber (Cornfield and Mantel, 1950). This technique makes no assumption about the distribution of eruption ages being normal, either arithmetically or logorithmically, but it does require that the sample include the entire age range of children who have for any tooth from 0 to 100 percent erupted. That is, Karber's solution is not recommended for incomplete data, (e.g., the oldest group of subjects only have 85 percent of a given tooth erupted).

A graphical solution is certainly the easiest and quickest method and is surprisingly accurate. It consists of plotting the percentage of teeth erupted against age on arithmetic probability paper. Since the distribution of tooth eruption ages is nearly normal, the plots assume a linear form and estimates of the mean and standard deviation are obtained from a "least squares" line of best fit.

Perhaps the most accurate approach is probit analysis, a statistical technique originally developed to estimate the dosage of a drug at which 50 percent of a given population subjected to the drug die. Here, the analogy is finding the median age for a dental eruption. This level of dosage is often called the median lethal dose (LD50). Estimating the LD50 is a difficult statistical problem since either the exposed subject does or does not die. By the same token, either the tooth is or is not erupted at a given age, so the two situations are parallel and the statistical methods developed for one are applicable to the other.

The advantage of the probit method is that complete data are not required. However, it is important to have values in the area of 40 to 50 percent of teeth erupted, but one need not be concerned with missing values below 16 percent or above 84 percent erupted.

The probit method as used in dental eruption studies has been examined by Hayes and Mantel (1958) and Gates (1966). For a more definitive explanation Finney (1952) is recommended. Simply put, the percentage of teeth erupted in each age group is transformed into probits which are essentially a type of standard score. When these are plotted against log age[1] to take out the positive skewness from late erupting teeth, the series of points appear linearly arranged. A straight line can be fitted to these points by eye or by the maximum likelihood method and tested for goodness of fit. When an adequate fit is found by either method, the probit regression line equation is then used to calculate the median age of eruption as well as the variance and standard error of the median.

[1]According to Hayes and Mantel (1950), the distribution age for a given tooth is so close to being normal that both theoretically and empirically, there is no need to use log age.

Hayes and Mantel (1958) found the different methods to give quite similar results. They suggest Karber's method as being best when complete data are available.

LONGITUDINAL VERSUS CROSS-SECTIONAL STUDIES

It is important to note that while the different methods of calculating the mean or median age of eruption give slightly different answers, comparing the results of longitudinal and cross-sectional studies cause much greater errors. Dahlberg and Menegaz-Bock (1958) pointed out that in longitudinal studies, the examiner sees the tooth only after it erupts and never before so that the time of eruption is always overestimated. As a result, the estimates of eruption age from longitudinal studies tend to be older than for cross-sectional ones. This can easily be adjusted for by subtracting from each subject's age of eruption one half the examination interval on the assumption of uniformily distributed eruption during that interval. Of course, if the interval between examinations is very short, then the degree of overestimation becomes negligible. Surprisingly then, cross-sectional studies generally give a better representation of the eruption age of a population than the longitudinal approach.

LOCAL FACTORS EFFECTING THE AGE OF ERUPTION

Relevant local factors include environmental situations in the oral cavity which influence the eruption of one or two teeth, relatively independent of general somatic development and maturation. There are innumerable local conditions which can effect the eruption of teeth such as x-radiation to the developing tooth, or direct trauma from accidents. From the point of view of population studies, it is evident that both of these are far too infrequent to be a major or even minor source of error in a large survey. Far more important are carious teeth and the extraction of carious teeth. Since almost all human populations are subject to dental decay these factors must be considered when determining eruption age.

Several workers have observed that extracting deciduous molars caused the premolars which erupt in the same space to appear earlier (Leslie, 1951). This is sometimes explained by noting that when the deciduous teeth are extracted, the hard and soft tissues above the permanent tooth are removed which reduces the physical impediments to eruption. While this explanation sounds reasonable it is not quite that simple. More specifically, Leslie observed that in certain situations the premolars erupt later rather than earlier than normal when the deciduous molars are extracted. He suggests that later eruption occurs when the deciduous molars are extracted very early so that the tissue overlying the permanent tooth has a chance to reorganize. This would tend to make eruption even more difficult than the normal situation where the resorbing deciduous root leaves a path for the permanent tooth to follow.

Another local factor effecting the age of premolar eruption is the mesial drift of the first permanent molar when the deciduous first or second molars are extracted. Some evidence suggests that if this occurs before the age of seven, there is ample time for mesial drift of the first permanent molar into the space where the premolars normally erupt, resulting in delayed eruption. On the other hand, after the age of seven, there is not enough time for the first molar to drift mesially and the premolars erupt at the normal time.

The extraction effect is not limited to deciduous teeth alone. Fanning (1962a) observed in Boston children that if one or more permanent teeth are extracted in the arch, the third molar erupts approximately 1.5 years earlier than normal. She pointed out that this finding may explain to some extent the early eruption of third molars reported by Chagula (1960), in a sample of East African school boys. In a later study, Fanning surveyed some of these children and found, in fact, that the younger ones had many carious and extracted teeth.

Even without extractions, carious teeth may be associated with earlier erupting permanent successors. Fanning (1962b) reported that in a study of 207 Ohio born children, root resorption of the deciduous molars in boys was accelerated in the presence of dental caries. The same trend was seen in girls, although the results were not significant. It is reasonable to speculate then, that the permanent tooth would follow the path of the resorbing deciduous root and erupt earlier than normal.

In summary, the extraction of deciduous molars has an effect on the eruption times of the permanent premolars due to the resulting mesial drifting of the first permanent molar and the reduction or increase in the amount of bone overlying the erupting tooth. As far as population studies are concerned, there is no way to adjust for differences in caries prevalence when comparing eruption in two or more populations, since the degree of retardation or acceleration is not known. As always, the safest course is to be conservative in any conclusions drawn from the data.

THE NUMBER OF ERUPTED TEETH

Besides the mean or median age of eruption for each type of tooth, a rough estimate of dental development can be made just from counting the number of erupted teeth. This is a simple procedure which takes little training. The only pitfalls are in distinguishing a deciduous from a permanent tooth and also in being sure that extracted or impacted teeth are not counted as missing. Needless to say, if there is a choice between evaluating the eruption age of each tooth and counting the number of teeth erupted, the former gives more information and is certainly to be preferred. A word of caution should again be given on the difference between the use of the median and mean. Because more teeth are retarded rather than advanced in eruption, the median number of erupted teeth is usually less than the mean number and gives a more accurate value for the population.

INTERRELATIONSHIP BETWEEN ERUPTING TEETH

The eruption times of different teeth in an individual are not independent of each other. If the central incisor erupts early, there is a good chance the remaining teeth will also be advanced. The actual correlations among the eruption of permanent teeth range between .34 and .83 with an average of about .65, indicating that there is considerable interdependence among the eruption times of different teeth (Sturdivant *et al.*, 1962). The highest correlations are between teeth in the same morphological class. For example, the correlation of I_1 with I_2 is .74, whereas I_1 with M_1 is .55, and this relationship seems to hold for all classes of teeth. It should also be noted that homologous teeth on the left and right sides of a jaw are highly correlated in eruption age (ranges between .77 to .94). This is also true for homologous teeth in the maxilla and mandible (ranges between .67 to .82).

From the viewpoint of field studies, the relatively high correlation between teeth in age of eruption means that one can feel safe in assuming that if a subject is advanced at age eight, he will also be developmentally ahead at later ages.

ERUPTION VARIATION

Since the permanent teeth erupt over a 16-year period, it is not surprising that the variation in time of eruption is not the same for every tooth. Those teeth which erupt at an older age are more variable in eruption time. This makes intuitive sense because of the scale effect. The variation in first molar eruption has to be less than that of the third molar, since the former has a lower age limit of 5 or 6 years and the latter of 17-21 years. While this is the most extreme case, it demonstrates the point and suggests that it is not legitimate to just compare the "raw" variance in eruption age for each tooth. As an example of this problem, Gates (1964) gives the median age of eruption and its fiducial range (the age at which it would be expected to find a given tooth erupted in 5 to 95 percent of the population from which the sample was drawn) in 5,660 Australian school children. The fiducial range increases as the median age of eruption increases—the notable exception to this is the second molar, which has a smaller range than expected. Unfortunately, there is little information available on the variation in the eruption of the third molars. This tooth usually erupts after the completion of compulsory education, so that many older adolescents are not available when school surveys of dental eruption are done.

One way to avoid the scale effect is to use the coefficient of variation, which standardizes the variance by the mean. Table 1 is an

TABLE 1

THE AVERAGE COEFFICIENT OF VARIATION FOR THE ERUPTION AGE OF INDIVIDUAL PERMANENT TEETH. BASED ON DATA TAKEN FROM DAHLBERG AND MENEGAZ-BOCK (1958), CATTELL (1928), KLEIN *et al.* (1938), COHEN (1928), EVELETH (1968) and AINSWOTH (1925).

Tooth	Males		Females	
	Mean	*Range*	*Mean*	*Range*
I^1	10.05	9.06-11.54	9.19	7.82-10.41
I^2	9.86	8.58-12.76	11.38	9.87-12.02
C	11.13	9.31-12.09	11.20	9.61-14.53
P^1	14.32	12.69-16.05	12.99	11.01-15.42
P^2	13.29	11.82-15.71	12.86	12.40-15.49
M^1	11.89	8.43-12.87	11.13	9.25-15.87
M^2	9.29	8.51-10.36	9.35	8.93-11.33
I_1	11.06	8.43-14.21	10.37	6.72-12.19
I_2	10.70	9.19-15.81	10.13	9.37-13.93
C	10.40	9.56-11.87	10.29	9.42-12.92
P_1	12.72	12.24-15.39	12.47	10.79-13.82
P_2	13.88	12.71-18.24	13.31	12.68-15.45
M_1	11.51	10.62-15.26	11.75	7.50-18.23
M_2	9.91	7.37-11.52	9.38	8.39-13.02

analysis of the coefficients of variation for the eruption age of permanent teeth in six populations. The mean and range of the coefficients are presented separatey by sex.

While there is some doubt about any one coefficient, a definite pattern is discernable. The first premolars (P1) and especially the second premolars (P2) in both the maxilla and mandible show more variation than the other teeth. The reasons for the high coefficients of variation for P2 might be their relatively high frequency of congenital absence — around four percent — which gives a positive skew to the distribution of eruption ages for this tooth. In a sense then, the upper age boundary for the eruption of P2 is infinite, and this results in a large value for the fiducial range. On the other hand, P1 is seldom congenitally absent, so that the high coefficient of variation for this tooth would appear to be real and probably due to the effect of caries and extractions of deciduous teeth, delaying or accelerating eruption. While the premolars are quite variable in eruption age, the second molars show the lowest coefficient of variation, although they approximate the variation seen in I1, I2 and C.

VARIABILITY IN THE SEQUENCE OF PERMANENT TOOTH ERUPTION

The sequence of permanent tooth eruption for a population can easily be determined by examining the median ages of eruption for each tooth. Although there is considerable variation, the most common sequence is:

Maxilla: M1, I1, I2, P1, C P2, M2
Mandible: (I1, M1) I2, C, P1, M2, P2

The parenthesis around I1 and M1 signify that these teeth erupt at about the same time and that their ordering is arbitrary. The above sequence holds for both left and right sides of the jaws. Of course, there are many deviations from these patterns. For example, Lo and Moyers (1953) Sturdivant *et al.* (1962) and Knott and Meredith (1966), found around 20 different sequences of eruption in the maxilla and mandible respectively in longitudinal studies of white males and females. Some of the more common sequences were:

JAW	*SEQUENCE*	*% OF SAMPLE*
Maxilla	M1, I1, I2, P1, C, P2, M2	16-26
	M1, I1, I2, P1, P2, C, M2	18-49
Mandible	(I1, M1) I2, P1, C, P2, M2	9-18

For both arches, the major source of variation is the eruption of the canine relative to the premolars (Sturdivant *et al.*, 1962) and, in this area, a sex difference has been noted by some workers. Adler and Godeny (1952) showed that in a large sample of Hungarian children the lower canine in girls erupts before the upper first premolars whereas in boys the reverse order predominates. Barrett *et al.* (1964) have devised a modified way to determine the statistical significance of the eruption sequence for any two teeth. While this test is of some interest, it will not be examined here since it has limited application in most field situations.

Between the mandible and maxilla there is also a definite ordering in eruption sequence. Most mandibular teeth erupt before their opposites or homologues in the maxilla. The actual percentage of times maxillary teeth erupt before the mandibular teeth has been reported by Sturdivant *et al.* (1962). Generally speaking, less than eight percent of anterior teeth erupt first in the maxilla; in the posterior teeth, however, 46 percent of first premolars, 44 percent of second premolars, 46 percent of first molars and 28 percent of second molars appear in the upper jaw first. Most other reports give the maxillary premolars a predominance over their mandibular counterparts in eruption.

The permanent teeth erupt in three distinct periods. In the first one, the first molars, central and lateral incisors; the second period, the canines, first and second premolars and second molars; and in the third period, the third molars appear.

For the most part, there is no overlap between the second and third periods, whereas the first and second do overlap in about 2-3 percent of the population (Adler and Adler-Hradecky, 1959). This may result from the upper lateral incisors being congenitally absent in about 2-3 percent of most populations so that the first premolar, the first tooth of the second period, erupts before the lateral (which in this case never erupts). These periods can be important when examining a limited group of children with respect to age and numbers. If they are between periods, not as much variation will be found within the population in tooth eruption compared to examining children in the middle of a given period.

DECIDUOUS TOOTH VARIATION
Compared to the permanent teeth variation in eruption of the de-

ciduous teeth is minimal. The sequence of deciduous tooth eruption can be listed as:

$dI_1, dI^1, dI^2, dI_2, (dM_1, dM^1), dC^1, C^1, C_1, dM_2, dM^2$

There is naturally some variability in the above sequence, and this can only be considered a general tendency. For example, Doering and Allen (1942) found that 12.2 percent of their 220 children had a different sequence. Most frequently dI^2 erupted after dM^1. Another general rule is that the mandibular teeth erupt before their maxillary counterparts. The notable exception to this is the lateral incisors where the reverse order is commonly seen (Rabinow *et al.*, 1942 and Barrett and Brown, 1966).

POPULATION VARIATION IN TOOTH ERUPTION

Trying to compare the eruption age of the permanent teeth in different populations is most difficult because few investigations have published comparable data. As pointed out previously, some investigations use the median age and others the mean age of eruption, and even if the same statistic is used, they are often calculated by different methods. In addition, there is the problem of longitudinal versus cross-sectional studies, wide disparities in sample size, different definitions of eruption, and finally, the prevalence of caries. With all these limitations, it becomes a legitimate question whether or not a comparison is possible. While there is no answer to this question, it may still be worthwhile to examine variation in tooth eruption, keeping in mind the serious problems in comparison and being conservative in any conclusions.

Based on the work of Friedlaender and Bailit (1969), perhaps the most striking observation is the relative homogeneity within major population groupings in age of eruption. While this does not hold true for all teeth in all populations, it is supported by most of the data. The second major observation, a corollary of the first, is that there does seem to be substantial differences between Africans and Melanesians, and Asians and Europeans. The former groups erupt their teeth earlier than the latter populations. This varies somewhat from tooth to tooth, with the anterior teeth being most accelerated. Whether or not the earlier eruption results from genetic or environmental factors is not really known, although there is some reason to believe the differences are of genetic origin (Friedlaender and Bailit, 1969).

ERUPTION OF DECIDUOUS TEETH

The primary dentition starts to erupt at six months of age and continues for the next 24 months or so. Relatively speaking, only a few studies have investigated the eruption of the deciduous teeth, but from the papers, it can be concluded that population differences appear to be minimal. Voors (1957) did an analysis of variance on the age of eruption of the first deciduous tooth to erupt and found no significant differences among children of varied ethnic backgrounds and socio-economic levels. He maintained that the eruption of the deciduous teeth can be used as a temporal landmark to compare the growth and development of children from different populations. Meredith (1946) in an exhaustive review of the literature also concluded that ethnic and racial differences in the deciduous teeth are minimal.

SEX VARIATION IN THE ERUPTION OF THE PERMANENT TEETH

Based on ten populations using cross-sectional sampling and the median age of eruption, the average percentage sex difference ((males-females) males) x 100 in the timing of permanent tooth eruption and its standard error are:

	I1	I2	C	P1	P2	M1	M2
Maxillar	$3.87 \pm .63$	$3.64 \pm .72$	$5.88 \pm .45$	$3.92 \pm .59$	$3.37 \pm .61$	$1.70 \pm .43$	$3.33 \pm .78$
Mandible	$2.84 \pm .60$	$3.25 \pm .11$	$8.85 \pm .66$	$5.89 \pm .35$	$3.36 \pm .54$	4.13 ± 1.15	$4.08 \pm .68$

The teeth with the greatest amount of sexual dimorphism in eruption age are the canines. On the average, females erupt these teeth six months earlier in the maxilla and eight months earlier in the mandible. It has already been noted that the early eruption of the canine in females results in a different sequence of permanent tooth eruption. In females the canine usually erupts before the first premolar and in males after the first premolar. The delayed eruption of the canine in males is also seen in most non-human primates, being very exaggerated in terrestrial monkeys such as the baboon. This sex difference in eruption may be due to the canine being much larger in males than females (in certain species) both in crown and root, and therefore, taking longer to erupt. As far as it can be determined, it is not because the rate of canine development in the males is slower than in females.

For the other teeth, females are about 3.5 percent earlier than males in eruption. The only variation from this is the first molars which show the smallest sex difference, around 2 percent. For different age groups, there is obviously going to be some with more sexual dimorphism in the number of erupted teeth than others. Children who are 5 to 6 years old and just erupting their first molars can be expected to show little differences between males in females, since the first molars only show a 1-2 percent sex difference. On the other hand, at age eleven the difference will be greatest since the canines are erupting. After the canines appear the degree of sexual dimorphism decreases, mainly due to the fact that most of the 28 teeth have erupted.

It is interesting that the teeth on either side of the canine, the lateral incisors and first premolar, show more sexual dimorphism than the more distal teeth in the same class, the central incisor and second premolar, respectively. This parallels the situation in tooth size according to Garn *et al.* (1966). These workers claimed a field effect of sex dimorphism in the M-D diameter around the canine, whereby the laterals and first premolars also showed a greater sex difference.

Bailit *et al.* (1968) was not able to demonstrate this field effect on examination of a larger group of populations, so that there is some doubt if a real sex gradient exists. However, if we assume that there is a tooth size sex difference gradient around the canine, then the difference in tooth eruption becomes clarified. That is, if I^2 is proportionately larger than I^1 in males versus females, then they would also be expected to erupt later, for the same reasons given for the canine. This would also be true of the premolars.

The age of eruption of the third molar has not been presented because there are so few data available. The few studies done so far suggest that there is little or no sexual dimorphism in the eruption of this tooth (Rantanen, 1967; Adler and Adler-Hralecky, 1962). This is somewhat remarkable, since it is the only tooth that does not erupt earlier in females.

SUMMARY AND CONCLUSIONS
Information on the eruption of the permanent dentition can pro-

vide anthropologists with some important insights into human populations. Since there seems to be significant racial differences in the age of eruption — Melanesian and African populations being decidedly advanced over European or Asian groups, these data can be used along with other serological and anthropometric measures to classify or determine the genetic affinities among populations. Secondly, tooth eruption does not seem to be influenced by environmental factors to the same extent as skeletal maturation so that dental age can be a useful predictor of chronological age.

Methodologically, eruption data can be collected at little expense in terms of specialized equipment or facilities. Cross-sectional sampling by age and sex may be the best method for obtaining accurate estimates of eruption age, and of the various methods for calculating the median age of eruption, probit analysis is preferred. When comparing tooth eruption data in different populations, care should be taken that the studies were cross-sectional, obtained data on the sexes separately, used the median versus the mean age of eruption and calculated the median by probit analysis.

The other major factor which can affect eruption age is the prevalence of caries in the populations. Generally, a high rate of caries and extractions lead to earlier eruption ages. Finally, there is considerable variation in the sequence of eruption within populations, and certain teeth are more variable than others. All these factors need to be considered when analyzing field data.

Bibliography

Adler, P. and Adler-Hradecky, C.
1959   Normal variability of the changing dentition. Acta Morph., *9:* 63-72.
Adler, P. and Godeny, E.
1952   Studies on the eruptions of permanent teeth. Acta Gent. et. Statis. Med., *3:* 30-49.
Ainsworth, N.J.
1925   Dental disease in children. Med. Research Council, Great Britain, Special Report, Series No. 97.
Bailit, H.L., DeWitt, S.J. and Leigh, R.
1968   The size and morphology of the Nasioi dentition. Am. J. Phys. Anthrop., *28:* 271-288.

Barrett, M.J. and Brown, T.
1966   Eruption of deciduous teeth in Australian Aborigines. Aust. Dent. J., *11:* 43-50.

Barrett, M.J., Brown, T. and Cellier, K.M.
1964   Tooth eruption sequence in a tribe of Central Australian Aborigines. Amer. J. Phys. Anthrop., *22:* 79-89.

Cattell, P.
1928   Dentition as a Measure of Maturity. Cambridge: Harvard University Press.

Chagula, W.K.
1960   The age at eruption of third permanent molars in male East Africans. Am. J. Phys. Anthrop., *18:* 77-82.

Cohen, J.T.
1928   The dates of eruption of the permanent teeth in a group of Minneapolis children: A preliminary report, JADA, *15:* 2337-2341.

Cornfield, J. and Mantel, N.
1950   New aspects of the applications of maximum likelihood to the calculation of dosage response curve. Am. Stat. Assoc. J., *45:* 181-210.

Dahlberg, A.A. and Menegaz-Bock, R.M.
1958   Emergence of the permanent teeth in Pima Indian children. J. Dent. Res., *37:* 1123-1140.

Doering, C.R. and Allen, M.F.
1942   Data on eruption and caries of deciduous teeth. Child Devel., *13:* 113-129.

Eveleth, P.B.
1966   Eruption of permanent dentition and menarche of American children living in the tropics. Hum. Biol., *38:* 60-70.

Fanning, E.A.
1962a   Third molar emergence in Bostonians. Amer. J. Phys. Anthrop., *20:* 339-346.

––––––––––

1962b   The relationship of dental caries and root resorption of deciduous molars. Arch. Oral Biol., *7:* 595-601.

Friedlaender, J.S. and Bailit, H.L.
1969   Eruption times of the deciduous and permanent teeth of natives of Bougainville Island, Territory of New Guinea: A Study of Racial Variation. Human Biol., *41:* 51-65.

Garn, S.M., Kerewsky, R.A. and Swindler, D.R.
1966   Canine "field" in sexual dimorphism of tooth size. Nature, *212:* 150-151.

Gates, R.E.
1964   Eruption of permanent teeth of New South Wales school children. II. Sequence of eruption and commencement and completion of the dentition. Austral. Dent. J., *9:* 380-386.

1966   Computation of the median age of eruption of permanent teeth using probit analysis and an electronic computer. J. Dent. Res., *45:* 1024-1028.

Hayes, R.L. and Mantel, N.
1958   Procedures for computing the mean age of eruption of human teeth. J. Dent. Res., *37:* 938-945.

Klein, H. and Palmer, C.E.
1938   Dental Caries in American Indian Children (Records from schools). Am. Dent. Assoc. J. and Dent. Cosmos, *25:* 996-998.

Knott, V.B. and Meredith, H.V.
1966   Statistics on eruption of the permanent dentition from serial data for North American White children. Angle Orthod., *36:* 68-79.

Leslie, G.H.
1958   A biometrical study of the eruption of the permanent dentition of New Zealand children. John McIndoe Ltd., New Zealand.

Lo, R.T. and Moyers, R.E.
1953   Studies in the etiology and prevention of malocclusion. I. The sequence of eruption of the permanent dentition. Am. J. Orthodont., *39:* 460-467.

Rabinow, M., Richards, T.W. and Anderson, M.
1942   The eruption of deciduous teeth. Growth, *6:* 127-133.

Sturdivant, J.E., Knott, V.B. and Meredith, H.V.
1962   Interrelations from serial data for eruption of the permanent dentition. Angle Orthod., *32:* 1-13.

Voors, A.W.
1957   The use of dental age in studies of nutrition in children. Docum. Medic. Georg. Trop., *9:* 137-148.

Wheeler, R.C.
1965   A Textbook of Dental Anatomy and Physiology. 4th edition, Philadelphia: Saunders.

FOUR

Biological Anthropology:
The Uses of Bone

The interpretation of human skeletal variation has long been a prerogative of the biological anthropologist in a field where many expertises impinge on his. Perhaps it is no surprise then that this section includes more chapters than any other. Human bones do yield much information, and they have that undeniable advantage of durability. Fossil bones link us directly with the past—no inferences needed—but their morphology must be interpreted. McHenry provides one sophisticated example of how this may be done. Subfossil and archaeologically-derived skeletons provide less evolutionary but more demographic potential. Two papers (Saul's and Edynak's) show the range of deductions that such material permits. Rightmire examines two complementary but sometimes conflicting methodologies for ascertaining phylogenetic distances among populations represented by osteological samples.

Study of the human skeleton has generated many approaches to personal identification—forensic anthropology—that can also assist in demographic assessment. McKern's paper on sexing pelves illustrates this genre, while Lombardi's study of Mexican crania uses factor analysis to look at size interrelationships among the skull's constituent parts.

Capping Section Four is Hursh's evaluation of methodologies available for the study of cranial form, including techniques not yet tried. Osteology's future seems assured by the vigor, diversity and potential of the methodologies tested in the following chapters.

1976 In   The Measures of Man edited by
Eugene Giles and Jonathan S. Friedlaender.
Peabody Museum Press, Harvard University,
Cambridge, Mass. Pp. 338 to 371.   Written in 1971

13. Multivariate Analysis of Early Hominid Humeri

Henry M. McHenry

Introduction

The announcement and analysis of the Kanapoi humerus in 1967 by Professors Bryan Patterson and William Howells showed the utility of multivariate analysis in paleoanthropology. Despite the warning by Straus (1948) that hominoid humeri, especially the distal ends, are difficult to distinguish from one another, they were able to separate quite effectively the humeri of chimpanzees and humans using discriminant analysis. Their method not only distinguished the two groups of humeri and classified the fossils, but it also led to a better interpretation of the morphology.

When the expedition led by Richard Leakey discovered a new and beautifully preserved early hominid humerus in 1970, I was fortunate

NOTES: I wish to thank Professor W. W. Howells for the valuable counsel throughout the preparation of this study. I am also grateful for the encouragement given to me by Dr. Bernard Campbell who first suggested the project. Richard Leakey generously permitted me to study the original East Rudolf material. Dr. C. K. Brain and his assistant Elizabeth Voigt gave me permission to study the South African early hominid material at the Transvaal Museum and were very helpful. The following people kindly permitted me to study the comparative skeletal material in their charge: Dr. Poll of the Musée Royale de l'Afrique Centrale in Belgium, Professor Vandebroek of to be given the opportunity to do a similar multivariate analysis (Leakey 1971). My intention was to expand the Patterson and Howells (1967) study to include all hominoid genera with a larger number of measurements and with the three best preserved early hominid humeri, those from Kromdraai, Kanapoi, and the new one from East Rudolf.

The new humerus from East Rudolf (KNM-ER 739) has been described preliminarily by Richard Leakey (1971) and more thoroughly by Leakey, Mungai, and Walker (1972). The bone is very significant for several reasons: (1) it is beautifully preserved, lacking only the proximal end; (2) it is older than 1.0 to 1.5 million years (Leakey 1972); (3) it is very robust indicating, perhaps, its affinity to the robust australopsithecine species; (4) we know little about the locomotor behavior of the robust australopithecine and the possibility still exists that they were knuckle-walkers like African great apes or at least their immediate phylogenetic predecessors were (Leakey 1971).

The latter possibility has stirred a good deal of private discussion in the last few years particularly just after the discovery of the new humerus. Certain features of the bone such as its striking rugosity and thickness give it a certain non-hominid appearance. In general robusticity it is comparable to a female gorilla although the distal articular surface is somewhat smaller. There are distinctive differences as well, including the shape and depth of the olecranon fossa which is more comparable to the human condition.

---

the Université du Louvain, Dr. Richard Thorington of the Smithsonian Institution, Dr. Barbara Lawrence and Mr. Charles Mack of the Museum of Comparative Zoology, Harvard University, Mr. Don Brothwell and Mrs. Prue Napier of the British Museum (Natural History), Mr. Barton of the Powell-Cotton Museum, and Professor Howells of the Peabody Museum, Harvard University.

Living expenses while working on the project were paid in part by a National Institute of Health Predoctoral Fellowship No. 1F01GM 43, 300-01. A grant from the Wenner Gren Foundation for Anthropological Research really made the study possible. Part of the travel expenses were paid by a prize from the Harvard Travel Service.

My greatest debt is to my wife who has aided me enormously from the first word of the grant proposal to the final conclusion.

With these considerations in mind, a multivariate analysis of the distal ends of the australopithecine humeri was undertaken. The analysis focused on the following basic question: Is there any indication in the shape of the fossil bones that any of these early hominids or their ancestors used their forelimbs differently from modern man? To answer this question, it is easiest to divide it into three smaller problems: (1) Are the overall shapes of the fossil distal humeri different from those of modern man? (2) Are they more like one of the other extant hominoids? (3) Are the differences accountable on the basis of function? While considering all these questions the knuckle-walking hypothesis will be examined — that is, do the fossils accord well with the theory that man passed through a knuckle-walking stage in his evolution?

MEASUREMENTS

Measurements were chosen with several factors in mind. Of course, the completeness of the fossils is a primary consideration. Although the East Rudolf humerus consists of most of a shaft as well as the distal joint surface, the majority of the measurements concentrate on the distal end of the bone so that the Kanapoi and Kromdraai humeri can be included in the analysis. Measurements were taken that seemed to describe best the overall shape of the bone. An attempt was made to have a balanced number of transverse and a-p breadths as well as some lengths and heights. Each measurement was repeated several times to insure accuracy. Experience by previous workers was not ignored. Straus (1948) defines ten dimensions of the distal humerus of which nine are incorporated into this study. Patterson and Howells (1967) define several new measurements which also are used here.

A great deal of thought went into the problem of the "functional significance" of the measurements. The excellent work of Oxnard and associates on the shoulder of primates (Ashton *et al.* 1965, Oxnard 1967) and by Day and Wood (1968) on the talus has demonstrated how useful a functional, quantitative approach to morphology can be. Indeed, Day and Wood were able to talk about the "total functional morphology" of the Olduvai talus and its "functional affinities" within the primates. These phrases are enormously appealing, but may be oversimplifications. I had intended to find dimensions of the distal humerus which varied among the higher primates according to locomotor adaptations. For example, Napier and Davis (1959) propose that the trochlear index (trochlear width/capitular width x 100) reflects to what extent the animal habitually assumes a suspensory posture. They speculate that primates which are more quadrupedal would have proportionately larger capitular surfaces (for the articulation of the radius) than those primates which habitually suspend themselves underneath branches. These latter primates (the semibrachiators and the brachiators) would have proportionately larger trochlear surfaces for the articulation of the ulna. Their argument is that the radius is important as a supportive structure and the ulna as a suspensory structure. Recent studies have shown, however, that the tensile forces incurred by activities such as suspension are not transmitted to any large extent through bone (Curry 1968, Oxnard 1971). For the specimens they measure, the index takes on the values that they expect, *Papio* with the smallest value and *Pan* with the largest. However, when one is dealing with just the hominoids, the pattern is just the opposite from the prediction. The most arboreal ape *(Hylobates)* has the lowest value and the most quadrupedal ape *(Gorilla)* has the highest figure.

This example is cited not to criticize Napier and Davis but to show the frustration behind trying to define measurements that will reflect the function of an isolated part of the skeleton. More will be said later on this subject.

The measurements are listed in Table 1 and shown in Figure 1. A full description of each is given elsewhere (McHenry 1972).

THE COMPARATIVE SAMPLE

Table 2 presents a list of the comparative sample. Eight genera are represented including all species of Hominoidea with the exception of the gibbons which are represented by only one species, *Hylobates lar*. I was very fortunate to obtain data from the rare and important pygmy chimpanzee, *Pan paniscus*, kept at the Musée Royale de l'Afrique Centrale in Belgium. The dimensions of the distal humerus of this species are on the average smaller than modern man, whereas the same measurements in *Pan troglodytes* are usually larger than man. Considering the very close resemblance between the distal humerus of chimpanzees and man, it may be important to know that any differences are not due simply to size. The extensive chimpanzee and gorilla collections at the Powell-Cotton Museum in England pro-

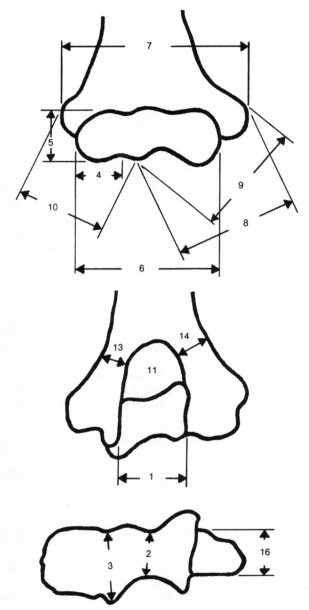

Figure 1. Diagram of the 16 measurements taken on the distal end of the humerus.

TABLE 1

MEANS AND STANDARD DEVIATIONS OF THE ORIGINAL MEASUREMENTS OF THE DISTAL HUMERUS.

Original Variables	Homo n=64 Mean	s.d.	P. troglodytes n=42 Mean	s.d.	P. paniscus n=16 Mean	s.d.	Gorilla n=66 Mean	s.d.	Pongo n=34 Mean	s.d.	Hylobates n=27 Mean	s.d.
1. Trochlear wd	21.9	2.61	21.6	1.86	19.5	1.20	30.7	3.99	22.5	2.69	10.9	0.83
2. Trochlear a-p diam	15.0	2.03	16.1	1.91	14.4	1.23	22.2	3.61	15.2	2.54	7.6	0.66
3. Lat trochlear ridge a-p diam	22.3	2.11	26.8	1.92	24.0	1.75	33.0	5.30	27.0	3.98	11.7	0.75
4. Capitular wd	15.7	1.55	18.2	1.40	16.0	0.8	21.5	4.34	17.6	2.14	8.2	0.65
5. Capitular ht	19.0	2.05	21.4	1.82	19.1	1.51	28.2	4.34	23.8	3.39	11.8	0.80
6. Articular surface wd	38.8	4.35	44.6	2.90	39.5	2.62	59.8	8.49	45.5	5.28	20.1	1.21
7. Biepycondylar wd	55.7	6.15	62.1	4.55	56.1	3.63	88.4	13.2	64.2	7.44	27.5	1.57
8. Trochlea to med epicondyle	38.6	4.48	43.7	3.26	41.6	2.76	64.3	9.92	48.1	6.21	18.1	1.23
9. Trochlea to supracondylar ridge	36.6	4.10	40.4	2.56	39.8	2.75	60.5	8.77	47.2	5.69	17.7	1.19
10. Capiate to lat epicondyle	26.5	2.34	30.8	2.65	29.4	2.52	43.7	6.01	34.6	4.27	14.5	1.03
11. Olecranon fossa wd	25.0	2.47	25.2	2.05	23.5	1.19	35.7	5.77	25.4	3.46	10.9	0.84
12. Olecranon fossa depth	6.7	0.90	9.3	1.12	8.2	1.18	12.7	2.30	8.1	1.40	4.1	0.31
13. Wd med wall of olecranon fossa	9.3	2.51	11.9	1.69	11.8	2.15	15.2	3.07	15.0	2.36	4.6	0.97
14. Wd lat wall of olecranon fossa	14.8	2.04	19.3	2.18	17.1	1.83	26.3	4.06	19.5	3.06	9.3	1.02
15. A-p diam shaft	14.7	1.82	17.4	1.42	15.2	1.18	22.3	2.85	15.9	2.57	7.7	0.69
16. Wd med epicondyle	12.0	1.74	12.6	1.31	11.5	1.37	16.5	2.48	13.8	2.46	5.1	0.50

Original Variables	Nasalis n=17 Mean	s.d.	Macaca n=20 Mean	s.d.	Presbytis n=24 Mean	s.d.	Kromdraai	East Rudolf	Kanapoi
1. Trochlear wd	12.0	1.37	8.7	1.05	8.9	0.55	20.0	24.7	24.6
2. Trochlear a-p diam	11.7	1.85	7.1	0.71	7.6	0.65	12.6	14.6	13.2
3. Lat trochlear ridge a-p diam	14.9	1.98	11.5	1.13	10.2	0.58	20.6	24.4	22.2
4. Capitular wd	11.3	1.23	6.7	0.80	7.2	0.43	16.5	17.3	16.3
5. Capitular ht	13.1	1.80	8.4	0.92	8.9	0.49	16.9	25.6	19.4
6. Articular surface wd	23.2	3.14	14.8	1.47	16.7	0.74	40.1	43.6	44.8
7. Biepycondylar wd	31.1	5.04	20.9	2.44	23.5	1.11	53.8	71.2	60.2
8. Trochlea to med epicondyle	19.9	2.87	12.9	1.57	14.1	0.68	34.1	49.7	41.8
9. Trochlea to supracondylar ridge	19.1	2.78	12.6	1.39	13.7	0.58	31.8	47.1	39.3
10. Capiate to lat epicondyle	19.0	1.97	11.8	0.98	13.4	0.70	24.9	34.3	27.6
11. Olecranon fossa wd	14.2	1.76	9.5	0.90	10.0	0.60	19.1	29.9	28.6
12. Olecranon fossa depth	6.0	0.83	3.1	0.40	4.0	0.34	6.4	8.1	8.2
13. Wd med wall of olecranon fossa	4.4	1.20	3.4	0.69	3.1	0.36	8.8	13.3	10.7
14. Wd lat wall of olecranon fossa	10.0	1.83	5.0	0.79	6.6	0.62	14.3	18.6	15.2
15. A-p diam shaft	9.2	1.41	6.1	0.67	6.9	0.31	13.1	17.3	15.7
16. Wd med epicondyle	7.2	1.28	6.8	0.85	5.6	0.54	10.4	13.3	13.5

343

TABLE 2

COMPARATIVE SAMPLE USED IN THE METRICAL COMPARISONS OF THE DISTAL HUMERUS.

Species	Total	Male	Female	Sex Unknown	Museum
H. sapiens	64	32	25	7	
Negro	1	1			Kenya National Museum
Bushman	7			7	Brit. Mus. Nat. Hist.
Amerindian	50	25	25		
Eskimo	5	5			Peabody Museum,
Australian	1	1			Harvard University
P. troglodytes	42	21	21		
East Africa	3	2	1		Kenya National Museum
West Africa	39	19	20		Powell-Cotton Museum
P. paniscus	16	6	8	2	Musée Royal de l'Afrique Centrale, Tervuren, Bel.
G. gorilla	66	25	41		
East Africa	2	1	1		Kenya National Museum
(*berengei*)	1	1			Mus. Compar. Zool., Harv. Univ.
West Africa (*gorilla*)	63	23	40		Powell-Cotton Museum
P. pygmaeus	34	14	20		
Sumatra	10	4	6		Smithsonian
Borneo	15	5	10		Smithsonian
	4	3	1		Brit. Mus. Nat. Hist.
	5	2	3		Mus. Compar. Zool., Harv. Univ.
H. lar	27	14	13		
Siam	25	12	13		Mus. Compar. Zool., Harv. Univ.
	1	1			Kenya National Museum
	1	1			Berkeley
N. larvatus	17	5	12		
Borneo	17	5	12		Mus. Compar. Zool., Harv. Univ.
M. fascicularis	20	10	10		
Borneo	20	10	10		Mus. Compar. Zool., Harv. Univ.
P. rubicundus	25	12	13		
Borneo	25	12	13		Mus. Compar. Zool., Harv. Univ.

vided an excellent sample of those species. Orangs were obtained mostly from the Smithsonian collections and gibbons from the Museum of Comparative Zoology, Harvard University.

The three monkey species were chosen to represent (1) the locomotor group called "semibrachiators" *(Nasalis larvatus* and possibly *Presbytis rubicundus)*, and (2) the locomotor group called "quadrupedal" *(Macaca fascicularis)* (Napier and Napier 1967). The semibrachiators were chosen simply because they have been singled out as forms analogous to the earliest hominoids by some workers (e.g. Napier 1963). *Macaca fascicularis* is a good generalized monkey that is equally at home on the ground, in the trees, and in the water (Furuya 1961). All of these monkey skeletons are kept at the Museum of Comparative Zoology, Harvard University.

SCREENING OF DATA

The data were first screened by calculating means, standard deviations, and coefficients of skewness and kurtosis. Large standard deviations or departures from normality are a good indication of errors in the data. Several mistakes were caught in this way before the data were edited using the Churchill multiple regression editing program.

The Churchill program allows the investigator to put the measurements into three member combinations which are used to calculate regression formulae. Each measurement of each individual is compared with the predicted value from the regression formula and if its deviation from the regression line is greater than a chosen value (here 3.0 standard deviations), then it is printed out. The program also prints out the predicted value of that measurement based on the original regression formula and predictions based on a second set of formulae. Care was taken to put each measurement in at least two combinations. Each species was run separately. Since orangs and gorillas show such marked sexual dimorphism, males and females were entered separately in these species. The whole process is costly and tedious.

The list of measurements exceeding 3.0 standard deviations was not excessive. Many of these were obvious mistakes such as reading the wrong first digit of the Helios Caliper. With the obvious mistakes corrected, less than one percent of the measurements exceed 3.0 standard deviations. Most of them were left. Some measurements were too far off to tolerate, and these were corrected using the predicted value from the regression equation with the largest multiple correlation coefficient. A very few aberrant specimens were dropped from further analyses such as one juvenile *Pan paniscus* zoo specimen.

DESCRIPTION OF BASIC DATA

The means and standard deviations are shown in table 1 along with the measurements on the fossils. There is nothing particularly surprising or informative about this table by itself but reference to it will be made during the interpretation of the multivariate analyses. Note that the Kromdraai specimen is usually smaller than man and the two species of chimpanzees, whereas the East Rudolf specimen is larger than most human means. Notice also the metrical resemblance between the East Rudolf fossil and the orang. The Kanapoi humerus follows the human pattern primarily. These means are very difficult to compare, however, because of the great size differences between the species.

Size is, of course, one of the major sources or variation among higher primates. The range from male gorilla to female *Macaca fascicularis* is so enormous that it probably obscures the recognition of other sources of variation. One simple way to equalize the sizes of all the subjects is to convert all the variables into z-scores. One simply subtracts the group mean from the variable and divides by the standard deviation. In this way the mean for each variable becomes 0 within each species and the standard deviation is 1.0. However, the mean and standard deviation for a single fossil is meaningless and therefore its z-score cannot be found.

Another method for reducing the effect of size is to form ratios between sets of variables. This method was used by Ashton and Oxnard (1964) and Day and Wood (1968) quite effectively. By forming ratios one can compare the means and standard deviations of the species directly. Devising ratios also provides one more chance to find the elusive "functionally meaningful traits." Ideally one could form a large number of ratios and then choose those that seem to vary in ways consistent with differences in function. For example, ratios that are homogeneous within locomotor groups but heterogeneous among different locomotor groups could be selected. The attempt to partial out the functionally significant variation in this way failed as will be explained below. Another possible advantage to using ratios is the reduction of within-group heterogeneity. For example, all 16 original variables are highly significantly heterogeneous between male and female gorillas. This heterogeneity is greatly reduced by using ratios. Only four out of the 15 ratios finally used in the multivariate analyses are as significantly heterogeneous between the gorilla sexes.

There are some disadvantages to using ratios in multiple discriminant analysis, which is the type of statistic to be used in this study. One is that the analysis can, in effect, make its own ratios by weighting variables in appropriate ways. Another disadvantage is that ratios are necessarily made up of at least two somewhat independently varying dimensions and their intercorrelations can differ from one species to the next. So, for example, a large value from the ratio of the width of the articular surface to the width of the shaft may mean either the former is large or the latter is small.

For these reasons both ratios and raw data are used in the multivariate analyses. The results can then be checked against one another. Fifteen ratios were finally adopted. The criteria for choosing the ratios were as follows: (1) how well the entire list of ratios described the shape of the bone; (2) the functional significance of the ratio; and (3) the amount of among-group heterogeneity. A list of the ratios follows:

1. Trochlear shape (Troch shape): troch wd/troch a-p.
2. Relative size of the trochlea (Troch size): troch wd/cap wd.
3. Posterior projection of the lateral trochlear ridge (Lat troch proj): lat troch a-p/troch a-p.
4. Shape of the olecranon fossa (Olec shape): (lat troch a-p + depth olec)/(troch wd + wd olec).
5. Relative size of the lateral trochlear ridge (Lat troch size): lat troch a-p/a-p shaft.
6. Shape of the capitulum (Cap shape): cap wd/cap ht.
7. Projection of the medial epicondyle (Med epi proj): troch-med epi/troch wd.
8. Width of the olecranon fossa (Wd olec): wd olec/biepi.
9. Flare of the medial border of the shaft (Shaft flare): troch-med epi/troch-sup epi.
10. Shape of the shaft (Shaft shape): a-p shaft/(wd olec + wd med olec + wd lat olec).
11. Relative size of the medial and lateral portions of the shaft (Med olec size): wd med olec/wd lat olec.
12. Relative width of the medial epicondyle (Med epi size): wd med epi/a-p shaft.

13. Relative depth of the olecranon fossa (Depth olec): depth olec/a-p shaft.
14. Relative height of the lateral epicondyle (Lat epi ht): cap-lat epi/cap ht.
15. Relative transverse diameter of the medial epicondyle (Trans med epi): (troch-med epi − troch wd)/wd med epi.

The mean value of each ratio is shown in table 3. As with the original variables, it is difficult to interpret the table by itself. The most striking feature is how similar the humeri of all these species are. The fossils show no obvious affinity to any one species. The interpretation of these values must await the multivariate analysis.

BACKGROUND TO MULTIPLE DISCRIMINANT ANALYSIS

The mathematical background to multiple discriminant analysis is dealt with in detail by several authors and will not be described here (see especially Cooley and Lohnes 1962, Seal 1964, Rao 1952). The method is excellent for analysing problems of the type presented here. First of all it reduces the information into smaller chunks that can be interpreted. Thus swarms of points in 16-dimensional space sometimes can be reduced with a minimum loss of information to a few linear functions. The method also produces a maximum separation of *a priori* groups which is ideal for this study, since the data are in definite natural groups (species), and knowledge of the uniqueness of each group is desired. The discriminant functions are orthogonal to one another which is an advantage in that it will partial out large sources of variation (such as size) on one function so that such sources will not dominate all functions. The weighting of each variable can be interpreted on each function making it possible to relate, for example, the separation of two groups to the variation of a few specific variables. Since the differences between group means on the discriminant functions are proportional to Hotelling's T^2, the multivariate generalization of Student's t-statistic, the significance of the discrimination can be found. This can be done using Wilks' lambda which tests the null hypotheses of equality of population centroids (Cooley and Lohnes 1962). Since the differences in group means on the functions are also proportional to Mahalanobis' D^2, the groups can be studied in terms of the distances between group centroids. Finally, as Fisher (1936) pointed out in his first paper introducing discriminant analysis, unclassified objects can be entered into the

TABLE 3

MEAN VALUES FOR THE HUMERAL RATIOS.

		East Rudolf	Kromdraai	Kanapoi	Homo	Pan troglodytes	Pan paniscus	Gorilla	Pongo	Hylobates	Presbytis	Nasalis	Macaca
1.	Troch shape	169	159	186	147	135	136	140	152	143	117	103	122
2.	Troch size	143	121	151	138	119	121	143	129	134	124	107	129
3.	Lat troch proj	167	164	168	150	168	167	149	183	155	135	128	162
4.	Olec shape	60	69	57	62	77	75	69	73	73	76	80	81
5.	Lat troch size	141	157	141	154	154	158	148	171	154	149	164	189
6.	Cap shape	68	98	84	83	85	84	77	74	70	81	87	80
7.	Med epi proj	201	171	170	177	203	214	210	214	168	160	159	149
8.	Wd olec	42	36	48	45	41	42	40	40	40	43	46	46
9.	Shaft flare	106	107	106	105	108	105	106	102	120	103	100	102
10.	Shaft shape	28	31	29	30	31	29	29	27	31	35	32	34
11.	Med olec size	72	61	70	61	62	70	58	78	49	47	44	68
12.	Med epi size	77	79	86	82	73	76	74	87	67	81	78	111
13.	Depth olec	47	49	52	46	53	54	57	51	53	59	66	52
14.	Lat epi ht	134	147	142	141	144	155	156	146	123	151	147	141
15.	Trans med epi	188	136	127	141	176	194	203	186	143	96	100	62

349

appropriate group. Theoretically, then, a fossil can be classified into its appropriate species. A great deal of caution must be used, however. More will be said about this later.

The assumptions made by multiple discriminant analysis are essentially the same as those of analysis of variance. Most of these are fulfilled by the osteometric variables used in this study. Within-group homogeneity is assumed which is not always strictly true of all species. When the sexes are pooled, the most heterogeneous group is gorilla in which the differences between male and female are highly significant for all of the original variables and several of the ratios. The ratios greatly reduce the sex differences within these species, thereby increasing the within-group homogeneity.

Another assumption behind this kind of analysis is that the variables are linearly related to one another. However, non-linear relationships between body measurements are common and indeed are the basis of the study of allometry. Body mass increases by the cube of body lengths. To maintain a constant relation between the strength of supporting columns (i.e. the limb bones) and body mass, the cross-sectional area of the supporting structures increases with the square of their length. If these relationships are not taken into account, many of the structural differences found could be simply the result of size differences.

One method for correcting for non-linearity is to convert measurements into natural logarithms. Ashton, Healey and Lipton (1957) used this method in their study of hominoid teeth. Experimental analyses were run, therefore, using log-converted data in this study. Very little effect can be detected. F-ratios among species are almost unaffected. Some of the correlation coefficients change a few hundredths up or down. Two pilot multiple discriminant analyses were run with and without the log conversion and no appreciable differences were found. This is not surprising: the measurements cover such a small area. They are essentially all widths of one kind or another. When the length of the humerus is compared with the width, then a non-linear relationship is clearly in evidence, but the length is not included in any of the following analyses.

Two multiple discriminant computer programs were used. One was written by Kenneth Jones (1964) as part of a package called the Multivariate Statistical Analyzer (MSA). The other was the BMDO7M of the BMD Biomedical Computer Programs (Dixon 1970). A comparison of the two programs showed that they gave essentially the same results (McHenry 1972).

The following multiple discriminant analysis used the 15 ratios on all of the species. This analysis is designed to test the following hypothesis: if the humeri of a series of higher primate species can be discriminated from one another, then the early hominid fossils will fall within the human range of variation. The fossil humeri are entered as a second sample: they are not used in the calculation of the functions. In addition to the fossils several other specimens are entered as a second sample to check the stability of the discrimination. Four humans including a Bushman and an Eskimo are treated in this way. Two members from each sex of all the other hominoid species are also part of the second sample as well as two members of each monkey species. Again, none of these specimens are used in the calculation of the discriminant functions so that their classification using those functions is a second check on the reliability of the analysis, although this procedure leaves many holes and cannot be depended on.

Removing these specimens from the original analysis reduces the sample sizes from the values shown in Table 4.

The actual programs used in this analysis were the DISCRI, MAHALA, and CLASSI parts of the MSA package. Eight discriminant functions were generated from the nine species. Judging by the value of Wilks' lambda (see Cooley and Lohnes 1962), all but the last function are highly significant. This means that the chance of producing group differences as large or larger than given by each of the first seven functions by drawing nine samples at random is less than 1 in 1000. The first seven functions account for almost 100% of the trace. The seventh function accounts for 1.7% of the trace (i.e. of total possible discrimination).

But the real interest is not in the significance of the discrimination since the groups are different species with clearly distinguishable morphologies. It is only with more closely related groups such as subspecies that the significance of the discrimination becomes particularly interesting.

The mean discriminant scores for each group and for each function are shown in Table 4 along with the projections of the fossils. The

TABLE 4

RESULTS OF THE 15 VARIABLE MULTIPLE DISCRIMINANT ANALYSIS. THE MEAN DISCRIMINANT SCORES FOR EACH GROUP AND FOR EACH FUNCTION ARE GIVEN AS WELL AS THEIR STANDARD DEVIATIONS.

		I	II	III	IV	V	VI	VII	VIII
	Eigenvalue	8.90	3.42	2.46	2.07	1.80	0.62	0.33	0.02
	% of trace	45.34	17.44	12.52	10.57	9.16	3.18	1.70	0.10
Homo n=60	Mean	30.03	171.59	19.96	-63.94	58.95	-40.91	43.95	75.49
	s.d.	2.30	3.14	1.50	3.80	1.48	2.77	1.16	3.69
P. troglodytes n=38	Mean	30.42	172.35	22.52	-53.12	63.89	-38.03	43.79	75.86
	s.d.	2.14	2.75	1.27	3.87	2.03	2.59	1.52	3.86
P. paniscus n=16	Mean	22.97	175.83	21.51	-51.21	61.79	-42.65	43.98	73.60
	s.d.	2.81	3.51	1.37	4.82	1.58	2.84	1.33	3.76
Gorilla n=62	Mean	21.66	174.77	17.25	-51.83	59.65	-40.01	44.56	75.62
	s.d.	2.80	3.37	1.46	2.94	1.81	2.97	1.26	3.91
Pongo n=30	Mean	25.52	175.33	22.88	-49.49	55.71	-42.61	43.26	75.91
	s.d.	3.39	3.38	1.39	3.57	2.22	2.58	1.64	4.30
Hylobates n=23	Mean	24.57	158.21	21.61	-52.79	56.00	-36.87	44.71	75.07
	s.d.	3.14	4.47	1.53	3.49	1.99	2.80	1.25	4.14
Nasalis n=15	Mean	38.75	158.13	20.20	-51.15	62.08	-45.93	45.45	75.95
	s.d.	2.56	3.72	1.37	4.02	1.88	3.00	1.29	3.17
Macaca n=19	Mean	55.05	179.81	19.74	-51.87	56.90	-38.57	45.00	75.42
	s.d.	3.99	4.12	1.52	3.11	2.66	2.66	2.23	3.53
Presbytis n=23	Mean	38.86	163.96	16.42	-51.15	59.67	-40.04	42.13	75.37
	s.d.	3.70	2.51	1.05	3.36	1.69	1.71	1.13	2.68
Kromdraai		29.60	167.62	21.13	-59.67	60.50	-38.20	41.94	78.85
East Rudolf		19.23	169.84	20.58	-57.30	54.43	-40.85	42.34	74.45
Kanapoi		26.06	173.76	21.85	-63.72	59.79	-44.41	44.81	78.23

352

degree to which each variable is associated with each function can be seen in Table 5. This table gives the correlation coefficients between the discriminant scores and the variables. A larger positive or negative value means that the variable is highly correlated with the function. This is not a measure of the actual weighting of the variable in the function, but can be thought of as its potential contribution.

By combining the information in tables 3, 4 and 5, a general picture emerges. Function I is primarily concerned with separating the hominoids from the monkeys, especially *Macaca*. The traits most strongly associated with it are the relative transverse diameter of the medial epicondyle (r=−0.53), projection of the medial epicondyle (r=−0.35), and the relative width of the medial epicondyle (r=0.31). The first two are very highly correlated with each other (r=0.89) and really represent the same piece of information: the extent to which the medial epicondyle projects outward away from the shaft. On inspection of the means in table 3 it is clear that the hominoids' projection index is consistently larger than the monkeys, especially *Macaca*. Both of these ratios are negatively correlated with the first function which is consistent: the group with the smallest values for the two ratios projects the highest on the function. The third most strongly correlated ratio, the relative width of the medial epicondyle, is positively correlated with the first function. The value for this ratio in *Macaca* is the largest of all species indicating this animal's characteristically wide medial epicondyle. The increased projection of the medial epicondyle in hominoids may be related to the power of the muscles that attach there such as the flexors of the hand and wrist and the supinator.

All of the fossil humeri fall well within the hominoid range.

Function II separates the gibbons from the rest of the hominoids. *Nasalis* projects like the gibbon with *Presbytis* half way between these two and the rest. Both the projection of the medial epicondyle and the relative size of the medial portion of the shaft are equally highly correlated with the function (r=0.37). There are four other traits almost as highly correlated making a simple interpretation difficult. The relation between the medial portion of the shaft to the lateral portion was originally thought to be associated with the kinds of stresses most commonly transmitted through the elbow. The compressive forces in the quadrupedal and terrestrial genera such as *Gorilla* and *Macaca* were thought to be transmitted primarily through

TABLE 5

ASSOCIATION OF EACH VARIABLE WITH EACH FUNCTION IN THE 15 VARIABLE ANALYSIS.

Ratios	F-ratio	Correlations Between Discriminant Scores and Original Variables							
		I	II	III	IV	V	VI	VII	VIII
1. Troch shape	22	-0.17	0.15	0.15	-0.23	-0.24	0.19	-0.15	-0.16
2. Troch size	31	-0.14	0.17	-0.29	-0.27	-0.31	0.29	0.25	-0.00
3. Lat troch proj	34	-0.05	0.28	0.47	0.14	-0.15	0.24	-0.29	-0.27
4. Olec shape	51	0.19	-0.07	0.21	0.67	0.21	0.14	0.04	0.07
5. Lat troch size	31	0.22	0.13	0.25	0.15	-0.27	-0.18	0.35	0.26
6. Cap shape	28	0.13	0.07	0.02	-0.22	0.50	-0.36	-0.15	-0.08
7. Med epi proj	65	-0.35	0.37	0.16	0.28	0.22	-0.14	-0.18	0.10
8. Wd olec	25	0.18	-0.04	-0.09	-0.36	0.03	-0.39	0.27	-0.36
9. Shaft flare	24	-0.11	0.18	-0.04	-0.19	0.37	0.52	-0.05	0.34
10. Shaft shape	30	0.24	-0.18	-0.20	0.01	0.13	0.37	-0.22	-0.40
11. Med olec size	26	-0.01	0.37	0.30	0.01	-0.15	-0.18	-0.25	-0.12
12. Med epi size	50	0.31	0.30	0.00	-0.04	-0.35	-0.23	0.00	0.75
13. Depth olec	27	0.01	-0.18	-0.23	0.42	0.23	-0.22	0.32	0.27
14. Lat epi ht	31	-0.05	0.24	-0.33	0.23	0.29	-0.45	-0.23	-0.09
15. Trans med epi	106	-0.53	0.32	0.11	0.23	0.23	0.01	0.10	-0.31

the radius, on to the capitulum, and down the lateral portion of the shaft. Therefore, the lateral portion of the shaft should be larger proportionately than the medial in species which habitually use the arms in a quadrupedal stance (and hence produce compressive forces). Like other "functional" explanations attempted by the author, this one failed miserably. By this theory, gorillas should have broad lateral shafts and gibbons, who rarely use their arms in a quadrupedal posture, should have relatively narrow lateral shafts. The opposite is true.

The fossils project with the great apes and man on function II although the Kromdraai specimen is very slightly moved toward the gibbon.

The gorillas are separated in function III from the rest of the hominoids. This is primarily a result of the small posterior projection of the lateral trochlear ridge in gorilla humeri. This trait is by far the most highly correlated with the third discriminant function (r=0.47). The original rationale for using this trait was the mistaken belief that knuckle-walkers had strong posterior projections on the lateral trochlear ridge associated with hyperextension of the elbow and locking of the olecranon. However, gorilla and chimpanzee are almost at opposite extremes in this trait which is another example of my frustration with making *a priori* arguments of functional significance in the distal humerus.

The fossils stay with the pack on function III. Despite the initial impression I had that the East Rudolf specimen looked gorilloid, it shows no inclination to follow that species on this function which separates the gorilla from the rest.

Function IV separates man from all of the other species. Table 4 shows that the mean projections of all the species except man range from −49 to −53, whereas man's centroid is −64. The variable that is by far the most strongly associated with the function is the olecranon shape (r=0.67), a ratio comparing the a-p diameter of the lateral trochlear ridge plus the depth of the olecranon fossa to the width of the trochlea plus the width of the olecranon. Primarily, this measures the depth of the olecranon fossa relative to its width. The shape of man's olecranon fossa is unique in this respect being very wide and very shallow. Presumably this is related to the fact that man is the only primate that does not use his upper limb in locomotion. Another trait with a high positive correlation with the fourth function is the ratio of the depth of the olecranon fossa with the a-p diameter of the shaft (r=0.42). This trait is obviously closely related to the olecranon shape.

The behavior of the fossils on this uniquely human function is very interesting. The Kanapoi specimen projects almost exactly on the human centroid. Its projection is −63.7 and the human centroid −63.9. The Kromdraai humerus is closest to man but closer to the other hominoids than Kanapoi (−59.7). The East Rudolf specimen is about midway between the human and ape projections (−57.3). The East Rudolf humerus resembles man, not the apes, in the traits most strongly correlated with the fourth discriminant function. Table 6 compares the fossil with the means for man and all the hominoids combined for the traits most highly correlated with the fourth function. The projection of the medial epicondyle is the only trait in which the East Rudolf fossil shows a marked divergence from man and affinity with the other hominoids. The Kromdraai and Kanapoi specimens are also shown in Table 6. Several of the individual traits are divergent from the human means despite the fact that the overall effect of this function brings these fossils closest to man. This is a shortcoming of comparing single traits one by one. Such comparisons

TABLE 6

TRAITS ASSOCIATED WITH FUNCTION IV
OF THE 15 VARIABLE MULTIPLE
DISCRIMINANT ANALYSIS.

MEANS

Traits with high correlation with function IV		East Rudolf	*Homo*	All Hominoids	Kromdraai	Kanapoi
Olec shape	(0.67)	60	62	70	69	57
Depth olec	(0.42)	47	46	52	49	52
Wd Olec	(−0.36)	42	45	42	36	48
Med epi proj	(0.28)	201	176	197	171	170
Troch size	(−0.27)	143	140	134	121	151

ignore the subtler and more complicated relations among the variables which produce the discriminant functions.

Function V is concerned with maximizing the chimpanzees and minimizing the Asian apes. The projection of the chimpanzee mean on this axis is 63.9, of orang 55.7, and that of gibbon 56.0. Man and gorilla are about the same (58.9 and 59.7, respectively). The pygmy chimpanzee is midway between chimpanzees and the projection of man and gorilla.

The most highly correlated variable with this function is the shape of the capitulum ($r = 0.50$) which is the width divided by height. Other important variables are the flare of the medial border of the shaft ($r = .37$) and the relative size of the medial epicondyle ($r = .35$). Orang and gibbon both have low capitular shape ratios. Both of these species also have small values for the shaft flare ratio. Curiously the relative width of the medial epicondyle is the smallest in gibbon and the largest in orang. The means for chimpanzee vary in the opposite way from the first two variables mentioned and is close to gibbon in the third.

The Kanapoi and Kromdraai specimens again do not depart far from the human centroid. The East Rudolf specimen is more interesting. It not only departs markedly from the human mean, but projects to the far side of the orang and gibbon range. Part of the reason for this is the fact that the capitulum is high and narrow in the East Rudolf specimen which seems to be a characteristic of the Asian apes. But with many of the other features associated with this function the fossil resembles the African apes and man (e.g. shaft flare, medial epicondyle size, trochlear size). The best explanation for the behavior of the East Rudolf humerus on this function is perhaps to say that on the particular combination of traits taken together that best distinguish the Asian apes from the chimpanzee, the fossil resembles the former. This is very different from saying the shape of the East Rudolf humerus is most like that of an Asian ape.

Functions IV and V are plotted together in Figure 2. The Kanapoi and Kromdraai humeri project very close to the human position while the East Rudolf specimen diverges markedly from all centroids.

Functions VI and VII are complicated and hard to interpret. Since they only account for 3.18% and 1.70% of the total trace, they probably are not very important. Function VI separates *Pan troglodytes* from *Pan paniscus* on the basis of the lateral epicondyle. There is a great deal of overlap of the 95% centours when these two functions

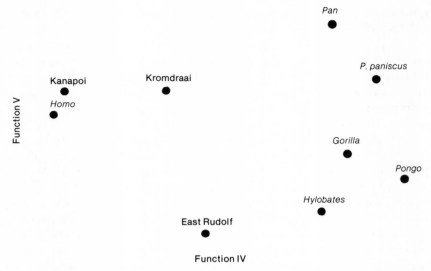

Figure 2. Distribution of humeral projections from the multiple discriminant analysis using 15 ratios of measurements taken on the distal end. Note the close proximity of the Kanapoi and Kromdraai specimens to the human position and the divergence of the East Rudolf fossil.

are plotted together. For these reasons it is assumed that these last few functions are simply picking up random fluctuations in the data.

The program CLASSI calculates the discriminant scores and Mahalanobis' D^2 distance from group centroids for each individual in the analysis. It also gives the chi-square value associated with group membership of each individual from which the probability of group membership is calculated (see Cooley and Lohnes 1962). This probability is deceptive: a subject may be an enormous distance away from any group centroid and still be assigned a 100% chance of belonging to the nearest group. This is particularly true of the fossils which may not fall close to any group centroid. On the basis of these probabilities, a classification matrix is set up giving the number of subjects properly classified.

Among the subjects used in the calculations of the eight discriminant functions (as opposed to those in the second sample), 98.95% are classified correctly, but one pygmy chimpanzee is assigned to the chimpanzee range and one, curiously enough, to the gorilla range. The only other misclassification is one gorilla that falls into the orang group. The second sample does not do as well: out of 24 subjects, six are classified incorrectly. These misclassifications include one human (Bushman) to the chimpanzee range, two chimpanzees to the pygmy chimpanzee range, two male orangs to gorilla, and one *Nasalis* to *Presbytis*. Clearly the classificatory power of the discriminant functions based on these probabilities is not perfect. But the misclassifications are understandable: human, chimpanzee, and pygmy chimpanzee humeri are very much alike, as are those of male orang and female gorilla. The chi-squares of these misclassified subjects relative to their correct centroids are only slightly greater than the chi-squares relative to the wrong centroid to which they are assigned by probability.

The location of the fossils in the eight-dimensional discriminant space relative to group centroids can be measured in terms of chi-square. The chi-square for the points in this space representing the Kromdraai and Kanapoi humeri relative to the human centour are 13.24 and 9.60 respectively. With eight degrees of freedom, chi-square would be larger than 15.51 in 5% of cases, 18.17 in 2%, and 20.09 in 1%. Clearly then these two humeri are closely associated with the human centour. The next nearest centour to the Kromdraai humerus is chimpanzee with a chi-square of 18.00. Kanapoi is also rather close to the pygmy chimpanzee centour with a chi-square of 9.60. The East Rudolf humerus is outside the 99% range of all groups. Its chi-square is 20.20 relative to orang, 22.99 to gorilla and 32.10 to man.

The exclusion of the East Rudolf humerus from any of the centours is intriguing. Given the similarity in shape of all hominoid humeri (at least their distal ends), it is quite a feat for the multiple discriminant analysis to separate them at all. The ability of this analysis to discriminate between the hominoid humeri indicates the enormous sensitivity it has to the most subtle shape differences. To the eye the distal end of the East Rudolf humerus appears to be very similar to certain human humeri such as those of the Greenland Eskimo used in the sample. One obvious difference is the shape of the capitulum which is more globular and less flattened than is the usual case in man. The diagnostic steep lateral wall of the olecranon fossa of the African ape humeri is absent in the East Rudolf specimen which alone excludes it from being a typical humerus of a knuckle-walker of extant type. The trochlea is not narrow and deep as is often the case in the orang humerus.

Perhaps the analysis is too sensitive to subtle shape differences and the East Rudolf humerus really does fit the human pattern. Its exclusion from the human group in this particular multivariate analysis may be due to minor variations which may be typical of the humeri of other human populations that were not included in the sample. Certainly, the shaft of the fossil can be matched with those of the Greenland Eskimo with their rugose delto-pectoral crests and overall robustness. But the fossil did not cluster with the five Eskimo humeri included in the analysis of the distal end.

On the basis of this analysis and on inspection of certain non-metric traits, it appears that the shape of the East Rudolf humerus does not fit the pattern typical of the knuckle-walking apes. Of the 124 African ape humeri examined, all had one distinctive trait which could separate them from all other hominoids: the flattened lateral wall of the olecranon fossa. Presumably this feature is related to the locking of the elbow in a hyper-extended position which is common among these apes when they are supporting weight on the knuckles. The olecranon fossa is also rather deep in these ape humeri although deep fossae can occur among other hominoids. The East Rudolf humerus has a very shallow olecranon fossa and no steep lateral wall or ridge.

In sum, then, the humeri of the primate species studied here can be discriminated fairly well and two of the fossils (Kromdraai and Kanapoi) fall within the human range. The humerus from East Rudolf, on the other hand, has a distinctively different shape from the human humeri sampled here. Although it falls outside the centours of all the species tested, the East Rudolf fossil approaches the orang more closely than the human range.

The exclusion of the East Rudolf humerus from the human range is an unexpected result. Even more surprising is its metrical resemblance to the orang humerus. Plotting the individual ratios in a diagram as in Figure 3, however, shows how remarkably the orang means correspond to the East Rudolf values. The only outstanding difference is in the relative size of the lateral trochlear ridge, a trait presumably related to side to side stability of the elbow joint particularly in the extended position. The fossil approaches the human condition in this feature.

The results of this analysis are quite inconsistent with the proposition that the East Rudolf specimen belonged to a knuckle-walking creature resembling any of the extant knuckle-walkers. The fossil is

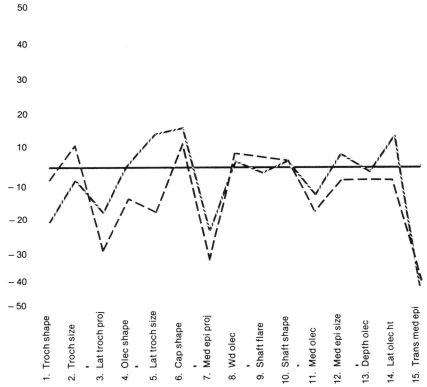

50

40

30

20

10

− 10

− 20

− 30

− 40

− 50

1. Troch shape
2. Troch size
3. Lat troch proj
4. Olec shape
5. Lat troch size
6. Cap shape
7. Med epi proj
8. Wd olec
9. Shaft flare
10. Shaft shape
11. Med olec
12. Med epi size
13. Depth olec
14. Lat olec ht
15. Trans med epi

Figure 3. Ratio diagram showing the close metrical similarity between the distal humeri of *Pongo* and the East Rudolf fossil. The straight line represents the human means. The dashed line follows the percent difference from the human means of the *Pongo* means. The dotted/dashed line is the East Rudolf humerus.

particularly unlike the chimpanzee or pygmy chimpanzee humeri sampled for this analysis. Its dissimilarities to the gorilla humeri are shown in the third function which separates the gorillas from all of the other hominoids including the fossil.

ANALYSIS USING ORIGINAL VARIABLES

Another multiple discriminant analysis was done using the original 16 variables before they were transformed into ratios. Primarily this was done as a check on the preceding analysis, but some new information was desired, particularly about the original variables themselves.

Again the MSA program was used but only the hominoid species were included. The monkeys were dropped partly because they proved to be so unlike the fossils and also because of their small size.

The results are similar to the previous analysis, except that the first function accounts for the major part of the trace (59%). This function is associated primarily with size: the gorilla projections are maximized and the gibbon discriminant scores are minimized. All of the variables are strongly and positively correlated with the discriminant scores which is another indication of its size association. The fossils line up according to their sizes: Kromdraai the smallest and East Rudolf the largest.

Function II is more interesting although it accounts for only 16% of the trace. In general it separates the Asian apes from man with the African apes falling in the middle. The Kanapoi and Kromdraai humeri fall in the overlapped ranges of human and chimpanzee ranges. The East Rudolf specimen projects outside the human range and is closest to gorillas and pygmy chimpanzees. Widths of the olecranon fossa, trochlea and capitulum are the most strongly associated variables with the function. None of the variables has a strong negative correlation with the function.

The third function is about equal in trace to the previous one (14%). The gibbons are again minimized as they are on the first four functions which account for 99% of the trace. *Pan* and *Pongo* are maximized with *Gorilla* and *Homo* falling in between. The East Rudolf fossil is midway between man and gibbon whereas the other fossils are close to man. The last significant function accounts for 9.5% of the trace and separates the chimpanzee from the rest. None of the fossils separates with the chimpanzee humeri.

My impression is that the effect of size is important in more than just the first function in this analysis since almost all of the variables are positively correlated with the functions (except for IV) and gibbons are always minimized. Even if this is untrue, the majority of the trace is lost in function I which is clearly dominated by the effect of size. The information gained by the analysis is therefore rather trivial since it is obvious that these species are very different in size.

Nonetheless, the fossils behave in a way similar to the previous analysis: the specimens from Kromdraai and Kanapoi are close to the human range while the East Rudolf humerus remains outside of it. It is interesting, however, that the Kromdraai specimen has almost the same chi-square relative to the chimpanzee and human centroids and in fact is slightly smaller in the former. The Kanapoi humerus is very close to the human centroid while the East Rudolf fossil again approaches the orang more closely than any other species.

LOCOMOTOR GROUPS ANALYSIS

One analysis is done that probably violates the assumption that the within-group variance is homogeneous. Species are lumped into groups according to their locomotor behavior. The first such analysis groups the knuckle-walkers *(Pan* and *Gorilla)* together and those apes with a habitual behavior best described as suspensory posture *(Pongo* and *Hylobates)*. The humeri of man form a group, representing the only primate that does not use his forelimbs in locomotion.

There is no really good statistical justification for lumping these very heterogeneous groups. Indeed, previous analyses show that the species to be lumped here are often separated by the first few discriminant functions which account for much of the trace. The considerable size difference alone between gibbons and orangs and between chimpanzees and gorillas makes them inappropriate bedfellows. At worst the results might only be a pictorial representation. Certainly any tests of the significance of the discrimination are dubious in this case.

But the purpose of lumping species into locomotor groups is important. As difficult as it has proved in the past, it is still hoped that some set of traits that will characterize the shape of the distal humerus of knuckle-walkers from those animals that habitually assume a suspensory posture. With such a set of traits, the fossils can be interpreted more confidently as belonging to creatures that behaved in a particular way.

The previous analyses show that the Kromdraai and Kanapoi humeri fall within the range of variation found in modern man. The East Rudolf specimen, however, is unique in that it does not correspond closely to any of the samples represented in the test. But it does resemble the large, arboreal, slow-climbing Asian ape, *Pongo pygmaeus* more closely than other species. Therefore a rephrasing of the hypothesis to be tested is in order.

The hypothesis can be stated as follows: if the distal end of the humerus of three hominoid locomotor categories, knuckle-walking *(Pan* and *Gorilla)*, forelimb suspension *(Pongo* and *Hylobates)*, and bipedalism *(Homo)*, can be discriminated from each other, then the fossil specimens from Kromdraai and Kanapoi will fall in the range of variation which includes the bipeds, and the specimen from East Rudolf will be included in the range of those hominoids whose locomotor behavior involves suspensory posture.

The traits in this analysis are the humeral ratios described above. The samples are the same as before only *Pan troglodytes*, *Pan paniscus* and *Gorilla gorilla* are combined into one group (the knuckle-walking) and *Pongo* and *Hylobates* are lumped into another (suspensory posture). The BMDO7M stepwise discriminant analysis is used (Dixon 1970). Discriminant scores for each individual are calculated by a special program written by the author from the coefficients of the discriminant function given by the BMD program. The means, standard deviations, and correlations of these scores with the variables is calculated by standard procedures.

The results are summarized in Table 7 and in Figure 4. The first function accounts for 55.48% of the trace and the second function for 44.52%. Function I is primarily concerned with separating the human humeri from the rest and function II discriminates the humeri of genera belonging to the knuckle-walking group.

The traits most closely associated with the first function are shown in Table 7 and include the shape of the olecranon fossa (r=0.479) and the relative width of the olecranon fossa (r=−0.399) both of which were primary in the "uniquely human" function IV in the previous analysis. The shape of the capitulum is the third most strongly correlated function. This ratio is the most important trait in distinguishing the Asian apes from the rest of the hominoids.

The second function is mostly concerned with separating the humeri of the knuckle-walking apes from the rest. The traits with the highest correlation with the function are also shown in table 7. The first three of these might be thought of as traits unique to knuckle-walkers. The relative height of the lateral epicondyle (r=0.391), the relative transverse diameter of the medial epicondyle (r=0.391), the relative depth depth of the olecranon fossa (r=0.349), and the projection of the medial epicondyle (r=0.312) are all larger in knuckle-walkers than other hominoids. The relative size of the medial epicondyle (r=−0.318) is smaller in knuckle-walkers.

The positioning of the fossils on the two functions is interesting. Function I shows the Kanapoi and Kromdraai humeri close to the

TABLE 7

THE ASSOCIATION OF THE 15 HUMERAL RATIOS
WITH THE DISCRIMINANT FUNCTIONS DERIVED FROM
THE ANALYSIS WHICH COMBINES SPECIES
INTO LOCOMOTOR GROUPS.

	Ratios	F-ratio	Correlations Between Discriminant Scores and Original Variables	
1.	Troch shape	10.52	−0.028	−0.219
2.	Troch size	7.84	−0.196	−0.110
3.	Lat troch proj	18.50	0.263	−0.114
4.	Olec shape	78.49	0.479	0.299
5.	Lat troch size	15.93	0.136	−0.232
6.	Cap shape	50.69	−0.334	0.242
7.	Med epi proj	49.39	0.259	0.312
8.	Wd olec	63.29	−0.399	−0.122
9.	Shaft flare	39.91	−0.160	0.347
10.	Shaft shape	5.21	−0.105	0.147
11.	Med olec size	1.04	0.054	−0.144
12.	Med epi size	15.29	−0.131	−0.318
13.	Depth olec	47.30	0.209	0.349
14.	Lat epi ht	45.28	−0.051	0.391
15.	Trans med epi	75.31	0.286	0.391
	% of trace		55.48%	44.52%

human mean and the East Rudolf specimen almost midway between the suspensory posture and knuckle-walking means. Function II which is primarily discriminating the knuckle-walkers from the rest has the Kromdraai and Kanapoi specimens close to *Homo*. The East Rudolf fossil projects in the opposite direction from the knuckle-walkers and is, in fact, very close to being equal to the mean for the suspensory posture group.

The classification matrix based on probabilities of group membership is not far off. One human is misclassified into the knuckle-walking range, 6.4% of the knuckle-walking humeri are misclassified and one specimen from the suspensory posture group is classified as a knuckle-walker. The Kromdraai and Kanapoi fossils are assigned to

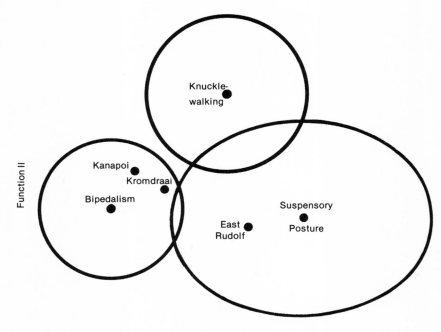

Figure 4. Results of the "locomotor-grouping" discriminant analysis of ratios from the distal end of the humerus. The humeri of the knuckle-walking group (*Gorilla, Pan troglodytes,* and *Pan paniscus*) presumably are adapted to withstanding a predominance of compressive forces. Those humeri included in the suspensory posture group (*Hylobates* and *Pongo*) are subject to more tensile forces. The bipeds (*Homo*) have forelimbs with no locomotor function at all.

the human range and are as close to the human means as many humans. The East Rudolf fragment is classified in the suspensory posture group. Its chi-square relative to the suspensory group is small, showing that the specimen is well within the range of that group. The chi-square of this fossil relative to the human and knuckle-walking groups is much greater. It must be remembered that these statistics may well be invalid because of the within-group heterogeneity. But they do correspond to what was found in previous analyses.

These results are consistent with the hypothesis: the locomotor groups can be discriminated from one another and the fossils fall within their expected groups.

By way of checking, an analysis very similar to this was done which lumps the species in the same groups except for the orangs and gibbons which were treated separately. The results are almost identical: the Kromdraai and Kanapoi humeri fall closest to man, and the East Rudolf specimen falls within the orang range. The chi-square for the latter relative to the orang centour is 6.298. With three degrees of freedom, chi-square would be larger than this in 10% of cases.

Summary and Conclusions

MULTIVARIATE ANALYSIS

The results of the multivariate analyses of the distal humerus can be summarized as follows:

1.   Multiple discriminant analysis using 15 ratios of measurements taken on the distal humerus of all hominoid genera (except *Symphalangus*) and three monkey species shows the close resemblance of the Kanapoi and Kromdraai humeri to the humeri of man. The new East Rudolf specimen appears to have a unique shape: its position in the eight-discriminant function space is outside of the ranges of all primates tested. Its projection on individual functions indicates that it is unlike the humeri of chimpanzee and gorilla, but similar in certain respects to those of man and orang. Its metrical resemblance to the orang distal humerus is demonstrated by its almost identical pattern in a ratio diagram (Fig. 3) and by its projection on function V. Its similarity to the human humerus is shown by its behavior on function IV which separates the human humeri from all others on the basis of traits such as the shape of the olecranon fossa.

2.   Similar results are obtained by using 16 original measurements (as opposed to ratios) in a multiple discriminant analysis of hominoids (excluding the three monkey samples). Again the Kanapoi and Kromdraai humeri fall close to man although the latter is equally close to chimpanzee. The East Rudolf specimen remains outside the centours of the other hominoid humeri.

3.   Lumping the hominoid humeri into locomotor categories (gorilla and chimpanzee as knuckle-walkers, man as a biped, and gibbon and orang as suspensory posture), confirms the human shape of the Kromdraai and Kanapoi humeri, but places the East Rudolf specimen in the suspensory posture group. Rearrangement of the groupings so that orangs and gibbons are entered separately, chim-

panzees and gorillas together, and man separately, places the East Rudolf fossil within the orang range of variation. The fossil consistently falls outside of the knuckle-walking group's range.

GENERAL CONCLUSIONS

The results of the multivariate analyses of the shape of the distal end of the East Rudolf humerus do not support the theory that it belonged to a knuckle-walking hominoid. In all analyses the fossil falls consistently outside the range of variation of the extant knuckle-walkers. This is particularly true when the knuckle-walking apes are entered into the analysis as one group. In several of the analyses one particular discriminant function separated either of the knuckle-walking apes from the rest of the hominoids and the East Rudolf humerus consistently clustered with the latter. These results confirm the impression based on the inspection of the non-metrical traits that most of the significant knuckle-walking traits of the humerus are not present. Of particular importance is the lack in the fossil of a steep lateral side of the olecranon fossa. This trait is present in all of the African ape humeri examined.

But the actual functional affinities of the East Rudolf specimen are hard to assess. The evidence is ambiguous and contradictory. In some multivariate analyses it fell with the orang humeri, but in others it was separated from all hominoids. These analyses, of course, consider only the metrical information from the distal end of the bone. In some non-metrical traits it resembles man, especially in the shape of the olecranon fossa. It is shallow, broad, and has gradually sloping sides. Presumably, this shape in man is related to the fact that the humerus is not used in locomotion. The well developed pectoral crest is not usually so strongly developed in the humeri of other hominoids.

The general robustness of the shaft of the East Rudolf humerus resembles a female gorilla. The circumference at midpoint is 84 mm in this fossil compared to a mean circumference in man of 56 mm, in chimpanzees of 71 mm, in pygmy chimpanzees of 60 mm, in female gorillas of 86 mm, in male gorillas of 108 mm, in female orangs of 61 mm and in male orangs of 78 mm. All of these values vary a good deal, but even the most robust Eskimo was much less than the fossil (76 mm). The length of the fossil humerus (perhaps 33 to 35 cm) is probably less than the mean length of female gorillas (38.1 cm). If the circumference at midpoint is divided by the length to get an index of robusticity, then the East Rudolf specimen exceeds the mean for all hominoid species measured. There is considerable variation in robustness of the humeral shaft, however.

The metrical resemblance of the distal end of the East Rudolf humerus to those of the orang is striking, particularly the shape of the capitulum. In orangs and in the fossil the capitulum is high and relatively narrow giving it a globular shape rather than the flattened oval typical of the other hominoids. The relative size, shape, and projection of the medial epicondyle are also similar. The shape of the olecranon and the size of its lateral ridge are quite different, however.

In conclusion, then, the overall morphology (metrical and non-metrical) of the East Rudolf humerus does not resemble the humeri of extant knuckle-walking apes except in the robustness of the shaft. Its functional affinities are ambiguous, showing some typically human traits and some typically orang traits. The Kromdraai and Kanopoi humeri are clearly hominid in shape.

References

Ashton, E. H., M. J. R. Healy, and S. Lipton
    1957   The descriptive use of discriminant functions in physical anthro-pology. Proceedings of the Royal Society (B), *146:* 552-572.
Ashton, E. H., M. J. R. Healy, C. E. Oxnard, and T. F. Spence
    1965   The combination of locomotor features of the primate shoulder girdle by canonical analysis. Proceedings of the Zoological Society of London (Journal of Zoology), *147:* 406-429.
Ashton, E. H., and C. E. Oxnard
    1964   Locomotor patterns in primates. Proceedings of the Zoological Society of London, *142:* 1-28.
Cooley, W. W., and R. Lohnes
    1962   Multivariate Procedures for the Behavioral Sciences. Wiley, New York.
Currey, J. D.
    1968   The adaptation of bones to stress. Journal of Theoretical Biology, *20:* 91-106.
Day, M. H., and B. A. Wood
    1968   Functional affinities of the Olduvai hominid 8 talus. Man, *3:* 440-455.

Dixon, W. J.
1970   Biomedical Computer Programs. University of California Press, Berkeley, Los Angeles, London.
Fisher, R. A.
1936   The use of multiple measurements in taxonomic problems. Annals of Eugenics, *7:* 179-188.
Furuya, Y.
1961   The social life of the silvered leaf monkeys *(Trachypithecus cristatus)*. Primates, *3:* 41-60.
Jones, K. J.
1964   The Multivariate Statistical Analyzer. Cambridge, Massachusetts.
Leakey, R.
1971   Further evidence of lower Pleistocene hominids from East Rudolf, North Kenya. Nature, *226:* 241-245.

———
1972   Further evidence of lower Pleistocene hominids from East Rudolf, North Kenya, 1971. Nature, *237:* 264-269.
Leakey, R., J. M. Mungai, and A. C. Walker
1972   New australopithecines from East Rudolf, Kenya (II). American Journal of Physical Anthropology, *36:* 235-252.
McHenry, H. M.
1972   Postcranial Skeleton of Early Pleistocene Hominids. Ph.D. Thesis, Harvard University, Cambridge, Massachusetts.
Napier, J. R.
1963   The Locomotor Functions of Hominids. In: Classification and Human Evolution. S. L. Washburn, ed. Aldine, Chicago.
Napier, J. R., and P. R. Davis
1959   The forelimb skeleton and associated remains of *Proconsul africanus*. Fossil Mammals of Africa. British Museum of Natural History, London, *16:* 1-70.
Napier, J. R., and P. Napier
1967   A Handbook of Living Primates. Academic Press, London and New York.
Oxnard, C. E.
1967   The functional morphology of the primate shoulder as revealed by comparative anatomical, osteometric and discriminant function techniques. American Journal of Physical Anthropology, *26:* 219-240.

———
1971   Tensile forces in skeletal structures. Journal of Morphology, *34:* 425-436.

Patterson, B., and W. W. Howells

1967 Hominid humeral fragment from early Pleistocene of north-western Kenya. Science, *156:* 64-66.

Rao, C. R.

1952 Advanced Statistical Methods in Biometric Research. John Wiley and Sons, New York.

Seal, H.

1964 Multivariate Statistical Analysis for Biologists. Methuen, London.

Straus, W. L., Jr.

1948 The humerus of *Paranthropus robustus*. American Journal of Physical Anthropology, *6:* 285-311.

14. Osteobiography: Life History Recorded in Bone

Frank P. Saul

Prologue and Introduction

Those of us who work with skeletons owe much to William Howells. He has helped us to make our measurements more precise in terms of reference points and he has encouraged us to be more selective in our choice of measurements, while on occasion supplying us with new and more useful measurements.

Throughout, the "where" of measurement has been subordinated to the "why" of measurement as in his techniques for the determination of sex in individual skeletal remains and for the estimation of biologic distance between skeletal populations.

For a situation where measurements were not applicable, as in the assessment of age at death, Professor Howells (with Dr. Orville

NOTE: In addition to those individuals and institutions acknowledged within the text, I thank the following: For professional guidance, Drs. R. E. W. Adams, G. R. Willey, A. L. Smith, W. W. Howells, A. Damon, H. B. Haley, A. K. Freimanis, A. Romano, M. T. Jaen, R. Morales, and N. Hammond. For financial assistance, The U. S. Public Health Service (DHEW-PHS Research Grant No. 5-S01-RR05700-02), The Milton Fund of the Harvard Medical School, The Pennsylvania State University and The Society of Sigma Xi.

Elliot) arranged and ordered the traditional criteria in regard to both effectiveness and age groupings that would better serve demographic and epidemiologic investigations.

In addition to using Professor Howells' specific techniques and methods in my own studies of the skeletal remains of the ancient Maya, I have sought to enlarge upon his continuing emphasis on meaningful—rather than mindless—measurement and observation.

For instance, I have coined the terms "osteobiography" and "osteobiographic analysis" in order to stimulate archeologists to think in terms of skeletons as life histories recorded in bone.[1] In line with this approach, I have tried to increase the dialogue and understanding between archeologist and biologic anthropologist with the aid of a simplistic diagram (Figure 1) that lists some of the kinds of data that can be obtained from skeletal remains in relation to their role in answering basic archeologic questions.

This approach seems particularly appropriate for the Maya area since cultural remains such as pottery and architecture have been much studied while skeletal remains have been virtually ignored owing to their poor preservation and frequent artificial deformation. However, even seemingly inadequate material can yield useful information if subjected to intensive reconstruction followed by intensive problem oriented examination as I have attempted to demonstrate using skeletons from Harvard's Peabody Museum expedition to Altar de Sacrificios (Saul 1972).

The presentation that follows will be based upon my intensive studies of Altar, Lubaantun (Saul, 1975) and Seibal (Saul, in preparation) as well as my surveys (1972 and 1973) of collections of Maya skeletal material located at the Peabody Museum (Harvard), the Museo Nacional de Antropologia (Mexico) and the Museo Nacional de Arqueologia y Historia (Guatemala), Museo de Tikal (Guatemala) and the Museo de Merida (Mexico).

Examples of osteobiographic data derived from these studies will be presented in relation to the phraseology of Figure 1.

Who Was There?

This question is answered initially in terms of the sex and age at

[1]Also, I had grown weary of talking about "aging," "sexing," "racing," etc. skeletons and wished to devise one word that would cover all these and other aspects of skeletal analysis.

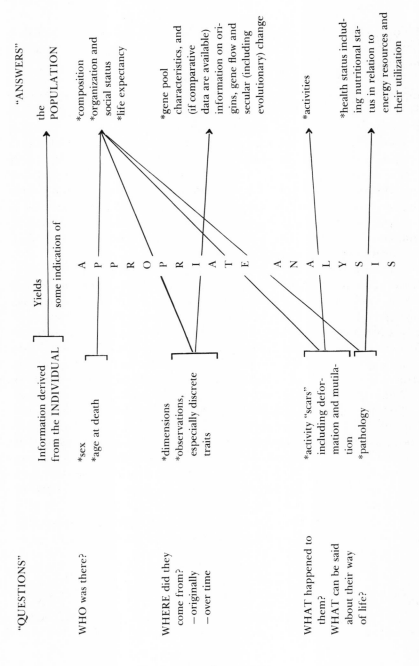

Figure 1. Some potential applications of osteobiographic analysis (from Saul 1972:4).

374

death of the individuals whose remains have been recovered. This is the basic question in more ways than one, and it must be answered before proceeding with any subsequent analyses for biologic purposes, inasmuch as so many biologic phenomena vary in relation to sex and age.

Sex estimates are based on observation and measurement of known sexual dimorphisms in the pelvis and other portions of the skeleton. The pelvis seems to provide the most reliable information since the shape and dimensions of the female pelvis have been subjected to generation after generation of natural selection for successful child birth. The accuracy of sex estimates in pre-pubertal individuals remains controversial.

The criteria used for age estimates vary according to the appropriate stage of the life cycle. They vary from diaphyseal ("shaft") length and degree of calcification of the deciduous dentition in the pre-natal period and early childhood, on through to the presence or absence of union between specific epiphyses ("joint ends") and their diaphyses during adolescence, and eventually include observations of bone remodeling and loss in older individuals. Some criteria can be observed with the naked eye whereas others involve radiologic and microscopic procedures.

Once obtained, these data can also be applied to the understanding of group or sub-group composition, organization and social status. In addition, life expectancy can be assessed and interpreted in relation to population energy levels and ecologic adjustment.

For example, sex and age data from Altar de Sacrificios show a low percentage of sub-adults, that together with an excess of males in the sex distribution, lends weight to the possibility of selective occupation of Altar for ceremonial purposes (with minimal family life). However, on at least one occasion, females played important roles in the ceremonial life of Altar as is shown by the nature and contents of the tomb occupied by Burial No. 128 (a 40-44 year old female, the main occupant) and Burial No. 96 (a 25-29 year old female, a presumed auto sacrifice to No. 128). Included among the tomb contents is the now famous Altar vase whose glyphs provide a date of 754 A.D. together with a pictorial record of the events surrounding the deaths of the tomb's occupants (Adams 1971:68-78).

Or for instance, Chichen Itza's legends of sacrificed maidens were lent only partial support by Hooton's (1940) examination of the sex and age of at least 42 individuals recovered from the Sacred Cenote in 1909. In addition to the anticipated female occupants (whose virginity was not ascertainable (p. 273)[2] there were at least 13 adult males (as opposed to 8 females) and perhaps more significantly, the cranial remains of at least 21 children aged 12 years or younger were also present. My recent survey of the 1960 and later remains recovered from the Sacred Cenote further supports the Maya emphasis upon child sacrifice (or at least "burial") in ancient times and in this place, since I determined that once more, at least one-half (29) of the occupants were children. Again, as in Hooton's study, more adult males (19) than females (10) were present.

However, at Lubaantun, the "Collective Tomb" consisted of the dental remains of 15 adults, both young and middle adult and both male and female, with the only evidence for selective inclusion being the total absence of sub-adult remains. This lack of sub-adult remains indicated that this was a very different situation from that reported from Yakalche by Pendergast et al. (1968) who estimated that a single cache of dental remains (348 teeth) included a minimum of 13 donors of deciduous teeth and 30 donors of permanent teeth. They further postulated that "the age range indicated in the Yakalche material points to the possibility of connexion between the tooth offering and rain ceremonies" (p. 642). The absence of children among the Lubaantun remains would appear to preclude those particular ceremonial connotations and rather suggest a family or similar reentombment over time of surviving portions of previous burials—a belief reinforced by similarities in dental morphology (Saul, 1975).

Again and again, aside from their well known demographic and epidemiologic applications, sex and age determinations can provide

[2]My most recent examination (September 1974) of the Chichen Itza material located at the Museo Nacional de Antropologia in Mexico City, suggests that at least one of the females had borne a child. This opinion is based upon the presence of a "scar of parturition" on the dorsal surface of a left pubic bone purported to have come from the Cenote. If the provenience assignment is correct, Hooton's statement (1940:273) that "the osteological evidence does not permit a determination of this nice point" (*i.e.* "virginity") is no longer completely accurate in the light of advances in osteobiographic methodology. (For a review of J. L. Angel's and T. D. Stewart's efforts along these lines, see "Identification of the Scars of Parturition in the Skeletal Remains of Females" by T. D. Stewart, pages 127-135 in *Personal Identification in Mass Disasters*, edited by T. D. Stewart and published by the Smithsonian Institution, Washington, D.C., in 1970).

important clues to the original function and nature of archeologic sites and/or cultural beliefs.

Where Did They Come From? Originally . . . and Over Time?

The fragmentary and often deformed nature of Maya skeletal materials makes it difficult to apply the biologic distance techniques that have been used in some other areas, so proper answers to the question of origins will require other and better samples from within and without the Maya area. In the meantime we do have the fairly complete skeleton of the earliest known lowland Maya, Altar de Sacrificios Burial No. 135, who dates to about 800 BC. Altar Burial No. 135, male, 20-24 years of age, is remarkably similar in dimensions and contours to the well known Tepexpan specimen from the Valley of Mexico (Saul 1972:9, 92). These individuals are widely separated in time and it would be foolhardy to suggest genetic continuity, but the striking resemblances do at least heighten such a possibility.

Origins aside, cultural discontinuities and findings of statural decreases from ancient to modern times (Stewart 1953, Haviland 1967, Saul 1972: 28-30) have led to speculations that the Maya area was subject to invasions that may have contributed to the collapse of Maya civilization in the 9-10th centuries A.D. (Sabloff and Willey 1967). No support for this suggestion can be found in the report of my former student and colleague, Donald Austin, who after analyzing genetically based characteristics and dimensions of teeth from Altar and Seibal declared

> Univariate analyses of all of the traits reveal that the populations show slightly more variation geographically than temporally. Multivariate analysis, in the form of a generalized distance function, of the discontinuous traits was also performed. The results indicate that, whether the individuals from the sites are considered as one population or as separate populations, there is greater genetic continuity through time than geographically. This does not support the postulate concerning large scale population intrusion into these two Maya communities during the Terminal Classic. Instead, the results suggest the persistence of local endogamy with relatively little change in the dental genes through time (Austin 1970:60-61).

Aside from minimizing the possibility of invasions of Altar and Seibal, these indications of genetic continuity lend weight to nutritional and similar disease oriented explanations for decreases in Maya stature from ancient to modern times, (Saul 1972:30-33 and below).

What Happened to Them? What Can Be
Said About Their Way of Life?

These are very broadly stated questions, and many bits and pieces of "answers" derived from Maya remains could be cited at this point.

For instance, new data on cranial deformation and dental decoration are being passed on to the archeologists for analysis as additional cultural traits (Saul 1972: 10-28: 1975).

However, the most significant replies to these questions are coming from the finding and interpretation of pathologic lesions that provide some indication of the health status of the ancient Maya.

The health of the ancient Maya has been a matter of speculation for some time as various disease based theories were offered in an attempt to explain the 9-10th century A.D. collapse of Maya civilization, while recently the poor health of the modern day Maya has been contrasted with the presumed good health of the ancient Maya (PAHO 1968:166). Unfortunately, all this speculation was accompanied by little examination of the skeletal record itself.

The study of their actual remains has produced much new and interesting data that for the purposes of this particular presentation I shall organize in terms of probable disease entity or diagnosis (especially as these relate to archeological context) while avoiding the lengthy descriptions and discussions to be found in my 1972 monograph.

TRAUMA AND VIOLENT INJURY

This is a category of potentially great interest to the Maya specialist in relation to postulations of invasions and/or civil warfare, aside from the known occurrences of ceremonial death.

There are at least three Maya sites that provide some indirect evidence for violence. I refer to the skeletal remains recovered from the Sacred Cenote of Chichen Itza, a mass burial found under the ball court at Seibal, and the previously mentioned presumed autosacrifice from Altar. In all three cases the location and other circumstances are suggestive of violent or at least unnatural death.

Unfortunately, the various remains do not manifest injuries that might have served as the immediate cause of death. Hooton did find some healed fractures among the people from Chichen Itza but a recent re-examination by me indicates that at least one of these was a congenital defect of the variety called an encephalocele (or herniation of the meninges and/or brain through what was once the anterior fontanelle of the skull). However, I have balanced this somewhat by noting a large partially healed bone flap lesion suggestive of a hacking cut in an individual recovered during the later operations at the Sacred Cenote.

Otherwise there seem to be few definite indications of violence. The Altar materials yielded only one individual with a healed clavicular fracture and another with a healed "parry" fracture of the ulna.

INFECTIOUS DISEASE

A number of specimens from Altar, Seibal and other sites bear witness of infections of uncertain origin that proceeded far enough to produce inflammation, and sometimes destruction of bone.

Of particular interest to the historians of medicine are those specimens that manifest the types of lesions that are associated with syphilis or yaws as seen today. Both Altar and Seibal have yielded several individuals with deformed tibiae of the variety called sabershin in deference to their anterior-posterior curvature. Individuals with this deformity were found in the mass burial under the ball court at Seibal and also at Altar, including the young lady (24-29 years of age) who is thought to be an auto-sacrifice to the older priestess (40-45 years) and shows a slight tibial sabering along with stellate lesions of the frontal bone. In the latter instance, the previously mentioned Altar vase dates the burial as having occurred about 754 A.D., but in all instances the specimens are certainly pre-Columbian, thus providing new perspective for arguments about the dating and origins of the treponemal infections.

MALNUTRITION AND CHILDHOOD DISEASE

Numerous specimens from Altar and Seibal and other sites show the cranial outer table porosities and diploic expansion previously found by Hooton in the first Chichen Itza collection and offered as an explanation for the decline of the Maya (Hooton 1940:275).

At that time this lesion was referred to somewhat inaccurately as "osteoporosis symmetrica" (Hrdlicka 1914; Hooton 1940) but now it is usually referred to as spongy or porotic hyperostosis (Angel 1967). Similar but more consistent lesions are found in modern day patients with hereditary anemias such as Thalassemia or Sicklemia, but those of the Maya are more likely to be due to iron deficiency anemia.

Children and women of child bearing age are especially prone to this condition (Saul 1972:38-42).

Periodontoclasia or periodontal degeneration is common and could be due to a number of prosaic causes including a lack of dental hygiene, but when it occurs in conjunction with subperiosteal hemorrhages as evidenced by ossified remnants at Altar and Seibal, the vitamin C deficiency ("scurvy" is its most extreme form) must be considered. Elsewhere (Saul 1972:56-66) I have discussed the specifics of this unexpected finding in a tropical "paradise" and have listed the cultural preferences and food preparation techniques that can and have resulted in its occurrence in modern Guatemala.

Numerous teeth, both deciduous and permanent, from many sites record growth interruptions of enamel formation. Similar arrested development in modern teeth has been related to a wide variety of systemic disturbances, including malnutrition and various other disease processes occurring during childhood. The locations of these lesions in the Maya indicate that they occurred most frequently at about 3-4 years of age. This timing is of special interest because this was the age at which weaning took place among the Maya at the time of first European contacts, according to Bishop de Landa (Tozzer 1941). Weaning is a critical period with many important ramifications as studies of modern highland Maya have shown:

> Weanling diarrhea was established by these studies as a classical example of synergistic interaction of malnutrition and infectious disease and, in developing countries, as probably the most important single factor in growth and development of children in their most formative years (Scrimshaw, Behar, Guzman, and Gordon 1969, p. 55).

The consequences of weaning might have been different in 3-4-years-old ancient Maya as compared with the 25-months-old (median age at completed weaning) modern Maya cited above but there is a strong possibility that there is a relationship between the rigors of weaning and the lesions I have recorded in ancient Maya teeth. If so, we might note that one of the "accomplishments" of modern civilization and its emphasis upon early weaning has been to lower the age at which Maya children lose access to a valuable nutritive and immunological supplement (Saul 1972:66-68).

CONCLUSION

In this brief presentation, I have reviewed some of the kinds of information that are recorded in the human skeleton. The variety and quantity of useful information that can be obtained from fragmentary Maya remains emphasizes the value of the problem oriented approach implicit in the term "osteobiography."

In particular, I would cite the potential importance of health status as recorded in the skeleton, as it relates to understanding the collapse of ancient Maya civilization (Saul 1972:72-73) and the roots of modern day health problems in Central America (Scrimshaw *et al.* 1968).

Bibliography

Adams, R. E. W.
    1971   The Ceramics of Altar de Sacrificios. Papers of the Peabody Museum, Harvard University, Vol. 63, No. 1, Cambridge, Massachusetts.
Angel, J. Lawrence
    1967   Porotic Hyperostosis or Osteoporosis Symmetrica, pp. 378-389, in Brothwell and Sandison, Editors. Diseases in Antiquity. Thomas, Springfield, Ill.
Austin, D. M.
    1970   Dental Microevolution in Two Ancient Maya Communities. Master's thesis, The Pennsylvania State University.
Haviland, William A.
    1967   Stature at Tikal, Guatemala: Implications for Ancient Maya Demography and Social Organization. American Antiquity, *32 (5):* 316-325.
Hooton, Earnest A.
    1940   Skeletons from the Cenote of Sacrifice at Chichen Itza. In: The Maya and Their Neighbors, C. L. Hay and others, eds., pp. 272-280. New York.
Hrdlicka, Ales
    1914   Anthropological Work in Peru in 1913, with Notes on Pathology of Ancient Peruvians. Smithsonian Institution Miscellaneous Collections, Vol. 61, No. 18.
P. A. H. O.
    1968   Food and Nutrition of the Maya before the Conquest and at the Present Time. In: Biomedical Challenges Presented by the American Indian, pp. 114-119. Scientific Publication No. 165. Pan American Health Organization, Washington, D. C.
Pendergast, D. M., M. H. Bartley and C. J. Armelagos
    1968   A Maya Tooth Offering from Yakalche, British Honduras. Man, *3:* 635-643.

Sabloff, J. A., and Gordon R. Willey
    1967   The Collapse of Maya Civilization in the Southern Lowlands:
    A Consideration of History and Process. Southwestern Journal of An-
    thropology, *23:* 311-336.
Saul, Frank P.
    1972   The Human Skeletal Remains of Altar de Sacrificios. An Osteo-
    biographic Analysis. Papers of the Peabody Museum, Harvard Uni-
    versity, Vol. 63, No. 2, Cambridge, Massachusetts.

    1975   The Human Remains. In: Lubaantun: A Classic Maya Realm,
    N. Hammond, Editor. Peabody Museum Monographs No. 2. Harvard
    University, Cambridge, Massachusetts.

    The Human Skeletal Remains of Seibal, and the Health Status of the
    Ancient Maya. Memoirs of the Peabody Museum, Vol. 13, No. to be as-
    signed, Cambridge, Massachusetts. In preparation.
Scrimshaw, N. S., Behar, M. A. Guzman, and J. E. Gordon
    1969   Nutrition and Infection Field Study in Guatemalan Villages,
    1959-1964, IX: An Evaluation of Medical, Social, and Public Health
    Benefits, with Suggestions for Future Field Study. Archives of En-
    vironmental Health, *18:* 51-62.
Scrimshaw, N. S., C. E. Taylor, and J. E. Gordon
    1968   Interactions of Nutrition and Infection. World Health Organiza-
    tion Monograph Series No. 57, Geneva.
Stewart, T. D.
    1953   Skeletal Remains from Zaculeu, Guatemala. The Ruins of
    Zaculeu, Guatemala, R. F. Woodbury and A. S. Trik, Editors. The
    United Fruit Company, Boston, pp. 295-311.
Tozzer, Alfred M., Editor
    1941   Landa's Relacion de las cosas de Yucatan. Papers of the Peabody
    Museum of Archaeology and Ethnology, Harvard University, Vol. 18.

15. Metric versus Discrete Traits in African Skulls

G. P. Rightmire

Introduction

Craniometry is surely one of the oldest pursuits in physical anthropology, and a great many early compilations of skull or head measurements now lie dusty and unused on library shelves, attesting to the fact that collection of such data has often been undertaken haphazardly and without any real goals, save simple cataloging of information. A number of schools (Pearson and the Biometric Laboratory in England, Hrdlička and Hooton in America) have advocated varying sets of "standard" measurements, though no one of these has ever really prevailed, and the question of which and how many measurements to take has always been an awkward one. Fortunately, recent factor analytic and discriminant surveys of the cranium are at last proving useful, in showing which dimensions or combinations thereof correspond to stable patterns of variation within and between

NOTES: For their kind permission to study collections of African skeletal materials, I am grateful to Professor Peter Sebuwufu, Department of Anatomy, Makerere University, and to Professor Phillip V. Tobias, Anatomy Department, University of the Witwatersrand. Both R. G. Matson and Henry Harpending contributed valuable suggestions during the planning of this work, and Jerome Kaplan provided assistance with computer programming. I am pleased to have had the support of the Research Foundation of the State University of New York.

human populations, and it is significant that these patterns do not always incorporate such time-honored measures as cranial or nasal indices (see Howells, 1969; 1972 for a review). Some of the traditional measurements might well be dropped and other new ones substituted, but this is beyond the scope of coverage here.

Early statistical approaches to anthropometric data were similarly beset with difficulties, so long as populations could be compared on the basis of only one trait or measurement at a time, and workable alternative multivariate procedures were only slowly formulated and sometimes too readily embraced. Pearson's famed Coefficient of Racial Likeness was of course severely flawed and, in its original form, suitably short lived. Further and much refined developments occurred later with the introduction of Fisher's linear discriminant function and Mahalanobis' generalized distance (D^2), but actual application of these statistics to anthropological work was (and may be still) hindered by a feeling that computational procedures are overly complex and time-consuming. Also, at various times queries have been raised concerning the "fit" of the anthropometric data themselves to (normal) distributions considered prerequisite to the use of the statistical methods, and recently the uncritical use of multivariate procedures has been questioned by Kowalski (1972). Possible discrepancies in the data must be allowed for, though several studies have suggested the problem to be minor (Talbot and Mulhall, 1962). Dissatisfaction generated on these several accounts has generally resulted in a resurgence of interest in simpler statistics, such as that proposed by Penrose (1954), as the more useful and convenient, especially when computer aids are lacking (see Huizinga, 1962, for historical treatment of distance coefficients and their popularity).

Given this background, it is not surprising that some anthropologists have tended to shy away altogether from measurements and the associated statistical procedures and rely instead on the array of discrete or non-metrical variants present in appreciable frequency in most human populations. The recognition and study of such traits is of course not new at all (Brothwell, 1965) nor is the feeling that monogenic characters generally, and the various blood polymorphisms in particular, are better suited than metrical or polygenic traits to the determination of genetic similarities or differences between groups; Boyd presented this view forcefully in 1950. It has also been stated, and as warmly denied, that polygenic characters, having a complex set of genetic determinants, are likely to be more stable over time (less subject to the action of selection and drift) and hence the better markers of population affinity. But controversy continues (see Bielicki, 1962, and the accompanying comments as a sample; de Villiers, 1968, has reviewed the literature to date), and simple resolution of this question is not likely to be forthcoming.

To return, there has been a relatively recent emphasis in skeletal studies on the use of discrete variants, at least some of which (e.g. metopism, palatine and mandibular tori) seem to be under simple genetic control. Others are less well understood and, while discrete or discontinuous in their phenotypic manifestation, are probably dependent on several interacting loci. These have come to be termed "quasi-continuous" after analogous variants long under study in mouse and other rodent populations (Berry, 1968). A number of these characters were used by Laughlin and Jørgensen (1956) to calculate simple distances between Greenlandic Eskimo isolates, and later Brothwell (1959) did the same for some 14 series of crania representing a rather larger portion of the world's populations. Further work along these lines has stressed either some version of Penrose's (1954) "size" and "shape" statistical approach (e.g. de Villiers, 1968) or a measure of divergence attributed to C. A. B. Smith and applied to diverse collections of skulls by Berry and Berry (1967) and Kellock and Parsons (1970a; 1970b). For the most part, unfortunately, one has little grasp of the meaning of the results obtained; samples of widely divergent groups of man are shown to be different, and that is not unexpected. Very few studies have been concerned only with contiguous, closely related populations, and of these, fewer still (e.g. Laughlin and Jørgensen, 1956; de Villiers, 1968) have included distances based on metrical traits as well as on discrete traits for comparison. Preliminary work of my own using both approaches has suggested some problems with discrete trait distances (Rightmire, 1972), and the present paper is an attempt to explore the situation further.

The Bantu-Speakers as a Test Framework

Skeletal materials representing the Bantu-speaking Negro peoples, now spread over much of Africa south of the Sahara, provide a kind of test framework, or at least an approach to what is required. This is true for several reasons. Firstly, well documented series of crania, mostly of dissecting hall origin, are available for study, and this is a rarity. Also important is the fact that the history of Bantu Negro expansion into East and South Africa, occurring over the last two millennia or earlier, is broadly known, in outline if not in all details. Here linguistic studies, archaeological investigations of Iron Age assemblages and their dating by radiocarbon, and in the later phases, oral tradition and eye-witness accounts left us by early explorers and traders, have all been utilized to trace the gradual diffusion of the metal working, Bantu-speaking farmers into regions previously peopled largely by "Late Stone Age" or "Mesolithic" communities alone (e.g. the Bushmen of southern Africa).

Linguistic evidence affords virtually the only source of information relating to the origins and early history of the Bantu-speakers. The 300 or so languages making up this group are closely related to each other, despite their current wide geographic distribution, and this has long suggested an earlier unity. Greenberg's (1949; 1963) well known linguistic analysis places Bantu as part of a larger "Benue-Congo" group of languages, which today are spoken almost exclusively in Nigeria and the Cameroons; and it is here, in a relatively restricted area, that Bantu must have originated and spread to the southeast. Murdock (1959) has carried Greenberg's conclusions several steps further and has attempted to document the Bantu advance first into the tropical rainforest and later into the great lakes region of East Africa and the southern grasslands. He sets the beginning of this great population expansion at the first century A.D.[1]

A rather different, but not necessarily contradictory picture has been presented by Guthrie (1962) and subsequently elaborated by Oliver (1966). Here, again on linguistic grounds, the early migrants are presumed to have occupied a roughly elliptical belt of lightly wooded land stretching south of the forests, from the mouth of the Congo River in the west to the Rovuma in the east. During this period,

[1]This date is almost certainly too late, as newer radiocarbon evidence suggests that iron and pottery had already reached parts of central and southern Africa prior to the start of the Christian Era. Although information from the Congo is as yet inconclusive, dates compiled by Stuiver and van der Merwe (1968) indicate early Iron Age occupation in Zambia during the first century A. D. and in Rhodesia only a century or two later.

the Bantu refined their metal technology and developed the African cereals introduced from the east. Then, as population increased, and with the aid of various imported Southeast Asian food plants (e.g. the banana), an expansion mainly to the north brought the Iron Age to Lake Victoria and the East African Interlacustrine region. A final wave (or waves) of population movement would then have introduced the Bantu-speakers into the remainder of their present habitat, including southern Africa.

Whatever the precise routes followed, it seems definite that the East African great lakes area was populated by Iron Age immigrants well before any appreciable movement of populations into South Africa occurred. Data recently obtained from Rwanda and other parts of East Africa fall within the first half and middle years of the first millennium A. D. (Sutton, 1971), while full-fledged Iron Age culture does not appear in the northern Transvaal until 800 A. D. (Stuiver and van der Merwe, 1968). So, the Interlacustrine Bantu tribes, including the Rwanda, Rundi and various others of Uganda and Western Kenya were probably settled prior to the penetration of Natal and the Cape Coast by Nguni groups and the occupation of Lesotho and the Transvaal by the Sotho.

The stages in the peopling of what is now South Africa by Bantu Negroes remain imperfectly known, though understanding of the local Iron Age sequences is increasing, and oral tradition in some instances proves useful. The Nguni groups, including both Zulu (Natal Nguni) and Xosa (Cape Nguni), have clearly been established south of the Drakensberg on the Natal coast for a long time; Nguni speakers were definitely identified there by the Portuguese late in the 16th century, and by their own tradition, Xosa peoples were in this region for generations before that (Wilson, 1969a). There are no obvious links in either language or traditions with other Bantu groups to the north of the Drakensberg (save only with some relatively recent migrants like the Rhodesian Ndebele, who came from the south), and this argues that the Nguni movement southward is an ancient one. Jeffreys (1967) has suggested a date of 1400 A.D. in this connection, and Inskeep (1969), on the basis of tentative ceramic associations, inclines toward an even earlier chronology.

The Sotho peoples also have had a long history of occupation in and around the present Transvaal, although records of eye witnesses start rather later than for the Nguni; early accounts (17th century) of a hearsay nature (information obtained from Nama Hottentot travelers) are numerous, but Sotho were not seen by European explorers prior to 1801 (Wilson, 1969b). Archaeological evidence, however, seems to associate the Sotho speakers with Iron Age settlements dating to the 11th century, and there is little reason to doubt that this group comprised the main body of early stone builders in the Transvaal (Inskeep, 1969; Mason, 1962; van der Merwe and Scully, 1971). Like the Nguni, with whom they have had much contact over several centuries, the Sotho must originally have come from the north, and the traditions of some of the tribes point strongly toward Tanzania and the lakes region. The details of these movements are lost, but, again, they are presumably ancient ones.

A final tribe of South African Bantu-speakers, the Venda, occupies the more northerly parts of the Transvaal and is of rather special interest because of a rich oral tradition linking it with the Interlacustrine groups of east central Africa. The Venda speak a language which is similar in some respects to Sotho, and also to Shona (a Rhodesian Bantu language), but certain items in its vocabulary "suggest that some of the speakers were from areas around the northern end of Lake Nyasa" (Westphal, 1963). Also on linguistic grounds, Jeffreys (1967) has concluded that the Venda reached southern Africa some time after the Nguni and Sotho but before the close of the 15th century. Others arguing on the basis of genealogies place this event much later, in the 17th or even in the 18th century; the date is thus uncertain, but the weight of evidence compiled from explicit tradition, as well as from ritual, economy and language, underlines a lacustrine connection, and a relatively recent one (see Wilson, 1969b).

To sum up, then: The Nguni and Sotho clearly have ancient roots tying them to their present South African territories. Each group has influenced the other, and there has been some movement back and forth across the common frontier, including absorption of Nguni populations by Sotho and vice versa. Also, both have been in contact with Bushman and Hottentot tribes, and most Nguni dialects now exhibit the effects of this interaction. The Venda, by contrast, appear to be more recent migrants into southern Africa and are more easily linked with the East African Interlacustrine groups to the north. For the several tribes considered, archaeological, linguistic and other *non-biological* sources of information thus suggest the approximate pattern of group relationships or "tree" represented in Figure 1.

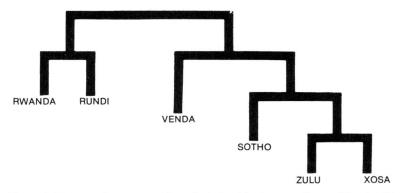

Figure 1. Diagramatic representation of relationships between East and South African Bantu-speaking tribes based on archaeological, linguistic and other non-biological sources of information. (This is meant to be approximate and descriptive only, and vertical distances shown in the "tree" carry no quantitative significance.)

Methods

SKELETAL MATERIALS

All skulls of Bantu-speaking Negroes examined during the course of this work are adult, male and at least complete enough to permit scoring of the non-metrical variants (next section). These materials fall into two broad groupings, as follows:

a. *East African Interlacustrine Bantu-Speakers.* Two major tribal divisions, the Rwanda and the Rundi, are here represented. Fairly extensive skeletal series of each are housed in the Galloway Collection of the Department of Anatomy, Makerere University, Kampala, and departmental records list age, sex, tribal affiliation and cause of death for all specimens. A full set of cranial measurements was taken on 40 Rwanda and 38 Rundi individuals, starting with those listed early in the catalog (begun in 1947) for which any chance of "detribalization" and possible blurring of tribal distinctions is very slight.[2]

[2]Some loss of distinction between tribes is still a possibility, for other reasons. The Rwanda and Rundi skeletons in the Galloway Collection represent migrant populations, largely male and foreign to Kampala. There is always a chance that some of these individuals were lumped together into a single category (e.g. "Rwanda") despite an actual diversity of tribal origins. Little (1971) has reviewed several instances where this sort of confusion occurs in East Africa and notes that "from the point of view of the individual, all tribes other than those from his particular home area tended to be reduced to three or four categories bearing the labels of those tribes who, at the coming of the Europeans, were the most powerful and dominant in the region."

Since scoring is a relatively rapid procedure, and some damaged skulls useless for measurement could be added here, observations of discrete traits were made on larger samples: 61 Rwanda and 41 Rundi, these last comprising the total number of specimens available.

b. *South African (Southern) Bantu-Speakers.* Materials falling in this second category were examined at the Medical School, University of the Witwatersrand, Johannesburg, where they make up part of the Raymond A. Dart Collection of Human Skeletons in the Department of Anatomy. Here, as in Kampala, information as to sex and tribal affiliation is retained for most incoming skeletons, and where questions arise, particulars can easily be cross-checked by reference to a separate listing kept for cadavers as these are transferred from hospital to medical school storage facilities. Documentation is thus not a problem of any import.

As indicated earlier, crania representing four tribal divisions were measured, these samples numbering 30 Zulu, 32 Xosa, 35 Southern Sotho, and 33 Venda males in all. Again, generally more skulls could be scored than measured, so that sample sizes are somewhat larger in the discrete traits analysis (see Table 3).

MEASUREMENTS AND OBSERVATIONS
The 37 cranial measurements utilized in the present study include a number of "standard" ones as well as others (subtenses and angles obtained with the aid of a coordinate caliper) designed especially to register aspects of midfacial protrusion, supraorbital projection, elevation of the nasal saddle, parietal and occipital curvature and so on. These form a slightly modified and expanded version of an earlier list published elsewhere (Rightmire, 1970) and need not now be redefined. All measurements, recorded to the nearest millimeter or whole degree, were transferred from mimeographed field blanks to computer punch cards and carefully scrutinized for error prior to analysis.

Non-metrical or discrete traits scored on all skulls number 18 and are among those commonly encountered in anthropological work. Most are cranial, but three mandibular features (numbers 16, 17, and 18) were also noted wherever possible. Brief descriptions follow:

1. *Metopic suture* Nasion to bregma when complete; may be partially closed. Present in low frequencies in adult crania.

2. *Wormian bones* Extra (sutural) bones of the skull most common in the lamboid suture though occasionally present at bregma, in the coronal suture, at lambda or asterion or elsewhere. Here, only ossicles *at lambda* are recorded.

3. *Epipteric bone* Sutural ossicle at pterion.

4. *Parietal notch bone* Ossicle found in the narrowest area of the incisura parietalis; this should be distinguished from a sutural ossicle at asterion.

5. *Inca bone* Refers to the formation of an independent bone in the occipital region; only those ossicles which can be readily distinguished from wormian (sutural) bones at lambda are counted.

6. *Os japonicum* The zygomatic bone may be divided by a horizontal suture into two parts, the lower of which is then termed the os japonicum.

7. *Accessory infraorbital foramen* Usually the infraorbital foramen is single, though accessory foramina may be present; the presence of such extra foramina (rarely numbering more than one) is noted.

8. *Zygomaticofacial foramen* Present approximately in the center of the malar (external) surface of the zygomatic bone.

9. *Foramen of Huschke* Occurs as a small gap in the floor of the external auditory meatus; usually obliterated after age five, but may persist into adult life.

10. *Auditory exostosis* Bony growth in the external auditory meatus. Medial and lateral exostoses are not treated separately.

11. *Palatine torus* May be defined as a bony elevation along the median or transverse sutures of the bony palate. Three classes or types of torus are recognized; these are a) ridge: narrow and uniform in width from anterior to posterior; b) mound: relatively wide and tapers anteriorly and posteriorly; c) lump: all other tori of irregular shape. These classes are not here treated separately.

12. *Torus maxillaris* Hyperostosis on the alveolar portion of the maxilla; usually confined to the lingual aspect in the molar region.

13. *Parietal foramina* Found near the lambdoid angle of the parietal, these may be present singly or in pairs; more than two is rare.

14. *Supraorbital foramina* Present near the superior orbital margin.

Complete foramina on each side are counted; in order to avoid excess tabulation, notches (incomplete foramina) are not considered.

15. *Ethmoid foramina* Usually found in the orbit, near the suture between ethmoid and frontal bones. Two per orbit (anterior and posterior) is common, but one or both may be absent, and multiple foramina do occur. The presence of *one* foramen only is recorded.

16. *Multiple mental foramina* The presence of more than one mental foramen per side is recorded.

17. *Mylohyoid arch* The formation of a bony arch over the mylohyoid groove on the internal aspect of the ascending ramus is noted.

18. *Mandibular torus* Bony growth on the lingual aspect of the mandible near the roots of the canine and premolar teeth.

DISTANCE STATISTICS

Two separate generalized (multivariate) distance statistics were applied to the data at hand; the first, Mahalanobis' D^2, was used to compute intergroup distances on a subset of the measurements taken, while a second measure of divergence appropriate to the treatment of discontinuous variables provided a matrix of distances derived from the non-metrical information.

a. *Mahalanobis' D^2*. Since there is a total of 37 cranial measurements available (Table 1), and a number of these are likely to be highly correlated among themselves (i.e. will not all supply new and independent information in strictly additive fashion), there is a problem of variable selection to be faced prior to the actual determination of D^2 values. Usually in this situation a set of correlation coefficients is obtained and a subset of apparently independent characters selected simply by inspection — a relatively unsophisticated procedure (Rightmire, 1969). However, better methods exist, as has been pointed out by Howells (1966); and here all measurements were first run on a program (BMDO7M, distributed by U.C.L.A.) capable of ranking them, in stepwise fashion, in an order reflecting their efficiency in distinguishing the particular groups examined. In effect, a given variable is chosen for its contribution to group separation *after* it has been adjusted for correlation with others entered before it, and this procedure is continued until ranking is complete (see Rightmire, 1971, for details).

TABLE 1

BANTU TRIBAL GROUP MEANS FOR THE
37 CRANIAL MEASUREMENTS USED IN THE ANALYSIS.

	Measurement	Rwanda (n=40)	Rundi (n=38)	Zulu (n=30)	Xosa (n=32)	Sotho (n=35)	Venda (n=33)
1.	Cranial ln.	183.64	183.28	186.33	188.28	187.17	186.21
2.	Glabella protrusion	4.97	4.94	5.10	5.12	5.11	5.18
3.	Basion-nasion[1]	98.25	99.50	102.00	101.53	101.34	100.45
4.	Basion-prosthion[1]	101.37	100.44	101.00	101.68	101.77	101.33
5.	Basibregmatic ht.[1]	128.87	128.36	134.43	132.15	131.91	133.39
6.	Max. cranial br.[1]	132.89	131.50	135.20	135.68	133.82	132.75
7.	Max. frontal br.	112.97	112.15	115.79	115.78	115.85	113.45
8.	Bizygomatic br.	128.64	127.39	129.79	131.00	130.28	129.45
9.	Biauricular br.[1]	114.17	113.05	113.13	114.43	114.74	114.69
10.	Subspinale subtense	24.70	25.28	23.93	23.90	23.54	24.42
11.	Max. malar ln.	53.45	53.47	55.73	55.37	55.22	55.81
12.	Malar subtense[1]	10.47	10.10	11.86	11.53	11.88	11.39
13.	Malar ht.	19.37	19.02	20.23	18.81	20.51	19.51
14.	Frontal sagittal chord[1]	110.37	109.92	112.63	112.87	113.25	113.45
15.	Frontal subtense	27.70	27.26	27.76	27.75	28.62	27.93
16.	Frontal angle	30.32	30.05	30.20	29.40	30.28	29.63
17.	Occipital sagittal chord	94.22	93.13	95.79	96.28	94.91	94.84
18.	Occipital subtense[1]	26.82	25.78	26.76	28.03	27.05	25.27
19.	Occipital angle	29.25	27.86	30.66	31.21	29.74	28.63
20.	Orbit br.[1]	39.95	39.78	38.86	39.81	39.34	40.51
21.	Orbit ht.[1]	34.67	34.39	33.46	33.75	33.51	33.66
22.	Inter-orbital br.[1]	22.92	23.71	24.46	23.84	22.91	23.81
23.	Nasal br.[1]	25.84	26.71	27.66	28.31	27.59	27.84
24.	Nasal ht.	48.72	48.68	49.56	49.78	50.00	50.54
25.	Nasion subtense	17.89	18.94	17.86	17.50	16.71	18.78
26.	Nasion angle[1]	19.67	20.89	19.16	18.81	18.08	20.27
27.	Palate ln.[1]	48.89	47.81	48.63	46.96	49.02	47.87
28.	Palate br.	38.62	38.15	39.39	40.34	39.45	40.09
29.	Mastoid ln.	26.95	27.39	28.53	28.25	28.28	27.30
30.	Supraorbital projection	6.10	5.92	6.20	6.21	6.14	6.24
31.	Nasion-prosthion	67.50	66.28	66.59	66.06	66.20	67.36
32.	Bimaxillary chord	94.75	94.02	96.23	94.65	95.05	96.15
33.	Prosthion subtense	37.14	36.92	34.93	34.75	34.51	36.09
34.	Mid-orbital chord	59.79	60.23	60.13	59.68	59.02	60.36
35.	Naso-orbital subtense	18.34	18.23	18.20	17.37	17.42	18.21
36.	Naso-orbital angle	31.39	31.15	31.03	30.28	30.48	31.00
37.	Biorbital chord[1]	99.77	99.34	102.73	102.59	101.91	101.63

[1]measurement used in the 15-variable D^2 analysis

A subset of 15 of the original 37 measurements was selected in this way, and using this subset, values of D^2 were computed for successive pairs of African Negro tribal groups, to a total of 15, set out in *Table 2*. These distances, obtained with the aid of program MAHALANOBIS' D^2 written by Jones (1964), should represent as statistically accurate and biologically correct a picture of tribal relationships as is likely to be realized from a combination of recent craniometric techniques and multivariate distance procedures based on continuous skeletal measurements. They may be compared with distances obtained using 30 variables (also in Table 2) and with the results of the discrete traits analysis, outlined below.

    b.   *Sanghvi's Chi-Square Distance (X^2 or G^2)*. A number of divergence measures are currently available for use with discrete variables. Both Penrose's (1954) approach and a more recent statistic devised by C.A.B. Smith (see Grewal, 1962) have been applied to non-metric skeletal data. Smith's distance especially has received considerable attention, though the results obtained with this simple arcsine transformation are of questionable value (Rightmire, 1972). Other distance measures have been developed for use with blood gene frequency information, and there is now on record a somewhat confusing array of claims and counterclaims championing or finding some fault with each. However, several of these distance formulations have been compared by Kidd and Sgaramella-Zonta (1971) and

TABLE 2

VALUES OF MAHALANOBIS' D^2 COMPUTED FOR SIX BANTU TRIBAL GROUPS USING 15 CRANIAL MEASUREMENTS (UPPER RIGHT AND ALSO 30 MEASUREMENTS (LOWER LEFT PORTION OF THE TABLE). ALL DISTANCES OBTAINED ARE STATISTICALLY SIGNIFICANT (P. .05).

	Rwanda	Rundi	Zulu	Xosa	Sotho	Venda
Rwanda	—	2.16	8.23	6.10	6.71	3.80
Rundi	2.99	—	6.91	8.64	11.35	3.45
Zulu	13.24	12.04	—	1.96	2.16	3.96
Xosa	9.67	14.74	4.97	—	2.46	3.42
Sotho	9.42	15.05	4.97	4.92	—	5.38
Venda	5.24	6.40	13.61	6.30	9.92	—

Sanghvi and Balakrishnan (1972), and in most instances results produced are largely equivalent.

In view of these findings, Sanghvi's original X^2 statistic, related to chi-square, seems appropriate for use with the African tribal data. Computation of this index, either in its earlier form (Sanghvi, 1953) or in a slightly shortened version as G^2 (Balakrishnan and Sanghvi, 1968), is quite straightforward. The percentage incidence (p) of each trait is calculated for each group (Table 3), and the distance between any pair of populations is then simply $(p_1 - p_2)^2 / \bar{p}$ summed over each class of all characters. Division by the total number of degrees of freedom is optional, and is intended to correct for situations involving missing data.

TABLE 3

BANTU TRIBAL GROUP FREQUENCIES (PERCENT[1]) FOR 18 DISCRETE TRAITS USED IN COMPUTING VALUES OF SANGHVI'S DISTANCE.

Trait	Rwanda (n=61)	Rundi (n=41)	Zulu (n=50)	Xosa (n=45)	Sotho (n=45)	Venda (n=35)
Metopic suture	0.0	0.0	2.0	2.2	4.4	0.0
Lambdoid Wormians	41.8	28.0	36.7	43.3	34.0	42.6
Epipteric bone	8.2	13.4	6.1	9.3	8.1	8.6
Parietal notch bone	9.0	9.7	12.0	12.5	12.2	17.1
Inca bone	1.6	0.0	8.0	0.0	8.9	0.0
Os japonicum	1.6	0.0	0.0	2.2	0.0	0.0
Acc. infraorbital foramen	4.9	8.5	9.0	13.3	7.8	11.4
Zygomaticofacial foramen	80.3	81.7	84.0	78.9	80.0	81.4
Foramen of Huschke	6.5	11.2	1.0	4.4	6.7	7.1
Auditory exostosis	0.0	0.0	1.0	0.0	0.0	0.0
Palatine torus	9.8	4.9	2.0	4.4	4.5	2.8
Torus Maxillaris	0.0	0.0	0.0	1.1	0.0	8.8
Parietal foramen	65.5	54.9	68.0	56.6	56.7	70.6
Supraorbital foramen	33.6	25.6	21.0	21.1	28.9	24.2
Ethmoid foramen single	2.5	2.5	5.1	3.6	1.2	6.0
Multiple mental foramina	9.5	11.2	14.2	6.5	21.8	8.0
Mylohyoid arch	6.0	7.5	14.2	16.9	14.9	3.2
Mandibular torus	0.0	0.0	0.0	0.0	0.0	0.0

[1]For traits which occur bilaterally, the number of sides, rather than the number of individuals, scored was used in calculating frequencies.

Distances computed in this way for all African Negro tribes and 12 discrete traits are given in Table 4; six characters, showing zero incidence in one or more populations, were omitted from the calculations. These constitute measures of what has been called "genetic" distance or difference between populations, and a preference for such determinations over those obtained from skeletal measurements is not uncommon.

DISCRIMINANT ANALYSIS

The distance relationships among the several tribal groups are more easily appreciated if these groups can be positioned in a space of reduced dimensionality. So, to facilitate interpretation of the Mahalanobis D^2 values, multiple discriminant analysis has been applied to the same subset of 15 selected measurements taken on each cranium.

The value of the discriminant approach to problems of human variation in cranial measurements has been widely documented in the work of Professor Howells, and no lengthy discussion of the method need be given here. In simple, general terms, the procedure is this: the original variables are used to determine a set of new compound measurements or axes, the discriminant functions, upon which each individual or group centroid can be plotted by means of its discriminant scores. These axes and scores are uncorrelated and have the property of maximizing between-group relative to within-group variation. Thus the first function extracted is the most "important" in the sense that this is the dimension along which maximum group separation occurs; the second axis portrays the largest differ-

TABLE 4

SANGHVI'S CHI-SQUARE DISTANCES (X^2 or G^2) BASED ON
12 DISCRETE TRAITS IN SIX GROUPS.

	Rwanda	Rundi	Zulu	Xosa	Sotho	Venda
Rwanda	—	1.14	1.84	1.63	1.49	1.24
Rundi		—	1.86	1.42	0.99	1.63
Zulu			—	1.08	1.26	1.48
Xosa				—	1.18	1.50
Sotho					—	2.27
Venda						—

ences not registered on the first, and so on, to a possible total of dimensions one less than the number of groups represented. Further, in this reduction to "discriminant space," there is often little loss of total information; only the first two or three functions computed may be necessary to construct a space in which essentially the original configuration of group centroids is retained.

Discriminant results, obtained with a much modified version of program EIDISC available at the SUNY Binghamton Computer Center, are outlined in Figure 2.

MULTIDIMENSIONAL SCALING

Unlike continuous measurements, the discrete trait data in the form of presence-absence scores for each character on each individual do not readily lend themselves to treatment by discriminant analysis. This approach has been tried, especially with blood group information (e.g. Friedlaender, 1969), but owing to the (unmet) assumption that the variables used in this sort of multivariate analysis be normally distributed, results are somewhat suspect.

However, as in the case of the Mahalanobis distances, the matrix of Sanghvi chi-square associations obtained from the discrete charac-

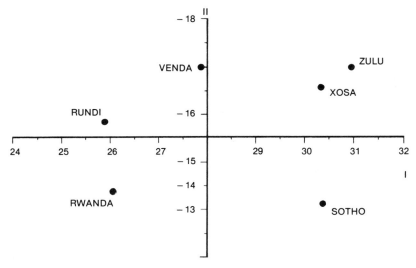

Figure 2. Bantu-speaking Negro group centroids on the first two of five computed discriminant functions as axes.

ter frequencies is rather hard to deal with as it stands. Some means of reducing the dimensionality of the space within which the groups are visualized would be desirable, and the method selected is non-metric multidimensional scaling. This technique as envisioned by Shepard (1962a and b) and further refined by Kruskal (1964a and b) deals directly with measures of proximity or dissociation (distance) between objects or groups; these measures may take a variety of forms, and there are no constraints placed on the nature of the data (metric or discrete) from which the measures are derived.

Given a set of experimental similarities or distances between groups, multidimensional scaling is used to find a configuration of groups in a space of some minimal number of dimensions, usually fewer than (groups − 1). The procedure is an iterative one, and within a space of specified dimensionality points or groups are moved about so as to obtain a monotone relationship between the original proximity measures and the actual distances in the configuration. The extent to which success is achieved in this endeavor is expressed as a measure of "stress." Stress is thus high when the fit of the new distances to the rank order of the original separations is poor, and becomes lower as this fit improves. Perfect or 0% stress implies that there is a precise monotone relationship between the two sets of co-efficients. When a series of iterations has produced a configuration showing minimal stress in some number of dimensions, the procedure is terminated. Spaces of successively fewer dimensions are then tried, and further configurations, each associated with a stress value, are computed until all programed possibilities are exhausted. Generally, configurations of higher dimensionality show lower stress than those arrayed on only one or two axes. The decision as to how many axes or dimensions to extract from the data may be an awkward one, but some guidelines are offered by Kruskal (1964a).

Multidimensional scaling has been applied extensively in psychological work and is now receiving some attention in other fields as well (see Rao, 1972). Within anthropology, the technique has been employed successfully by archaeologists. For example, Hodson *et al.* (1966) were able to group a series of bronze brooches from La Tène cemetery in Switzerland, and True and Matson (1970) found a meaningful configuration of 20 Chilean preceramic sites, each represented by 74 characters used in computing coefficients of association. Scaling appears to be equally applicable to measures of biological distance or similarity, though to date there has been only passing mention of its potential in the literature.[3]

The program executed with the present data in MDSCAL, available as part of the OSIRIS group of routines distributed by the Inter-University Consortium for Political Research, Institute for Social Research, University of Michigan. Results obtained by scaling for the Sanghvi X^2 distances are presented in Figures 3 and 4.

Results and Discussion

When the results of the 15-variable Mahalanobis' D^2 analysis presented in Table 2 are examined, the two East African tribes, Rwanda and Rundi, are seen to be closely allied, though even this distance (2.16) is statistically significant ($p<.05$) when tested by the chi-square

[3]Attention has rather centered around the use of principal components analysis to provide genetic maps of populations. However, in the cases either of classical principal components drawn from an R-type matrix or of principal coordinates (Gower, 1966) derived from a Q-type matrix, the data should normally be in the form of correlations or covariances. Where these conditions are met, results using components analysis or multidimensional scaling should be similar; where they are not, scaling is still available as the more general procedure.

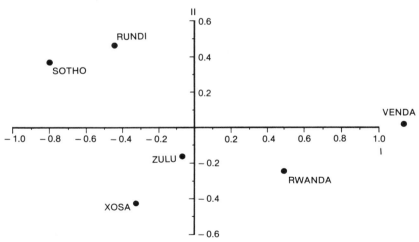

Figure 3. Bantu-speaking Negro tribal groups plotted on the first two dimensions of a three dimensional configuration obtained by multidimensional scaling of the Sanghvi distances. Stress associated with this configuration is only 0.1%.

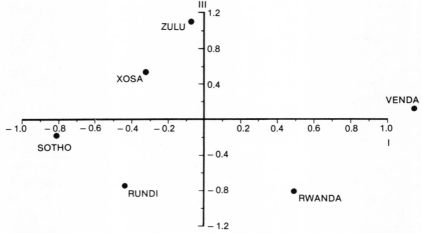

Figure 4. Groups plotted on dimensions I and III of the three dimensional configuration obtained by multidimensional scaling of the Sanghvi distances. See also Fig. 3.

procedure of Talbot and Mulhall (1962). The D^2 values separating both of these populations from the Nguni and Sotho tribes of South Africa are considerably greater, and the Rundi-Sotho distance is the greatest recorded; the Rundi thus seem to be rather more closely linked with the Nguni, while the Rwanda are more or less equidistant from the three Southern Bantu groups. The Rwanda-Venda and Rundi-Venda separations, finally, represent a kind of middle ground. These are greater than the distance between the two East African tribes but smaller than the D^2 values relating the Interlacustrine peoples to the Nguni and Sotho speakers to the south. In other words, the Venda here occupy an intermediate position, at least in absolute terms; direction cannot easily be determined from inspection of the table.

If the South African tribes are considered alone, lesser distances are again encountered. In particular, the two Nguni groups are close together (the D^2 value here of 1.96 is the lowest computed) as is not surprising given their linguistic affinities and long period of geographic proximity along the southeast African coast. Zulu-Sotho and Sotho-Xosa separations are on a par with those observed in the Rwanda-Rundi pairing and, not unreasonably, suggest about the same degree of biological relationship. The Venda are relatively more distant from the Nguni and Sotho tribes than are any of these latter among themselves; this observation is quite compatible with the Venda-East African Bantu separation discussed above and again argues for an intermediate placement of these peoples, whose traditions clearly link them with the lakes region.

When 30 rather than only the first 15 selected variables are used to compute distances, results are similar. All of the D^2 values are somewhat larger, and here the Rwanda-Rundi separation is the smallest, followed by the distances relating Nguni and Sotho among themselves. However, the position of the Venda is obscured slightly, as this tribe is greatly removed from the Zulu group (though not radically displaced relative to the other South Africans). The Venda position is still more or less intermediate, but the addition of more measurements has certainly not clarified this issue. Some of these "new" variables, entered last in the selection process, are appreciably correlated with those in the original subset and cannot contribute much useful information; their inclusion may actually be detracting in a small way (as unnecessary "noise") from the accuracy of the distance approach.

So, all things considered, the D^2 analysis based on cranial measurements yields results which are quite in harmony with the picture of tribal relationships obtained from linguistic and historical sources. Discriminant analysis of these same measurements reinforces this conclusion and permits plotting of each group on each of five successively less important functions or axes. The first two dimensions extracted alone account for over 76% of total variation, and group centroids on these axes indeed indicate the Venda to be intermediate between East and Southern Bantu-speakers, in cranial form as well as in geographic terms (Figure 2). Preliminary interpretation of the scaled vectors associated with these functions suggests that the first is emphasizing breadths (e.g. biorbital, biauricular), and the second braincase height or something like it. Absolute intergroup differences in most characters are small, and the discrimination registered on each axis is evidently based on the subtle covariation of several related measurements.

If now the Sanghvi measures of divergence derived from discrete traits are considered, a rather different interpretation emerges. The Rwanda and Rundi tribes are again closely linked, and the relationships of the Rwanda with the several southern nations are about as expected. However, the Rundi and the Sotho are too close; this is the lowest value of X^2 recorded, indicating less separation even than between Rwanda and Rundi or Zulu and Xosa. Distances within the Nguni and Sotho constellation are about right (that is, lower than those relating Interlacustrine tribes to this cluster). But the Venda location appears anomalous. These people are properly less distant from the Rwanda than are other South Africans, though they are quite noticably removed from the Rundi. Their position with respect to the Sotho is extreme, as this distance is substantially larger than any other in the table.

Multidimensional scaling of the Sanghvi distances yields configurations of the six groups in spaces of one to five dimensions. The configurations of greater dimensionality show the lowest stress values (stress = 0.0% and 0.1% for five and four dimensions, respectively), while the one and two dimensional representations are least acceptable (stress = 34.5% and 14.8% respectively). According to general guidelines laid down by Kruskal (1964a), stress values of 10% to 20% are only "fair" to "poor" and reflect a relatively imprecise fit of the original (X^2) distances to those pertaining in the computed configuration. Therefore both the one and two dimensional arrays were set aside, and the results plotted (Figures 3 and 4) are obtained by scaling in a three dimensional framework. The associated stress is low (0.1%), and there is thus a nearly perfect monotone relationship between the X^2 values and the new interpoint distances.

In terms of the first axis or dimension only, the Venda are contrasted to the Sotho, while both Eastern Bantu-speakers and Nguni groups are intermediate. This axis has a high Spearman rank correlation coefficient with the incidence of both parietal foramina (r_s = 0.77) and a single ethmoid foramen (r_s = 0.75), but the biological relevance of this observation, if any, is unclear. It is certainly quite doubtful that this dimension can be interpreted as reflecting the changing frequency of any single gene (for foramen formation, say) from one population to the next. Still, the Venda and the Sotho are antipodal in their respective incidences for these traits (see Table 3), and it is apparent that the distance between them is in large part dependent on this.

Axis II (associated with lambdoid Wormian bones and the foramen of Huschke!) does little to separate Interlacustrine from South African groups, and it is only with the addition of the third dimension that the configuration begins to resemble the earlier discriminant placement of points or centroids. This third axis places the Rundi and Rwanda together below the plane defined by dimensions I and II, and the Zulu and Xosa lie above this surface. The Venda here fall in between, so that they are more or less intermediate but not in direct line with the other populations when the configuration is visualized in three dimensions. The Sotho are still too close to the Rundi (or vice versa), but this is of course the X² result and indicates no fault with the scaling procedure.

Conclusions

Clearly then there is a serious lack of correspondence between the two series of biological distances as here set out. The D^2 values and associated plot are in close agreement with expectations concerning tribal relationships derived from linguistic and other non-biological sources, while the divergences calculated by Sanghvi's method and scaled in three dimensions are somewhat out of step, and it is hard to make much sense of them. However, the scaling procedure holds some promise for use with biological distance measures and should be explored further.

This is not to say, of course, that patterns of biological variation must always match or complement those of linguistic change and cultural diffusion. Biologically diverse peoples may share a common language, and vice versa. But in the present study there is an appreciable weight of evidence—not only linguistic and archaeological but consisting of oral tradition and eye-witness accounts as well—suggesting that the Interlacustrine and Southern Bantu-speaking Negro tribes are related, and can be presumed to show genetic affinities, according to the scheme outlined earlier in Figure 1. That the non-metrical data (or at least the distance estimates derived from these) do not adequately reflect this picture certainly does nothing to support claims that such determinations are to be preferred as more accurate, or whatever, than conclusions stemming from the study of continuous measurements. One might rather take the opposite view, as this work supports the continued application of distance and related statistics based on craniometric data to problems of population history and affinity.

Bibliography

Balakrishnan, V. and L.D. Sanghvi
    1968   Distance between populations on the basis of attribute data. *Biometrics, 24:* 859-865.

404 *The Measures of Man*

Berry, A.C. and R.J. Berry
1967 Epigenetic variation in the human cranium. Journal of Anatomy, *101:* 361-379.
Berry, R.J.
1968 The Biology of non-metrical variation in mice and men. In: The Skeletal Biology of Earlier Human Populations. D.R. Brothwell, ed., Pergamon Press, Oxford, pp. 103-133.
Bielicki, T.
1962 Some possibilities for estimating inter-population relationship on the basis of continuous traits. Current Anthropology, *3:* 3-8.
Boyd, W.C.
1950 Genetics and the Races of Man. Little, Brown, Boston.
Brothwell, D.R.
1959 The use of non-metrical characters of the skull in differentiating populations. Bericht über die 6 Tagung der Deutschen Gesellschaft für Anthropologie, pp. 103-109.

1965 Of mice and men. Epigenetic polymorphism in the skeleton. In: Homenaje a Juan Comas en su 65 Aniversario, Vol. II, pp. 9-21.
de Villiers, H.
1968 The Skull of the South African Negro. Witwatersrand University Press, Johannesburg.
Friedlaender, J.S.
1969 Biological Divergences over Population Boundaries in South-Central Bougainville. Unpublished Ph.D. Thesis, Harvard University.
Gower, J.C.
1966 Some distance properties of latent root and vector methods used in multivariate analysis. Biometrika, *53:* 325-338.
Greenberg, J.H.
1949 Studies in African linguistic classification. Southwest Journal of Anthropology, *5:* 309-317.

1963 The languages of Africa. International Journal of American Linguistics, *29* (Part II): 1-171.
Grewal, M.S.
1962 The rate of genetic divergence of sublines in the C57BL strain of mice. Genetic Research, *3:* 226-237.
Guthrie, M.
1962 Some developments in the prehistory of the Bantu languages. Journal of African History, *3:* 273-282.
Hodson, F.R., P.H.A. Sneath and J.E. Doran
1966 Some experiments in the numerical analysis of archaeological data. Biometrika, *53:* 311-324.

Howells, W.W.
1966 The Jomon population of Japan: a study by discriminant analysis of Japanese and Ainu crania. Papers of the Peabody Museum, *57:* 1-43.

1969 Criteria for selection of osteometric dimensions. American Journal of Physical Anthropology, *30:* 451-458.

1972 Analysis of patterns of variation in crania of recent man. In: Functional and Evolutionary Biology of Primates: Methods of Study and Recent Advances. R.H. Tuttle, ed. Aldine, Chicago, pp. 123-151.
Huizinga, J.
1962 From DD to D² and back. The quantitative expression of resemblance. Proceedings. Koninklijke Nederlandse Akademie van Wetenschappen, *65:* 1-12.
Inskeep, R.R.
1969 The archaeological background. In: The Oxford History of South Africa. M. Wilson and L. Thompson, eds. Oxford University Press, pp. 1-39.
Jeffreys, M.D.W.
1967 Pre-Columbian maize in Southern Africa. Nature, *215:* 695-697.
Jones, K.
1964 The Multivariate Statistical Analyzer. A System of FORTRAN II Programs to be Run Under 7090-4 FORTRAN Monitor System.
Kellock, W.L. and P.A. Parsons
1970a Variation of minor non-metrical cranial variants in Australian Aborigines. American Journal of Physical Anthropology, *32:* 409-421.

1970b A comparison of the incidence of minor non-metrical cranial variants in Australian Aborigines with those of Melanesia and Polynesia. American Journal of Physical Anthropology, *33:* 235-239.
Kidd, K.K. and L.A. Sgaramella-Zonta
1971 Phylogenetic analysis: concepts and methods. American Journal of Human Genetics, *23:* 235-252.
Kowalski, C.J.
1972 A commentary on the use of multivariate statistical methods in anthropometric research. American Journal of Physical Anthropology, *36:* 119-131.
Kruskal, J.B.
1964a Multidimensional scaling by optimizing goodness of fit to a nonmetric hypothesis. Psychometrika, *29:* 1-27.

1964b Nonmetric multidimensional scaling: a numerical method. Psychometrika, *29:* 115-129.

Laughlin, W.S. and J.B. Jørgensen
1956   Isolate variation in Greenlandic Eskimo crania. Acta Genetica et Statistica Medica, *6:* 3-12.

Little, K.
1971   Some Aspects of African Urbanization South of the Sahara. McCaleb Module, Addison-Wesley, Reading.

Mason, R.
1962   Prehistory of The Transvaal. Witwatersrand University Press, Johannesburg.

Murdock, G.P.
1959   Africa. Its Peoples and Their Culture History. McGraw-Hill Book Company, New York.

Oliver, R.
1966   The problem of the Bantu expansion. Journal of African History, *7:* 361-376.

Penrose, L.S.
1954   Distance, size, and shape. Annals of Engenics, *18:* 337-343.

Rao, C.R.
1972   Recent trends of research work in multivariate analysis. Biometrics, *28:* 3-22.

Rightmire, G.P.
1969   On the computation of Mahalanobis' generalized distance (D^2). American Journal of Physical Anthropology, *30:* 157-160.

_____   1970   Iron Age skulls from Southern Africa re-assessed by multiple discriminant analysis. American Journal of Physical Anthropology, *33:* 147-168.

_____   1971   Discriminant function Sexing of Bushman and South African Negro crania. South African Archaeological Bulletin, *26:* 132-138.

_____   1972   Cranial measurements and discrete traits compared in distance studies of African Negro skulls. Human Biology, *44:* 263-276.

Sanghvi, L.D.
1953   Comparison of genetical and morphological methods for a study of biological differences. American Journal of Physical Anthropology, *11:* 385-404.

Sanghvi, L.D. and V. Balakrishnan
1972   Comparison of different measures of genetic distance between human populations. In: The Assessment of Population Affinities in Man. J.S. Weiner and J. Huizinga, eds., Clarendon Press, Oxford, pp. 25-36.

Shepard, R.N.
1962a   The analysis of proximities: multidimensional scaling with an unknown distance function. I. Psychometrika, *27:* 125-139.

1962b   The analysis of proximities: multidimensional scaling with an unknown distance function. II. Psychometrika, *27:* 219-246.

Stuiver, M. and N.J. van der Merwe
1968   Carbon-14 dating. II. Radiocarbon chronology of the Iron Age in sub-Saharan Africa. Current Anthropology, *9:* 54-58.

Sutton, J.E.G.
1971   The interior of East Africa. In: The African Iron Age. P.L. Shinnie, ed. Oxford University Press, pp. 142-182.

Talbot, P.A. and H. Mulhall
1962   The Physical Anthropology of Southern Nigeria. Cambridge University Press.

True, D.L. and R. G. Matson
1970   Cluster analysis and multidimensional scaling of archeological sites in Northern Chile. Science, *169:* 1201-1203.

van der Merwe, N.J. and R. T. Scully
1971   The Phalaborwa story: archaeological and ethnographic investigation of a South African Iron Age group. World Archaeology, *3:* 178-196.

Westphal, E.O.J.
1963   The linguistic prehistory of Southern Africa: Bush, Kwadi, Hottentot and Bantu linguistic relationships. Africa, *33:* 237-265.

Wilson, M.
1969a   The Nguni people. In: The Oxford History of South Africa. M. Wilson and L. Thompson, eds. Oxford University Press, pp. 75-130.

1969b   The Sotho, Venda and Tsonga. In: The Oxford History of South Africa. M. Wilson and L. Thompson, eds. Oxford University Press, pp. 131-182.

16. Life-Styles from Skeletal Material: a Medieval Yugoslav Example

Gloria Jean Edynak

Introduction

Traditionally, human typology and classification were the primary concerns of physical anthropologists. Nowhere was this more plain than in osteological investigations of both humans and non-human primates. More recently, both the approach and subject matter of physical anthropology have come to encompass newer and broader interests, including natural selection in human populations, medical aspects of human variability, growth and maturation studies, primate behavior, and population genetics. Yet all these new interests are compatible with physical anthropology if one accepts the basic concern of the discipline as biological variation in primate populations in time and space.

NOTE: The author sincerely appreciates the criticisms and suggestions offered on the original manuscript by Dr. David Hamilton and Dr. Philip Evans of the Department of Anatomy, Harvard Medical School, Dr. Sandy Marks, Jr., and Dr. Sam Clark, Jr., Department of Anatomy, University of Massachusetts Medical School. Considerable thanks go to Jack Sepkoski, Department of Geology, Harvard University, who helped me throughout my using the QUAJAC program and to Dr. Stephen Gould of the Department of Geology, Harvard University who suggested the possibility of using cluster analyses on these data. The Department of Anthropology, Harvard University provided the funds to carry out the computer calculations.

Because of this great expansion of physical anthropology, "traditional" subjects such as skeletal morphology began to appear obsolete to some, perhaps because the genetic control of morphological variation is much less understood than the transmission of blood proteins and red cell antigens, but also because the study of bones had come to be associated with the "old" typological physical anthropology.

However, as early as 1930 osteologists had begun to approach their material from a population viewpoint. In his *The Indians of Pecos Pueblo*, Hooton introduced into American phsical anthropology the concept of demography and demonstrated that the decline in population size and change in structure correlated with historical factors. Hooton-trained osteologists continue his interest in demography, but in addition a few such as Lawrence Angel apply a knowledge of functional anatomy to the study of certain kinds of morphological variation. For example, Angel (1947, 1956 and 1972) correlates changes in length of life, pathology and dental attrition to the rise and fall of Greek culture from the Bronze Age to modern times. In Yugoslavia the patterns of longevity, population structure, pathology, dental disease and attrition from the Iron Age through the medieval period differ from those in the Greek population (Edynak, 1974). I suggest that these patterns correlate with age-sex specific role behavior within each group and with events that initiate cultural change.

Besides Angel there are other physical anthropologists who are interested in correlating functional variation in individual human skeletons with cultural behavior. Saul (1972) and Hoyme and Bass (1962) relate the anatomy and pathology of individuals within American Indian populations to archaeological and literary data on sex and age-related subsistence and cultural activities. These studies, however, do not employ quantitative techniques which would allow for a more clear definition of patterns and testing of hypotheses derived from ethnographic data.

In this paper I wish to ask if life-styles can be inferred from human skeletal remains. Do quantifiable anatomical data exist which reflect differences in age and sex specific role behavior? The following points guided my procedure. (1) The anatomical variables chosen for the analysis (eg. degnerative arthritis, intervertebral disc herniation, and dental attrition) are essentially functionally produced traits. (2) The population chosen for study is culturally homogeneous, technologically simple, and age and sex role differences have been extensively described in the ethnographic literature (3) The data can be coded and

treated quantitatively. (4) The object of study is the individual configuration, not the population frequency of a trait.

The first step in the analysis is to quantify the pattern of traits of each
skeleton. A similarity coefficient is calculated for each possible pair of
individuals based on the concurrence of their traits. Then pairs of individuals are sequentially grouped into clusters based on the degree of
similarity (Sokal and Sneath 1963). Each cluster of individuals is
characterized by a particular pattern of traits. This pattern can be interpreted in functional anatomical terms, i.e., how the body was used.
The functional anatomical interpretations are then related to the
ethnographic data.

Methods

The skeletal material comes from four small burial mounds in the
watershed of the Trebišnjica River near Trebinje, Yugoslavia.[1] The
graves are assigned to the fourteenth through sixteenth centuries
and were used exclusively by a transhumant population (Beslagić,
1962). This population engaged primarily in raising cattle, sheep and
horses, some agriculture, and in caravan transport. Palavestra (1971),
Vukanović (1962) and Wenzel (1962) provide general information
on the population in this region.

1. VARIABLES
Degenerative arthritis   Variables are chosen which reflect physical
stress, the most important of which is degenerative arthritis of the
joints. This disease is characterized by destruction of the articular
cartilage and subchondral bone accompanied by bony spurs of lipping (A.R.A. Primer, 1964). Experimental evidence shows that impact loading or absorption of shock directly by the joint surface causes
rapid degeneration of the joint (Radin and Paul, 1971; Simon and
Radin, 1972). Studies on industrial workers show that occupational
behavior such as bending and lifting heavy material by miners causes

[1]The skeletons came from a series of joint excavations conducted by the Zemaljski
Museum in Sarajevo and Stanford University during 1968-1970 field seasons. My
participation was supported by the following travel grants: In 1968, the Sheila Oliver
Award, granted by the Women's Travel Club associated with the Department of Anthropology, Harvard University; in 1970, by the International Research and Exchanges
Board and the Wenner Gren Foundation; and in 1971, by the National Science Foundation.

a specific pattern of degenerative arthritis (Kellgren and Lawrence, 1952), as does the use of pneumatic tools by ship builders (Rostock, 1936; Hunter et al., 1945). Degenerative arthritic changes of a bony joint were recorded on a scale from one to five (1=no bony lipping, 2=slight bony ring around the rim of the articular surface of a long bone, 3=protruding bony ring around the rim of the joint surface, 4=bony projections or osteophytes passing inferiorly or superiorly from the rim of the articular surface of a long bone, 5=ankylosis or fusion of the bony joint).

Trauma, fractures and bone infections Trauma to the skeleton occurs as healed fractures (Plate 1) or "slashes" (Plate 2). The specific bone, and location of the trauma on the bone (proximal, distal) are recorded. Wells (1964) considers a distal fracture on the long bones of the forearm or leg to be accidental (fall fracture), and a midshaft fracture of a long bone to be the result of violent or intentional trauma. A fracture of the distal ulna or radius is recorded as present = 2, or absent = 1. This is the model for all other fractures and "slashes." In addition to trauma there are bone infections, either of the blood supply of the bone (osteomyelitis), or of the periosteum (periosteitis). Long bones having a beaded cortical surface without any obvious areas of drainage from the medullary shaft are presumed to be cases of periosteitis (Plate 3); if there appears to be drainage from the medullary shaft, it is labelled osteomyelitis (Boyd, 1953). These infections are frequently associated with fractures in the medieval Yugoslavian material.

Osteoporoses Osteoporosis is defined as a reduction in the amount of bone (Frost, 1966; Eighteenth Rheumatism Review, 1968; Nordin et al., 1970). This reduction of bone mass is seen grossly as larger empty spaces in the cancellous bone of vertebrae, head of the humerus and femur, ilium and ribs in comparison with normal bones.

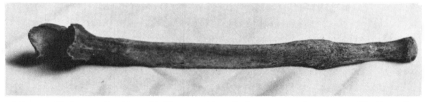

Plate 1. Skeleton of a 40 to 50 (?) year old male from mound 11, grave 20. Note the accidental distal fracture of the right ulna.

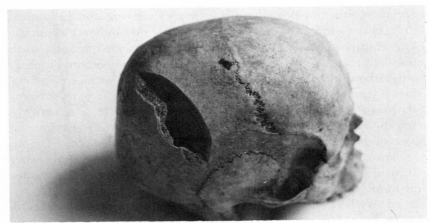

Plate 2. Cranium of a 45 to 55 year old male from mound 11, grave 6, with a "slash" trauma.

Plate 3. Right tibia and fibula showing periosteitis in a 37 to 46 year old male from mound 11, grave 10, with a mid shaft fracture of the femur.

There are larger spaces between the trabeculae of cancellous bone, and the trabeculae themselves are thinner. What causes osteoporosis in various disease states is not altogether clear, but may be an altered remodelling rate in favor of resorption (Frost, 1963; *Eighteenth Rheumatism Review*, 1968; Nordin et al., 1970). This may be true particularly in post-menopausal osteoporosis, in which the drop in estrogen no longer tends to inhibit bone resorption (estrogen-parathyroid antagonism) (Nordin et al., 1970). On the other hand, surface area/volume relationships may be a more important physical factor in senile osteoporosis because of (1) a higher rate of turnover in cancellous bone than cortical bone, (2) a larger surface to volume ratio in trabecular bone, and (3) a lack of replacement of trabecular bone in the adult (whereas periosteum does replace cortical bone in the adult) (Frost, 1966). Pathologic osteoporosis is associated with "dowager's hump," vertebral collapse, vertebral fractures, and ballooning of the intervertebral discs, or "Schmorl's nodes," in living adult white females (Urist, Gurvey and Fared, 1970). In the Yugoslav population, osteoporotic vertebrae are frequently associated with wedged-shaped vertebrae and Schmorl's nodes (Plates 4, 5, 6 and 7). Osteoporosis of the cancellous bone in the vertebral column is recorded present = 2, or absent = 1. Osteoporosis of the cranium (Plate 8) is recorded as a separate variable as it may suggest anemia (Murray and Jacobsen, 1971).

Dental pathologies Diseases of the dentition and alveolus were recorded according to the numerical system of Acsádi and Némeskeri (1970; pp. 121-122). This numerical system applies to periodontal disease (Plate 7), deposition of calculus (Plate 8), alveolar abscesses, and dental attrition. In addition, carious lesions were graded on a scale of one to five (1 = no carious lesions, 2 = small lesion present, 3 = lesion at the root/enamel junction, 4 = large carious lesion in root, 5 = carious lesion encompassing two teeth). Finally, a unique wear pattern of the anterior teeth (see drawing) was recorded as present = 2 or absent = 1.

2. AGING AND SEXING

The method of estimating age and sex follows Acsádi and Nemes-kéri (1970). This method provides criteria estimating age in infants (root and crown development in the dentition), children and adolescents (tooth eruption and epiphyseal union), and adults (changes

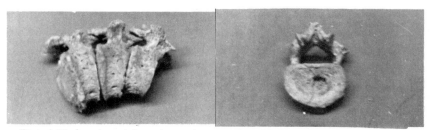

Plate 4. Wedge-shaped thoracic vertebrae numbers 10, 11, and 12 of a 55 to 59 year old female from mound 6, grave 35.

Plate 5. Wedge-shaped lumbar vertebrae of a 45 to 55 year old female from mound 6, grave 15.

Plate 6. A posterior view of the vault of a 30 to 34 year old male from mound 6 grave Ia. A possible case of anemia derived osteoporosis.

in the pubic symphysis, degree of endocranial suture closure and medullary resorption in the head of the femur and humerus).

3. CLUSTER ANALYSIS

Data were collected into a matrix comprised of eighty-four rows (representing each individual skeletal specimen) and thirty-six columns representing the variables. IBM cards were punched for each row, so that all variables pertaining to any one individual were on one card. Each variable was recorded either as present/absent or ordered (1,2,3,4,5). A list of variables is presented in Table 1 with a statement of how it was recorded.

A computer program written by Jack Sepkoski, Jr., (1970) for Q-mode hierarchical cluster analysis was used to reveal patterns of non-congenital pathologies within the medieval Yugoslav population. The analysis consists of calculating similarity coefficients among all pairs of individuals and clustering by the pair group method. Sepkoski's computer program has an option which transforms mixed scale data (the recording states of the variables in this study) to a percent of a common range for all variables. This transformation equalizes the weights of all variables. In this study I choose the quantified simple matching coefficient to express similarity between two individuals. In this case both presence and absence of a trait were important in establishing similarity. The simple matching coefficient is given as

$$S_{SM} = \frac{c+a}{c+a+u}$$

where, c = number of positive matches between two individuals;
a = number of negative matches between two individuals;
u = number of mismatches between two individuals.
The quantified simple matching coefficient is given as

$$q\,S_{SM} = \frac{\Sigma \min (X_{ik}, X_{jk}) + \Sigma [\max(X_{ok}) = \max (X_{ik}, X_{jk})]}{MAX(X_{ok})}$$

in which the frequency of positive matches between two individuals is transformed to

$$c = \sum_{k=1}^{11} \min (x_{ik}, x_{ij}),$$

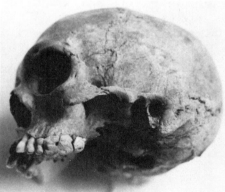

Plate 7. Periodontal disease as indicated by alveolar resorption in a 40 to 50 year old male from mound 11, grave 20. Note premortem tooth loss on the right side of the mandible.

Plate 8. Heavy calculus deposit and periodontal disease around the left maxillary molars in a mature male.

the frequency of negative matches between two individuals is transformed to

$$a = \sum_{k=1}^{n} [MAX (x_{ok}) - max (x_{ik}, x)],$$

and the frequency of mismatches is transformed to

$$u = \sum_{k=1}^{n} (max (x_{ik}, x_{jk}) - min (x_{ik}, x_{jk})].^2$$

Clustering is accomplished by finding those pairs of individuals (or clusters of individuals) that have the highest coefficient of association in both their columns. In Sepkoski's computer program this is done by finding the highest association $S_{A,B}$ in each column A. The list of these n coefficients $S_{A,B}$ (where n is the number of individuals and/or cluster in the matrix of coefficients) is then reviewed to determine if the highest coefficient $S_{A,B}$ of column A is also the highest coefficient of column B. If not, the coefficient is eliminated from the list; if so, individuals (or clusters) A and B are linked together at level $S_{A,B}$ to form a new cluster, A (where A is the lower of the two individual or cluster numbers). This clustering method is called the pair-group method because only one group or sample can enter a given cluster during a single cycle. (A cycle is a single pair of operations of finding the highest coefficients and then recomputing the matrix of coefficients). During a cycle there is a possibility of two to n (where n is an even integer, n-1 if n is odd) individuals and/or clusters being

[2] Let MAX (x_{ok}) be the largest value that the kth attribute can take. For binary data coded as 0 and 1, MAX (x_{ok})=1. In other cases, MAX (x_{ok}) can be the maximum value observed for the kth attribute, or it can be a theoretical maximum, such as 100 for data expressed as percents. For the kth attribute of objects i and j:

$$min (x_{ik}, x_{jk}) = \begin{cases} x_{ik}, \text{ for } x_{ik} \leq x_{jk} \\ x_{jk}, \text{ for } x_{ik} > x_{jk} \end{cases}$$

$$max (s_{ik}, x_{jk}) = \begin{cases} x_{jk}, \text{ for } x_{ik} \geq x_{jk} \\ x_{jk}, \text{ for } x_{ik} < x_{jk} \end{cases}$$

These algorithms are taken from Sepkoski, 1973, pp. 4-6.

TABLE 1

VARIABLES USED IN LIFE-STYLE ANALYSIS.
AGE AND SEX OF EACH INDIVIDUAL WERE NOT
INCLUDED AS VARIABLES IN THE CLUSTER ANALYSIS.

Variable	*Recorded State*
(1) "slash"	absent/present
(2) fracture of distal radius or ulna	absent/present
(3) fracture of cranium	absent/present
(4) fracture of midshaft of the femur	absent/present
(5) fracture of distal femur	absent/present
(6) fracture of clavicle	absent/present
(7) fracture of sacrum	absent/present
(8) osteomyelitis	absent/present
(9) periosteitis	absent/present
(10) degree of right hip degenerative arthritis	ordered $(1, 2, 3, 4, 5)$
(11) degree of left hip degenerative arthritis	ordered $(1, 2, 3, 4, 5)$
(12) degree of degenerative arthritis in cervical vertebrae	ordered $(1, 2, 3, 4, 5)$
(13) degree of degenerative arthritis in thoracic vertebrae	ordered $(1, 2, 3, 4, 5)$
(14) degree of degenerative arthritis in lumbar vertebrae	ordered $(1, 2, 3, 4, 5)$
(15) degree of right knee degenerative arthritis	ordered $(1, 2, 3, 4, 5)$
(16) degree of left knee degenerative arthritis	ordered $(1, 2, 3, 4, 5)$
(17) degree of right shoulder degenerative arthritis	ordered $(1, 2, 3, 4, 5)$
(18) degree of left shoulder degenerative arthritis	ordered $(1, 2, 3, 4, 5)$
(19) degree of right ankle degenerative arthritis	ordered $(1, 2, 3, 4, 5)$
(20) degree of left ankle degenerative arthritis	ordered $(1, 2, 3, 4, 5)$
(21) Schmorl's nodes	absent/present
(22) vertebral osteoporosis	absent/present
(23) sacro-iliac degenerative arthritis	ordered $(1, 2, 3, 4, 5)$
(24) right elbow degenerative arthritis	ordered $(1, 2, 3, 4, 5)$
(25) left elbow degenerative arthritis	ordered $(1, 2, 3, 4, 5)$
(26) right wrist degenerative arthritis	ordered $(1, 2, 3, 4, 5)$
(27) left wrist degenerative arthritis	ordered $(1, 2, 3, 4, 5)$
(28) vertebral collapse	absent/present
(29) osteoporotic cranium	absent/present
(30) degree of carious lesions	ordered $(1, 2, 3, 4, 5)$
(31) degree of periodontal disease	ordered $(1, 2, 3, 4, 5)$
(32) alveolar abscess	absent/present
(33) degree of dental attrition	ordered $(1, 2, 3, 4, 5)$
(34) calculus deposit	ordered $(1, 2, 3, 4, 5)$
(35) deformation of anterior, upper teeth	absent/present
(36) premortem tooth loss	absent/present

clustered to form 1 to n new groups, respectively. The matrix of coefficients of association is recalculated after this operation so that each individual and/or cluster is now compared to the new groups. In this study the new matrix is calculated by the unweighted pair-group method, in which each individual in the two clusters is given equal weight in the computation. Thus, the cluster containing the larger number of individuals has the greatest weight. If cluster A contains q number of individuals, cluster B, r individuals, and cluster C, s individuals, where $q + r + s$ is greater than or equal to 3 and less than or equal to n, then the coefficient of association between AB and cluster (or individual) C is

$$S_{AB,C} \quad \frac{(s \bullet q) \bullet S_{A,C} + (s \bullet r) \bullet S_{B,C}{}^3}{s \bullet (q + r)}$$

The output of this program includes a printed dendrogram of the clusters, and a histogram in which the degree of expression of each variable based on the percent range transformation is given for each cluster. The only problem with this analysis is that lack of data on individuals can result in spurious associations. However, such misplaced individuals can be explained by reviewing the original data matrix.

Figure 1 and Table 2 present the results of the cluster analysis using the quantified simple matching coefficient. The dendrogram can be read from left to right with decreasing overall similarity as larger groups are formed. There are seven clusters:

1)   11-5A to 6-6 is a cluster consisting of children with almost no behaviorally determined variables, but having some erupted teeth, plus some adults with missing data.

2)   P-7 to 6-39 is a relatively heterogenous group which can be subdivided into a subgroup of middle-old adults (over fifty years old) and a subgroup of young females. What relates the subgroups is the high frequency of culturally deformed anterior upper teeth and considerable premortem tooth loss. The young females show moderately heavy dental attrition and very little to moderate degenerative arthri-

---

[3] The explanation of the clustering procedure in the QUAJAC program is taken from Sepkoski, 1971, pp. 10-12, unpublished manuscript, Department of Geology, Harvard University.

tis of the joints. The middle-old adults, which consist of both females and males, differ from the young females in having a high degree of vertebral and shoulder osteoarthritis, as well as possessing moderately heavy lipping in the hip, knee, elbow and wrist.

3) The next interpretable cluster is P-2 to 6-16. This consists of middle-age adults (twenty to fifty years old) of both sexes who differ

TABLE 2

CLUSTERS AND GROUP VARIABLES BASED ON SOKAL AND
MICHENER SIMPLE MATCHING COEFFICIENT AND
UNWEIGHTED PAIR-GROUP CLUSTERING

Dendrogram Order	Estimated Age	Sex	Group Characteristics
11-5a	6 mo.-1 yr.		
11-1	6 mo.		
11-5b	1 yr.		
11-7	nb.		
11-12	f.		Children
6-26b	1 yr.		
D68-a	12-13	M	
P-5	30-40	M	
11-14	4-5	M?	
11-15	7-8	M?	
6-19	65	M	
6-21a	40-50	M	High degree of simularity based on
6-27b	12	M	high number of negative matches
P-10	12-13	M	and much missing data; little to no
P-3a	60-70	M	degenerative arthritis of joints;
6-29a	12	F	presence of deciduous upper
1-4	12-13	M	canine and premortem tooth loss
6-3	8	M?	
1-6	7	M	
6-11	10	F	
p-3b	7	M	
6-28	3-6	F?	
11-9	7-8	M?	
6-6	2	F	
P-7	35-45	F	Middle-old Adults
P-la	70-75	M	High vertebral o-a (50%), esp. L;
6-31	50-55	F	40% r + l hip o-a; 40% r + l knee
6-18	55-65	F	o-a; 70% r+l sh o-a; 40% elb.+wr;
6-10	55-65	M	ant. teeth def.; high tooth loss

TABLE 2 *(Continued)*

CLUSTERS AND GROUP VARIABLES BASED ON SOKAL AND MICHENER SIMPLE MATCHING COEFFICIENT AND UNWEIGHTED PAIR GROUP CLUSTERING

Dendrogram Order	Estimated Age	Sex	Group Characteristics
6-33	40-50	M	Young Females
6-27a	17-20	F	0 or 20% r + 1 hip o-a; 30% vert.,
6-13	20-30	F	knee, ankle o-a; r+1 sh. elb. + wr.
1-7a	20-25	F	o-a = 20%; mod. caries + perio-
D68-b	25-30	F	dontosis attrition = 40%; 4/7
6-4	18-20	F	= def. ant. teeth; 5/7 = tooth loss
6-39	35-45	F	
6-12	25-30	F	
P-1b	50-55	F	Scant Data
6-7c	?		
6-37	?		
6-29b	6	F	
P-2	25-30	M	Middle-Age Adults
6-7b	30-34	F	Var. hip o-a; C = 20%, Th = 30%,
11-8	44-53	M	var. L; sh., kn., ank. =30-40% o-a;
6-24	30-40	M	s-i=40% + elb., wr.=30%; severe
6-16	35-40	F	caries, 3/5=tooth loss; 1/5=def. ant. teeth
6-40	40-50	F	Middle-Age Females
6-2a	50-54	M	Var. hip o-a = 30-40%/vert. o-a =
6-36	40-50	F	50%; sh. o-a=30-40%; s-i=20%;
6-14	40-50	M	kn., ank.=20%; elb., wr.=20-40%;
6-23a	25-29	F	1/2=disc hern.; 5/12=vert. osteop.;
6-7	27-34	F	caries = 40%; 7/12 = abscess; attri-
P-6	35-40	F	tion=70%; 1/3=def. ant. teeth;
6-15	45-55	F	2/3=tooth loss
6-21b	35-39	F	
11-13a	44-50	F	
6-5	25-29	M	
1-8	45-55	F	
P-9a	50-54	M?	Old Males
P-4a	55-60	F	Frac. cran. + cl.; hip o-a=50%+;
6-8	55-60	M	C = 50%; Th = 50%; L = 60%
6-23b	50-60	M	o-a; kn.=60%; sh., ank.=40-60%;
P-4b	50-55	F	s-i=45%; + o-a; 1/9=disc her.;
6-17	60-70	M	8/9=vert. osteop.; elb.=60%; (var.);

TABLE 2 *(Continued)*

CLUSTERS AND GROUP VARIABLES BASED ON SOKAL AND MICHENER SIMPLE MATCHING COEFFICIENT AND UNWEIGHTED PAIR GROUP CLUSTERING

P-9c	50-60	M?	r wr.=50%, l wr.=80%; o-a;
6-1b	60-70	M	3/7=abscess; attrition severe;
6-7a	60-70	F	2/2=heavy calculus; 4/4=def. ant. teeth; premortem tooth loss
6-22b	30-34	M	Middle-Age Males
11-10	37-46	M	Frac. dist. rad., cran., midshft.
11-20	40-50	M	femur; osteomye. + perios; hip o-a = 40%; little joint o-a; elb., wr=20% (no dyssyn.); heavy periodontosis; mod. severe attrition, cement; 3/3=def. ant. teeth; 2/3= premortem tooth loss
11-6	45-55	M	Middle-Age Adults
6-35	55-59	F	Frac. cran.; osteomye.; hip o-a 20%
11-16	26-35	M	to 100% (var.); scant data on joints;
6-26a	2-4 mo.		vert. o-a=40%; r sh.=20%' s-l=
6-1a	30-34	M	50%; elb. wr.=30%; 5/6= disc
6-9	35-44	M	her.; 2/5=vert. osteop.; attrition=
6-34	25-30	F	40%; calculus=30%; 3/7=def. ant. teeth; no mortem tooth loss; periodontosis=40%
11-13b	15	M?	Scant Data
6-38	1½-2		
6-2b	2-3		
6-30	2		
7-1	40-50	F	
6-32	60-70	M	
1-5	75+	M	

The percentage means the degree of expression of the trait. In the case of degenerative arthritis of the joints, 0% means no lipping and 100% means ankylosis. Symbols: o-a = degenerative arthritis, sh. = shoulder, elb. = elbow, s-i = sacroiliac, wr. = wrist, C = cervical vertebrae, Th = thoracic vertebrae, L = lumbar vertebrae, osteop. = osteoporosis, osteomye. = osteomyclitis, perios. = periosteitis, disc. hern. = intervertebral disc herniation, kn. = knee, ank. = ankle, attrition = dental attrition; def. ant. teeth = deformed anterior teeth; dyssym. = dyssymmetry. frac. = fracture = have.

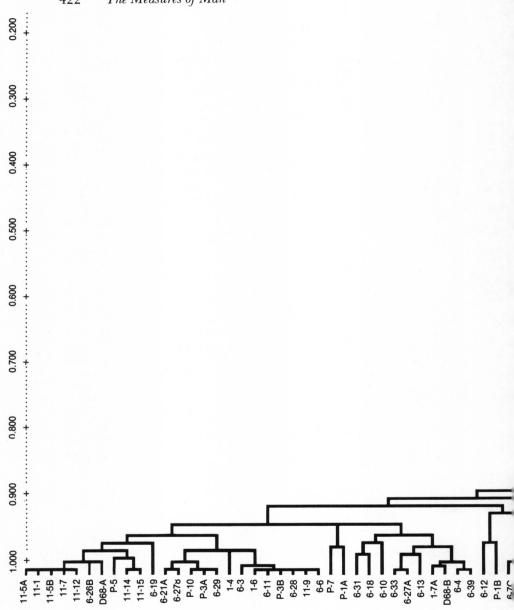

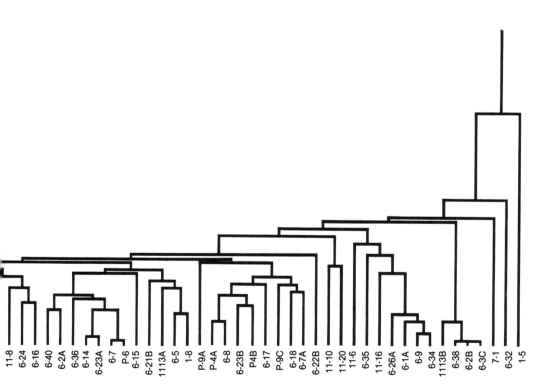

from the older group of mixed adults only in the degree to which the characteristics are expressed. Degenerative arthritis of the joints is moderate; two-fifths have osteoporotic crania; there are severe carious lesions, premortem tooth loss and less dental deformation. If this group had been older they might have been indistinguishable from group 2 middle-old adults.

4)   The next cluster runs from 6-40 to 1-8 and consists almost entirely of middle-age females. These females are characterized by little or variable hip degenerative arthritis and little extremity arthritis. Vertebral degenerative arthritis, however, is severe and occurs with Schmorl's nodes and moderate shoulder degenerative arthritis. Furthermore, there is a high frequency of vertebral osteoporosis — mainly in the over forty-year-old adults. The dentition in this group is noteworthy for its severe attrition, relatively severe degree of carious lesions, high frequency of alveolar abscesses, dental calculus, periodontal disease, premortem tooth loss and dental deformation.

5)   The next cluster consists of a discrete group of old males, P-9A to 6-7A. They are characterized by healed fractures, strong hip and vertebral degenerative arthritis with the strongest lipping in the lumbar vertebrae, hip joint, and sacro-iliac articulation. There is only one incidence of Schmorl's nodes, but almost all individuals have vertebral osteoporosis. Degenerative arthritis of the joints of the extremities is advanced, with the left wrist much more severely affected than the right in all cases. Dental pathology is extreme, with severe attrition, deposition of calculus, fifty percent occurrence of abscesses, high degree of premortem tooth loss and deformed anterior upper teeth.

6)   Individuals 622B to 11-20 are highly correlated with the preceding group. They are younger males in their thirties and forties, and have several examples of "slashes," healed fractures (cranium, midshaft of the femur) and bone infections. They have much less degenerative arthritis of the joints of the extremities than the older group, but hip changes are moderately severe. The pattern within the cluster is comparable to that in clusters comprising older males. The teeth display heavy periodontal disease, deposition of calculus, moderately severe attrition, and some individuals have premortem tooth loss. All individuals have deformed anterior upper teeth.

7)   The last cluster, 11-6 to 6-34, consists of four males and two females who are middle-aged adults. There are three cases of

"slashes," a cranial fracture and one case of osteomyelitis. Hip degenerative arthritis is highly variable, while vertebral degenerative arthritis is moderately severe. There is little data on the other joints, except that the right shoulders, elbows, and wrists seem to be lightly to moderately affected. All individuals have Schmorl's nodes except one. Periodontal disease, deposition of calculus and dental attrition have developed to a moderate degree. Carious lesions are small; only half of the group shows deformation of the anterior upper teeth, and none have lost teeth premortem.

There are a number of peculiar groupings as well as "misplaced" individuals within clusters. In all cases these individuals or clusters can be explained by a large amount of missing data with an association based primarily on negative matches, or an association based on positive association using only a few variables.

Discussion

It is clear from the cluster of children, based largely on negative associations, that information relating to physical stress can not be obtained from juvenile skeletons. In fact, physical stress affects only the adult skeletons as a result of patterned behavior during the adult's life. The patterns found within the adult clusters are interpreted in terms of functional anatomy and then related to adult roles based on ethnographic data.

Much of the ethnographic information comes from a symposium edited by Filipović (1963), particularly his own article (Filipović, 1963), and publications by Dinić (1937) and Kovačević (1961). This population comes from the mountainous area near Trebinje, about thirty miles inland from the Dalmatian Coast, and represents a transhumant stock-raising group that flourished in the Middle Ages. The population was organized into settlements or *katuns* consisting of a few to one hundred households. Each *katun* originally had summer pastures in the mountains and winter pastures in the valleys of rivers or along the Dalmatian Coast. Men were concerned primarily with stock-raising, soldiering and caravan transport. The sources give less information about women, but they were responsible for household horticulture, making cheeses and other products derived from the stock, and repairing the stone houses and walls.

The dentition of young females shows significant wear, while degenerative changes on the young female skeletons are not particularly evident (of course age is a factor here). Culturally deformed anterior teeth are not unique to the females but are also found in young males. Otherwise, female dental attrition and disease is advanced over that of the male at the same age. The higher degree of attrition in young females may have resulted from a diet which included more plant material than that of males. The high rate of attrition in young females facilitated entry of microorganisms that resulted in more abscesses, periodontal disease and more premortem tooth loss than in young males. Data are lacking on whether women used their teeth in preparing leather, although leather export from *katuns* was high. The high rate of dental attrition in Eskimos is related to chewing hide in the preparation of clothing (Brothwell, 1968). On the other hand, men, who spent most of their time with the herds (either up in the mountains, on transhumance, or on caravans), probably relied more on meat and milk derivatives for nutrition than the females. Inhabitants of the mountainous areas of Hercegovinia today rely mainly on milk-derived products, potatoes, bread and mutton for food; men and guests are offered meat first.

Mature female skeletons are further characterized by heavy vertebral and moderately heavy shoulder degenerative arthritis, whereas hips and extremities are considerably less affected. Furthermore, the vertebral column shows evidence of intervertebral disc herniation and osteoporosis. This pattern seems indicative of chronic stress or compression of the joints of the spine as in weight bearing, bending and lifting (shoulder degenerative arthritis), such as would occur during hoeing, lifting rocks in clearing gardens, or repairing fences and houses. (Southern Hercegovinia is limestone karst, dusty, rocky terrain.) The occurrence of vertebral osteoporosis in older females suggests post-menopausal osteoporosis.

Old and young males share the same pattern to different degrees. This pattern includes "slashes" (undoubtedly the cause of death in a few cases), healed violent or intentional fractures (nose, cranial vault, clavicle, midshaft of the femur), osteomyelitis and periosteitis. Furthermore, all pelvic joints are more severely affected by degenerative arthritis than are other joints, and degenerative changes appear earlier in the hip. In addition to the pelvis, the lumbar vertebrae are most severely affected by degenerative arthritis and in old males, the left wrist is consistently more affected than the right. Schmorl's nodes are infrequent in this group. The osteoarthritic pattern suggests more direct absorption of shock on the male pelvis and lumbar joints than in the female. Furthermore, the relative absence of evidence of disc herniation suggests that the shocks originated at the pelvic level and travelled upward. This could be consistent with the role of soldier within the *katun*. Vlach[4] men were organized into pastoralists (sheep and cow herders) and soldiers, who were responsible for horse rearing, defending the *katun*, and caravan transport. The latter were frequently hired out as mercenaries to the feudal lords. It seems that the pelvic-lumbar degenerative arthritis relates to absorption of shock from below, as in horseback riding. Affliction of the knee and ankle joint may also be related to this activity. The occurrence of violent trauma and fracture is consistent with the behavior of a vlach soldier defending the *katun's* herds, fighting for a feudal lord, or plundering a coastal village. The high degree of arm-forearm arthritis is probably related to fighting, skinning, wooling and handling cargo. The higher degree of affliction of the left wrist over the right wrist is possibly related to carrying a shield on the left wrist. Vertebral osteoporosis occurs exclusively in the older males and probably belongs to the class of senile osteoporoses. The young men suffered from severe periodontal disease, deposition of calculus, premortem tooth loss, and moderately severe attrition. However, it is not until old age in males that teeth are severely worn with concomitant caries and abscesses. This pattern in males is probably due to a diet with higher meat content than that of females and to the possibility that females used their teeth for cultural purposes which led to earlier attrition.

The remaining two groups are very difficult to interpret. They are adult groups of both sexes with patterns somewhat intermediate between the previous groups. The first consists of the two original clusters in the dendrogram, consisting of middle-old adults and middle-aged adults. They share heavy vertebral, shoulder, hip, and extremity degenerative arthritis. In addition, they have severe carious lesions and a high rate of premortem tooth loss. These individuals

---

[4]*vlach*—A person engaged in stock-raising, particularly sheep, and seasonal rounds in the Dinaric zone of Yugoslavia. During the late medieval period, they transported raw materials (especially metals) from Bosnia to Dubrovnik and other Dalmatian coast cities and brought back salt and manufactured products by caravan.

may have occupied themselves with activities around the settlement, rather than travelling (with flocks or caravan) or soldiering.

The second group of mixed middle-aged adults is next to the last cluster in the dendrogram. It consists of young and older females and males who are characterized by a high frequency of "slashes," healed fractures (cranium) and osteomyelitis. There are few data on extremity degenerative arthritis in this cluster, but hip and vertebral degenerative arthritis are relatively high and there is a high frequency of Schmorl's nodes. The only marked dental pathology is periodontal disease, and carious lesions are few and small; there is no premortem tooth loss. It is possible that this pattern is indicative of intra-group hostility, whether between or within households. Studies of more recent clan organizations in southern Hercogovinia, Montenegro and Albania show the frequency of household conflicts—often over stolen animals, defense of the clan's honor, a blood-feud, or adultery. The vertebral pattern within this mixed middle adult group suggests chronic stress like that in females, but the dental pattern suggests more the male diet. It is possible that some of these individuals engaged in pasturing sheep and cattle as well as in activities around the settlement (as distinct from the soldiers who reared horses and travelled with caravans or were mercenaries). The low rate of dental attrition, carious lesions and abscesses indicates less dependence on plant foods.

Conclusions

This study was designed to explore the possibility of using patterns of non-congenital skeletal and dental pathologies as indicators of human behavior and lifestyles. Variables were chosen which result from degenerative processes on the bony joints and dentition. Patterns relating to different age and sex categories were extracted by cluster analyses, and functional interpretations were offered. Possible lifestyles have been suggested on the basis of these interpretations and the ethnographic evidence. Thus, young and middle-aged women can be functionally differentiated from each other, and females can be clearly differentiated from young and mature males. The major differences between the sexes relate to lifestyles in which women were subjected to chronic back stress and to severe dental attrition in their youth. These anatomical data correlate well with the ethnohistorical inferences that women engaged in household horticulture, repairing stone houses and fences, and possibly the preparation of hides by chewing. Women might have consumed a diet containing more vegetables than that of man which in addition probably included grit as a result of stone grinding. Men, on the other hand, exhibit a functional pattern that is related to more direct stress on all joints, than was apparent in women, but particularly on the pelvic and lumbar joints. In addition there is ample evidence of violence and non-accidental fractures in the male population. This functional pattern correlates well with the ethnographic description of stock-rearing, horse-back riding, and soldiering.

Bibliography

Acsádi, Gy., and J. Nemeskéri
   1957   Paläodemographische Probleme am Beispiel des frühmittelalterlichen Graberfeldes von Halimba-Cseres, *Homa, 8:* 133-147.

   1970   History of Human Life Span and Mortality. Akademiai Kiado, Budapest.
Angel, J.J.
   1947   The length of life in ancient Greece. Journal of Gerontology, *2:* 18-24.

   1950   Population size and microevolution in Greece. Cold Spring Harbor Symposia on Quantitative Biology, *15:* 343-351.

   1969a   The bases of paleodomography. American Journal of Physical Anthropology, *30:* 427-437.

   1969b   Paleodemography and evolution. American Journal of Physical Anthropology, *31:* 343-354.
A.R.A. Primer
   1964   Primer on the rheumatic diseases, prepared by the American Rheumatism Association, Journal of the American Medical Association, part II, *190:* 441-444.
Beslagić, Š.
   1962   Srednjovjekovni nadgrobni spomenici-stecci (Medieval grave monuments-stecci). Nase Starine, *8:* 17-36.

Boyd, W.
1953   Text Book of Pathology, 6th edition, Lea and Febiger, Philadelphia.
Dinić, M.
1937   Dubrovacka Srednjevekovna Karanvanska Trgovina (The Medieval Caravan Trade of Dubrovnik). Beograd.

1968   Eighteenth Rheumatism Review for the years 1965 and 1966, Arthritis and Rheumatism, vol. 11, no. 3, supplement, pp. 628-630.
Filipović, M.
1963   Struktura i organizacija srednjovekovnix katuna (Structure and organization of medieval *katuns*). In: Simpozijum o Srednjovjekovnom Katuna (Symposium on Medieval *Katuns*), M.O. Filipović, ed., pp. 45-120, Osolobodene, Sarajevo.
Frost, H.M.
1963   Bone Remodelling Dynamics. Charles C. Thomas, Springfield, Illinois.

1966   The Bone Dynamics in Osteoporosis and Osteomalacia, Charles C. Thomas, Springfield, Illinois.
Hoyme, L.E., and W. M. Bass
1962   Human skeletal remains from the Tolifero (Ha 6) and Clarksville (M C 14) sites, John H. Kerr Reservoir Basin, Virginia. Bulletin of the Bureau of American Ethnology. Bulletin 182, Smithsonian Institution, Washington, D.C., pp. 329-400.
Hodson, F.R.
1970   Classification by Computer. In: Science in Archaeology, D. Brothwell and E. Higgs, eds., pp. 649-660, Praeger Publishers, New York.
Hooton, E.A.
1930   The Indians of Pecos Pueblo. A study of their skeletal remains. Published for the Department of Archaeology, Phillips Academy, Yale University Press, New Haven.
Hudson, E.H.
1965   Treponematosis and man's social evolution. American Anthropologist, *67:* 885-901.
Hunter, D., A.I. McLaughlin, and K.M. Perry
1945   Clinical effects of the use of pneumatic tools. British Journal of Industrial Medicine, *2:* 10-16.
Kellgren, J.H., and J.S. Lawrence
1952   Rheumatism in miners. Part II: x-ray study. British Journal of Industrial Medicine, *9:* 197-207.
Kovačević, D.
1961   Trgovina u Srednjovjekovnaj Bosni (Trade in Medieval Bosnia). P. Grinfelder, Sarajevo.

Murray, R.O., and H.G. Jacobson
    1971   The Radiology of Skeletal Disorders. Chapter 7, Halmopoietic Disorders. The Williams and Wilkins Co., Baltimore, Maryland.
Nordin, B.E., M.M. Young, L. Bulusu, and A. Horseman
    1970   Osteoporosis re-examined. In: Osteoporosis, Uriel S. Barzel, ed., Grune and Stratton, New York, pp. 47-67.
Palavestka, V.
    1971   Folk traditions of the ancient populations of the Dinaric region. Wissenschfliche Mitteilungen des Bosnisch-Herzegowinischen Landesmuseums, vol. 1, part B, Oslobodenje, Sarajevo, pp. 13-98.
Radin, E.L., and I.L. Paul
    1971   Response of joints to impact loading. I, *in vitro* wear. Arthritis and Rheumatism, *14:* 356-362.
Rostock, P.
    1936   Gelekschäden durch Arbeiten mit Pressluftwerkzeugen und andere schwere körperliche Arbeit. Medizinische Klinik, *36:* 341-343.
Saul, F.P.
    1972   The human skeletal remains of Altar de Sacrificios, an osteobiographic analysis. Papers of the Peabody Museum of Archaeology and Ethnology, vol. 63, no. 2, pp. 1-123.
Sepkoski, J.J.
    1970   Quantified coefficients of association and the QUAJAC computer program for performing Q-mode hierarchical cluster analysis. Unpublished manuscript, Department of Geology, Harvard University.

    1971   Report on the Q-mode Cluster Analysis program for the classification of qualitative and semi-quantitative data. Revised version, unpublished manuscript, Department of Geology, Harvard University.

    1973   Quantified coefficients of association and the measurement of similarity. Submitted to the Journal of the International Association for Mathematical Geology, May, 1973.
Simon, S.R., and E.L. Radin
    1972   The response of joints to impact loading. II, *in vivo* behavior of subchondral bone. Journal of Biomechanics, *5:* 267-272.
Sokal, R.R., and P.H. Sneath
    1963   Principles of Numerical Taxonomy, San Francisco, W.H. Freeman and Co.
Urist, M., M.S. Gurvey, and D.O. Fared
    1970   Long-term observations on aged women with pathologic osteoporosis. In: Osteoporosis, Uniel S. Barzel, ed., Grune and Stratton, New York, pp. 3-37.

Vukanović, T.P.
    1962   Les Valaques, habitants autochtones des Pays Balkaniques. L'Ethnographie, n.s., *56:* 11-41.
Wells, C.
    1964   Bones, Bodies and Disease, Ancient Peoples and Places series, vol. 37, Dr. Glyn Daniel, ed., Frederick A. Praeger, New York.
Wenzel, M.
    1962   Bosnian and Herzegovinian tombstones—who made them and why. Sudost Forshungen, *21:* 102-143.

17. Sexual Dimorphism in the Maturation of the Human Pubic Symphysis

Thomas W. McKern

Introduction

Estimation of chronological age from the maturational status of unknown skeletal remains has long been an important problem to identification experts in their efforts to aid federal and local law enforcement agencies as well as those scientists who attempt to reconstruct and describe man's distant ancestors.

Formerly, the information utilized in this area was derived primarily from textbooks of anatomy. In such sources, however, unsubstantiated statements were to be found regarding the ages at which maturational events occur. The placing of definite dates on such events is in keeping with the general practice of oversimplifying anatomical descriptions for teaching purposes. Variation was minimized and central tendencies became the working standards.

Among those areas of the skeleton where morphological changes demonstrate direct relationship to age, the symphyseal face of the pubic bone is undoubtedly one of the most reliable. Descriptions of maturational activity began early. Hunter (1761), Aeby (1858), Henle (1872), and Cleland (1889) described gross changes in the pubic symphysis during the life of an individual. It was not until the 1920's, however, that some of the anthropologically-oriented anatomists began to re-examine skeletal maturation with greater reference to variability.

433

Of these, perhaps the greatest contribution was made by T. Wingate Todd, who had access to a large and unusually well-documented skeletal collection. Todd's meticulous observations of this sample revealed that the symphyseal face of the pubic bone undergoes a regular metamorphosis from puberty onward (1920, 1921). In order to represent this transformation, he identified a succession of ten phases involving a number of easily recognized bony features. These pubic phases proved fairly satisfactory for aging purposes. But though Todd was aware of the role of variation in maturational events, he still tended to fall into the traditional anatomical trap of simplification.

In 1955, Brooks tested the method on a series of California Indian skeletons and a sample of male and female skeletons from Western Reserve University, the same utilized by Todd. She found that for all ages over 20 years the phases consistently yielded a higher-than-actual age, and concluded that the phases needed modification.

The first good opportunity to test current aging techniques had been provided by the Memorial Division of the Office of the Quartermaster General. Following World War II, the Memorial Division established identification laboratories at various sites in Europe and in the Pacific, where American war dead were identified and processed for shipment back to the U.S. Even greater opportunities came in 1953 when, following the Korean conflict, Operation Glory was initiated. T. Dale Stewart of the Smithsonian Institution was selected to direct research on identification problems in connection with the recovery of American war dead in Korea. At the Central Identification Laboratory located at Kokura, Japan, Stewart was able to record a vast amount of evidence for skeletal age changes in 450 individuals. These data were later forwarded to the Smithsonian Institution in Washington, D.C.

In 1955, the author joined Stewart in an intensive analysis of these data. For the first time, detailed information was available for a large, well-documented sample of male skeletons between the ages of 17 and 50 years. Standard aging criteria could be checked, the reliability of techniques used for age estimation could be tested, and research for new methods could be initiated. Results of the analysis were published in a detailed report which, among other things, introduced a new method of age identification based on the metamorphic activity of the symphyseal face of the pubic bone (McKern and Stewart, 1957).

Male Pubic Symphysis

Todd was essentially correct in his selection of cases to typify successive age periods, but the result was a static method of age determination. The variability of each feature was lost, and only those pubic bones which are close to the typical in morphology can be aged with reasonable accuracy.

A more reliable and realistic analysis of symphyseal maturation should take into account all feature variations. Rather than divide, then, the whole course of symphyseal metamorphosis into ten typical phases, McKern and Stewart devised a method that made it possible to translate a large number of morphological combinations into chronological terms.

Separate components of the symphyseal face were recognized as was the fact that each of these components undergoes transformation by stages. The result is expressed as a formula which can be translated easily into chronological age.

The idea of summarizing complete morphology by means of a formula is not new to biological science. A well-known example is the somatotype formula introduced by Sheldon (1940). In this case a formula, consisting of three components of seven grades each, described the body type of an individual. Such a procedure not only forces the observer to analyze the composition of a structure but, once formulated, enables anyone to visualize what the original structure looked like. Moreover, a formula is a convenient device for comparative purposes.

After some experimentation with elements involved in metamorphosis of the symphysis, McKern and Stewart found that the most reliable results were obtained from a formula consisting of three components with five subdivisions or stages each.

The search for the main elements began with Todd's description of the changes in the pubic symphysis:

1. Ridges and furrows
2. Dorsal margin
3. Ventral beveling
4. Lower extremity
5. Superior ossific module
6. Upper extremity
7. Ventral rampart
8. Dorsal plateau
9. Symphyseal rim

Obviously, a formula of nine digits, necessary if all nine features were utilized, would prove too cumbersome. It was decided, therefore, to locate recognizable combinations of these features.

At age 17, the starting point of the McKern-Stewart series, the most prominent feature of the symphyseal face is a pattern of transverse ridges and furrows (Todd's Feature 1). The pattern is often interrupted by either a longitudinal ridge or groove bisecting part or all of the symphyseal face and dividing it into dorsal and ventral halves. This division is important because it foreshadows events that are restricted to one or the other side. For convenience in referring to this division, the terms "dorsal demi-face" and "ventral demi-face" are used.

Since ridge and furrow obliteration is retrogressive in character, gradually disappearing into other features, it is not considered to be a separate feature but a part of succeeding features.

Next, the analysis of the McKern-Stewart series revealed that the lower symphyseal extremity (Todd's Feature 4) occurs in combination with the expansion inferiorly of the dorsal margin; that the upper extremity (Todd's Feature 6) is closely associated with the development of the ventral border; and that the so-called ossific nodule (Todd's Feature 5), which is found in only a small number of cases and even then quickly loses its identity, is but the upper part of the ventral rampart. Such features are included in the descriptions of the two demi-faces.

Lastly, Todd's Features 2 and 8 (dorsal margin and plateau) were combined, as were his features 3 and 7 (ventral beveling and rampart). This combining was based on the recognition of the dorsal and ventral demi-faces. It was felt that the functional relationship of dorsal margin to dorsal plateau and ventral beveling to ventral rampart are extremely close and thus may be considered as interrelated metamorphic features.

This leaves only one of Todd's features (No. 9, the symphyseal rim), and it is distinct from the demi-faces. Actually, it involves the face as a whole but only after the original subdivision of two demi-faces has disappeared. In this way, McKern and Stewart arrived at three components that are considered diagnostically reliable in their chronologic behavior: (1) the dorsal plateau, (2) the ventral rampart, and (3) the symphyseal rim.

Because metamorphosis is not always in the same direction, the components do not represent a succession of structural changes. A structure such as a dorsal plateau develops gradually, becomes complete, and then proceeds to break down and disappear. On the other

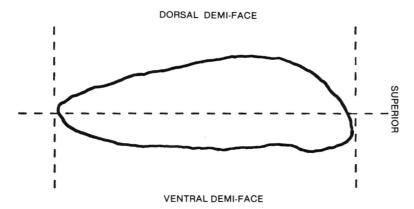

Figure 1. Diagram of the articular surface on the left side of a male pubic symphysis divided into dorsal and ventral demi-faces.

hand, the symphyseal rim, having reached its peak in the mid-thirties, thereafter gradually disintegrates and eventually is replaced. Thus the numbers used in designating the stages (and hence the formula) ignore the changes in direction. Having the numerical sequence of the stages parallel the direction of the structural changes would only complicate the visual usefulness of the formula. Therefore the active stages of all three components have been numbered from 1 to 5. In addition to the five active developmental stages, a preliminary stage (0), denoting absence of the feature in question, precedes each set of stages. The three components and their developmental stages are defined as follows:

THE SYMPHYSEAL COMPONENTS

1. *Dorsal Plateau.* Between the ages of 17-18, the grooves near the dorsal margin begin to fill in with finely-textured bone and the ridges show the first evidence of resorption. Coincident with this process, a delimiting dorsal margin appears which eventually outlines the entire demi-face.

Starting in the same general area, the interacting processes of resorption and fill-in spread over the dorsal demi-face until the ridge and groove pattern has been obliterated. Ultimately, this gives to the demi-face a flat, platform-like aspect and for this reason the component has been given the name "dorsal plateau."

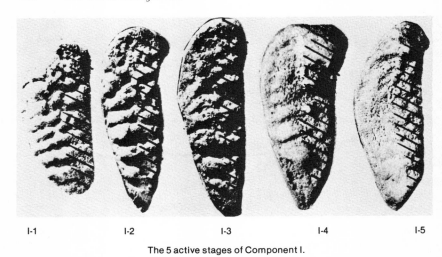

I-1   I-2   I-3   I-4   I-5

The 5 active stages of Component I.

Figure 2. The 5 active stages of Component I (From McKern and Stewart, 1957, Fig. 39).

The six (0-5) stages of Component I follow:

0. Dorsal margin absent
1. A slight margin formation first appears in the middle third of the dorsal border.
2. The dorsal margin extends along entire dorsal border.
3. Filling in of grooves and resorption of ridges to form a beginning plateau in the middle third of the dorsal demi-face.
4. The plateau, still exhibiting vestiges of billowing, extends over most of the dorsal demi-face.
5. Billowing disappears completely and the surface of the entire demi-face becomes flat and slightly granulated in texture.

2. *Ventral Rampart.* Early in the development of Component 1, differentiation of dorsal and ventral demifaces becomes pronounced due to the breakdown, by rarefaction, of the ventral half. Over this porous, beveled surface an elongated and more or less complete epiphysis or rampart forms. This rampart is produced by the extension of ossification from upper and lower extremities aided, at times, by independent ossicles along the line of the future ventral margin. Obviously, however, the pattern is variable and the rampart may remain incomplete even in later age groups (the hiatus is usually in the middle two-thirds of the ventral border, or may bridge only certain portions of the beveled surface).

The six (0-5) stages of Component 2 are as follows:

0. Ventral beveling is absent.
1. Ventral beveling is present only at superior extremity of ventral border.
2. Bevel extends inferiorly along ventral border.
3. The ventral rampart begins by means of bony extensions from either or both of the extremities.
4. The rampart is extensive but gaps are still evident along the earlier ventral border, most evident in the upper two thirds.
5. The rampart is complete.

3. *Symphyseal Rim.* The final stages of symphyseal maturation are characterized by the formation of a distinct and elevated rim surrounding the now level face. At the same time, the bony texture of the face begins to change from a somewhat granular to a more finely-grained or dense bone and, although vestiges of the ridge and groove pattern still may be recognized in the lower third of the dorsal demi-face, it is sometimes difficult to tell whether they are merely regular undulations of the smooth bony surface or true remnants of the earlier ridge and groove pattern.

Following the completion of the symphyseal rim, there is a period during which changes are minute and infrequent. Ultimately the rim is worn down or resorbed and a smooth surface extends to the margins. As the face levels off it undergoes erosion and erratic ossification, the bone becomes more porous, and the margins may be lipped.

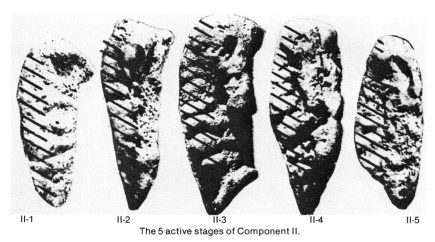

II-1   II-2   II-3   II-4   II-5

The 5 active stages of Component II.

Figure 3. The 5 active stages of Component II (From McKern and Stewart, 1957, Fig. 41).

Metamorphosis of the symphysis in the last decades of life is characterized by further breakdown of the bony tissue. However, because of the small number of older individuals present in the McKern-Stewart series, last stages could not be defined.

The six (0-5) stages of Component 3 are as follows:

0. The symphyseal rim is absent.
1. A partial dorsal rim is present, usually at the superior end of the dorsal margin; it is round and smooth in texture and elevated above the symphyseal surface.
2. The dorsal rim is complete and the ventral rim is beginning to form. There is no particular beginning site.
3. The symphyseal rim is complete.The enclosed symphyseal surface is finely-grained in texture and irregular or undulating in appearance.
4. The rim begins to break down. The face becomes smooth and flat and the rim is no longer round but sharply defined. There is some evidence of lipping on the ventral rim.
5. Further breakdown of the rim (especially along superior ventral edge) and rarefaction of the symphyseal face; there is also disintegration and erratic ossification along the ventral rim.

To arrive at an age estimate, each of the three components is scored by associating the appropriate component stage with that of the symphysis to be identified. These three scores are then added and the predicted age for that sum can be read from Table 1.

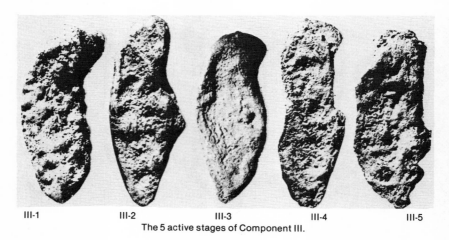

III-1   III-2   III-3   III-4   III-5
The 5 active stages of Component III.

Figure 4. The 5 active stages of Component III (From McKern and Stewart, 1957, Fig. 42).

TABLE 1

CALCULATED MEAN AGE, STANDARD DEVIATION AND AGE RANGES FOR THE TOTAL SCORES OF THE SYMPHYSEAL FORMULAE*

Total Score	No.	Age Range for the Scores	Mean Age	Standard Deviation
0	7	-17	17.29	.49
1-2	76	17-20	19.04	.79
3	43	18-21	19.79	.85
4-5	51	18-23	20.84	1.13
6-7	26	20-24	22.42	.99
8-9	36	22-28	24.14	1.93
10	19	23-28	26.05	1.87
11-12-13	56	23-39	29.18	3.33
14	31	29+	35.84	3.89
15	4	36+	41.00	6.22

*From McKern and Stewart, 1957, Table 27.

Instead of depending upon static, typical symphyseal phases, the McKern-Stewart system of components allows for individual variation. The resulting age estimations of unknown skeletal remains are more realistic, more accurate and more dependable. It must be pointed out, however, that since this method was derived from a male skeletal sample, it can be used with confidence only in the identification of male cases.

Female Pubic Symphysis
Since the female skeleton demonstrates various growth spurts at younger ages than do male skeletons, it is necessary to apply two separate standards, male and female, to skeletal development in cases of age identification. However, development of a method similar to that produced by McKern and Stewart has been frustrated by one important barrier: the scarcity of adequate samples of well-documented female skeletons.

Although the McKern-Stewart technique for aging male pubic symphyses has proven reliable, it was never intended to be utilized in cases of female skeletal identification. It has been so applied, nonetheless, with questionable results due to the unique nature of the metamorphic changes in the female pubic bone.

Metamorphic differences between male and female pubic symphyses have been recognized by a number of scholars but, again, it was Todd who first developed female standards for symphyseal metamorphosis (1921). His attempt failed only because his sample was deficient both in age range and in proper age documentation.

Using Todd's system in her analysis of a California Indian series, Brooks (1955) showed female mortality curves which were inordinately higher than curves for the males in the same population and urged the necessity of establishing more reliable aging standards for females. Stewart (1970) suggested that some of the inconsistencies found in the Brooks' study may have been due to traumatic changes in the female pubic symphysis resulting from childbirth. Whatever the reasons, sexual dimorphism in the pattern of maturative changes in the symphyseal face of the pubic bone is a fact. And male criteria cannot be used on female pubes with any real anticipation of accurate age assessment.

Since 1960, McKern and Gilbert have collected female pubes of known age, primarily from anatomy and pathology laboratories in various parts of the U.S. By 1971, a total of 130 cases had been accepted. Table 2 gives the age distribution for this sample along with known parity information (Gilbert and McKern, 1973).

It is both interesting and significant that the entire range of metamorphic activity found in the male symphysis is also found in the female. It is only the chronology of the various maturative events that differs. Thus most of the terminology introduced by the McKern-Stewart system could be applied in the analysis of the Gilbert-McKern sample.

Observations of the age changes in the female pubic bone resulted in the establishment of the following three components:

THE SYMPHYSEAL COMPONENTS
1. *Dorsal Demi-Face.* From birth to about age 16, the dorsal demi-face is made up of ridges and furrows of very finely-grained bone. About the age of 16 years, the mid-third of the dorsal demi-face begins to flatten as the area of contact between the two symphyses increases. A dorsal margin extends both superiorly and inferiorly from the mid-third, and the ridges and furrows continue to flatten

TABLE 2

AGE DISTRIBUTION AND PARITY OF THE
GILBERT-MCKERN SAMPLE

Age	Known Parity	Unknown Parity	Total
10-15	3	0	3
16-20	7	0	7
21-25	4	0	4
26-30	3	0	3
31-35	6	0	6
36-40	6	1	7
41-45	4	1	5
46-50	10	1	11
51-55	5	2	7
56-60	11	2	13
61-65	6	9	15
66-70	5	3	8
71-75	4	7	11
76-80	4	10	14
81-85	3	6	9
86-90	1	5	6
91-95	0	1	1
Total	82	48	130

and fill in as the total dorsal demi-face spreads ventrally. The last stage of development in the dorsal demi-face is characterized by the completion of the dorsal margin, and the extension of the flattened area along the ventral edge of the dorsal demi-face.

2. *Ventral Rampart.* The ventral rampart (demi-face) is beveled and slopes away from contact with its opposite, unlike the dorsal demi-faces which oppose one another. The ventral rampart undergoes flattening and fill-in at a protracted rate. This fill-in and flattening of ridges and furrows begins first along the inferior end and proceeds superiorly. Next, it begins at the superior end and proceeds inferiorly. Finally, the ventral rampart is complete, its lateral border an arcuate line from the pubic crest to the inferior ramus. The rampart may be flat and solid or irregular and pitted.

The arcuate line was recognized early by Cleland (1889) as forming the lateral border of the ventral rampart and he used it as a rough sex-and-age criterion: "The distance between the lines marking the inner limit of attachment of the femoral muscles on the right and left sides is considerably greater in the female than in the male. In a middle-aged or old female the line in question will always be seen marked by a distinct ridge, with a flattened surface extending inwards from it, covered in the recent stages by the superficial ligament of the symphysis; and the distance between the two ridges of opposite sides will be found to increase as the pubic arch is approached."

3. *Symphyseal Rim.* Dorsally, the rim is evident from about age 22, but it is only after the complete development of the dorsal demi-face that the rim becomes apparent ventrally. It is then a line of separation between the dorsal demi-face and the ventral rampart. The ventral aspect of the symphyseal rim develops slowly and is not usually complete until the end of the third decade; then, about the middle of the fifth decade, this portion of the rim may begin to break down or simply disappear through rounding so that there may no longer be a clear dividing line between the dorsal demi-face and the ventral rampart.

The six (0-5) stages of metamorphic change in the three components are shown in Figure 5. All symphyseal faces shown in Component 1 are from the left side. Those for Component 2 are: 0, 2, 4, right side, and 1, 3, 5, left side. For Component 3, the pubes represent: 0, 2, 5, right side, while 1, 3, 4 are left side. An explanation of the stages of metamorphic activity for each of the components are as follows:

Component 1:
0. Ridges and furrows very distinct. Ridges are billowed, dorsal margin undefined.
1. Ridges begin to flatten, furrows to fill in, and dorsal margin begins in mid-third of demi-face.
2. Dorsal demi-face spreads ventrally, becomes wider as flattening continues. Dorsal margin extends superiorly and inferiorly.
3. Dorsal demi-face is quite flat. Margin may be narrow or indistinct from face.
4. Demi-face becomes complete and unbroken, is broad and very fine-grained, and may exhibit vestigial billowing.
5. Demi-face becomes pitted and irregular through rarefaction.

Component 2:
0. Ridges and furrows very distinct. The entire demi-face is beveled up towards the dorsal demi-face.
1. Beginning inferiorly, the furrows of the ventral demi-face begin to fill in

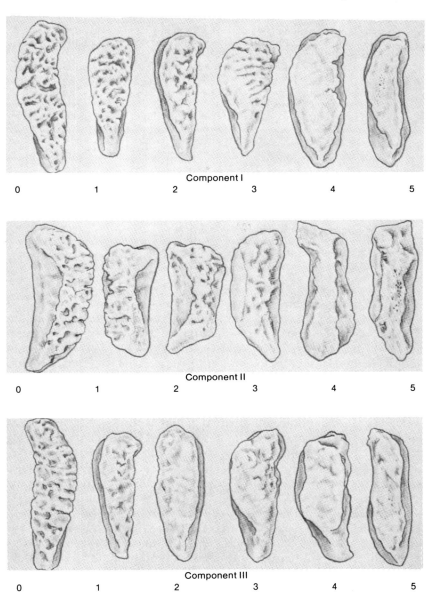

Figure 5. The 6 maturative stages of Components I, II and III (From Gilbert and McKern, 1973, Fig. 1).

forming an expanding beveled rampart, the lateral edge of which is a distinct arcuate line extending the length of the symphysis.

2. Fill-in of furrows and expansion of demi-face continue from both superior and inferior ends. Rampart spreads laterally along its ventral edge.
3. All but about one-third of the ventral demi-face is filled in with fine-grained bone.
4. The ventral rampart presents a broad, complete, fine-grained surface from the pubic crest to the inferior ramus.
5. Ventral rampart may begin to break down, assuming a very pitted and perhaps cancellous appearance through rarefaction.

Component 3:
0. The rim is absent.
1. The rim begins in the mid-third of the dorsal surface.
2. The dorsal part of the symphyseal rim is complete.
3. The rim extends from the superior and inferior ends of the symphysis until all but about one-third of the ventral aspect is complete.
4. The symphyseal rim is complete.
5. Ventral margin of dorsal semi-face may break down so that gaps appear in the rim, or it may round off so that there is no longer a clear dividing line between the dorsal demi-face and the ventral rampart.

Although the combined sample ranged in age from 13 to 97 years, it became apparent that no regular metamorphic activity could be found beyond about 55 years. An 80-year-old individual cannot be distinguished from one who is a decade younger or older by this morphoscopic method. One hundred and three individuals were analyzed and scored according to their stages of development. As in the McKern-Stewart method, an individual is scored 1-1-0 for a toal score of 2 if only Components 1 and 2 are active and these have only begun to develop. Similarly, an older individual might be in Stage 3 of Component 1, Stage 2 of Component 2, and Stage I of Component 3, yielding a score of 3-2-1 for a total of 6. Age limits of the component stages are shown in Table 3 and the calculated mean ages, standard deviations, and age ranges for total scores derived from these 103 individuals are presented in Table 4.

Special attention must be placed on the possible effects of birth trauma to the female pubis. Angel (1969) and Stewart (1957, 1970) describe fully the appearance of the dorsal aspect of the female pubis which has suffered damage as a result of childbirth. As the fetus develops and eventually emerges, the inter-pubic ligaments may be pulled to the point of hemorrhage and herniation, leaving permanent pits or grooves on the dorsal surface of the pubis. During the last week of pregnancy, the pubes seperate at the symphysis as much as 10 mm.,

TABLE 3

AGE LIMITS OF THE COMPONENT STAGES*

		Component I		
0	3		14-24	18.00
1	23		13-25	20.04
2	27		18-40	29.81
3	16		22-40	31.00
4	27		28-59	40.80
5	15		33-59	48.00
		Component II		
0	11		13-22	18.63
1	21		16-40	22.52
2	25		18-40	29.64
3	19		27-57	38.77
4	28		21-58	40.90
5	9		36-59	48.50
		Component III		
0	30		13-25	20.23
1	8		18-34	25.75
2	14		22-40	32.00
3	21		22-57	35.60
4	27		21-58	39.90
5	11		36-59	49.40

*From Gilbert and McKern, (1973), Table 1.

and the inter-pubic ligaments attach more and more laterally from the symphysis with each succeeding pregnancy.

After examination of some 140 cases of known parity, it does not seem presently possible to determine the number of pregnancies an individual has experienced simply by noting the degree of damage done to the pubic bone. Indeed, some of the cases with only one pregnancy show much more extensive trauma then do some multiparas. However, the degree of traumatic change observed in the Gilbert-McKern combined sample indicated that only rarely is a pubis rendered impossible to age. Several cases demonstrated involvement of the ventral aspect of the rim and ventral demi-face were undamaged, yielding an accurate age assessment. But caution is always indicated with unknown pubes characterized by excessive parity damage. They may be much younger than they appear.

TABLE 4

CALCULATED MEAN AGE, STANDARD DEVIATION* AND AGE
RANGES FOR THE TOTAL SCORES OF THE SYMPHYSEAL FORMULAE

Total Score	No. Cases	Age Range	Mean	Standard Deviation
0	2	14-18	16^5	2^5
1	12	13-24	19.8	2.76
2	13	16-25	20.15	4.97
3	4	18-25	21.50	5.36
4-5	7	22-29	26.00	5.70
6	8	25-36	29.62	6.86
7-8	14	23-39	32.00	5.54
9	5	22-40	33.00	9.00
10-11	11	30-47	36.90	7.73
12	12	32-52	39.00	8.54
13	8	44-54	47.75	7.57
14-15	7	52-59	55.71	8.07
Total	103			

*From Gilbert and McKern, (1973), Table 2.

Summary

Since Todd's system of typical phases for both males and females served only those symphyses that conform to his concept of typical, new methods have been proposed in which symphyseal metamorphosis is evaluated in terms of combinations of its component parts. Thus for both the McKern-Stewart and the Gilbert-McKern techniques, three components have been selected, each sub-divided into five developmental stages which when combined as a formula for any pubic symphysis will yield an age range and the probable age of the individual. In comparison with Todd's system, the symphyseal formula expresses the true nature of symphyseal variability and does not confine the observer to the narrow limits of "typical" phases.

There is no doubt that separate metamorphic standards exist between the sexes. Even though the entire range of male activity can be demonstrated in the female pubic bone, there exist some very crucial differences. For example, the dorsal surface of the male and female symphysis is the site of the earliest metamorphic change; however, the female pubis undergoes flattening of the dorsal demi-face at a much faster rate than does the male. On this basis alone, a female pubic symphysis aged 25 has the appearance of a male of 35 years.

Another major difference is found in the development of the ventral rampart, Component 2. In the male, the ventral rampart is a bony extension along the ventral demi-face. Something similar is seen in the female, but it is actually the symphyseal rim which divides the dorsal and ventral aspects in the female pubic face. In the male, the two demi-faces are separated by an imaginary line whereas in the female the ventral rampart (demi- face) is beveled away from the dorsal demi-face. Because of this structural difference, a female pubis in Stage 3 of Component 2 would be aged about 38 years, while a male pubis in the same category of the male standard would be aged about 23 years. The major problem is in the location and definition of the ventral demi-face. In the male, the symphyseal rim encloses both dorsal and ventral demi-faces. In the female, it actually separates the two demi-faces.

Of course there are limitations to both the McKern-Stewart and the Gilbert-McKern methods. But each represents a more thorough knowledge and a better control of the variability in individual maturative features and thus represents an important advance in identification procedure.

What of future research in this area of age identification? It would seem that we have done fairly well in our understanding of the complex maturation of the male pubic symphysis. We have only begun to understand the same process in the female. Yet it has become increasingly apparent that, in mass disasters as well as individual deaths from general causes, females comprise an increasingly greater majority of victims other than in the case of war. Although studies of the female skeleton are particularly inhibited by lack of extensive documented samples, there is an immediate need for new studies as well as for the constant refinement of existing techniques in this relevant field.

Bibliography

Aeby, C.
1858 Ueber die Symphyse ossium pubis des Menschen nebst Beitragen zur Lehre vom hyalinen Knorpel und seiner Verknocherungen. Zscher f. rationelle Med., Reihe 3, *IV:* 1-77.
Angel, J. L.
1969 The bases of paleodemography. American Journal of Physical Anthropology, *30:* 427-437.

Brooks, S. T]
1955   Skeletal age at death: The reliability of cranial and pubic age indicators. American Journal of Physical Anthropology, *13:* 567-597.
Cleland, J.
1889   On certain distinctions of form hitherto unnoticed in the human pelvis, characteristic of sex, age and race. Memoirs and Memoranda in Anatomy, *I:* 95-103.
Gilbert, B. M. and T. W. McKern
1973   A method for aging the female *os pubis.* American Journal of Physical Anthropology, *38:* 31-38
Henle, J.
1872   Bander Zwischen beiden Huftknochen. Handbuch der Banderlehre des Menschen (Handbuch der systematischen Anatomie), 2e Aufl., 121.
Hunter, W.
1761   Remarks on the symphysis of the *ossa pubis.* Medical Observations and Inquiries, *2:* 333.
McKern, T. W. and T. D. Stewart
1957   Skeletal age changes in young American males. Quartermaster Research and Development Command. Technical Report EP-45, Natick, Mass.
Sheldon, W. H.
1940   The varieties of human physique, an introduction to constitutional psychology. New York.
Stewart, T. D.
1957   Distortion of the pubis symphyseal surface in females and its effect on age determination. American Journal of Physical Anthropology, *15:* 9-18.

1970   Identification of the scars of parturition in the skeletal remains of females. In: Personal Identification in Mass Disasters, T. D. Stewart, ed. United States National Museum, Washington D. C.
Todd, T. W.
1920   Age changes in the pubic bones. I: The male white pubis. American Journal of Physical Anthropology, *3:* 285-334.

1921   Age changes in the pubic bones. II: Pubis of male negro-white hybrid. III: Pubis of white female. IV: Pubis of female negro-white hybrid. American Journal of Physical Anthropology, *4:* 1-70.

18. Size Integration of Craniofacial and Dental Dimensions

A. Vincent Lombardi

Introduction

To the student of human evolution, the teeth have been important elements in tracing the origin of man and in establishing relationships among populations, both recent and ancient. But while data have been amassed on tooth size in a number of populations, little is known about the nature of dental associations within the individual. Important questions to be answered are whether tooth size is correlated with skeletal craniofacial dimensions and, if so, how and to what extent they are related. The assumption running through much of the anthropological literature is that there is overall coordination between dental and skeletal dimensions, but the available evidence is only general in nature.

Garn and Lewis (1958) studied the association in recent and ancient man to test the validity of "giant" ancestral forms, consideration being given to the relationship among species, among races and among individuals. Focusing on selected tooth measurements they found no significant correlation between tooth size and stature. Considering head width and head length as well as stature, Filipsson and Goldson (1963) found a low positive correlation (0.20) between crown length and head width, but no correlation could be demonstrated between crown length and head length or stature. The problem of dental and skeletal associations was reconsidered by Garn, Lewis and Kerewsky (1968) because of persistent allusions to such associations in the literature. Pooling the correlations for both sexes of a sample drawn from a modern population, they arrived at a mean *r* of 0.16 as an estimate of the magnitude of the relationship between dental and skeletal dimensions. Solow (1966) in a factor analytic study of craniofacial and somatic skeletal dimensions included dental variables other than individual tooth size. Dental arch length, width and circumference, as well as axial inclination of the teeth and measures of occlusion and tooth alignment, were among the variables considered. Some of the resultant factors associated incisor inclination with length of the mandible, circumference of the dental arches with maxillary prognathism, dental arch width with maxillary width, and molar occlusion with mandibular length.

The present study pursues further the way in which dental and craniofacial dimensions are integrated within a single population. Factor analysis was used to simplify comprehension of the associations among a large number of dental and craniofacial measurements. The value of factor analysis in this instance is its capacity to reduce the information in a correlation matrix to a relatively small number of "factors" which account for the correlations among the measurements. Factor analytic methods have been used by numerous investigators (Howells, 1951, 1957, 1972; Schwidetzky, 1960; Landauer, 1962; Brown, Barrett and Darroch, 1965; Solow, 1966; Brown, 1967; Kanda and Kurisu, 1967, 1968; Kanda, 1968) to determine the axes of morphologic variation in the craniofacial skeleton of man. While similar in approach, the generation of craniofacial factors beyond those previously identified was not an objective of this study. This investigation differs from Solow's by considering measurements on individual teeth rather than dental arch variables.

Materials and Methods

A series of 66 adult skulls from Mexico City intact with mandibles and good dentitions, representative of a broad population best described as modern Mexican Indian, was used in the study. No attempt was made to consider the sexes separately because of the small sample and the lack of supporting material to confirm sex assignments. Crown length (mesiodistal diameter) and crown width (buccolingual diameter) measurements were made on the individual teeth in addition to 28 measurements on the craniofacial skeleton. Crown indices were computed for the teeth following the formula: crown index = buccolingual diameter x 100/mesiodistal diameter. To assure a linear relationship among the variables, the raw data were transformed into natural logarithms. Third molar measurements were excluded from analysis because of the high frequency of third molar agenesis in the skulls; thus, a total of 70 variables were subjected to the iterative principal factors analysis routine (BMDO3M) of the Biomedical Computer Programs package.[1] Initial communality estimates were the squared multiple correlation coefficients, and the Varimax rotation was used to transform the initial factor solution to the terminal solution. Factor analysis was run on the craniofacial dimensions alone as well as combined respectively with crown length, crown width and the crown index.

Results

Each rotated factor had its strongest correlations with dimensions of the craniofacial skeleton or of the teeth but not with both; therefore, each factor could be identified by its principal loadings as either a craniofacial or dental factor. A number of factors, however, revealed morphologic integration between the skeleton and the dentition by having secondary loadings for the other tissue system. These factors are of principal interest here, but the factors derived from the analysis of the craniofacial dimensions taken separately are first described to set the parameters of skeletal variation.

CRANIOFACIAL ANALYSIS

Factor analysis of the craniofacial dimensions alone resulted in eight factors which account for 74 per cent of the total variance (Table 1). It is apparent from previous studies that these are not all the factors operating on craniofacial variation.

I. *Cranial base breadth.* The measurements which loaded most highly on this factor, which was the most important in terms of variance accounted for, were those which crossed the cranial base. Similar factors were found by Howells (1957) and Kanda and Kurisu (1967).

II. *Maxillary prognathism.* The midfacial lengthening characterized by the high loadings for palate length and basion-prosthion length suggests a factor of maxillary prognathism. Cranial base length and nasal breadth had lower but strong loadings and orbit height had a negative correlation with the factor; measures of mandibular size had smaller loadings. Howells (1972) using different measurements also identified a prognathism factor as did Brown (1967).

[1] Dixon, W. J., editor, 1970 **BMD: Biomedical Computer Programs,** University of California Press, Los Angeles.

TABLE 1

ROTATED FACTOR MATRIX OF CRANIOFACIAL MEASUREMENTS

Variable	I	II	III	IV	V	VI	VII	VIII	Communalities
Maximum cranial le.	0.19	0.25	0.26	0.08	0.46	0.58	0.09	0.07	0.74
Maximum cranial br.	0.49	-0.13	0.09	-0.09	-0.05	0.57	0.10	0.11	0.62
Bizygomatic br.	0.76	0.19	0.20	0.15	0.36	0.17	0.21	0.23	0.94
Biauricular br.	0.82	0.08	0.12	0.15	0.26	0.27	0.11	0.08	0.87
Minimum cranial br.	0.69	0.16	-0.02	0.15	-0.03	0.29	0.23	0.14	0.67
Bimaxillary br.	0.53	0.25	0.19	0.17	0.56	0.04	0.15	0.18	0.77
Basion-bregma ht.	0.33	-0.00	0.15	0.02	0.33	0.71	0.19	0.03	0.78
Basion-nasion le.	0.33	0.46	0.22	-0.10	0.43	0.55	0.11	-0.00	0.88
Basion-prosthion le.	0.14	0.73	0.08	0.06	0.43	0.22	0.12	0.11	0.82
Nasion-prosthion ht.	0.12	0.17	0.72	-0.05	0.23	0.21	0.40	0.09	0.83
Nasion-gnathion ht.	0.23	0.11	0.52	0.01	0.32	0.27	0.64	0.10	0.92
Nasal ht.	0.17	0.11	0.82	-0.05	0.26	0.13	0.07	0.19	0.85
Nasal br.	0.24	0.42	-0.09	0.15	0.16	-0.03	-0.11	0.44	0.49
Orbit ht.	0.02	-0.37	0.43	0.40	-0.07	0.26	-0.09	-0.13	0.57
Orbit br.	0.52	0.16	0.37	0.20	0.16	0.32	0.00	-0.17	0.62
Interorbital br.	0.19	0.19	0.21	-0.03	0.18	0.16	0.21	0.70	0.71
Palate br.	0.33	0.17	0.11	0.38	0.40	0.23	0.37	0.21	0.69
Palate le.	0.15	0.76	0.21	0.12	0.19	-0.04	0.23	0.15	0.77
Bicondylar wi.	0.72	0.19	0.17	0.23	0.19	0.18	0.12	0.31	0.82
Bigonial br.	0.64	0.02	0.05	-0.12	0.56	0.06	0.10	0.02	0.74
Ramus ht.	0.25	-0.13	0.22	0.18	0.31	0.16	0.47	0.21	0.54
Minimum ramus br.	0.06	0.24	0.14	-0.17	0.76	0.06	0.14	0.11	0.72
Symphyseal ht.	0.18	0.29	0.06	0.14	0.13	0.13	0.78	0.06	0.78
Pogonion-gonion le.	0.25	0.17	0.30	0.07	0.78	0.24	0.12	0.06	0.87
Mental foramen br.	0.18	0.19	0.16	0..8	0.59	0.23	0.15	0.19	0.63
Minimum frontal br.	0.24	0.04	0.23	0.09	0.05	0.61	0.28	0.46	0.78
Maxillary intercanine br.	0.19	0.28	-0.07	0.44	0.46	0.02	0.22	0.03	0.57
Mandibular intercanine br.	0.17	0.07	-0.04	0.78	-0.02	-0.05	0.11	0.05	0.65
Trace	4.36	2.32	2.41	1.55	3.92	2.66	2.09	1.40	20.71
Per cent of common variance	21.0	11.2	11.6	7.5	18.9	12.8	10.1	6.8	

NB Communalities are for 8 factors

III. *Upper face height.* Vertical dimensions of the face, especially of the upper face, correlated strongly with this factor. This is independent of lower face height which loaded on another factor. Orbit breadth as well as orbit height loaded on this factor suggesting that general orbit size and nasal height are important determinants of upper face height. Length of the body of the mandible also correlated with this factor. Factors of face height were found previously by Howells (1972), Brown (1967), Solow (1966) and, perhaps, Kanda and Kurisu (1967).

IV. *Dental arch breadth.* This factor was defined by the loadings for intercanine breadth in both dental arches. The smaller loading for palate breadth indicates that it is to some extent secondary to dental arch breadth. Mental foramen breadth and other breadths of the mandible did not load significantly. Orbit height but not orbit breadth also correlated with this factor.

V. *Facial massiveness.* Lengths and breadths of the face predominated on this factor; however, maximum cranial length, cranial base length and maxillary intercanine breadth also loaded significantly, suggesting a factor of general skeletal size. Orbital and nasal dimensions did not load on this factor. Correspondences with factors previously described are tentative (Howells, 1972; Brown, 1967; Kanda and Kurisu, 1967; Landauer, 1962).

VI. *Cranial vault size.* The measurements which loaded on this factor relate to the brain case, indicating a factor of cranial vault size. Cranial height, length and breadth loaded in descending order. Minimum frontal breadth correlated strongly, as did cranial base length. This factor corresponds well with the *F1* factor of Kanda and Kurisu (1967), which along with height, breadth and length had a high loading for cranial capacity, although base length did not load on their factor.

VII. *Lower face height.* This appears to be clearly a factor of lower face height, with vertical dimensions involving the mandible loading most highly. Coordination with midfacial dimensions is suggested by the loadings for nasion-prosthion height and palate breadth. There may be some correspondence to the *ramus height* factor of Brown, Barrett and Darroch (1965) but the measurements are different.

VIII. *Interorbital breadth.* This is considered a local factor, as signaled by the dominant correlation with inter-orbital breadth. Minimum frontal breadth and nasal breadth loaded strongly, however, and perhaps indicate that the factor is more general in nature, relating to upper face width but not including bizygomatic or bimaxillary dimensions. This seemingly corresponds with the factor of the same name found by Howells (1972).

CRANIOFACIAL AND DENTAL ANALYSIS

The craniofacial dimensions then were factored with crown length, crown width and the crown index separately. In the crown length and crown width analyses, nine factors were interpreted which account for, respectively, 73 and 75 per cent of the total variance (Tables 2 and 3). The craniofacial-crown index analysis resulted in twelve identifiable factors encompassing 73 per cent of the variance (Table 4).

The craniofacial factors described above appeared essentially unchanged in the analyses with the dental dimensions, except for the *interorbital breadth* factor (Factor VIII) which did not occur. The variables subsumed on this factor instead loaded more strongly on other factors in the presence of dental variables.

Of principal interest in this investigation were those factors which

TABLE 2

ROTATED FACTOR MATRIX OF CRANIOFACIAL MEASUREMENTS AND CROWN LENGTH

Variable	I	II	III	IV	V	VI	VII	VIII	IX	Communalities
Maximum cranial le.	0.21	0.16	0.02	0.28	0.07	0.15	0.06	0.43	0.60	0.73
Maximum cranial br.	0.45	0.01	-0.06	0.13	-0.03	0.09	0.00	0.70	0.01	0.72
Bizygomatic br.	0.75	0.15	0.09	0.19	0.19	0.24	-0.04	0.13	0.42	0.92
Biauricular br.	0.79	0.18	0.01	0.12	0.17	0.07	-0.05	0.26	0.29	0.86
Minimum cranial br	0.72	0.10	0.14	0.01	0.10	0.27	0.08	0.23	0.01	0.69
Bimaxillary br.	0.53	0.09	0.11	0.09	0.15	0.23	0.02	-0.08	0.63	0.79
Basion-bregma ht.	0.38	0.27	-0.17	0.16	-0.07	0.20	0.07	0.52	0.42	0.77
Basion-nasion le.	0.38	0.15	0.24	0.27	-0.14	0.15	0.05	0.34	0.59	0.81
Basion-prosthion le.	0.21	0.05	0.55	0.20	0.07	0.15	0.18	0.07	0.57	0.78
Nasion-prosthion ht.	0.12	0.07	0.01	0.77	0.01	0.29	0.11	0.18	0.31	0.83
Nasion-gnathion ht.	0.22	0.29	-0.02	0.60	0.05	0.51	0.05	0.14	0.34	0.89
Nasal ht.	0.19	-0.05	-0.07	0.76	-0.02	0.11	0.01	0.12	0.37	0.78
Nasal br.	0.31	-0.22	0.48	-0.10	0.20	0.13	0.02	0.01	0.26	0.50
Orbit ht.	0.14	-0.14	-0.68	0.19	0.11	0.05	0.17	0.06	-0.00	0.59
Orbit br.	0.65	0.06	-0.14	0.33	-0.02	-0.01	0.18	0.06	0.25	0.65
Interorbital br.	0.20	-0.01	0.19	0.09	-0.01	0.66	-0.06	0.16	0.30	0.63
Palate br.	0.36	0.10	0.05	0.18	0.45	0.34	0.08	0.14	0.43	0.70
Palate le.	0.24	0.06	0.58	0.36	0.14	0.21	0.18	-0.16	0.30	0.74
Bicondylar wi.	0.76	0.07	0.06	0.09	0.18	0.31	-0.08	0.08	0.29	0.83
Bigonial br.	0.52	0.32	0.04	0.04	0.01	-0.06	-0.06	0.11	0.52	0.67
Ramus ht.	0.26	0.11	-0.20	0.23	0.21	0.49	-0.11	0.03	0.30	0.56
Minimum ramus br.	0.02	0.19	0.18	0.14	-0.11	0.13	0.01	-0.05	0.78	0.73
Symphyseal ht.	0.22	0.37	0.21	0.29	0.16	0.58	0.03	-0.07	0.11	0.69
Pogonion-gonion le.	0.25	0.17	-0.01	0.30	0.10	0.07	-0.02	0.08	0.82	0.87
Mental foramen br.	0.27	0.03	-0.01	0.13	0.18	0.24	0.18	0.00	0.66	0.64
Minimum frontal br.	0.31	-0.04	-0.06	0.18	0.02	0.59	0.15	0.52	0.20	0.82
Maxillary intercanine br.	0.15	0.12	0.22	-0.01	0.59	0.09	0.17	0.05	0.46	0.67
Mandibular intercanine br.	0.26	0.09	-0.07	-0.04	0.72	0.08	0.26	-0.11	-0.06	0.68
M2	0.07	0.86	0.08	0.13	0.13	-0.04	0.06	0.09	0.08	0.80
M1	0.05	0.77	0.08	0.15	0.32	-0.14	0.13	0.23	0.04	0.82
P/	0.03	0.77	0.03	-0.08	-0.07	0.00	0.24	-0.08	0.05	0.67
P1	0.24	0.63	-0.27	-0.11	-0.15	0.03	-0.44	-0.18	0.14	0.81
C	0.30	0.50	-0.15	0.41	-0.05	-0.12	0.50	-0.01	0.03	0.79
I2	0.04	0.40	0.18	0.01	0.03	0.16	0.45	-0.16	-0.01	0.44
I1	0.01	0.39	-0.03	0.04	0.23	0.08	0.70	0.12	0.06	0.73
M2	0.04	0.84	0.02	0.14	0.06	0.10	0.10	0.07	0.20	0.79
M1	0.16	0.69	-0.17	0.09	0.24	0.20	0.22	0.04	0.23	0.75
P2	0.02	0.81	0.12	-0.11	-0.08	0.17	0.26	0.06	0.07	0.79
P1	0.24	0.63	-0.02	-0.07	-0.31	0.20	0.36	-0.07	0.14	0.74
C	0.32	0.55	-0.09	0.33	-0.03	0.00	0.49	-0.03	0.11	0.77
I2	-0.06	0.33	-0.02	-0.00	0.03	-0.16	0.76	0.13	0.10	0.74
I1	-0.08	0.27	0.01	0.08	0.22	0.02	0.71	-0.00	0.00	0.63
Trace	5.07	6.32	1.90	2.84	1.85	2.61	3.14	1.85	5.31	30.88
Per cent of common variance	16.4	20.5	6.1	9.2	6.0	8.4	10.2	6.0	17.2	

NB Communalities are for 9 factors

associated craniofacial and dental variables. Dimensions of the canines loaded on four craniofacial factors:

Cranial base breadth (Factor I, Table 2).   In the craniofacial-crown length analysis, this factor was correlated with the mesiodistal diameter of the maxillary and mandibular canines. They were the only teeth correlated with this factor.

Upper face height (Factor IV, Table 2).   This factor was correlated with the maxillary canine and the mandibular canine in the craniofacial-crown length analysis. No other teeth loaded on this factor; it may be relevant that the canine is the human tooth with the longest root (Wheeler, 1958). Two dimensions of the jaws also had moderate loadings on this factor: palate length and pognion-gonion length.

Facial massiveness (Factor III, Table 4). As described above, this factor was characterized by high loadings for lengths and breadths of the facial skeleton. The canines were the only teeth to correlate with this factor in the craniofacial-crown index analysis. The loading for the maxillary canine was moderate, while the correlation with the

TABLE 3

ROTATED FACTOR MATRIX OF CRANIOFACIAL MEASUREMENTS AND CROWN WIDTH

Variable	I	II	III	IV	V	VI	VII	VIII	IX	Communalities
Maximum cranial le.	0.24	0.21	0.22	0.15	0.02	0.14	0.56	0.14	0.46	0.75
Maximum cranial br.	0.13	0.08	0.40	-0.10	0.03	-0.05	-0.03	-0.07	0.73	0.74
Bizygomatic br.	0.18	0.17	0.80	0.22	0.14	0.24	0.24	0.06	0.21	0.93
Biauricular br.	0.09	0.15	0.80	0.05	0.16	0.10	0.19	0.09	0.32	0.85
Minimum cranial br.	0.03	0.11	0.64	0.24	0.13	0.07	-0.15	0.19	0.39	0.71
Bimaxillary br.	0.20	0.16	0.66	0.28	0.15	0.16	0.42	-0.00	-0.01	0.80
Basion-bregma ht.	0.14	0.29	0.31	-0.03	-0.05	0.20	0.35	0.27	0.61	0.80
Basion-nasion le.	0.19	0.19	0.32	0.35	-0.15	0.11	0.54	0.18	0.44	0.85
Basion-prosthion le.	0.11	0.12	0.17	0.67	0.10	0.05	0.50	0.03	0.17	0.80
Nasion-prosthion ht.	0.76	0.21	0.13	0.18	0.02	0.26	0.20	0.05	0.20	0.82
Nasion-gnathion ht.	0.53	0.29	0.25	0.14	0.01	0.57	0.24	0.10	0.22	0.90
Nasal ht.	0.80	0.06	0.22	0.09	-0.04	0.12	0.28	-0.03	0.13	0.81
Nasal br.	-0.09	-0.20	0.31	.0.58	0.14	0.01	0.12	0.12	0.03	0.53
Orbit ht.	0.45	-0.01	0.06	-0.45	0.21	-0.06	-0.09	0.18	0.17	0.52
Orbit br.	0.34	0.08	0.51	0.02	-0.01	-0.01	0.18	0.38	0.23	0.60
Interorbital br.	0.26	0.07	0.31	0.42	0.02	0.33	0.06	-0.27	0.27	0.60
Palate br.	0.21	0.13	0.42	0.24	0.40	0.31	0.27	0.06	0.21	0.67
Palate le.	0.26	0.29	0.25	0.75	0.15	0.09	0.17	0.04	-0.03	0.75
Bicondylar wi.	0.13	0.07	0.76	0.23	0.13	0.24	0.09	0.11	0.23	0.80
Bigonial br.	0.03	0.35	0.69	0.02	-0.03	0.04	0.37	0.05	0.01	0.75
Ramus ht.	0.18	-0.01	0.32	-0.08	0.12	0.67	0.25	0.08	0.13	0.70
Minimum ramus br.	0.17	0.30	0.19	0.28	-0.09	0.10	0.67	-0.03	-0.09	0.71
Symphyseal ht.	0.12	0.28	0.17	0.36	0.10	0.66	0.00	0.22	0.10	0.75
Pogonion-gonion le.	0.33	0.24	0.39	0.15	0.06	0.12	0.69	0.09	0.08	0.85
Mental foramen br.	0.26	0.18	0.33	0.28	0.22	0.11	0.43	0.20	0.10	0.58
Minimum frontal br.	0.27	0.11	0.25	0.16	0.06	0.34	0.06	0.00	0.67	0.74
Maxillary intercanine br.	-0.06	0.11	0.21	0.22	0.63	0.16	0.46	0.13	0.02	0.75
Mandibular intercanine br.	0.03	0.01	0.18	0.07	0.77	0.05	-0.12	0.15	-0.00	0.67
M2	0.05	0.84	0.03	0.08	0.08	0.14	0.16	0.06	0.05	0.78
M1	0.10	0.83	0.12	0.03	0.22	0.09	0.10	0.18	0.11	0.83
P2	0.09	0.83	0.12	0.09	-0.13	-0.04	0.05	-0.01	0.02	0.73
P1	0.03	0.80	0.17	0.09	-0.03	-0.19	-0.07	0.02	0.08	0.72
C	0.23	0.73	0.15	0.12	-0.03	0.03	0.10	0.45	0.07	0.84
I2	-0.07	0.38	0.17	0.14	0.05	0.23	0.01	0.58	-0.07	0.60
I1	0.02	0.65	0.11	0.04	0.26	-0.04	-0.08	0.43	-0.01	0.70
M2	0.03	0.82	-0.04	0.02	0.12	0.23	0.35	0.08	0.04	0.86
M1	-0.01	0.81	0.13	-0.01	0.24	0.19	0.16	0.14	0.13	0.82
P2	0.12	0.89	0.02	-0.01	-0.18	0.07	0.08	0.00	0.09	0.86
P1	-0.08	0.67	0.20	-0.10	-0.26	0.14	0.18	0.17	-0.00	0.65
C	0.24	0.63	0.21	0.03	0.08	0.08	0.19	0.44	0.19	0.78
I2	0.07	0.45	0.22	-0.04	0.25	0.06	0.11	0.69	0.10	0.81
I1	0.06	0.55	-0.01	-0.03	0.19	0.08	0.15	9.60	0.07	0.73
Trace	2.74	8.21	5.24	2.71	1.89	2.17	3.47	2.46	2.61	31.50
Per cent of common variance	8.7	26.1	16.6	8.6	6.0	6.9	11.0	7.9	8.3	

·NB Communalities are for 9 factors

TABLE 4

ROTATED FACTOR MATRIX OF CRANIOFACIAL MEASUREMENTS AND CROWN INDEX

Variable	I	II	III	IV	V	VI	VII	VIII	IX	X	XI	XII	Communalities
Maximum cranial le.	0.29	0.02	0.40	0.17	0.01	-0.02	0.29	0.08	0.00	0.61	0.12	0.20	0.79
Maximum cranial br.	0.61	-0.02	-0.06	-0.09	0.39	-0.05	0.12	-0.02	-0.00	0.42	0.02	-0.20	0.77
Bizygomatic br.	0.81	0.07	0.32	0.07	-0.00	0.02	0.20	0.12	-0.02	0.09	0.23	0.26	0.94
Biauricular br.	0.87	0.10	0.20	0.02	-0.01	-0.06	0.13	0.13	0.01	0.16	0.06	0.10	0.89
Minimum cranial br.	0.71	0.18	0.01	-0.19	0.24	0.06	0.07	0.21	-0.14	0.14	0.08	0.10	0.73
Bimaxillary br.	0.57	-0.00	0.55	-0.00	-0.09	0.11	0.18	0.15	0.06	-0.00	0.20	0.26	0.81
Basion-bregma ht.	0.45	0.16	0.25	0.00	-0.05	0.08	0.19	0.01	-0.05	0.68	0.12	-0.05	0.82
Basion-nasion le.	0.41	0.12	0.37	-0.04	0.06	-0.00	0.31	-0.13	0.10	0.55	0.05	0.37	0.90
Basion-prosthion ht.	0.19	-0.03	0.42	-0.14	0.04	-0.02	0.25	0.10	0.15	0.26	0.02	0.65	0.82
Nasion-prosthion ht.	0.20	0.05	0.24	-0.06	0.13	0.07	0.80	0.05	0.02	0.18	0.21	0.03	0.84
Nasion-gnathion ht.	0.30	0.14	0.32	-0.16	0.03	0.00	0.64	0.07	-0.01	0.22	0.46	0.03	0.92
Nasal ht.	0.27	-0.11	0.20	0.20	-0.08	-0.08	0.78	-0.06	-0.06	0.13	0.07	0.09	0.82
Nasal br.	0.26	-0.03	0.10	0.08	-0.00	0.12	-0.15	0.12	-0.08	0.03	0.08	0.64	0.55
Orbit ht.	0.11	-0.04	-0.13	0.20	-0.25	0.25	0.25	0.34	-0.00	0.21	-0.03	-0.48	0.65
Orbit br.	0.57	0.08	0.12	0.05	-0.26	-0.02	0.32	0.08	0.07	0.28	-0.01	0.04	0.60
Interorbital br.	0.29	-0.12	0.15	-0.01	0.20	0.31	0.20	0.01	-0.33	0.12	0.42	0.36	0.74
Palate br.	0.41	0.04	0.38	0.03	0.07	0.02	0.23	0.48	-0.02	0.14	0.26	0.16	0.72
Palate le.	0.14	0.06	0.22	-0.14	0.08	0.07	0.41	0.20	0.02	-0.00	-0.02	0.69	0.79
Bicondylar wi.	0.76	0.12	0.12	0.14	-0.11	0.08	0.13	0.15	-0.07	0.10	0.26	0.31	0.87
Bigonial br.	0.62	0.16	0.60	0.01	0.05	0.01	0.03	-0.08	-0.03	0.01	-0.00	0.02	0.78
Ramus ht.	0.34	0.05	0.21	0.05	-0.28	-0.02	0.23	0.07	0.01	0.10	0.67	-0.01	0.75
Minimum ramus br.	0.08	0.04	0.78	-0.02	0.08	0.09	0.19	-0.13	0.04	0.10	0.13	0.21	0.76
Symphyseal ht.	0.15	0.35	0.16	-0.30	0.07	-0.03	0.32	0.25	-0.04	0.10	0.48	0.22	0.73
Pogonion-gonion le.	0.32	0.07	0.73	0.15	-0.04	0.06	0.36	0.09	-0.07	0.24	0.03	0.14	0.88
Mental foramen br.	0.26	0.05	0.56	0.09	0.00	0.23	0.24	0.32	-0.08	0.20	0.06	0.18	0.69
Minimum frontal br.	0.40	-0.12	-0.01	0.05	0.21	0.18	0.21	0.10	0.00	0.53	0.50	0.09	0.84
Maxillary intercanine br.	0.21	0.08	0.47	-0.14	-0.03	-0.19	-0.01	0.52	0.26	0.07	0.15	0.24	0.75
Mandibular intercanine br.	0.20	-0.05	-0.04	-0.08	-0.13	-0.56	-0.04	0.76	-0.12	-0.03	0.03	0.09	0.67
M2	-0.05	0.07	0.07	0.08	0.05	0.81	0.03	-0.02	0.16	0.04	-0.02	0.06	0.70
M1	0.08	0.17	0.05	0.05	0.03	0.78	0.11	-0.07	0.26	-0.03	0.04	0.00	0.74
P2	0.18	-0.02	0.12	0.32	0.37	0.17	0.22	-0.23	-0.41	-0.02	0.10	-0.04	0.60
P1	0.01	0.08	0.04	0.17	0.81	0.09	0.03	-0.10	0.12	0.02	-0.08	0.12	0.75
C	-0.04	0.51	0.37	0.05	0.15	0.48	-0.07	-0.01	-0.01	0.22	0.12	0.09	0.73
I2	0.13	0.30	0.09	0.57	-0.02	0.26	-0.06	0.09	0.05	0.13	-0.07	0.05	0.55
I1	0.11	0.73	-0.01	0.04	0.08	0.20	0.04	0.02	0.05	-0.10	-0.21	-0.04	0.64
M2̲	-0.10	-0.09	0.04	0.11	-0.02	0.19	-0.01	0.04	0.60	-0.00	0.06	-0.02	0.54
M1̲	0.00	0.17	-0.05	-0.01	0.18	0.20	-0.02	-0.11	0.54	0.03	-0.14	0.05	0.43
P2̲	-0.02	-0.03	0.01	0.55	0.14	0.11	0.41	-0.28	0.28	-0.02	-0.06	-0.18	0.70
P1̲	-0.10	0.28	0.13	0.65	0.16	-0.04	-0.01	-0.08	0.05	0.01	0.03	-0.08	0.56
C̲	0.05	0.40	0.30	0.23	0.25	0.30	-0.03	0.15	0.12	0.35	0.12	-0.05	0.63
I2̲	0.21	0.67	-0.02	0.37	0.06	-0.00	0.06	0.13	-0.12	-0.05	0.15	0.03	0.69
I1̲	0.11	0.61	0.10	0.13	-0.12	0.02	-0.04	-0.20	0.07	0.19	0.13	-0.00	0.52
Trace	5.65	2.37	3.85	1.82	1.58	2.18	3.18	1.89	1.45	2.35	1.85	2.47	30.67
Per cent of common variance	18.4	7.7	12.6	5.9	5.2	7.1	10.4	6.1	4.7	7.7	6.0	8.1	

NB Communalities are for 12 factors

mandibular canine was low but substantially higher than the loadings for the other teeth.

Cranial vault size (Factor X, Table 4).   Also in the craniofacial-crown index analysis, the mandibular canine correlated with cranial vault size, which indicates the extensive range of integration between the craniofacial skeleton and the canines.

The factors described above indicate that certain dimensions of the canines are integrated with development of the facial skeleton, cranial base and cranial vault. Some craniofacial factors had loadings with other teeth, although they did not form a consistent pattern:

Facial massiveness (Factor VII, Table 3). This factor in the cranio-facial-crown width analysis had its strongest loadings for mandibular dimensions. In addition, the crown width of the mandibular second molar correlated with the factor. As noted earlier, when the craniofacial dimensions were factored separately, maxillary intercanine breadth had a strong loading on *facial massiveness*.

Dental arch breadth (Factor V, Table 2). In the craniofacial-crown length analysis, the mesiodistal diameter of the maxillary first molar correlated with intercanine breadth. Inexplicably, the crown length of the mandibular first premolar had a negative loading on this factor.

Jaw size (Factor VII, Table 4). This craniofacial factor was identified only in the craniofacial-crown index analysis. It is characterized by high loadings for dimensions of the maxilla and mandible, especially but not exclusively the vertical dimensions of the jaws. The crown index of the mandibular second premolar loaded on this factor that seems to reflect jaw size.

Five factors of predominantly a dental nature had loadings for craniofacial dimensions:

General tooth size (Factor II, Tables 2 and 3). This factor was identified in both the craniofacial-crown length and craniofacial-crown width analyses. It is characterized by correlations with teeth in all regions, although there appears to be a diminishing posterior-anterior gradient. Two mandibular dimensions are, in part, secondary to and dependent on tooth size: symphyseal height and bigonial breadth, although the former loaded weakly in the crown width analysis. Minimum ramus breadth also loaded in the crown width analysis.

Anterior tooth size (Factor VIII, Table 3). The second factor associated with tooth size found in both the crown length and crown width analyses had a high correlation with the anterior teeth and to a lesser extent, with regard to crown length only, with the first premolars. The meaning of this factor *per se* is not clear; however, when considered with the factor for general tooth size, there seems to be a tendency for tooth size to differentiate along an anterior-posterior axis. In the crown width analysis, orbit breadth loaded on this factor, suggesting integration between orbit breadth and anterior crown width.

Anterior tooth crown index (Factor II, Table 4). This factor had high loadings for the upper and lower incisors and canines, with the maxillary lateral incisor loading the least. Also, symphyseal height correlated with this factor; greater symphyseal height seems to be associated with anterior teeth which have a high crown index. This factor would appear to be similar to the factor of *anterior tooth size* found in the crown length and crown width analyses.

Maxillary premolar crown index (Factor V, Table 4).   The upper first premolar had the highest loading on this factor, with the second premolar loading less intensely; but maximum cranial breadth also loaded on this factor, with a slightly higher correlation than that of the second premolar. This factor suggests an association between wide upper premolars and maximum cranial breadth. The zero-order correlation coefficient between the maxillary first premolar and maximum cranial breadth was 0.29 (p < 0.01).

Maxillary molar crown index (Factor VI, Table 4).   This factor was identified by its high loadings for the maxillary molars, especially the second molar, but interorbital breadth also had a moderate correlation.

Finally, it is of interest on what factors dental measures did not load. In this study, *maxillary prognathism* was independent of any of the dental variables. Solow (1966) found maxillary prognathism to be associated with arch circumference, but he also found a factor of maxillary prognathism independent of dental variables. In addition, *dental arch breadth* did not correlate strongly with crown dimensions, although the crown length of the maxillary first molar had a moderate positive correlation. Solow identified the same factor but found it associated with maxillary arch circumference.

Discussion

The purpose of this study was to ascertain the patterning of the statistical associations between dimensions of the teeth and craniofacial skeleton by means of factor analysis. For the most part, the craniofacial factors described here correspond to those found in previous investigations. Differences seem largely attributable to the variation in the kind and number of measurements considered. It should be noted too that factors are mathematical models of biologic organization and as such they are subject to modification or rejection in the light of new information. Nonetheless, the results of this study indicate that there are factors which integrate the dental and craniofacial skeletal systems.

The *interorbital breadth* factor appears at first inspection to be simply a factor of the craniofacial skeleton; however, when the craniofacial dimensions were factored with the dental variables, the *interorbital breadth* factor disappeared and the component variables loaded on other factors. Minimum frontal breadth loaded on *lower face height* in the crown length and crown index analyses, and it loaded with *cranial vault size* in the crown width analysis. Nasal breadth loaded more highly on *maxillary prognathism* in the crown width and crown index analyses, but on *cranial breadth* in the crown length analysis. Interorbital breadth itself follows minimum frontal breadth and correlates with *lower face height* in the crown length and crown index analyses and follows nasal breadth in loading on the *maxillary prognathism* factor in the crown width analysis. In summary, it appears that in certain circumstances minimum frontal breadth, nasal breadth and interorbital breadth are related to dimensions of the lower face and, indirectly, to dental dimensions.

Other craniofacial factors manifested direct associations with dental dimensions. The factors *cranial base breadth, facial massiveness, upper face height* and *cranial vault size* had loadings for canine dimensions. *Facial massiveness* and *dental arch breadth* were associated with molar size, and premolar size was correlated with *dental arch breadth* and *jaw size* factors. Dimensions of the incisors did not load significantly on any craniofacial factor. It may be inferred that since the loadings clearly identify the factors as factors of the craniofacial skeleton with secondary dental correlations, the dimensions of individual teeth *may* be dependent upon the size of the craniofacial skeleton. (While cause-effect relationships can not be ascertained from statistical tests of association, the factors are suggestive of the possibility.) Of the individual teeth, the size of the canines seems to relate to and reflect most intensely craniofacial dimensions. Moreover, the skeletal parameters that correlate with canine size are general in nature and not necessarily topographically associated with the canines: *cranial base breadth,* which in terms of common variance determined is statistically the most important factor; *facial massiveness,* which is characterized by overall size of the facial skeleton, predominantly but not exclusively dimensions of the mandible and maxilla; *upper face height,* with which the roots of the maxillary canines are associated topographically; and *cranial vault size,* which is most probably a function of brain development. Crown dimensions of the canines thus appear related to overall size of the craniofacial skeleton. The molar and premolar associations are less clear, but they seem to reflect some integration with the craniofacial skeleton.

Where skeletal dimensions appear secondary to dental factors, it is apparent that dimensions of the mandible correlate most frequently and load on the factors that account for the most variance. The factors which correlate symphyseal height, bigonial breadth and ramus breadth of the mandible with individual tooth dimensions account for up to 26.1 per cent of the common variance in their systems. In the maxilla, the degree of integration is less; craniofacial-dental integration was on a single factor that accounts for only 7.5 per cent of the variance: palate breadth was correlated with intercanine breadth.

Dimensions more remote to the dentition have correspondingly less association with individual tooth dimensions. Orbit breadth correlated with crown width on a factor which accounted for 7.9 per cent of the common variance. The factor which correlated interorbital breadth with the crown index of the maxillary molars determined 7.1 per cent of the variance, and maximum cranial breadth loaded with the crown index of the upper premolars on a factor responsible for 5.2 per cent of the common variance.

Overall, it seems that dimensions on the mandible are most closely associated with tooth dimensions, followed by those on the maxilla and by dimensions on the upper face and cranial vault. In general, the parts of the craniofacial skeleton nearest to the dentition had the highest dimensional associations and the anterior face had more than the deeper structures.

The craniofacial dimensions noted varied in a positive relationship with crown length, crown width and the crown index. While it is easy to believe that increased crown length and crown width might be accompanied by larger craniofacial dimensions, the association with the crown index is less obvious. It may be that the crown index, that is, the relative width of a tooth, measures more than tooth shape and is correlated with occlusal area, thus reflecting the amount of chewing surface on the tooth, but this is open for further study.

It is likely that the increased dimensions secondary to tooth size found in this study represent a strengthening of the skeleton to withstand and dissipate the masticatory stresses that arise from the greater occlusal area of larger teeth. If this is so, it remains to be determined whether the increased skeletal dimensions are a consequence of individual development related to functional experience or whether they are population adaptations resulting from selection pressures.

These findings are largely in agreement with Moss' functional matrix concept of skeletal development (Moss and Young, 1960). Moss (1960, 1964) asserts that the dentition comprises a functional matrix which bears on mandibular development, but development of the maxilla is influenced primarily by the functional matrix that relates to respiration, with the teeth a subordinate influence. Dimensions of the teeth in this study related more with dimensions of the mandible than with those of the maxilla, which accords with Moss' hypothesis.

The significance of the secondary associations of canine size with general dimensions of the craniofacial skeleton is unclear. The canines are the teeth with the greatest sexual dimorphism in size, but whether this is a consequence of differences in skeletal size as this study would appear to suggest is yet to be proved. The necessary inclusion of both sexes in the same analysis obscures any direct inferences.

In short, some of the factors that seemingly identify developmental axes of the craniofacial skeleton were correlated with crown dimensions of the canines and, to a much less extent, molar and premolar dimensions. Conversely, the dental factors that apparently bear on development of the dentition as a whole were most closely integrated with mandibular dimensions, followed by the parts of the craniofacial skeleton nearest to the dentition. This suggests that development of the dentition and of the craniofacial skeleton influences each other in independent ways that are related to different adaptive or functional mechanisms.

Finally, to maintain proper perspective, it should be recognized that the correlations between craniofacial and dental dimensions account for only a small portion of the dimensional variance in the two organ systems. The craniofacial skeleton and the teeth are relatively independent developmentally. Compared to the skeleton the teeth have virtually no ontogeny, since the crown dimensions of all the permanent teeth except the third molars are determined by age six (Wheeler, 1958); whereas the skeleton has yet to achieve its growth spurt, and growth will continue actively for another decade.

Bibliography

Brown, T.
1967 Skull of the Australian Aboriginal. A Multivariate Analysis of Craniofacial Associations. Dept. of Dent. Science, University of Adelaide, Adelaide.
Brown, T., M. J. Barrett and J. N. Darroch
1965 Craniofacial factors in two ethnic groups. Growth, *29:* 109-123.
Filipsson, R. and L. Goldson
1963 Correlation between tooth width, width of the head, length of the head, and stature. Acta Odont. Scand., *21:* 359-365.
Garn, S. M. and A. B. Lewis
1958 Tooth size, body size and "giant" fossil man. Am. Anthrop., *60:* 874-880.
Garn, S. M., A. B. Lewis and R. S. Kerewsky
1968 The magnitude and implications of the relationship between tooth size and body size. Archs. Oral Biol., *13:* 129-131.

Howells, W. W.
1951   Factors of human physique. Am. J. Phys. Anthrop., *9:* 159-192.

1957   The cranial vault: factors of size and shape. Am. J. Phys. Anthrop., *15:* 19-48.

1972   Analysis of patterns of variation in crania of recent man. In: The Functional and Evolutionary Biology of Primates. R. H. Tuttle, ed. Aldine- Atherton, Chicago, pp. 123-151.

Kanda, S. and K. Kurisu
1967   Factor analytic studies on the Japanese skulls. Med. J. Osaka Univ., *18:* 1-9.

1968   Factor analysis of Japanese skulls, part 2. Med. J. Osaka Univ., *18:* 315-318.

Kanda, S.
1968   Factor analysis of Japanese skulls, part 3. Med. J. Osaka Univ., *18:* 319-330.

Landauer, C. A.
1962   A factor analysis of the facial skeleton. Hum. Biol., *34:* 239-253.

Moss, M. L.
1960   Functional analysis of human mandibular growth. J. Pros. Dent., *10:* 1149-1159.

1964   Vertical growth of the human face. Am. J. Orthodontics, *50:* 359-376.

Moss, M. L. and R. W. Young
1960   A functional approach to craniology. Am. J. Phys. Anthrop., *18:* 281-292.

Schwidetzky, I.
1960   Faktoren des Schädelbaus bei der vorspanischen Bevölkerung der Kanarischen Inseln. Homo, *10:* 237-246.

Solow, B.
1966   The Pattern of Craniofacial Associations. A morphological and methodological correlation and factor analysis study on young adult males. Acta Odont. Scand., *24:* supplement 46, Copenhagen.

Wheeler, R. C.
1958   A Textbook of Dental Anatomy and Physiology. 3rd ed., W. B. Saunders Co., Philadelphia.

19. The Study of Cranial Form: Measurement Techniques and Analytical Methods

Thomas Mercer Hursh

Introduction

The history of the study of cranial form has seen a variety of innovative ideas. The bulk of these have been new measurements or new methods for measurement or analysis. However, cranial measurements taken today still conform in large part to the Frankfort Convention of 1882 and their analysis is chiefly characterized by univariate tests. The purpose of the discussion which follows will be to examine many of the proposals for measurement procedures and analytic methods with respect to their utility, meaning, and possible implementation within Biological Anthropology. The focus will be on the interaction between measurement techniques, analytic procedures, the data to be measured, the problems posed, and the overall set of structured expectations which the experimenter might have.

The background against which my own observations ought to be viewed involves at least two assumptions. Firstly, the specific historical development of a field is an important area of study in itself; a great deal can be learned about the current state of a field from its historical progression. The "culture" of the scientist is itself an important factor in his perception and analysis of data. Secondly, the role of measurement in the biological and physical sciences is quite different. The physical scientist tends to believe that the data which he observes have some special value in and of themselves. This value is derived from their repeatability, lending them a semblence of absoluteness or "truth" so that even if the researcher makes no "great" advances he has at least contributed to our store of "true" things known about the world. The expectation of extensibility is founded on a belief in the logic and order of the universe and assures the experimenter that his "facts" have potential utility for higher order observations on the laws of the universe. However, the biological scientist is possessed of no similar security. The ecosystem-specific and ideohistorical influences on any given organism or population are so unique that no biological scientist can be assured of repeatability or extensibility except in the most trivial cases. One might say that it is this uncertainty, this unpredictability, more than any other single factor which defines a living organism and the higher the organism the more unpredictable. Thus, the biological scientist must be extremely careful in the choice of his methods and area of study if he is to hope to acquire repeatable or extensible information at all.

The Historical Development of the Measurement Problem

The earliest descriptive or classificatory systems were based upon the philosophical foundation of Aristotelean science. Each natural group was recognizable as a group because of some common ideal configuration which the individual organisms approximated. It was their conformity to this ideal that made them recognizable as members of the group. Deviations from this ideal were seen more as errors than as a desirable part of the natural scheme. The attributes of this ideal were often left quite imprecise or were concerned with the features which distinguished similar groups. The main parameters were often not discussed or considered interesting since they were thought to be obvious to any observer. Furthermore these ideals were seen as being more "real" than the physical manifestations of the group members, since their variation was "error." Finally, these ideals were perceived as invariate over time. (Russell, 1945; Aristotle, 1910).

Whatever deviations might have existed in Greece away from this 'ideal'-oriented system largely disappeared under the influence of the Romans and the Medieval church. Jointly they added the justification of divine sanctification to this perceived order, so that the thought of a changing or blending nature became heretical (Russell, 1945; Pliny, 1893; Lyell, 1835; Alphonin, 1781). Description of natural forms during this period was relatively simple since it was merely necessary to class a new specimen as either another example of an existing group, an example of a previously unrecognized group, or a monster. The ideal was known and obvious and errors were unfortunate deviations introduced by the profane world on a divine order.

The age of exploration produced something of a crisis in classification. It was no longer obvious to the observer where the boundary lines lay between diverse groups and how large a collection ought to be considered representative of a single taxon. Since the Aristotelean model of the world still persisted, this developing science of taxonomy focused on the derivation of simple measures which would aid the eye in forming the categories which were "known" to exist in nature. (Linnaeus, 1781; Cuvier, 1829).

These measures and the analytic methods which accompanied them did not meet with resounding success. In many cases simple measures of skin color, head length, stature, and the like imposed divisions on natural variation which ran counter to the intuitive judgments of the observer with respect to the overall "racial" affiliation of the groups (Penniman, 1935). This led to developments both in the complexity of analytical and measurement method as scientists realized that biological variation was inadequately described by simple distances and angles. Most of these surface or volume oriented methods arose "in vacuo" with respect to the preparedness of the scientific community to analyze the data they gathered. The main thrust of measurement and analysis was focused on the more well understood area of conventional statistics. It is undoubtedly not coincidental that conventional statistics are founded upon the notion of the central tendency, with what seems often only a grudging concession to the fact of variance. Central tendency is of course quite reminiscent of the Aristotelean 'ideal.'

One very important factor in the development of biological measurement has been the complexion of the analytic methods available and the culture or goals of the investigators. During an era in which variation is uninteresting and analysis is essentially limited to the trait list, little measurement exists. When measurement is needed to solve a classificatory dilemma it arises, but the main thrust is confined to measures of discrimination. Researchers were at one time confident that simple centroids must exist since the model was so obviously correct. This simple solution to the descriptive problem was not confirmed and analytic procedures were pushed toward greater complexity, but the foundation model remained essentially intact. It might be worth noting that even the evolutionists were often trapped into this conformity. One notable exception was Lamarck:

"these . . . devices, commonly used in natural science, are purely artifical aids which we have to use in the arrangement and division of the various observed natural productions; to put us in the way of studying, comparing, recognizing, and citing them. Nature has made nothing of the kind: and instead of deceiving ourselves into confusing our works with hers, we should recognize that Classes, Orders, Families, Genera, and nomenclatures are weapons of our own invention." (Lamarck, 1914 (1808)).

Simple Distances, Angles, And Indices

Naturally enough, the first measures to arise were quite simple in terms of definition, equipment, and/or analysis. The original core of biological measurements parallels the kinds of measurements already derived in the physical sciences. The foundation of modern craniometry is based on measures such as length, width, height, and distances connecting distinguishing features. For the purpose of discussion these can be considered as being in three classes.

The first class might be called the box measurements. These measures treat the skull as a sort of box or container whose size is to be determined. All of these are measures of the extremes of the skull rather than being oriented toward specific points. One end of the caliper may be placed on a defined point by convention, but the other end is typically moved back and forth until the largest distance is found. In a number of cases, such as cranial breadth, both ends are free to move with only the orientation of the caliper being defined as fixed. This class of measures must be regarded with some suspicion in modern Biological Anthropology as the value of size as a taxonomic indicator has been questioned in recent years. (Lovejoy et al, 1973; Wolpoff, 1973). Any Anthropologist with experience in measuring skulls is aware that changes in skull form often result in strange deviations in these measures and in the migrations of the points they are based upon. This uncertainty is clear when one tries to make comparisons across taxa boundaries. In many cases the changes in shape of the cranium result in a box type measurement being taken across two very different regions of the skull. Comparability and/or equivalency are lost in such measurement situations.

The second class might be called the sutural measurements. These are derived from the distance between two points, at least one of which is defined by a suture line or similar feature. Suture lines, foramina, notches and the like appear with some frequency in the definitions of measurements. The justification is that these features provide readily identifiable landmarks upon which to fix the calipers; they provide repeatability. At first glance such features seem to offer a welcome aid to measurement since, being fine lines or points, they are often fairly unambiguous locaters of position. They might also appeal as reflecting some biologically or structurally significant feature of the skull. For example, the meeting point of the sagittal and lambdoid sutures is a sort of centroid of three growth centers. However, some of this appeal disappears in skulls whose sutures have closed so completely that their location has been eradicated, or whose intrasutural bones mock the convenience of the suture's fine line. Any experienced osteometrist will have experienced at least one, and probably many, skulls which were overall quite normal in appearance, but which possessed some "anomaly" which rendered one of the measurements on that skull less than faithful to its intent. Various conventions have arisen to deal with the more frequent problems (this alone testifies to their frequency), but one can easily question, by Occam's razor, a procedure which requires such patching.

The third class of measures is those that are based upon points defined by extremes of curvature, or regions of maximum change in curvature. Superficially these points seem to be just as prey to hazard as the former two classes, and to some degree this is of course true. However, the worst that can happen to a point defined by curvature is that there is no curvature or the change in curvature is flat or uniform. However, this uncertainty as to the location of the point is not necessarily as bad as it might seem, nor in my experience is it as frequent an occurrence as the problems associated with sutures and foramina. These points are also those which hold the most information about the shape of the skull. This is perhaps most easily understood if one thinks in terms of predicting one part of a skull when one knows another part. If an area is relatively uniform, i.e., the shape of the curve is consistent, then knowing the shape in one place will give one a high degree of ability to predict it in another place. Knowing the center and one point on the surface of a sphere one can "predict" all of the other points. If a surface is highly variable then one's ability to predict drops off accordingly. Additional points located in regions of sharp change in curvature tell the most about the shape of the curve; they have the highest information value. It would seem that distances which were based on this class of points should themselves in turn have the highest information value. Points which are located by means of sharp changes in curvature are in practice just as precise as the sutural or foraminal ones. Points which on a given specimen happen to fall on a region of gradual or even curvature might seem to provide a dubious basis for a distance determination. However, if the distance is taken more or less perpendicular to the surface, then the uncertainty over the exact location of the point will have little effect on the distance derived. For example, when determining head length according to the usual technique the exact point on the occipital is not too important since the distance will not be greatly affected by minor movements around the region. Thus, while the points of this class might seem to have some special appeal it is clear that they too can be problematic, especially when used to define distances.

In addition to the use of these three classes of points to define distance measurements, they are also used to measure angles and indirectly for the derivation of indices. Some practitioners favor the use of angles and ratios very highly over simple distances on the argument that they are more indicative of proportion and structure and thus more useful in taxonomy than are distances (Lovejoy et al, 1973; Wolpoff, 1973).

Angles have been used primarily to judge the relative positions of cranial parts or the nature of their attachment. For example, the facial angle is a measure of the relationship the face has with the rest of the skull and the gonial angle relates the jaw and perhaps the masticatory musculature to the skull. Indices have been used to judge the relative proportions of cranial parts, either as a measure of shape or indirectly of function.

Indices and angles might be intrinsically superior to distances as a measure of skull form in some ways, but they are derived from the distances and subject to their same foibles. If an index is computed as a porportion of two distances and those two distances are based on suture lines which are not comparable across taxa boundaries then the index is not likely to be comparable across taxa boundaries. If the distances used have no biological significance, if they vary randomly in a population, or if there is so large an individual variation that functional differences can not be perceived, then the same is likely to be true of the index derived from them.

In recent years a number of authors have made a clear effort to sharpen their evaluation and to increase the information value of their measurements. This is perhaps most clearly indicated in concern over biological function. Results now seem more often readily interpretable in terms of the capabilities and operation of the organism compared with the more hollow statistics of yesteryear. I would, however, like to question whether this has also meant a substantial improvement in the quality of our vision of evolutionary realities. Certainly functional performance is one of the base understandings necessary to evaluate the evolutionary record, but what of our understanding of the nature and pattern of variation? The question of function is probably one which can be studied with considerable effect with quite simple measures and analysis. Whether the question of patterns of variation is best explored in this way is not so clear.

COORDINATE POINTS

One simple alternative technique is the direct acquisition of two- or three-dimensional coordinates of the points to be measured, the locations of the points themselves being the data, not the means to the data (e.g., Giles, 1971). This technique does imply the need for different equipment, with its associated expense. However, this equipment can be quite simple, such as a diagraph and simple coordinate plane. This instrument has a needle which can be placed on the point to be measured. A vertical scale measures the height over the coordinate plane. A second needle, fixed so that it is perpendicularly below the measurement needle, touches the coordinate plane, providing two additional coordinates. This device is neither significantly more expensive than anthropometric calipers nor particularly difficult to use. Another more expensive but probably more convenient and useful device is the acoustical tablet (Irwin and LaJeunesse, 1973). One should expect that current technological developments will provide a number of alternative devices with rapidly falling costs.

In my own experience, if the point set is well defined to begin with, many points turn out to be less ambiguous than corresponding measurements. For example, prosthion typically varies in position according to the convenience of caliper placement for the particular measurement (facial or basal) from the front to the underside of the alveolar margin. When placing a needle this kind of directional ambiguity is more or less eliminated. Needless to say, considerable variance in possible patterns of the use of points exists, from the simple application of traditional points to the definition of totally new points based on new criteria. If the former extreme is followed then the possible virtues of the coordinate point method are limited to the conveniences of the procedure itself. If new points are included, as well as redefinition of old points, then important parameters to be measured could be easier to define with points than with distances, since one can concentrate directly on the features of interest without concern for an opposing point on which to base a measurement.

The major question about the utility of coordinate points relates to their analysis, if they are to be considered as locations, not the limits of distances. The possibilities in this regard will be discussed in the section on analysis, but it is possible to mention one way in which they can be used as a simple alternative to traditional caliper measurements. This is through the conversion of the data after acquisition from locations into a set of interpoint distances. A large number of distances can thus be produced in a relatively small measurement period. The number of possible distances produced is given by the formula:

$$D = \frac{P x\,(P\text{-}1)}{2}$$

Where 'D' is the number of distances produced and 'P' is the number of points used. For example, if 50 points are used then 1225 distances will result. Whether or not this is considered an advantage depends in large part on the analysis intended and the opinion of how meaningful all the derived distances might be. One might have some questions about the accuracy of this method since the distances are computed. I have tested this with some of my own data and found that the confidence level on the derived distances is about plus or minus 2 millimeters, a figure which is certainly adequate for most work and in fact exceeds the repeatability of many workers with caliper derived measurements.

The use of coordinate points has a certain appeal since it allows a more direct conceptualization of the form of the cranium in terms of the locations and relations of its defining features. Certainly the information content of the points which can be gathered in a given time interval greatly exceeds the information content of the measurements which could be taken in the same period, especially when one considers all of the angles, indices, surfaces and volumes which are defined by the points in addition to the distances. The chief obstacle would seem to be in retrieving any significant amount of this information, a matter which will be discussed further under analytic techniques. Blind acquisition of points as data is of course no more virtuous than measurement of distances since in neither case has the tool been invested with the meaning which only careful consideration can provide.

Surface Determining Methods

Interest in this category of measurement is derived from the same disappointment with simple measures which produced more elaborate analysis techniques, only here the proposed solution complicates the measurement process. The basis of these, as well as later techniques, lies in an attempt to extract a more complete representation of the measured object. The empirical limitation has been the expense of the equipment required and the apparent lack of analytic procedures adequate to make significant use of the greater information extracted. These still are a set of aspirant procedures rather than a realized set despite the fact that some of them have existed for some time. In a few cases the problem is one of projected, but not fulfilled, technological developments.

CONTOURING TECHNIQUES

This group makes linear or planar extractions from the object in much the same way that coordinate points are a point-based extraction or representation of the object. In both cases the purpose of the technique is to derive a representation of the object which is simplified from the object itself, but which maximizes the information content of the extraction.

All of the techniques are based upon some manipulation of light as a means of measurement. Light has several possible advantages over calipers as well as some potential weaknesses. The property of light which makes it usable as a measurement vehicle is the combination of its high speed and tendency to travel in a straight line under non-refractive conditions. Light passing around or bouncing off a subject forms a remote "description" of a subject. The differences between these procedures lie principally in the nature of the manipulation of the light in order to control the nature of the equivalency. One advantage is that the contact period with the specimen is reduced since the representation is captured photographically for later analysis. Some doubt has been raised in the literature about the virtues of photographs as a measurement intermediary (Clarke and Howell, 1972), but this criticism can only be directed at non-standardized processes and poor quality reproductions since the potential error factor of photogammetry on skull-size objects is on the order of a fraction of a millimeter.

Perhaps the greatest obstacle to these procedures is the problem of the analysis of the data they generate. Only volume and distance information has been relatively easy to extract. This represents such a severe condensation of the information extracted that the greater expense of the procedure seems hardly justified. To this point then, these procedures have been successful mostly as a kind of elegant display mechanism rather than a serious measurement tool in craniometry.

SHADOW PROFILES

The basis of this procedure is the derivation of profiles of the object to be measured from several different perspectives. The techniques of shadow outlines has a long history in craniometry and related sciences, principally as a means of deriving distance measurements in a particular plane, such as the sagittal, which are not so easily gauged on the real specimen. Frequently, of course, it is a part of the procedure by which scale drawings are produced. Its use to describe whole rounded contours depends on the taking of several of these shadow profiles from different perspectives which can later be assembled into a whole. If one imagines slicing an object in several planes, and making a cardboard model of each section, and then fitting together the cardboard pieces in the orientations corresponding to the relative direction of cut, one gets something of an idea of how the procedure might work. The effect is rather like a Thanksgiving crepe foldout decoration which comes flat but unfolds to make a three-dimensional turkey or pilgrim. Another similar technique, known as *Lichtschnitteverfahren,* uses the projection of thin slits of light perpendicular to the line of sight to define the contours (Stenger, 1939).

There are two serious limitations to these techniques other than the general ones referred to above. The approach is not capable of representing negative (concave) contours such as the sockets of the eye, since light is blocked from passing through those regions from all directions. Also the technique utilizes multiple events for measurement, i.e., turning the camera or specimen between each profile, and this raises a serious problem of fitting together the images with confidence.

STEREOCONTOURING

The process of stereocontouring on a biological specimen is essentially the same as that utilized for the production of contour maps. Two or more photographs are taken from known orientations. These photographs are subsequently projected by specialized equipment which restores the orientation of the taking cameras. The image that results varies in its point of focus according to the differences of height in the original specimen. The trained operator can follow this point of focus with a special device along lines of equal elevation. These correspond to the contour lines. In its established and conventional form this procedure can be carried to rather high degrees of accuracy; on the order of 99% confidence of being within one contour interval. The possible size of the contour interval varies with the equipment and situation, but frequently it is quite reasonable to talk of an interval of one or at most a few millimeters for the largest objects. This clearly is competitive with caliper measurement (Gruner, 1970; Herron, 1972).

One of the possible limitations of this technique is the expense of the projection apparatus, but often local Departments of Geography or map making firms will have this equipment and will allow its use for far less than the purchase price. The expense problem with respect to the camera equipment is, however, potentially serious; little work has been done on the production of lightweight and less expensive devices for the biological sciences. Certainly even an optimistic estimate would have to be in the thousands of dollars. Another less serious limitation is the availability of adequately trained operators, since it is now possible to make the extraction of the contour lines by computer. This implies its own expense and difficulties, but the most serious question is what to do with contour lines once you have them.

INFERROMETRIC AND MOIRE FRINGE CONTOURING

These two procedures are like stereocontouring except that a projection is made upon the subject itself as a means of determining the shape of the surface. Both use a kind of projection which produces a change in the visible pattern based on the height of the viewed or reflective object. In its simplest and least effective form one can imagine the use of projection of a grid on the object to be measured. The appearance of this grid would be distorted by the differences in elevation of the object. The use of interference patterns, which are the kind of striped patterns one sees in oil slicks, as a sensitive measure of distortion has a well developed history in physics and chemistry. However, its chief utility lies in the measurement of extremely small distances or changes such as those that might be measured in angstroms or microns, rather than in centimeters. While I am not aware of any extensive testing of it as a biometric technique my expectation is that the problems of the varying reflective characteristics of bone, bone's rather rough surface, the need for a different sort of accuracy, and its expense limit its probable utility.

Another approach of the same sort is the use of moire fringe patterns to provide a varying pattern on the surface of the object according to distance differences. Moire fringe patterns are created by the interaction of gratings and are capable of significant magnification as well as the representation of differences. While this procedure might be less expensive than some it is not at all clear that its promise of accuracy and representation of detail warrants its pursuit (Oster and Nishijima, 1963; Takasaki, 1970).

This whole class of linear and planar extractions tends to impose an outside extraction on the variation of the skull. In some cases the visual displays which these abstractions are capable of producing are quite striking, and certainly do closely resemble the original. However, it might be also said that they miss the point, i.e., if the apex of the curve of the brow ridge of an individual happens to fall between contour lines, or between regions on the inferrometric-type pattern, then the procedure is not "smart" enough to notice. It was shown before that such apexes are points of maximum information so it seems distressing that the techniques are extracting more information than we seem capable of analyzing, but are potentially missing the most important points. While not a rigorous objection this does point out the possibility that the human eye may have certain advantages over these arbitrarily imposed extractions. A procedure which allowed more direct modeling on the part of the experimenter might well be more desirable.

Full Surface or Volume Methods

In addition to the linear and planar techniques, there are some techniques which extract a full surface or volumetric representation. All of the cautions and difficulties with respect to expense and analysis hold with greater emphasis for these procedures. However, there is a possibility that if they can be made technologically convenient that they will overcome some of the limitations of their simpler relatives. There is serious question at the moment as to the convenient or practical feasibility of using these techniques. They are included, however, since it is quite reasonable to expect that they could actually be utilized, given determination and financial backing, in the near future.

FULL SURFACE STEREOMETRICS

As the name implies this is simply the extension of the stereometric procedure used to extract contour lines to the extraction of the full surface. This is the sort of extraction which could only be carried out by a machine since it implies the derivation of the distance level for all resolvable points on the surface. The limitation here is, of course, the resolution of the camera and film system used. While this approach might overcome some of the criticisms of arbitrariness which planar stereometrics contain, it is if anything further removed from analytic utility. Some possible uses in an analytic framework will be alluded to later.

Holography

Holography has occasioned considerable excitement in several contexts with its promise of full three-dimensional pictures and freedom from the restrictions of parallax. Holography is a "photographic" process which involves the use of one or more coherent light sources (laser light) reflected off the object and combined with a reference source and recorded on film. The reflected and reference sources interact in much the same way as waves interact to produce a pattern which is diagnostic of the reflecting object. This pattern of wave interactions which is recorded in the film can be projected with another laser to produce an image which is perceived by the eye as being fully three dimensional. This illusional dimensionality is so complete that if one changes one's position with respect to the image, then the image changes in the same way that it would if in fact the objects were actually present. The quality of these images is limited, but improving rapidly, to the extent that they are now starting to be competitive with photographic images.

Holographic representations, at least in terms of display, would seem to be far superior to other methods. Several difficulties limit their utility so far. It has been true that the exposure times required for making an holographic image were long, this itself posing problems such as vibration that tended to require a very special environment. This problem would seem to be passing with the development of much brighter sources. The expense has also been a significant obstacle, but the price of production laser equipment has been plummeting in recent years to the point that it might become competitive with many scientific camera arrangements. The most severe problem is again input to analysis. This is more severe since the holographic image is not subject to analysis in the same way as conventional photographs by computer image scanning equipment. However, there has been considerable development toward both computer reading and generation of holographic images so this may not long remain a barrier. (Leith and Upatnicks, 1965; Smith, 1969). The potential utility of many of the techniques explored was limited by the availability of analytic techniques to exploit their information or economic factors. The mechanical imposition of an extractive process may not yield as good quality information as a human observer. All of this seems to tarnish the supposed bright features of many of the proposed developments of measurement technology. The requirements of the problem to be studied should be the prior and primary factor in the derivation of a measurement scheme, limited only by the necessities of practicality and return for investment. The nature of experimentation in the biological sciences is such that the researcher has a mandate to try to maximize his information return and this cannot be done by the mere blind acquisition of data along traditional lines. This follows as a consequence from the large degree of environmental, populational, and individual variation in biological organisms. The traditional measurements were derived during an era when the world view of much of biological science was wrestling with a crisis of taxonomy brought on by dramatically increased experience. Currently this same set, or similar derived measurement schemes, have been used well by a number of authors to study the isolated function of bodily parts. However, some doubt can certainly be raised as to whether these same schemes will be adequate to deal with the variation of whole bodily systems or of whole organisms in populations, a focus defined as important by the contemporary evolutionary orientation of biological science. This might well imply the necessity of pursuing some of these more exotic measurement procedures despite their potentially greater expense, providing the return seems promising and analytic techniques are shown to exist. One technique which seems the most accessible in this respect is the use of coordinate relations.

The future of measurement in craniometry is dependent on the development of advanced technology in the same fashion as our use of some of the more elaborate statistical techniques had to await the development of computational machinery of sufficient power to make their use reasonable. Two such areas seem to stand out at the moment. One of these is the general development of automated picture processing techniques. This offers significant potential as a vehicle by which large volumes of information on skull form could be acquired rapidly and input to a suitable computing device. The availability of relatively inexpensive picture processing devices is advancing at such a rate that the only real limitation to their use could be the question of defining the data extraction process and the analysis.

The other area, which is not quite as developed but which also seems close at hand, is the interface between computational analytic equipment and holographic images. The development of holographic images is such that serious consideration should be given to their possible use since they represent a means of describing and extracting the whole surface of the crania for analysis. Indeed, ultrasound holography (Meterell, 1969) might make possible holographs of the interior of the skull as well.

Analytic Methods

The need for appropriate analytic procedures both to support and to define measurement techniques has been pointed out frequently above. The variety of analytic procedures in fairly current usage is rather more diverse than the measurement techniques which feed them. The following discussion will consider some of the impacts of this relationship as well as the nature of the analytic techniques themselves. This discussion will consider both the internal nature, that defined by the procedure itself, and the external nature, that defined by its pattern of use. In addition, some techniques which are not in wide use will also be discussed because of their possible utility for some of the measurement techniques described above. There is no pretense made here that this discussion is exhaustive of all possible analytic procedures. In fact, the author is himself aware of many others which will not be mentioned, since their immediate applicability to problems in skull form is not certain. The selection offered here are those which have a proven or clear potential utility for the analysis of cranial form. To some extent it will be necessary to lump together whole classes of procedures in order to make the discussion of a manageable size.

Univariate Measures

The earliest measures by Quetelet and Ammon included a perception of several forms of central tendency and the observation that biological variables tended in many cases to a standard form of distribution (Penniman, 1935). This led quickly to a comparison between central tendencies by such workers as Galton and Fisher and this in turn suggested comparisons with allowances made for the amount of variation which was present (Penniman, 1935).

All of univariate statistics might be characterized by these simple features: an interest in central tendencies, a comparison of central tendencies with possible controls for variation, and non-parametric equivalents of these such as the degree of conformity of a nominal distribution to expectation. The initial concern for central tendency is clearly derived from the Aristotelean (and Linnean) model of the world in which natural variations were represented by their ideals. The addition of variation to this consideration was undoubtedly motivated by the empirical force of gathered data showing overlapping distributions with clear differences in means, combined to some degree with the esthetic appeal of the recurring 'normal' distribution. Giving concern to variation would seem to herald the shift in the model of biology from static to evolutionary, from ideal to varying. I would like to suggest, however, that its role in univariate statistics is subordinate to that of central tendency both in theory and in practice.

A survey of statistical tests and procedures in use suggests that they are predominately some form of "means test" so that the role of variation is simply to validate or invalidate the conclusion suggested by the relationship of the means. Thinking from within a "statistical" framework it is not clear what kind of alternatives might exist to this preference. That such an orientation is not dictated by the structure of the data themselves is made clear, however, by a fairly cursory examination of some of the other analytic procedures which have rarely been applied in biological anthropology. One such group of techniques is graph theory. Graph theory deals with the connectedness of networks of relationship (Witz, 1966); the focus is on the structure of relationship or on the degree of interconnection, not on any notion closely related to a "mean." While it is not certain that graph theory would provide a useful analytic model for judging the structure of evolving populations (I suspect it might with some development), its existence points out that the focus of the statistical model is not mandated by the data, but by the disposition of the analytic culture of the experimenter.

A discussion of the current utility of univariate statistics for the study of cranial form is made difficult since the nature of their perceived utility depends entirely on the conceptual framework in which one views the problems facing the field. Univariate statistics do or can provide a certain service within some contexts. They can conveniently serve as a sort of catalogue number that gives a rough idea of the nature of the group. They can serve as a check on assumptions and as a possible foundation for more complex analyses. Furthermore, many of the problems posed by contemporary craniometry, at least in the form in which they are stated, are ones whose solution is defined by a simple statistical test. This includes a whole category of taxonomic proposals which are questions of the probability of two distributions belonging to different samples. It also includes functional proposals in which the test is concerned with the possible relationship of patterns of performance and functional ability to observed anatomical variations. In this sense it would seem that these statistical tests are providing a more metrical and thus standardized form of what would otherwise be provided by inspection.

There are three principal ways in which these simple statistical tests fail the requirements of the field. First, as many will freely admit of themselves, statistics are not very well understood by a significant number of people in the field. This lack of depth of understanding of exactly what is implied by a statistical test and what its requirements are leads to unfortunately frequent misuse or error. Often these errors are matters of nicety, where the statistical implications are technically in error, but the direction of the conclusion would probably not be changed. In some other cases, of course, the problem is more serious, and not necessarily realized.

Second, they are sometimes not complex enough to test the proposed model. Here one must change to another form of test. Even in this circumstance they may have some utility as a preliminary to the more complex task. Third, there may be a significant discrepancy between the implications of the statistical model and the assumptions of the evolutionarily directed culture of the contemporary biological scientist. There are many features of the statistical model which seem to correspond rather well with the evolutionary one. The foundation of statistics on the principals of probability and distribution would seem to mirror the conclusions of the genetic model of inheritance. However, there are two major ways in which this correspondence should be questioned. First, as mentioned before, the focus of univariate statistics both in theory and more so in practice seems to be central tendency. Even though the focus of statistics is not patterns of variation some suggest that it is quite possible to talk about and analyze variation within the statistical model. However, it is difficult to manipulate the possible structuring of variation with simple statistics, and the use of a model which is type-oriented will tend to make one's thinking type-oriented. The use of an analytic model which is at odds with one's hypothesis of the structure and process of reality is difficult to support. The deviations which are imposed by life forms are far from random or probabilistic; they are typically structured often in quite complex and not necessarily survival-oriented ways. One lesson we should have learned from the current distribution of species is that natural selection is not deterministic in the sense that there is only one possible equilibrium solution to any given environmental problem. Furthermore, the structure of organisms themselves distorts the accuracy of the simple probabilistic models since any component of an organism is part of an operating system. We have become sensitized in recent years to the fact that systems exhibit behaviors which are not explicable from the isolated character of their parts and so we should not expect the selection and inheritance of organisms to be discussable with any accuracy unless the whole of the systematic framework is considered. Some acknowledgment of this is present in contemporary genetics in such concepts as linkage and pleiotropy, but this area of investigation has hardly been approached. Since simple statistics are not at all oriented toward a systemic analysis it seems quite doubtful that they should be regarded as the proper foundation for this kind of investigation.

MULTIVARIATE STATISTICS

The use of multivariate statistics brings with it a special model which in its complexity and somewhat different assumptions is quite distinct from its univariate cousin. Multivariate statistics were developed from the 1890's to the 1920's and 1930's as a response to the shortcomings of univariate statistics. One might divide the researchers of the present and the past into two categories: those who felt the course of biology should follow the building and testing of simple models until broader competence would allow consideration of larger problems, and those who were anxious to approach the more complex problem of the description and analysis of human variation in populations as soon as possible. The first group is largely satisfied with univariate statistics or some other relatively simple analytic procedure such as tabulation since the questions asked are simple in structure. The second group was quickly disillusioned with the efficacy of univariate measures since the patterns which it imposed on variation often did not correspond with intuitively perceived relationship. The inability of the human observer to judge and quantify relationships among many variables at once and the inability of univariate statistics to consider but one variable at a time demands multivariate statistics.

In order to discuss the current utility of multivariate statistics I would like to impose two categories on multivariate statistics. The first category might be called *reductive* and its principal form is usually called factor analysis (c.f. Harman, 1970). The purpose of this group of techniques is to take the complex variation of many variables in a population and simplify the representation of that variation into a small number of created variables which account for the bulk of the variation. These created variables are composites of the original variables and hopefully are to some degree interpretable in terms of some common effect, trend, or factor with respect to the organism. For example, if one had taken a large number of measurements on some set of skulls then a factor analysis would examine the correlations among each of the variables in order to discover which of them tended to vary in the same or related ways. These correlations would then be used to make up new supervariables, combinations of the original measurements, along lines of high correlation explaining a relatively high percentage of the total variation in the original set. The first factor which is often derived (they are produced in order of the percent of the variance which they explain) from unadjusted measurements is one which is a combination of everything. This factor is usually explained as representing that part of the variance due to size. Another factor might include major contributions from those measures which tend to lie parallel to the sagittal plane and the Frankfort Horizontal. This factor would be explained as "head linearity" or some similar concept. Factor analysis then is a way to describe a complex pattern of variation in a more simple form. The hypothesis testing form of this class might be said to be multivariate analysis of variance (Sokal and Rohlf, 1971). This technique, which has not yet been used with great frequency in biological anthropology, begins with a model of the major contributing factors to the variation and a relationship between the variables and these factors. The observed variation is then analyzed to assess the degree to which each factor contributes to the overall pattern.

The other class of multivariate statistical technique might be called *distortive*. This term would seem to be rather pejorative, but it is used since the characteristic which defines this class is that the purpose of the analysis or description is the computational selection of ways to rearrange the variables measured in order to identify differences, in other words, to purposely distort the variable space. The most familiar form of this technique in anthropological circles is the so-called discriminant function analysis. This procedure performs an examination of the overall variation in much the same way as factor analysis except that the purpose is the selection of supervariables which identify the differences between two or more groups. Thus a factor analysis over a set of measurements might well identify size as an important factor in explaining the pattern of overall variation, but if two groups within this same sample were close in size then some other factor, such as linearity of features, would emerge as the principal discriminant. The purpose of this kind of analysis is to investigate the nature of the relationship between two or more groups rather than to explain the nature of the variation as a whole.

These techniques have enjoyed fairly extensive use in biological anthropology and have demonstrated considerable power. They present a possibility for the descriptive manipulation of quantities of data which could not be considered with univariate techniques. Wide use of these techniques was dependent on advances in the availability of sufficiently powerful computing devices. The nature of the description is quite different from that which is represented by a mere tabulation of all the differences and similarities, both because all are considered at once and because intercorrelations are accounted for. It would seem to some people that this is the solution to the univariate dilemma—consideration of wholes and complex relationships.

Such enthusiasm must, however, be subject to some quite significant limitations. In some sense these techniques can be thought of as being too powerful. This overpowering character derives in large part from a lack of any baseline of comparison and control and in part from the difficulty of extracting testable or applicable hypotheses from probabilistic arrays. The difficulty is that discriminant function analysis will find differences even when they are not there. This does not actually mean that it creates differences, but that it is so good at detecting differences that it will be able to discriminate with high levels of accuracy on differences which are not attributable to causal origins, but rather to happenstance. The descriptive power of this technique is such that there is an enormous temptation, all too often succumbed to, to consider the discriminant functions themselves as an adequate endproduct of analysis. When this happens, no hypothesis is generated to guide further work, no testing of the conclusions in another context takes place, and no model building is engaged in other than the preparation of attractive displays of the group centroids.

Part of the difficulty is certainly attributable to the very complexity which gives these techniques their power. This complexity makes the interpretation of the results of such an analysis quite difficult, especially for persons who are not even completely comfortable with the mathematical foundations of univariate statistics. Part of the difficulty, though, is inherent in the procedures themselves, in that they operate quite blindly ignorant of any structural model. It might be said that such procedures as multivariate analysis of variance are exceptions to this criticism. To some extent this is true in that some controls, some structure, is imposed by the researcher, but they still allow neither control over the extractions made from the individual variables nor do they allow the detection of alternatives to the model with which the experimenter may have begun.

The chief problem with the utility of multivariate statistics is their correspondence to the cognitive model of the experimenter. The multivariate statistical model, while different in some respects from the univariate one, still is based on a probablistic foundation. Thus, some of the same doubts and questions which were raised above with respect to the desirability of this model for work in contemporary evolutionary biology pertain as well to this more sophisticated class of techniques. Furthermore, the difficulties experienced with statistical models of deriving a meaningful test for an hypothesis are multiplied exponentially in multivariate statistics. Also the problem of deriving a hypothesis from a multivariate description for later testing is exponentially more difficult in most cases than for simple statistics. On the other hand one should not conclude from these difficulties that multivariate statistics have no utility at all. Some researchers (e.g. Day and Wood, 1969) have shown an occasional ability to notice patterns from multivariate analysis which might not have occured to them otherwise and these have formed testable hypotheses. They can serve a kind of forensic function when this is required or desired, such as in their use for sex identification (Giles, 1970). It is even arguable that for those who are interested in investigating such large scale questions as migration patterns in the Pacific Basin that some temporary utility could be derived from these techniques in the absence of the identification of a more suitable procedure. The guideline is once again the careful and thoughtful application of the technique with understanding of its consequences.

Response Surface Modeling

Response surface methodology is a class of procedure which is characterized by an attempt to derive curves of one or more dimensions in response to a set of observed data. It differs in this respect from statistics in that it does not so much attempt to extract parameters of description as to model the observed variation itself. As such, it is applicable only to those problems where the researcher's model or the underlying phenomena are suitable for representation as a curve. This is, however, quite a large class of phenomena and one which could be used with some frequency in the study of cranial form. One of the distinguishing features of response surface methodology as a technique is that it is in some sense non-deterministic. That is, the technique allows one to make a series of educated guesses as to what kind of curve would best explain the data. There is full freedom to try many different approaches to a solution corresponding to different possible models or explanations. For example, if one believes that the effect of increasing the overall size of an organism is that there will be an exponential increase in occlusal surface area, then one could try to fit observed data with an exponential curve. The response surface approach is actually a kind of series of modeling approximations. Approximating stops when either the fit is close enough, the complexity of the model seems too great, or the approximation does not seem appropriate (Myers, 1971).

The response surface approach implies a rather different attack on problems than might be made with a statistical approach. First, the assumptions are largely vested in the experimenter, not in the technique. If the experimenter understands the significance of the class of curve which he is trying in given circumstances then he has rather direct control over the relationship between the raw data and the model or conclusions. Second, the use of a response surface approach implies the prior existence of a fairly clearly defined model since it is not possible to simply measure a number of variables and see what comes out. Third, the goal of the procedure is a specific relation between defined variables, with less possibility of simple description as an end.

There are a number of classes of response surface; two of the most common of these are polynomial and Fourier. Polynomial surfaces are generated as a result of an equation which has the form of an additive series of terms, each term being a successive set in a series of powers of the base variable. For example:

$$Y = ax^{\circ} + bx^{1} + cx^{3} \ldots ix^{n}$$

A Fourier equation has the form of a series of similar terms only the transformations of the base variable are in terms of trigonometric functions. For example:

$$Y = a \sin(x) + b \sin(2x) + c \sin(3x) \ldots$$

Each exists in a wide variety of basic patterns, each a variant on this same structure, but using different transformations of the base variable(s). Polynomial functions are characteristically used to describe non-repeating phenomena, change with respect to size for example, while Fourier functions are used for harmonic functions.

It is difficult to assess the possible utility of these procedures in the study of cranial form since they have been used so little. They suggest some promise for discrete, small scale investigations of the relationship between distances, angles and such. They would even seem to have greater utility in this respect than comparable statistical studies since their output would be a description of the pattern of the variation, not just the identification that a covariance existed. More interesting is the possibility that they might be used to study the form·of bone surfaces themselves. Since these are surfaces, i.e. curves, it would be possible to attempt modeling of the bone surfaces with some kind of equations. Such studies as those by Lestrel (1973) promise that the coefficients of response surface equations may be quite interpretable in biological terms. Response surface methodology is not oriented toward the study of distributional variation. However, if response surfaces are developed, the distributional patterns of the coefficients or of the different equation forms would likely be more fruitful than the study of the patterns of the raw variables since the results would be more interpretable. The possibility also exists of combining a morphologically oriented response surface with a geographically oriented response surface directly as a means of studying this kind of variation (geographically oriented response surfaces are often known as trend surfaces and at least one way of combining them is the principal components trend surface analysis [Monmonier, 1972] although this does not really fulfill what was suggested above.) The principal danger would therefore be the possibility of excess due to over-zealous application when it is not appropriate. It would seem that response surface methodology holds considerable promise for the analysis of the locational-type data which would result from one of the point or surface oriented techniques described above.

Experiment and Analysis

The emphasis in this paper so far has been exclusively on research focused on the empirical description and explanation of naturally occuring patterns of variation. This neglects a whole category of approach to the study of cranial form—the controlled experiment to observe and test the influence of various factors on bone growth and modification. Part of the justification of this neglect, other than simple preference, is that the contribution of this class of study is likely to be limited in the immediate future. The factors which influence the developmental and modificational patterns of such a complex structure as the cranium are likely to be sufficiently complicated that the kind of single-variable understanding which is derived from such experiments is useful more as a guideline than as a result. Nevertheless, it is important for the student of cranial form to consider the impact of such studies in his modeling process. One example of this kind of possible influence is seen in the change in assumptions which result from developing awareness of the plasticity of bone even after maturity is reached. Anyone who has thought about the implications of the toothpick-thick edentulous jaw which exist in quite "normal" individuals would realize that some of the simple discriminations which have been proposed for size differences in fossils need to be questioned. All of this serves to re-emphasize the mandate for the researcher to carefully consider the culture from which his orientation is derived, the existing information on a research area, the definition of the problem he wishes to study, the impact of the measurement procedure and analytic technique he will use, and the interrelationship of these factors with respect to his study.

Concluding Statements

In honor of the occasion which this volume celebrates, I here would like to suggest that the hope of this article is to a significant degree personified in W.W. Howells. I do not pretend to suggest, even in the euphemistic context of a dedication, that Dr. Howells has in every moment of his professional career managed to conform to the very difficult standard which I have proposed in the preceding pages. Indeed, considering the fact that his training occurred before the recent burst of culture-relativistic concern, it is to some extent amazing that he displays any of these qualities at all. The secret behind this achievement is that Dr. Howells is an Anthropologist first, and then a student of fossil and modern human variation. The contrast between his orientation and that of a number of the other members of the field was recently displayed in the 1972 Yearbook of Physical Anthropology.

Reading the various authors' opinions of what the focus and purpose of physical anthropology should be, one could easily wonder if they were in the same field.

I think we can see, both from the diversity of problems and techniques which Dr. Howells himself has followed and from the diversity of his students' work that he must indeed have an open mind to alternative possibilities. He has not only been open but actively searching for better solutions to the analytical dilemmas he found in his work and that of the field. This openness and critical appraisal of the achievements which have been made lie at the heart of the position which has been advocated in this article. Perhaps in the final analysis the careful consideration of the impact of one's culture is not so much a new philosophic tradition as it is a standing principle of the anthropologist. In this light it would seem worth repeating that it is very important even for those of us who study the most biological of man's aspects to remember the broader context of man's cultural side and not to fall into the trap of believing that we are somehow different from those we study.

Bibliography

Aphonin
    1781   On the Use of Natural History. In: Linneaus, Selected Dissertations from Amoenites Academicae, translated and published by F.J. Brand, London.
Aristotle
    1910   Historia Animalium. Translated by D'Arcy Thompson, Clarendon Press, Oxford.
Clarke, R.J. and Howell, F.C.
    1972   Affinities of the Swartkrans 847 hominid cranium. American Journal of Physical Anthropology, *37:* 319-336.
Cuvier, G.
    1829   A Discourse on the Revolutions of the Surface of the Globe and the Changes Thereby Produced in the Animal Kingdom. Whittaker, Treacher and Arnot, London.
Day, M.H. and Wood, W.M.
    1969   Hominoid tali from east africa. Nature, *222:* 591-592.
Giles, E.
    1970   Discriminant function sexing of the human skeleton. In Personal Identification in Mass Disasters, T.D. Stewart Ed., Smithsonian Institution, Washington, D.C.

1971   Pers. Comm. Conversations and informal memoranda concerning the use of coordinate digitizing equipment (OSCAR) for the study of skull form.

Gruner, H.
1970   Short range and mono photogrammetry. Bausch and Lomb Spotlight, R. McHail Ed., *2:*1 ff.

Harman, Harry H.
1970   Modern Factor Analysis. University of Chicago Press, Chicago.

Herron, R.E.
1972   Biostereometric measurement of body form. Yearbook of physical anthropology, *16:*80-121.

Irwin, H.T. and Lajeunnesse, R.M.
1973   Descriptions and Measurements in Anthropology: acoustical computer techniques. Presented at the IXth International Congress of Anthropological and Ethnological Sciences, Chicago.

Lamarck, J.B. de
1914   Zoological Philosophy: an Exposition with Regard to the Natural History of Animals. Translated by H. Elliot, Macmillan, New York.

Leith, E.N. and Upatnicks, J.
1965   Photography by laser. Scientific American, *212*(6): 24-35.

Lestrel, P.E.
1973   Fourier analysis of cranial shape: a longitudinal study. Presented at the Annual Meetings of the American Association of Physical Anthropology.

Linnaeus, C.
1781   Select Dissertations from Amoenites Academicae. Translated and published by F. Brand, London.

Lovejoy, C.O., Heiple, K.G. and Burstein, A.H.
1973   The gait of Australopithecines. American Journal of Physical Anthropology, *38:*757-780

Lyell, C.
1835   Principles of Geology. John Murray, London.

Metherell,A.F.
1969   Acoustic Holography. Scientific American, *221*(4):36-53.

Monmonier,M.
1972   A spatially-controlled principal components analysis. Geographical Analysis, *4*(4):392-406.

Myers, R.H.
1971   Response Surface Methodology. Allyn and Bacon, Boston.

Oster, G. and Nishijima, Y.
1963   Moire patterns. Scientific American, *208*(2):56-70.

Penniman, I.K.
1935   A Hundred Years of Anthropology. Duckworth, London.

Pliny (the Younger)
1893 The Natural History. Translated by J. Bostock and H. Riley. George Bell, London.
Russell, B.
1945 History of Western Philosophy. Simon and Schuster, New York.
Smith, H.M.
1969 Principles of Holography. Wiley, New York.
Sokal, R. and Rohlf, J.
1971 Introduction to Biostatistics. Freeman, San Francisco.
Stenger, E.
1939 The History of Photography. Mack Printing, Easton, Pa.
Takaskai, H.
1970 Moire Topography. Applied Optics, *9*:1467.
Witz, K.
1966 Notes on Mathematical Models in the Social Sciences. Wiley, New York.
Wolpoff, M.H.
1973 The evidence for two Australopithecine lineages in South Africa. Yearbook of Physical Anthropology, vol. 17, (in press).

FIVE

Biological Anthropology:
The Cultural Context

Most biological anthropologists physically are in a cultural context. Very few anthropology departments sustain more than two or three biological anthropologists among their stable of cultural anthropologists; the biological presence is strictly a minority representation. Thus it often surprises other academics that many, perhaps most, biological anthropologists feel at home in such a milieu, and not just because they have known no other. Among the characterizations of American anthropology has been the tenacity with which it maintains a holistic view. Exceptions exist no doubt, but real mutual interest typifies the inter-subdisciplinary activities of anthropologists of most stripes. Biological anthropologists have much to give and much to learn, and there are many to learn from.

In this concluding section the papers are weighted toward "incoming": one archaeologist (Lathrap) and several sociocultural anthropologists (Ogan, Nash and Mitchell and Ross) show from their own research and thinking materials and ideas that depict what they can offer us and how we may have influenced them. In partial return Seaford's contribution shows an unexpected way in which a biological anthropologist can step back and forth across that boundary which keeps us together.

20. Radiation: the Application to Cultural Development of a Model from Biological Evolution

Donald W. Lathrap

Introduction

This essay has a curious history, and has held a special place in my written output. Almost all of my later publications have in one sense or another been elaborations of the paper's themes, or further wrestlings with problems left unresolved here. I was still a graduate student at Harvard when it was originally written as an exercise for a seminar given by Dr. Cora DuBois during the fall semester of 1956. The subject of the seminar was "Evolutionary Theory in Anthropology." I had planned to do a critique of the evolutionary thinking of a cultural anthropologist who was widely regarded as a leader in that area of theorizing. Having read with care the total of that scholar's "Evolutionary Writings," I prepared an oral critique for the seminar; but I felt that as a corpus the man's writings were so vacuous as to be an insufficient excuse for a 30 page exegesis: incidently, I still am underwhelmed by the "Evolutionary Writings" of Leslie White. Dr. DuBois graciously permitted me to substitute an essay on another subject, and after a full semester of thrashing around, I finished the present paper. Dr. DuBois' reaction was generally favorable, but she felt that the paper should be expanded into book-size and should include *all* evidence from the Old World. Her final comment: "I like very much the start you have made, and hope you will go on fussing with all this," can at this late date be viewed either as an exhortation or a curse, but it was certainly an accurate prophecy.

The late Clyde Kluckhohn next read the paper and was far less gentle. It was his considered opinion that the whole ought to be boiled down to twenty manuscript pages which really said what I wanted to say. It was this total disagreement between these two expert opinions which lead me to put the manuscript aside "temporarily." Philip L. Phillips and Gordon R. Willey also read the effort. Phillips was totally negative, while Willey liked it and publicly acknowledges having used the manuscript in the preparation of his own essay "Historical Patterns and Evolution in Native New World Cultures" (1960: 129). Since 1957 I filed the manuscript away bringing it out only rarely and showing it to a select few. On one such occasion a junior colleague suggested that I burn it. In 1972 John Pfieffer generously agreed to look at it, and it was he who convinced me that even now it was worth publishing. At about the same time Dr. Heinz Von Foerster also expressed a strong interest in the manuscript.

The paper is being published more or less as written in 1957. If I were writing it today, many things would be changed; but in rereading the attempt, I don't see too much to regret given the state of knowledge in 1957. A revision in terms of the increments in knowledge over the last 16 years would be a different paper.

Editorial changes have usually involved sentences which Dr. DuBois did not understand; clearly in these instances the failure in communication was mine. I have added a few asides, in brackets, which introduce new material or ideas. Kluckhohn found the original coda insufferably pompous, an opinion with which I now heartily concur; and a new ending has been prepared.

To me, at least, the position of the paper seems compatible with considerable recent writing in Anthropology, particularly the volume *Population Growth: Anthropological Implications*, edited by Brian Spooner, 1972, and most especially with the essays of Don Dumond (1972 a,b) in that volume. On the other hand my paper is out of step with much of what has been explicitly labeled "New Archaeology," particularly the moiety of "New Archaeology" which Kent Flannery has called "Law and Order" (1971).

The paper seems to me an appropriate offering to William Howells. In a trivial sense it is appropriate because he was the only senior professor at Peabody, with whom I was working closely, who did not get a look at it in 1957. In a more significant way, I would hope that it reflects Howells' insistence that Anthropology, as a whole, is a meaningful field of study; and that the problems of the archaeologist may well receive clarification from concepts drawn from human biology and biological evolution. This is a lesson I internalized from his graduate teaching; and from watching his consistently brilliant and integrated presentation of human evolution and culture history in the freshman course Anthropology IA, in which I had the privilege of serving as teaching assistant.

The purpose of the paper is simple: it is an attempt to reduce certain thought patterns to their most explicit form. These are ideas I have found covertly stimulating my own thinking and which I seem to find in the works of various writers who are dealing with the problems of cultural development. I am curious to see the full implications of several of these ideas once they are taken from the ranks of unstated premises, changed from a nebulous to a concrete form, and placed in juxtaposition. Bald statements of faulty premises will be more ridiculous than cleverly dressed presentations of the same ideas. Since this exercise is largely a stock taking of premises, the statements will be kept as bald as possible in order to make that which is foolish most easily recognizable.

More specifically in the paper I wish to push the analogy between the process known as radiation in biological evolution and what may be similar features in the course of cultural development. The type of developmental scheme set up by those anthropologists, who have been styled evolutionistic, is not particularly close to anything to be found in the well developed theory of Biological Evolution. If the idea of Cultural Evolution is to be continued as part of the working arsenal of the twentieth century, it might be interesting to see if there would be any advantages in bringing the conceptual scheme of Cultural Evolution more closely in line with that of Biological Evolution.

No claim of a high degree of originality is made for any of the ideas expressed in this paper; what may be new are details of organization. This being the case it is only fair to give an introductory statement of gratitude to those authors who have done the most to shape my thinking, since these debts are both larger and less specific than can be acknowledged by the standard form of citations. The most significant intellectual debt is to the writings of Kroeber, and as far as this particular paper is concerned specifically to chapters XII and XIII of the original edition of *Anthropology* (1923). There are also influences from *Cultural and Natural Areas of Native North America* (1939). From the point of view both of abstract formulation and of concrete data this paper has been in large measure an outgrowth of the paper by Willey and Phillips titled: *Method and Theory in American Archaeology II:*

Historical-Developmental Interpretation (1955). Though it originally was not so intended, the final form of my paper is in many of its parts little more than a commentary on the Wiley and Phillips paper. Eiseley's paper *The Paleo Indians: Their Survival and Diffusion* (1955) gave final form to my ideas on subsistence patterns as adapting and radiating entities. The paper by Birdsell on gene flow in Austrailia gave me the idea of progressively evolving abstract models for whole continents (1950) (*in other words, the idea of simulation*). The ideas concerning Biological Evolution which I have used or abused in this paper are largely from Simpson's book *The Meaning of Evolution* (1949).

If the above mentioned sources are the most significant to the formulation of this paper, several others, read concurrently with its composition were also influential, though to a lesser degree. A paper by Meggers, "Environmental Limitations on the Development of Culture" (1954) was certainly provocative, as were all four articles in the memoir *Seminars in Archaeology: 1955* (1956).

The Radiation of Subsistence Patterns, an Abstract Formulation

The point of departure for this discussion lies in viewing each society as an adapting organism. This view point necessitates taking a restricted range of cultural phenomena under consideration, in that interest is focused only on those patterns which structure the food quest and the distribution of food within a society. It should be made clear that this restriction of attention does not imply a lack of interest in other of the patterns involved in a total culture. The limitation is made with the hope of deriving a more simplified model by treating certain factors as constants, even though one must suspect that they are variables and exercise a considerable influence over the situation.

Likewise it should be made clear that a conceptual scheme which treats societies as if they were organisms does not necessarily mean a capitulation to the point of view that the individual is unimportant. Such a scheme is used only to see if certain, *highly limited* aspects of cultural development can be treated as if the individuals involved in a society were a constant.

If a society is to be treated as an adapting organism, then what it is adapting to is largely its geographical environment. Within a given environment a given subsistence pattern will support only a certain density of population. Any change in either the environment or the subsistence pattern may influence the population density one way or the other. The relative efficiency of a particular cultural pattern of subsistence and of the society maintaining it can be stated in terms of the population density which it can support in a given environment. It should be superfluous to add that such a statement of efficiency has nothing to do with the question of "good" societies or "bad" societies or the whole question of normative values within Anthropology. Such a statement of efficiency can be made on purely objective grounds. A subsistence pattern and the society maintaining it can be said to be adapting to a particular environment, when the total of changes becoming stabilized in the total cultural pattern tend to increase the efficiency of the subsistence pattern. It is here suggested that a large percentage of the changes which occur in a culture, especially within its subsistence patterns are adaptive in the sense of the word just defined.

If they behave as biological organisms in certain limited respects, societies with a particular subsistence pattern should continually extend their geographical range up to the limits beyond which their particular subsistence patterns could not be practiced, or in other words beyond which the efficiency of the pattern becomes zero. The reason for this is obvious, for if the population is increasing and the subsistence pattern remains constant the maximum efficiency of the pattern at a given level of adaptation will soon be reached and as long as there is unoccupied land adjoining the areas of excess population, the excess people will tend to move outward rather than starve, and the range of societies with a particular cultural pattern will thus be expanded.

The interrelated working out of the two sets of tendencies mentioned above takes its most simple form if we picture the peopling of an uninhabited continent. On the one hand there will be progressive adaptation to the area originally occupied and on the other there will be the continual radiation into other areas with somewhat different environments.

Let us picture an hypothetical continent extending through a wide range of latitudes and exhibiting a wide range of life zones. This continent is previously uninhabited by man. Let us introduce onto this continent at any point a small society with a subsistence pattern which is somewhat generalized (the meaning which "generalized" has in this discussion should become clear as the reader proceeds). The first thing which would be expectable is that the society should radiate and gradually send offshoot societies into all geographical areas of the continent which can be effectively utilized by the subsistence pattern of the original society, that is all areas in which the original subsistence pattern could be practiced at a level of efficiency higher than zero. The result would be to spread a number of similar societies with similar cultures over a large portion of the continent and into a fairly wide range of geographical life zones. Except under conditions of well developed empire or under modern means of communication, the societies would tend to lose contact with one another. In the course of time it would be expectable that the societies in the various regions of the hypothetical continent would become progressively more distinct. Part of this change should be strictly adaptive to the range of environments into which the parent society spread and part could be considered as the cultural analogue of genetic drift. That is to say that there would be random loss of certain cultural traits due to the smallness of the spreading groups and the development of new traits which would not spread rapidly because of the lack of extensive contacts.

It would also be expectable that many of the originally uninhabitable areas of the continent would become inhabited. This last development would progress as follows. Societies in areas which were marginal with respect to the original subsistence pattern, that is areas in which the pattern could be practiced at a level of efficiency only slightly higher than zero would undergo changes in their subsistence pattern toward greater efficiency in terms of the immediate environment and these changes in subsistence pattern would then permit the penetration of adjoining areas which previously could not have been utilized.

It is easy to visualize the long term results of the process just outlined, that is assuming that no further complicating factors intervened. After a long period of time the hypothetical continent should be almost completely occupied. Each society should be well adapted to its own immediate geographical environment. All of the societies should share a number of cultural elements due to the fact that all had diverged from a single cultural tradition, but in the course of time the shared cultural content should become progressively less due to cultural drift. The subsistence economies, though originally all of one pattern should show progressively greater divergence as each became more completely adapted to its own limited environment.

It would be well to examine closely the nature of a society which has been adapting to a particular environment over a long period of time. Within the limitations of the basic kind of subsistence pattern originally established in the area, the subsistence aspects of the culture will tend to approach maximum efficiency for the immediate environment.

Of course the maximum efficiency conceivable under these circumstances will be approached as a limit and there are reasons why the limit can not be attained. Such an adaptation will involve the progressively greater emphasis on the most efficient food sources within the particular environment, and progressively more efficient mechanisms for the procuring and processing of these food sources. Some resources, such as the bitter acorns, will remain unusable until elaborate processing patterns are developed. A few specific examples might help to clarify this discussion.

The societies which flourished on the Northwest Coast of North America are an example of a hunting and gathering economy which was able to support a high density of population because of the efficient utilization of certain localized and abundant sources of food, especially the salmon. The cultural patterns were highly adapted to the environment, not only with respect to the catching and preservation of salmon, but also to other features of the environment less directly concerned with food production but important in that they lead to a high efficiency in all aspects of survival. Notably there was the pattern of woodworking technology which was beautifully adapted to the processing of soft but strong woods with straight, widely spaced grain. Such a technology could be practiced only within the range of a couple of species of trees, namely the red cedar and the coast redwood. In their specific adaptation the societies of the Northwest Coast attained a high degree of efficiency but as a consequence their possible geographic range was restricted. Their subsistence patterns and the surrounding patterns in other aspects of culture could be practiced only at the mouths of rivers with heavy salmon runs and within the fog belt forest immediately adjacent to the coast, which contained either cedar or redwood. These theoretical limits closely correspond to the actual limits attained by societies practicing the specialized type of culture which is traditionally called "Northwest Coast". This range was from Humboldt Bay in California to Yakatat Bay in Alaska.

California offers other examples of relatively efficient societies which were limited in their geographical range. In Central California there were a number of societies which were dependent for a major part of their subsistence on one or two species of oak. With this efficient utilization of the acorn as a food source went a number of other cultural patterns and all of these acorn based societies were similar in various other aspects of culture. The range of these culture patterns was determined by the range of the particular oaks.

The Southern California Coast, from Point Concepcion to slightly below Los Angeles offered conditions permissive to the development of efficient deep sea fishing. These conditions involved both a rich marine fauna and a relatively sheltered stretch of ocean behind the Channel Islands. Again there was a specialization in subsistence pattern, a great increase in population, and a development of specific complexes in other aspects of culture which were seldom diffused beyond the area in which this particular economic adaption was possible.

Such societies are in a position which is immediately advantageous but which from the point of view of long term survival is a precarious one. In this way they are comparable to the most highly specialized organisms in the biological world. Such creatures have come to make increasing better use of environmental niches which are progressively more narrow. A particularly spectacular example in Zoology is the round worm which lives only in the felt mats placed under beer steins in Bavarian taverns (Buchsbaum, 1938: 157). It is for these reasons that societies which have reached nearly maximum adaptation to a highly limited geographical range will be spoken of as specialized societies.

The specialized society can be expected to function well only as long as there are no major changes in the environment. It can not spread outside of the environment to which it has limited itself and in its tendency to concentrate on a single food source, it may itself radically alter the environment by destroying its own basis for existence. Also it tends to lose the ability for radically new developments since specialization is largely in terms of emphasising certain alternatives which were present in the original culture and in discarding others.

The results of continued adaptation undisturbed by other factors, such as environmental change or the introduction of an entirely new type of subsistence pattern, would be a continent with cultural areas which coincide almost exactly with natural areas and with only slight cultural differences to be noted as one passed from one society to its neighbor. Except where cut by sharp geographical boundaries, the ethnographic map should show the sort of gradual village to village shift in traits which has been observed in the detailed analysis of California ethnographic data (Kroeber, in Klimek 1935: 10-11). This is also the sort of ethnographic map hypothesised by Ford in his excellent discussion on typology (1954). By borrowing a term from geology we might call such a condition, a mature ethnographic profile. The characteristics of the mature ethnographic profile would be the high correspondence between cultural and geographic boundaries and the lack of

sharp cultural boundaries which are not paralleled by marked geographic boundaries. In such a situation random and long continuing
diffusion of traits would tend to reduce to a minimum differences between adjoining groups.

If no disturbing factors are introduced, the system of the hypothetical continent should drift toward a cultural and demographic equilibrium in which subsistence economies so closely approached their maximum efficiency and population densities so closely approached their
limits under the particular pattern that variations would tend to become random and minor.

Of course such a static situation would not often be reached in actual conditions. Shifts in climate, the extinction of various forms of
life, and partial or complete destruction of societies through disease
are constantly expectable. Any of these factors could completely upset
the equilibrium. More effective than these factors would be the appearance of a completely new pattern of subsistence economy on the continent. Such an event is likely to take place long before the continent
approaches equilibrium. If such an introduction is to be effective the
new pattern must be of significantly greater efficiency [i.e. capable of
supporting a denser population] than the pattern already established
in the continent.

The introduction of a pattern of food production into an area in
which previously only hunting and gathering had been practiced is of
particular interest to the student of culture history. The case in which
societies with different subsistence patterns are in competition for the
same geographical areas is more complex than that in which societies
with a single type of subsistence pattern are spreading over a previously uninhabited area. The basic rule which ought to be applicable
would be that in a given locality where two societies with different
basic subsistence patterns were brought into contact, the more efficient
of the two societies, in the sense defined above, would eliminate the less
efficient. In this case the relative efficiency of the two societies must be
judged in terms of the immediate geographical environment. Thus the
geographical spread of societies with a new subsistence pattern is limited not just by purely geographical factors, as in the first case studied,
but by geographical factors and the efficiency of the subsistence patterns already occupying the various areas into which the new societies
might spread. It might be illuminating to run through another
hypothetical radiation.

Starting with the hypothetical continent again, it is assumed that the continent has run through the full course of the spread of societies with hunting and gathering patterns and that throughout the continent the ethnographic map has attained a mature profile. Now it is assumed that at some point on this continent a subsistence pattern involving agricultural practices develops. One might even hazard a guess as to where such a development might take place upon the continent. It will probably be in an area where no variant of the original subsistence pattern ever reached a very high level of efficiency. In other words it would be an area unblessed with any major satisfactory source of natural food so that the members of the society inhabiting it were forced to continue to use all available resources, such as they were, and to continue to experiment with them. Such an area would force the societies within it to remain more or less generalized in their subsistence pattern in order to eke out a bare existence.

It might be expected that the beginnings of agriculture would involve only minor additions to a meager subsistence economy. Indeed these are the patterns of incipient agriculture which are indicated by recent work both in the Chicama valley in Peru (Bennett and Bird, 1949. 116-123), and in Tamaulipas in Northern Mexico (MacNeish, 1957). In these beginning stages agriculture would be of some aid to the hard pressed inhabitants of these difficult regions but it would not pose a challenge to the efficiency of hunting and gathering economies in more favored regions of the continent. Only after long periods of time under cultivation would the cultivated plants change sufficiently from their wild ancestors to be markedly more efficient food sources. than uncultivated plants. It would be at this time when agriculture would cause a violent upward swing in the amount of food produced, and consequently in the population of the society involved. In theory an outward push of offshoot societies carrying an agricultural pattern of subsistence should follow.

These migrations will be impelled by the same force which caused the original spread throughout the uninhabited continent but will be moving against obstacles. In the first place, the society by the time it starts to send out offshoots will be to a slight degree specialized to its original location. This may mean that it has a number of cultural traits which are neutral or detrimental with regard to efficiency in the adjoining environments. The agricultural societies will be migrating into regions to which they are either only moderately or even poorly pre-adapted but in which the non-agricultural societies are already fully adapted. The probable final results of the outward migrations of societies with an agricultural subsistence pattern against already established, nonagricultural societies can best be estimated if the hypothetical continent is divided into zones.

There will be zones in which hunting and gathering societies can exist at varying degrees of efficiency but which cannot support agriculture even at a low level of efficiency and after extensive adaptation. Agricultural societies will not penetrate into these zones and here hunting and gathering societies will continue to flourish. Such regions can be identified in a general way as to specific environment. Some will be extreme deserts lacking major rivers which might make irrigated agriculture possible. Others will be areas of cold climate and short growing season making the usually cultivated crops uneconomical.

The second group of zones will include those which can support hunting and gathering societies at a low level of efficiency but which can support agricultural societies at a much higher level. In these zones it would be expected that the hunting and gathering societies with their low populations would be quickly swamped by the intruding agricultural societies with their higher population densities. One such type of area would be desert crossed by rivers sufficiently large to make riverine agriculture possible.

The third group of zones would be those in which the existing hunting and gathering societies are operating at a moderate to high efficiency. The intrusive agricultural societies initially will not be adapted to these zones. [The extreme sensitivity of the tropical grass, maize, to the lengthened photoperiod in temperate zones, meant that maize agriculture was initially an impossibility North of Mexico and that the agricultural pattern could become productive only after maize had genetically adjusted to the new conditions. The necessity for agricultural systems to readjust gradually to new niches is not just a hypothetical possibility.] Until adaptation has had time to progress the efficiency of the intruding societies will be about equal to the indigenous societies. The situation in this last group of zones will be complicated by trait-unit diffusion. Though both resident and intrusive cultures may retain their individuality for a long period of time they may exchange a large number of cultural traits. Thus the resident societies may become to a greater or lesser degree agricultural by adopting individual cultigens without taking over either the full agricultural pattern or other complexes in the total cultures of the invading societies. On the other hand the invading societies may take traits from the original residents which might be of aid toward increased ease of survival in the particular environment. Thus diffusion would tend to equalize the efficiencies of the two competing societies and the contest would thus be prolonged. In cases where the scales are so equally balanced, ultimate survival of one or the other of the societies may depend on other factors than sheer economic efficiency. One probable outcome of such situations is the fusion of the two traditions, but this may take a long time. Specific situations of this type were given attention in the *Seminar in Archaeology on Culture Contact Situations,* (Lathrap, ed. 1956) and can be found there under the classifications of A-2 and A-3.

During the long period while societies of the two patterns preserve their cultural integrity, zones of this third kind will exhibit a distinctive ethnographic map. Societies with divergent cultural patterns will be in juxtaposition and there will be sharp cultural boundaries which follow no obvious geographical boundaries. In contrast to the condition earlier described this set of circumstances will be called an immature ethnographic profile.

At the end of this second round of radiation, the picture of our hypothetical continent is considerably more complex. In the hearth area of the agricultural pattern the process of adaptation, which was already well begun before the outward spread from this region, is continuing, probably at an accelerated rate. In the regions where agricultural societies easily replaced the earlier societies there will be cultural patterns which were originally similar to those of the hearth area both in subsistence pattern and in non-subsistence aspects of culture. But as these societies become established in their new home the process of regional specialization produces progressively greater divergence. In the intermediate zones where immature ethnographic profiles are a continuing feature, further adaptation may be more in response to the problem of the co-existence of two hostile subsistence patterns than to the actual geographical environment. In other words adaptive changes may be more in the relms of organization and military effectiveness than in the relm of economics. The fusion which may be the end product in these regions may be quite different from either of the parent cultural traditions. In areas where agricultural societies could not penetrate, hunting and gathering societies will continue to perfect their specialization in exploiting available resources. These marginal societies may still preserve some shared cultural features which point back to their common origin at a time before their continuous distribution was broken by the spread of agricultural societies.

In the hypothetical continent just discussed the picture has been kept simple by holding the number of distinct patterns and the consequent cultural radiations at two. In an actual situation the picture will become progressively more complicated as a larger number of subsistence patterns come into existence and spread further layers of relatively uniform culture over the already complex ethnographic map.

Subsistence Patterns and Cultural Stages, a Problem of Definitions.

The matter of the productivity of a particular subsistence pattern in a particular region can be approached in another way. In the earlier section of this paper the efficiency of a subsistence pattern has been defined in terms of the density of population which it could support. This kind of efficiency is related to but not identical to statements concerning the number of man-hours which are necessary to provide a person with an adequate diet, under given conditions of subsistence pattern and environment. This second index will give the proportion of a man's time which must be devoted to subsistence activities, or the number of full time specialists, in non-subsistence activities, who can be supported by a single full time food producer. This is a question of the amount of food surplus which the individual worker in subsistence activities can produce.

The amount of food surplus produced is partially related to the permanence of the community in the geographical sense. At one end of this scale will be groups of hunters and gatherers who seldom accumulate food beyond what is consumed on a day to day basis. They are likely to be dependent on the products of a wide range of plants which will become available at different seasons of the year and each of which will be most plentiful in a different part of the range of the group. This situation will lend to an annual round of migrations with camp sites located so as to take maximum advantage of each of the species producing important plant foods. Such a picture is not purely hypothetical but the actual condition of the Panamint Shoshoni (Colville, 1892; Lathrap and Meighan, 1951). In areas of sparse game there will be a tendency to exhaust game within the immediate vicinity. Again frequent movements of camp will be necessary.

If any particular food source can be made to yield a large food surplus which can be stored against the time of year when that source is non-poducing, there will be a progressive tendency to settle permanently at those spots where that particular food source is most available. A food surplus must be stored and is usually too bulky to carry around continually. Its caching requires permanent structures as protection both against animals and other societies. When caching becomes customary there is a high probability that a base camp will develop and will be manned on a year round basis by at least part of the population.

At the other end of this range is the large city which produces none of its food and which requires not only a very high index of food surplus but efficient means of transportation.

The relationship of subsistence patterns to various kinds of settlement patterns both temporary and permanent has been reviewed in detail by one of the *Seminars in Archaeology;* 1955 (Beardsley, et. al., 1956) and it would serve no purpose to review completely the work of that group.

The amount of food surplus is also closely linked with the various formulations of cultural stages which have been advanced by anthropologists and others for at least the last century. As a society advances from a lower to higher stage there is an elaboration of institutions. Such elaboration of institutions may be religious, governmental, military, commercial, or even artistic but implies a group of full time specialists who produce no food, and who are supported by the food surplus built up by others.

It is not the purpose of this paper to review all of the stage schemes from Lubbock on in terms of food surplus. The system of stages proposed by Willey and Phillips can be taken not as an average example of such conceptual schemes but rather as a particularly successful and sophisticated one. The authors are quite frank in admitting the mixed nature of the criteria used for demarking various steps of their schemes. In general they treat their scheme as one dimensional or linear in that they work as if their stages were segments of a single continuum (Willey and Phillips 1955; 788). Since there are two or possibly three groups of criteria used at various points in the scheme, it might be instructive to view this stage setup as a two dimensional diagram. The two most important axes in such a plotting would seem to be the pattern of producing food and the success, in terms of food surplus, which a culture achieves. Since they were dealing with New World prehistory it is only fair that this examination of their work should continue along the same lines.

One of the axes which will be used in this diagramming will be the amount of food surplus produceable by a full time worker in subsistence activities. This is obviously a continuous variable and any divisions (*scaling*) along this axis will be purely arbitrary. Four such divisions will be marked off. The first will include those situations which approach a zero food surplus. This is the situation in which the productive members of a family must work nearly full time on subsistence tasks just to meet the day to day needs of the family. There is little or no time for any kinds of manufactures which are not strictly utilitarian from the point of view of subsistence economy and little non-essential elaboration of these necessary manufactures. The small band wandering from camp site to camp site is a common but perhaps not necessary feature of this situation. Societies in surplus level one would lack both elaborate means for the preservation of food and the food surplus which they could so preserve.

The second segment of the food surplus axis would include those societies which could build up an appreciable food surplus above the day to day needs and store it against those times of the year when food was scarce. There would be sufficient spare time for the artistic elaboration of functional artifacts and for the manufacture of goods which were not directly related with subsistence pursuits. Part time specialization of labor would be probable. There would be a tendency for societies in this segment of the food surplus axis to have a fairly permanent central settlement near the most significant source of food. Storage of food surpluses will tend to inhibit movements by the group.

The third segment of the food surplus axis would include those groups which produce a surplus in a quantity which would permit: 1. the maintenance of a limited number of full time specialists in religion and/or industry; 2. the production of a considerable volume of nonfunctional manufactures which would be consumed in dedication to temples, as grave furniture, in destruction to gain prestige, etc.; 3. the devotion of considerable energy in the construction of features which were of a community nature and which were not strictly for subsistence purposes.

The fourth segment of the food surplus axis would contain societies whose food surplus was sufficient to maintain large bodies of full time specialists in manufacturing, religion, government, and war on a permanent basis so that these bodies of specialists could be organized into elaborately structured, hierarchial and self-perpetuating institutions. In societies within this segment of the axis the amount of energy expended on public works is greatly increased.

The second axis concerns itself with the means of food production rather than what is achieved through these means. Though several means may add to the subsistence economy of a single society this is less clearly a continuous variable than the other axis. The means of subsistence is the same concept as the subsistence pattern which was so belabored in the earlier section of this paper. If the Willey-Phillips scheme is now to be discussed in these terms it is necessary to pass from a hypothetical to specific treatment of subsistence patterns and to come to grips with the problem of how many specific subsistence patterns were significantly involved in the PreColumbian development of culture in the New World.

The first major distinction of subsistence pattern is between food production and merely living off the food provided by the unmodified environment. That is the distinction between the cultivation of plants and/or the raising of domesticated animals on the one hand and what is called by the vague and general term of "hunting and gathering" on the other. In the New World it is probably safe to concentrate attention on the cultivation of plants and neglect domesticated animals since it seems unlikely that in PreColumbian times any New World group derived a really major portion of its diet from domesticated animals, at least not to the extent of having its settlement patterns and yearly rounds of activity largely governed by the needs of its domesticated animals. [I now think this statement too strong.]

Under the general heading of "hunting and gathering" at least three patterns can be recognized which give promise of proving to be basic when more is known about New World pre-history. The first includes those societies which on the basis of archaeological evidence appear to have derived a major part of their subsistence from the hunting of large, land animals. In practice, if not in theory, this group is largely coterminous with the Early Lithic stage of Willey and Phillips. The empirical criteria for recognizing archaeological assemblages which belonged to societies in this grouping are a predominance of large, well flaked projectile points of a generally lanceolate form and of skin working tools and an absence or scarcity of stone tools suitable for the preparation of vegetable foods.

The second subsistence pattern under "hunting and gathering" contains those preagricultural societies which have recently been placed together under the title of "Desert Cultures" (Jennings et. al. 1956: 69-72). According to the usage of this paper it seems more reasonable to refer to this as the Desert subsistence pattern. Since the publication of the Willey-Phillips stage scheme, workers have evidently felt the necessity of a grouping on the same level of magnitude as Early Lithic and Archaic to embrace materials not logically compatible with either group. This category accomodates a large number of archaeologically known societies, mainly in Western United States but extending well into Mexico, whose diagnostic artifact is the unshaped hand stone and hand mill (mano and metate in the usage wide spread among western archaeologists). Large core tools, including a form often called a scraper-plane are a frequent but not invariable concomitant feature. Projectile points and other examples of controlled stone flaking are generally rare at least when compared to the bulk of grinding tools. This emphasis on flat stone mills suggests a high degree of dependence on small, hard seeds both from grasses and plants in the genera *Chenopodium* and *Amaranthus*. It is this feature, the dependence on seed collecting which should be regarded as the basic element of the subsistence pattern which had been called "Desert."

What is included in the Desert pattern is largely stolen from the Archaic stage of Willey and Phillips, but some groups were to be found in their Early Lithic Stage. Typical archaeological assemblages within this pattern include the Cochise series of Arizona and Oak Grove of the Santa Barbara Coast of California (Rogers 1929).

For the third pattern the term Archaic will be retained from the Willey and Phillips system. It must be openly admitted that this category is in part residual. From the point of view of dirt archaeology an "Archaic" assemblage is often identified by the presence of polished stone tools, but this usage is frequently violated. In practice any site which is non-ceramic, has a large number of large stemmed or notched projectile points, and lacks both large numbers of hand mills and projectile points which are of specific "Early Lithic" type, is in danger of being classified as "Archaic". There are also difficulties when a definition is attempted on the basis of pattern of subsistence economy. On the one hand there is the tendency to make progressively greater use of riverine and marine resources where these are available. This takes the form both of the collecting of shell fish and of fishing. On the other hand there is an emphasis on the use of nuts for food, especially acorns where these are available. In Tropical Forest environment various palm nuts may be substituted. Finally hunting of medium and small sized land animals is usually maintained as a significant though perhaps not a major source of food.

There is perhaps no logical relationship among all the various traits mentioned above for Archaic, though certain functional groupings do appear. The extensive use of mortars and pitted stones seems related to the processing of nuts and a high frequency of mortars might be considered a good diagnostic of Archaic sites. Willey and Phillips have related the presence of heavy wood working tools, usually of polished stone, to the necessity of clearing and living in heavily wooded environments (1955: 740). In spite of the fact that not all of these traits show a logical association at first glance, they do seem to hang together as some sort of a complex in widely separated parts of the New World. Cultures which are archtypical to the average archaeologist's concepts of "Archaic" are found in such widely separated parts of the New World as Eastern United States, and the Central Valley of California, and on the East Coast of Brazil.

For purposes of this paper the "Archaic" pattern will be defined as non-agricultural, specialized neither in the direction of Big Game Hunting nor of seed gathering, and where possible specialized in the direction of the utilization of riverine and marine food resources. Cultures such as those of the Eskimo and the Northwest Coast Indians are so highly specialized within certain segments of the possibilities inherent within the basic Archaic pattern that it might be better to treat them separately, but for the sake of simplicity this will not be done.

The major category of agriculture in the New World can be similarly subdivided. There were two major patterns of agricultural subsistence in the New World which appear to have had, at least in their earlier phases of development, independent histories. These are the pattern of seed crop agriculture with maize as the major crop and the pattern of root crop agriculture with manioc as the staple. The sum of available evidence is less than conclusive but strongly suggests a Mesoamerican origin for the former (Mangelsdorf, 1954) and an independent South American origin for the latter (Rouse, 1957). It is not certain that manioc was the original crop with which the incipient agriculturalists of South America experimented but at an early date, and probably before the introduction of maize into South America, it was a staple crop which made efficient agriculture possible in lowland South America (*Ibid.*).

The situation is similar for maize. While it may not have been the earliest crop in Mesoamerica, it was the crop which led to really efficient agricultural patterns and permitted the expansion of Meso-american patterns of culture North into the United States and South into western South America.

On the basis of available evidence it would seem that the maize and manioc patterns of agriculture ran separate courses up to about 800 B.C. at which time they came into close contact, merged, and mutually reinforced each other through parts of their range (Bird, 1951, 40; Larco Hoyle 1947, 150).

The objection might be raised that the quinoa-potato pattern of the extreme highlands of the Central Andes should be given the status of a third major division. This will not be done since it seems most likely that this pattern represents the successful attempt to extend the range of a mixed maize and manioc agriculture beyond the useful geographical limits of both plants, with quinoa being substituted for maize and potatoes for manioc.

Beyond the two major groupings just discussed, hunting and gathering on the one hand and agriculture on the other, there is another sort of pattern which is less obvious and not strictly comparable to the other two. That is a pattern of parasitism. By this is meant the supporting of part or all of the specialists of one society, who produce no food, on the economic surplus built up by another society. Like all forms of parasitism in nature this requires the most delicate kind of adjustment. Not only must the parasite subdue the host but it must extract only a limited part of the surplus available in the host. If this limit is exceeded the host society will become completely disorganized and cease to be productive. It is obvious that this kind of parasitism, which we may call militarism or empire, requires a period of experimentation before a truly successful pattern can be reached. It is also clear that there are minimums of economic surplus which limit the temporal and spatial distribution of empire. Initially there must be sufficient surplus in the conquering society to support the non-productive mechanism of subjugation, the army. Also there must be considerable surplus in the host society or the whole enterprise is not worth the effort. Empire is a secondary kind of economic pattern which is possible only after the primary economic pattern of a group of societies in a region has reached a high level of surplus, usually that level which has been designated four in this discussion.

It is now possible to set up a two dimensional diagram combining these two axes (Fig. 1).

The ideal procedure would be to plot all known societies of the aboriginal New World, including both those known through ethnography and those known through archaeology on this graph and see how they are distributed. If a unilinear conception of stages is to be accepted as completely accurate, then the distribution of individual societies should be completely linear. In other words the correlation between measurements of the societies on both axes should approach 1. Stated in still another way the position of any society on one axis should absolutely determine its position on the other.

The ideal procedure will not be followed here as it would take a full scale monograph to complete the task. The alternative will be to make an estimate of the perimeter of the swarm of points. The shaded area on Fig. 1 gives such an estimate of the outline of the swarm. It should not be necessary to give a detailed defense of these general limits to anyone even slightly familiar with the data of New World archaeology and ethnography. The two extreme positions included within the outline will be discussed briefly. These are squares C-3 and E-1. Certain California cultures fulfill certain of the requirements of level 3 in the food surplus axis and are completely non-agricultural. Among these would be the Gabrileño and Chumash on the south coast and the Pomo-Patwin Valley block in Central California. These societies present some of the criteria which were set up for segment 3. These included vast amounts of nonfunctional trade goods, a degree of specialization of labor in the manufacture of such trade goods. In Central California relatively large communal, religious structures were maintained. Various groups within the climax region of the Northwest Coast area would also qualify as C-3.

Likely candidates for the E-1 square would be the archaeologically defined societies inhabiting the Tamaulipas Caves and showing only primitive vestiges of agricultural practices (MacNeish, 1957).

On the basis of this distribution it seems clear that there is a definite tendency with which the proponents of Cultural Evolution have long grappled. Since some of the societies which diverge most markedly from this tendency are those which have figured in the discussion of specialization in culture which has just been completed, it would seem that specialization might be useful auxiliary concept in the aresenal of the cultural evolutionist.

It is now time to discuss in a more precise way the connection between the two separate kinds of systems with which this paper has

	1	2	3	4
	Hand to mouth existence. No storage.	Storage Central Town with some population all year round. Some craft specialization.	Much craft specialization. Full time political leaders. Specialized religious structures.	Hierarchies of Political, Religious and Military Specialists.
F Parasitism "Empire"	Early Tamaulipas Complexes •			
E Maize Agriculture		Zuni •	Cahokia •	• Inca • Aztec • Huari • Teotihuacan Chavin de Huantar • • Tikal
D "Root crop horticulture" with	Siriono •	• Amahuaca	Sitio Conte (Cocle) •	• Omagua "Kingdoms"

514

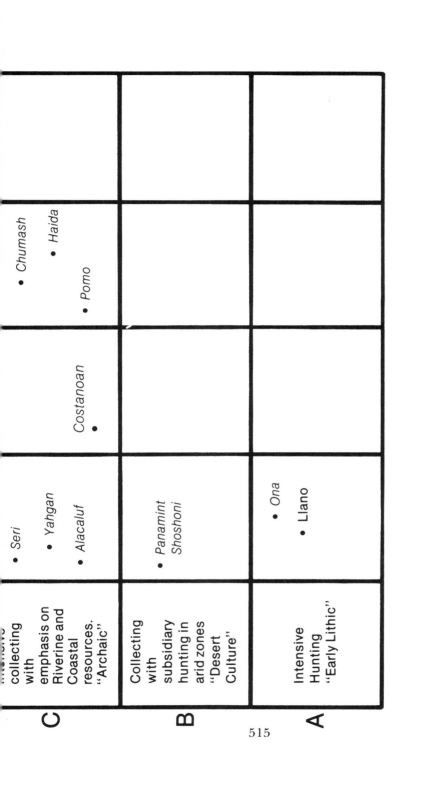

C collecting with emphasis on Riverine and Coastal resources. "Archaic"	• Seri • Yahgan • Alacaluf	• Costanoan	• Chumash • Haida • Pomo	
B Collecting with subsidiary hunting in arid zones "Desert Culture"	• Panamint Shoshoni			
A Intensive Hunting "Early Lithic"	• Ona • Llano			

515

been dealing. Though the efficiency of a subsistence pattern defined in terms of the number of people supported per unit area is not the same as the measure of food surplus available to support elaboration of institutions, it is difficult to imagine that there could be a major increase along one of these scales without a significant increase along the other. As we have seen a new stage is marked either by the introduction of a new pattern or by a great increase in food surplus. Either of these conditions is likely to be associated with a disruption of demographic balance which will trigger a radiation of the type described in the second section of the paper. The ultimate implication of this relationship is a strong tendency for cultural stages to coincide with major historically related traditions. As long as one is staying within the framework of a single continent or hemisphere, the old term, *Kulturkreise,* is equally appropriate for these units of relatedness. This set of circumstances explains Willey and Phillips' lack of success in suppressing another set of criteria for stages which were constantly tending to creep into their system. These are criteria of historical relatedness among societies to be classified together in a stage.

Cultural Radiations, Cultural Stages, and Problems of New World Culture History

In this section I will compare at a few important points the facts concerning cultural development in the New World with the abstract workings out of the systems discussed in the two preceding sections.

The Early Lithic Stage of Willey and Phillips contains those societies which were responsible for the original peopling of the New World. The characteristics of these societies as they entered and spread through the New World is of theoretical interest. If those "Early Lithic" societies regarded as typical, are in fact the earliest "Early Lithic" societies, then highly specialized groups initially peopled the New World. The "typical" Early Lithic assemblages, those characterized by a high frequency of beautifully flaked, lanceolate points, showing various distinctive features, i.e. fluting, suggest societies which were specialized as to food source and environment. The high percentage of projectile points in these complexes argues that large land animals were the major source of food. Where faunal remains have accompanied such artifacts this impression of intensive utilization of particular mamalian species is confirmed (Sellards, 1952). The dependence on large herds of big game involved an environmental restriction to those areas where such herds were found, specifically to grass land and tundra regions. The big game hunting groups must be considered as highly specialized in relation to a specific environment, but an environment of a type which is wide spread in a large land mass.

Eiseley has made out a very good case that this specialized form of Early Lithic was in fact the first form of human society to enter the New World (1955). Indeed it is his theses that it was this specialization, this mastery over a particular food source, which permitted the peopling of the New World. Krieger has criticised this view on the grounds that it will not cover some facts in the small but growing corpus of data relating to the earliest known inhabitants of the New World (Krieger, 1956). However this question is ultimately decided, Eiseley's discussion of the nature of the early, big game hunting societies stands as valid. Whether these groups represent the original inhabitants of the New World or a secondary specialization, taking place either in the New World or the Old, their efficient subsistence pattern caused the spread of a relatively uniform culture over much of the New World. This is more easily seen for North America where the evidence is fairly abundant; even in South America the limited finds so far uncovered support this picture (Rouse and Cruxent 1957 b).

[I do not now believe that the specialized, big game hunters could have been the first inhabitants of the New World. There are now simply too many demonstrably ancient complexes which do not fit the pattern. Oddly, the archaeological record from South America and the Arctic has produced more and more convincing evidence than temperate North America. It is interesting and significant though that Paul S. Martin has recently (1973) argued for the viability of a model such as I have presented above. Even more interesting from the point of view of this paper is the case which Martin makes for what, in the terms of this paper, might be called an explosive radiation. By combining the dated distribution of obviously related "big game hunting" complexes on the grasslands of North and South America with some most ingenius model building, Martin presents a convincing picture of how these groups very rapidly expanded their range by migration through all areas of the New World which could support their economic pattern at the same time exterminating the large herds of grassland megafauna on which they were totally dependent. Using Joe Ben Wheat's (1972) reconstruction of an actual Bison kill which indicates both hunting strategy and the minimum size of the group involved, as a basis of argument, it is easy to see how such a spread would come about. It is more efficient for organized groups to hunt large herds of megafauna than for solitary hunters, but large, organized groups must be fed by more frequent and larger harvests of game. Communal hunting methods will be more destructive of the game, since a total herd is likely to be eliminated in a single drive. Such a drive is likely to produce more meat than the group can immediately eat or process, so that there will be considerable waste of meat. All of these tendencies mean that the game resources of a particular territory will be depleted more rapidly, and various hunting bands will be placed in competition for the remaining grassland still stocked with game. Military effectiveness will be enhanced by still larger and more tightly organized groups, which will require still more frequent and efficient hunting, and so on . . . In other words, we have a system in which all loops give positive feedback so that the upward spiral toward larger groups and more destructive hunting practices is continuously accelerating. It is not surprising that this economic system devoured the resources on all the grasslands of the New World with a rapidity, which in the time scale of the archaeologist resembles that of a fire-storm.]

Archaeological evidence is lacking which would permit a clear picture of the nature of any societies which might have existed in the New World earlier than the specialized early hunters. It is beyond the scope of this paper to evaluate the evidence for and against the existence of such societies. If they did exist, it is possible to imagine their nature. One can dimly visualize a low level and very generalized kind of hunting and gathering economy using most readily available sources of food, but doing so not very efficiently. It has been argued that if such societies did enter the New World, they must have done so during a period of warm climate and not during the height of the Fourth Glacial advance (Mather, 1954).

The origins of the Desert pattern of subsistence are explicable in terms of either of the two candidates for the earliest kind of society in the New World. If specialized big game hunters were the earliest inhabitants, then the manner in which the Desert pattern developed among them has already been described, in purely theoretical terms, in the first section. It is a case of an expanding group of societies reaching the edges of regions where their original subsistence pattern was not practicable in this case desert areas deficient in the big game on which they were depending. At the peripheries of these areas the subsistence pattern would be modified to take advantage of more readily available food sources, in this case grass seeds, and once this modification in subsistence pattern had progressed sufficiently far the whole region would be occupied.

If on the other hand we start with an unspecialized hunting and gathering group, all that is necessary is an emphasis on certain aspects already present in the subsistence pattern, in other words a slight specialization to meet the requirements of a rigorous environment.

The geographical range of the Desert Culture pattern is continuous and it requires no very great leap of the imagination to see it taking its characteristic form in one part of this range and from there spreading by migration throughout the rest of its range. [Walter Taylor's excellent essay on the historical relationship between the Hokaltecan languages and the spread of the Desert economic pattern [1961] is in total agreement with the position which I take here. This parallel involves both Taylor's epistemology in approaching the problem and his substantive conclusions. This concurrence is gratifying, in that Taylor's attack on the problem was totally independent of my own.] Considering the present state of our knowledge concerning the earlier South American cultures, it would be difficult either to affirm or to deny that groups with this pattern of subsistence ever migrated into the Southern part of the New World.

It is probable that societies of the Desert pattern reached their maximum extent around 6000 years ago. Since that period there has been a progressive encroachment on their range by Archaic pattern groups from the North and West and by groups practicing maize agriculture from the South. Of those groups which survived up to the period of White contact perhaps the Panamint Shoshoni might be considered the best example of a Desert Pattern culture. It is also possible that the Desert Pattern culture somewhere within its range gave rise to the pattern of maize agriculture, which is a specialization with regard to a particular grass seed.

The Archaic pattern of subsistence is difficult to treat in terms of this system. If there was a generalized hunting and gathering pattern functioning very early in the New World, then the various Archaic groups may represent nothing more than societies which have maintained the more balanced subsistence patterns of their ancestors without the extreme specializations of either the big game hunters or the seed gatherers. If big game hunting was the original subsistence pattern in the New World then the Archaic pattern societies may represent a number of independent attempts to meet the collapse of the big game hunting

The Measures of Man

economy as climate changed, or key species were exterminated by over-hunting. Certainly some of the groups placed inside their Archaic stage by Willey and Phillips represent one or the other of these possi-bilities. All of this discussion points up the residual nature of the Ar-chaic pattern.

The similarities between the block of "Archaic" cultures in Eastern United States and those of California, and between both of these and the Sambaquís remains of Eastern Brazil have led to speculation that there may have been an historical connection among them. In a num-ber of cases the similarities are quite specific (Willey, 1949; Baerreis, 1950). It would be tempting to suggest that these similarities are the result of migrations from one of these areas into the other two and in the light of the orientation of this paper it would be helpful if such a migration could be tied to the spread of a particularly successful eco-nomic pattern. If one were to pursue this line of thinking, one would probably suggest that an economy oriented toward the collection of molluscs would be the one most likely to have caused such a spread. These speculations had best be dropped since at present it is difficult to reconstruct the time and nature of the Archaic connections between Eastern and Western United States, if indeed they do exist. No connect-ing links have turned up archaeologically.

When the problem of suggesting a date and a route for a migration which would connect the Archaic of Eastern United States and that of Brazil is examined, the difficulties are found to be even more formid-able. At any particular time Archaic and Desert patterns seem to have had a complementary distribution in space, so the Southwest of the United States and Mexico seem to have been blocked as a route south for most of the time prior to the arrival of Columbus. Indeed no com-plexes of the "classic" Archaic type, with the full assmeblage of pol-ished stone artifacts, have been found in these areas. The West Indies offer the alternate route and this area, before the spread of societies with the manioc pattern of agriculture out of South America, did have a subsistence pattern which must be called Archaic. However it was a very watered down Archaic and almost all the specific traits which sug-gest connections between Eastern United States and Brazil are missing in this intermediate area. In these cases, however, we are speaking largely from ignorance rather than from any very thorough knowledge of the nonceramic cultures of the areas involved.

The abstract speculations in an earlier section of this paper suggest why there should be societies with incipient agriculture, which were of long duration and localized distribution. Agricultural societies will not start spreading outward until their subsistence economy has markedly surpassed that of their non-agricultural neighbors. This will not occur until the cultivated plants have been improved as a response to long cultivation. Such improvement is dependent on genetic changes within the plants and so may be slow in coming. If there were not evidence for such societies we would have to imagine their existence. Luckily there are several sites which admirably fullfill these theoretical expectations. The Tamaulipas Caves and Bat Cave (Mangelsdorf, 1954), give us good pictures of incipient maize agriculture, while Huaca Prieta and other coastal sites in Peru showing a non-maize agriculture of long standing suggest one branch of the early agricultural experimentation in South America which in other regions of South America seems to have led to the effective domestication of manioc. In these cases we have what is certainly the early experimental beginnings of agriculture. Societies of this type form part of those grouped in the "Preformative" of Willey and Phillips. If the stage is to be strictly developmental, then they are the only examples which should be so classified.

The other societies placed in this stage by Willey and Phillips are largely agricultural societies of low or moderate efficiency but the level of efficiency is not related to the experimental nature of the agriculture as such. In some cases they seem to be dealing with agricultural groups who had recently pushed or had been pushed into areas for which their agricultural and total subsistence patterns were poorly adapted. These societies represent periods of secondary readaptation of pattern which were already adapted to other areas, rather than periods of original experimentation. Such periods may be followed either by better adaptation to the particular environment or by complete failure. In other cases they seem to be dealing with societies which have received individual cultigens or complexes of cultigens as diffused traits and are in the process of integrating these traits into their originally non-agricultural pattern. The theoretical model for both of these situations has already been touched on briefly in the second section of this paper and will not be belabored a second time. The attribution of Adena-Hopewell to a "Preformative" stage will be discussed in the next part of this section.

The societies which Willey and Phillips have placed in the "Formative" stage are most interesting because they show behavior which is close to that expectable on the basis of the theoretical considerations covered in this paper. The position will be defended that maize-based "Formative" cultures and manioc-based "Formative" cultures are two separate entities, at least when viewed historically. For the present, attention will be focused on maize "Formative" for it is better known. The criterion used by Willey and Phillips to separate "Formative" from "Preformative" is the presence of stable village life. It is here suggested that an equally useful criterion would be one of efficiency in the sense defined in the opening section of this paper. One might start the "Formative" at the time when the efficiency of the agricultural societies had so far surpassed that of their neighbors that rapid expansions through migration was the result. With recent advances in our knowledge of the prehistory of both North and South America it seems likely that there are historical connections among various of the maize based Formative cultures of the New World. These historical connections are so close as to strongly suggest migration.

Krieger developed the implications of this position most thoroughly for the groups in the Eastern United States (Newell and Krieger, 1949: 231-232). Whatever the ultimate outcome of the present arguments concerning the exact dating of the earliest Caddoan materials, Krieger's demonstration of the relationship of these materials to the Middle to Late Formative materials of Mesoamerica is hard to demolish. The artifacts of Caddoan and Mississippian Culture also suggest a peculiar kind of conservatism in Formative Cultures which have migrated into an environment different from the one in which they developed. Such conservatism is found in such features as ceramics and art style. The explanation which suggests itself is that during the period in which the subsistence economy is adjusting to the new environment there is less free energy to be devoted to nonfunctional, technological and artistic elaboration.

The possibilities of migrations of maize based Formative societies from Mesoamerica to South America have been developed by the recent writings of Portar (1953), Willey (1955), Evans and Meggers (1957), and the Reichel-Dolmatoffs (1956). It now seems likely that the development of high civilization in Peru was more the result of the intrusion of Mesoamerican type Formative culture into the region at about 800 B.C., than of the long agricultural development which preceded this event on the Peruvian coast.

[More recent work increases the probability of these migrations, but also indicates that the direction was from South America to Mesoamerica and that manioc agriculture was the economic impetus. (Lathrap 1971, 1973, 1974,; Green and Lowe 1967)].

It seems likely that the historical unity as well as the developmental unity of the maize based Formative cultures in both continents strongly colored the working definition of Formative used by Willey and Phillips. Perhaps unconsciously this covert historical criterion was allowed to outweigh the others which are overtly set forth in the definition. Their placement of the Adena-Hopewell materials in Preformative rather than Formative seems explicable because this cultural tradition is not in the Mesoamerican Formative mold. It is harder to justify in terms of economic surplus or settlement pattern.

It is now possible to turn to the manioc based Formative pattern. There are several lines of evidence which indicate that fully developed and highly productive manioc cultivation is at least as old in South America as any form of the cultivation of maize. [The remainder of my 1957 discussion of the beginnings of Tropical Forest Agriculture is so totally superceded by my 1970 book, The Upper Amazon, that it has been omitted. I now suspect that the beginnings of horticulture in tropical riverine zones of South America are to be sought in the 10-15, 000 B.C. range].

The societies placed by Willey and Phillips in their "Classic" stage represent no change in subsistence pattern. They do represent the full realization of the potentialities of a subsistence pattern which extends back in time to the Preformative. The differences among Preformative, Formative, and Classic are purely of degree along the scale measuring food surplus. They are not differences of pattern. The full realization of potentialities suggests a high degree of adaptation to the particular environment. We might expect the Classic Stage societies to arise in those areas where Formative stage societies had been established for a considerable period of time and thus had had the opportunity of adapting and elaborating the subsistence patterns to a form most specialized in terms of the conditions of the particular environment.

The Classic stage societies in the New World arose only out of maize based Formative societies. [I would now greatly modify this statement]. In the Mesoamerican region their emergence can be explained in terms of a long period of adaptation for here maize based Formative societies seem to have their greatest time depth. The situation in Peru is less easily disposed of but can be partially explained in terms of preadaptation to the particular environment and by the ease with which the incoming Formative societies displaced or at least dominated the sparse indigenous populations.

Only two areas of the New World had societies which attained the type of organization which Willey and Phillips have called "Post-Classic." It would seem that this pattern of organization was reached more or less independently in Mesoamerica and Peru. It might be suggested that the most practical criterion to use for its definition would be in terms of subsistence pattern. The dominant "Post-Classic" society of an area is parasitic in that it partially supports its non-producing specialists on the food surplus taken from other societies. It is to be noted that "Post-Classic" cultures arose only out of a basis of maize agriculture in the New World. It is further to be noted that they arose only in areas which had already attained what Willey and Phillips have called a "Classic" stage of development. The reason for this is obvious. It is only the "Classic" society which initially will have the large body of economically non-productive specialists necessary to subdue and parasitize another "Classic" culture, and in the days before extreme industrialization with its extensive and peculiar needs for exotic raw material, it is only the "Classic" stage culture which is worth tapping for its surplus.

These simplistic observations stand in an interesting relationship to the idea of the "Co-Tradition" which has been successfully applied by Bennett and others. This is basically the idea of a cultural area through time but has other interesting side features. We are now in a position to say how the boundaries for such culture areas are originally set and subsequently maintained in the two regions where the concept has been most successfully applied, in Peru and Mesoamerica (Bennet 1948; Levine 1958). The original spread of Formative Culture through the incipient co-tradition area provides the uniform cultural base out of which it is to grow. The limits of the area are set geographically in terms of environments which will most quickly permit the Formative base to reach high efficiency. Within these limits there will first appear a series of "Classic Stage" societies. Within this block of Classic Stage societies one or more will embark on a path of conquest and one will ultimately conquer most of the societies worth conquering. Ideally this should take in the whole block of Classic societies. Such an Empire will have the effect of bringing a degree of cultural uniformity throughout the region. Like all parasitic adjustments the empire requires a very delicate balance between the parasite and the host. Because of this fact the first experimentations along these lines are likely to have a success which is ephemeral, at least when viewed in the anthropologist's time perspective. The collapse of an empire will lead to a period of regional rediversification after which another society will succeed in establishing at least temporary hegemony over the block of highly productive societies. The total extent of any of these empires is likely to be slightly different from that of any other, but they will all tend to be congruent with the total block of productive societies which had already reached a "Classic Stage." In this way the boundaries of the co-tadition are maintained through time. The other result is that within the co-tradition area there will be a regular rhythm between periods of cultural unity and periods showing a high degree of regional diversification. The Mesoamerican co-tradition shows at least three periods of unification, with the unifying cultures being, from earliest to latest, Teotihuacan, Tula and Aztec (Lathrap 1957). The expansive periods in Peru were only two, Tihaunaco and Inca. [One could also make a case for Chavin]. Rowe has commented on this rhythm in his recent discussion of Andean prehistory (1956). It is interesting to note in the Peruvian co-tradition that there are instances of what appears to be revivalistic nationalism in the wake of crumbling empires (Lathrap, ed. 1956, 18-19). These cases seem completely comparable to the sort of "Nationalism" which was rampant in late nineteenth century Europe. This nationalistic pattern seems to come into being as soon as an empire has been established and would seem to be an important factor in leading to rapid regional diversification as soon as an empire collapses.

V. *Summary.*

If there can be said to be any subject matter in this paper, it is the series of difficulties arising out of the treatment of New World Archaeological data by the Willey and Phillips stage scheme. I do not claim that recognizing these difficulties is an innovation, for the authors of that scheme explicitly demonstrate that they were well aware of them. One of these difficulties is the lack of complete correlation between criteria of food surplus and criteria of means of food production, the problem of reducing a two dimensional system to a linear system. The other complication is the tendency of criteria of historical relatedness to creep into the system and partially or completely to replace criteria of the other two kinds.

A model which attempts to relate distribution in time and space to the appearance of elaboration of institutions may shed some light on the difficulties noted above. The core of this scheme lies in its insistence that a clear distinction be maintained at all times between the economic basis for a society and what is produced by means of this basis, either in terms of efficiency, the level of population maintained, or in terms of food surplus, and the number of non-productive specialists maintained. The economic basis of any society is called its economic pattern. It is the contention of this paper that in the culture history of any continent the number of basic economic patterns is finite and definable. In fact it should be a rather small number. With sufficient archaeological work the point of origin of each pattern can be determined and from that point on the subsequent history of the pattern can be specified.

I further contend that such economic patterns, once they are established, will behave in certain respects like radiating species in biology. By migration of societies they will tend to extend their limits to the maximum. Their success in this will be determined by certain principles already discussed. These patterns, as they expand through migration, tend to spread relatively uniform culture over wide areas. In part, the patterns discussed in this paper as important in New World culture History have agreed with the stage concept as proposed by Willey and Phillips; and the correspondences and lacks of correspondences have been mentioned. It must be emphasized that the economic patterns of this paper ought to represent historically valid entities, though at the present state of our knowledge it is not always possible to show that they do.

The subsistence pattern also behaves like a biological organism in that it too may adapt and become highly specialized to a particular limited environment. This possibility may mean that a society with a pattern generally regarded as less efficient may become so highly specialized to a particular geographical niche that it is able to maintain itself against the pressures of societies with later and basically more efficient economic patterns, but patterns which are not yet adapted to the specific niche into which they are trying to penetrate. It is this kind of situation which gives rise to the anomalies in rigidly conceived schemes of cultural evolution. The ethnographic picture of California stands as a fine example of such misfits.

A particularly successful specialization within an economic pattern will also tend to spread outward by migration. The migration will be less sweeping, however, as the limits will be set by the extent of the specific kind of environment which was responsible for the specialization. A good example of this is the spread of Northwest Coast societies,

I am assuming that Northwest Coast culture was brought to Northern California by a migration of Yurok and Wiyot speaking peoples.

[As population builds up and the number of discrete societies competing for the same segment of "living room" increases, the manner in which such competition is resolved may require a more complex analysis if it is to be understood. I have argued as if the resolution would always be in favor of the society with a larger population, a denser population, and a more complex social organization, but even a casual familiarity with the record of New World culture history suggests a few contrary examples.] A classic instance would be the migration of the Athapascan peoples from North to South. A demonstration that these migrations were accompanied by the spread of the bow and arrow as a weapon in warfare might offer a partial understanding of the migration in terms of an increase in military efficiency. However, I do not think that the sum of available archaeological evidence would support such an explanation. If one were placed in the position of having to set up a theoretical model which would cover a large number of such cases, where people are moving against a more efficient and specialized subsistence pattern, an argument in terms of the refilling of only partially utilized land might be plausible. The generalized hunting and gathering society tends to use its full territory about equally; as it becomes specialized around certain food resources or should it develop or be replaced by an agricultural economic pattern, there will be an increasing utilization of certain small areas of the groups territory, i.e., the mouths of rivers, major groves of oak trees, or the best agricultural land. The utilization of the rest of the territory will be progressively less intense. The result of these processes will be to create a partially demographic vacuum which will draw in peoples from other areas, who may still be sufficiently generalized as hunters and gatherers to take full advantage of the "empty" land. This is not to say that these movements will not be resisted by the original owners of the lands. It may ultimately seem to them, however, that the effort of keeping out the invaders is more than the possession of these lands, which have now become marginal to their way of life, is worth.

In this paper I attempt to show how the so called historical approaches; *Kulturkreise,* "Age-Area," migration studies, etc., can be related to the so called evolutionary approach. Perhaps no pseudo-issue has muddied the pool of anthropological thinking more than the distinction between history on the one hand and "pure" Cultural Evolution on the other. It seems unlikely that the issue is entirely dead yet. If the model proposed by this paper is insufficient as a demonstration of how these two approaches interlock it may at least show the direction in which more adequate synthesis should turn.

One of the recurrent themes of this paper has been the emphasis on the spread of cultural patterns by the migrations of societies, this emphasis has been determined by the total orientation of the paper. That migrations were important in New World culture history is indicated by what has long been known about the relationships among New World languages. The linguistic data, especially when mapped, clearly cries out for our acceptance of numerous and wide spread migrations, and with the recent development of lexico-statistical methods, which at the very least can give us some idea of the relative order of various migrations, it would seem time to try to face the problem constructively.

[Migration as an expression of demographic disequilibrium is a process and is as amenable to an analysis based in a uniformitarian world view as any of the processes of geology or sub-human biology. I am arguing that an understanding of this process is a, perhaps the, major precondition for an understanding of cultural evolution. Cultural evolution is an adaptive process with societies adapting to their environment. The first groups entering a continent may be free to adapt solely to the geographical environment, but as the continent or hemisphere becomes filled with competing societies and their markedly different economic patterns, this competition forms the major part of the environment to which a society must adapt. It is the ongoing process of demographic growth and migration which sets up these confrontations.]

References

Baerreis, D.A.
    1950   Comments on South American archaic relations. American Antiquity, *16:* 165-166.
Beardsley, R.K., et. al.
    1956   Functional and evolutionary implications of community patterning. Memoirs of the Society for American Archaeology, No. 11: 192-157.
Bennett, W.C.
    1948   The Peruvian co-tradition. Memoirs of the Society for American Archaeology, No. 4: pp. 1-7.
Bennett, W.C., and J.B. Bird

1949 Andean culture history. American Museum of Natural History, Handbook Series No. 15, New York, New York.

Bird, J. B.
1951 South American radiocarbon dates. Memoirs of the Society for American Archaeology, No. 8, Salt Lake City, Utah.

Birdsell, J. B.
1950 Some implications of the genetical concept of race in terms of spatial analysis. Cold Spring Harbor Symposia on Quantitative Biology, Cold Spring Harbor, New York, *15*.

Buchsbaum, R.
1938 Animals Without Backbones. University of Chicago Press, Chicago, Illinois.

Coville, F. V.
1892 The Panamint Indians of California. American Anthropologist, *5:* 251-261.

Dumond, D. E.
1972 Population growth and political centralization. In: Population Growth—Anthropological Implications. B. Spooner, ed. The MIT Press, Cambridge, Massachusetts, pp. 286-310.

1972b Prehistoric population growth and subsistence change in Eskimo Alaska. In: Population Growth—Anthropological Implications. B. Spooner, ed. The MIT Press, Cambridge, Massachusetts, pp. 311-328.

Eiseley, L. C.
1955 The Paleo-Indians: their survival and diffusion. New Interpretations of Aboriginal American Culture History, Washington, D. C., pp. 1-1.

Evans, C., and B. J. Meggers
1957 Formative period cultures in the Guayas Basin, Coastal Ecuador. American Antiquity, *20:* 235-247.

Flannery, K. V.
1971 Archaeology with a capital S. Paper Read at the 70th Annual Meeting of the American Anthropological Association, New York.

Ford, J. A.
1954 The type concept revisited. American Anthropologist, *56:* 42-54.

Green, D. F., and G. W. Lowe
1967 Altamira and Padre Piedra, early preclassic sites in Chiapas, Mexico. Papers of the New World Archaeological Foundation, No. 20, Brigham Young University, Provo, Utah.

Huxley, J.
1964 Evolution: the modern synthesis. Science Editions, John Wiley and Sons, Inc., New York.

Jennings, J. D., et. al.

1956   The American Southwest: a problem in cultural isolation. Memoirs of the Society for American Archeology, No. 11, pp. 59-127.

Klimek, S.
1935   Culture element distributions: I. The structure of California Indian Culture. University of California Publications in American Archaeology and Ethnology, *37:* 1-70.

Krieger, A. D.
1956   Review: New interpretations of aboriginal American culture history. American Anthropologist, *58:* 939-941.

Kroeber, A. L.
1923   Anthropology. Harcourt, Brace and Company, New York.

1939   Cultural and natural areas of native North America. University of California Publications in American Archaeology and Ethnology, *38:* 1-242.

Larco Hoyle, R.
1947   A culture sequence for the north coast of Peru. Bureau of American Ethnology Bulletin 143, Washington, D. C., pp. 149-176.

Lathrap, D. W.
1957   The classic stage in Mesoamerica. The Kroeber Anthropological Society Papers, No. 17, pp. 38-74.

1970   The Upper Amazon. Thames and Hudson, London.

1971   The tropical forest and the cultural context of Chavin. In: Dumbarton Oaks Conference on Chavin. E. Benson, ed. Dumbarton Oaks Research Library, Washington, D. C., pp. 73-100.

1973a   Complex iconographic features shared by Olmec and Chavin and some speculations on their possible significance. Primer Simposio de Correlaciones Anthropologicas Andino-Mesoamericano, 25-31, Julio, 1971, Guayaquil. In Press.

1974   The arid lands, the moist tropics, and the emergence of great art styles in the New World. In: Art and Environment in Native America. I. Traylor and M. E. King, eds. Texas Tech. University, Lubbock, Texas. pp. 115-158.

Lathrap. D. W. (editor)
1956   An archaeological classification of culture contact situations. Memoirs of the Society for American Archaeology, No. 11, pp. 1-30.

Lathrap, D. W., and C. W. Meighan
1951   An archaeological reconnaissance in the Panamint Mountains. Reports of the University of California Archaeological Survey, No. 11, pp. 11-32.

Levine, M. H.
1958 An area co-tradition for Mesoamerica. The Kroeber Anthropological Society Papers, No. 18, pp. 1-47.

MacNeish, R. S.
1957 Some implications of the Tamaulipas archaeological sequence. Paper Read before Mesa Cuadrada, February 21, 1957, Cambridge, Massachusetts.

Mangelsdorf, P. C.
1954 New evidence on the origin and ancestry of maize. American Antiquity, *19:* 409-410.

Martin, P. S.
1973 The discovery of America. Science, *179:* 969-974.

Mather, J. R.
1954 The effect of climate on the New World migration of primitive man. Southwestern Journal of Anthropology, *10:* 304-321.

Mayr, E.
1942 Systematics and the origin of species. Columbia University Press, New York.

Meggers, B. J.
1954 Environmental limitation on the development of culture. American Anthropologist, *56:* 801-824.

Newell, H. P., and A. D. Krieger
1949 The George C. Davis Site, Cherokee County, Texas. Memoirs of the Society for American Archaeology, No. 5, Menasha, Wisconsin.

Portar, M. N.
1953 Tlatilco and the pre-classic cultures of the New World. Viking Fund Publications in Anthropology, No. 19, New York.

Reichel-Dolmatoff, G., and A. Reichel-Dolmatoff
1956 Momil, excavaciones en el Sinu. **Revista Colombiana de Antropologia**, Bogota, Colombia, *5:* 109-334.

Rogers, D. B.
1929 Prehistoric man of the Santa Barbara coast. Santa Barbara Museum of Natural History, Santa Barbara, California.

Rouse, I.
1957 Lowland South America. American Antiquity, *26:* 412.

Rowe, J. H.
1956 Cultural unity and diversification in Peruvian archaeology. Paper Read before the 5th International Congress of Anthropological and Ethnological Sciences, September 2, 1956, Philadelphia, Pennsylvania.

Sellards, E. H.
1952 Early Man in America. University of Texas Press, Austin, Texas.

Simpson, G. G.
1949 The Meaning of Evolution. Yale University Press, New Haven.

1953   The Major Features of Evolution. Yale University Press, New Haven.
Spooner, B. (editor)
1972   Population Growth: Anthropological Implications. The MIT Press, Cambridge, Massachusetts.
Taylor, W. W.
1961   Archaeology and Language in Western North America. American Antiquity, *27:* 71-81.
Wheat, J. B.
1972   The Olsen-Chubbuck Site: A Paleo-Indian Bison Kill. Memoirs of the Society for American Archaeology, No. 26.
Willey, G. R.
1949   The southeastern United States and South America: A comparative statement. The Florida Indian and His Neighbors, pp. 101-116.

1955   The interrelated rise of the native cultures of Middle and South America. New Interpretations of Aboriginal American Culture History, Washington, D. C., pp. 28-45.

1960   Historical patterns and evolution in native New World cultures. Evolution After Darwin. Sol Tax, ed. University of Chicago Press, Chicago, pp. 111-144.
Willey, G. R., and P. Phillips
1955   Method and theory in American archaeology. II: Historical-developmental interpretation. American Anthropologist, *57:* 723-819.

21. Culture Change and Fertility in Two Bougainville Populations

Eugene Ogan, Jill Nash and Donald Mitchell

Introduction

Among W. W. Howells' manifold contributions to anthropology is his ability to cut across subdisciplinary boundaries. He has awakened in students an appreciation of the complementarity between biological and social anthropology, of the ways in which an ethnographer may inform and, in turn, be enlightened by the methods and findings of his colleague in physical anthropology. Recent cross-disciplinary field studies in the Solomon Islands are an elaborate development of this appreciation. However, following Howells' leads, even a lone ethnographer can pursue certain topics often ignored by social anthropologists trained in narrower approaches.

The present contribution is modest, indeed, compared to the kinds of team research carried out today with increasing frequency. In the first instance, this paper records some specific data about cultural practices affecting fertility in two related Bougainville populations. These data gain greater significance against the background provided by Bulmer (1971) and others on population trends in Papua New Guinea. Finally, the data are related to current social and political change in Bougainville, in the hope that the emerging leaders of that island may come to appreciate the potential problems of population increase.

Samples have been drawn from speakers of two non-Austronesian languages, Nasioi and Nagovisi, resident in southern Bougainville. The two languages represent one family of a southern Bougainville non-Austronesian stock (Allen and Hurd, n.d.). Field work in these areas was carried out at different (but overlapping) times, by different individuals, and under differing conditions. Thus, the material gathered is not strictly uniform. In particular, the Nasioi data do not permit use of the innovative statistical techniques associated with W. W. Howells' own work. (Such treatment of the richer Nagovisi material is in preparation.) Nevertheless, findings from the two groups may be usefully related to each other, as well as to other Melanesian populations.

The Nasioi[1]

The Nasioi live in the Kieta Subdistrict of Bougainville in habitats ranging from the beach to altitudes of 3000′ above sea level. Material about both traditional and changing Nasioi life has been published elsewhere (e.g., Ogan 1972); only limited discussion is appropriate here.

There were approximately 13,000 Nasioi in 1970, an increase of some 30 percent since 1963, if Department of District Administration Reports are to be accepted at face value. Nasioi nearer the coast have been in continuous contact with Europeans since the establishment of a Roman Catholic mission at Kieta in 1901. German administration and copra plantations followed in 1905 and 1908 respectively, and some Nasioi men began working as far from their homes as German Samoa before World War I. While some mountain-dwelling Nasioi were able to avoid contact for a number of years, there is no doubt that considerable social change has taken place even in the more remote areas. Japanese occupation and Allied military operations during World War II were particularly upsetting to Nasioi life.

During first field work in 1962, it was obvious that Nasioi were notably dissatisfied with their situation *vis-a-vis* Europeans, and were striving to improve their perceived situation by means both secular and supernatural. Their distress was further aggravated by the discovery and subsequent development of a multi-billion dollar copper mine at Panguna in a mountainous part of Nasioi area (Momis and Ogan 1972; Ogan 1970). The future of Nasioi in particular and of Bou-

[1] Field work among the Nasioi since 1962 has been variously supported by a Pre-Doctoral Fellowship from the National Science Foundation; a Sinclair Kennedy Fellowship from Harvard University; grants from the University of Minnesota Office of International Programs) and the American Philosophical Society (Penrose Fund); and a Research Fellowship from the Australian National University. E. O. is most grateful to Dr. Donald McTavish for methodological guidance; Laurie Lucking provided clerical assistance. Neither is responsible for any deficiences in the finished paper.

gainville as a whole remains problematical as of mid-1973 (cf. Ogan 1973).

TRADITIONAL PRACTICES AFFECTING FERTILITY

Because of all the changes which have taken place since 1901, especially the influence of the Catholic mission which claims approximately 80 percent of Nasioi as adherents, reconstruction of traditional practices having to do with sexual activity is difficult. What seems certain is that, as in many societies in what is now Papua New Guinea (Bulmer 1971:145), the most important single cultural factor directly affecting fertility was a postpartum tabu on sexual relations.

Nasioi today and presumably in the past share with many other New Guineans (Bulmer 1971:144-45, 150) the belief that multiple acts of intercourse are necessary to produce pregnancy, and the failure to appreciate that nine months constitute the normal gestation period. What they did appreciate was the practical problem of providing adequate care for children born too close together (cf. Wray 1971: 406, 454). This was usually phrased in terms of the necessity for prolonged breastfeeding to insure a child's health, and the potential danger if a subsequent pregnancy interrupted lactation. The earliest ethnographic description of Nasioi life states that children were breastfed up to and beyond the age of four (Frizzi 1914: 20), which would suggest a postpartum tabu of not less than two years, and birth intervals of three or four years. Besides the postpartum tabu, one other traditional restriction of sexual activity was of some, albeit secondary, significance: a widow was not supposed to remarry until a pig feast had been given for her deceased spouses's clansmen. The only other restriction reported—that a man preparing a special sago dish should abstain from sexual relations during this work—is unlikely to have had much effect on fertility.

While there seems to be no doubt about the traditional significance of a postpartum tabu among the Nasioi, there *is* considerable ambiguity about the use of contraceptives or abortifacients, and the practice of infanticide. Frizzi (1914: 20) argues strongly that both abortion ("Kindesmord") and infanticide ("der direkte Kindesmord") were responsible for rapid depopulation in the area. Certainly, modern informants speak of the use of a plant material called *bisira* (literally, "barren"; Frizzi refers to "Bischira") as a means of population control. However, since the use of such material would be *prima facie* evidence of illicit sexual activities—in much the same way as is the presence of a package of condoms in a middle-class American husband's wallet—accurate information is hard to come by. Because informants' descriptions are unclear as to whether the effects of *bisira* are contraceptive or abortifacient or both, and whether its use would be regarded by a Westerner as magical or medicinal, and because the efficaciousness of plant substances in this regard is still open to question (Bulmer 1971:151), it is difficult to agree with Frizzi as to any major effect on population growth. In any event, informants today state that using *bisira* also interferes with lactation, which would be just as injurious to the nursing child as his mother's succeeding pregnancy.

Similarly, one is reluctant to credit Frizzi's emphasis on infanticide. He was, after all, a white male who had a relatively brief stay in the area (six months in all of Bougainville and Buka). Further, the fact that his most detailed description of infanticide is not from Nasioi but from a Buin informant does not create greater confidence in his report. As Bulmer (1971:154) has noted, it is difficult to draw a line between deliberate infanticide and selective neglect of an infant. Whereas modern Nasioi deny that the former was ever normative, they do admit that, in the case of twins, a mother would not attempt to nurse both but would either give one child (the boy in a mixed-sex pair) to a wetnurse or, if none were available, would allow the child to starve.

BIRTH INTERVAL DATA

Modern Nasioi still claim that a postpartum tabu should be observed until the nursing child "is old enough to walk." Actual children pointed out as being of the appropriate age suggested a tabu of 15 months. While relatively brief by both traditional Nasioi and other New Guinean (Bulmer 1971:148) standards, this would, if strictly observed, keep births spaced at intervals of at least two years.

To test the degree to which the tabu was observed, E. O. attempted to collect data on birth spacing from four adjacent villages in the Aropa Valley. Efforts were, of course, hampered by women's reluctance to speak in detail of such matters to a white male. Further, use of the records of Tubiana Catholic mission (all villagers were nominally Catholic and resident in Tubiana parish) in conjunction with detailed census and other ethnographic investigation showed that mission records had to be treated with considerable caution.[2] In fact, baptismal records were notably unreliable for births which occurred before the 1950's; subsequent records, when cross-checked with ethnographic material, can be regarded with much greater confidence.

In preparing to analyze these data, certain intervals were removed

---

[2] Tubiana has probably had more turnover of parish priests than many other mission stations in Bougainville.

from consideration. These included children born to Nasioi women by non-Bougainville spouses; children born to couples who had grossly abnormal marital histories (e.g., long periods of physical or mental illness and hospitalization by one or both parents); and intervals following early neonatal deaths.

Table 1 shows the data grouped by five-year periods, calculated in years and hundredths of years, and assigned to the five-year period in which the midpoint of the interval fell. The data show that there has been no statistically significant change in birth intervals in the sample since 1955, but that modern intervals are shorter than those inferred for traditional Nasioi society.

On the other hand, Table 1 provides some support for the idea that many Nasioi are still observing a postpartum tabu of 15 months. Since there is no evidence that nontraditional methods of birth control were being practiced during the time period in question (see below), the likelihood is great that widespread failure to observe the tabu would have resulted in an appreciable proportion of birth intervals of less than 24 months. In fact the figures are:

> 1955-59 1 interval less than 24 months (3.8 percent)
> 1960-64 5 intervals (12.2 percent)
> 1965-69 4 intervals (9.8 percent)

These figures become more meaningful when compared with Epstein's Tolai data (quoted by Bulmer 1971:148). Although observation of a traditional Tolai tabu would have likewise spaced births at least two years apart, in fact 46 percent of the sample of 139 successive births in Matupit were at shorter intervals.

DISCUSSION

Any examination of ongoing social life among the Nasioi is faced

TABLE 1

Year Period	No. Intervals	Mean Interval	Standard Deviation	Range
1955-59	26	2.98	.73	1.50-4.58
1960-64	41	2.71	.76	1.08-5.08
1965-69	41	2.75	.74	1.42-4.83
	108	2.80	.75	1.08-5.08

with both a wide array of variables and what sometimes appears to be a continually accelerating process of change. If, as seems to be the case, there have been changes in cultural practices affecting fertility, how may these be most usefully assessed?

It is, perhaps, easiest to begin with some obvious effects of European contact. Catholic missionization operated to eliminate any infanticide or "artificial" methods of birth control (traditional or European), and gave positive support in its teachings to the joys of parenthood. Priests and nuns provided medical services of varying quality over the years and not infrequently took over temporarily the raising of orphaned or ailing children. Individual clergy appeared to have been distressed by the depopulating effects of World War II (but see van de Kaa 1971a: 51) and to have explicitly urged their parishioners to produce large families. At the same time, there is no evidence that the mission ever tried systematically to impart Western theories of conception and pregnancy,[3] or to teach the acceptable rhythm method of birth control either separately or as a modification of the postpartum tabu.

The second most significant European influence on Nasioi life in general, at least until 1960, were the plantations. Their effect on Nasioi fertility, however, would have been indirect. Presence of these plantations in Nasioi territory provided opportunities for wage labor without the disruption of cohabitation for long periods which presumably had effects on population elsewhere (cf. van de Kaa 1971a: 41). Undoubtedly, some Nasioi males did leave Bougainville for wage labor, both before and after World War II, but they were not under the same pressures to do so that affected the Nagovisi (see below).

While some medical services were provided by the Australian administration in the Kieta Subdistrict before World War II, these were expanded in the postwar period (cf. van de Kaa 1971a;16-20) and, especially, after 1960. Most important of these for fertility was the malaria eradication program (van de Kaa 1971a:19-20) which began in 1960 by spraying village buildings with a DDT solution. Mass drug administration began in 1962. Parasitological tests carried out by the government noted a sharp reduction in parasite rate between 1962 and 1964. Although official censuses cannot provide information adequate for statistical tests, the effects on Nasioi population must have been

3 It is frequently observed — however accurately or inaccurately — by staff at the University of Papua New Guinea that, because teachers at Catholic girls' schools in Bougainville and elsewhere in New Guinea have never corrected their pupils' belief that only multiple acts of intercourse will produce pregnancy, alumnae of these institutions are at highest risk of unwanted pregnancy when they come to urban centers for further education.

remarkable. Everything known about malaria eradication in Melanesia (e.g., Pirie 1971:7) and elsewhere (e.g., Newman 1965) would support this contention. Furthermore, there appear to be some remarkably subtle relations between malaria and lowered fertility (e.g., Eaton and Mucha 1971) which enhance the significance of the eradication program for this discussion. However, since 1967, political tension has caused some Nasioi to successfully resist the spraying of their houses.

A government program of infant and maternal welfare clinics began in the Subdistrict in 1965. Unlike teams of workers in the malaria eradication program, who take their spraying equipment and medication to remote villages, the welfare nursing teams usually visit only those villages accessible by vehicle. Women from the four sample villages normally attend these clinics, at least on occasion. Participation depends a great deal on the age of the woman (younger women tend to be more responsive) and her proximity to the site of the clinic. As of 1970, maternal welfare clinics did not provide birth control information or materials.

Since improved medical services have undoubtedly lowered Nasioi mortality—and probably most affected infant and maternal mortality—one may raise the question of this demographic change on Nasioi beliefs and attitudes. Unfortunately, one here enters a realm of speculation. *If* such traditional practices as the postpartum tabu drew some strength from Nasioi empirical observations that well-spaced children were more likely to survive (cf. Wray 1971: 454), then it is conceivable that lowered mortality (i.e., higher survival) might lead to some doubts as to the necessity for observing the tabu strictly. But while many Nasioi appreciate that much larger numbers of children now fill the villages than before 1950—and at least some state that this situation is due in part to Western medicine—there is no clearcut evidence that this new observation has directly weakened traditional practice, despite the apparent plausibility of such a speculation.

What *is* clear is that modern political developments have led a number of Nasioi to express a desire for rapid population growth. This is in large part a direct, if unanticipated, response to pressures exerted by the Australian administration. Part of the remarkable "hard-sell" campaign in the early 1960's to establish a Local Government Council in the Kieta Subdistrict (Ogan 1972: 77-8) was phrased in terms of threats to Bougainville by the more populous New Guinea Highlands. Administration officers would say: "The Chimbu have a Council and there are lots more of them than there are Nasioi. If you don't get a Council, too, they'll come over here and kick your arse." This threat must have been remembered when hordes of mainland New Guineans arrived to work on construction of the copper project.

A similar government ploy was attempted when Nasioi (and other Bougainvilleans; see Anis *et. al.* 1972) began to demand a referendum to assess support for Bougainville's secession from Papua New Guinea. Administration officers scorned the notion of Bougainville independence by pointing out the District's small size. While a number of Nasioi were sufficiently aware of the existence of the tiny island Republic of Nauru to know that large size is not a necessary prerequisite for political independence, the whole argument further strengthened the equation in Nasioi minds of population size with political strength.

Space limitations preclude a more detailed discussion of the present Nasioi situation. Suffice it to say here that a variety of factors have operated to change traditional cultural practices affecting fertility, and the overall effect has been both to increase actual fertility and to implant the idea of population growth as desirable. Progress toward this goal (however deplorable to a Western observer) is indicated by government estimates of natural growth rates ranging from 3.5 to 4.8 percent in different parts of the Nasioi territory.

The Nagovisi[4]

The Nagovisi live on the lower slopes of the Crown Prince Range on the west coast of south central Bougainville. They numbered about 7000 in 1970, a figure which is approximately double that of the pre-World War II population. In comparison to their closest linguistic relations, the Nasioi, the Nagovisi have had much less direct contact with Europeans. Although Nagovisi men had worked on plantations in other parts of Bougainville, New Britain, New Ireland and Manus since the early part of the century, their home area was not penetrated by Christian missionaries and government personnel until the mid-1920's, and the regular operation of these agencies did not get under way until the early 1930's. There are no European-owned plantations or other businesses in Nagovisi.

However, the Nagovisi did not escape the trauma of World War II; on the contrary, they suffered considerable depredation from the Japanese occupation and American bombings. The pace of acculturation

[4] Field work among the Nagovisi since 1969 has been supported by Pre-Doctoral Fellowships and Field Research Grants from the U.S. Public Health Service, National Institute of Mental Health, and a Research Fellowship from the New Guinea Research Unit, Australian National University.

quickened after the war, especially with regard to medical care. A hospital was established at the Sovele Roman Catholic mission in the 1950's. During the 1960's, Nagovisi began extensive cocoa plantings, with consequent markedly increased participation in a money economy (Mitchell 1971). Construction of the copper mine at Panguna and rapid expansion of a road system have further accelerated social change in recent years.

TRADITIONAL PRACTICES AFFECTING FERTILITY

Traditional Nagovisi forms of family limitation are quite similar to those reported for the Nasioi, and certain differences in these data are as likely to represent the failure of Nasioi to report in full such practices as infanticide as any marked contrasts in the two groups' respective precontact situations. Like the Nasioi, Nagovisi typically believe that multiple copulations are necessary to produce pregnancy and are unaware of the normal length of gestation.

Prior to the end of tribal warfare in the early 1930's, a lengthy postpartum sex tabu was observed. According to informants, births were spaced four to seven years apart. The stated reason for the long interval was that there should not be two small children to carry to and from the gardens, lest the father be prevented from protecting his family in case of ambush. It was thought that the youngest child should be able to walk long distances unaided before a younger sibling replaced him.

In the past, this postpartum tabu was enforced by a system of fines *(nomma)* paid by the offending couple in shell money or, later, Australian currency to their opposite-sex siblings. In addition to claiming *nomma* payments, the siblings—enraged that the violation had endangered the health of the mother and the replaced child—might destroy property belonging to the couple, such as household utensils, pigs, coconut trees and the walls of their house, "so that they could no longer hide there and copulate."

Other than the postpartum tabu, there were relatively few stringent restrictions on copulation in traditional Nagovisi society. Marriage for both sexes was both normative and statistically normal; there was no cultural provision for permanent bachelorhood or spinsterhood. Adultery, if discovered, was a cause of conflict and litigation, but not necessarily of divorce. It was not considered proper for a widow to remarry before an appropriate period of mourning (at least a year) had been completed. However, insofar as can be inferred from present mortality patterns, widowhood was probably relatively rare among women of childbearing age, and it seems unlikely that this restriction was a major factor in family limitation.

Nagovisi informants also reported the use of plant materials to produce sterility and/or abortion, and the practice of infanticide. The
plant, *wano,* also used to stun fish in a fish drive, might abort the fetus
or, according to some informants, might merely blind or otherwise
deform it. A second plant, *kawawala,* was said to produce sterility
until such time as the affected woman took the antidote. A number of
practices (e.g., ritual prohibitions) associated with *kawawala* usage
suggest supernaturalism rather than medicine to a Westerner.

Infanticide was practiced in the case of twins, or when the second
birth followed the first too closely. The most common method reported
was crushing the infant's head with a rock, although one informant
said that the child might also be smothered in the ashes of the fireplace
or stepped on. Many people admitted to the practice of infanticide
during World War II, when the necessity of hiding in the bush pre-
cluded the normal care of babies.

BIRTH INTERVAL DATA

In 1970, J. N. collected data on the number and spacing of births
among 86 Nagovisi women, living in contiguous villages, who could be
interviewed. Actual dates of birth were taken from the Infant Welfare
Clinic records at the Sovele Hospital, or from the Stati Animari of
Sovele Mission (through the courtesy of Fr. Denis Mahoney, S.M.).
For the most part, the interview data were used to establish stillbirths
and spontaneous abortions. In 1972, D. M. obtained additional records
which brought the total number of usable intervals up to 300, spanning
a time period from about 1925 to July 1972. The dates in the early
years are subject to errors, but there are few reasons to doubt the accuracy of the dates from 1950 to the present, most of which are known
to the month and day of birth.

In preparing the data for analysis, intervals following early neonatal
deaths and stillbirths were not included. Where data are available, in
such cases conception took place again an average of .5 year after the
death. Obviously such intervals represent special cases (cf. Bulmer
1971:148). Intervals were calculated as years and hundredths of years,
and were assigned to the five-year period (e.g., 1950-54) in which the
midpoint of the interval fell. They were then grouped according to the
estimated age of the women (as of 1972) by five-year periods.

A variety of statistical techniques may be applied to these data in
order to extract a maximum amount of information and, indeed, this
treatment is the subject of a separate paper (Mitchell and Nash, n.d.).
One can only state here—in unadorned fashion, without providing
detailed support—the most important result of this intensive analysis

of the Nagovisi material alone: the emergence of the women themselves (i.e., the composition of the reproducing population) as the
most powerful explanatory variable relevant to all the changes revealed in the data since 1950.

However, the goal of the present paper is different: the description of
the very considerable non-measurable cultural and historical variables
involved, especially as these can be briefly but meaningfully compared
to the situations of the Nasioi and other groups in Papua New Guinea.
For this purpose, Table 2 should suffice.

Table 2 shows that for the sample population there have been statistically significant decreases in the mean interval between births (between the periods 1955-59 and 1960-64 [5%] and between 1960-64 and
1965-72 [1%]) and that there has likewise been a significant drop in the
variability of these intervals. The latter point becomes clearer if the
data are grouped into periods of 1925-49, in which variances are quite
large; 1950-64, in which variances are smaller and similar to each
other; and 1965-72, where variances are smallest of all. Grouped in this
way, all differences are significant at least to the .01 level. It now remains to look at historical and cultural changes acting on the Nagovisi population.

DISCUSSION

Infant and maternal welfare services were introduced into Nagovisi
in the early 1960's. Included in the program are prenatal care, delivery

TABLE 2

Year Period	No. Intervals	Mean Interval	Standard Deviation	Range
1925-29	1	8.00		
1930-34	3	5.00	2.65	3.00- 8.00
1935-39	6	3.50	1.38	2.00- 6.00
1940-44	8	5.38	2.26	3.00- 9.00
1945-49	15	4.30	2.52	1.59-12.00
1950-54	33	3.71	1.42	2.04- 8.04
1955-59	56	3.68	1.34	2.00- 9.12
1960-64	71	3.16	1.21	1.58- 7.75
1965-72	107	2.68	.78	1.05- 5.83
	300	3.31	1.44	1.05-12.00

of babies at the mission hospital with an obstetrical nurse in attendance, postpartum rest and care for the mother, and monthly clinics held in the village for the first five years of the child's life. In the clinics, infants and children are examined for signs of illness and inoculated, and mothers are given instructions on infant care, e.g., washing, feeding solid foods, etc. The earlier feeding of solid foods is in contradiction to traditional ways, which might keep certain infants under food tabus (especially with regard to protein foods) for years, until the tabus were ritually removed.

Malaria eradication also began in the early 1960's. Since the pre-eradication extent of malaria is not known, it is difficult to gauge the effectiveness of the program. However, in 1970, none of the women in the sample, who were examined by the Harvard Medical Expedition, showed malaria or signs (e.g., enlarged spleens) of past malaria.

As mentioned above, Nagovisi men began to accept work on plantations before 1914. According to a 1929 census, an average of nearly 20 percent of all married men in the area of the present sample were absent on such work. Early postwar censuses show about 20 percent of adult men absent at work, and this figure rose steadily to some 53 percent from the sample area in 1955. Census records are not available for consultation after that date, but informants state that men continued to go to plantations throughout the 1950's.

In the early 1960's, two things happened which acted to deter men from going away and staying away for long periods. First was the beginning of cash cropping: the planting of cocoa on a large scale by individuals began at this time, and the first cocoa began to bear by the middle 1960's. By 1968, nearly every household had cash income from the sale of cocoa beans. The ability to earn a small but steady income at home decreased the desire of married men to seek employment outside the Nagovisi area (cf. the model relating migration to cash cropping in Ward 1971:85-87).

Along with cocoa planting, the early and mid-1960's brought new kinds of opportunities for wage labor with the construction of the copper mine at Panguna, within walking distance of Nagovisi. Between 1964 and the end of the construction phase in 1971, many Nagovisi men worked there in a variety of unskilled jobs, without contracts. Usually men would work for six months or so; they were often able to return home for short periods during their employment. So many jobs were available at this huge project that men felt no compunction about walking off a job, to return later and find another one. Working at Panguna was thus most unlike plantation labor.

Some Nagovisi have said, "Having children very close to each other ᵥbegan with the cocoa." Later, in response to the anthropologists' hypothesis, informants agreed that cocoa planting had allowed men to remain at home and still earn money—and that propinquity naturally led to shorter periods elapsing between the birth of a baby and the resumption of copulation.

There is clear evidence for the breakdown of customary sanctions and observation of the postpartum tabu. In recent times, *nomma* fines have been neither asked nor paid. For example, when in 1971 it became apparent that the mother of a young baby was without question pregnant, one of the woman's clan brothers asked her mother if they ought not to destroy her coconuts. No action was taken, and the woman gave birth to her second child after an interval of 1.25 years. She was 19 years of age at the time.

Such indiscretions are still regarded as in some sense scandalous and immoral, but these days little note is taken of birth intervals which are barely over two years. Such intervals do, at least, conform with the norm that the earlier baby should "walk" before copulation is begun; in this case, the criterion "walk" has been redefined in a way which is comparable to Nasioi practice.

Since all the women in the sample profess adherence to Roman Catholicism, they are discouraged to practice any form of "artificial" birth control, whether traditional or European. Both women and their husbands are for all practical purposes entirely ignorant of the only approved method, that of rhythm. Some prolific Nagovisi state that, by having many children, they are doing "good work for God." Still other men occasionally say that everyone ought to have many children, in order to "fill up" Papua New Guinea so that Europeans won't take it over, and so that the country will be "strong."

Conclusion

Traditionally, Nasioi and Nagovisi shared cultural practices which had important effects on fertility, yet the available data suggest notable differences in more recent times. Doubtless many factors are relevant to these differences, but one may make a plausible argument for assigning considerable weight to different histories of culture change.

On the one hand, the Nasioi (especially in the Aropa Valley whence the birth interval data for this paper were drawn) came into early and relatively close contact with a Christian mission which forbade any traditional contraceptives, abortifacients, or acts of infanticide. At the same time that Nasioi men were drawn deeper and deeper into a money economy, local plantations provided opportunities for wage labor without long-term (i.e., more than one year) disruption of family life. Since they were close to a center of European population,[5] Nasioi could take early advantage of whatever governmental medical facilities were available. Resulting lowered infant and child mortality was inconsistent with the belief that a long birth interval was absolutely necessary for children's survival. All these influences tended toward abandonment of early practices which limited fertility, without providing functional substitutes.

Nagovisi, on the other hand, were missionized more than a quarter of a century later. When seeking cash, Nagovisi men were, until about 1960, compelled to undertake contract labor which removed them from their homes—a practice perfectly consonant with maintaining the traditional postpartum sex tabu. Particularly since cash cropping and new forms of wage labor permitted uninterrupted domesticity to be combined with participation in a money economy have birth intervals shown notable declines.

Against this background one can look again at Tables 1 and 2 to note the manner in which the most recent birth interval data from Nagovisi come to approximate ever more closely that from the Aropa Valley Nasioi. (However, even in the most recent of the three comparable periods, the difference between the respective mean intervals remains statistically significant.) It is perhaps not too far-fetched to see the Nagovisi, in respect to cultural practices affecting fertility,[6] as moving along behind—and most recently, beginning to draw abreast of—the Nasioi on the same path of culture change.

Still further speculation is possible by comparing both groups against the Tolai of New Britain, for Bougainville District is second only to New Britain in estimated rates of population growth since 1961 (van de Kaa 1971a:65). The Tolai are generally regarded as the most acculturated or Westernized group in Papua New Guinea; data have already been cited above to suggest their still more complete abandonment of a traditional postpartum sex tabu. Could one argue that the Nasioi, followed by the Nagovisi, are moving rapidly toward a nexus of cultural practice and population explosion now represented by the Tolai?

[5] Kieta was Bougainville District Headquarters from 1905 until World War II, and again became the administrative center as the result of mining developments in the latter 1960's.

[6] And perhaps in other respects as well, but such considerations go beyond the scope of this paper.

This metaphor of movement leads to painful consideration of Bougainville's future, for the population and land problems of the Tolai are fairly described as critical (cf. Granger 1971). One possible solution for both islands is a program of family planning, but here the prognosis is at least as grim for Bougainville as for the rest of Papua New Guinea (van de Kaa 1971b:20-22). Not only is there no substantial interest in family planning expressed by local leaders; on the contrary, concern at the village level for population growth as leading to political strength has already been noted. Indeed, during the sitting of the second Papua New Guinea House of Assembly, the Member for South Bougainville—a man most deeply respected by the majority of both Nasioi and Nagovisi (Ogan 1971)—all but accused the administration of genocide for including a small sum for family planning in the public health budget.

Given the history of culture change in southern Bougainville, this is a perfectly understandable response. As Benedict (1973:1046) has recently pointed out: "Birth control succeeds or fails insofar as people see their own individual life chances in terms of more or fewer children. . . . These estimates depend not only on the intimate relations between men and women but on the political, economic, and social relations within the whole community." Changing cultural practices affecting fertility among the Nasioi and Nagovisi demonstrate the interplay of all these factors. It remains for anthropologists and others concerned with the future of these people to show the villagers themselves how to make estimates of their life chances based on the best information Western science can provide; however, the final decisions rest with Bougainvilleans.

References

Allen, J., and C. Hurd
    n.d.   Languages of Bougainville District. Ukarumpa: Summer Institute of Linguistics.
Anis, T., E. Makis, T. Miriung, and E. Ogan
    1972 Toward a New Politics? The 1972 House of Assembly Election in Bougainville. Ms.
Benedict, B.
    1973   Review of The Khanna Study and The Myth of Population Control. Science, *180:* 1045-1046.
Bulmer, R. N. H.
    1971 Traditional forms of family limitation in New Guinea. In: Population Growth and Socio-Economic Change. M. W. Ward, ed. New Guinea

Research Bulletin No. 42, Australian National University Press, Canberra, pp. 137-162.

Eaton, J. W., and J. I. Mucha

1971 Increased fertility in males with the Sickle-Cell trait? Nature, *231:* 456-457.

Frizzi, E.

1914 Ein Beitrag zur Ethnologie von Bougainville und Buka, mit Speziell-er Beruchsichtigung der Nasioi. Baessler-Archiv Beiheft VI, Leipzig and Berlin, B. G. Teubner.

Granger, K. J.

1971 Population and land in the Gazelle Peninsula. In: Population Growth and Socio-Economic Change. M. W. Ward, ed. New Guinea Research Bulletin No. 42, Australian National University Press, Canberra, pp. 108-121.

Kaa, D. J. van de

1971a The Demography of Papua and New Guinea's Indigenous Population. Ph.D. thesis, The Australian National University, Canberra.

————

1971b The future growth of Papua New Guinea's indigenous population. In: Population Growth and Socio-Economic Change. M. W. Ward, ed. New Guinea Research Bulletin No. 42, Australian National University Press, Canberra, pp. 16-30.

Mitchell, D. D.

1971 Gardening for Money: Land and Agriculture in Nagovisi. Ph.D. thesis, Harvard University, Cambridge, Massachusetts.

Mitchell, D. D., and J. Nash

n. d. Nagovisi Birth Intervals. Ms.

Momis, J., and E. Ogan

1972 A view from Bougainville. In: Change and Development in Rural Melanesia. M. W. Ward, ed. Australian National University Press, Canberra, pp. 106-118.

Newman, P.

1965 Malaria eradication and population growth. Bureau of Public Health Economics, Research Series No. 10, University of Michigan, Ann Arbor.

Ogan, E.

1970 The Nasioi vote again. Human Organization, *29:* 178-189.

————

1971 Charisma and race. In: The Politics of Dependence. A. L. Epstein, et. al., eds. Australian National University Press, Canberra, pp. 132-161.

————

1972 Business and cargo: Socio-economic change among the Nasioi of Bougainville. New Guinea Research Bulletin No. 44, Australian National University Press, Canberra.

1973 Cargoism and politics in Bougainville. Paper Presented at the Central States Anthropological Society Meeting, St. Louis.

Pirie, P.

1971 Population developments in the Pacific Islands. In: Population Growth and Socio-Economic Change. M. W. Ward, ed. New Guinea Research Bulletin No. 42, Australian National University Press, Canberra, pp. 3-15.

Ward, R. G.

1971 Internal migration and urbanization in Papua-New Guinea. In: Population Growth and Socio-Economic Change. M. W. Ward, ed. New Guinea Research Bulletin No. 42, Australian National University Press, Canberra, pp. 81-107.

Wray, I. D.

1972 Population pressure on families: family size and child spacing. In: Rapid Population Growth: Consequences and Policy Implications. National Academy of Sciences. Johns Hopkins Press, Baltimore, pp. 403-462.

22. Bush Fallow Farming, Diet and Nutrition: a Melanesian Example of Successful Adaptation

Harold M. Ross

Introduction

Besides producing a large proportion of America's leading physical anthropologists of this generation, Professor William Howells also played a major role in forming the professional and intellectual *personna* of a great many social or cultural anthropologists. Like many who took his courses at Wisconsin and Harvard and learned to appreciate his patrician wit and catholic interests, we learned from him to have an open and inquiring mind, to cultivate an avid curiosity, to practice meticulous scholarship, to appreciate actively human ecology

NOTE: Research on Malaita, Solomon Islands, has been supported by National Science Foundation Graduate Fellowship (12419) for 1962-65; Public Health Service Research Fellowship (MH-30017) and concurrent National Institute of Mental Health Research Grant (MH-12647) for 1966-68; and a grant from the Center for International Comparative Studies, University of Illinois (Joseph B. Casagrande, Director), for the summer of 1972. Constructive criticism of earlier drafts by Professor Donald Lathrap of the University of Illinois and Dr. Matthew Cooper of McMaster University of Ontario was highly useful and is gratefully acknowledged. Darlene Graves, of the Department of Anthropology at the University of Illinois, provided secretarial support most effectively. Ben Parker, University of Il-

and evolution, and to be aware of the biological realities that relate to human beings and their many cultures. I carried this academic heritage into the field with me when I did my own ethnographic research. Professor Howells' long-standing (Howells 1937 and 1943) and continuing (Oliver and Howells 1957, Howells 1972 and 1973) interest in Oceania and in Melanesia in particular stimulated interest in that part of the world. As recently as 1968, Professor Howells lived and worked with me for almost two months (Photograph 1) among the Lau

Photograph 1.   Professor Howells doing anthropometry at Maana'afe, Lau Lagoon, Malaita, Solomon Islands, in July 1968.

linois, did the photographic processing and arranging. This work is related to a research project of the Peabody Museum and Department of Anthropology, Harvard University, supported by grant no. GM 13482 of the N.I.G.M.S., U.S. Public Health Service. It is also part of the Human Adaptability section of the International Biological Program. The work was conducted with the permission and invaluable assistance of the Administration of the British Solomon Islands Protectorate.

and Baegu people of Malaita, Solomon Islands, in an extremely isolated and undeveloped part of Melanesia, as part of the Harvard University project conceived and sponsored jointly by himself, Albert
Damon, and Douglas Oliver. This combined anthropological-biologi-
cal-medical project made the research and analysis reported below possible, and it will in time be recognized as a highly productive and
significant enterprise (Damon 1970).

Traditional Tropical Forest Farming

In the millenia since the advent of the Food-Producing Revolution
(Childe 1936 and Braidwood 1952) ended the epoch or more of hominid hunting and gathering, much of mankind has relied upon a relatively mobile sort of farming involving short-term use of gardening
sites, frequent shifts of cultivation loci over wide areas, and (often)
widespread population dispersal and movements. This mode of food
production is still particularly common in the world's tropical forest
regions, such as Melanesia. During the "benevolent imperialism" af-
termath of the Colonial Era, government officials and agricultural experts trained in the progress/efficiency oriented (and frequently ethno-
centric) traditions of Western Civilization have denounced this kind of
traditional farming as inefficient (the cardinal sin), wasteful, and environmentally destructive; incapable of supporting large populations
or of being a formative base for "high" civilizations. General allega-
tions (made so often as to defy precise attribution) against this traditional kind of tropical forest farming center around the theme that it is
an adaptation *manqué,* maintained in ignorance, which (if it were not
for the perverse pig-headedness of "natives") should be abandoned as
soon as "better" western models appear. Specific charges against it are
that: (1) The tradition-bound people who practice it do not know what
they are doing; (2) It takes too much work and costs too much; (3) It is
not productive enough and too much land is required; (4) It fails to
satisfy nutritional needs; (5) It is wasteful and environmentally destructive; (6) It is an inferior form of ecological adaptation; (7) It leads
to nomadic populations, hard to administer and control, and who destroy more than their share of public resources; (8) It cannot support
large, settled populations; (9) It cannot support "high" or complex
civilizations; and (10) It cannot accommodate cash economies or modernization and development programs, and therefore has no place in a
modern or developing nation. Consequently, attempts to anchor shifting tribesmen to the land and to replace "wasteful" traditional meth-

ods with western-oriented "scientific" ones have been features of agricultural modernization schemes in developing tropical countries. Objective ethnographic and archaeological studies of functioning ecosystems of people living in customary ways on their own land, however, suggest that in fact traditional tropical forest farming is ecologically non-destructive, is quite efficient, can support sizeable populations, can meet their nutritional requirements, and can lead to impressive cultural developments. If this be so, then perhaps rationalization of the system would be a better (more "rational") goal than simple termination.

What I have, for want of a better name, called traditional tropical forest farming has many names. Pelzer (1945) and others speak of "horticulture" or "gardening" to emphasize contrasts with the disimilar European field agriculture system dominated by cereal grain farming and herd mammal husbandry. Dibble farming and the *Hackbau* of the German ethnologist Hahn (Heine-Geldern 1964) take their names from the common tools that are supposed to have preceded plow technology in an evolutionary sequence. In anthropological parlance, "slash-and-burn" farming stresses the characteristic process of clearing the land, just as "shifting cultivation" accents (perhaps erroneously) the moving of garden plots and/or people. Specialists in particular geographic or cultural areas may prefer loan words or terms with local meanings; thus "swidden" agriculture (Izikovitz 1951) is common in Europe and Southeast Asia, while "milpa" farming is found in Mesoamerica. It is known as "caiñgin" in the Philippines, "ladang" in Indonesia, "taungya" in Burma, "rai" in Indo-China, "djum" in India, and "chitimene" in parts of Africa (Conklin 1954:134). Economists and agronomists may call it "forest fallow" or "bush fallow" cultivation (or alternatively speak of "long-term fallowing" as opposed to "short-term fallowing" systems, or "extensive" as opposed to "intensive" agriculture) in the manner of Boserup (1965). Among the more felicitous usages has been ethnobotanist Barrau's (1959) description of the complex as a "bush-fallowing system," designating the crucial factor that such practices maintain fertility by letting old fields lie fallow, permitting the forest biome ("bush" in the vernacular English of the South Pacific) to regenerate at least partially before it is cultivated again.

Swidden or bush fallow farming is a spatially and temporally widely distributed complex of many techniques and beliefs. In a summary article, David Harris (1972:246) gives as its universal characteristics and minimal definition, "(a) partial or complete clearance of the vegetation cover by cutting or burning, (b) the temporary cultivation of crops in the cleared area, and (c) the abandonment of the plot to fallow under regenerating vegetation for a longer period than the preceding phase of cultivation." As general attributes of swidden cultivation, he states that it is a small-scale form of agriculture (plots are rarely larger than 2.47 acres and often less than an acre in size), it is "land-extensive" but "labor-intensive" (involving wide tracts of land for fallowing and intensive use of human hand labor), it can be highly productive in the sense that such systems can produce high yields per unit of labor, it is usually associated with low human population densities, and it is usually associated with dispersed settlement patterns of village or hamlet units (D. Harris 1972:246-8). As lesser or secondary attributes, he explains that swidden cultivation can be "monocultural" (with one regionally preferred staple crop) or "polycultural," sometimes referred to as "intercropping," (with a diverse assemblage of useful trees, shrubs, and herbs as a single plant community); that it can operate in a "pioneering" mode (where population and gardens "shift" in a linear way following an expanding frontier) or a "cyclical" mode that is more stable and features habitual re-use of the same land; and that there is an inverse correlation between the population size of the settlement unit (hamlet or village) and the distance between adjacent units, with "pheric distance" or travel time (Vayda 1961) being a more realistic measure than mere linear or geographic distance (D. Harris 1972:246-9).

The canonical form of swidden or bush fallow cultivation varies. In the classic Indo-Pacific Maritime region (coastal East Africa and the African river valleys, southern India, mainland and insular Southeast Asia, and Oceania) it typically features heavy reliance upon root and tree crops propagated vegetatively; minimal emphasis on practical animal husbandry; a preference for forest soils; and shifting cultivation (of garden plots) utilizing natural plant succession to maintain fertility through a recurring cycle of land clearance, use, abandonment, and movement to a new plot, while the tropical forest biome regenerates on the old one through a succession sequence of pioneer species (grasses, ferns, and weeds), herbaceous shrubs and bamboos, pioneer softwood trees, and (if allowed to go to a stable climax) primary tropical forest hardwoods. In general, the subsistence basis in this form of farming features a large *carbohydrate component* providing the bulk of the caloric requirements; a smaller *supplemental vegetable foods component* of lesser vegetables, nuts, and fruits providing essential fats, vitamins, and minerals; and a critical but usually small *animal protein component* as an ancillary source of proteins supplementing the usual vegetable protein sources. *A cash crop component* can be added to this basic assemblage where feasible and when desired.

Throughout Oceania (the area I know best), taro, yams, bananas, breadfruit, and coconuts are the staple elements with other cultigens such as sugar cane, sago, pandanus, fruits or nuts, and one or more green leafy vegetables being locally important. Sweet potatoes enjoyed paramount importance in some regions, such as Maori New Zealand and the New Guinea highlands. Pigs and chickens, kept with a greater or lesser degree of care and ritual importance, are the domesticated sources of animal proteins. Fishing in the open sea, lagoons, lakes, and rivers is highly important, wherever it can be done in Oceania; and the hunting of birds and small mammals is locally important where game resources permit. Some protein intake comes from desultory or even systematic utilization of various reptiles, amphibians, arthropods, worms, and mollusks.

Outside the Indo-Pacific region similar practices characterize farming in many forested and semi-forested tropical environments, such as equatorial and western Africa south of the Sahara and the Sudan. In the western hemisphere, much of Mesoamerica south of the Valley of Mexico, the Circum-Caribbean area, the Amazon-Orinoco riverine systems, the Montaña region along the eastern Andean piedmont, and much of the rest of tropical South America outside the Andean Cordillera highlands exhibit similar subsistence practices. The specific plant and animal elements of the various dietary components are not always the same. Manioc (both sweet and bitter forms), sweet potatoes, true arrowroot *(Maranata arundinacea),* and some other root crops are the carbohydrate bases of the South American variant. Cereal grains may join or replace tree and root crops as the main caloric component in some areas, as maize, beans, and squash do in the Americas; as sorghums, legumes, and melons do in Africa; and as rice does in southern and eastern Asia and small parts of Micronesia (the Marianas). On a world-wide scale, and considering groups more complex than the tribal level of socio-cultural integration, such as peasants and urban civilizations (Steward 1955), cereals are more important than root vegetables. Elements of the supplemental vegetable foods component vary widely, with variety being provided both by unique autocthonous species and nowadays by the ubiquitous garden vegetables spread by European imperialism. While pigs and chickens are the leading domestic animals in Oceania and parts of Africa, goats and water buffaloes become important in Asia, and cattle rank high in Africa. Hunting and gathering may replace animal husbandry altogether in much of the Americas, where the cameloids, guinea pigs, dogs, turkeys, and some waterfowl were the only domesticated animals, whose range was at best severely limited. Hunting was also locally important in Africa. Fishing exists wherever suitable water is accessible.

Although the Pacific people whom I know best seem to prefer to use humid tropical forest soils (rain forests), the same techniques can be applied in drier tropical forests, monsoon areas, scrub forests, and deciduous woodlands (but rarely in savannahs or grasslands). Even if in the ethnographic present this kind of farming seems most suitable for humid tropical forest regions, there is good historical and archaeological evidence for its once much greater extent. Krader (1968:67), citing Tacitus (1948), claims that the ancient pre-Christian Slavs practiced shifting cultivation in the temperate deciduous forests of eastern Europe in historic times. The Danubian farmers of Neolithic Europe in the 5th-6th millenia B.C. may have helped spread village agriculture from the Mediterranean into temperate central and western Europe using a form of shifting cultivation of the pioneering or frontier mode (Clark 1962:126 and Neustupny 1961). There is some evidence that the Erteb∮lle peoples used slash-and-burn farming in the birch and alder forests of the Baltic and North Sea areas when farming was first introduced into sub-boreal northern Europe in the 3rd millenium B.C. (Becker 1955:749-67). Shifting agriculture was also characteristic in relatively humid parts of wooded eastern North America during Middle and Late Woodland times after 800 A.D., possibly even around the great Cahokia heartland of Illinois and Missouri and particularly associated with Middle Mississippian expansion into marginal areas, such as is manifested by the Steed-Kisker site, in western Missouri and eastern Kansas (Caldwell 1958).

Conklin (1961:27) estimates that in the present day swidden farming occupies an area of 14 million square miles inhabited by 200 million people; and Dobby (1950:349) believes that it consumes one-third of all agricultural land in southeast Asia.

Although it is by now sorely in need of updating, Conklin's (1961) article, with its componential or topical outline and extensive bibliography, remains the best summary and comparative description of this kind of farming.

In some ways traditional tropical forest farming of Oceania may be the most interesting and archetypal of all, because it may be a marginal relict of the oldest farming complex in hominid evolution. Because of its Austronesian language phylum affinities (Grace 1955) and certain cultural traits summarized in Suggs (1960), one may be justified in regarding Oceania as in some ways an extension of the insular southeast Asian culture area (Kroeber 1947:322-330). Sauer (1952) prophesied that agriculture based on vegetative (clone) cultivation of root crops may have occurred earlier in Southeast Asia than anywhere else in the world, and Vavilov (1951) proposed a Southeast Asian center of origin and dispersal for such typical plants as taro, yams, and bananas that still are the subsistence basis in Oceania. Womersley (Barrau 1961:6) has proposed a Melanesian or New Guinea center of origin for the sago palm *(Metroxylon* sp.), the "fehi" banana *(Musa troglodytarum)*, sugar cane *(Saccharum officinarum)*, the "pitpit" grass *(Saccharum edule)*, and the edible hibiscus *(Hibiscus manihot)*, which are all associated with the traditional tropical forest farming complex in Oceania and Southeast Asia. Reports of incredibly early archaeological discoveries in Thailand's Spirit Cave and related sites in Thailand and Indo-China in Hoabinhian contexts dating from 9700 B.C. and earlier of the remains of plants that are still grown today by bush fallow methods and used by farmers in Southeast Asia and Oceania (Gorman 1969:672-3, Solheim 1971:338), and the possibility of slash-and-burn associated with a Cord-Marked Pottery horizon in Taiwan in the period *circa* 9000 B.C. (Chang 1966, Chang and Stuiver 1966, Solheim 1967:898) make a case for extremely early farming of cultivated plants in this part of the world (possibly the earliest anywhere) that is intuitively or viscerally compelling, even if it may be weak on certain formal logical and probabalistic grounds (Harlan and De Wet 1973:52). This farming technology, using these same plants, continues today in the Melanesian islands of Oceania.

A Melanesian Example: The Baegu of Malaita, Solomon Islands

During 1966-68 I spent about 16 months living with and learning from a Melanesian people in northern Malaita Island (Ross 1973a). The Baegu are a physically variable people of Melanesian-Papuan race (Garn 1961: 130-32, Coon and Hunt 1965:175-7) who speak one dialect of an Austronesian (Malayo-Polynesian) language (Capell 1954). They live in tiny hamlets in the forested interior mountains, tilling the soil with bush fallow methods and supplementing production with hunting, gathering, and fishing on a small scale, and barter marketing with their neighbors (Ross 1973b). Traditional Baegu believe in and practice an animistic paganism, requiring filial piety for and the propitiation of ancestral spirits. About half of the population still practice the pagan religion; the remainder have converted to one of several competing Christian sects. Socially they recognize bilateral kinship obligations, patrilineal land-owning clans, and co-residential neighborhood groups. As in much of Melanesia, there is a marked sexual role difference with men having generally higher status and semi-monopoloy on sacred affairs, while women handle routine drudgery and ritually profane situations. So far there has been little foreign influence, thanks to the unsuitability of the area for commercial exploitation. Their customary values, social organization, and subsistence economy are still intact and viable.

Being a high continental island, Malaita provides a variety of habitats varying with altitude and distance from the shoreline. The island (Map 1), lying in the southwestern Pacific about 1000 miles northeast of Australia and 6000 miles southwest of California, is centered at 9°S latitude and 161°E longitude near the southeastern end of the Solomon Islands. It is a thin island about 120 miles long and 10-15 miles wide near its northern end where the Baegu live, rising to an elevation of 3200 feet in that vicinity. It is the most densely populated island of the Solomons, being "home" to about 40% of the British Solomon Islands Protectorate's estimated population of 121,000.

Malaitamen exploit all ecological zones to some degree. Starting with the furthest one to seaward, these are a pelagic zone, a reef and lagoon area (an offshore barrier reef encloses an extensive lagoon off northeastern Malaita while there is a fringing reef on the northwestern coast), a littoral zone with alternating stretches of strand forest and mangrove or sago palm swamp, a lowland or intermediate forest zone below 2000 feet elevation (where most gardens are) covered with secondary forest and a few remaining sacred groves of virgin primary hardwood rain forest, bamboo thickets above 2000 feet, and a palm-cycad-moss forest along the island's mountain backbone where perpetual cloud cover creates a somber region of fog and drizzle. Brooks in the highlands and moderate sized rivers lower down provide a variable freshwater habitat. Rugged terrain, rocky land, and heavy rainfall make riverine systems fast-flowing, cold, and clean. Along the coast typical daily temperature maxima are in the 80° F's, and minima in the 60° F's, with normal temperature lapse rate and perpetual cloudiness reducing these averages in the hills. Average yearly rainfall exceeds 120 inches near the shore, and is over 200 inches per year at higher altitudes.

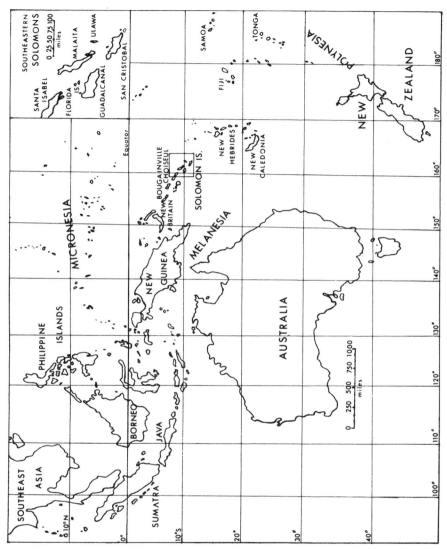

Map 1. The Southwestern Pacific, showing the location of Malaita and the Solomon Islands, adapted from Fox (1925:i). Melanesia includes New Guinea, the Bismarck Archipelago, the Solomon Islands, the New Hebrides, New Caledonia, and Fiji. Melanesia, Micronesia, and Polynesia together comprise the culture area called Oceania. (Drawing by Susan Binder, University of Illinois.)

In terms of human ecology, there are two life styles in the area that together form a single economic system. The interior mountain people such as the Baegu grow root crops and forage in the woodlands. The coastal people and offshore islanders (particularly the Lau people) fish extensively and cultivate some coastal garden plots. An extensive barter trade, conducted at a series of regular market places along the beach, unites the two (Ross 1973b).

Good ethnographic descriptions of Malaitan tribes (Map 2) are available, particularly Ross (1970 and 1973a) for the Baegu; Hogbin (1939) for the Toabaita; Ivens (1930) and Maranda and Maranda (1970) for the Lau; Russell (1950) and Guidieri (1972 and 1973) for the Fataleka; Cooper (1970, 1971, and 1972) for the Langalanga; Keesing (1965, 1967, 1968a, 1968b, 1970a and 1970b) for the Kwaio; de Coppet (1968, 1970a, and 1970b) for the 'Are' are; Ivens (1927) for Sa'a; and Zemp (1971, 1972a, and 1972b) for ethnomusicological description of the entire island.

BAEGU FARMING TECHNIQUES

Baegu farming techniques grow out of an impressive body of traditional lore and practical experience. Barrau (1958) is perhaps the best comprehensive description of Melanesian farming in general. The Baegu recognize four types of soil corresponding well with classifications made empirically by European agronomists. Coastal areas have brown soil *(gano u'udi)* with much sand and gravel, said to be best for coconuts and yams. This belongs to the coastal people of the Lau Lagoon, and the Baegu make little use of it. In the hills there are lateritic red soils *(gano mele)*, very hard when dry and having an embarrassingly slippery hardpan when wet with rain, poor for gardens but offering the best hamlet sites. Interior valley lowlands have wet black soils *(gano bulu)* of alluvium, too soggy and unstable for any crops but swamp taro *(Cyrtosperma chamissonis)*. The best soil for gardening is a dry black soil *(gano fufu'u)*, friable and easily worked, and rich in humus, which tends to lie on moderate slopes at altitudes between 500 and 2000 feet. Soils in higher altitudes are thin and red.

A Baegu gardener begins by selecting a plot of land, which he either owns outright as a member of an agnatic descent group *('ae bara)*, or on which he can claim usage rights through ramifications of cognatic kinship or usage privileges through affinal alliances or patron-client relationships (Ross 1973a:154-175).

It should be on a moderate slope with good drainage. Topsoil horizons should be deep and dark with plenty of organic content giving it a "greasy" *(unganalae)* feel. Deeper horizons in the soil profile should

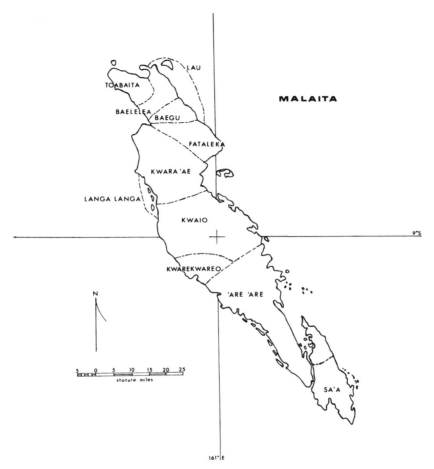

Map 2.   Tribal locations in Malaita, Solomon Islands (Ross 1973a:48-49). (Drawing by Susan Binder, University of Illinois.)

contain weathered limestone fragments. Other things being equal, Malaitans prefer to use land in an advanced stage of secondary growth (approximately 10-25 years after its last use). Older fallow land has primary hardwood growth, that is too hard to clear, while younger fallow has only shrubs and pulpy secondary softwoods that do not add enough "grease" *(ungana)* to the soil to produce good crops. The diagnostic criterion is that no manmade traces of former cultivation (fences or lean-to shelters) remain.

The gardener then clears the ground *(talia gano)* around the intended periphery, letting brush and saplings lie where they may fall (Photograph 2). Brush in the center is piled after clearing *(ungainia);* and the gardener fells small and medium sized trees *(taba 'ai ki),* sparing forest giants and economically useful or magically significant species. Some large trees are left standing for shade and so that their roots will help hold the soil against erosion. Felled trees are sectioned *(kada 'ai ki)* for easier handling, and the branches lopped off *(fifisia 'ai).* Once done laboriously with stone adzes *(ile nagi)* and bamboo *(ile 'au)* or shell *(ile karongo)* knives, the Baegu now use steel bushknives (machetes) and axes acquired through trade or purchased with plantation labor wages earned abroad.

As the next step, the gardener erects a log fence *(labua sakale)* between the just cleared area and the surrounding forest (Photograph 3). Some build upright palisades of saplings *(labua biru),* particularly around sub-divisions of the garden. Meticulous gardeners neatly subdivide their fields, with rectangular internal beds and rows neatly laid

Photograph 2.   A Baegu farmer, Afuga of Walelangi, clearing secondary growth for his new garden plot.

Photograph 3. Afuga and Singiala building a log fence around the newly cleared garden's periphery.

out with log borders *(labua biutoli)*. Compulsive ones will build little fences *(labua tobi)* around big trees and rocks inside the garden.

During the fence-building phase, the cut rubbish is drying in the sun. The gardener next burns *(suu gori'ai)* his (or her) brush piles and burns off *(suu fuli'ere)* the remaining superficial ground cover (Photograph 4). By means of mechanical destruction and chemical reaction, fire converts the recently cut vegetation to nutrients in forms useable by growing crops and restores them to the soil. Fire also helps fell large hardwoods by girdling, weakening, and eventually killing them. Rubbish not converted to ash by burning is used as a mulch.

Although steel cutting tools have all but replaced traditional ones, the Baegu still prefer their own digging sticks *(kwata)* to western shovels or hoes. Using these sharpened and sometimes fire-hardened (charcoal tipped) dibbles, they plant their crops, setting taro stems into holes *(kilua alo)* and making small mounds for yams *(faasia kai)* or sweet potatoes (Photograph 5).

Depending upon growing conditions and his own energy, a gardener will weed his fields *(laua ni ole)* one to four times before he begins

Photograph 4.   Kwaomata of Walelangi burning dried brush in his garden site on a steep Malaitan hillside.

harvesting four to six months after planting, pulling weeds out by hand *(failia)*. The regeneration of extirpated weeds *(laua e'eo)* is an indication that the garden is ready for harvest *(fiu busu)*. Most people are conscientious, talented farmers whose finished gardens *(ole)* are in their own way works of art (Photograph 6). It is interesting to note that they put far more care into taro fields (Photograph 7), which have certain masculine and ritual associations, than they do into sweet potato fields (Photograph 8), which grow rampantly and choke out all but the boldest weeds.

Yams *(Dioscorea* sp.) are a seasonal crop, but all others can be grown throughout the year. Certain "wild foods;" notably *Canarium* nuts, *Spondias dulcis* fruits, and the *Saccharum edulis* cane; are also harvested only seasonally.

They may replant a field once, but rarely more. While harvesting, people clear land for a new garden, timing their work so that the new garden begins bearing just about the time the old one is exhausted. An abandoned field soon sprouts with annual weeds, ferns, and grasses; then with a shrub and fast-growing softwood cover; and ends with a tall stand of timber. The Baegu will re-use an old field after traces of earlier use (lean-to shelters, fences, or bed dividers) have vanished by rotting, but usually before the land reverts to hardwood forest, which they say is harder to clear, the previously cited 10-25 year cycle of usage.

Magic, while not as pervasive as Malinowski (1935) described among Melanesians of the Trobriands, is still an integral part of agricultural technology. The fence around a newly cleared field is largely symbolic (separating human cultivation from natural jungle) or magical, since such fences are usually so low and fragile that they could not seriously deter even moderately hungry swine. Other magical techniques include sacred dracaena or cordyline *(sango)* plants *(Cordyline termi-nalis)* set in the four corners of their rectangular gardens or planted near the center, in which case the garden is said to be "protected" *(sango na)*. Some men set a magical rock *(fau aabu)* at the up-hill edge of the garden, a practice borrowed from their Fataleka and Kwara'ae neighbors to the south. Pagans plant a small patch of taro dedicated as a first fruits offering in the center of the garden. Accompa-

Photograph 5. Kwaomata planting taro with his dibble or digging-stick in a hill-side garden (Ross 1973a:82).

Photograph 6.   Maefasia's garden in Uradaue district, showing elaborate care and aesthetic layout.

Photograph 7.   Lebefiu's taro garden in Walelangi, well tended and weeded, with fences and bed dividers.

Photograph 8. Sulaofia's sweet potato garden in Gwaikafo district. Luxuriant growth retards weed infestation.

nying most phases of gardening activity, pagans pray for success to the ghosts *(akalo)* of their ancestors; Christian Malaitans, who continue to believe in the existence of the ancestral spirits and dieties (Hogbin 1939 and Keesing 1967), address much the same prayers to Jesus or the Virgin Mary.

Certain formalities are observed, particularly with taro gardening. The first three taro shoots are planted *(kilu asua)* with prayers. One should make a first fruits offering before the garden is ready for use or "open" *(mole na)*. Pagans offer ten taro corms and maybe a fish to a priest *(fata'aabu* or *wane ni foa)* Christians give a similar offering to the Church for distribution to the sick or old. The first lot of taro thereafter harvested is taken home and formally cooked and served *(sakafa lufi)* in a leaf and stone oven *(bii)* as a taro-coconut pudding *(gwasu)* or a taro-Canarium almond pudding *(kate)* at a communal meal. After this harvesting *(kwaia alo)* is secular and routine.

As part of the major Baegu pagan religious ceremonial cycle (a series of mortuary feasts called *maoma* honoring recently dead priests), hill clans cultivate ritual taro gardens, performing all cultivation steps

with ritual precision and using a special metaphoric vocabulary to refer to their activities. These culminate in a spectacular pig sacrifice,
communal feast, and display of traditional epic songs *('ae ni mae)*,
panpipe concerts, and dances *('au 'agae)*, in honor of the ancestral
ghosts.

There are no general puberty rites as such, but a "nobleman" *(arai)*
who wished to enhance the status *(faabaita)* of an adolescent son could
give a special feast in his honor. The youth would live in isolation,
shunning baths and letting his hair grow while he planted a special
taro garden. When the taro crop matured, it was cooked and served at a
feast where the father distributed shell money *(malefo)* and valuable
ornaments to the guests.

Although men usually do the backbreaking work of tree felling and
disposal and women spend more time weeding, gardening tasks are
not identified with either sex. During the clearing phase groups of
people may work together, but on the whole the Baegu see gardening
as an individual task and in fact use their gardens as places of escape
when they want privacy. Sacred taro gardens planted for mortuary festivals *(maoma)* are, however, a communal male project. Scheffler
(1965:11) says that in Choiseul Island gardening is invariably cooperative, and Raulet (1960) argues that bilateral descent is a Melanesian
adaptation to the exigencies of communal taro gardening.

Attitudes and ambition greatly affect the amount of time devoted to
gardening, but horticulture of this sort need not be too time consum-
ing. Table 1 summarizes observations based on random selection (all
adults in a single neighborhood) of 19 Baegu men and 21 women over
a three month period. During a four hour gardening effort, men will
work about 190 minutes; fiddle with pipe and tobacco about 15 minutes; chew betel quids about 15 minutes, and spend about 20 minutes
leaning on their sticks, looking at things, or relieving their bladders.
Communal garden work means more time spent in conversation or
argument.

Crop failures are rare, and the hill people expect their farming to be
successful. Given the high rainfall, drought or brushfires are impossible. Locust or caterpillar plagues occasionally do some local damage,
and in the 1950's a series of *Phytophthora colocasia* (Coursey 1968:27)
taro blights did cause widespread crop destruction. The most common
agricultural hazards are mud and rock slides or soil slumping following the torrential rains of tropical cyclones or severe thunderstorms.
Prayer and magic are cautiously optimistic, asking protection from
extraordinary catastrophes, not enhanced fertility on a routine basis.

TABLE 1

WORKING TIME DEVOTED TO VARIOUS ACTIVITIES BY BAEGU MEN AND WOMEN. A "WORKING DAY" IS ABOUT EIGHT HOURS LONG. MONTHLY DATA ARE GIVEN TO SHOW THE POSSIBLE EXISTENCE (OR LACK OF) SEASONAL VARIATION.

Activity	Sample Number	Man-Days Worked January 1967	Man-Days Worked June 1967	Man-Days Worked September 1967	Average Work Days Per Man Per Month
Men	19				
Gardening		154	197	201	9.68
Foraging		17	19	15	.89
Marketing		28	26	24	1.37
Hamlet Work		26	16	14	.98
Resting[1]		281	241	267	13.84
Travel-Visits		83	71	49	3.56
Women[2]	21				
Gardening		214			10.19
Foraging		17			.81
Marketing		71			3.38
Hamlet Work		19			.90
Resting[1]		258			12.29
Travel-Visits		72			3.43

[1]"Resting" is perhaps a bad category. It includes time spent at home on rainy days gossiping, singing, chewing betel, or just sitting; but it also involves a great deal of babysitting, child supervision, and house or tool maintenance.

[2]Kathryn Penstone Ross, wife and field assistant, collected the data on Baegu women.

THE BAEGU DIET

Although American palates would find the Baegu diet bland and monotonous, there is a variety of plants available for food. Table 2, adapted from Ross (1973a:78), is a list by broad nutritional categories roughly equivalent to the essential components produced by typical tropical forest farming, of the foods available to the Baegu, ranked within each category according to expressed Baegu taste preferences. Baegu names are given in parentheses following common English names; pronunciation follows approximately the standards for International Phonetic Alphabet symbols modified as explained in Ross (1973a:293). Linnaean taxonomic identifications were taken from the

TABLE 2

BAEGU FOODS ARRANGED IN ORDER OF INFORMANTS EXPLICITLY
STATED PREFERENCES WITHIN BROAD NUTRITIONAL CATEGORIES
CORRESPONDING ROUGHLY TO THE GENERAL "COMPONENTS" OF
TROPICAL FOREST FARMING PRODUCE.

Nutritional Category	Domesticated Foods (Gardens and Hamlets)	Semi-Domesticated Foods (Owned by Persons or Groups)	Wild Foods (Hunted and Gathered) or Trade Items
Proteins	Swine (boso) Jungle Fowl (karai) *Pole Beans (bini) Dog (kuri) *Cat (fusi) Human Flesh (wane)	Feral Swine	Fish (sekwari) *Tinned Meats Wild Birds (saaro) Cuscus Opossum (futo) Other Sea Foods (mollusks, marine worms, echinoderms, crustaceans, and aquatic reptiles) Land Arthropods (insect larvae and spiders) Bats; especially the giant "flying fox" (sakwalo) Rodents Land Reptiles and Amphibians
Carbohydrates	Taro (alo) (Colocasia esculenta) Yams (kai) (Dioscorea sp.) Sugar Cane (ofu) (Saccharum officinarum) *Sweet Potato (kai rogi) (Ipomea batatas) *Manioc (kai 'ai) (Manihot dulcis) *Maize ('ade 'ade) (Zea mays) *Pumpkin and Squash (bumakani) (Cucurbita sp.)	Swamp Taro (kakama) (Cyrtosperma chamissonis) Bush Taro (edu) (Alocasia indica or macrorhiza) Breadfruit (rau 'ai) (Artocarpus altilis) Sago or Ivory-Nut Palm Pith (sao) (Metroxylon salomonensi) Cordyline or Draecena Root (sango) (Cordyline terminalis)	*Polished Rice (raisi) *Bread (baredi) "Pitpit" Cane (losi) (Saccharum edule) Wild Yams (fana) (Dioscorea sp.) Palm Hearts Fern Rhizomes Cycad Pith (kwae) (Cyathea sp.) *Polynesian Arrowroot (Tacca leontopetaloides) Screw Pine (kaufe or tare) (Pandanus sp.) Miscellaneous Roots and Tubers from the Forest
Lesser Vegetables	Edible Hibiscus Leaf (dee) (Hibiscus manihot) Taro Leaf (abana alo) (Colocasia esculenta) *Tomatos (tomata) *Chinese Cabbage (karabasi) *Water Cress (wata kabisi) *Cucumbers (kukaba) *Scallions (saletisi)	Betal Pepper Leaf (ofe) (Piper betel)	Fern Fiddleheads Wild Greens Edible Fungi Mangrove Pods (koa)
Nuts	Areca Palm Nuts (agero) (Areca catechu) Coconut (malinge or niu) (Cocos nucifera)	Canarium Almond (ngali) (Canarium indicum)	Pacific Chestnut (alite) (Terminalia copelandii) Wild Varieties of Canarium Nuts (Canarium sp.) Miscellaneous Forest Nuts
Fruits	Banana (bou) (Musa sp.) *Papaya ('ai asi) (Carica papaya) *Pineapple (bainabu) *Melons (meloni)	Mango (takare) (Mangifera indica) Malay Apple (kabarai) (Eugenia malaccensis) "Inikori" Fruit (Spondias dulcis) *Citrus Fruits; pommelao (bobolao) and lime (laimo)	*Wild Thimbleberry (toto)* *(Rubus rosaefolius)* Miscellaneous Tree and Bush Fruits of the Forest
Cash Crops and Special Items	*Tobacco (firi) *Cocoa (koko) *Chili Peppers (roketo) *Peanuts (binuti) *Kapok (kabaki)		

*Introduced crops and foods of foreign origin.

standard Solomon Islands forest guide (Whitmore 1966) with generous help from employees of the Protectorate Secretariat's Forestry and Agriculture Departments at Honiara, Guadalcanal. When two or more closely related species are used, or where specific identification is unsure, only generic names are given.

Starchy tubers, corms, and roots are the basic garden crops of the carbohydrate component, the staple element of the diet, and the favorite vegetable food. They particularly relish taro *(Colocasia esculenta)*, recognizing a complex folk taxonomy of a couple of dozen or more varieties discriminated by appearance and culinary properties, that I never did master. In sacred contexts, taro is a "male food," grown in gardens dedicated to the ancestral dieties of the filial piety cult to be eaten only by male communicants. Sweet potato *(Ipomea batatas)*, imported by students returning from Anglican Mission schools in Norfolk Island and New Zealand in the last century, make an even larger contribution to dietary intake but are less favored. Several kinds of native yams *(Dioscorea* sp) and sweet manioc *(Manihot dulcis)*, introduced from the Americas at an unknown date, grace the table more rarely. On the other hand, yams thrive in the sandy soils near the coast, where they are the leading garden crop of the Lau people of the coast and lagoon area, and where they replace taro as the sacred vegetable food for sacrifices (the pagan *maoma* ceremony).

Taro leaves *(Colocasia esculenta)* and the edible hibiscus *(Hisbiscus manihot)* provide the bulk of the leafy green vegetable dietary component.

Most gardens include some plants particularly valued for their flavors or useful as auxiliary food supplies. Indigenous ones are sugar cane, bananas *(Musa* sp.), and a cane-like grass *(Saccharum edule)* called "pitpit" in New Guinea Pidgin that has an edible immature inflorescence. Recently introduced foreign crops include maize, squash, pumpkins, watermelons, pineapples, papayas, and citrus fruits. A few farmers grow and eat tiny quantities of European garden vegetables: tomatoes, cucumbers, pole beans, Chinese cabbage, watercress, and scallions.

In groves around hamlets people plant coconut palms *(Cocos nucifera)* and their favorite narcotics, the areca nut palm *(Areca catechu)* and betel pepper leaf *(Piper betel)* combination (chewed as a quid with coral lime), and imported tobacco.

Individuals or family groups "own" some forest trees used in various ways. Sago palms *(Metroxylon salomonensi)* provide thatch for houses; its pith is fed to pigs or left to ferment and breed a highly relished beetle larva, being used directly for human food only in emergency conditions. The breadfruit tree *(Artocarpus altilis)* bears a starchy fruit frequently eaten.

People crave and industriously harvest Canarium almond nuts *(Carnarium indicum)* and occasionally collect Pacific chestnuts *(Terminalia copelandii)*. They exploit native fruit trees: mangos *(Mangifera indica)*, the Malay apple *(Eugenia malaccensis)*, and a local fruit called "inikori" identified by government foresters as *Spondias dulcis*.

Foraging in the woodlands supplements these plant products and lets the Baegu tap a reservoir of wild foods in emergency situations. When it is necessary or they are in the mood to do so they gather and eat wild (possibly feral) yams, cycad pith, wild palm hearts, fern fiddleheads, wild greens, mushrooms, bracket fungus, and large red raspberries. Swamp taro *(Cyrtosperma chamissonis)* and a hardy bush taro *(Alocasia sp.)* grow untended in boggy areas, available for use between garden crops and as emergency rations. The Baegu use pandanus leaves for mats and umbrellas, but only rarely eat the fruits, used as staples on Pacific atolls in Micronesia.

Meat is not plentiful. Pork is a high prestige festival food, served only three or four times a year by Pagans at mortuary feasts *(maoma)* and by Christians at weddings or Church holidays. Pigs are important ritually and economically, but Malaitans do not control or husband them as carefully as some Melanesians, such as the Siuai of Bougainville, described by Oliver (1955), or the Tsembaga Maring of New Guinea, described by Rappaport (1968), do. Semi-domesticated jungle fowl (chickens) and their eggs, often partially hatched, are occasionally eaten. Marine fish from ocean or lagoon, obtained by barter trade from the Lau people (Ross 1973b), form the greatest bulk of animal foods consumed. The Baegu hill people do, however, spear eels and freshwater fish in rivers; gather prawns and snails from streams; and collect some seafoods (crabs, langoustes, sea slugs, and shellfish) from the beach and mangrove swamp areas. Some men will not eat crustaceans or mollusks, because there is a belief that these foods will destroy a man's magical powers or make him sexually impotent. White men's appetite for such foods as lobster and oysters is a source of ribald humor for Malaitans. A few Baegu men hunt the large "flying fox" bats *(sakwalo)*, cuscus opossums *(futo)*, and birds, particularly the Pacific wood pigeon *(bole)* and native duck *(a'arongo)*; but most seem to consider hunting scarcely worth the effort. Foraging on land yields a number of edible beetle larvae, caterpillars, and spiders that, while small in single portions, may form a significant protein dietary supplement (Kessing 1965:367). Only in emergencies will they eat dogs, cats, native wood rats *(kiki i tolo)*, the giant rat *Mus rex (furingale)*, small bats *(tarawedi)*, lizards, or frogs; which they say all "taste bad."

There are food taboos, usually regarding the quasi-totemic animal (snake or bird) said to be the putative ancestor of one or more clans; but these taboos affect only those clans, not the population in general. However, the prohibition against killing or eating the sea-eagle seems to be Malaita-wide.

Epicurean cannibalism and "insult anthropophagy" of slain enemies (you eat them and then you defecate them) was once common in Malaita, but was suppressed by the 1930's through Christian mission teachings and British police power. There are persistent rumors, however, that some downed Japanese aviators and the garrison (who mysteriously disappeared after the Guadalcanal campaign) of a Japanese weather station in northern Malaita may have met an alimentary end during World War II.

European trade foods are too hard to get and too expensive to be of much practical use. Chinese merchants sell polished white rice, which is a taste acquired by Malaita men during periods of contract labor on commercial plantations, where it is the basic refectory ration. Most rice is imported from Southeast Asia, but some is grown locally by Guadalcanal Plains Limited, a private investment and development corporation owned and financed by Europeans resident in the Solomons. (In Solomon Islands parlance, all white men, regardless of nationality, are "Europeans.") A few Malaitans have also learned to like and to bake bread from Australian flour. Tinned meats (fishes, corned beef or mutton, poultry, and sausages) are an extremely expensive luxury item purchased occasionally for conspicuous consumption on special occasions from Chinese traders; most are imported from Australia or New Zealand, but there are some Asian (mainly Japan and Mainland China) goods. Malaitans now and then buy (when they can afford it) tea, coffee, black/white pepper, and curry powder from Chinese stores or trade vessels.

Attempts at cash cropping have by and large been failures, because there is no suitable way to transport and market crops. Few if any Baegu have realized any profits from the cash crops sponsored by the administration, and they tend to resent government attempts to stimulate production of them.

Baegu people eat a large morning and evening meal with frequent small snacks between. Cookery is simple, but not unpalatable. They bake taro, maize, breadfruit, and sweet potatoes directly among embers or steam them in leaf-wrapped packets. Leafy vegetables and green maize ears are boiled in bamboo joints or tradeware utensils. They steam pork or fish in leaf ovens, smoke eels and canarium nuts, and broil grubs and shellfish on open coals. Grubs, crustaceans and mollusks may also be boiled in bamboo joints. Fruits, coconuts, and some vegetables are of course eaten raw. The Baegu do make one interesting boiled dish of edible hibiscus leaves with coconut cream and diced taro, some near the coast make a mangrove pod and shellfish chowder, and they produce a variety of starch and nut puddings for festival occasions; but these offerings just about exhaust their efforts at culinary elegance.

Salt comes from seawater gathered by women on the beach and carried in hollow joints of bamboo. They sometimes use betel pepper leaves as condiments, and they use pepper or curry powder, if they can afford them. Wild ginger *(fiu)* is used for magic and curing, and people occasionally nibble it for its sharp flavor; it is not, however, a regular part of the cuisine.

According to my 1968 census about 1880 Baegu inhabit a roughly triangular area of 55.3 square miles in the interior of northern Malaita. This does not include the coastal strip below 500 feet exploited by others. There are roughly 34.0 persons per square mile with each having potential use of 18.8 acres of land (Ross 1973a:94-99).

The mean size of intact nuclear biological families in the hills is 4.7 persons (two persons with 2.7 children living with them (Ross 1973a:207). A nuclear biological family (parents with children) is the usual Baegu domestic social unit exploiting a set of gardens by pooling the produce for subsistence. Other forms of households (sibling pairs, mature children with aged parents, affiliated widows or widowers, etc.) may, of course, sometimes replace nuclear families in this function (Ross 1973a:216-222).

Surveying 24 currently productive gardens, I found that the average married adult's garden covers about 21,900 sq. ft. or .503 acres. Since people start a new garden before they have finished harvesting an old one, a person will have between 21,900 and 43,800 sq. ft. under cultivation at any given time. Considering that a man and wife will each have a garden; and given that the average parental pair has 2.7 dependent children, this would mean that it takes between 43,800 and 87,600 sq. ft. or 1.006 and 2.012 acres of garden to support an average Baegu hill family. On an individual basis it requires mean values of 9,319 to 18,638 sq. ft. or .214 to .428 acres per capita under cultivation at a time. Rounding off for significance and using divisors of 4 and 5 (since decimal persons are a pragmatic absurdity), this would mean that a Baegu person needs an acreage in the range of 0.2 to 0.6 acres for subsistence.

Lacking any means of transport but slithering about on foot in the mud and having no means of weighing large harvests, I was unable to find out directly how much food a garden produces. At present I can approach this only crudely and indirectly by way of typical daily food consumption.

In February 1967 I made a dietary survey of three families over a nine day span, and repeated this in June 1968. This cohort included eight adults, four juveniles (ages 6-12 years), and two weaned small children. Tables 3 and 4, adapted from Ross (1973a:79), give the results of this dietary study showing portions in grams per person per day and percentages of types of food by weight.

Since Baegu farming approaches the conditions of an ideal closed system (nuclear biological families and other households live on the produce of their own gardens directly consumed or used in trade only marginally supplemented by foraging), one can estimate the annual productivity. Adding the total food eaten daily by an adult male, an adult female, two juveniles, and one weaned small child, one finds that an average intact nuclear biological family of 4.7 people will eat about 8.559 kilograms of food per day. On a yearly basis they would consume at this rate 6887 lbs. (3124 kg.) or 3.44 tons (3.124 metric tons) of food. Since an average family lives on the produce of 1.006 to 2.012 acres of garden land, these acreages should represent approximate maxima and minima of productivity. Dividing the annual consumption of food by an average Baegu family first by the larger acreage necessary for subsistence, then by the minimum acreage needed, suggests that garden land in northern Malaita will (when cultivated by traditional methods) yield between 1.71 and 3.42 tons per acre (3.86-7.62 metric tons per hectare) of foodstuffs per year. This is of course an imprecise estimate (better only than no estimate at all).

BAEGU NUTRITION

The first surprising thing about these figures (Table 3) is their gross size. At first I declined to accept my own figures, but close follow-up observations (my persistent nosiness causing a certain amount of irritation) convinced me that an adult Baegu male does eat about a kilogram of taro and sweet potatoes per day. Children seem to eat almost as much, but I suspect the fact that I was watching them made them want to show off by stuffing themselves. It may also be worth noting in passing that women appear to eat less of the highly valued vegetable foods.

TABLE 3

AVERAGE PORTIONS OF FOOD EATEN DAILY BY BAEGU INDIVIDUALS ALL PORTIONS ARE IN GRAMS.[1]

Food	Adult ♂	Adult ♀	Juvenile (6-12 yrs) ♂	Juvenile (6-12 yrs) ♀	Weaned Small Children (<6 yrs)
Proteins					
Meat and Fish	34.02	50.41	47.26	94.49	0
Carbohydrates					
Taro *(Colocasia)*	185.21	88.20	37.79	0	103.96
Swamp taro *(Cyrtosperma)*	134.18	179.54	264.59	349.64	0
Bush taro *(Alocasia)*	32.12	25.20	0	0	0
Sweet potato	653.95	683.55	590.62	321.29	623.70
Manioc (Cassava)	100.16	157.51	212.63	387.46	0
Maize	15.11	15.76	23.62	51.97	0
Breadfruit	30.25	0	33.08	0	0
Lesser Vegetables					
Edible hibiscus leaf	260.82	346.49	354.38	231.53	321.29
Taro leaf *(Colocasia)*	37.79	18.91	0	0	0
Tomato	0	0	14.18	18.91	0
Other leafy vegetables	41.59	88.20	127.58	165.37	0
Nuts					
Coconut	47.26	81.90	113.40	170.10	0
Canarium almonds	170.10	62.99	0	0	0
Fruits					
Banana *(Musa)*	166.33	72.46	61.43	0	18.91
Papaya	39.69	0	0	0	0
Total Daily Ration	1948.58	1871.12	1880.56	1790.76	1067.86

[1]Foods were measured in "finished" form, cooked or raw but ready for consumption, just prior to eating, with the exception of green, leafy vegetables (usually boiled), which for obvious reasons I weighed before cooking.

TABLE 4

PERCENTAGES (BY WEIGHT) OF VARIOUS TYPES OF FOODS COMPRISING THE BAEGU DAILY DIET.

Food	Adult ♂	Adult ♀	Juvenile (6-12 yrs) ♂	Juvenile (6-12 yrs) ♀	Weaned Small Children (<6 yrs)
Animal Proteins	1.7	2.7	2.5	5.3	0
Carbohydrates	59.1	61.4	61.8	62.0	68.3
"Garden" vegetables	17.5	24.2	26.4	23.2	30.1
Nuts	11.2	7.7	6.0	9.5	0
Fruits	10.6	3.9	3.3	0	1.8

The second surprising thing about the Baegu diet is their reliance upon predominantly starchy foods, particularly taro and sweet potatoes, and the proportionately small protein intake. Intuitively, it seems obvious that there will be some adaptive value for a largely carbohydrate foods diet among an active, highlands-dwelling population whose livelihood entails high energy demands. Analysis of Pacific subsistence crops done for the South Pacific Commission has determined the nutritional constituents of tropical crops such as the Baegu use. Table 5 summarizes these food values, originally published by the Commission in separate issues of their *Quarterly Bulletin* (Peters 1954, Malcolm and Barrau 1954; Massal and Barrau 1954, 1955a, 1955b, 1955c, 1955d, 1956a, 1956b, and 1956c). Sweet potato *(Ipomea batatas)* tubers for example yield about 1.7% proteins by weight, while *Colocasia esculenta* taro corms average 1.9%. Both have only small amounts of vitamins and essential minerals. Both are mostly water (70.8% and 72.5%) with carbohydrate components of 28.5% and 24.0% respectively. Apparently the Baegu, who live on a diet of starch rich but protein poor vegetable foods, maintain adequate nutritional standards by eating massive amounts. Table 6 estimates (by combining information from Tables 3 and 5) the nutrients available in the Baegu daily diet.

The total caloric intake reported in Table 6 seems rather low for an active farming people, whose agility on muddy mountain trails continually embarrassed me (despite some experience in scholastic and collegiate basketball and track). I think people eat quite a bit more than I observed, and that the error is due to practical shortcomings of

TABLE 5

CONSTITUENT FOOD VALUES OF 100 GRAM PORTIONS OF PACIFIC AREA SUBSISTENCE CROPS COMPILED FROM ANALYSES DONE BY JACQUES BARRAU, SHEILA MALCOLM, AND EMILE MASSAL FOR THE SOUTH PACIFIC COMMISSION, NOUMEA, NEW CALEDONIA.

Nutrient	Taro (Colocasia)[1] Tubers	Taro (Colocasia)[1] Leaves	Sweet Potato	Manioc (Cassava)	Breadfruit	Banana (Musa)	Coconuts	Yams	Sago
Calories	100	0	100	130	105	90	350	103	250
Water (g)[2]	72.5	87.0	70.8	67.0	70.0	75.9	48.0	72.5	26.4
Proteins (g)	1.9	3.5	1.7	1.2	1.6	1.0	3.8	2.0	0.2
Fats (g)	0.2	0.8	0.3	0.3	0.3	0.5	34.0	0	0
Carbohydrates (g)	24.0	7.4	25.0	30.0	25.0	19.7	13.5	23.5	71.6
Ash (g)	1.3	1.5	1.0	1.2	1.2	0.7	1.0	1.0	0.35
Fiber (g)	0.8	2.0	3.3	1.5	?	1.0	3.2	?	0.4
Calcium (mg)[2]	30.0	150.0	35.0	0.13	33.0	6.6	21.0	10.0	10.0
Phosphorus (mg)	80.0	59.0	50.0	0.1	32.0	33.0	98.0	69.0	12.5
Iron (mg)	1.0	1.0	0.8	0.8	1.1	traces	2.0	0.9	1.5
Vitamin A (iu)[2]	30	0	2500	0	40	400	0	traces	0
Thiamin (mg)	0.04	0.1	0.1	0.04	0.15	0.05	0.11	0.1	traces
Riboflavin (mg)	0.03	0	0.05	0.075	0.03	0.08	0.01	0.05	traces
Niacin (mg)	0.4	0	0.7	0.6	0.9	0.6	0.2	0.4	traces
Vitamin C (mg)	10.0	25.0	25.0	25.0	23.0	10.0	3.0	5.0	0

[1]Lacking detailed analyses of the food value of Alocasia or Cyrtosperma tubers, I assume in Table 6 that these two genera of taro have approximately the same constituents as Colocasia tubers.

[2]Grams, milligrams, or international units as appropriate.

TABLE 6

ESTIMATED BAEGU DAILY NUTRIENT INTAKE BASED ON AVERAGE FOOD CONSUMPTION.[1]

Nutrient[2]	Adult ♂	Adult ♀	Juvenile (6-12 yrs) ♂	Juvenile (6-12 yrs) ♀	Weaned Small Children (< 6 yrs.)
Calories	2825	2193	1910	2107	842
Proteins (g)[3]	76.3	60.8	49.5	57.7	22.4
Fats (g)	129.2	75.3	47.9	70.9	4.0
Calcium (mg)[3]	911.1	889.4	834.1	680.9	572.0
Phosphorus (mg)	1657.1	1263.6	1030.7	1029.8	561.9
Iron (mg)	25.8	27.5	28.0	27.3	15.6
Vitamin A (iu)[3]	26313	30588	29823	20455	25339
Thiamin (mg)	2.57	1.97	1.56	1.33	0.99
Riboflavin (mg)	1.64	1.45	1.39	1.33	0.94
Niacin (mg)	30.77	18.31	11.02	11.60	5.86
Vitamin C (mg)	428.8	475.0	495.7	427.3	328.9

[1]Based on mealtime consumption, which omits most between meals snacking.

[2]Values for typical Pacific subsistence foods come from Table 5; those for conventional garden vegetables and fruits from USDA Special Publications (1945:8-15); and those for meats, fish, leafy vegetables, and nuts are estimates using average values for those categories from USDA Special Publications (1945:8-15).

[3]Grams, milligrams, or international units as appropriate.

my dietary survey. As just one person, I could not follow the entire cohort around on their twice weekly trips to market or their several days in their respective gardens. There are also times when tact indicates that an observer would not be welcome. I really had control over my sample only when they were around the hamlet; this means I could weigh their food intake only at normal meal times, or if I was lucky enough to catch them trying to snack during the daytime while in my sight. Men often carry a fiber bag of roasted taro or a leaf-wrapped packet of smoked fish with them, and everyone eats fruit or grubs if they find them in the forest or garden. If someone tried to gobble a quick snack enroute to market or garden, I suspect I missed it.

Small children, whose mealtime calorie intake of only 842 from Table 6 seems especially low, are incorrigible snackers, eating constantly between meals and sucking on sticks of sugar cane all day long.

Finally, there is the distinct possibility (Durnin 1970) that the Baegu and other Melanesians can get by perfectly well (by means either of evolutionary mutation and selection or of adaptive plasticity in a single life-time) on a lower caloric level than could European or American populations from different environments with different genetic endowments, evolutionary histories, and nutritional experiences.

Table 7 compares average Baegu daily nutrient intake with minimum physiological requirements and recommended daily allowances for other parts of the world.

Protein nutrition is an especially complex problem. Proteins, the basic matter of living tissues, are extremely complex molecules of nitrogen, carbon, hydrogen, and oxygen. They are formed from "building blocks" of amino acids by complex reactions involving a number of different enzymes and organic catalysts. Protein metabolism and breakdown is likewise complex, ending typically with the excretion of nitrogen in urea. Living organisms constantly synthesize and metabolize proteins as part of their life processes.

As Stini (1971:1021-2) points out, human beings need some twenty-odd different amino acids that are listed in Table 8. Eight (isoleucine, leucine, lysine, methionine, phenylalanine, threonine, tryptophan, and valine) are critical or essential to dietary regimes, because they cannot be synthesized by the body itself and must be provided as food intake. Not only must there be a sufficient level of total protein intake, but foods eaten should provide some of all the amino acids needed. Furthermore, there are problems of amino acid imbalance, in that certain complementary amino acids must be ingested at the same time in order for the body to absorb and synthesize proteins properly. Within limits the human body can compensate for protein deficiencies and imbalances. It can synthesize itself or convert all but the eight critical amino acids, and it can buffer the effects of imbalances by secreting the individual's own proteins into the intestinal lumen, where the essential amino acids permit uptake of the rest (Stini 1971:1021).

Man, as a result of a million or more years as a hunter, has evolved into an animal dependant to some degree upon meat (Stini 1971:1023). It has been alleged that plant foods cannot alone sustain human life, because they may not contain all the essential amino acids. This is not correct, as Table 8 shows, but there still are complications with plant-rich, meat-poor diets. One species of plant may in fact lack some essential amino acids. Hence to satisfy protein nutritonal requirements, people must use a wide variety of plant foods. Amino acid imbalances in plant species may interfere with proper protein synthesis and me-

TABLE 7

COMPARISON OF BAEGU DAILY NUTRIENT INTAKE WITH ESTABLISHED NUTRITIONAL STANDARDS.

Nutrients	BAEGU INTAKE Adult Males	BAEGU INTAKE Adult Females	Adult Minimum Daily Requirements[2]	Recommended Daily Allowances[1] PHILIPPINE ISLANDS STANDARDS Adult Males	PHILIPPINE ISLANDS STANDARDS Adult Females	UNITED NATIONS FAO STANDARDS Adult Males	UNITED NATIONS FAO STANDARDS Adult Females	U.S.A. STANDARDS Adult Males	U.S.A. STANDARDS Adult Females
Calories	2825	2193	1224-4082	2400	1800	3200 5	2300	2800	2000
Proteins (g)	76.3	60.8	18-40	53	46	46	39	65	55
Fats (g)	129.2	75.3	29-85	—	—	—	—	—	—
Calcium (mg)	911.1	889.4	364-910	500	500	500	500	800	800
Phosphorus (mg)	1657-1	1263.6	605-1511	—	—	—	—	800	800
Iron (mg)	25.8	27.5	10-15	—	—	—	—	10	18
Vitamin A (iu)	26313	30588	2500	5000	5000	—	—	5000	5000
Thiamin (mg)	2.57	1.97	1.0	1.2	0.9	1.3	0.9	1.4	1.0
Riboflavin (mg)	1.64	1.45	1.2	1.2	0.9	1.8	1.3	1.7	1.5
Niacin (mg)	30.77	18.31	10	—	—	21.1	15.2	18	13
Vitamin C (mg)	428.8	475.0	30	70	70	—	—	60	55

[1] Recommended daily allowances are established by public policy and "afford a margin of sufficiency above average physiological requirements" determined by empirical research (Altman and Dittmer 1968:95). Standard allowances set by the Food and Nutrition Board, National Research Council-National Academy of Sciences for the United States in 1943 and updated periodically, and allowances for other countries determined by the Food and Agriculture Organization, United Nations, are adapted from Altman and Dittmer (1968:95-97) and NRC-NAS (1968:68-69).

[2] Minimum daily requirements determined by empirical physiological research are calculated from results reported in Wohl (1945)

581

TABLE 8

AMINO ACIDS NEEDED FOR HUMAN PROTEIN FORMATION AND THEIR
PRESENCE AND CONCENTRATION IN PLANT FOODS, ADAPTED FROM
COURSEY AND HAYNES (1970:264), MEYER (1960:139-141), AND WATER-
LOW AND STEPHEN (1957:7).

| Amino Acids | Leaves[1] | Spermatophytes | | Thallophytes[1] (Edible Fungi) |
		Seed Crops[2]	Root Crops[3]	
Alanine	4.4- 5.1	—	—	—
Amide	4.7- 6.0	—	—	—
Arginine	12.4-14.0	5.8-9.9	—	4.9-13.3
Aspartic Acid	4.7- 5.4	—	—	—
Cystine	1.1- 1.6	0.6-2.0	1.1-2.8	—
Glutamic Acid	6.4- 7.8	—	—	4.9-5.8
Glycine	0.4	5.3-5.6	—	—
Histidine	3.6- 4.0	1.5-2.6	—	1.4-7.4
Hydroxy Proline	—	—	—	—
*Isoleucine	3.6- 7.3	3.1-5.3	1.8-3.8	1.1-4.0
*Leucine	3.6- 7.3	5.0-9.0	2.9-6.2	2.7-4.9
*Lysine	5.0- 6.8	2.0-5.8	3.8-4.8	3.9-9.1
*Methionine	1.2- 1.6	1.3-3.4	1.0-2.0	0.4-0.9
*Phenylalanine	2.4- 2.6	5.4-6.9	2.1-5.2	1.1-1.9
Proline	3.1	—	—	—
Serine	—	—	—	—
*Threonine	3.0- 4.0	1.5-4.5	2.8-5.4	2.0-3.7
*Tryptophan	1.4- 1.9	1.0-1.6	0.9-1.0	0.6-1.0
Tyrosine	2.3- 2.7	3.2-5.6	1.6-4.2	1.1-2.3
*Valine	3.3- 4.5	3.7-7.1	2.6-6.6	2.2-4.0

[1]Expressed as per cent protein nitrogen (Meyer 1960:139).

[2]Calculated to 16.0 grams of nitrogen; considers cotton seed meal, linseed meal, peanut flour, soybean meal, oats, and rice (Meyer 1960:141).

[3]Expressed as percentage of a "reference protein," said to approximate whole egg protein and to be ideal for human nutrition, which is in turn expressed as percentage composition of yams, taro, manioc, and sweet potatoes (Coursey and Haynes 1970:264).

*Essential amino acids that cannot be synthesized directly in the human body (Waterlow and Stephens 1957:7). Coursey and Haynes (1970:264) also list cystine and tyrosine as essential amino acids. Altman and Dittmer (1968:53) and Wohl (1945:926) include histadine in the list.

tabolism, if sufficient variety is not available. The worst problem is that amounts of protein in plant foods tend to be small, and the fiber in plant tissues limits the amounts that human beings can eat (Lawrie 1970:53), since we are not equipped by nature to digest cellulose.

Melanesians may compensate for this in several ways. Rather far out is the suggestion reported in the *South Pacific Bulletin* (1970:46) review of work on nutrition among New Guinea highlanders, who subsist almost exclusively on sweet potatoes, that they may in fact use nitrogen-fixing micro-organisms inhabiting the human intestine, which convert atmospheric nitrogen and fermented (partially digested) carbohydrates into bacterial proteins in the gut itself. Nitrogen-fixing bacteria inhabiting the root systems of legumes do perform such syntheses. Hipsley and Bergerson report the isolation of such bacteria in the human intestines, and Oomen and Corden estimate that they may provide as much as 16 grams of protein per day for their hosts *(South Pacific Bulletin* 1970:46). Another possible role for intestinal microflora, is that some species of bacteria may help break down cellulose fibers in plant foods, permitting Melanesians to eat the vast quantities of vegetables that the Baegu do, Table 3. Man's adaptation to his own intestinal micro-flora is still only poorly understood.

Durnin (1970:135) more realistically suggests that assumed standards of nutritional adequacy for maintenance of health (including protein intake) are based upon well-fed European populations, and that people who live habitually on a different nutritional plane, such as Melanesians, may have satisfactorily adapted to a consistently lower intake.

As Heggen (1972) once pointed out, the protein consumption data in the Baegu dietary survey (Tables 3, 4, and 6 above) do not make sense in some respects. First, the level itself is astonishingly low, and second, one would expect adult males (out of hunger or due to custom) to get the largest proportion of high prestige meat foods. Apparently they do not. As Table 7 shows, however, the Baegu do in fact get enough protein, largely from the plant foods they consume in massive amounts to meet any existing nutritional standards, although the meat they eat is too scarce for our tastes. Then, too, I think they on the whole eat more meat or fish than Tables 3 or 6 survey results show. My data were routine daily feedings, not ceremonial feastings, and meat and fish tend to be ceremonial rather than daily foods. Meat is a "special occasion" food for festive occasions. Pigs are butchered for pagan sacrifices or Christian feasts. Fish are served at weddings, for lesser sacrifices, and as formal gifts *(felenga)* from a new bridegroom to his affines. People will splurge on costs and eat massive amounts of pork, fish, or tinned meats on festival occasions (pagan mortuary festivals, weddings, or church holidays) and then go without meat for days. Second, they snack frequently on edible snails, caterpillars, or spiders, which they find while working in their gardens and consume raw on the spot. Though small in unit size, these foods can in the long run provide important additions of animal protein, particularly the eight critical amino acids, which the human body cannot synthesize.

Heggen (1972) says that the fact that Baegu males appear from Tables 3 and 4 to eat only half as much protein as females is consistent with the observable greater retardation in skeletal maturation of males over females, reported by Damon (1970), when compared with white American standards. Again, however, I think that in the long run men may eat more protein than they seemed to do in my dietary survey reported in Tables 3 and 6. At ceremonial feasts, not included in the study, women get only small portions, while men and boys eat like hogs (no pun intended). Routine daily feeding data are biased for two reasons. Women, who prepare the morning and evening meals, do nibble a bit, and since my survey favored formal meals rather than desultory snacking throughout the day, one would expect Tables 3 and 6 to reflect an emphasis on meal-preparation nibbling. Male snacking along trails and in gardens would be under-represented. Second, Baegu hill people catch a lot of riverine prawns *(dengi)*. Because of the belief that crustaceans and mollusks cause impotence, some men prefer to forego these routine mealtime proteins in favor of ceremonial pork/ fish feasting or of snacking on "safe" caterpillars or spiders snatched in the garden. Finally, even fish (which men *do* eat more of than women according to my subjective observations) obtained at market from the Lau people is expensive, and people do not trade for fish every week. My dietary study was so short of duration that it may well have covered a time when the families I observed were not trading for fish.

Children, too, have a significant other source of proteins. Young boys will spend hours or even days damming and diverting small hill streams to collect prawns *(dengi)* from exposed pools in the old channel and broiling them in small bankside cooking fires.

The indication in Tables 3 and 4 that children under 6 years of age get no animal protein at mealtimes, and the consequent low protein intake of 22.4 grams daily listed in Table 6, is however probably correct. The Baegu believe that meat and particularly fish are bad for small children, and will not permit them to eat these foods until they are 4-6 years of age and have been "strengthened" *(faaramoelae)* by magical techniques in the men's house *(beu)*. Small children do get the crustaceans and mollusks that are avoided by adult men. "He ate fish" *(ania sekwari)* is the usual folk diagnosis for most infantile and younger juvenile cholic, diarrhea, or abdominal pains. Similar beliefs are common in the Solomon Islands, as Hogbin (1964:32) reports for Guadalcanal. This animal protein deprivation in early childhood may have some effect in helping people adapt to a relatively low protein diet, and a reliance upon plant rather than animal proteins.

People fear for the health of children, and try to protect them from eating foods defined as "dangerous." On the other hand, children and women are more innovative where foods are concerned, willing to try **foreign or unusual foods, while adult men (who fear for their piety and** sacred powers) are more conservative and reluctant to experiment.

Finally, the variety of the Baegu diet helps. Nuts, fruits, small game, and various different vegetables provide small amounts of amino acids of different kinds. These small amounts add up to a respectable total protein intake, when added together as they are in Table 6.

Likewise, the small unit amounts of nuts, fruits, garden vegetables, and odd bits of meat combine to provide, as Tables 6 and 7 show, adequate intake of the fats needed by the body to assuage hunger and to utilize vitamins and minerals properly, and of the various vitamins and minerals themselves needed for good health. Again, the variety of different foods eaten to supplement to basic root starch diet is probably at least as important as the cumulative amount.

Baegu salt, other than that contained in meat or fish and the pigs' blood puddings they cook in bamboo tubes at mortuary festivals *(maoma),* comes from the seawater that women carry up from the beach after markets. As seawater, it should have more potassium salts (as opposed to the familiar sodium chloride salt) and should contain more trace elements and ions than from land sources. Baegu cooks use it to season green vegetables and some root puddings, but they use it seldom and sparingly, and salt intake in the diet is low. Damon (1970) and Page (1973) attribute their relative freedom from coronary and circulatory diseases to this low salt diet that is forced upon them by the logistic difficulties in getting seawater several thousand feet up into the mountains using bamboo joints.

An Evaluation of Bush Fallow or Swidden Farming

This factual material on Baegu farming and comparative data culled from anthropological literature can be used to counter the ten specific charges against or objections to bush fallow or swidden farming mentioned by way of introduction.

That the people who practice it do so in ignorance. The Baegu know Malaitan soil and its properties; know the value of firing ash and mulch as fertilizers; know the value of a few standing large trees for shading and reducing rain force with their leaves and with their roots holding soil against mechanical erosion; and know the value of short cultivation periods with long fallow periods for forest regeneration (hence fertility restoration). Ollier, Drover, and Godelier (1971) cite the sophisticated and complex soil knowledge of the Baruya, a Kukukuku group of eastern New Guinea. Rappaport (1971:350) says the Tsembaga Maring of the central highlands of New Guinea recognize the importance of regenerating trees, calling them *"duk mi"* or "mother of gardens." Reina (1967) describes the impressive and systematic modern Mayan knowledge of all phases of *milpa* agriculture. Cowgill (1961:13-29) and Reina (1967:9) report that Mayan peasants of the Peten area of Guatemala know the land should rest. Conklin (1954) implies that the Hanunóo of the Philippines know that mixed cropping improves production and helps maintain fertility longer. Ogan (1971) describes Nasioi of Bougainville land disputes as examples of a Melanesian people's appreciation for land, their major productive factor, and Allan (1957:v and 213) describes the Solomon Islanders' general "paranoia" and fear of losing their land to the government. Leach (1959:64) asserts that the shifting cultivation practiced by the Shan Hills tribesmen of Burma, the Iban of Sarawak, Borneo, and the Sinhalese of the dry zone in Ceylon is rational economic behavior, recognizing that swidden farming offers greater and easier economic rewards than terraced field, sedentary cultivation.

That it is too much work and costs too much. Table 1 indicates that the Baegu do not put into their gardens that much more work on subsistence than hunters and gatherers do for subsistence (Lee and Devore 1968), about 500-1000 man-hours per year (Sahlins 1968:30). Using the Table 1 datum of about 10 man-days work per month gardening on the 15 man-days per month value for gardening-foraging-marketing by women, one can calculate that the Baegu expend 960-1440 man-hours per year on subsistence.

Nor is their style of gardening an onerous burden. Initial clearance may be hard, but they need do little weeding. People use their gardens for privacy when they want to be alone to think, and most of them regard farming as a pleasant activity. Old people putter in their gardens as long as they are able. Conklin (1954) mentions that swidden cultivation is carried out effectively by a small labor force with little capital expenditure. Rappaport (1971:348-9) computed energy expenditures for Tsembaga Maring (New Guinea) gardening totaling 561,307 kilocalories per acre, broken down for specific activities as shown in Table 9. He estimated that the biomass of crop yield support-

TABLE 9

ENERGY FLOW AND BALANCES IN TSEMBAGA MARING GARDENING, CENTRAL HIGHLANDS OF NEW GUINEA (RAPPAPORT 1971:348-9). ALL FIGURES ARE IN ESTIMATED KILOCALORIES PER ACRE INPUT/OUTPUT FOR A TYPICAL PAIR OF GARDENS.

INPUTS		OUTPUTS	
Activity (Work Expenditures)	Energy Inputs	Use of Product (Gross Profits)	Biomass of Crop Yield
Clearing Underbrush	56,628	Uphill Gardens (Sweet Potatoes)	
Clearing Trees	22,650	Human Consumption	2,434,495
Fencing Gardens	34,164	Pig Feeding	2,147,399
Weeding and Burning	18,968	Downhill Gardens (Taro and Yams)	
Placing Soil Retainers, Etc.	14,476	Human Consumption	3,716,755
Planting and Weeding Until Harvest	180,336	Pig Feeding	1,480,546
Other Maintenance of Gardens	46,000		
Sweet Potato Harvest	44,835		
Taro Harvest	5,608		
Cassava Harvest	2,184		
Yam Harvest	15,700		
Cartage (From Gardens to Hamlet)	119,764		
TOTAL INPUT[1]	561,313	GROSS OUTPUT[1]	9,779,195
		NET OUTPUT[1]	9,217,882

[1]Computations do not agree with the totals shown in Rappaport (1971:348-9), but the errors are trivial.

ing humans and pigs was 9,218,188 kilocalories. His output/input ratios (crop yield divided by total energy expended in kilocalories) were 16.5 to 1 for taro-yam gardens and 15.9 to 1 for sweet potato gardens for nucleated settlement patterns or 20.1 to 1 and 18.4 to 1 respectively for dispersed settlement patterns (Rappaport 1971:351). In view of Conklin's (1961:28) warning about the gross difficulties of measurement in shifting cultivation settings, however, I suspect that Rappaport's figures should be taken with a hefty grain of salt; as if, perhaps, each raw number contained about one significant figure. Marvin Harris (1971:203-217) calculates an $E = m \times t \times r \times e$ Food Energy Formula (Annual Food Energy Calorie Output equals number of food producers in the labor force times hours of work per food producer times calories expended per hour per man above basal metabolism rate times the techno-environmental efficiency ratio of average number of calories of food produced for each calorie expended in food production) for slash-and-burn Tsembaga Maring farmers of:

$$150,000,000 = 146 \times 380 \times 150 \times 18.0$$

as compared with corresponding values for Kalahari Bushmen hunter-gatherers of:

$$23,000,000 = 20 \times 805 \times 150 \times 9.6$$

or for Genieri (West African) hoe using cereal cultivators of:

$$460,000,000 = 334 \times 820 \times 150 \times 11.2$$

or for Yunnanese (China) peasants growing irrigated rice and other crops of:

$$3,788,000,000 = 418 \times 1129 \times 150 \times 53.5$$

or for mechanized United States of America agriculture of:

$$260 \text{ trillion} = 5,000,000 \times 1,714 \times 150 \times 210$$

which is not a particularly unfavorable comparison. Techno-environmental ratios are high, yields are high, and work is low.

Efficiency is perhaps the ultimate arbiter and the mathematical expression of the input and output relationship. In a matrix solution of:

$$e_i = \sum_{j=i}^{n} p_{ij} \quad r_i$$

where P is the production matrix with elements p_{ij}, r the respiration vector, e the direct energy flow vector, and n the number of system components; that considered all aspects of ecosystem energy flow (production, respiration, direct, and indirect) and which involved comparison of New Guinea horticultural, Silver Springs, Old Field, Salt Marsh, and New England Spring ecosystems; Hanon (1973:7) concluded that the New Guinea system was 40 times more energy efficient than modern American agriculture and food processing.

That it is not productive enough, and that too much land is required. Baegu gross yields of 1.7 to 3.4 tons of foodstuffs per year are impressive, as are Cowgill's (1961:21) measurement of initial yields for Mayan *milperos*. Conklin (1957) and Gourou (1956) report that swidden rice production in the Philippines compares favorably with Indo-Chinese irrigated padi fields on a per unit of labor basis, and Leach's (1959) similar data have already been mentioned. Rappaport's (1971) estimates of crop yield biomass and output/input ratios for Tsembaga farming also are good productivity indicators. Baegu needs of 0.2 to 0.6 acres of garden land per person at any one time are not excessive. Rappaport (1971:345) reports the Tsembaga using 0.2 acres per person with 90% lying fallow Barrau (1959:54) reckons that throughout Melanesia 0.2 to 0.5 acres per head of land will suffice. Given that the bush fallow cycle tends to run from 10 to 20 years, this would imply that demands for the system are a mere 2 to 10 acres per person. Even the upper Baegu limit of 0.6 acres under cultivation and a 25 year bush fallow period would still require only 15 acres per head, well within the Baegu potential of 18.8 acres available.

That it fails to satisfy nutritional needs. Even with some quibbling about the quality of the diet and whether or not plant proteins can so completely replace animal protein sources, the figures in Table 7 indicate that the Baegu are adequately nourished. Their diet meets or exceeds minimum daily requirements and recommended daily allowances in every nutrient category. Damon's (1970:8) pediatric studies showed no overt evidence of malnutrition of any form (cheilosis, stomatitis, glossitis, hair defects, xerophthalmia, or small body size) among Baegu children. Minor parotid enlargement did occur among 20% of Baegu children. Hemoglobin levels appeared normal after correction for endemic malaria. Kwasiorkor protein deficiency is not evident, and the male puberty rituals that Whiting (Whiting, Kluckhohn, and Anthony 1958) associates with kwasiorkor via a complex chain of reasoning beginning with early protein deficiencies and compensatory mother-child nursing and sleeping arrangements do not occur in northern Malaita; although Ivens (1927:130-159) description of the *malaohu* boys' ritual among the Sa'a, South Malaita and Fox's (1925:186-190) portrayal of the *maraufu* seclusion and initiation rite in the Arosi area of San Cristobal Island suggest that male puberty rituals were not unknown in the Southeastern Solomons. Nutritional data presented in Tables 3, 5 and 6 indicate that even with a starch-rich, meat-poor diet people can get adequate protein, fat, vitamin, and trace mineral intake by eating large quantities of the foods that are available and using a wide variety of species as supplementary or auxillary foods. Gross caloric intake appears satisfactory. Very few of the Baegu hill people are truly skinny, although body build tends to be thin and wiry. (Obesity is a severe disadvantage in mountainous terrain where all travel is by foot.) There is little or no overt evidence of childhood malnutrion; young people die of malaria, dysentary, respiratory epidemics, or traumatic injuries. The Baegu people appear healthy and well-fed despite clinical evidence (Damon 1970) of endemic and chronic malaria and intestinal parasitism at around 25% frequency, indicating that food scarcity is not a critical public health factor.

While it cannot be proved through citation of literature, my intuitive impression is that malnutrition and poverty are less characteristic of "primitive" or "tribal" man, who eats a varied diet of traditional foods, than they are of overpopulated yet technologically inefficient high civilizations (traditional India and China) uprooted by the horrors of war; or partially acculturated peoples who have acquired the craving but not the wherewithal for western luxury goods (Africa, rural Latin America, and most of the "Third World"), and who give up the variety of their own diets for high prestige but nutritionally unsatisfactory imported foods.

That it is wasteful and environmentally destructive. One of the first obvious points to be made is that the "waste" (or fallow) land associated with bush fallow farming is not in fact wasted. For the Baegu, as shown in Table 2, it is an important resource for hunting and foraging. From it they derive game (feral swine, oppossums, wild birds, and flying foxes) to augment their animal protein foods larder; grubs and spiders for relishes to upgrade their daily amino acid intake; wild plant foods to support life in emergency times; and almost their entire daily supply of firewood. As Conklin (1954:140-1) points out, land not being cropped is not wasted, but is in the essential stage of fallowing to restore soil fertility, a sort of crop rotation.

In tropical rain forests such as Malaita, with over 200 inches of rain per year (Ross 1973a:32-33), soil erosion is inevitable and continuous, regardless of the agricultural technology employed. Bush fallow farming, by short croppings and long fallowing during forest regrowth, minimizes this loss. The Baegu try to ameliorate the situation by leaving standing in garden plots some hardwood trees, whose foliage reduces the force of tropical downpours, whose shade slows moisture loss by evaporation and prevents hardpan formation and fast runoff, and whose root systems hold the soil against mechanical water erosion overcoming Lafont's (1959:57) criticism. They also systematically avoid cultivation directly on stream banks, which prevents stream pollution by mud from spoiling freshwater fisheries, thereby negating Tubb's (1959:68) objection to shifting cultivation on that ground. Cowgill and Hutchinson (1963:42) found only negative evidence in their search in El Bajo de Santa Fé in the Peten for lacustrine evidence of erosion and loss of soil fertility due to milpa farming; the *bajo* (a shallow lake with a swamp forest) was not formed by choking due to farming and erosion.

Soil fertility inevitably declines with any form of agricultural use; the second law of thermodynamics says you cannot get something for nothing. As David Harris (1972:245) points out, continuous cultivation systems maintain productivity through direct soil enrichment (edaphic systems) or water control (hydraulic systems). Bush fallow systems, like the Baegu's, do so by leaving land lie fallow long enough (10-25 years) to restore fertility through forest regrowth and decay of vegetation.

Nor does bush fallow cultivation destroy the forest itself. As Conklin (1954:140-1), Goodenough (1955), and Frake (1956) point out, swidden gardeners prefer to re-use second growth because it is easier to clear; they do not continue to clear and destroy primary forest, unless they operate in a "pioneering mode" (D. Harris 1972:249). Bush-fallow cultivation can, with overuse, lead to permanent savannahs, such as characterize the New Guinea highlands, with a permanent cover of *Imperata* grasses which are hard to clear and which do not add essential nutrients to the soil (D. Harris 1972:253); but even this may be an overrated danger. Barrau (1959:53) rates drought and firing as the major etiology of grasslands. Conklin (1959a:61) blames dry weather, inferior natural forest cover (*Acacia* or *Casuarina* sp.), unsuitable use of topography (ridges or steep slopes), frequent firing, and over-grazing by cattle or goats for grassland spread. Guadalcanal and the Florida (Nggela) Islands in the Solomons have extensive grasslands on hills and ridges; in neighboring Malaita, where farmers do not use ridges, hilltops, or steep slopes, grasslands are absent.

That it is an inferior form of ecological adaptation. Rappaport (1971:345) argues that other types of farming are more ecologically disruptive than swidden systems; and that swidden systems are less destructive, because they let an ecosystem (through bush fallowing and polycultural cropping) reach a more mature stage (Rappaport 1971:355-6).

Certainly the very longevity of bush fallow systems argues that they *are* ecologically suitable. In northern Malaita there is no evidence for declining soil fertility. Almost all the interior land is in some stage of secondary forest growth, but the continual regeneration of primary forest (when people permit the cycle to complete itself) suggests that long range quality is maintained. Soil cultivated in this manner does not wash away or lose its fertility, and can (seen in longer perspective) be used over and over again. Archaeological evidence of human occupation of the New Guinea Highlands by 8,000 B.C. (Bulmer and Bulmer 1964, Golson 1968) and settlement of the New Hebrides by 905 B.C. (Shutler and Shutler 1968) implies that men have been exploiting the tropical rain forest environment of the Solomon Islands for a long time without destroying the area ecologically. Traditional tropical forest agriculture is even older in other parts of the world. Solheim (1967) reports pollen indications of its existence in Taiwan since 10,000 B.C., and Gorman's (1969) excavations in Thailand suggest that the practice may be older yet in mainland Southeast Asia. All of these lands remain productive despite long human use, somewhat better than our own experiences in North America.

Cowgill *et al* (1966:122) report that paleoecological analysis of the Laguna de Petenxil in Guatemala by geologists and lacustrine biologists shows that slash-and-burn milpa farming has been practiced in the area since 3900 B.C. with no permanent depletion of soil fertility. Soil fertility, they say, is cyclical; apparent decline is naturally reversible and not permanent. They even suggest (Cowgill *et al:* 1966:123) that milpa cultivation may help the spread of tropical forests into savannah areas, rather than vice versa.

There is no reason to assume that traditional tropical forest agriculture is ecologically destructive. Arguing from the Maori archaeological record and the palynological profile in New Zealand, Simmons

(1969:29) concludes that "the effect of man's clearing activities in the form of uncontrolled fires and slash and burn agriculture is not irreversible, unless the tendency to nonreversion is already present," and that vast ecological changes will occur only "if the existing biosphere is predisposed to such changes." *If* there is a bush fallow period for forest regeneration, the soil will as Freeman (1955) reported from his research in Sarawak, Borneo remain productive indefinitely despite repeated cultivation.

In part there is a prejudice against bush fallow cultivation stemming from western cultural biases. Boserup (1965) reflects our assumption of a value-graded evolutionary scale, with "superior" intensive methods centering around water control and artificial fertilization properly replacing "more primitive" extensive ones using bush or forest fallow techniques. Yet Forde (1934) long ago pointed out that human ecological adaptation is a complex relationship of society, habitat, *and* economy including the level of technology available to the population; that is, there is no simple "better" or "worse" absolute way to adapt to the environment. The human habitat includes material culture (technology), social organization, and ideologies or beliefs, ours and those of other peoples; and we as a population must adapt to these as well as to the physico-chemical and biotic properties of the environment (Flannery 1968). What is a good adaptation for people with tractors and chemical fertilizers might be a terrible one, or not even possible at all, for people using hand tools and having no chemical industry to support them. We also tend to value progress as an end in itself (DuBois 1955); hence adaptations that do not accord with our notions of progress are by definition inferior and unsuitable. Yet Geertz (1963) has shown that traditional village horticulture is a viable and satisfying adaptation in rural Indonesia.

Bush fallow cultivation is of course not satisfactory for all situations. It is eminently suitable for hand tools and relatively small groups without much financial capital. Cheap and readily available power machinery and artificial fertilizers give the advantage in productivity to more intensive forms of agriculture. As David Harris (1972:251-256) demonstrates convincingly, certain ecological factors condition its use. It has its greatest potential value in tropical areas where drought or cold do not curtail growing seasons (and where forest regeneration is most rapid). Soil fertility under such use remains greater longer in areas with a dry season, however, which permits better burning and conversion of plant materials to useable ashes, than it does in rain forests. Its tool arsenal is well suited to clearing woodlands; they are poor for grassland clearance. Wide use of livestock (who graze and browse the richer vegetation removing nutrients) undermines swidden farming utility. Root crops remove nutrients from the soil (in harvesting) in less concentrated forms than cereal crops do, hence root crop swiddens can persist longer. In summary, swidden or bush fallow cultivation is most stable and most effective in tropical forests, with brief dry periods, with a vegecultural tradition of root-crop planting with hand tools and human labor (D. Harris 1972:254).

That it leads to wasteful and nomadic populations that are hard to administer and control. Fundamental to this notion is the assumption that swidden cultivation has deleterious effects on soil fertility that force a population to move on to richer areas after exhausting an old garden. Use of land for cropping uses its nutrients. Cowgill (1961:30-33) clearly shows that Mayan milpa yields decline to 1/2 or 1/3 their original value after two or three years of cropping, but that fallow periods of rest restore them to original productivity after a few years. The Baegu recognize that it is the organic component, the humus that gives soil its "greasy" *(unganalae)* feel, that is lost quickly; which they give as their rationale for shifting garden sites to let the land lie fallow and forest regeneration to restore the organic component of the soil to its original value. Cowgill (1961:45-46) reports that potassium and magnesium content of the soil increase as a result of burning; that sodium content and the *pH* level stay the same (or increase slightly); and that nitrogen, phosphorus, and calcium content decline slightly. As a result of continuing cultivation, the *pH* value of the soil and its content of organic material, nitrogen, phosphorus, potassium, sodium, magnesium, and calcium all decline (Cowgill 1961:48). Popenoe (1959:73-4) giving data from Central America suggests that the crucial losses associated with declining fertility and yield are of organic material and nitrates. Barrau (1959:54) agrees, with data from Fiji, that while phosphates and potash (potassium compounds) are retained, nitrogen loss may be the real problem. Cowgill (1961:8) does not find the nitrate losses too significant, and she argues (Cowgill 1961:34) that yields decline due to losses of trace elements like boron, phosphorus, and zinc.

At any rate, the point in bush fallow or swidden cultivation is that soil fertility is restored by letting land rest while reforestation restores fertility.

Cowgill suggests some other causes for abandonment of used garden sites by the Maya, such as the marked increase of insect pests in the second year of cultivation (Cowgill 1961:48) or competition from weeds, which do not take up too much space or too many nutrients, but which may take needed moisture from crops (Cowgill 1961:36 and 49). Rappaport (1971:348-351) rates weeding as the single most demanding and onerous labor input required in Tsembaga, New Guinea, gardening. The Baegu, I think, move to new gardens largely because of weeds choking the old ones. When using only hand tools, and lacking hoes or other soil cultivating implements, weeds simply become uncontrollable after a few months. It is a question of the labor involved in weeding, rather than of weed competition with crops, which may explain why sweet potatoes (that choke out weeds) have replaced taro in so many places.

Freeman (1955) for the Iban of Sarawak, Borneo, and Carneiro (1960) have questioned the tacit assumption that swidden cultivators must move because they exhaust the soil available to them. Carneiro pointed out that there is no simple regression relationship between declining land fertility and population movement, and that in fact villages are relocated for a variety of natural and supernatural reasons. Using his formula for how large a population can be supported permanently in one locale:

$$P = \frac{\dfrac{T}{(R + Y)} \times Y}{A}$$

where population equals total area of arable land, divided by fallow years plus cultivated years, times cultivated years, divided by area of cultivated land needed to support one person for a year; his formula for how much land is needed to support a village in one locale:

$$T = \frac{P \times A}{Y} \times (R + Y)$$

where land needed equals population times area of cultivated land needed to support one person for a year, divided by years of cultivation, times fallow years plus cultivated years; and his formula for how long a community can remain in the same place before being forced to move by soil depletion:

$$L = \frac{T}{(P \times A)/Y}$$

where length of time a village may remain in the same locale equals total area of arable land available; divided by population times area of

cultivation needed to support one person for a year, divided by cultivated years for a plot; Carneiro (1960:232-3) concluded that among the
Kuikuru of the upper Xingu basin of Brazil, 2000 people could live
where only 145 now do, that the present population need use only 7%
of the arable land now available to them, and that it would take them
nearly 400 years to plant and exhaust all the land available to them.
Hence, there is nothing incompatible between Kuikuru swidden cultivation and permanent, sedentary settlement patterns.

There is no logical necessity for swidden or shifting cultivation to
imply population movements.

While the locus of gardening activity obviously shifts, relationships
of people, residences and gardens are not constant. In some cases only
garden sites are moved, while people continue to live at the same old
village; in others people move their villages, but continue to till the
same fields; while elsewhere people simultaneously establish new villages and gardens in new areas. Only when population exceeds carrying capacity, estimated by Carneiro (1960:233) to be about 500 people
per village are population movements necessary, and only in the pioneering mode of swidden cultivation (D. Harris 1972:249) does shifting
cultivation necessarily entail shifting populations.

There is also a matter of value judgments. If shifting cultivators are
in fact destroying (that is, modifying) forest resources needed by other
people, then national governments or colonial administrations may
have a duty to try to change their mode of life to accommodate other
interests. But mere administrative convenience (for police control,
censuses, media access, taxation, etc.) is scarcely justification for
policies forbidding swidden cultivation and forcibly settling populations in sedentary settlement patterns.

That it cannot support large, settled populations. Malaita Island
is populous (50,659 people in 1750 square miles for a population density of 28.95 people per square mile according to the British Solomon
Islands Protectorate's 1971 decennial census) and probably always has
been. The present extent of secondary forest (almost universal except
for sacred groves that are never cut) suggests that for at least two generations the population has been just about at the limit set by the carrying capacity of the land under prevailing conditions. Lacking resources for exploitation and having rather warlike inhabitants, the island was spared the worst excesses of population decline and subsequent expansion that followed European contact elsewhere in the
Pacific. There was no effective medical program to control the natural
death rate on the island prior to the World Health Organization's anti-

yaws campaign in 1958 and the establishment of a few Rural Health Clinics by the British Administration and the Malaita Council (a local self-government group) during the 1960's. My census figures of 2.7 living children per parental pair, with oral genealogical records confirming this as the normal family size from the past, imply that to date there has been no baby boom in the Malaitan interior. People there expect to lose at least half their children by premature death from natural causes.

Yet this population without excessive effort remains adequately fed. They are generous with food, they do not hoard it, and hunger is not a major theme in Baegu mythology. They expect to eat well, relying upon hunting and gathering in the forest to see them through crises following natural disasters.

The carrying capacity of the land, the base for large settled populations, obviously relates to the yield and productivity facts cited above. Cowgill (1961:8) simply asserts that slash-and-burn farming can support a rather large and sedentary population. Although the Peten region of Guatemala now has a population density of maize cultivators of about 1.5 per square mile (Cowgill 1962:278), she calculates that the Peten could potentially support 100-200 persons per square mile with one-half the adult population as full-time non-agricultural specialists (Cowgill 1961:40). Lafont's (1959:57) estimates of only 3.0 persons per square mile at a subsistence level only are demonstrably too low. Rappaport (1971:345-6) reports the Tsembaga Maring in New Guinea living at a population density of 64 per square mile, 97 per square mile in terms of arable land only, and 124 per square mile in terms of all land that was ever in present or past used for cultivation. In absolute terms, this represents 204 people who own a mere 3.2 square miles. He estimates the maximum carrying capacity of the land to be in excess of 200 persons per square mile (Rappaport 1971:346). Udo (1965:55) gives a population density of root crop swidden farmers of over 400 per square mile for southeastern Nigeria, Ibo and Calabar areas, and Brookfield and Brown (1963:105-122) describe Chimbu swidden farmers in the central New Guinea highlands living at a density of 524 persons per square mile. Carneiro's (1960:233) estimate of 500 people per village as a potential maximum also applies.

Conklin (1959b:63) provides formulae for calculating carrying capacities and population-land balances under traditional tropical forest agriculture. Critical population size is given by:

$$Cs = \frac{L}{AT}$$

where critical population size equals maximum cultivable land available, divided by minimum average area for clearing required per person per year times minimum average duration of the full cultivation-fallow cycle; and critical population density is given by:

$$Cd = \frac{Cs}{L} \times 100$$

where critical population density equals critical population size divided by maximum cultivable land available, times 100.

In a way this criticism of swidden agriculture, that it cannot carry large populations, is an arbitrary expression of unwarranted techno-logical determinism. Boserup (1965), after all, argues that population growth may precede technological and social change. David Harris (1972:256-7) argues that socio-cultural factors may be more important than techno-environmental ones. The characteristic social organization of swidden farmers is as simple (often segmentary) tribes living as decentralized autonomous communities in small dispersed communities; and they frequently have trouble transforming themselves into dependent peasantries under centralized control, because of traditional difficulties (socio-culturally, not ecologically, imposed) of generating social controls appropriate for integration into larger populations. I have suggested (Ross 1973b) that ritual warfare concomitant with formal trade relations may serve as such an areal integration institution, permitting Malaita Island (especially the inland Baegu and the coastal Lau) to develop larger integrated cultural systems numbering some 15,000 or more people.

That swidden cultivation cannot serve as formative base for or support high civilizations. This same argument (Ross 1973b) can be used in this context, too. Lathrap (1970:45-67, 84-112) demonstrates most convincingly that the Tropical Forest Culture of the Amazon basin, practicing swidden cultivation of root crops and featuring extensive trade networks, played a major role in the development of South American civilization and may indeed have been formative for the later rise of high civilizations in South and Central America, perhaps including even the Andean region (Lathrap 1970:107). Sauer (1950 and 1959) also argued that cultivation of root crops such as manioc and sweet potato *(Ipomea batatas)* preceded potato *(Solanum tuberosum)* and grain cultivation in the Andean highlands.

Cowgill's (1961:40) estimate of a Peten population density of 100-200 per square mile with half of the adult population as full-time non-agricultural specialists leads her to assert that the collapse of lowland Mayan civilization was not due simply to depletion of the soil by slash-and-burn farming. Bronson (1966) in fact suggests that root crops grown on swiddens contributed to lowland Mayan subsistence, permitting them to develop a stratified and centralized theocratic civilization that could integrate large populations and control land rights and cultivation shifts in a swidden or milpa technological environment. Root crops have more nutritional and economic potential (Coursey and Haynes 1970:261) than our Euro-American orientation to cereal grains will let us perceive.

That it cannot accommodate cash economies in modern or developing nations. While it cannot be denied that plantation agriculture of major market crops is more efficient and profitable for large-sale investors, there is no reason why individual small-scale land owners cannot produce some crops for a cash income, if they have adequate support and an economic infrastructure provided by local governments. Geertz (1963) shows that Indonesian peasants can cope with cash cropping on a small scale, even in the face of plantation competition and government development schemes. Salisbury (1970), describing the highly successful Melanesian Tolai people of rural New Britain in the Bismarck Archipelago, proves that pre-industrial agricultural economies need not be stagnant and unchanging. Lockwood's (1971) study of Samoan village economy demonstrates that there is some "cushion" in subsistence productivity (which depends upon demand for subsistence produce) in such cultures; that participation in the market sector of the economy varies with the "incentive factor" (which depends upon an effective linkage with the market sector); and that market production supplements, not substitutes for, subsistence production. Subsistence economies can, therefore, produce considerable goods for marketing in a cash economy, without affecting subsistence level itself, if there is access to markets. The economist Fairbairn (1971:102) argues that Pacific islands nations should assign high priority to upgrading agricultural production, particularly subsistence agriculture, which is hard to estimate in national income accounting but which is fundamental to population survival, in order to reduce dependence upon costly imported foodstuffs. Economic development in commercial agriculture or manufacturing industries is futile if profits earned are lost through balance of trade deficits by importing foreign foodstuffs in order to meet local demands, or if increased reliance upon imported staples and loss of traditional variety in diets cause widespread malnutrition.

Implications for the Planning and Administration
of National Development Programs

Many ambitious development schemes in the tropical world have faltered under conditions of insurrection, civil war, or local opposition. (On the other hand, there are, of course, bureaucratic insensitivity, managerial incompetence, corruption, and oppression.) An emphasis on development projects that work within local traditional concepts of land tenure, land usage and farming practices may be useful in avoiding needless opposition and in simplifying the whole process. Economic development is proving to be a slow and painful process at best. Only if the governments of developing countries can hold the loyalty of their populations (by meeting the people's needs in ways they themselves understand and appreciate) can these nations maintain the integrity and commitment needed to achieve modernization and better lives for their citizens.

If these traditional forms of tropical agriculture are as effective as I think I have shown they can be, and if the criticisms against them prove as unfounded as I think they are, then perhaps agricultural and economic planners should re-examine their goals. For the foreseeable future, we can safely assume that for many of the developing nations money, heavy machinery, chemical fertilizers, and well-trained technical experts (and even mere operators) will be scarce or non-existent. Administrators and planners in developing countries, many of whom have an important subsistence farming component based on traditional techniques in their national economies (Fairbairn 1971:81-2), and officials from wealthier nations who direct aid programs, could profit from a "bird in hand" (supposed to be worth two in the bush) approach, seeking development within this traditional context for more conservative rural areas at least in the interim, deferring efforts to transform this into "scientific" or "business-like" agriculture on a western model until they have the technical and educational bases to support such aims. They should work with, rather than against, the facts of life.

This will require, first, knowledge. Knowledge will come from objective and problem oriented studies by agronomists, anthropologists, economists, food scientists, geographers, and other scientists, doing both basic and applied research. More important, there should be comparative studies on a worldwide basis to establish the potential of this kind of farming and the parameters of its permissable variations. Most important of all, this knowledge must be disseminated among the officials and technical experts who need to know it. De Schlippe (1959:67) has suggested regional training centers for this purpose, funded perhaps by the United Nations.

Second, it should be a part of national policies to maintain suitable ecological balances for traditional farming methods in areas where they are practiced. They should allow for bush fallowing to maintain fertility where the soil engineering and fertilization techniques (needed for stable intensive field agriculture) are not likely to be available), recognizing that so-called "waste" forest land is essential as fallow to the whole cultivation process. They should permit cultivators to live in dispersed settlement patterns for easier access to gardens. European peasantries and American farmers live on single family farmsteads; why should Melanesians or Asians be forced to live in nucleated villages? To maintain this balance, they must control population-on-the-land levels either through birth control programs or by providing for migration to towns and employment there for the excess.

Third, land (the primary productive factor) should be equitably and rationally distributed. Land surveys and title search and registration programs should assign title to tracts that include both current farms and adequate forest land for bush fallow and foraging practices. Where suitable (because of traditional tenure practices) title should be given jointly to communal groups (villages, clans, or tribes) rather than singly to individuals. This will permit more local control and flexibility for use of land in the owners' best interests, and for better fit of population to the land available at any one time. Owners should be allowed to live in villages, hamlets, or single farmsteads as they see fit.

Fourth, planners and administrators should avoid forcing people to adopt methods beyond their understanding. In technical assistance programs, let them keep their own basic technology. As a first step provide better hand tools of high quality, such as machetes, axes, adzes, knives, scythes, saws, hoes, rakes, shovels, files, iron digging bars, wedges, pry-bars, mattocks, picks, augers, and hand garden cultivators; then gradually introduce relatively small power tools such as mowers, tillers, pumps, and miniature tractors. As in the *Ugly American* (Burdick and Lederer 1958), a bicycle-powered pump is a better device than a sophisticated (and expensive) electric or diesel one, when engineering and mechanical skills are minimal. Utilize existing traditions of joint or cooperative ownership when introducing expensive machinery or equipment. Emphasize the use of mulch or compost to supplement firing ash, if chemical fertilizers are not readily available. Barrau (1959:55) suggests improving farming techniques by rotation of subsistence plants, manuring the land (compost), and planting the fallow with legumes to increase fertility.

Fifth, we should sponsor introduction of new crops that people can grow with existing skills. Following Barrau (1959:55), new crops can add variety to, and improve, the diet; facilitate production and preservation of foods; and increase overall production. Immediate nutritional improvements would come from a greater variety of crops that offer more and different amino acids, fats, vitamins, and minerals. For improved protein nutrition, this may mean relying upon plants rather than animal foods among people who are excellent practical botanists, but who take animal husbandry casually. Some nutritional possibilities are avocados, beans, peas, soybeans, cowpeas, black-eyed peas, and peanuts. One could introduce new domesticated animals such as pigeons, ducks, geese, guinea hens, turkeys, rabbits, or guinea pigs that are cheap, easy to care for, and similar to existing meat foods. Introduction and improved breeding of pigs, cattle, or goats are also possible. Polycultural, as opposed to monocultural, cropping can increase overall production and has vast potential. Montgomery (1960) reports twenty or more crops in a single Chimbu garden in New Guinea, and Conklin (1957:147) has counted over forty different crops in Hanunóo fields in the Philippines.

Sixth, cash crops are required, whether we like it or not, to provide means for purchasing the western goods that the entire world now desires and to pay the taxes needed for financing development projects. Commercial plantations do not satisfy these needs for the people. Where cash crops are sponsored, they should be suitable for at least some small scale production by individuals using adapted traditional methods. Trees and bushes capable of vegetative propagation will require the least readjustments. A greater variety of cash crops would be a hedge against price fluctuations inherent in international commodities such as copra or cocoa. Spices, pyrethrum daisies, tea, coffee, oil and wax palms, toddy palms, rubber, areca palms (betal nut), tobacco, chicle, jute, sago, and various tropical fruits and nuts should all be tried.

Seventh, local education and agricultural training programs should aim initially at rationalizing and improving traditional farming, rather than attempting an immediate transition to western methods. We should teach local populations to use bush fallow methods as effectively as possible (given financial, material, and technical shortages); teach them practices learned from other bush fallow cultivators around the world; and teach them how to integrate some small scale cash cropping in their production. In essence, we should diffuse knowledge and practices useful in traditional agriculture developed in one region to others who could use them.

There are also improvements to be made in more complex and difficult fields of social engineering. If bush fallow farmers really are destroying land belonging to others or needed for lumbering or pulpwood industries, and if it is really advisable to make them more sedentary, Barrau (1959:55) advises positive methods. Give them title to plantations for long-lived cash crops as an incentive to stay in a given area. Valuable tree crops may help transform a pioneering mode of shifting cultivation into a cyclical one tied to a single locale. As Leach (1959:66) notes more knowledge of what incentives and disincentives will work is needed before we can educate shifting cultivators to settle.

Bush fallow cultivators could be integrated more fully into certain industries. For example, lumber and pulpwood (paper) industries could work together with bush fallow farmers. They could integrate their production into the bush fallow cycle, planting valuable hardwoods or pulpwood species seedlings on newly abandoned (fallow) gardens, cutting the grown trees while helping cultivators clear garden land some years later, and sharing profits on a negotiated royalties basis.

National governments will have to provide a suitable infrastructure for either cash cropping or advanced subsistence farming to support growing urban areas. Transport from farm to market is fundamental, because rural areas need radically better farm to market access. Improved trails and bicycle tracks will have more initial value than will automobile roads, although urban areas and their hinterlands will eventually need road networks. Access roads into rural areas will stimulate production. Ultimately, there must be dependable transportation and pick-up services in the form of buses, trucks, or boats, run by governmental subsidies or agencies if necessary.

Governments can improve the interface between farm and market, enabling rural populations to serve the burgeoning towns and to contribute to the national economy. Production and marketing cooperatives will permit accumulation of more efficiently marketable quantities. Local collection and preliminary processing points with proper storage and preservation facilities in rural areas, served by government subsidized truck or boat transport, will improve the quality and availability of cash crop produce for marketing or of subsistence foods for sale in urban areas. Producers must be trained to grow and prepare cash crops for sale. They must have both transport and access to marketing outlets, such as regular farmers' market sites in cities and towns. National and regional marketing boards can help control supply and demand (through accumulation and planning) to take advantage of price fluctuations in international markets. Finally, some in-country processing of commodities will improve the balance of payments situation in international finance, will offer employment to rural populations migrating to urban developments, will create a pool of skilled workers, and will enhance the people's confidence and pride of identity by letting them gain new competences.

Conclusions and Summary

The Baegu of Malaita are successful tropical forest farmers who produce more than enough for their own needs, who eat well, who enjoy good health, and who conserve and protect their land and its resources.

Properly handled swidden or bush fallow cultivation can be an effective and ecologically well-adapted way of using tropical forest land, albeit one which Europeans or Americans (attuned to a cultural stereotype of sturdy yeomen living for generations on the family farm) find hard to accept. Comparative, historical, and quantitative empirical data suggest that traditional tropical forest agricultural methods are well-suited to the environment, productive, and nutritionally adequate for the people who practice them. They know their own land intimately and have evolved their subsistence techniques over many millenia.

National development schemes and programs for economic and social change should consider human values as well as material ones; after all, economics can and should be more than just a mechanistic means-end relationship (Sahlins 1972). Even well-meaning attempts to replace traditional human adaptations with supposedly better western or modern ones can be cruel or foolish. Until we understand tropical conservation problems more fully, and until truly massive financial and trained human resources are available on a worldwide scale, foreign aid representatives and indigenous government officials can do more real good by working with, not against, local cultural traditions. In areas where swidden or bush fallow cultivators live, the initial goals of development schemes should be to improve the productivity and effectiveness of their subsistence ways, not to force them into ours or someone else's. Quite apart from the moral issues of personal and ethnic liberty, it makes economic and political sense to help people maximize their own potential.

References

Allan, C. H.
1957 Customary Land Tenure in the British Solomon Islands Protectorate. Western Pacific High Commission, Honiara, Guadalcanal, British Solomon Islands.
Altman, P. L., and D. S. Dittmer (editors)
1968 Metabolism. Federation of American Societies for Experimental Biology, Bethesda, Maryland.
Barrau, J.
1958 Subsistence agriculture in Melanesia. Bernice. P. Bishop Museum Bulletin 219, Bernice P. Bishop Museum Press, Honolulu.

1959 The "bush fallowing" system of cultivation in the continental islands of Melanesia. Proceedings of the Ninth Pacific Science Congress of the Pacific Science Association 1957, 7: 53-55. Secretariat, Ninth Pacific Science Congress, Bangkok.

1961 "Introduction". Plants and the Migrations of Pacific Peoples. Jacques Barrau, ed. Bernice P. Bishop Museum Press, Honolulu, pp. 1-6.
Becker, C. J.
1955 The introduction of farming into northern Europe. Journal of World History, 2: 749-767.
Boserup, E.
1965 The Conditions of Agricultural Growth: The Economics of Agrarian Change under Population Pressure. Aldine-Atherton, Inc., Chicago.
Braidwood, R. J.
1952 The Near East and the Foundations for Civilization. University of Oregon Press, Eugene, Oregon.
Bronson, B.
1966 Roots and the subsistence of the ancient Maya. Southwestern Journal of Anthropology 22:251-279.
Brookfield, H. C., and P. Brown
1963 Struggle for Land: Agriculture and Group Territories Among the Chimbu of the New Guinea Highlands. Oxford University Press, Melbourne.
Bulmer, S., and R. Bulmer
1964 The prehistory of the Australian New Guinea highlands. American Anthropologist, 66: 39-76.

Burdick, Q., and W. J. Lederer
1958 The Ugly American. Norton, New York.
Caldwell, J. R.
1958 Trend and Tradition in the Prehistory of the Eastern United States. Illinois State Museum, Springfield, Illinois.
Capell, A.
1954 A Linguistic Survey of the South-Western Pacific. South Pacific Commission, Noumea, New Caledonia.
Carneiro, R.
1960 Slash-and-burn agriculture: a closer look at its implications for settlement patterns. In: Selected Papers of the Fifth International Congress of Anthropological and Ethnological Sciences. Anthony F. C. Wallace, ed. University of Pennsylvania Press, Philadelphia, pp. 229-234.
Chang, K. C.
1966 Preliminary notes on the excavations in Formosa, 1964-1965. Asian Perspectives, *9:* 140-149.
Chang, K. C., and M. Stuiver
1966 Recent advances in the prehistoric archaeology of Formosa. Proceedings of the National Academy of Sciences, *55:* 539-557.
Childe, V. G.
1936 Man Makes Himself. C. A. Watts and Co., London.
Clark, J. D. G.
1962 World Prehistory: An Outline. Cambridge University Press, New York.
Conklin, H. C.
1954 An ethnoecological approach to shifting agriculture. Transactions of the New York Academy of Sciences, Series II, *17:* 133-142.

1957 Hanunoo agriculture in the Philippines. Food and Agriculture Organization, United Nations, Rome.

1959a Shifting cultivation and succession to grassland climax. Proceedings of the Ninth Pacific Science Congress of the Pacific Science Association 1957, Secretariat, Ninth Pacific Science Congress, Bangkok, *7:* 60-62.

1959b Population-land balance under systems of tropical forest agriculture. Proceedings of the Ninth Pacific Science Congress of the Pacific Science Association 1957, Secretariat, Ninth Pacific Science Congress, Bangkok, *7:* 63.

1961 The study of shifting cultivation. Current Anthropology, *2:* 27-61.
Coon, C. S., and E. E. Hunt, Jr.
1965 The Living Races of Man. Borzoi Books, Alfred A. Knopf, New York.

Cooper, M.
1970 Langalanga Ethics. Unpublished Ph.D. dissertation, Department of Anthropology, Yale University, New Haven.

1971 The economic context of shell money production in Malaita. Oceania, *41:* 266-276.

1972 Langalanga religion. Oceania, *43:* 113-122.
de Coppet, D.
1968 Pour une étude des échanges céremoniels en Mélanésie. L'Homme, *8:*45-57

1970a Cycles de meurtres et cycles funéraires: ésquisses de deux structures d'échange. In: Échanges et Communications: Mélanges Offerts à Claude Levi-Strauss, J. Pouillon and P. Maranda, eds. Mouton, s'Gravenhague, Netherlands, and Paris.

1970b 1, 4, 8, 9, 7. La monnaie: presence des morts et mesure du temps. In: L'Homme, *10:* 17-39.
Coursey, D. G.
1968 The edible aroids. In: World Crops, *20:* 25-30.
Coursey, D. G., and P. H. Haynes
1970 Root crops and their potential as food in the tropics. In: World Crops, *22:* 261-265.
Cowgill, U. M.
1961 Soil fertility and the ancient Maya. Transactions of the Connecticut Academy of Arts and Sciences, New Haven, *42:* 1-56.

1962 An agricultural study of the southern Maya lowlands. American Anthropologist, *64:* 273-286.
Cowgill, U. M., and G. E. Hutchinson
1963 El bajo de Santa Fé. Transactions of the American Philosophical Society, New Series, Philadelphia, *53:* 1-51.
Cowgill, U. M., C. E. Goulden, G. E. Hutchinson, R. Patrick, A. A. Racek, and M. Tsukada
1966 The History of Laguna de Petenxil. Memoirs of the Connecticut Academy of Arts and Sciences, New Haven, *17:* 1-126.
Damon, A.
1970 Human Ecology in the Solomon Islands. Unpublished manuscript prepared for the Department of Anthropology and Population Center, Harvard University, and the U. S. Public Health Service, National Institute of General Medical Sciences.
Dobby, E. H. G.
1950 Southeast Asia. University of London Press, London.

DuBois, C.
    1955 The dominant value profile of American culture. American Anthropologist, *57:* 1232-1239.
Durnin, J. V. G. A.
    1970 How do some New Guineans survive on what they eat? Pacific Islands Monthly, *41 (12):* 133-135.
Fairbairn, I. J.
    1971 Pacific Island economies. Journal of the Polynesian Society, *80:* 74-118.
Flannery, K. V.
    1968 Archaeological systems theory and early Mesoamerica. In Anthropological Archaeology in the Americas. B. J. Meggers, ed. Anthropological Society of Washington, Washington, D. C., pp. 67-87.
Forde, C. D.
    1934 Habitat, Economy, and Society. Methuen and Co., Ltd., London.
Fox, C. E.
    1925 Threshold of the Pacific. Alfred A. Knopf, New York.
Frake, R.
    1956 Malayo-Polynesian land tenure. American Anthropologist, 58: 170-173.
Freeman, J. D.
    1955 Iban agriculture. Her Majesty's Stationery Office, London.
Garn, S. M.
    1961 Human Races. C. C. Thomas, Springfield, Illinois.
Geertz, C.
    1963 Agricultural Involution: The Processes of Ecological Change in Indonesia. University of California Press, Berkeley.
Golson, J.
    1968 Archaeological prospects for Melanesia. In: Prehistoric Culture in Oceania. I. Yawata and Y. H. Sinoto, eds. Bernice P. Bishop Museum Press, Honolulu, Hawaii, pp. 3-14.
Goodenough, W. H.
    1955 A problem in Malayo-Polynesian social organization. American Anthropologist, *57:* 71-83.
Gorman, C. F.
    1969 Hoabinhian: A pebble-tool complex with early plant associations in Southeast Asia. Science, *163:* 671-673.
Gourou, P.
    1956 The quality of land use of tropical cultivators. In: Man's Role in Changing the Face of the Earth. W. L. Thomas, ed. University of Chicago Press, Chicago, pp. 336-349.
Grace, G. W.
    1955 Subgrouping of MalayoPolynesian: a report of tentative findings. American Anthropologist, *57:* 337-339.

Guidieri, R. I. A.
1972 Fathers and sons: ritual cannibalism in Malaita. Nouvelle Révue francaise de Psychoanalyse, *6*. (Reference given by Solomon Islands Research Register, Number 2, 1973).

1973 Road of the dead: ancestor worship in Malaita. Revue des Oceanistes, *32*(1). (Reference given by Solomon Islands Research Register, Number 2, 1973).

Hannon, B.
1973 Cropping the Ecosystem. Unpublished manuscript, CAC Document 99. Center for Advanced Computation, University of Illinois, Urbana.

Harlan, J. R., and J. J. J. de Wet
1973 On the quality of evidence for origin and dispersal of cultivated plants. Current Anthropology, *14:* 51-62.

Harris, D. R.
1972 Swidden systems and settlement. In: Man, Settlement and Urbanism. P. J. Ucko, R. Tringham, and G. W. Dimbleby, eds. Schenkman Publishing Company, Cambridge, Massachusetts, pp. 245-262.

Harris, M.
1971 Culture, Man, and Nature: An Introduction to General Anthropology. Thomas Y. Crowell Company, New York.

Heggen, P.
1972 Personal letter of September 8, 1972, from Department of Anthropology, Peabody Museum, Harvard University.

Heine-Geldern, R.
1964 One hundred years of ethnological theory in the German-speaking countries: some milestones. Current Anthropology, *5:* 407-418.

Hogbin, H. I.
1939 Experiments in Civilization. George Routledge and Sons, London.

1964 A Guadalcanal Society: The Kaoka Speakers. Holt, Rinehart, and Winston, Inc., New York.

Howells, W. W.
1937 Anthropometry of the natives of Arnhem Land and the Australian race problem. Peabody Museum Papers, Harvard University, Cambridge, *16:*1-97.

1943 The racial elements of Melanesia. In: Peabody Museum Papers, Harvard University, Cambridge, *20:*38-49.

1972   **Computerized clues unlock a door to Polynesia's past. In: Pacific Islands Monthly, *43(5(:*67-69.**
1973   **The Pacific Islanders. Scribner's, New York.**

Ivens, W. G.
  1927 Melanesians of the South-East Solomon Islands. Kegan Paul, Trench, Trubner & Co., Ltd., London.

————
  1930 Island builders of the Pacific. Seeley, Service, and Co., London.
Izikovitz, K. G.
  1951 Lamet: hill peasants in French Indochina. Ethnologiska Studier 17, Etnografiska Museet, Göteborg, Sweden.
Keesing, R. M.
  1965 Kwaio Marriage and Society. Unpublished Ph.D. dissertation, Department of Social Relations, Harvard University, Cambridge, Massachusetts.

————
  1967 Christians and pagans in Kwaio, Malaita. Journal of the Polynesian Society, *76*:82-100.

————
  1968a Chiefs in a chiefless society. Oceania, *38*:276-280.

————
  1968b Nonunilineal descent and contextual definition of status: The Kwaio evidence. American Anthropologist, *70*:82-84.

————
  1970a Shrines, ancestors and cognatic descent: the Kwaio and Tallensi. In: American Anthropologist, *72:* 755-775.

————
  1970b Kwaio fosterdge. American Anthropologist, *72*:991-1091.
Krader, L.
  1968 Formation of the State. Prentice-Hall, Inc., Englewood Cliffs, New Jersey.
Kroeber, A. L.
  1947 Culture groupings in Asia. Southwestern Journal of Anthropology, *3*:322-330.
Lafont, P. B.
  1959 The "slash-and-burn" *Ray* agricultural system of the mountain populations of central Vietnam. Proceedings of the Ninth Pacific Science Congress of the Pacific Science Association 1957, Secretariat, Ninth Pacific Science Congress, Bangkok, *7*:56-59.
Lathrap. D. W.
  1970 The Upper Amazon. Ancient Peoples and Places Series, Glyn Daniel, ed. Thames and Hudson, New York.
Lawrie, R. A. (editor)
  1970 Proteins as Human Food. The AVI Publishing Company, Westport, Connecticut.
Leach, E. R.
  1959 Some economic advantages of shifting cultivation. In: Proceedings of the Ninth Pacific Science Congress of the Pacific Science Association 1957, Secretariat, Ninth Pacific Science Congress, Bangkok, *7:* 64-66.

Lee, R. B., and I. Devore (editors)
1968 Man the Hunter. Aldine Publishing Company, Chicago.
Lockwood, B.
1971 Samoan Village Economy. Oxford University Press, Melbourne.
Malcolm, S., and J. Barrau
1954 Pacific subsistence crops: yams. South Pacific Commission Quarterly Bulletin, *4*(3):28-31
Malinowski, B.
1935 Coral Gardens and Their Magic. American Book Company, New York.
Maranda, P., and E. K. Maranda
1970 Le crâne et l'uterus: deux théorèmes Nord-Malaitains. In: Échanges et Communications: Mélanges Offerts à Claude Lévi-Strauss, J. Pouillon and P. Maranda, eds. Mouton, s'Gravenhague, Netherlands, and Paris, pp. 829-861.
Massal, E., and J. Barrau
1954 Pacific subsistence crops: breadfruit. South Pacific Commission Quarterly Bulletin, *4*(4):24-26.

———— 1955a Pacific subsistence crops: sago. South Pacific Commission Quarterly Bulletin, *5*(1):15-17.

———— 1955b Pacific subsistence crops: taros. South Pacific Commission Quarterly Bulletin, *5*(2):17-21.

———— 1955c Pacific subsistence crops: sweet potato. South Pacific Commission Quarterly Bulletin, *5*(3):10-13.

———— 1955d Pacific subsistence crops: cassava. South Pacific Commission Quarterly Bulletin, *5*(4):5-18.

———— 1956a Pacific subsistence crops: the banana. South Pacific Commission Quarterly Bulletin, *6*(1):10-14).

———— 1956b Pacific subsistence crops: the coconut. South Pacific Commission Quarterly Bulletin, *6*(2):10-12.

———— 1956c Pacific subsistence crops: some lesser-known Pacific food plants. South Pacific Commission Quarterly Bulletin, *6*(3):17-18.
Meyer, L. H.
1960 Food Chemistry. Reinhold Organic Chemistry and Biochemistry Textbook Series, Calvin A. VanderWerf, ed. Reinhold Publishing Company, New York.
Montgomery, D. E.
1960 Patrol of the Upper Chimbu Census Division, Eastern Highlands. Papua and New Guinea Agricultural Journal *13*:1-9.

National Research Council-National Academy of Sciences, Food and Nutrition Board
1968 Recommended Dietary Allowances (Seventh Edition). National Academy of Sciences, Washington, D.C.

Neustupny, E. F.
1961 Czechoslovakia before the Slavs. Ancient Peoples and Places Series, Glyn Daniel, ed. Thames and Hudson, New York.

Ogan, E.
1971 Nasioi land tenure: an extended case study. Oceania, *42*:81-93.

Oliver, D. L.
1955 A Solomon Island society: kinship and leadership among the Siuai of Bougainville. Harvard University Press, Cambridge.

Oliver, D. L., and W. W. Howells
1957 Micro-evolution: cultural elements in physical variation. American Anthropologist, *59:*965-978.

Ollier, C. C., D. P. Drover, and M. Godelier
1971 Soil knowledge amongst the Baruya of Wonenara, New Guinea. Oceania, *42*:33-41.

Page, L.
1973 Salt looms as villain in civilized societies' diet. In: Enterprise Science News Release by W. J. Cromie, ed. April 11, 1973.

Pelzer, K.
1945 Pioneer settlement in the Asiatic tropics: studies in land utilization and agricultural colonization in southeastern Asia. American Geographical Society Special Publication 29. International Secretariat, Institute of Pacific Relations, New York.

Peters, F.
1954 Analysis of South Pacific foods. South Pacific Commission Quarterly Bulletin, *4*(1):6-7.

Popenoe, H.
1959 The influence of the shifting cultivation cycle on soil properties in Central America. Proceedings of the Ninth Pacific Science Congress of the Pacific Science Association 1957, *7:*72-77.

Rappaport, R. A.
1968 Pigs for the Ancestors. Yale University Press, New Haven, Connecticut.

———
1971 The Flow of energy in an agricultural society. In: Biology and Culture in Modern Perspective: Reprints from Scientific American, J. G. Jorgenson, Introduction. W. H. Freeman and Company, San Francisco. pp. 344-356.

Raulet, R. H.
1960 Social Structure and Ecology in Northwest Melanesia. Unpublished Ph.D. dissertation, Department of Anthropology, Columbia University, New York.

Reina, R. E.
   1967 Milpas and milperos: implications for prehistoric times. American Anthropologist, *69:*1-20.
Ross, H. M.
   1970 Stone adzes from Malaita: an ethnographic contribution to Melanesian archaeology. Journal of the Polynesian Society, *79:*411-420.

   1973a Baegu: social and ecological organization in Malaita, Solomon Islands. Illinois Monographs in Anthropology, Number 8. University of Illinois Press, Urbana and Chicago.

   1973b Areal Integration and Barter Markets in Malaita, Solomon Islands. Paper Read at Social Anthropology in Melanesia Symposium, Central States Anthropological Society Annual Meeting. St. Louis, March 29, 1973, Edwin A. Cook, Chairman.
Russell, T.
   1950 The Fataleka of Malaita. Oceania, *21:*1-13.
Sahlins, M. D.
   1968 Tribesmen. Prentice-Hall, Inc., Englewood Cliffs, New Jersey.

   1972 Stone Age Economics. Aldine Publishing Company, Chicago.
Salisbury, R. G.
   1970 Vunamami: Economic Transformations in a Traditional Setting. University of California Press, Berkeley.
Sauer, C. O.
   1950 Cultivated plants of South and Central America. In: Handbook of South American Indians. Bulletin of the Bureau of American Ethnology 143, Smithsonian Institution, Washington, D. C., *6:* 487-543.

   1952 Agricultural Origins and Dispersals. American Geographical Society, New York.

   1959 Age and area of American cultivated plants. In: Actas XXXIII Congresso International de las Americanistas 1958, International Congress of Americanists, San Jose, Costa Rica, *1:* 215-229.
Scheffler, H. W.
   1965 Choiseul Island Social Structure. University of California Press, Berkeley.
de Schlippe, P.
   1959 Systems of land tenure among shifting cultivators. In: Proceedings of the Ninth Pacific Science Congress of the Pacific Science Association 1957, Secretariat, Ninth Pacific Science Congress, Bangkok, *7:* 71.
Shutler, R., Jr., and M. E. Shutler
   1968 Archaeological excavations in southern Melanesia. In: Prehistoric Culture in Oceania. I. Yawata and Y. H. Sinoto, eds. Bernice P. Bishop Museum Press, Honolulu, pp. 15-17.

Simmons, D. R.
1969 Economic change in New Zealand prehistory. Journal of the Polynesian Society, *78*:1-34.

Solheim, W. G.
1967 Southeast Asia and the West. Science, 157:896-902.

———

1971 New light on a forgotten past. National Geographic, *139*:330-339.

South Pacific Bulletin
1970 **Living on Air (Book Review of SPC Technical Paper 162, Metabolic Studies in New Guinea by E. H. Hipsley, and SPC Technical Paper 163. Nitrogen Metabolism in Sweet Potato Eaters by H.A.P.C. Oomen and M.W. Corden). In: South Pacific Bulletin, *20 (4):*46.**

Steward, J. H.
1955 Theory of Culture Change: The Methodology of Multilinear Evolution. University of Illinois Press, Urbana and Chicago.

Stini, W. A.
1971 Evolutionary implications of changing nutrition patterns in human populations. American Anthropologist, *73:*1019-1030.

Suggs, R. C.
1960 The Island Civilizations of Polynesia. The New American Library, Mentor Books, New York.

Tacitus
1948 On Britain and Germany. Translated by H. Mattingly. Penguin Classics, London.

Tubb, J. A.
1959 Shifting cultivation and inland fisheries. In: Proceedings of the Ninth Pacific Science Congress of the Pacific Science Association 1957, Secretariat, Ninth Pacific Science Congress, Bangkok, *7:* 68-70.

Udo, R. K.
1965 Disintegration of nucleated settlement in eastern Nigeria. In: Geographical Review, *55:* 53-67.

United States Department of Agriculture, Bureau of Nutrition and Home Economics
1945 Tables of Food Composition in Terms of Eleven Nutrients, USDA Miscellaneous Publication Number 527, Government Printing Office, Washington, D. C.

Vavilov, N. I.
1951 The Origin, Variation, Immunity, and Breeding of Cultivated Plants. Ronald, New York.

Vayda, A. P.
1961 Expansion and warfare among swidden agriculturalists. American Anthropologist, *63:*346-358.

Waterlow, J. C., and J. M. L. Stephen (editors)
1957 Human Protein Requirements and Their Fulfillment in Practice.

Food and Agriculture Organization and World Health Organization, United Nations, New York.

Wharton, C. R. (editor)
1969 Subsistence Agriculture and Economic Development. Aldine Publishing Company, Chicago.

Whiting, J. W. M., R. Kluckholn, and A. Anthony
1958 The function of male initiation ceremonies at puberty. In: Readings in Social Psychology. E. E. Maccoby, T. M. Newcomb, and E. L. Hartley, eds. Henry Holt and Company, New York, pp. 359-370.

Whitmore, T. C.
1966 Guide to the Forests of the British Solomon Islands. Oxford University Press, London.

Wohl, M. G. (editor)
1945 Dietotherapy: Clinical Application of Modern Nutrition. W. B. Saunders Company, Philadelphia.

Zemp, H.
1971 Instruments de musique de Malaita (1). Journal de la Société des Oceanistes, *27:* 31-53.

1972a Instruments de musique de Malaita (II). Journal de la Société es Oceanistes, *28:* 7-48.

1972b Fabrication des flûtes de Pan aux Îles Salomon. In: Objets et Mondes, *12:* 247-268.

23. Cultural Facial Expression

Henry W. Seaford, Jr.

Introduction

> I venture to predict that another couple of decades may establish, upon a rigorously scientific base, some rather astounding associations of physiognomy with behavior . . . If the behavior of an individual arises principally from the structure and functioning of his own organism and is only secondarily modified by his cultural environment, there is some hope for a future science of individual anthropology of which physiognomy would be a part. If, however, as many believe, the mentality, personality, and behavior of individuals and groups are determined almost wholly by environment—if, in short, there is no relation between body and behavior—the study of the human face in its wealth of variations is still of interest to the geneticist, the physiologist, the pathologist, and the feeble aesthete (Hooton 1954:176).

In 1772 J. C. Lavater published his *Essays on Physiognomy*. Lyrical in creationist perspective, these volumes were laudably written "for the promotion of the knowledge and the love of mankind" (Lavater, 1789), and by the beginning of the 19th century had been published in at least 55 different translations (Graham 1966). It was the French physician, G. B. Duchenne, who considered Lavater's approach limited in that it did not deal with the dynamics of facial muscle contraction,[1] a deficiency he remedied in 1862 with his own *Mécanisme de la Physion-*

---

[1] Lavater himself, however, pointed out that it was his purpose to deal only with "physiognomy" which "teaches the knowledge of character at rest" as contrasted with "pathognomy" treating "character in motion" (1789, 1:20).

omie Humaine (Duchenne, 1876), a fascinating work of considerable contemporary utility (cf. Ekman *et al.*, 1971).

One hundred years after Lavater, in 1872, another influential book of similar genre was published, *The Expression of the Emotions in Man and Animals*. In that seminal treatise its insatiably curious author, Charles Darwin, with less poetic flair but not without felicitous prose, suggested that it was more intellectually stimulating to seek understanding of facial expressions from an evolutionary rather than a special creation point of view. He maintained that although some expressions could be learned like speech, or result from innate proclivities modified by various social conventions,[2] "all the more important ones, are . . . innate or inherited" (Darwin, 1955).

For the first part of the 20th century the consensus of American scholarship disagreed (Izard, 1968; Ekman *et al.*, 1972). Innate behavior did not accord with the zeitgeist of the psychology of those days (as Izard aptly expresses it), and anthropologists, embued with the stimulating perspectives of cultural relativity (Boas, 1938; Efron, 1941; La Barre, 1947; Birdwhistell, 1952), emphasized cultural variations in facial expressions.

Today, psychologists have demonstrated pan-sapient regularities in interpreting facial expressions (Izard, 1968; Ekman, 1968; Ekman *et al.*, 1969; Ekman *et al.*, 1972), and some anthropologists—among whom one of the earliest was Earl Count (1958)—share interests with ethologists.[3] Universals are again scientifically respectable. But their delineation amid the cultural matrix in which they occur has proceeded with extraordinary slowness since the time of Darwin, the scientific attitudes cited above having played their part.

One of the most sophisticated treatments of the interrelation of innate and learned facial behavior is Paul Ekman's (1972) "Universals and Cultural Differences in Facial Expressions of Emotion." Eschewing both the Scylla of doctrinaire relativism and Charybdis of unexamined universalism, Ekman steers a straight course with his "neurocultural theory." Founded firmly on empirical evidence that personnel of different cultures similarly express the emotions of happiness,

---

[2] Darwin uses the example of kissing, which did not seem to be a universal according to his data, but which, he suggests, must be based on a biological pleasure of contact (1955:352). Eibl-Eibesfeldt suggests that kissing may be more widespread than earlier, deficient observations indicated (1970:427-428).

[3] Studies of the face in physical anthropology were summarized by Goldstein (1936), and have been given expression more recently by Steegman (1965, 1967, 1970a, 1970b, 1972; Steegman and Platner, 1968).

anger, disgust and sadness, as well as the interpretations thereof, he theorizes that culture nevertheless affects the elicitation of emotions, the social situations in which they should occur, and the consequences of their arousal. The "display rules" which determine the expression of emotion in a given social setting, however, are conceived primarily in terms of one emotion's masking another; e.g., happiness masking sadness when the expression of the latter is culturally improper. Two emotions occurring simultaneously represent a "blend." Thus the Darwinian and psychological tradition of studying expressions of emotion is perpetuated.

This study, in contrast, focuses upon cultural aspects of facial muscle contractions, at least some of which may not be associated with the expressions of emotions *per se*. Rather, they appear to resemble such ethnosyncratic phenomena as linguistic dialect. If, for example, there is *triangularis* contraction during a smile, this is not to be interpreted as a blend of sadness and happiness (nor am I at all sure that Ekman would so interpret it); it is simply a behavioral artifact related to propriety rather than affect—an anthropological rather than a psychological datum in the traditional sense. Other expressions to be discussed, though related to cultural processes, may function to engender rapport in social interaction; they may be expressions of the emotion of friendliness (consisting of the primary dyad of joy and acceptance according to Plutchik, 1968:117).

In a study of primate facial expression, R. J. Andrew (1963:1041) has called for the assistance of anthropologists in distinguishing cultural from more genetically based behavior: "The detailed study of human facial displays promises to be the most difficult, as well as the most important, area of this field of investigation. Cross-cultural studies by anthropologists will be essential." Partly as a response to this challenge, I began to consider more seriously some of my long-standing hunches about regional facial expression. It appeared the most economical and expeditious source of data would be school annuals. Examination of some 10,000 yearbook photographs from various parts of the United States revealed a striking difference in the frequency with which certain expressions occurred in the south compared with other parts of the country (Seaford, 1966). Significant at greater that the .01 level were frequencies of contractions of the *orbicularis oris,* the *triangularis* and the *depressor labii inferioris* during smiling. The complex of these contraction configurations was called "the Southern Syndrome." In spite of all the limitations of deriving information from small yearbook photographs, the results were encouraging enough to warrant further investigation.

The yearbook study having suggested that frequencies of the various constituent patterns of the Southern Syndrome were highest in Georgia, South Carolina, Virginia, and North Carolina (in that order), a field survey of these states was made during the summer of 1968. In the process of collecting data, there developed what ultimately became an informal, 15-minute, taped interview consisting of a dialect reading (Muri and McDavid, 1967) to corroborate provenience, and general conversation about family background and personal interests. Simultaneously, with a Leica M-3 fitted with 90 mm. lens, I photographed what seemed to be—based on the earlier study—the regional facial contraction patterns as they occurred. Since the shutter sound was recorded on tape, I could usually tell, with relative accuracy in data analysis, whether or not the photographed contraction was merely an articulatory artifact. By the end of the summer I had decided that patterns, for all intents and purposes, were as plentiful in Virginia as elsewhere and that the proximity of that state to home-base in Pennsylvania would make it an ideal location. The University of Virginia kindly furnished facilities,[4] and the control sample was taken at Dickinson College, Carlisle, Pennsylvania.

Because attracting informants proved more time-consuming than originally anticipated, the total of 62 in each of the samples fell short of the initial goal of 100. To minimize variables, all data used in the statistics came from white informants, although one black student, who graciously responded, was interviewed. Frequent observations of people in public places of both geographic areas led me to believe that my samples, taken largely from academic communities, were satisfactorily representative. Most of the data were gathered during the summers of 1969-70.

Some of the patterns figuring prominently in the work had been anticipated from the initial yearbook study. Others were suggested during the photography, and as my three assistants and I studied the results. Precise determination of some facial behaviors was not always easy, and, in a very few cases, impossible. For example, it was not always possible to determine whether the lips were rolled slightly between the teeth or merely clampled together by the *orbicularis oris.* Other patterns were more easily described. Observer reliability, measured by the percentage of agreement of observers with my judgments, approached 69% for three observers and 84% for two. Many of the patterns proved to be significantly Virginian, but some did not. In fact,

[4] In 1917 this institution hosted Ales Hrdlicka who was studying pigmentation in "old Americans" (Hrdlička 1918).

two of them turned out to be more characteristic of Pennsylvania (Table 1).

Muscle contractions were determined by observing changes in facial topography. Contractions usually occurring simultaneously were placed in pattern categories which were developed as the work progressed, and will be discussed below. After covering literature on facial muscle contraction (Duchenne, 1876; Gray, 1959; Huber, 1931; Lightoller, 1925, 1928a 1928b; Shapiro, 1947; Subtelny, 1965; Subtelny and Subtelny, 1962; Virchow, 1908, *inter alia*), observing dissections on a few dozen cadavers, watching my own contractions in a mirror, and palpating the muscle *(cf.* Darwin, 1955:149), I attained a

TABLE 1

FREQUENCIES OF CONTRACTION CONFIGURATION
IN VIRGINIA AND PENNSYLVANIA SAMPLES,
EACH CONTAINING 62 INFORMANTS.

Pattern	Virginia n	Pennsyl- vania n	Z test: level of significance
Orbicular Clamp	216	144	> .01
Purse-Clamp	38	14	> .01
Pursed Smile	98	45	> .01
Inferior Press	12	8	—
Inferior Press Smile	21	10	—
TOTAL Inferior Presses	33	18	> .01
Angle Depression	16	3	—
Angle Depression Smile	94	15	—
TOTAL Angle Depressions	110	18	> .01
Tongue Display Type A	116	103	< 5.0
Tongue Display Type B	25	3*	—
Tongue Smile	15	5*	—
Mandibular Thrust	17	5	—
Mandibular Thrust Smile	10	1	—
Inferior Inversion	25	35	> 1.0
Double Inversion	19	54	> .01

Chi-square test of differences between samples exceeds P=.01.

*One occurrence in each of these categories effected by informant both of whose parents are Virginians.

satisfying consistency in describing cutaneous movements. The case of *m. risorius* is one outstanding exception. Although it appears I can contract my own, it is difficult, if not impossible, to descry a separate contraction of that muscle apart from the *zygomaticus* and or *platysma* in the photographs of informants.[5] Initially, electromyography was considered (not only for the *risorius* region, but for others as well), but ruled out mainly because it would have made the fieldwork too complicated.

The following discussion of facial muscle contractions deals only with the circumoral area. It is quite possible that future study will reveal contractions of other muscles of expressions which are also relevant. The names of the various patterns, as I have noted, were devised during the course of this study *(cf.* Fig. 1).

The Orbicular Clamp (Pl. 1-1, 2; Pl. 2-2, 3) is formed by contractions of the *orbicularis oris superioris* and *inferioris* joining the lips together with varying degrees of firmness. This clamping action is frequently assisted by *m. mentalis.* When the lips are moved perceptibly mesially by contractions of the *caninus* and *triangularis* and/or the *modiolus* in addition to the above, a Purse Clamp results (Pl. 1-3, 4; Pl. 2-1). The Pursed Smile (Pl. 3-1) is obviously the sphincterial contraction of the *orbicularis oris,* along with contractions of the zygomaticus major and the various heads of the *quadratus labii superioris.* On occasions when the latter pattern occurs, the *quadratus labii inferioris* arranges the lower lip against the mandibular alveolus and teeth, a configuration referred to here as the Inferior Press Smile (Pl. 3-2). Angle Depression (Pl. 3-3, 4) is mainly the function of the *triangularis'* action on the corner of the mouth, although *m. platysma* may assist occasionally. This depressor action frequently accompanies smiling in Virginia. As laboratory analysis proceeded, it was considered taxonomically more elegant to divide Tongue Display into two types. Type A (Pl. 4-1, 2) consists of a tongue discretely protruded by the posterior fibers of the

[5] Frequently I have observed lateral retractions of the angles of the mouth on southern faces. The fleeting movement suggests the designation, "risorius tic." However, *m. risorius* seems to be one of the most variable muscles of expression (Lightoller, 1925:17-2; Gray, 1959:419), and one demurs in specifying its contraction with the name of a pattern. To avoid this Angle Retraction was chosen as an apt description of what the *risorius* does anyway (Seaford, 1971). Whether, therefore, it be the *risorius per se* or a *risorius* like contraction of the *platysma,* the pattern is adequately described. I have not listed Angle Retraction in the tables of this paper because it occurred with surprisingly low frequency in my samples. Thus, although my general field observations indicate its presence in the subcultures of the south, further study must precede further comment on this pattern.

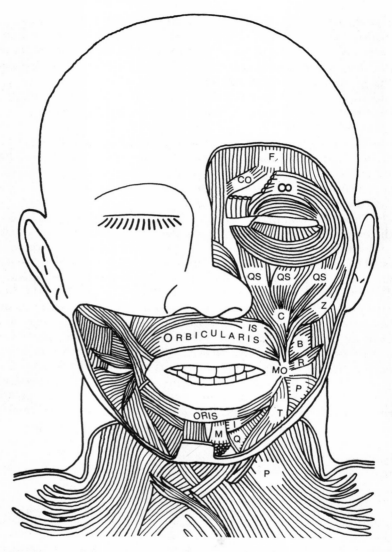

Figure 1. Selected Facial Muscles — Buccinator (B); Caninus (C); Corrugator (CO); Frontalis (F); Incisivus Inferioris (I); Incisivus Superioris (IS); Mentalis (M); Modiolus (MO); Orbicularis Oculi (00); Orbicularis Oris; Platysma (P); Quadratus Labii Inferioris (Q); Quadratus Labii Superioris (QS); Risorius (R); Triangularis (T); Zygomaticus (Z). Orbicularis Oculi cut to show Corrugator. (After Grant 1951: figs. 448 and 499 with omissions and modifications from Sharpiro 1947 and Gray 1959).

Plate 1-1.   Virginia Orbicular Clamp

Plate 1-2.   Virginia Orbicular Clamp

Plate 2-2.   Virginia Orbicular Clamp (Weddell 1930); cf. Pl. 1-1
Plate 2-3.   Virginia Orbicular Clamp (Weddell 1930); cf. Pl. 1-2

Plate 1-3.   Virginia Purse-Clamp

Plate 1-4.   Virginia Purse-Clamp

Plate 2-1.   Virginia Purse Clamp (The Christian Science Monitor 1971); cf. Pl. 1-3
Plate 3-1.   Virginia Pursed Smile

Plate 3-2. Virginia Inferior Press Smile

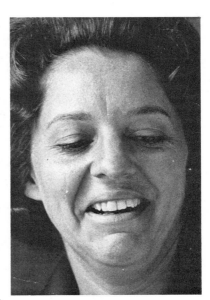

Plate 3-3. Virginia Angle Depression Smile
Plate 3-4. Virginia Angle Depression Smile

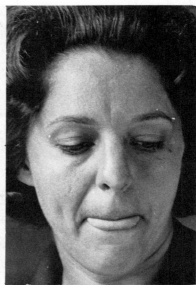

Plate 4-1.   Virginia Tongue Display Type A
Plate 4-2.   Virginia Tongue Display Type A

genioglossi with the apex spread by the *verticalis* as it passes through the lips. Type B pattern is formed when either the tip of the tongue is placed against the upper incisors, or the tongue is curled behind the teeth, the latter apparently involving the various contractions of the *longitudinalis.* Although smile contractions can accompany either type, they are characteristically associated with Type B in Virginia and in other southern states, a configuration called Tongue Smile (Pl. 4-3, 4). Mandibular Thrust (Pl. 5-1, 2) is self-explanatory. Inferior Inversion consists of rolling the lower lip over the teeth, while Double Inversion is placing both lips between the teeth. In exaggerated cases of the last pattern, the *risorius* and/or *platysma* retract the angle of the month (*cf.* Gray, 1959:418-420, 1234-1236).

The last two configurations, Inferior Inversion and Double Inversion, appearing not infrequently in Virginia, are more characteristic of Pennsylvania (Table 1). Since both patterns came to my attention during the southern fieldwork, I anticipated their being constituents of the Southern Syndrome, but data from the control sample proved this guess wrong. All the other patterns listed in Table 1 are characteristically Virginian and probably southern in general.

A procedural oversight must be mentioned in regard to the record-

Plate 4-3. Virginia Tongue Smile
Plate 4-4. South Carolina Tongue Smile

Plate 5-1. Virginia Mandibular Thrust
Plate 5-2. Virginia Mandibular Thrust

ing of Orbicular Clamps and Type A Tongue Displays. Although most of the other patterns—i.e., ones not evoked by articulation and/or simple smiling—were recorded,[6] various occurrences of these two configurations in the Virginia sample were not. Clamps and Type A Tongue Displays were so frequent that at the time it appeared superfluous to record all of them. When the Pennsylvania data began accumulating, however, it became evident that there was a startling number of Orbicular Clamps and Type A Tongue Displays, and every case of these two patterns was recorded for comparison with the Virginia sample. Fortunately the frequencies of Orbicular Clamps turned out about as anticipated; i.e., in spite of failure to record all of the ones in the Virginia sample, the difference between those recorded and their much lower incidence in the Pennsylvania sample (where virtually all were recorded) is highly significant (Table 1). The Type A Tongue Displays however, did not conform to a neat statistical pattern since nearly as many of these patterns were found in Pennsylvania as had been *recorded* in Virginia. A retroactive estimate of the frequency of these patterns can be made however: approximately two-thirds of the occurrences were recorded in Virginia. If all had been recorded, then, the pattern would have been demonstrated significantly Virginian. One factor determining the frequencies of this facial behavior could have been a temperature-humidity differential. Some of the Pennsylvania interviews were conducted in an air-conditioned room, whereas none of those in the Virginia sample was. My judgment is that this factor was not of primary importance.

Obviously, these problems could have been mitigated by using a motion picture camera or videotapes—techniques seriously considered in the planning stages of the research. It was decided, however, that enough patterns could be captured with the Leica to provide the data needed. Motion pictures would have involved more expense, would have entailed problems of retrieval, and, in my estimation, would have

---

[6] Occasionally my reaction time was too slow to catch some of the more ephemeral expressions of film. This was true of both samples. Since I was more aware of missing more while working with Virginia informants, however, any bias in the data favors the already impressive statistical significance of the high incidence of patterns in the southern example.

[7] A Leica IIIf with 135 mm. Hektor lens was used occasionally as an auxilliary camera. The maximum aperture (f/4.5) of the lens, however, often made exposures with available light impossible. To avoid flood lights because of possible informant discomfort, an electronic flash fitted to the M-3 was used under adverse lighting conditions. The reduced image in the Imarect finder on the IIIf. however, proved less satisfactory than that of the M-3 with its 1 to 1 magnification.

been technological overkill. At the same time they would have made possible a more sophisticated analysis, especially regarding description of the waxing and waning of the various configurations. Motion pictures of a dozen or so Virginia informants electromyographically wired could provide valuable additional data.[8]

Speculation about the origin of some of these patterns might furnish leads for future investigation. Historic priority of the Virginia colony and its importance in the diffusion of the plantation economy throughout other regions of the south (Wood, 1963) suggest how early Virginia subculture with its eastern dialect diffused to other areas (McDavid, 1958). Considering the major role played by English dialects and other aspects of that culture during colonial days (McCormick, 1900; Stanard, 1917; Bean, 1938), it would seem likely that some traditional kinesic phenomenon, such as the orbicular restraint of the English, may have been imported as well. Darwin (1955: 212) noted the use of the *triangulares* during smiling by one of his contemporaries *(cf.* "Angle Depression Smile" in Table 2). A limited examination of colonial portraiture yielded nothing on *triangularis* contraction, but some orbicular activity was detected in paintings of the Madisons. A portrait by Stuart Gilbert of the younger Madison suggests a Purse-Clamp (Pl. 2-1), while one in later years depicts an Orbicular Clamp (Pl. 2-2). A portrait of Dorothea Payne Todd Madison (Pl. 2-3) shows a slight Orbicular Clamp. One could speculate that various facial muscle contraction configurations may have diffused across the Atlantic to be elaborated by Virginians as part of a regional etiquette imitated by all who felt rewarded by the exercise of social graces. Through time, the behaviors apparently spread through neighboring regions and, with the collapse of the plantation system, through various socio-economic levels of the society.

The available ethological literature provides other interesting perspectives for considering the possible provenience of some of the patterns of the Southern Syndrome. The infrahuman primate behavior with which to compare Tongue Display (especially Type A) is, quite naturally, tongue display as in lip-smacking, the predominant communicative function of which is apparently to promote amicable approach between individuals (van Hooff 1969: Chevalier-Skolnikoff 1973b *inter alia).* Van Hooff (1969) cites Zuckerman's (1932) observation of its use in greeting behavior of *Papio hamadryas,* and Carpenter

[8] Having recently observed the recording of visual data at the laboratory of Human Interaction and Conflict, University of California, I have decided that videotape could have added many desirable dimensions to my study.

TABLE 2

VIRGINIA AND PENNSYLVANIA PATTERNS ACCORDING TO SEX; RATIO
OF MEN TO WOMEN, 30:32 and 32:30 RESPECTIVELY; NUMBER OF INFOR-
MANTS RESPONSIBLE FOR PATTERNS IN PARENTHESES.

	Virginia		Pennsylvania	
Patterns	men	women	men	women
Orbicular Clamp	113(26)	103(30)	78(23)	66(21)
Purse-Clamp	15(9)	23(11)	9(4)	5(3)
Pursed Smile	41(16)	57(22)	13(8)	32(16)
Inferior Press	4(2)	8(7)	3(3)	5(4)
Inferior Press Smile	4(3)	17(12)	8(5)	2(2)
Angle Depression	9(6)	7(6)	1	2(2)
Angle Depression Smile	28(13)	66(33)	5(4)	10(8)
Tongue Display Type A	55(16)	61(19)	74(22)	29(12)
Tongue Display Type B	4(2)	21(8)	1	2(2)
Tongue Smile	2(2)	13(7)	1	4(4)
Mandibular Thrust	10(7)	7(6)	0	5(4)
Mandibular Thrust Smile	3(3)	7(6)	0	1
Inferior Inversion	14(8)	11(8)	16(8)	19(11)
Double Inversion	4(4)	15(7)	33(10)	21(6)

(1940) mentions tongue protrusion in hylobatid hellos, incidentally associated with bared teeth. (One can hardly refrain from thinking of the Tongue Smile). Even the possibility of interspecific communication is suggested by Bolwig's (1959) calming of a vexed vervet by lip-smacking to it *(cf.* Cullen, 1972:120-122; van Hooff, 1972: 233). The description of slow tongue display during cordial grooming sessions of *Pan troglodytes* by Goodall (1965: 470) and van Hooff (1969: 53)—while differing from the frenetic lip-smacking of monkeys—is not dissimilar to what I have observed in *Homo sapiens.*

Is it possible that tongue display has a similar communicative function throughout the various families of Anthropoidea? Perhaps whenever we humans wish to engender rapport in social interation, this basic primate behavior is one of the communicative devices we have at our disposal. Moreover, if a salient value of an entire culture or subculture happens to be the desirability of warm, personal relationships—a characteristic of the culture area of the southern United States

(Odum, 1930:77-8)—many individuals raised there would not surprisingly include tongue display in their repertoire of facial expressions, thus accounting for the high incidence of this contraction pattern in the Virginia sample.

So far tongue display has been treated as if it were a unitary behavior. Whenever the show of tongue has indicated friendly intention by ego to alter, sophisticated categories concerning other details of performance have been eschewed. The suggestion advanced is that the most significant feature of all these behaviors may be the visibility of the tongue. It is still necessary to consider possible variations in the "message" (Smith, 1965) of tongue protrusion as affected by the degree of extension, as well as interpretations of that message by workers in the field.

Eibl-Eibesfeldt (1970: 424) brings us face to face with the probability that a maximally extended tongue among humans has its own message which is patently not one of cordiality. Such a prominent negative signal is this behavior that it has surfaced in our lexicon. Perhaps a system of classification analogous to the linguist's "distinctive features" will be necessary to differentiate the meaning one receives from this expression compared with that involving the more discreet extension of the tongue. These "distinctive features" could be based on muscle contractions; e.g., strong contraction of the posterior fibers of the *genioglossi* protruding the tongue maximally imparts a negative aspect to the message, while moderate contraction, occasionally associated with *verticalis* action, spreading out the apex of the tongue (Gray, 1959:1236), signals the opposite.

Even when the tongue is not maximally extended there seems to be some ambivalence in the information content of the display, and/or its association with other behaviors. Hinde and Rowell (1962:15) mention a slight element of fear or aggression, while van Hooff (1969: 68) relates it to a tendency to flee. A recent study by Smith, Chase and Lieblich (1974) focuses on this possibly negative aspect of tongue display.[9] After observing "tongue showing" in nursery school children,

[9] The presence of conflicting tendencies in the sender, of course, is always a possibility (cf. Cullen 1972). But Smith (1969) would prefer to emphasize the heavy load each message" must bear, since it is a component of so many contexts. Ambiguities are not easily avoided. Commenting in this same vein, Andrew (1972) calls attention to the degree of recognition between sender and recipient as an important contextual element (cf. Miller 1971; Chevalier-Skolnikoff 1973a). He prefers not to appeal to conflict between two tendencies, and properly concludes: "Animal communication is so complex and involves so many levels, that it is usually possible for a worker to find examples of whatever he expects to find" (1972:204).

some individuals of differing cultural backgrounds, gorillas and orang-utans (the pongids aping the hominids so closely that an homologous relationship between the behaviors is suggested), these authors gather substantial evidence of this behavior's association with what could be interpreted as *aversion* to social interaction. Tongue showing occurs if the performer seems to be avoiding on-going social interaction for one reason, or another, or if he is alone but engrossed in some activity involving skill, which presumably could be interrupted by social interaction. Support from the literature is found, for example, in Moynihan's (1967: 244) statement that an element of risk is always involved in body contact (thus, reluctance to interact socially), and van Hooff's (1969: 51) impression that the "true lip-smacking face" is more indicative of amicable approach than the "tongue-smacking face" (the latter, being, therefore, possibly a signal of mild aversion). There are obviously several "variants" in tongue showing, one of which is the "taunting" gesture of the fully extended tongue, which is an extreme form of the attitudes attributed to the displayer of the more moderate forms viz., "reluctance" to engage in, "aversion" to, "negation" or "rejection" of social interaction. On the face of it, the tongue is hardly a sanguine signal for cordial communication. What appears contradictory because of the emphasis on the aversion-rejection theme, however, seems less so when the authors occasionally interpret the behavior as indicating "hesitance," a word they seem to use synonymously. For example, they speculate about two other variants of tongue showing: "cyclic" (repeated protrusions) and "noncyclic," which might be ontogenetically related to ingestion and satiety (hence, rejection), respectively. Despite diametrically opposed origins, both of these expressions might indicate *hesitance* to approach.[10] The authors summarize: "the communicator may . . . behave *hesitantly* if required either to accept or initiate a social interaction" (my italics and omission of the word "avoid"). If hesitation is what is involved-not aversion or rejection (except when a human "sticks out his tongue" at someone)—the interpretation Smith and his colleagues have placed on their data is easier for me to understand. How many social situations, indeed, are fraught with apprehension—mild fear, desire to flee? That at least one of the participants would express hesitance is hardly a

---

[10] Chevalier-Skolnikoff (1973b) presents a cogent case for the ontogenetic relationship in *Macaca arctoides* of lip-smacking and other expressions to "the infantile sucking reflex." Finding that "the tongue is not shown in any avoidance situation" (personal communication), she concludes simply that the display is one of friendliness. Her arguments are parsimoniously appealing.

wonder. What could better signal desire to communicate than a dis-arming hesitance—the antithesis of aggressive design?

Van Hooff has suggested that the "silent bared-teeth" display, which formerly may have expressed flight tendency, developed into an approach-engendering signal in many species of primates (1969: 43). Most interestingly, this expression "alternates with *the lip-smacking face* . . . performed during, or followed by, smooth approach" (1969: 45). There is, therefore, some rationale for saying that moderate tongue showing—cyclic or otherwise, whatever ambivalence it might indicate— functions to establish rapport.

Recent comment on the positive function of lip-smacking has been made by Chevalier-Skolnikoff (1973b), who provides further evidence from her study of *Macaca arctoides* that the "puckered-lips expres-sion" is also one of cordiality. She pictures two macaques; one, with "the puckered-lips expression, a friendly expression"; the other, "the adult lip-smacking expression, an intense (sic) friendly expression." The muscle contractions depicted strikingly resemble both the tongue displays and pursing expressions of the friendly hominids interviewed in my own fieldwork. Chevalier-Skolnikoff suggests that these expres-sions along with the "mutual mouthnibble" developed "ontogeneti-cally from the infantile sucking reflex" (1973b: 517). Both tongue dis-play and pursing could be, then, by-products of mammalian heritage, especially elaborated by primates with their complicated facial mus-culature.

In sum, it might be not unreasonable to hypothesize that if tongue display and pursing are, in fact, signals used by other primates to ex-press friendly intent, man too might have a proclivity to use the same motor patterns for the same purpose. If members of a whole society value friendliness, they might as well display tongues and purse lips to show it.

Some tentative conclusions of this study can now be summarized. A regional complex of facial muscle contractions called the Southern Syndrome consists of a tendency for the *orbicularis oris* to clamp the lips together, sometimes assisted by *m. mentalis.* The former, with sphincteral contraction, frequently accompanied by action of *m. trian-gularis,* opposes contractions of the levators of the upper face. Oc-casionally the *orbicularis oris inferioris* and/or the *quadratus labii in-ferioris* press the lower lip against the teeth. In addition to patterns formed by the muscles of expression proper, there are discrete protru-sions of the tongue by the *genioglossi,* or its placement behind the teeth in smiling. Also present is a tendency to thrust the mandible forward during speech or simply as social interaction occurs. Table 2 indicates the greater frequencies with which women effect most of these patterns.[11] Pensylvania faces, while manifesting most of the patterns of the Southern Syndrome, do so less frequently. Furthermore, the tendency to roll the lips between the teeth appears to be much more characteristic of that state than it does of Virginia.[12]

In whatever way these configurations of facial muscle contractions might be related to phylogenetic proclivities, ontogenetic development, and /or sapient psychological processes, they appear ultimately conditioned by culture. They are unlike expressions of emotion as these are usually studied,[13] but affect—e.g., friendliness—could be responsible for some patterns. Whether some of them are the function of certain habitual muscle contractions necessitated by dialect, or whether they serve as ingroup signs are matters to be investigated.[14] We have presented here a few of what Darwin would consider less "important" facial expressions, the disparate areal frequencies of which are probably the result of socially standardized behavior. At the same time, not wishing to ignore "the more important ones," we have speculated that, though elicited by compatible norms of a subculture communication system, Type A Tongue Display and Pursed Smile might ultimately relate to behavior shared by various taxa of Anthropoidea.[15]

[11] Some allowance must be made for the slightly greater number of women in the Virginia sample.

[12] Although data gathered in the interviews corroborate this statement, and although I have observed these expressions on Pennsylvanians not being interviewed, I am not as conscious of *anticipating* their occurrence as I am of Orbicular Clamps, Tongue Displays, Pursed or Angle Depression Smiles in southern faces. I do not wish to speculate on the reason for this; I merely indicate my own uneasiness with the finding.

[13] Also, it should be noted, whereas Virginians pursed only slightly more than Pennsylvanians when not smiling (Seaford 1971), they pursed significantly more when they did (Table 1). At least we have here a southern embellishment of the expression of happiness.

[14] It might not be inappropriate to mention here that in the yearbook study, patterns of the Southern Syndrome were virtually not discernible on children younger than 15 years of age. On other occasions, however, I have noted them (which ones, I am not now sure) on a few individuals somewhere between ages 6 and 15. The enculturation of these behaviors is projected for future investigation.

[15] Invaluable perspectives have been gained through conversations with Julia Chase, Suzanne Chevalier-Skolnikoff, Paul Ekman, who kindly read an earlier version of this paper and offered helpful suggestions, and John Smith, all of whom must be completely exonerated from any of the informational and theoretical aberrations I may have promulgated. My thanks again to those immortal Pennsylvanians and Virginians. This research was supported by NSF Grant GS-2338, and grants from the Faculty Research Fund at Dickinson College.

Bibliography

Andrew, R. J.
1963 Evolution of Facial Expression. Science, *142*:1034-1041.
1972 The Information Potentially Available in Mammal Displays. *In* Non-Verbal Communication, R. A. Hinde, ed. Cambridge: The University Press, pp. 179-204.

Bean, R. Bennett
1938 The Peopling of Virginia. Boston: Chapman and Grimes. Birdwhistell, Ray L.
1952 Introduction to Kinesics: An Emotivation System for Analysis of Body Motion and Gesture. Louisville: University of Louisville Press.

Boas, Franz
1938 The Mind of Primitive Man. New York: Macmillan.

Bolwig, N.
1959 A Study of the Behaviour of the Chacma Baboon. Behaviour *14:*136-163.

Carpenter, C. R.
1940 A Field Study in Siam of the Behavior and Social Relations of the Gibbon. Comparative Psychology Monographs 16 (5).

Chevalier-Skolnikoff, Suzanne
1973a Facial Expression of Emotion in Nonhuman Primates. In: Darwin and Facial Expression: A Century of Research in Review, Paul Ekman, ed. New York: Academic Press.

1973b Visual and Tactile Communication in *Macaca arctoides* and Its Ontogenetic Development. American Journal of Physical Anthropology *38*:515-518.

The Christian Science Monitor
1971 Assaults on the Ageless Piece of Aging Parchment. January 20.

Count, Earl W.
1958 The Biological Basis of Human Sociality. American Anthropologist, *60*:1049-1085.

Cullen, J. M.
1972 Some Principles of Animal Communication. In: Non-Verbal Communication, R. A. Hinde, ed. Cambridge: The University Press, pp. 101-122.

Darwin, Charles
1955 (1872) The Expression of the Emotions in Man and Animals. New York: Philosophical Library.

Duchenne, G. -B.
1876 (1862) Mecanisme de la Physionomie Humaine. Paris: Librairie J. -B. Bailliere et Fils.

Efron, David
1941 Gesture and Environment. New York: King's Crown Press.

Eibl-Eibesfeldt, Irenäus
1970 Ethology: The Biology of Behavior. New York: Holt, Rinehart and Winston.

Ekman, Paul
1968 The Recognition and Display of Facial Behavior in Literate and Non-Literate Cultures. Paper presented at the Symposium, "University of the Emotions" American Psychological Association.
1972 Universals and Cultural Differences in Facial Expressions of Emotion. In: Nebraska Symposium on Motivation, James Cole, ed. Lincoln, Neb: University of Nebraska Press.

Ekman, Paul, ed.
1973 Darwin and Facial Expression: A Century of Research in Review. New York: Academic Press.

Ekman, Paul, Wallace V. Friesen and Silvan S. Tomkins
1971 Facial Affect Scoring Technique: A First Validity Study. Semiotica, 3:37-58.

Ekman, Paul, Wallace V. Friesen and Phoebe Ellsworth
1972 Emotion in the Face: Guidelines for Research and an Integration of Findings. New York: Pergamon Press.

Ekman, Paul, E. R. Sorenson, and W. V. Friesen
1969 Pan-cultural Elements in Facial Displays of Emotions. Science, 164:86-88.

Goldstein, Marcus S.
1936 Changes in Dimensions and Form of the Face and Head with Age. American Journal of Physical Anthropology, 22:37-89.

Goodall, J. van Lawick
1965 Chimpanzees of the Gombe Stream Reserve. In: Primate Behavior, Irven, DeVore, ed. New York: Holt, Rinehart and Winston.

Graham, John
1966 Character Description and Meaning in the Romantic Novel. Studies in Romanticism, 4:208-218.

Grant, J. C. Bioleau
1951 An Atlas of Anatomy. Baltimore: William & Wilkins.

Gray, Henry
1959 Anatomy of the Human Body. Twenty-seventh Edition. C. M. Goss, ed. Philadelphia: Lea and Febiger.

Hinde, A. and T. E. Rowell
1962 Communication by Postures and Facial Expressions in the rhesus Monkey *(Macaca mulatta).* Zoological Society of London. Proceedings 138:1-21.

Hooff, J.A.R.A.M. van
1969 The Facial Displays of the Catarrhine Monkeys and Apes. In: Primate Ethology. Desmond Morris, ed. Garden City: Doubleday.
1972 A Comparative Approach to the Phylogeny of Laughter and Smil-

ing. In: Non-Verbal Communication, R. A. Hinde, ed. Cambridge: The University Press, pp. 209-238.

Hooton, Earnest A.
1954   Up from the Ape. Revised Edition. New York: Macmillan.

Hrdlička, Ales
1918   Anthropological Studies on Old American Families. Smithsonian Miscellaneous Collection, 68 (12) 49.

Huber, Ernst
1931   Evolution of Facial Musculature and Facial Expression. Baltimore: Johns Hopkins Press.

Izard, Carroll E.
1968   The Emotions as a Culture Common Framework of Motivational Experiences and Communicative Cues. Technical Report No. 30. Office of Naval Research.

La Barre, Weston
1947   The Cultural Basis of Emotions and Gestures. Journal of Personality, *16*:49-68.

Lavater, J. C.
1789   (1772) Essays on Physiognomy; for the Promotion of the Knowledge and the Love of Mankind. (Translated from German by Thomas Holcroft.) London: G. G. J. and J. Robinson.

Lightoller, G. S.
1925   Facial Muscles. Journal of Anatomy, *60*:1.
1928a   The Action of the M. Mentalis in the Expression of the Emotion of Distress. Journal of Anatomy, *62*:319.
1928b   The Facial Muscles of Three Orangutans and Two Cercopithecidae. Journal of Anatomy, *63*:19.

McCormick, S. D.
1900   Survivals in American Educated Speech. Bookman, *11*:446-450.

McDavid, Raven I., Jr.
1958   The Dialects of American English. In: The Structure of American English, Francis W. Nelson, ed. New York: The Ronald Press Company.

Miller, R. E.
1971   Experimental Studies of Communication in the Monkey. In: Primate Behavior: Developments in Field and Laboratory Research, II. L. A. Rosenblum, ed. New York: Academic Press.

Moynihan, M.
1970   Some Behavior Patterns of Platyrrhine Monkeys II. *Saguinus geoffroyi* and Some other Tararins. Smithsonian Contributions to Zoology, *28*:1-77.

Muri, John T. and Raven I. McDavid, Jr.
1967   Americans Speaking: A Dialect Recording Prepared for the National Council of Teachers of English. Champaign, Ill.: National Council of Teachers of English.

Odum, Howard W.
    1930   An American Epoch: Southern Portraiture in the National Picture.
    New York: Henry Holt.
Plutchik, Robert
    1968   The Emotions: Facts, Theories, and A New Model. New York:
    Random House.
Seaford, Henry W., Jr.
    1966   The Southern Syndrome: A Regional Pattern of Facial Muscle
    Contraction. Paper delivered at the Annual Meeting of the Pennsylvania
    Sociological Society.
    1971   The Southern Syndrome: A Regional Patterning of Facial Muscle
    Contraction. Ph.D. Thesis. Harvard University.
Shapiro, Harry W.
    1947   Applied Anatomy of the Head and Neck. Philadelphia: J. B.
    Lippincott.
Smith, W. John
    1965   Message, Meaning, and Context in Ethology. The American Nat-
    uralist, *99*:405-409.
    1969   Messages of Vertebrate Communication. Science, *165*:145-150.
Smith, W. John, Julia Chase, and Anna K. Lieblich
    1974   Tongue Showing: A Facial Display of Humans and Other Pri-
    mate Species Semiotica, *11*:201-246.
Stanard, N. M.
    1917   Colonial Virginia, Its People and Customs. Philadelphia: J. B.
    Lippincott Company.
Steegmann, A. T., Jr.
    1965   A Study of Relationships Between Facial Cold Response and Some
    Variables of Facial Morphology. American Journal of Physical Anthro-
    pology, *23*:355-362
    1967   Frost Bite of the Human Face as a Selective Force. Human Biology,
    39:131-144.
    1970a   Cold Adaptation and the Human Face. American Journal of Physi-
    cal Anthropology, *32*:243-250.
    1970b   Reliability Testing of a Facial Contourometer. American Journal
    of Physical Anthropology, *33*:241-248.
    1972   Cold Response, Body Form, and Craniofacial Shape in Two Racial
    Groups of Hawaii. American Journal of Physical Anthropology,
    37:193-221.
Steegmann, A. T., Jr. and W. S. Platner
    1968   Experimental Cold Modification of Craniofacial Morphology.
    American Journal of Physical Anthropology, *28*:17.
Subtelny, J. Daniel
    1965   Examination of Current Philosophies Associated with Swallowing
    Behavior. American Journal of Orthodontics, *51*:161-182.

Subtelny, J. Daniel and Joanne D. Subtelny
  1962   Malocclusion, Speech, and Deglutition. Reprinted From American
  Journal of Orthodontics, *48*:685-697.
Virchow, Hans
  1908   Geischtsmuskeln und Gesichtsausdruck. Archiv fur Anatomie und
  Physiologie. Anatomische Abteilung, S. 371-436.
Weddell, A. W., ed.
  1930   A   Memorial   Volume   of   Virginia   Historical   Portraiture.
  Richmond: The William Byrd Press.
Wood, Gordon R.
  1963   Dialect   Contours   in   the   Southern   States.   American   Speech,
  38:243-256.
Zuckerman, S.
  1932   The Social Life of Monkeys and Apes. London: Routledge & Kegan
  Paul.

Subject Index

Adaptation, cultural, 496–528, 552–605

Africa(ns), 214, 218–221, 223–227, 326, 331, 334, 338, 385

Age: dental, 321–334; from bones, 373, 413–414, 433–449; in sexual dimorphism, 196–209; in stature, 144. *See also* Growth

Agriculture, 503–528, 552–605; associated ceremonies, 565–568; crops, 555, 564; effectiveness, 585–599; techniques, 560–565

Alcohol, 234–235

Alouatta. See Howler monkey

Altitude, high, 250–254

Americans, 185, 202–209, 434, 442, 619–634

Andes, 232

Anglos, 202–209

Arthritis, 144, 410–411, 418–429

Asians, 331, 334

Australopithecines, 339–346, 351–369

Bantu, 385–389

Behavior, 62–67, 74–75, 77–104, 617–634; reproductive, 8–10, 24, 26, 29–30, 43–49, 535–547. *See also* Culture, Social organization

Birds. *See* Parrots

Blacks, American, 202–209

Blood groups, 218, 220

Bone. *See* Crania, Culture, Humerus, Paleopathology, Pubic symphysis, Osteology, Teeth

Borneo, 8–9

Bougainville, 145–146, 280, 533–547

Breeding structure. *See* Population structure

Buffering, in growth, 188–191

Canalization, growth, 182–191

Canonical analysis, 194–209

Carabelli's cusp, 168

Cluster analysis, 414–418

Coca, 234–235

Cold stress. *See* Stress

Computer simulation, 14–19; ORANG program, 20–49

Contouring techniques, 473–476

Cook Islands, 164

Coordinate points, 471–472

Correlation, 181–191; sib-pair, 282

Crania, 378, 383–403, 451–463, 465–489

Cross-sectional method, 144–160, 196–209, 245–249, 325

Culture, 233–256 *passim*, 375–381, 409, 425–429, 465–466, 500–528, 535–547, 552–605, 617–634; change, 537–540, 543–547, 599–604; and fertility, 535–547; history (New World), 516–528; inferences from bone, 375–381, 409, 425–429; of scientists, 465–466. *See also* Behavior

Demography, 502, 528, 535–547, 574–575, 596–598. *See also* Paleodemography

Dentition. *See* Teeth

Dermatoglyphics. *See* Fingerprints, Palmprints

Design, research, 232–233, 255–256

Development: cultural, 496–528; motor, 246–249

Diet, 57–58, 172, 175–178, 497–528, 569–574. *See also* Nutrition

Dimorphism. *See* Sex dimorphism

Discriminant function analysis, 194–209, 348–369, 396–403, 483–485

Disease, 171–172, 538–541, 544; hypertension, cardiovascular, respiratory, 253–254. *See also* Paleopathology

Distance measures. *See* Genetics, Statistics

Ecology, 3–5, 67–69, 553, 557–560, 592–594

Encephalization, avian, 55–56

Author Index

645